CLINICAL EXPERIENCES IN COUNSELING

Bradley T. Erford

Loyola University Maryland

PEARSON

Boston   Columbus   Indianapolis   New York   San Francisco   Upper Saddle River
Amsterdam   Cape Town   Dubai   London   Madrid   Milan   Munich   Paris   Montreal   Toronto
Delhi   Mexico City   São Paulo   Sydney   Hong Kong   Seoul Singapore   Taipei Tokyo

Vice President and Editorial Director: Jeffery W. Johnston
Senior Acquisitions Editor: Meredith Fossel
Editorial Assistant: Janelle Criner
Vice President, Director of Marketing: Margaret Waples
Senior Marketing Manager: Darcy Betts Prybella
Production Project Manager: Jennifer Gessner
Development Project Management: Aptara®, Inc.
Procurement Specialist: Pat Tonneman
Senior Art Director: Jayne Conte
Cover Designer: Karen Noferi
Cover Photo: © terry.runion, Fotolia
Media Project Manager: Noelle Chun
Full-Service Project Management: Mohinder Singh/Aptara®, Inc.
Composition: Aptara®, Inc.
Printer/Binder: LSC Communications
Cover Printer: LSC Communications
Text Font: 10/12, ITC Garamond Std

Credits and acknowledgments for material borrowed from other sources and reproduced, with permission, in this textbook appear on the appropriate page within the text.

Every effort has been made to provide accurate and current Internet information in this book. However, the Internet and information posted on it are constantly changing, so it is inevitable that some of the Internet addresses listed in this textbook will change.

Library of Congress Cataloging-in-Publication Data
Clinical experiences in counseling / [edited by] Bradley T. Erford, Loyola University
Maryland.—First edition.
    pages cm
  ISBN-13: 978-0-13-701724-9
  ISBN-10: 0-13-701724-3
  1. Counseling. I. Erford, Bradley T.
  BF636.6.C55 2015
  158.3—dc23

                                    2013039780

ISBN 10:   0-13-701724-3
ISBN 13: 978-0-13-701724-9

This effort is dedicated to
The One: the Giver of energy, passion, and understanding,
who makes life worth living and endeavors worth pursuing and accomplishing;
the Teacher of love and forgiveness.

—*BTE*

PREFACE

Clinical Experiences in Counseling provides much more than a basic review of practicum and internship. In this text, students will experience a series of "ah-ha" moments where issues, only partially understood before, are brought to life in practical situations; where the information from one's course of study comes together to form a complete picture; and where a student understands the counseling profession and process holistically. A special feature of the text is the frequent integration of self-assessments of personal beliefs, professional knowledge, and personal characteristics used to identify areas of strength, as well as areas in need of further improvement. Thus, *Clinical Experiences in Counseling* serves as a road map to assist the student in optimizing the practicum and internship experience, allowing the student to draw confidence from a knowledge base, continually self-assess in every area pertinent to competent practice, and integrate theory into intentional practice under supervision.

Clinical Experiences in Counseling emphasizes a number of issues often overlooked in clinical seminars and experiences, yet repeatedly experienced by the beginning counselor, including

(a) clarification of the confusion surrounding the counseling profession;
(b) the importance of goodness of fit between student skills and placement;
(c) the importance of understanding and operating from a theoretical perspective;
(d) the essentials of the initial meeting with a client;
(e) common ethical dilemmas experienced in counseling practice;
(f) multicultural issues related not only to ethnicity, but also to gender, religion, sexual orientation, and disability;
(g) how to respond to large-scale crises;
(h) how to respond to a client who intends to harm self or others;
(i) how to deliver evidence-based practice; and
(j) management of counselor self-care.

Chapter 1: *Matching Goals, Developing Skills, and Getting the Most Out of Clinical Placements,* by Rachel M. Hoffman and Bradley T. Erford, introduces the student to the wonderful world of the counseling field experience. We differentiate between practicum and internship experiences, focusing on the goals of each, and then discuss helpful orientation information such as working in multidisciplinary teams and matching your assets with preferred client populations and sites. A specific focus is placed on self-reflection, self-assessment, and identification of personal strengths and areas of challenge. Finally, we review where you are heading, including information related to certification, licensure, and employment.

In Chapter 2: *The Supervision Process,* Catherine Y. Chang, Caroline O'Hara, and Lindy K. Parker unveil the supervision process as a complicated process that involves various individuals (i.e., supervisor, supervisee, and client) and organizations (i.e., the university and the practicum/internship agency or school) and transpires through various stages. In this chapter, we explore supervision processes, the various roles you will hold as you begin your practicum–internship sequence, and also what you can expect from your on-site and university supervisors. We will also cover the development of positive supervision relationships and learning goals as well as the differences between supervision and counseling. In addition, we will discuss barriers to effective supervision, different theoretical approaches, and ways of making case presentations. Throughout this chapter, several self-assessment activities are provided to help students identify strengths, growing edges, needs, and goals.

Chapter 3: *The Many Details of a First Impression,* by Robin Wilbourn Lee, Jennifer Jordan, Kristi Gibbs, and Jeannine R. Studer, portrays entrance into the clinical experiences of practicum and internship as a time of excitement because it is an opportunity to work with real clients rather than practicing counseling skills by role-playing skills with peers. It may also be a time of trepidation, as many trainees ask themselves questions like, "Do I really have the skills for this?" or, "What if my supervisor doesn't like me?" or, "What if I have a client with issues I can't handle?" All these questions are a normal part of entering a new experience. An important goal for students at this point is to prepare for the anxiety one may experience as the student moves from practice to real-life situations.

Chapter 4: *Integrating Theory into Practice,* by Dana Heller Levitt, Alissa Darnell, Bradley T. Erford, and Ann Vernon, answers the question, Why do professional counselors study theories? Whether working with individuals, families, or groups, regardless of the setting, professional counselors have a professional responsibility to develop a foundation and clear rationale for their theoretical orientation to serve clients best. Professional counselors operate out of theories that best fit their personal philosophies of human change and the counseling process, but also choose approaches that effectively address the client's issues. Selecting a theoretical orientation is a career-long process that begins during professional training. In Chapter 4, the significance of integrating theory into counseling practice is explored, and a brief overview of the major theoretical paradigms is presented. Students also begin to explore their own initial preferences for theoretical orientation with the intent of continuing one's personal and professional exploration to discover a personal, integrated counseling style.

Chapter 5: *Record Keeping: What to Include and What to Leave Out,* by James Jackson and Charlotte Daughhetee, asserts that appropriate clinical record keeping is essential to ethical practice. When documenting counseling services, it is imperative that counselors be mindful of the legal, ethical, and agency requirements regarding documentation. Good comprehensive record keeping promotes quality treatment and also documents that treatment falls within accepted standards of care, thereby providing protection from liability risk. By following standard therapy note-writing formats and by allowing time for note writing immediately following a session, counselors can produce precise yet thorough documentation of their practice. In addition to client records, counselors engage in other types of professional writing, including communication with other professionals and the production of practice marketing materials. The ability to write professionally is vital to professional responsible practice.

Chapter 6: *Putting Ethics and Law into Practice,* by Lynn E. Linde and Bradley T. Erford, addresses some ethical and legal issues in counseling commonly encountered by counselors-in-training. Professional counselors must always remember that how one conducts oneself personally and professionally reflects not only on oneself, but also on colleagues and the counseling profession. Knowledge and understanding of the issues reviewed in this chapter on ethics and laws are only a starting point. Counselors must keep up to date with the laws, ethics, policies, and procedures that govern professional practice in your state and workplace. The implementation of professional responsibilities will require undivided attention every day of one's professional life.

Chapter 7: *Special Populations and Issues,* by Victoria E. Kress, Matthew J. Paylo, and Nicole A. Adamson, provides ample evidence that professional counselors are regularly faced with myriad complex client or student presenting issues that require the synthesis of information spanning multiple areas. The topics presented in this chapter cover a variety of issues and populations that counselors will confront in practice. The topics presented in this chapter are those that were likely not addressed in detail in other areas of the counseling curriculum and, as such, will hopefully prove to be helpful. In approaching these topics, an emphasis was placed on presenting basic, practical information that may help counselors navigate their work with these populations. The presentations provided are intended to serve as a starting point for considering one's work with the indicated populations.

Chapter 8: *Multicultural Counseling and Its Multiple Applications,* by José A. Villalba, will enhance the reader's clinical experiences by exploring the historical and contextual nature of cultural sensitivity, examining the development of the American Multicultural Counseling and Development Multicultural Counseling Competence standards, delving into the reader's self-awareness and the role their self-awareness plays when working with individuals identifying with different societal groups, and finally, emphasizing the benefits of working with clients from a strengths-based approach. To facilitate the readers' heightened multicultural counseling competence while in their clinical placement, each of the four sections of Chapter 8 concludes with a series of self-assessment activities and case study scenarios related specifically to the content of a particular chapter section.

Chapter 9: *Assessing and Intervening with Clients in Danger and Crisis,* by Linda Foster, Paul Hard, Laura L. Talbott, and Mary L. Bartlett, focused on assessment and intervention of clients in crisis. Counselors must be prepared to assess and intervene with clients who may be a danger to themselves (i.e., suicidal), others (i.e., homicidal), or have experienced traumatic events due to either natural disasters or man-made events. Topics of suicide, homicide, and large-scale shock can be uncomfortable for counselors-in-training, so self-assessment examples and activities were included to help students gain insight and create a personal philosophy for working with these issues.

Chapter 10: *Practicing Professional Responsibility,* by Stephanie G. Puleo, Charlotte Daughhetee, and Jason M. Newell, explored the theoretical foundations of ethical, proficient counseling practice and the developmental process of ongoing advancement of therapeutic expertise. In particular, the chapter discusses the sacred nature of the counseling relationship and the professional behaviors that are expected of the counselor in service of that relationship. Clients entrust aspects of their lives to counselors, placing a daunting amount of responsibility on them. The counseling relationship and the welfare of the client are contingent on professional, responsible practice by the counselor; therefore, the continuing improvement of one's counseling practice is fundamental to best practice. A major key to proficient counseling practice is the self-awareness of the counselor and the counselor's ability to assess areas of personal and professional growth. Commitment to continuing competency as a lifelong professional value is stressed, and the importance of advocacy for the profession and for clients is posited as essential to responsible professional practice.

Chapter 11: *Wrapping It Up,* by Nicole A. Adamson and Bradley T. Erford, focuses on how best to terminate therapeutic relationships or transition clients from intern care to the care of another mental health professional. Clinical experiences also offer opportunities to reflect on what has been learned and to provide formative and summative performance evaluations of the student, supervisor, and training program.

Chapter 12: *Other Pertinent Issues in Counseling Practice,* by Elisabeth Bennett, provides an overview of other pertinent issues/roles in counseling practice, including consultation, academic advising and career guidance, and advocacy. Supportive and collaborative services such as psychological, educational, and vocational assessment; compliance support for the psychopharmacological regimen set by the medical professional; and practice consistent with the requirements of third-party payers or managed care companies are also discussed. Understanding the role and function of the counselor is imperative in maintaining an ethical position and providing best practice throughout one's counseling career. A self-assessment at the end of each section will assist the reader in the application of knowledge in each area to the practice of counseling.

Up until this chapter, the focus has been on your relationship and interactions with clients, how to provide outstanding services, and how to get the most out of your practicum and internship. In the final two chapters, the focus shifts and is now squarely on you as the counselor in training. Chapter 13: *Counselor Self-Care,* by Kerry Thon, reviews the importance for all counselors to have an effective self-care plan to help prevent burnout and to deal with the stressors inherent in the counseling field. Clinical supervision allows you to seek advice and consultation from experienced counselors as you might seek knowledge from others who have gone before you. This can assist you in side-stepping common pitfalls and mistakes made by beginning counselors and provide much needed support as you come to the limits of your competence. Your self-care plan is much like your protective gear, which can help you weather the storms as you navigate through your first counseling experiences. Many professionals have tools of their trade that they need to keep in tip-top shape. As counselors, we are our own best therapeutic tool, so we have an obligation to keep ourselves in shape mentally, physically, and spiritually. What you learn about stress and wellness not only applies to your clients, but to yourself as well.

Finally, Chapter 14: *From Envisioning to Actualization: Marketing Yourself in the 21st Century,* by Daniel S. Testa, Jessica A. Headley, and Nicole A. Adamson, addresses the importance of finding your place in the counseling market as a 21st-century counselor. Section One (*Temet Nosce*) will address the significance of self-evaluation and reflection, using the SELF acronym. Section Two (Understanding the Field around You) will highlight current trends and opportunities in the field. Section Three (Securing a Job the Old-Fashioned Way) will cover the logistics of the job search and traditional self-promotion strategies. Section Four (Carving Out Your New-Age Niche) will outline how social media can be used to establish counselor identity and credibility. Finally, Section Five (The Advantages of Continued Learning) will discuss how advanced training and postgraduate education can increase your marketing opportunities. Ultimately, the integration of information from all these sections will enhance your ability to promote yourself to potential employers and clients, giving you the edge you need to compete in this current market.

In summary, *Clinical Experiences in Counseling* emphasizes understanding one's roles as a counseling practicum student or intern, practicing competently, continuing to assess what is not yet understood, and understanding the duty to continually grow and learn as a professional counselor.

ACKNOWLEDGMENTS

Meredith Fossel, my editor at Pearson, deserves special mention for her stewardship during the writing and production of this book. Additional thanks go to Karen Slaght, an outstanding copy editor; to Jennifer Gessner, my project manager at Pearson, and Mohinder Singh and Linda Clark, my project managers at Aptara, for their outstanding service. I am also grateful to the reviewers for their helpful and supportive comments: Charlene Alexander, Ball State University; Virginia B. Allen, Idaho State University; Mark Davis, Northwestern Oklahoma State University; Paul F. Granello, The Ohio State University; William M. King, Argosy University, Chicago; John J. Lemoncelli, Marywood University; and Angie D. Wilson, Texas A&M University–Commerce.

ABOUT THE EDITOR

Bradley T. Erford, PhD, LCPC, NCC, LPC, LP, LSP, is the 2012–2013 President of the American Counseling Association (ACA) and a professor in the school counseling program of the Education Specialties Department in the School of Education at Loyola University Maryland. He is the recipient of the American Counseling Association (ACA) Research Award, ACA Extended Research Award, ACA Arthur A. Hitchcock Distinguished Professional Service Award, ACA Professional Development Award, and ACA Carl D. Perkins Government Relations Award. He was also inducted as an ACA Fellow. In addition, he has received the Association for Assessment in Counseling and Education (AACE) AACE/MECD Research Award, AACE Exemplary Practices Award, AACE President's Merit Award, the Association for Counselor Education and Supervision's (ACES) Robert O. Stripling Award for Excellence in Standards, Maryland Association for Counseling and Development (MACD) Maryland Counselor of the Year, MACD Counselor Advocacy Award, MACD Professional Development Award, and MACD Counselor Visibility Award. He is the editor/coeditor of numerous texts, including *Orientation to the Counseling Profession* (Pearson Merrill, 2010, 2014), *Group Work in the Schools* (Pearson Merrill, 2010), *Transforming the School Counseling Profession* (Pearson Merrill, 2003, 2007, 2011, 2015), *Group Work: Processes and Applications* (Pearson Merrill, 2010), *Developing Multicultural Counseling Competence* (Pearson Merrill, 2010, 2014), *Crisis Intervention and Prevention* (Pearson Merrill, 2010, 2014), *Professional School Counseling: A Handbook of Principles, Programs, and Practices* (PRO-ED, 2004, 2010), *Assessment for Counselors* (Cengage, 2007, 2013), *Research and Evaluation in Counseling* (Cengage, 2008, 2014), and *The Counselor's Guide to Clinical, Personality and Behavioral Assessment* (Cengage, 2006); and coauthor of three more books: *35 Techniques Every Counselor Should Know* (Merrill/Prentice-Hall, 2010, 2015), *Educational Applications of the WISC-IV* (Western Psychological Services, 2006), and *Group Activities: Firing Up for Performance* (Pearson/Merrill/Prentice-Hall, 2007). He is also the General Editor of *The American Counseling Association Encyclopedia of Counseling* (ACA, 2009). His research specialization falls primarily in development and technical analysis of psychoeducational tests and has resulted in the publication of more than 60 refereed journal articles, 100 book chapters, and a dozen published tests. He was a member of the ACA Governing Council and the ACA 20/20 Visioning Committee. He is Past President of AACE, Past Chair and Parliamentarian of the American Counseling Association–Southern (US) Region; Past Chair of ACA's Task Force on High Stakes Testing; Past Chair of ACA's Standards for Test Users Task Force; Past Chair of ACA's Interprofessional Committee; Past Chair of the ACA Public Awareness and Support Committee (Co-Chair of the National Awards Sub-committee); Chair of the Convention and Past Chair of the Screening Assessment Instruments Committees for AACE; Past President of the Maryland Association for Counseling and Development (MACD); Past President of Maryland Association for Measurement and Evaluation (MAME); Past President of Maryland Association for Counselor Education and Supervision (MACES); and Past President of the Maryland Association for Mental Health Counselors (MAMHC). He was also associate editor and board member of the *Journal of Counseling & Development*. Dr. Erford has been a faculty member at Loyola since 1993 and is a Licensed Clinical Professional Counselor, Licensed Professional Counselor, Nationally Certified Counselor, Licensed Psychologist, and Licensed School Psychologist. Prior to arriving at Loyola, Dr. Erford was a school psychologist/counselor in the Chesterfield County (VA) Public Schools. He maintains a private practice specializing in assessment and treatment of children and adolescents. A graduate of the University of Virginia (Ph.D.), Bucknell University (M.A.), and Grove City College (B.S.), he has taught courses in Testing and Measurement, Psychoeducational Assessment, Life-Span Development, Research and Evaluation in Counseling, School Counseling, Counseling Techniques, and Stress Management, as well as practicum and internship student supervision.

ABOUT THE AUTHORS

Nicole A. Adamson, MSEd, is a doctoral student and graduate assistant at the University of North Carolina at Greensboro. She is a licensed school counselor and licensed professional counselor and has provided services in schools, community mental health agencies, and hospitals. She has published more than 15 peer-reviewed journal articles, book entries, and book chapters and has served the profession through leadership positions in Chi Sigma Iota International and the American Counseling Association.

Mary L. Bartlett, PhD, LPC-CS, NCC, CFLE, earned her doctorate in counselor education from Auburn University. She presently holds the position of Vice President of Behavioral Sciences for a national consulting firm and serves as an independent consultant, suicidologist, and international speaker. With 15 years clinical and teaching experience, she is an authorized trainer for the Suicide Prevention Resource Center and the American Association of Suicidology and is a qualified master resilience trainer. In addition, Dr. Bartlett assists leadership of the U.S. Department of Defense on the prevention of suicide and other mental health–related topics.

Elisabeth Bennett, PhD, is a counselor educator at Gonzaga University, where she is an associate professor, program director, and department chairperson. She has been providing counseling services to the community for nearly 30 years in various settings, including hospital, agency, school, clinic, and private practice. Her education, training, and experience range across several specialties, including neuropsychology and assessment, gerontology, child and adolescent development, marriage and family services, postpartum issues, and organizational consultation. Her greatest educational pleasure remains with her students and their clinical training.

Catherine Y. Chang, PhD, is professor and program coordinator of the counselor education and practice doctoral program in the Counseling and Psychological Services Department at Georgia State University. Her research interests include multicultural issues in counselor training and supervision and Asian-American and Korean-American concerns. More specifically, she has published articles related to racial identity development, privilege and oppression issues, and multicultural counseling competence. Dr. Chang has been honored with the Alumni Excellence Award from the University of North Carolina at Greensboro, the American Counseling Association Research Award, and the Pre-tenure Counselor Educator Award from the Southern Association for Counselor Education and Supervision.

Alissa Darnell, LAPC, is a doctoral student in counselor education at Ohio University. Her areas of interest include theory development, multicultural issues in counseling, and counselor wellness. Research and professional presentations have explored the connection between graduate training and practice, including how theories are employed in community counseling and the relationship between wellness and burnout. Alissa is currently counseling in a community mental health setting in North Georgia, serving individuals with severe and profound mental illness.

Charlotte L. Daughhetee is a professor in the graduate program in counseling at the University of Montevallo. She is an NCC, LPC, and LMFT. She has counseling experience in K–12, university, and private practice settings. She earned her MEd in school counseling in 1988 and her PhD in counselor education in 1992 from the University of South Carolina. She has experience in crisis intervention in school and university settings and has presented and published on crisis intervention. She is the program coordinator for the University of Montevallo Counseling Program, and she coordinates the school counseling track.

Linda H. Foster, PhD, NCC, NCSC, LPC-S, is an assistant professor at Troy University Montgomery. She received her undergraduate degree from Samford University, master's and education specialist degrees in Community Counseling from the University of Alabama in Birmingham, and a PhD in Counselor Education at Mississippi State University. She worked as a school counselor for over 10 years at the elementary, middle, and high school levels and is now entering her fifth year as a counselor educator. She has served on local, state, national, and international counseling boards and editorial boards. Her research interests include professional identity of counselors, clinical supervision of school counselors, counselor education faculty dynamics, personal development, leadership styles and personality types among counselor educators, and the use of single-subject research methods by counselors. She has presented on various topics at the state, national, and international levels and has published numerous articles in peer-reviewed journals, as well as several book chapters.

Kristi A. Gibbs, PhD, is an associate professor and director of the counselor education program at the University of Tennessee at Chattanooga. She has 15 years of clinical experience in various settings, including residential treatment facilities, hospitals, community agencies, college counseling centers, and private practice. She has published and presented at conferences primarily in the areas of counseling children and ethics.

Paul F. Hard, PhD, LPC-S, NCC, is an associate professor of counselor education at Auburn University at Montgomery. He has provided individual and group counseling in both private practice and community agency settings focusing on addictions, relationship counseling, sexual minorities, and trauma. His research interests have been in the areas of ethics, counselor/professional impairment and wellness, complicated grieving in pre- and postnatal loss, professional credentialing and advocacy, sexual minority issues in counseling, and ministerial termination.

Jessica A. Headley, MA, PC, is completing her PhD in the counselor education and supervision program at The University of Akron. She holds a graduate certificate in gerontology and has clinical experience in community mental health and hospital settings. She currently serves as the Assistant Editor of *Psychology of Women Quarterly* and holds various leadership positions within Chi Sigma Iota. She has authored and coauthored various journal articles, book chapters, and newsletters in the field of counseling.

Rachel M. Hoffman, PhD, is a clinical director at a behavioral health organization and adjunct faculty member in the counseling programs at Youngstown State University and Walden University. She has authored over 15 scholarly journal articles and book chapters, and she has presented over 70 times at national, state, and local conferences and workshops. She has experience working in a variety of settings, including addictions treatment, community-based mental health, inpatient psychiatric services, and college counseling.

James L. Jackson, Jr., PhD, LPC, NCC is an assistant professor and coordinator of the clinical mental health counseling track at the University of Montevallo in Montevallo, Alabama. His clinical experiences include therapy and advocacy services with abused children and adolescents in schools, foster homes, and group homes, as well as serving adults and families through private practice and community mental health agencies.

Jennifer Jordan, PhD, LPCS, NCC, is an associate professor in the counseling and development program at Winthrop University. She is past president of the Southern Association for Counselor Education and Supervision (2011–2012). She specializes in group counseling and working with children and adolescents.

Victoria E. Kress, PhD, is a clinic director, professor, and the coordinator of the clinical mental health, addictions, and college counseling programs at Youngstown State University. She has over 20 years of clinical experience in various settings, including community mental health centers, hospitals, residential treatment facilities, private practice, and college counseling centers. She has published over 60 journal articles and numerous book chapters, and coauthored a book on cultural and ethical issues that relate to counselors' use of the *DSM*.

Robin Wilbourn Lee, PhD, LPC, NCC, is an associate professor in the professional counseling program at Middle Tennessee State University. She received her doctoral degree in counselor education and supervision from Mississippi State University. Her interests include counselor training issues, ethical and legal issues, counseling supervision, women's issues, and generational characteristics.

Dana Heller Levitt, PhD, is an associate professor of counselor education at Montclair State University. She received her master's and doctoral degrees from the University of Virginia. Dr. Levitt's research focuses on ethics and counselor development, eating disorders, and body image.

Lynn E. Linde, EdD, is Coordinator of Clinical Experiences in the school counseling program at Loyola University Maryland. She received her doctorate in counseling from The George Washington University. She is a former Branch Chief for Pupil Services at the

Maryland State Department of Education. She was the 2009–2010 President of the American Counseling Association and 2012–2103 Treasurer. She was the Southern Region representative to ACA Governing Council and 20/20 Committee, Past Chair of the ACA—Southern Region, and Past President of the Maryland Association for Counseling and Development and has served on several committees and task forces, including the 2014 ACA Ethics Revision Task Force. She is an ACA Fellow, is a recipient of the Carl Perkins Award, and has received a number of awards from ACA, its entities, and the State of Maryland.

Jason M. Newell, PhD, LCSW-PIP, is an assistant professor of social work in the Department of Behavioral and Social Sciences at the University of Montevallo. His research and specialty areas include clinical practice with the mentally ill (adult, adolescent, and child); treatment of anxiety and mood disorders; traumatic and secondary traumatic stress; self-care and the prevention of professional burnout; practice with veterans and military families; and child welfare. He teaches introductory courses in social welfare and social work practice, human behavior and the social environment, research methods, practice with individuals and families, and mental health issues and services.

Caroline O'Hara, EdS, MS, is a doctoral student in the Counselor Education and Practice program at Georgia State University (GSU). She is a Licensed Professional Counselor and a National Certified Counselor. Caroline has published and presented at the national level in the areas of identity development, social justice counseling, sexual and gender diversity, multicultural competence, counseling supervision, and advocacy (both client and professional). She served as President of the Chi Epsilon Chapter of Chi Sigma Iota (CSI) and as a member of the CSI Advocacy Committee nationally. In addition, Caroline served as the managing editor of the text, *Professional Counseling Excellence through Leadership and Advocacy* and editorial assistant for a special issue of *Counselor Education and Supervision* focusing on social justice. Caroline has been awarded the ACA Courtland C. Lee Multicultural Excellence Scholarship Award and the CSI International Leadership Fellow and Intern Award.

Lindy K. Parker, EdS, is a licensed professional counselor, instructor, and academic advisor for counseling and psychology graduate programs at Georgia State University. She has clinical experience in multiple settings, including college counseling centers, psychiatric hospitals, substance abuse programs, adolescent outpatient facilities, alternative schools, and private practice. She has conducted research in the areas of gatekeeping, career counseling, professional advocacy, animal-assisted therapy, and school counseling. She is currently a doctoral student in the counselor education and practice program at Georgia State University.

Matthew J. Paylo, PhD, is an assistant professor and director of the student affairs and college-counseling program at Youngstown State University. He has over 10 years of clinical experience in various settings, including community mental health centers, prisons, hospitals, residential treatment facilities, and college counseling centers. He has published numerous journal articles and book chapters on trauma, offender treatments, social justice counseling, and the implementation of the *DSM*.

Stephanie Puleo, PhD, LMFT, LPC, NCC, is a professor in the Department of Counseling, Leadership, and Foundations at the University of Montevallo in Montevallo, Alabama. She is certified by the American Red Cross in Disaster Mental Health. Dr. Puleo earned her PhD in counselor education at the University of Alabama. She also has earned master's degrees in community counseling and in school psychology. In addition to coordinating the marriage and family counseling program track at the University of Montevallo, she provides counseling and psychometric services to individuals, couples, and families in the Birmingham and central Alabama area.

Jeannine R. Studer is a professor of counselor education at the University of Tennessee, Knoxville. She was previously a school counselor in Ohio, California, and Tennessee. She has published numerous articles and book chapters and is the author of three books that relate to the profession of school counseling.

Laura L. Talbott, PhD, MCHES, is an associate professor in the Department of Human Studies at the University of Alabama at Birmingham. She has served as a prevention specialist with general college student health issues and director of substance abuse prevention programs at a large university. Her research interests include the prevention of substance abuse, education and early intervention with potentially suicidal persons, and other public health issues that impact young adult health.

Daniel S. Testa is a doctoral student in the counselor education and supervision program at the University of Akron. He graduated from Malone University in 2010 and earned his PC licensure while gaining exposure in community mental health programs. He currently serves as President-Elect of the University of Akron's Chi Sigma National Honor Society chapter.

Kerry Thon, MA, LCPC, is clinical director of a residential treatment program for adolescents and has over 12 years of direct clinical experience with children, adolescents, and families. She has worked in residential treatment facilities, therapeutic day schools, private practice, and within community agencies. She is an adjunct instructor at several university counseling programs and serves on the board of the Illinois Mental Health Counselors Association. She facilitates retreats that focus on the health and well-being of counselors.

Ann Vernon, PhD, NCC, LMHC, is professor emeritus and former coordinator of counseling at the University of Northern Iowa and a counselor in private practice, where she works extensively with children, adolescents, and their parents. Dr. Vernon is the former Director of the Midwest Center for REBT and Vice-President of the Albert Ellis Board of Trustees. She is the author of numerous books, chapters, and articles, including *Thinking, Feeling, Behaving* and *What Works When with Children and Adolescents*.

José A. Villalba, PhD, received his doctorate in counselor education from the University of Florida. He is an associate professor in the Department of Counseling at the Wake Forest University. His teaching interests include multicultural counseling, counseling in school settings, and health and human services. His research interests include addressing Latina/o health disparities in emerging Latino communities. He has published several articles and book chapters, presented at several scholarly conferences, and served as keynote speaker for various organizations looking to promote multicultural competence and awareness.

BRIEF CONTENTS

CONTENTS

**Chapter 9   Assessing and Intervening with Clients in Danger
and Crisis**
■ **Linda Foster, Paul Hard, Laura L. Talbott,
and Mary L. Bartlett   188**

CHAPTER 1

Matching Goals, Developing Skills, and Getting the Most Out of Clinical Placements

BY RACHEL M. HOFFMAN AND BRADLEY T. ERFORD

PREVIEW

This initial chapter introduces you to the wonderful world that awaits in your counseling field experience. We differentiate between practicum and internship experiences, focusing on the goals of each, and then discuss helpful orientation information such as working in multidisciplinary teams and matching your assets with preferred client populations and sites. A specific focus is placed on self-reflection, self-assessment, and identification of personal strengths and areas of challenge. Finally, we review where you are heading, including information related to certification, licensure, and employment.

BEGINNING YOUR CLINICAL EXPERIENCE

Congratulations! You are embarking on one of the most exciting periods of your graduate training: the field experience! Your practicum and internship experiences afford you the opportunity to interact with clients and put all the knowledge and skills that you've learned in the classroom into practice. Practicum and internship experiences give you an opportunity to practice counseling skills and techniques under supervision. It's important that you are prepared to take full advantage of the field experience. This chapter and text will help provide you with resources to make the most of your practicum and internship placements. This text is designed to be read in its entirety; yet, it will also be helpful as a reference for special issues in the future. Each chapter will help inform a different aspect of your practicum and internship experiences.

A few years ago, an intern stated, "I wish I knew exactly what my client was going to say *before* I went into session. That way, I could be prepared with exactly how to respond." The idea of feeling unprepared to work with client concerns is one of the most common themes we hear as counselor supervisors. Trainees often feel overwhelmed at the thought of finally putting all their education into practice. Feeling overwhelmed is natural and can actually be helpful in motivating you to be more effective as a counselor trainee. After all, it would probably be concerning if you weren't at least somewhat anxious about your first experiences working with a client.

Although anxiety is normal, there are steps that you can take to prepare for your field experience (see Think About It 1.1). Being proactive in developing good relationships with supervisors, coworkers, and peers can be especially helpful in ensuring a successful field experience. The intent of this text is to impart strategies for a successful field experience. This chapter will provide a brief overview of the field experiences (i.e., practicum and internship) and will serve as the foundation for the rest of the text. Now, let's dive right into the wonderful world of the field experience!

THINK ABOUT IT 1.1

As previously mentioned, many students experience anxiety when considering their first practicum experience. Reflect on the following questions:

1. *What am I most anxious about with regard to my field experience?*
2. *What am I most looking forward to with regard to my field experience?*

Now consider and reflect on your goals for field experience.

3. *How do you define a successful field experience?*
4. *What skills will you hope to develop during your field experience?*
5. *What steps can you take to ensure that you'll develop these skills?*

DIFFERENTIATING BETWEEN THE GOALS AND OBJECTIVES OF PRACTICUM AND INTERNSHIP

Practicum and internship are often referred to as the field experiences. Combining the two field experiences can often lead students to believe that these experiences are quite similar. However, it's important to note that practicum and internship serve very different functions in counselor training. In this section, we will review the differences between practicum and internship experiences.

Practicum

In most counselor education programs, practicum represents the first introduction to the field experiences. In some cases, students may complete practicum experiences *on-site* (e.g., at a university counseling center under faculty supervision) or *off-site* (e.g., at a community-based agency). Regardless of the location, the practicum experience is designed to serve as an introduction to the practice of working with clients. During practicum, you will learn how to complete client-related documentation (e.g., progress notes, individualized service plans) and become oriented to your practicum location and the field of counseling.

Orientation is ordinarily an overreaching goal of the practicum experience. Practicum is a time for you to learn about your site's policies and procedures, become familiar with standards of practice, and basically become acclimated to the site and your supervisor's expectations for your performance. Your practicum experience also provides you with the opportunity to observe client sessions. Many practicum students find this helpful, as it allows an opportunity to see other professionals interact with clients. Finally—at long last—practicum experiences allow students to counsel real live clients with real presenting concerns.

For students who are enrolled in a Council for Accreditation of Counseling and Related Educational Programs (CACREP) accredited program, all field experiences will follow the requirements set forth by the CACREP (2009) standards. These requirements include the provision of at least 100 practicum clock hours, 40 of which must include direct service (i.e., face-to-face contact) with clients. The other 60 hours can be accrued in a variety of ways, including researching treatments, reviewing site policies and procedures, and completing client documentation.

CACREP requirements also provide specific direction related to the provision of counselor trainee supervision. Later in this chapter we will discuss the purpose of supervision and how you can maximize the effectiveness of your interactions with your supervisor. For now, it is important to mention that CACREP standards require 1 hour per week of on-site supervision with an approved clinical supervisor. In addition to on-site supervision, you are also required to complete a minimum of 90 minutes of group supervision with an approved faculty member from your university. This weekly group supervision usually takes place in the classroom, with a faculty member providing group supervision to students who are enrolled in the practicum course for that particular term.

Internship

Internship generally represents a full foray into the counseling profession—living the life of the counselor. Most internship sites will require interns to complete all the responsibilities generally associated with the counseling position, such as documentation, billing, and productive counseling practice. In schools, interns will run groups and conduct classroom guidance activities. Students who are enrolled in a CACREP-accredited program will be required to complete at least 600 clock hours of internship work (1000 for clinical mental health counselors), which will typically occur over the course of two to three semesters or three to four quarters. Of these hours, at least 40% must occur in direct-service activities, whereas the remaining hours can result in nondirect care. Supervision requirements remain the same as in the practicum, with students receiving at least 1 hour of individual supervision on-site and an average of 90 minutes of group supervision weekly, usually provided in a group seminar on a university campus.

In internship, you will generally be assigned a caseload of clients. Caseloads will vary according to your setting; outpatient interns might be responsible for 5 to 10 clients at a time, whereas inpatient interns might be responsible for only 2 to 3 patients at a time. In schools, an intern will generally share responsibility for student cases from the supervising school counselor's caseload. It is important to have open discussions with your supervisor related to the number of active clients with whom you feel comfortable working. Whether enrolled in practicum or internship, field experiences will help you to hone your counseling skills with real clients and students who present with real life challenges.

VOICES FROM THE FIELD 1.1   Practicum Versus Internship, by Danielle Geigle, Doctoral-Level Counseling Intern

In my experience, the practicum, which may be thought of as a beginning framework for professional development, allows students to directly apply the knowledge they have obtained through the classroom into the workforce, yet with limited responsibility and expectations. The duties of the practicum trainee include observation, record-keeping and documentation, providing assistance to other counseling professionals, and in some cases the student may facilitate individual or group counseling. Naturally the duties of each practicum student will vary according to area of specialization and the supervisor's method for training. Regardless, the student is able to acquire professional competencies at the novice level.

Because many beginning counselors face anxiety and uncertainty during these beginning stages, perhaps the greatest advantage of the practicum experience is the acquisition of personal and professional confidence. From my experiences, many beginning counselors strive for perfection. This is problematic for two reasons: (a) the more they are focusing on perfection, the less they are focusing on their efforts and what they have already achieved; and (b) as humans, being perfect is impossible! My point is that you should use the practicum phase of your training to not only learn "the basics," but also to reflect on your own personal strengths and weaknesses before moving on toward internship.

The internship, which may be referred to as a more comprehensive experience that encompasses all aspects and responsibilities of the counseling role, is a time in which students should seek advancement in developing the competencies of applying professional skills and knowledge. Because at this level students are now transitioning from students to professionals and are preparing for licensure and/or certification, it is important to make the most of your internship experience; seek out extra opportunities for professional development, take the initiative to start new projects or to complete tasks, set personal goals for what you want to accomplish during and after the internship experience, and most important, remember why you entered the counseling field to begin with. Doing so will allow you to continue enjoying what you do and keep you motivated and enthusiastic while working in the "real world"!

VOICES FROM THE FIELD 1.2   My Internship Experience, by Rick Fawcett, Master's-Level Clinical Mental Health Counseling Intern

---

I remember sitting in my first internship counseling session. I was dressed nicely, seated in the proper SOLER position (sit Squarely, Open posture, Lean slightly, Eye contact, Relax), and I was absolutely terrified as I waited for the client to arrive. The room felt like a sauna, and I was sweating bullets as I waited for the session to begin. Would the client cry? Would I cry? Would my faculty and site supervisors cry when they saw my sessions? I felt like the session began and ended within the span of 5 minutes, and the client and I both survived tearlessly.

I became more comfortable as my internship progressed. My internship site, a residential addiction treatment facility, was intimidating at first. I had never worked with clients in the community, much less with clients who have such a critical issue to deal with, one that could actually kill them. The counselors and staff at the facility were very helpful. I asked a great number of questions, but they were always there to help. When in doubt, I asked the question, and they were always available with an answer, probably recalling their own days as an intern.

Humility and ambition have been very important in my internship. I had to have a lot of humility to realize exactly how much I did not know. My professors had done a great job preparing me, but there is no substitute for real experience. If I was unsure, I asked. Sometimes my hunch was right, but sometimes it was wrong, so it was best to ask. Ambition helped me to make my own opportunities, which was crucial. I could have sat in an office all day, but I sought out opportunities in co-counseling, group counseling, assessments, and getting involved in other areas. I asked for more responsibilities, and that made my experience more valuable and enriching.

HELPFUL THINGS TO KNOW AS YOU START YOUR FIELD PLACEMENT

Some on-site supervisors meet with students during the semester prior to their practicum or internship experience. The purpose of this meeting is to provide a brief overview of the agency, give the practicum student or intern a tour of the facility, and basically answer any questions. Often, students will want to know how they should prepare for the field experience. It is helpful to provide students with some information about the agency, assign some readings that will be helpful, and impart some general logistical information (e.g., dress code, where to park, how to gain access to the building). As you begin your field experience, think about your placement site and what information you will need to have to successfully acclimate to the work environment. One of the most important pieces of feedback we give interns is to treat their internship placement as a job. In other words, even though most practicum and internship placements are unpaid, it is important that interns devote the same level of effort and energy that they would to a paid position. Unfortunately, we have supervised interns who have viewed their internship as a time when they could amend their schedule to best suit their needs or call off their internship if something better came up. I (RH) once had an intern call me at 7 a.m. on a Tuesday to tell me that she had secured Dave Matthews Band tickets and would be unable to facilitate her scheduled group at 9 a.m. Obviously, this was not okay with me, and it is not representative of the professionalism an intern should possess in that stage of development as a counseling professional. In a nutshell, be professional, be on time, and don't treat your internship work any different than you would a real job.

So now that you know what *not* to do, let's focus on how you can make the most of your clinical experience. In the following sections, we will review some important components of a successful field experience. However, attending to seemingly minor details can also lead to a smooth field experience (see Personal Reflection 1.1).

There are many components to a successful internship. In the following sections, we will provide a brief overview of some of the major areas of practicum and internship work. However, it is important to note that all field placement sites are unique; thus, it's important to talk with your site supervisor about important policies, procedures, and expectations specific to your site.

PERSONAL REFLECTION 1.1

I completed my doctoral internship at a private, for-profit, psychiatric hospital that provided acute care to children and adolescents. Although the facility was new to me, I was a licensed counselor, and I had worked in the field for a couple of years. On my first day, a Friday, I went to the agency dressed in my typical business attire. I was surprised, however, to notice that all the staff were dressed rather casually with most—even the psychiatrists—wearing jeans and casual shirts. Although I was surprised, I noted that several area hospitals had adopted an informal dress code policy, and I assumed that perhaps this hospital had decided to follow suit. In retrospect, I should have checked with my supervisor; however, it felt trivial to ask him about dress code when I had so many other pressing issues to address during our brief meeting that first day. So, instead, I returned to my internship on Monday dressed in jeans and a sweater. You can imagine my surprise (and horror!) when I noticed that everyone was dressed in business attire. I quickly approached my supervisor to apologize for my casual attire and explain my mistaken assumption that the hospital endorsed a casual dress code policy. My supervisor chuckled and reminded me that my first day had been a Friday, which meant that the staff members were dressed for *casual Friday*. Naturally, I spent the rest of the day completely uncomfortable with my attire and wishing that I would have just asked my supervisor about appropriate dress during my first day. The moral of the story? *Nothing* is too insignificant to talk about with your supervisor. If you're confused, if you have a question, or if you need clarification, then you need to speak with your supervisor. Remember, your supervisor signed on to work with you knowing that you are new to the profession; thus, the supervisor expects that you will have a lot of questions about the internship process.

WORKING WITH A MULTIDISCIPLINARY TEAM

A multidisciplinary team, sometimes referred to by other names, such as a treatment team, consists of a group of professionals from various professional backgrounds working together in the interest of effective client care. Depending on your field placement, you may be expected to work closely with a multidisciplinary team for the purposes of integrated coordination of client care. Multidisciplinary teams may consist of counselors, physicians (e.g., general practitioners, psychiatrists, pain management specialists), nurses, psychologists, social workers, occupational therapists, rehabilitation specialists, vocational specialists, supportive case managers, and paraprofessional support staff. Again, the type of setting that you work in and the client population that you serve will generally dictate the variety of team members assigned to work with the client. For example, counseling interns at an addiction treatment facility work as part of a team with an addictionologist (i.e., MD with a specialty in addiction medicine), nurses, social workers, case managers, and family counseling specialists. Another example of coordination of client care might include working with a client who has an eating disorder. In this example, it would be important for the counselor to work with the client's primary care physician to ensure proper management of the physical effects of the eating disorder. It would also be necessary to coordinate meal planning services and weight restoration with a nutritional counselor. Last, psychiatric services might be needed to help alleviate comorbid symptoms of depression or anxiety.

Working as part of a multidisciplinary treatment team has both advantages and challenges. In terms of advantages, working as part of a treatment team allows for different perspectives, which can contribute to a better overall understanding of the client and the presenting concern. Conversely, treatment teams can often make it difficult for some professionals, especially new professionals, to feel comfortable contributing to the team and advocating for the client. As part of a multidisciplinary treatment team, you must be prepared for all team meetings and be able to effectively articulate your clients' needs (see Case Study 1.1). As noted earlier, your internship is an opportunity to begin to transition from the role of the student to the role of the professional counselor. It is important that you work to develop skills to effectively work and interact with other professionals.

CASE STUDY 1.1

Shannon

Imagine you are a counseling intern in an outpatient counseling center who has been assigned to work with Shannon, a client who has, in the past, demonstrated resistance to the counseling process and has been a frequent no-show for her counseling appointments. During a recent team meeting, Shannon's psychiatrist noted that she had missed an appointment with her last week, and the case manager also reported that Shannon has been late to several of her scheduled sessions. As Shannon's primary counselor, you know that her car recently broke down, and she's been having difficulty getting to her appointments on time; however, when she does attend her appointments with you, she seems motivated and willing to work on counseling goals. During the meeting, the case manager and psychiatrist wonder if perhaps Shannon should be discharged from treatment for noncompliance. Would you feel comfortable advocating for her continued involvement in treatment? Explain.

KNOWING AND MATCHING YOUR HELPER ASSETS WITH YOUR PREFERRED SETTING AND POPULATION

Often, interns will mention populations with which they *never* want to work. For example, one intern indicated that she never wanted to work with sexual offenders, another with people who abuse narcotics or other street drugs, and yet another with suicidal clients. Obviously, it's important to be aware of potential challenges that you might experience with various populations; however, it is equally important to work on developing skills and competencies to work with challenging client populations.

Many interns assume that they can simply refer clients with whom they do not wish to work. However, referring clients is not always a clear-cut process, and there are times when the referral might not be in the best interest of the client. Consider the case of Carlos (Case Study 1.2). It can be helpful to remember you are not expected to always *agree* with your clients' thoughts and behaviors. In fact, it is not necessary to be in agreement with your clients; it is, however, necessary to understand and validate the worldviews of clients.

CASE STUDY 1.2

Carlos

Carlos is a 46-year-old Hispanic male who presented for counseling services with depression. Carlos is initially quite guarded and hesitant to open up to a counselor. After meeting for several sessions with Carlos, you've developed a good rapport with him, and he begins to open up about his past. Carlos reports to you that he used to be addicted to heroin, and while in his active addiction, he sexually assaulted a female. Carlos expresses remorse and regret over the event and identifies the experience as contributing to his current feelings of depression. Imagine if, as the assigned counselor, you informed Carlos that you would be facilitating a referral to another provider because you refused to work with sexual offenders.

What effect might this notification have on Carlos?

Is it possible that such behavior would damage the trust Carlos had placed in his counselor and potentially impact his future relationships with treatment providers?

What would be a proper course for the intern to take?

Carlos's case illustrates that it is important for counselors to be prepared to deal with complex client cases and demonstrate compassion and good judgment, even under trying circumstances.

Although professional counselors are expected to demonstrate competency working with various populations, it is important to note that there are times when a referral might be necessary. A referral should be made when a counselor does not believe that she can effectively work with the client because she lacks experience or competence in working with the client's presenting problem *or* when the client might need a higher level of care than what the counselor offers. For example, an outpatient counselor working with a client on anxiety issues might need to refer that client if it becomes apparent that the client is abusing her prescription benzodiazepines and needs a medical detoxification. Another reason for a referral might be when the counselor experiences significant countertransference toward the client. Put simply, countertransference occurs when the client evokes unresolved, serious issues within the counselor. For example, a counselor may experience a strong unpleasant reaction toward a client. After further reflection, the counselor might notice that a client reminds him of his mother, and thus, he is experiencing a countertransference reaction toward the client due to unresolved issues in his own personal relationships. A final situation that might involve the need for referral would occur if there was a potential conflict of interest between counselor and client. For example, consider a scenario in which a counselor realizes that her new client is also her son's middle school teacher. In this situation, it would be best for the counselor to refer this client to another provider to avoid any potential dual relationship issues.

When a referral is necessary, the counselor should inform the client about the referral and provide a rationale for the referral. The counselor should also provide the client with the contact information for at least three other providers believed able to provide effective counseling services based on the client's presenting problem.

The bottom line is that practicum and internship provide opportunities to expand your horizons and provide services across a diverse range of clients and client issues in a protected environment under the supervision of qualified professional counselors. Also, it is important for all counselors to meet clients where they are and to develop therapeutic relationships with even the most challenging clients under very challenging circumstances. Finally, recent ethics and court cases have made it clear that counselors in training may not refer clients because of personal self-held beliefs that may constitute discrimination. For example, it is not acceptable to refuse to see a client or refer a client because they are a sexual minority or espouse religious beliefs different from one's own. Such discriminatory behavior is a clear violation of the *American Counseling Association (ACA) Code of Ethics*.

Hopefully, by this point in your professional development, you've considered areas that you consider personal strengths, as well as potential areas for growth or how to improve on demonstrated weaknesses. At this time, read Think About It 1.2, and consider what additional growing edges you need to develop.

THINK ABOUT IT 1.2

- *What personal and professional learning experiences have you had that will contribute to your field experience? What do you do well? What strengths have you developed that will be helpful in working with your clients, supervisor, and coworkers?*
- *What personal and professional learning experiences will you need to continue your development as a counseling professional? In what areas do you need to grow? What will be the most difficult part of working with your clients, supervisor, and coworkers?*

VOICES FROM THE FIELD 1.3   Maintaining Balance and Engaging in Self-Care, by Julie Lenyk, Doctoral-Level Counseling Intern

The process of being a counselor intern requires a lot of extra work both during scheduled hours and on your own personal time. During internship I learned that in the counseling profession, it is easy to become overinvolved with work and lose sight of taking care of your own

(Continued)

well-being. However, over time I have learned that to be an effective counselor, it is important to be invested in your work, but it is also important to find a balance between your professional and personal life.

When I first started my internship, I realized that it was not going to be easy. I had to put in a lot of work to develop my skills as a counselor and a professional in this field. I spent a lot of time during regular work hours and outside work researching, practicing interventions, and prepping for my sessions. I also spent a lot of time completing the necessary paperwork, including progress notes and treatment plans. I found that on most days I had to come to work early and leave work late just to maintain all my professional responsibilities.

What I didn't realize at the time was that along with developing my professional skills and my passion for counseling, I was also developing poor self-care habits. Most days I would not take a lunch break or take time off to take care of my basic needs. I also spent many weekends studying and thinking about my clients. This did not offer me much time to engage in fun activities or interact with family and friends. I often put these things to the side because I did not think they were necessary for me to become a better counselor.

What I have learned is that self-care not only affects your personal well-being, but that it also affects your professional well-being and your ability to be an effective counselor. Self-care is just as important as researching interventions and preparing for sessions. It may take some time to develop a balance between work and personal priorities, but it is important to start maintaining a balance even before internship begins.

I now practice better self-care and engage in activities that enhance my overall well-being. I take time in between sessions to laugh with a colleague, meditate for a few minutes, or just get something to eat. I also spend time outside work practicing yoga, spending time with family and friends, and walking my dogs. It is important to make time for yourself and find what works for you. Maintaining a balance between work and leisure and engaging in self-care are important factors to ensure your success as a counselor.

WHERE ARE YOU HEADING? CERTIFICATION, LICENSURE, AND EMPLOYMENT

It is important to be aware of the various professional associations, accrediting organizations, and credentialing bodies associated with the counseling profession. As a student, learning the difference between state licensure and state and national certification can be somewhat confusing. In the following section, we will provide an overview of the accreditation process, the importance of professional organizations, and credentialing processes.

The American Counseling Association

With over 55,000 members, the American Counseling Association (ACA) is the world's largest professional counselor association. The ACA provides numerous opportunities for professional growth, networking, and development of professional counselors, counseling students, and counselor educators. For example, the ACA produces two publications: the news magazine *Counseling Today* and the scholarly publication *Journal of Counseling & Development* (JCD), aimed at increasing the knowledge base of ACA members. Each year, the ACA also hosts a professional development conference with over 500 sessions that cover a multitude of counseling topics and are attended by about 4,000 counselors. Attendees can earn continuing education credits (CECs), develop competencies, and network with other professionals. This conference is also a great opportunity for job seekers to learn about employment opportunities across the country.

The ACA is composed of numerous divisions and branches. ACA has 20 divisions that focus on specific work setting and passion areas of counseling practice. These divisions have their own leadership teams (e.g., officers) and include the American College Counseling Association (ACCA), American Mental Health Counselors Association (AMHCA), American Rehabilitation Counselors Association (ARCA), American School Counselor Association (ASCA), Association for Adult Development and Aging (AADA), Association for Assessment in Counseling and Education (AACE), Association for Counselor Education and

Supervision (ACES), Association for Counselors and Educators in Government (ACEG), Association for Creativity in Counseling (ACC), Association for Child and Adolescent Counseling (ACAC), Association for Lesbian, Gay, Bisexual and Transgender Issues in Counseling (ALGBTIC), Association for Multicultural Counseling and Development (AMCD), Association for Specialists in Group Work (ASGW), Association for Spiritual, Ethical, and Religious Values in Counseling (ASERVIC), Counseling Association for Humanistic Education and Development (C-AHEAD), Counselors for Social Justice (CSJ), International Association of Addiction and Offender Counselors (IAAOC), International Association of Marriage and Family Counselors (IAMFC), National Career Development Association (NCDA), and National Employment Counseling Association (NECA). Membership in any of these 20 divisions usually includes access to members-only features, such as a division journal and access to workshops or other professional development opportunities. Each division has special rates available for student memberships, which allow students access to division privileges at a discounted rate.

For representation purposes, the ACA divides the United States into four regions (i.e., Midwest, North Atlantic, Southern, and Western), and each region is composed of branches from states and territories. The purpose of the branches is to provide a local connection for counselors. Many branches organize local workshops, trainings, advocacy days, and other ways to connect with counselor professionals.

An additional important counseling organization that counseling students and professionals should be aware of is Chi Sigma Iota International (CSI). CSI is a professional honor society that provides opportunities for professional development and leadership among counseling students and professionals. More information about CSI can be found at www.csi-net.org.

The National Board of Certified Counselors

The National Board of Certified Counselors (NBCC) is a national credentialing body dedicated to the advancement of the counseling profession. NBCC sets standards of national counselor certification and provides a standardized test to assess the knowledge components provided by training programs in a variety of counseling-related disciplines (i.e., addictions counseling, clinical mental health counseling, school counseling). Many counselors obtain the National Certified Counselor (NCC) credential to demonstrate that they meet a high standard of professional counselor preparation. For further information about NBCC and the NCC, see www.nbcc.org.

State Certification and Licensure

Credentialing provides counseling professionals with the opportunity to meet the rigorous standards associated with the profession and, thus, to receive a state certification to engage in the practice of counseling. State certification is commonly required for school counselors employed in a state's public schools. (Note: Some state boards of education call it "licensure," but it is equivalent to certification as defined here because it does not allow the school counselor to engage in independent practice for remuneration.) Professionals meeting specific standards (e.g., education, training, supervision) can apply for state certification through a designated certification board, usually housed within the state board of education.

Licensure represents another type of state credentialing that restricts the practice of professional counseling to laws and regulations constructed by individual states or territories (Erford, 2013). Counseling licensure laws exist in all 50 states and the District of Columbia, but vary substantially according to state laws and regulations. Licensure laws govern both the practice of counseling (i.e., scope of counseling work) as well as the title of the counselor. For example, in Ohio, there are two tiers of licensure: Professional Counselor (PC) and Independently Licensed Professional Clinical Counselor (PCC); whereas next door in New York, the title is Licensed Mental Health Counselor (LMHC), and it is Licensed Professional Counselor (LPC) in Pennsylvania and Licensed Clinical Professional Counselor (LCPC) in Maryland.

Regardless of the title, it is important for counselor interns to become familiar with their state's credentialing and licensing process during the fieldwork experience. In fact, some internship placements may require students to earn a trainee, or counselor trainee, designation from the state regulatory board. In this case, students often need to prepare several months before their actual internship to ensure that all paperwork is completed and registered with the state regulatory board.

All states also require potential licensees to pass one of the comprehensive examinations produced by the National Board of Certified Counselors (NBCC). In addition to completion of the exam, state regulatory boards also require a specific number of indirect and direct supervised client hours. Your internship requirements generally work toward fulfilling this requirement. One last state requirement involves a professional disclosure statement. Nearly all state licensure boards require that all licensed or registered individuals provide a written statement that contains, at minimum, the following information: (a) the counselor's name, title, business address, and phone number; (b) the counselor's formal education; (c) the counselor's scope of competence; and (d) a sentence explaining that the professional disclosure statement is required by the state regulatory board. An example template for a professional disclosure statement is provided in Table 1.1, and an exemplar is provided in Chapter 6 during a more extended discussion of consent.

TABLE 1.1 Professional disclosure statement

Jane Doe, Licensed Professional Counselor (C.000000)

Counseling Agency

1 Counseling Way

Anytown, OH 55555

(555) 555-5555

Formal Professional Education

Anytown University	M.S.Ed	2012-2014
	Mental Health Counseling	
Anytown University	B.A.	2008-2012
	Psychology	

Areas of Competence

- Child, Adolescent, and Adult Counseling
- Mental Health Counseling
- Group Counseling
- Addictions Counseling
- Diagnosis and Treatment of Mental and Emotional Disorders under the Supervision of Dr. Carl Counselor (E.00000)

Ethical Standards

I subscribe to the code of ethics of the American Counseling Association (ACA). Copies are available and will be discussed upon request, or you may access the ACA Code of Ethics listed on the ACA Web page: www.counseling.org.

Limits of Confidentiality

All information in counseling will be treated as confidential except for the instances when the client becomes a serious threat to self (for example, suicidal) or others (for example, homicidal) or when mandated by law (for example, reporting of child abuse or neglect).

This information is required by the Ohio Counselor, Social Worker and Marriage and Family Therapist Board, which regulates all licensed and registered counselors and social workers.

The State of Ohio Counselor, Social Worker, and Marriage and Family Therapist Board

77 South High Street, 16th Floor

Columbus, OH 43215-6180

(614) 466-0912; www.cswmft.ohio.gov

One last point of importance to mention as you consider your future work as a professional counselor is license reciprocity. Reciprocity, or portability, refers to the acceptance of one's licensure credentials by regulatory boards in multiple states; currently, portability does not exist, but ACA, the American Association of State Counseling Boards (AASCB), and about 30 other counseling organizations are working to make it happen (Kaplan & Gladding, 2011). In other words, if you move from one state to another, it is possible that your license may not automatically be recognized in another state. In those situations, you would be required to meet any additional requirements, which could include additional course work or field experience hours. If you are considering moving after graduation, it can be very helpful to become familiar with licensure requirements for the state in which you wish to live. Now complete Self-Assessment Activity 1.1.

SELF-ASSESSMENT ACTIVITY 1.1 DEFINING THE COUNSELING PROFESSION

"So, you're kind of like a psychologist?" If I had a nickel for every time someone asked me that, I would have at least 75 cents! Articulating the differences between the counseling profession and other helping professions can be difficult. However, a couple of notable elements differentiate the counseling profession. Counseling is based on a strengths-oriented approach. In other words, counselors see clients as capable of making changes within their life. We use strengths-based approaches to help empower client change. "Counseling is a professional relationship that empowers diverse individuals, families, and groups to accomplish mental health, wellness, education, and career goals" (ACA, 2011). Consider this definition of counseling. What are your thoughts about the definition? Does it align with your ideas about the role of the counseling professional? Does anything need to be added to the definition?

In addition to the preceding definition, the committee *20/20: A Vision for the Future of Counseling* identified the following principles for unifying and strengthening the profession:

A. Sharing a common professional identity is critical for counselors.
B. Presenting ourselves as a unified profession has multiple benefits.
C. Working together to improve the public perception of counseling and to advocate for professional issues will strengthen the profession.
D. Creating a portability system of licensure will benefit counselors and strengthen the counseling profession.
E. Expanding and promoting our research base is essential to the efficacy of professional counselors and to the public perception of the profession.
F. Focusing on students and prospective students is necessary to ensure the ongoing health of the counseling profession.
G. Promoting client welfare and advocating for the populations we serve is a primary focus of the counseling profession (Kaplan & Gladding, 2011).

As you consider beginning your work as a counselor trainee, consider how you will incorporate the previously listed goals into your practice. If possible, try to make space for advocacy activities as part of your internship. For example, attend your state branch counseling association's annual state legislation day. This opportunity, sponsored by your local branch of ACA, allows counselors and counseling students the opportunity to work with the branch's legislative consultant to develop advocacy skills. This can be a great activity to complete during your internship experience, as it helps provide you with skills to advocate for clients.

VOICES FROM THE FIELD 1.4   Having Realistic Expectations, by Stephanie A. Fellenger, Master's-Level Counseling Intern

Before I started my internship, I had an ideal in my mind of how it would go. All my clients would love me, I would be able to help everyone I worked with, and I would leave with a feeling of

(Continued)

accomplishment every day. In reality, I've come to realize the good days are fantastic, and the bad days are truly terrible. Luckily, each day is a new day and a chance to start fresh.

Literally every worst-case scenario I could conjure in my mind about working in residential drug and alcohol treatment has happened during my year of internship. The short list includes having to negatively discharge a client from treatment, learning that a previous client overdosed and was found dead, and having to tell a client that her significant other lost his own battle with addiction. I have also had a client tell me she didn't want to work with me anymore, and I assessed a client who was having such strong suicidal ideation she had to be taken to the hospital via ambulance. These experiences are enough to cause distress for a seasoned counselor, let alone an intern.

It was unreasonable to assume that every day at my internship site would be wonderful or that I could make progress with every client. If I've learned nothing else, it is that counseling is a complicated process, with the counselor being only a fraction of the equation that leads to success for a client. Addiction counseling is particularly challenging because the clients are dealing with a multitude of problems at once, but at the same time, there is an opportunity to make a very real difference in a person's life in this field. None of that can happen without the clinician first taking the proper steps to safeguard his or her own well-being.

These experiences have helped me recognize some areas where I need to take better care of myself to be effective for my clients. Whether it's taking a quick break to grab some fresh air, closing my eyes for a few moments at my desk, or putting a "Do not disturb" sign on my door to catch up on paperwork, I've learned how important it is to first take care of myself, or I will have nothing to offer my clients. Every day won't be great, but every day will present opportunities to learn and grow, both personally and professionally.

VOICES FROM THE FIELD 1.5   Identifying Your Strengths and Areas in Need of Improvement, by Phillip Isco, Master's-Level Counseling Intern

"You will be evaluated." This sentence is perhaps the most frightening collection of words that could be said to an intern or even the most seasoned of counselors. Outside the phrase "I'm suicidal," nothing raises anxiety quite like the knowledge that your counseling skills will be evaluated in front of professors, peers, and supervisors. As I began my internship, I found myself terrified of the collection of forms used to evaluate graduate-level counseling students. These forms are full of boxes that need to be checked, Likert-type scales that need to be filled out, and the ever important "Is there any reason why you would not consider this person for licensure?" question.

In addition to being evaluated, I was regularly asked, "What do you feel that you do well?" and "What do you feel you could have done better?" I always struggled with this question in my internship, mainly because I felt I was doing everything wrong. I wasn't able to "fix" my client during my session? There is a weakness. A client is being resistant during session? That is all my fault. I asked too many close-ended questions? Time for a career change; maybe I should become an accountant.

Early in my internship, I found that it was easy to ignore strengths that I had been using all along. The ability to use humor in session and my willingness to accept feedback were both strengths that I had been ignoring. I found that "strengths" do not necessarily equate to "operating out of a theoretical orientation" or "an ability to complete an assessment on the first try." Instead, they could be qualities that I already possessed that assisted me in helping my clients feel more comfortable and allowed me to positively interact with my fellow colleagues.

As I progressed through my internship, I realized that "areas in need of improvement" do not equate to me being a "bad counselor." I quickly learned that there is no such thing as a "perfect counselor," and identifying areas in need of improvement and strengths would contribute to personal and professional development. It is not possible, nor is it realistic, to expect to know everything on the first day. Oftentimes I found myself being overly critical because a session did not go as well as I would have liked. It is important to recognize that much like clients, even counselors have a bad day. Sometimes you aren't "on your game," and it is easy to view everything as a weakness. I found that it is completely reasonable to ask for help when needed and that having areas in which I needed to improve was simply part of learning how to be an effective counselor.

Summary

The field experience is a time to begin practicing your skills, while under supervision, with the intent of learning and growing from your experiences. If you expect to be perfect as a counselor trainee, then you will likely be disappointed to learn that we all have areas in which to grow. The field experience is the perfect time to seek supervision, guidance, and support from your site-based supervisor and your faculty supervisor. This initial chapter differentiated between practicum, an initial experience in which one observes and works to develop basic counseling skills, and the internship experience, in which the intern dives deep into the counseling role and lives the life of the professional counselor. We discussed helpful orientation information such as working in multidisciplinary teams and matching your assets with preferred client populations and sites. Multiple opportunities were provided for self-reflection and self-assessment to identify personal strengths and areas of challenge.

Finally, we reviewed the services provided by, and importance of, professional counseling organizations like the American Counseling Association, its divisions and branches, and Chi Sigma Iota, the international counseling honorary society. We encourage all professional counselors to obtain the National Certified Counselor (NCC) credential offered by the National Board for Certified Counselors (NBCC), as well as the relevant state certification or licensure to attain and maintain employment opportunities as a professional counselor—to take your rightful place as a member of the counseling profession.

CHAPTER 2

The Supervision Process

BY CATHERINE Y. CHANG, CAROLINE O'HARA, AND LINDY K. PARKER

PREVIEW

The supervision process is complicated and involves various individuals (i.e., supervisor, supervisee, and client) and organizations (i.e., the university and the practicum/internship agency or school) and transpires through various stages. In this chapter, we explore supervision processes, the various roles you will hold as you begin your practicum–internship sequence, and also what you can expect from your on-site and university supervisors. We will also cover the development of positive supervision relationships and learning goals, as well as the differences between supervision and counseling. In addition, we will discuss barriers to effective supervision, different theoretical approaches, and ways of making case presentations. Throughout this chapter, we will provide several self-assessment activities to help you identify your strengths, growing edges, needs, and goals.

YOUR ROLES AS A CLINICIAN AND A SUPERVISEE: WHERE THE STUDENT AND PROFESSIONAL ALIGN

Entering practicum and internship is an exciting time for any professional counseling student. This experience marks the beginning of your transition from didactic learning in the classroom to supervised experience with real clients. One shift includes the addition and integration of field learning into your classroom learning. You will be shifting from learning *what* and *why* to learning *how*. You will also experience role shifts from being exclusively a student to becoming a clinician (a student–intern) and supervisee. As you start your clinical experience, consider the questions in Think About It 2.1.

As a counseling practicum student or intern, you may counsel individuals, couples, families, or groups in several settings. Regardless of where you are working as an intern (e.g., school, hospital, community health center, correctional facility, private practice, college counseling center), you will be employing your counseling skills and using the knowledge you have gained from your program of study. It is common for students entering the field to feel excited about finally being able to apply all that they have learned!

During practicum and internship, you will learn and gain experience as you counsel clients in a real-world setting under the supervision of established professionals. To understand what this means, we will begin by examining some important terms.

Supervision has been defined by Bernard and Goodyear (2009) as

an intervention provided by a more senior member of a profession to a more junior member or members of that same profession. This relationship is evaluative and hierarchical, extends over time, and has the simultaneous purposes of enhancing the professional functioning of the more junior person(s); monitoring the quality of professional services offered to the clients that she, he, or they see; and serving as a gatekeeper for those who are to enter the particular profession. (p. 7)

THINK ABOUT IT 2.1

As you begin your clinical training, reflect on the following questions:

1. *What are you most excited about?*
2. *What are your greatest fears about working with a client?*
3. *What client population do you think you will have the most difficult time counseling?*

Supervision formats include individual, triadic, or group sessions (Association for Counselor Education and Supervision [ACES], 2011; Gillam & Baltimore, 2010). It is common for interns to participate in both individual and group supervision at their university and both individual and group supervision on-site.

Supervisors are generally more experienced professionals who guide and evaluate other, often newer, professionals in their counseling work. Supervisors may be located on-site and/or at the student's university. Commonly, supervisors are professionals in the same field as their supervisees; however, many supervisors you will encounter are in other mental health fields (e.g., psychology, social work). Supervisors will work with you to ensure client welfare and facilitate your development as a professional counselor.

Supervisees are those individuals who participate in supervision and are evaluated by one or more supervisors. Supervisees may include both students who are in graduate training programs and individuals who have finished graduate studies (Bernard & Goodyear, 2009). Often, counselors who have finished their program of study are in supervision as they seek licensure.

Your Role as a Counseling Practicum Student and Intern

As a counseling practicum student and intern, your role as a clinician involves the practice of professional counseling with clientele while under supervision at your university and on-site. Interns may engage in many facets of counseling including, but not limited to, (a) conducting intake or follow-up assessments; (b) providing group, individual, couples, and family counseling; (c) documenting case notes; (e) attending in-services and treatment team meetings; and (f) providing psychoeducational and outreach workshops. In this role, counseling students gain experience and increase competence as they engage in behaviors of professional counselors in the field.

YOUR ROLE AS A SUPERVISEE.   In addition to your counseling activities, you will participate in regular supervision. As a supervisee, you will use supervision to explore client concerns and issues relating to your own development. In supervision, supervisees discuss their caseload of clients, provide evidence of performance in sessions (commonly by audio or video recordings or self-report), and process supervisor feedback (Bernard & Goodyear, 2009). Commonly, individual and triadic supervision sessions are about 1 hour long, and group supervision sessions are about 2 hours long.

A common expectation, especially during group supervision, is for supervisees to conduct case presentations about their clientele. A case presentation is more than just playing a section of a counseling session recording and processing feedback. Case presentations frequently involve a discussion of client demographics and characteristics, goals, interventions, assessment tools, the impact of client and counselor culture, conceptualization, ethical concerns, and theoretical orientation. We will discuss case presentations more fully later in this chapter.

On-Site Supervision and Your Site Supervisor's Role

The main role of the on-site supervisor is to ensure client welfare and attend to the needs and policies of the site. In this capacity, the site and the on-site supervisor are primarily concerned with service delivery (Bernard & Goodyear, 2009). In other words, the main goal of the site is the quantity and quality of services offered to the population they serve. The on-site supervisor typically has administrative and managerial responsibilities in addition to client care and is often classified as an **administrative supervisor**. For example, on-site supervisors may also deal with fiscal concerns of the site, personnel issues, and site regulations. Commonly, on-site supervisors are case managers, program coordinators, or other professionals in leadership positions.

It is important to remember that practicum students and interns are guests of their sites and should adhere to all site protocols. Sites expect that interns will comply with the rules and regulations of the site and follow standards for client care, crisis management, termination of services, and other situations. It is the responsibility of the site and site supervisor to provide the practicum student or intern with an orientation and any training materials regarding expectations, site policies and procedures, and emergency/crisis protocols (Bernard & Goodyear, 2009). In addition, sites and on-site supervisors typically expect that practicum students and interns will perform their duties during the site's normal hours of operation. Many universities have periods of time where classes are not held. However, do not expect that your site will mirror your university semester schedule. In fact, taking weeks away from your counseling work (e.g., during university breaks) could raise ethical concerns. If you do not see your clients for an extended period of time, this may be considered abandonment. Furthermore, your site may not be aware of or sympathetic to additional pressures on you from your university (e.g., exam weeks).

University Supervision and What You Can Expect

As previously discussed, university supervision and on-site supervision have areas of overlap and differences. Whereas on-site supervisors are primarily concerned with site needs (service delivery) and client care, university supervisors are primarily concerned with the education and skill development of the student (Bernard & Goodyear, 2009). University supervisors usually hold the role of a **clinical supervisor**. Thus, they are primarily focused on your growth and development as a professional counselor as well as the client care you provide. University supervisors are responsible for developing evaluation standards and disclosing to the student the ways in which grades are assessed.

As with any professional endeavor, it is wise to keep accurate, up-to-date, and succinct records summarizing your supervision sessions. Your university supervisor may prompt you to provide this information, but you should keep careful records regardless of which type of supervisor directs you to do so. Licensure boards may require you and your supervisor(s) to provide documentation of the dates, hours, and brief synopses of your supervision for you to obtain licensure. It is also possible that professional agencies may audit your records and request such documentation throughout your career. Please refer to Chapter 4 for more information on record keeping.

It is important that you know that university supervisors will not **cross-supervise**. This means that, generally, they will not tell you to do something that goes against the direction of your site supervisor or the policies of your site. The idea here is that university supervisors do not want to "step on anyone's toes" at the site, and vice versa. They do not want to tell on-site supervisors how to do their jobs. However, it is possible that a situation may arise in which there is an ethical or legal disagreement between supervisors or an emergency situation that requires action (see Think About It 2.2). If these concerns are unresolvable or urgent, your university supervisor may intervene.

For example, supervisors may disagree about mandated reporting and breaking confidentiality regarding a certain client. Perhaps the on-site supervisor has explored the issue with the supervisee and does not think reporting is necessary, but after exploring the issue with the supervisee, the university supervisor does think reporting is necessary. If we take this example further, then the university supervisor will weigh the concerns of the client, the supervisee, the site, and ethical and legal codes. If the university supervisor deems it necessary to report, he or she will aid the supervisee in how to do this, even though the on-site supervisor did not deem it necessary. This is an instance in which a university supervisor would be going against the on-site supervisor. Hopefully, these occasions are rare.

THINK ABOUT IT 2.2

As previously mentioned, during the course of your internship, you will likely have multiple individual and group supervision sessions each week. As a result, it is also likely that you will discuss some of your clients in multiple supervision settings.

- *What happens if one supervisor makes one suggestion and a different supervisor makes another suggestion?*
- *What if you receive feedback from your university group supervision that you could develop more of a discussion about the impact of cultural differences between you and a particular client, and yet, you receive feedback from your on-site group supervision that you are on just the right trajectory with this same client?*
- *How do you proceed?*

Part of the answer may depend on your theoretical orientation, of course. However, one method of approaching this conundrum is to discuss the differences in feedback with all parties involved before proceeding with your client. On the other hand, this may take some time, and it may be that you have another appointment scheduled with this client before you are able to discuss all feedback with all parties. In general, it is a good idea to (at the minimum) discuss any changes you intend to make in your approach with clients with your on-site supervisor before doing so.

University supervisors may facilitate discussions about many topics, such as your reactions to clients, your use of basic counseling skills, case conceptualizations, professional identity, and your theoretical orientation. University professors will want to observe you with a wide variety of clients and across a wide range of activities. For example, if you have been counseling female clients and have had limited opportunities to counsel male clients, your university supervisor may encourage you to obtain more diversity in your clientele. Or if you have had the opportunity to counsel clients with a high socioeconomic status (SES), can you also have the opportunity to counsel clients with limited financial means? Also, your supervisor will need to observe you demonstrating proficiency at different stages in the counseling process. In other words, how do you typically open an initial session, how do you work with clients after several sessions, and how do you terminate with clients? These are examples of the types of objectives that will contribute to your evaluations and grades.

Developing Positive Relationships with Your Supervisors

As a professional counselor, part of your training includes the development of interpersonal skills. These skills, such as active listening, reflecting, and clarifying, can help you build relationships in many spheres of your life, including supervision. In general, the characteristics expected of a competent professional counselor can also be applied to develop a positive **supervisory alliance** (working alliance with your supervisor), such as the ability to manage conflict, genuineness, and respect (Bernard & Goodyear, 2009; Borders & Brown, 2005). In addition, several other factors contribute to the supervisory alliance: supervisee attachment style, shame avoidance, anxiety level, need to feel and appear competent, and transference (directed toward the supervisor; Bernard & Goodyear, 2009).

To develop positive relationships with your supervisors, it is helpful to know what they need and expect (e.g., attending weekly treatment team meetings, providing two tapes per week for review). Conversely, it is also important for your supervisors to know what you need and expect (e.g., ability to maintain the required number of clinical hours, explanation of site crisis protocols). Thus, one of the paramount goals of a positive relationship is explaining, clarifying, and understanding expectations from the beginning and throughout your journey through practicum and internship. In many ways, this parallels principles of informed consent. However, your supervisor should ideally be providing information and asking questions to help initiate and facilitate this process, especially because you are new to counseling and supervision.

Haynes, Corey, and Moulton (2003) reported on a study that gathered information from supervisors regarding supervisee characteristics that facilitated successful supervision experiences. Several factors emerged, with the supervisee's desire to learn, grow, and improve being rated as the most helpful and important. Other ideal factors included nondefensiveness, openness, appropriate knowledge and clinical skills, preparedness, initiative, and the willingness to take risks. Conversely, participants reported that poorer supervisory alliances and outcomes resulted with supervisees who exhibited the opposite of these traits.

OPENNESS ABOUT CONCERNS, MISSTEPS, AND FEEDBACK.   One of the foundations of a positive supervision relationship is to share your concerns and missteps as early and often as possible. Even in a trusting environment, this is easier said than done. In other words, if you have a question on how to proceed or how to make a decision about a certain client, ask your supervisor early. If you wait several days or weeks, the situation may become more difficult to resolve and may place additional stress on you, your clients, your supervisor, and your site. Supervisors know that you are learning, and they are there to support you in your work. Use their expertise and perspectives.

Giving and receiving feedback are also key elements in building and maintaining a positive supervisory relationship (see Personal Reflection 2.1). In essence, feedback is communication that can affirm something done well or critique something that could have been done differently. Remember that although you will be receiving regular feedback from your supervisors, you also can and should provide feedback to them as well. According to Ivey, Ivey, and Zalaquett (2010), feedback provides information about how someone perceives another person. Ideally, effective feedback includes the following guidelines: (a) the receiver should be in charge, (b) feedback should focus on strengths and positive assets, (c) the topic should be something the receiver can change, (d) feedback should include concrete and specific ideas, (e) feedback should be nonjudgmental, (f) present tense feedback is ideal, and (g) feedback should be concise. After feedback is offered, the sender and receiver should confirm that they accurately understand each other. See also the later section entitled, Barriers to Supervision, which explores feedback processes in supervision.

PERSONAL REFLECTION 2.1

When I was a young child, I can recall some of my mother's guidance around household stains and spills. She would tell me that she would vastly prefer if I would tell her early rather than hide something until later. I remember her reassuring me that she would not be angry with me, but that it would be easier to clean a mess when it was freshly made than after it had set. She even demonstrated her claim by cleaning something just after a spill and showing me how easy it was. She contrasted this with stains that would not clean because they were not attended to quickly. Thus, through her explanation, demonstration, and reassurance, I felt confident that I could inform her if I made a mess without feeling guilty or fearful. As I hope you can tell, this story represents a parallel with supervision. Although your supervisors are not your parents or caregivers, they are in a position to guide and support you if you make a misstep or if something does not feel right. As with my childhood lessons, I urge you to inform your supervisors early if anything might need a quick spot clean.

SUPERVISEE RESPONSIBILITIES.   Another major aspect of building positive supervision relationships is to fulfill your responsibilities as a supervisee. Some of these responsibilities include being prepared for supervision sessions, actively engaging in self-reflection and increasing your self-awareness, identifying/developing your goals and asking for what you need, and completing tasks and commitments in a timely fashion. As with any professional meeting, supervisors expect that you will come prepared with specific questions or concerns to address and not waste time trying to think of something to talk about after you begin your session (Haynes et al., 2003). One way to avoid this is to keep a notebook, binder, or electronic file that can store notes, questions, and reflections that you have for supervision. This could include anything related to your direct work with clients or even the field of professional counseling. For instance, if your client asks you a question you do not know how to answer, you could document this in your list of questions or reflections to be ready to address during your next supervision session. You could also discuss reactions you are having to your clients, theory and technique questions, self-care strategies (for some ideas, see Think About It 2.3), roadblocks you are experiencing, and ways to advocate for clients and the counseling profession. Truly, supervision is what you make of it, and the possibilities are endless.

THINK ABOUT IT 2.3

As professional counselors, we discuss the importance of self-care as a central part of professional practice. But what does this abstract term really mean when self-care can vary so much from person to person? When professional counselors are able to engage in self-care, we have observed what an asset it can be in promoting wellness among counselors and clients alike. We have also witnessed, unfortunately, when self-care is pushed aside for various internal or external reasons to the detriment of the counselor and client. So what does all this mean? In the spirit of our prevention-oriented wellness model, we suggest that you (ahead of time) consider:

1. *What does self-care represent to you?*
2. *What does self-care specifically look like for you?*
3. *What are the benefits and obstacles to self-care?*
4. *What happens when you are not able to engage in self-care?*

Some examples might include setting boundaries around work; making time for regular eating, sleeping, and exercising; and noticing the physical aches and pains you carry in your body when you are stressed. Try to generate concrete examples about thoughts, feelings, behaviors, and circumstances/contextual factors. After considering your specifics, discuss your reflections with other students, instructors, supervisors, and loved ones to develop ideas about how to strengthen your self-care practices. Once you have a solid awareness and foundation, you will be able to rely on this existing knowledge when you are being tested during your practicum and internship experiences.

Another way to build positive relationships with your supervisor is by actively engaging in self-reflection and discussions to increase your self-awareness (Carroll & Holloway, 1999). It may be helpful to ask yourself what you hope and expect from supervision. Do you expect your supervisor to have "all the answers," and is this what you prefer? What do you know about yourself as a multicultural being (e.g., sexual identity, ability status, religious affiliation, race) and how might this affect your work with your supervisor(s) and your clients? Consider how you would like to assess and monitor your supervision relationship. It also may be helpful to reflect on how you approach, manage, and resolve interpersonal conflict (Bernard & Goodyear, 2009).

An additional aspect of fulfilling your responsibilities as a supervisee includes identifying and developing your goals and asking for what you need. This may be easier or more difficult, depending on a number of factors such as interpersonal style, personality, topic, nature of your supervision relationship, and contextual factors such as race and gender (Bernard & Goodyear, 2009). One way to take a preventative approach is to communicate clearly your program's requirements and your particular goals in your first interview at your site or your first meeting with your on-site supervisor. At that time, it is important and appropriate to explain the requirements of your program (e.g., how many direct service hours you need each semester) and your specific objectives and interests (e.g., equal experience with individuals and groups, but no interest in couples or children). This way, if you are into your third week at your site and still have not seen any individual clients, you could refer back to the initial conversation to prompt your supervisor so that he or she can work toward making changes to the clients assigned to you. Taking this example further, you may also discover that you want to work with couples, and so you will need to bring this to your supervisor's attention to see what changes might be made and what additional opportunities you may have at your site. Remember, it may or may not be possible for you and your supervisor to work out different arrangements, but it will help your supervisory relationship if you can be aware of your needs and communicate them clearly (and often).

By completing tasks and commitments quickly, regularly, and efficiently, you also build a positive relationship with your supervisor. When your site assigns you clients, when you meet with clients, and when you document your sessions, your on-site supervisor must "sign off" on your activities. For instance, during staff meetings, your supervisor might need to know the status of each of your clients before assigning you additional clients. If you fall behind on your documentation, it is difficult for your supervisor to have the information needed to make decisions about altering your case load. Not only can this be a nuisance for your supervisor to have to follow up with you, but it may be a legal, ethical, or site protocol violation to be slow or late in providing documentation. For these reasons, supervisees should complete paperwork and case notes on a regular basis. One suggestion is to designate a specific time slot daily or weekly to attend to the administrative parts of professional counseling. If you build this time into your schedule, you are more likely to complete paperwork in a consistent and timely fashion.

Developing Learning Goals with Your Supervisors

Initially, your goals for supervision may be broad and include things like becoming a competent counselor, developing autonomy, and being properly prepared for your future career as a counselor (Bernard, 1979; Morgan & Sprenkle, 2007). As supervision progresses and you become more self-aware of your own development as a counselor, you will likely add more specific goals and objectives to your list. Your university and on-site supervisors may also be able to suggest some learning goals for you.

Learning goals help to focus the efforts of your own work and development. They can also focus the content of the supervision session. For example, a supervisor who knows the supervisee has a goal of becoming more multiculturally competent will likely provide extra psychoeducational material relating to diverse cultures and multicultural counseling. The supervisor may even become acutely attuned to any biases the supervisee might display, and the supervisor can point those out to the supervisee as areas for potential growth.

Borders and Brown (2005) suggested creating a separate contract with your supervisors that is composed entirely of your stated learning goals (see Self-Assessment Activity 2.1). Sharing your stated goals and collaborating with your supervisors on any possible additions to the goal contract can help your supervisors get to know you more and likewise help you to better know your supervisor. This two-way interaction enriches the supervision relationship, which in turn leads to an enhanced supervision experience.

SELF-ASSESSMENT ACTIVITY 2.1 LEARNING GOALS

Learning goals are the agreement between the supervisor and supervisee and help focus the supervision sessions. Learning goals can include specific clinical interventions or techniques, relationship issues, cognitive skills related to conducting counseling, self-awareness, and so on. List three to five learning goals that you have for your supervision experience.

Supervision Versus Counseling

During supervision, you may notice your supervisor using techniques that look similar to the counseling skills you have recently acquired. You may also find the supervision experience feels therapeutic at times. Still, it should be clear that supervision is not intended to be personal counseling for supervisees. For example, consider the situation in Think About It 2.4. Although supervisees may find that personal issues arise during their practicum and internship sequence, a supervisor is only to address those issues that influence the supervisee's work with clients (Bernard & Goodyear, 2009). Anything beyond that, where a supervisor begins to act as the supervisee's personal counselor, is an ethical violation (Borders & Brown, 2005). That being said, supervisees in need of their own professional counseling are encouraged to seek that counseling from their university counseling center or another qualified professional in the field.

THINK ABOUT IT 2.4

Imagine you are a supervisee dealing with the loss of your mother. Your mother has been ill for some time, so her death was not unexpected, yet you are finding yourself having a difficult time dealing with her death. As a part of your clinical experience, you find your-self working with many women who remind you of your mother. You openly discuss your grieving process and your reactions to your clients with your supervisor.

- *How appropriate is it for your supervisor to assist you in your grieving process?*
- *How much time should the supervisor spend in discussing your reactions to your female clients?*
- *How receptive would you be to your supervisor referring you to a counselor to assist in your grieving?*

Bernard and Goodyear (2009) stated that evaluating supervisees is the most important difference between supervision and professional counseling. Unlike professional counseling, where most counselors refrain from evaluating their clients, evaluation of a supervisee is required. And although this evaluation can include some of the supervisee's stated goals, it is largely based on criteria outlined by professional standards. Moreover, practicum and internship supervision is generally conducted within a prescribed time frame, during which supervisees must achieve the required objectives and meet the professional standards; counseling, on the other hand, usually progresses at the client's pace (Gallon, 2002). Finally, the option to enter supervision is usually not optional, per se, whereas the decision to enter counseling usually is. To achieve counseling career goals, a supervisee should be required to receive supervision during training, and supervisors are often assigned to supervisees at the outset of their supervision process (Bernard & Goodyear, 2009). In other cases, supervisees may have some freedom in choosing a supervisor (see Personal Reflection 2.2).

PERSONAL REFLECTION 2.2

Less than a year into my counselor training program, my cohort, including myself, was required to choose which supervisor we would have for our practicum internship experience. We made this choice by registering for that supervisor's course section of practicum internship. Although some of my cohort members registered for the section offered at the most convenient time, a mentor of mine advised me against this common mistake. Instead, before registration began, I reviewed the curriculum vitae of the available supervisors. I also attended my university's Chi Sigma Iota chapter meetings with the objective of speaking to more advanced students in the program and soliciting their feedback on the potential supervisors. I narrowed down the list of possible fits with my chosen client population and interests, and I even made appointments with some of those potential supervisors. Being proactive and investing this time was invaluable to my training, as it informed my choice and helped create a supervision experience that was extremely positive for me.

Barriers to Effective Supervision

When done well, supervision can facilitate one of the most rewarding and enjoyable parts of your counselor training program. There are, however, numerous potential barriers to effective supervision that can originate from multiple sources (e.g., the supervisee, the supervisor, the site), despite each entity having only the best intentions. Being mindful of some of the common barriers is the first step toward preventing them and puts you on a path toward your best potential supervision experience.

One of the most straightforward barriers is lacking competence, from either the supervisee or the supervisor or both. Although it is nearly impossible for a supervisor to be knowledgeable about every clinical situation and possible client population, a supervisor should be competent and experienced in the area in which his or her direct supervisee is working (ACES, 2011). All efforts should be made to remedy mismatched supervisees and supervisors. To facilitate this, supervisees should gather as much information about their field placement as possible so that a fully informed match can be made with available supervisors.

Also, supervisors should be trained and should have achieved competence in the skill of supervision itself in advance of taking on a supervisee of their own. Before entering into a supervision relationship, prudent supervisees will seek assurance that their potential supervisor is both trained in supervision, as well as competent in his or her chosen clinical population. Still, even with adequate planning and preparation, supervisees may find themselves in negative supervision relationships, either with their university supervisor or site supervisor. Although these situations do appear to be rare, they can be stressful and confusing for the supervisee (Nelson & Friedlander, 2001). Some supervisees have had some success in resolving these conflicts in supervision by discussing them directly with their supervisor. Many supervisees use their own coping strategies to navigate and endure these supervision conflicts and also seek the support of peers and partners (Baird, 2010; Nelson & Friedlander, 2001). Other supervisees have had to involve a neutral third party—perhaps a site director or university clinical internship coordinator or faculty member—to facilitate a change in supervisor or internship placement (Baird, 2010). Of course, each situation is different and should be handled with thoughtful care. In all cases of a suspected ethical violation by a supervisor, though, a supervisee should consult with a trusted faculty member and/or senior staff member at his or her site on the appropriate reporting policies and procedures. Although being in a negative supervision relationship can be discouraging, supervisees should be reminded that the field facilitates multiple supervision relationships and opportunities—so hopefully one problematic supervisor will be only one among many positive supervisors a supervisee (and ultimately novice professional counselor) will encounter and learn from within their counseling career.

It is unreasonable to expect a supervisor to be competent in every type of clinical population and counseling setting (see Personal Reflection 2.3). It is equally unreasonable to expect a supervisee to be able to deliver best counseling practice to their chosen population at the start of their practicum and internship experience. There would be no need for supervision if this were the case. Throughout the practicum and internship experiences, you will undoubtedly be confronted with gaps in your counseling knowledge, as well as counseling skill areas that need further development. Yet, in an effort to appear competent, some supervisees may not readily express these readily identified shortcomings. It is in the best interest of both yourself and the clients you serve that you identify and express these areas to your supervisors and perhaps even make them working goals for the supervision relationship. Any supervisory relationship that lacks openness and space for the supervisee to express these doubts and vulnerabilities is facing a barrier to truly effective supervision.

Discussions about the supervisee's underdeveloped skills or even incompetence are likely inevitable, so a supervisee who is unable or unwilling to hear feedback from a supervisor will not experience an effective supervisory relationship. It is not uncommon for a supervisee to experience some level of anxiety, especially around these critical discussions (Borders & Brown, 2005). Yet being unable to receive and make use of feedback can impair

PERSONAL REFLECTION 2.3

I immediately developed a strong supervisory relationship with my postmaster's supervisor. I felt safe to share my incompetence, and she knew just the right ways to push me toward growth and best counseling practice. I was also extremely proud to call her my supervisor, as her reputation was well respected in the field.

When an entry-level opportunity to work at a child and adolescent treatment center was presented to me, I jumped at the chance to get experience in this area of counseling. Yet my supervisor expressed concerns about me having her as my only supervisor as I took on this new client population. Her concern was grounded in her knowledge that, although she had some past training and experience working with children, it had been many years, and her current practice was now focused exclusively on adults. Just weeks into my new practice, we mutually agreed that I needed to seek other supervision, specifically with a supervisor who had more competence in the area of children. Although I was saddened to leave that supervision relationship, I was soon matched with a supervisor who actively worked with children in her own ongoing practice, and we also developed a wonderful working alliance. It was an invaluable training experience.

In hindsight, it was my fear of the unknown and my resistance to change that almost got in the way of some crucial growth and learning. Although most in the field hope for students to have one valuable and impactful supervisory relationship, I now expect students to have at least two.

development. Equally, a supervisor that has not invited feedback from supervisees is also doing a disservice to the supervisory process. Being able to express to your supervisor what works and does not work for you is essential to creating a better, more productive working alliance (see Self-Assessment Activity 2.2).

SELF-ASSESSMENT ACTIVITY 2.2

Is feedback an area that makes you anxious? One way to alleviate that anxiety is to express to your supervisor the way you most like to receive feedback. Perhaps you like to hear things directly, along with concrete examples of ways to improve. Or maybe you prefer to receive feedback on opportunities for improvement when that feedback is presented along with identified areas in which you are excelling.

- How do you like to receive feedback?
- How can you communicate this preference to your supervisor(s)?
- Do you know the way in which your supervisor(s) prefers to give and receive feedback?

Perhaps the part of supervision that has the greatest potential to create anxiety and unease for both supervisor and supervisee is evaluation. Although you may be accustomed to evaluation coming only at the end of a course, evaluation should be ongoing throughout your supervision experience (Bernard & Goodyear, 2009; Campbell, 2006). Because the ability to remain on your chosen counseling career path can depend on the evaluation of your supervisor, as a supervisee, you should know exactly how your supervisor currently evaluates your performance and that you are doing what is necessary to receive a final endorsement toward licensure or certification. Although supervisors are ultimately responsible for providing this ongoing evaluation, supervisees should have a full understanding of when and how their supervisor will conduct and provide these evaluations, as well as the criteria used in those evaluations. If you are unsure about the criteria on which you will be evaluated, when evaluations will occur, if a specific evaluation instrument will or will not be used, or how evaluations will be communicated to you, then you are at risk of encountering a barrier to supervision.

One area of growing concern in the research literature is cultural self-awareness in the supervision relationship. Specifically, both supervisors and supervisees must be able to articulate their own cultural values and beliefs, as well as recognize those of others. Counselors in training are often lacking in multicultural competencies and may even hold biases toward racial, gender, and sexual orientation identifications of others (Ancis & Ladany, 2010; Ancis & Sanchez-Hucles, 2000). Other research has shown that when appropriate and sufficient attention is given to cultural issues in supervision, the supervisee has a more positive supervision experience (McLeod, 2008). Although it is preferable for these discussions to originate with the supervisor at the beginning of the supervisory relationship, supervisees should feel increasingly comfortable discussing multicultural issues during supervision, and eventually supervisees can initiate those conversations (Chang & Flowers, 2009; McLeod, 2008). Ignoring cultural issues—either your own, your client's, or your supervisor's—will likely be a barrier to effective supervision.

LEARNING FROM DIFFERENT PHILOSOPHIES AND THEORETICAL ORIENTATIONS: GROWING AND CHANGING

As a part of both the counseling and supervision processes, you will be exposed to a great deal of information (e.g., client demographic information; client behavior and attitude; your reaction toward the client and supervisor; the interaction among you, your clients, and your supervisor). This information can become overwhelming if you do not have a mechanism to assist you in organizing and interpreting that information. Counseling theories help us to make sense of this potentially overwhelming information. Schermer (2002, p. XI) stated, "The facts never just speak for themselves. They must be interpreted through the colored lenses of ideas: percepts need concepts." Theory can serve as these lenses to help us focus our attention and to assist us in organizing the multitude of information that we gather during a counseling session (Bernard & Goodyear, 2009). As a part of your clinical development, you will be encouraged to develop your own theoretical orientation and to apply that theory when appropriate to your client work. As you begin your journey to developing your own theoretical approach to your work with your clients, consider the following questions: How do you think people change? How do you make changes in your own life? In the next chapter, you will be introduced more thoroughly to the importance of integrating theory into practice with a focus on developing your own theory.

As you are encouraged to develop your theoretical orientation, it is important to remember that your supervisors also have their own theoretical orientations that guide their practice with their clients as well as their practice with their supervisees. In fact, many supervisors operate from a theoretical orientation that guides how they conceptualize client and supervisee change as well as a supervision model that guides how they structure their supervisory process. Your supervisors' theoretical orientations and supervision models will also guide how they structure and process case presentations.

Bernard and Goodyear (2009) described three broad categories of supervision models: (a) models grounded in psychotherapy theory, (b) developmental models, and (c) social role models. To these three categories, we suggest adding multicultural supervision models. Models grounded in psychotherapy theory include psychodynamic supervision, person-centered supervision, cognitive-behavioral supervision, systemic supervision, and constructivist supervision. Developmental models include the integrated developmental model (IDM; Stoltenberg, McNeill, & Delworth, 1998) and the Loganbill, Hardy, and Delworth model (1982). Examples of the social role models include the discrimination model (Bernard, 1979) and the systems approach to supervision model (Holloway, 1995). Examples of multicultural supervision models include the racial identity developmental model (Chang, Hays, & Shoffner, 2003) and the heuristic model of nonoppressive interpersonal development (HMNID; Ancis & Ladany, 2010). It is outside the scope of this chapter to discuss each of these supervision models; however, it is important for you as a beginning counselor to understand that many supervisors operate from a particular supervision model and that their model for supervision will influence the supervisory process and your relationship. Therefore, it is important for you to inquire about your supervisor's approach to supervision and how that may affect your supervisory process and alliance. Although, we believe it is the responsibility of supervisors to discuss their supervision models with supervisees at the beginning of the supervisory relationship, if your supervisor does not initiate this discussion, you can do so with the following questions: (a) What supervision model do you follow? (2) What is your approach to organizing the supervision session? and (c) What is your approach to providing feedback?

VOICES FROM THE FIELD 2.1   Becoming Myself, by Julia Whisenhunt

Prior to my doctoral studies, I had not considered the importance of having a theory of supervision. As part of my graduate education, I had trained in clinical supervision and even engaged in the supervision of supervisors. I was familiar with the process—the multiple roles the supervisor plays, the legal and ethical responsibilities, and ways to facilitate growth in my supervisee. I had the critically important knowledge and skills necessary to supervise another counselor. I was competent in supervision, but my style was inconsistent, and I didn't rely on a conceptualization of my supervisee to inform our process.

The doctoral program I attended at Georgia State University requires an intense supervisory training experience. At the beginning of the experience, I felt relatively confident in my supervision skills; I knew basically what do to and how to do it. Throughout my first 2 years in the program, my major professor had stressed the importance of approaching every professional role (i.e., counseling, supervision, teaching, and research) from a theoretical perspective. She believes that one's theory should be consistent across the professional domains—an idea that I had only partially endorsed. So, I knew I would be expected to demonstrate how what I did during my supervision sessions was reflected in my theory.

I began my supervision sessions with the explicit thought that I needed to balance the roles I played—consultant, teacher, and counselor—and integrate my counseling theory throughout. It was choppy and unnatural. I was generally doing and saying the "right" things, but I was so focused on my performance that I was missing some underlying themes and opportunities to facilitate awareness in my supervisees. I knew something had to change. My next approach was to enter each session relaxed, abandoning my mission to "perform" well, and demonstrate my theory. As each session progressed, though, I found myself reverting to the familiar stereotypic roles. It became clear to me that I wasn't allowing *myself* to be in the session. My professor even commented once "this doesn't sound like the Julia I know." I was acting out the role of what I expected of myself and what I thought was expected of me. How was I supposed to be natural in my supervision sessions and still uphold my responsibilities as a supervisor? For me, the answer came through letting go.

At that point in my professional development, I had already integrated my counseling theory and felt confident in my ability to let my theory guide me during counseling sessions without being cognitively preoccupied with evaluating myself and justifying each intervention. I came to the realization that I had to trust myself in supervision as well. I had the fundamental knowledge and skills in supervision. And, through my counseling theory, I knew how I conceptualized the process of growth and change. My task, then, was to modify my counseling theory to fit the supervision relationship. I began analytically evaluating how the components of my counseling theory fit or do not fit into the supervision relationship. It wasn't long until I realized that the components fit equally well into both relationships. My major professor was right! My theory *is* consistent across the professional domains. Once I accepted that my counseling theory also guides my supervision, I was free to be natural in sessions because I knew that what I was doing was informed by my theory and guided by my beliefs about growth and change.

This isn't to say that I am a counselor to my supervisees. Rather, my point is that, in my opinion, the process of supervising another counselor is essentially a process of facilitating development, which is not altogether very different from the underlying goal of counseling. And, just like in counseling, if I were not guided by a theory of how development occurs, my work with supervisees would be haphazard. As my major professor says, it's great if an intervention works well once, but how can you be expected to replicate those results if you don't know why you're doing what you're doing?

MAKING CASE PRESENTATIONS

Making case presentations is an essential skill to the development of a supervisee. Case presentations are an important learning tool because they not only provide a structure for helping us articulate our work with our clients, but they also provide us a structure for seeking supervision and consultation. Your supervisor's theoretical orientation and model of supervision will also influence the structure of case presentations. Table 2.1 provides sample guidelines for developing a case presentation.

TABLE 2.1 Guidelines for an oral or written case presentation

In preparing for your group presentation, select a client with whom you are having some difficulty or challenge. Prior to the meeting, organize information about your client and your experiences. Please include a brief audio/video presentation of the session. Your introduction and review of the tape should last no more than 15 to 20 minutes. This leaves the majority of the time for feedback and comments from your peers and supervisor. Your case presentation should include the following information:

1. Description of client.
2. Statement of the problem/concern.
3. Cultural information.
   a. What cultural biases might you have toward your client?
   b. What cultural biases might your client have toward you?
   c. What cultural values might enhance or impede your relationship with this client?
4. Your theoretical approach to working with this client.
5. Assessment/diagnosis.
6. Your treatment goals for this client.
7. Your goal for this session.
8. Are there any ethical considerations for working with this client?
9. Solicit feedback. What questions do you have for the supervision group?

VOICES FROM THE FIELD 2.2   The Importance of Those Intimidating Case Presentations, by Amber Cleveland Lewter

In my opinion, case presentations were an extremely helpful part of group supervision. They gave me the rare opportunity to hear what others were doing in session; it helped me learn vicariously through their experiences. As an intern, I often felt unprepared and concerned with whether I was "doing counseling exactly right." By being able to present my own work and get feedback from multiple people, it expanded my perspective. By hearing about others' work, I got to see different ways of doing things and integrate variety into my practice.

Borders (1991) provided a systemic approach to peer group supervision, which can be used to structure the case presentations. This model was adapted by Lassiter, Napolitano, Culbreth, and Ng (2008) to include a greater focus on multicultural counseling competence. The structured peer group format is designed to encourage skill development, conceptualization skills, supervisor feedback, and self-monitoring. According to Borders (1991), the structured peer group procedure includes the following steps:

1. The supervisee solicits specific feedback about his or her counseling performance.
2. Peers in the group are assigned or choose a specific role, perspective, or task to focus on while reviewing the counseling tape segment. These tasks may include observing

counselor or client nonverbals, assuming the role of the counselor or the client, viewing the segment from a specific theoretical orientation, or generating a metaphor for the counseling process.

3. The supervisee presents the taped segment.
4. The group members provide feedback based on their roles or tasks.
5. The supervisor facilitates the discussion serving as both moderator and process observer.
6. The supervisor summarizes the feedback and the discussion.

A modification to this process that we have made in supervision groups is that we end the discussion with "If this were my client I would. . . ." This stem offers the counselor trainee with specific things to consider in their future work with their clients while keeping in mind that this is from the perspective of their peer-group members.

Summary

The process of supervision is complex and multifaceted involving multiple individuals and agencies. In this chapter, we have discussed your transition from being a classroom-bound student to a counseling practicum student or intern. As you move into your practicum and internship, you will experience both excitement at the opportunity to put into practice your classroom learning and anxiety at having to put into practice your classroom learning. As a counselor trainee, you will be expected to be involved in all aspects of the counseling profession under supervision including, but not limited to, conducting intake interviews; providing individual, couples, and group counseling sessions; keeping accurate documentation; and participating in in-service and treatment team meetings.

A part of the supervisory process includes working with both your university supervisor and your on-site supervisor. Although both supervisors are concerned with client welfare and your development as a professional counselor, each will have different foci as their primary emphasis based on their role as either your university supervisor or your on-site supervisor. On-site supervisors are also often referred to as your administrative supervisor because they are concerned with the quantity and quality of services offered to the clientele that the agency serves. Your university supervisor may also be referred to as your clinical supervisor. Your clinical supervisor is concerned with your growth and development as a professional counselor. It is important that both the site and university supervisors work collaboratively to provide an optimal supervisory environment that will enhance your training.

An important aspect of the supervisory process is the relationship (i.e., supervisory alliance) that you will develop with both of your supervisors. To develop a positive supervisory alliance it is helpful for both you and your supervisors to be clear about your expectations and needs from the supervisory process. In addition, in conjunction with your supervisor, you will want to create an atmosphere of openness where concerns and missteps can be shared.

Developing learning goals with your supervisors assists in fostering the supervisory alliance. Learning goals help to establish the agreement between your supervisors and yourself, and they help to provide structure for your supervisory sessions. The learning goals can include specific clinical interventions or techniques, relationship issues, cognitive skills related to conducting counseling, and goals related to self-awareness. It is important to note that these learning goals are specifically related to your development as a counselor and are separate from your treatment goals that you will establish with your clients.

Effective supervision results in a positive growth experience for both supervisees and supervisors. However, there are barriers to effective supervision that you must be aware of and work toward preventing. These barriers include supervisor and supervisee competence, lack of effective and timely feedback, and cultural competence. Being mindful of these potential barriers to effective supervision is the first step toward preventing them.

This chapter has focused on the various aspects of the supervision process. It is important to note that how supervisors choose to structure the supervisory process is largely influenced by their theoretical orientation and their supervision model. Theory provides a lens to filter and organize the vast amount of information that you will gather in the counseling and supervision processes. Just as you are encouraged to develop your theoretical orientation for your work with your clients, your supervisors are encouraged to apply a supervision model to their approach to supervision. Your supervisors' theoretical orientation and their supervision model will influence how they use case presentations in your supervision. In this chapter, we presented the structured peer group model as one method for processing the case presentation. The supervisory process is a dynamic process that involves multiple individuals and agencies. To achieve a successful outcome in supervision, it is incumbent on both the supervisor and the supervisee to actively engage in the supervisory process, being mindful that both the supervisor and the supervisee are responsible for a successful supervision experience.

CHAPTER 3

The Many Details of a First Impression

BY ROBIN WILBOURN LEE, JENNIFER JORDAN, KRISTI GIBBS, AND JEANNINE R. STUDER

PREVIEW

Entering the clinical experiences of practicum and internship is often a time of excitement because it is an opportunity to work with real clients rather than practicing counseling skills by role-playing skills with peers. It may also be a time of trepidation, as many trainees ask themselves questions like, "Do I really have the skills for this?" or, "What if my supervisor doesn't like me?" or, "What if I have a client with issues I can't handle?" All these questions are a normal part of entering a new experience. An important goal for you at this point is to prepare for the anxiety you may experience as you move from practice to real-life situations. But remember, this is what you have trained for in your many classes and experiences. In addition, this is your career choice, and hopefully, you are excited about finally being able to begin your career as a professional counselor.

THE BEGINNING: STARTING WITH YOUR CLIENTS

Cormier and Hackney (2004) suggested that you can approach the first session with a client from two different perspectives. First, you may consider focusing on relationship dynamics, with the goal of the session being to develop a rapport with your client. Or you may consider focusing on collecting information that will be required for your site and record-keeping, thus focusing on the intake. Although you may focus on establishing the relationship first, you will still need to gather information related to the client's situation in future sessions.

Focusing on Relationship Dynamics

If you choose to focus primarily on building the relationship in the initial session, there are several key elements to consider, which include building rapport, characteristics of helpers, and developing and using your counseling skills.

DEFINING THE COUNSELING RELATIONSHIP. A quotation attributed to Albert Camus is enlightening when considering the counseling relationship: "Don't walk in front of me, I may not follow; Don't walk behind me, I may not lead; Walk beside me, and just be my friend."

Although you will not be developing a friendship with your client, you will be developing a very intimate relationship. It is important to distinguish the difference between a friendship and a counseling relationship. A friendship is based on mutual needs, whereas the counseling relationship is always based on the needs of the client. One important aspect to consider when conceptualizing your role in the counseling relationship is that it is always about your client and never about you.

Developing a relationship with your clients will be one of the first and most important goals that you must accomplish. Every theoretical approach and model of counseling accentuates the essential nature of the relationship, although some emphasize it more than others. Certainly, the relationship will be a key element when working from a client-centered approach. But even when using a behavior approach, you still need to have a relationship with your client. However, it is important to remember that developing the relationship will not be your only goal. The development of the relationship is, as Egan (2010) stated, "a means to an end" (p. 42).

Several terms are used to describe the counseling relationship. The *therapeutic* or *working alliance* not only describes the relationship that will be formed, but also indicates that both parties (client and counselor) will work hard to accomplish the goals of helping. You can consider the relationship you will develop as a collaboration between you and your client for a shared purpose (Hackney & Cormier, 2013). The process of developing the relationship is the beginning of your journey with your client. Let's rephrase the preceding quote to better represent the counseling relationship—walk beside your client, not in front or behind, and your goals will be more easily accomplished.

BUILDING RAPPORT.   Building rapport is a skill used not just by helping professionals, but also by many professionals whose goals are connecting with another person. For example, people in sales attempt to connect with potential buyers by identifying common interests, often engaging in "chitchat." Health-care professionals attempt to develop rapport with their patients by reviewing records for personal information prior to an exam and making sure to use the patient's correct name. You will begin developing rapport with your clients from the moment you meet them, which may begin when you retrieve them from the waiting room in an agency setting or a teacher's classroom. According to Hackney and Cormier (2013), rapport is defined as "the psychological climate that emerges from the interpersonal contact between you and your client. Consequently, good rapport sets the stage for positive psychological growth, whereas poor rapport leads to undesirable or even counterproductive outcomes" (p. 43).

Developing rapport is based on mutual trust between you and your client. It is important to recognize that your client is sharing his or her most intimate details with you and deserves your respect. Be willing to express your genuine interest in what your client is sharing, and rapport will naturally develop.

CHARACTERISTICS OF HELPERS.   Counselor educators have made many attempts to identify the personality characteristics of successful counselors. Yet, identifying characteristics that facilitate counseling is difficult due to the numerous definitions associated with these traits. Characteristics such as age, gender, religious beliefs, theoretical orientation, training and experience, and personality are known to be contributors to positive counseling outcomes (Reupert, 2006), with researchers debating which elements are most influential in this process.

Personality characteristics such as empathy and rapport, genuineness and congruency, understanding, valuing a counselee's ability to solve problems, and self-disclosure are identified as essential to positive counseling outcome. Although there is no general agreement on the most effective traits of successful counselors, there is agreement that it is the "self" of the counselor that is instrumental in establishing a therapeutic relationship (Reupert, 2006).

The characteristics, knowledge, and skills each counselor brings to the counseling relationship enable the counseling relationship to move forward in an intentional direction (Schmidt, 2002). As a novice counselor transitioning into the clinical experience, you are committing to the profession, and it is easy to get discouraged when your client does not change in the manner you hoped. Keep in mind that change takes time, and some clients are more resistant and uncooperative than others. Recognize client diversity as each individual represents a personal culture that needs to be understood. Furthermore, counseling requires being composed when your client expresses painful emotions, and patience is desired when working in ambiguous situations (Kottler & Brown, 2000). Skills you have already developed serve as a foundation for your entry into the profession. Use these skills, enhance them, and become skilled with more advanced approaches as you begin your journey into the counseling profession. Let's briefly define several important characteristics that will help when you are developing relationships with clients. After you have reviewed these characteristics, also consider the questions in Self-Assessment Activity 3.1.

Empathy.   You may consider empathy an innate characteristic of yours: the ability for you to have a deep level of understanding of the client. You have probably heard it described metaphorically as "walking in your client's shoes" (Hutchinson, 2007, p. 122). Empathy is considered a "staple" characteristic, comparing it to those staple items you may need to prepare a meal such as salt, sugar, flour, or butter. However, it is important to consider empathy as a characteristic that needs to be honed. As you begin to work with clients, always remember to remain empathic as a core condition necessary for developing a relationship.

Genuineness. Hackney and Cormier (2013) refer to genuineness as a "counselor's state of mind" (p. 69), which implies that counselors have the ability to be their true selves as they develop relationships with their clients. Congruence is a term related to genuineness. According to Gladding (2006), congruence is defined as "a consistency between the way people feel and the way they act" (p. 34). If you put these two characteristics together, you have a person who can be himself or herself consistently.

Unconditional positive regard. Rogers believed unconditional positive regard was one of the conditions necessary for clients to change (Gladding, 2006). Unconditional positive regard entails accepting the client for who he or she is, without any conditions. One distinction that is typically made regarding unconditional positive regard is that counselors accept the client as having worth but do not have to agree with or accept the behaviors of the client. Because of this, Wilkins (2000) suggested that unconditional positive regard is the most difficult characteristic to develop. We interact with people in our world with conditions, such as values, biases, temperaments, personalities, and personal experiences, but we do not always agree with what our clients are saying or doing. However, allowing the client the opportunity to experience a safe environment is a key, and unconditional positive regard will help to develop that safe environment. Wilkins suggested that understanding unconditional positive regard might be easier by considering the opposite. He defined *conditional positive regard* as ". . . the offering of warmth, respect, acceptance, etc. only when the other fulfills some particular expectation, desire or requirement" (p. 26). Wilkins also defined other extremes. *Unconditional negative regard* is a condition that indicates the person will hate or despise regardless of what is said or done. Wilkins also defined *unconditional positive disregard* as ". . . when one person refuses to enter into a relationship of any kind with another. It is paying no attention to and being neglectful of another whatever they say or do, or however they act" (p. 26). Although conditional positive regard may allow the client to demonstrate some growth, it is only due to the counselor's agenda. Pleasing the counselor becomes the motivation. Unconditional negative regard and unconditional positive disregard are both harmful and should be avoided.

Other characteristics. Additional characteristics of effective counselors include self-control, sympathy, flexibility, sensitivity, and an ability to create a safe environment (Jennings & Skovholt, 1999). In addition, Jennings and Skovholt investigated the personality characteristics of master counselors and found emotional well-being, humility, confidence, willingness to experience and process emotional and cognitive dissonance, nondefensiveness, and willingness to seek feedback as aspects that create an inviting counseling relationship. In a separate study, Gazzola, Smith, King-Andrews, and Kearney (2010) identified counselor values associated with work satisfaction that include helping others, using abilities and knowledge, growing and developing as a person, achieving, creating and innovating, interacting with others, variety in work, comfort in working space, autonomous decision making, financial security, career advancement, admiration, risk-taking, and managing and directing others.

SELF-ASSESSMENT ACTIVITY 3.1 PERSONAL HELPING CHARACTERISTICS

Write down the personal helping characteristics that you believe you possess and compare your list with those listed earlier. What are some of your traits that you believe may detract from establishing healthy counseling relationships? Which of the characteristics listed can you develop and/or improve on? How can you develop or improve on them?

DEVELOPING AND USING BASIC COUNSELING SKILLS.   As discussed earlier, your counseling skills will be another key step to developing relationships with your clients. Your use of these skills, both basic and advanced, will help you begin to communicate effectively with your clients as well as begin the process of helping. Following is a review of skills that will assist you in accomplishing those goals.

Attending.   Considered the most basic skill, attending is the foundation of the basic counseling skills. Metaphorically, it can be considered the foundation of a house, providing the stability that the home needs to continue the building process. Because attending is the most basic skill, once you understand and develop your attending skills, it should require less focus. Attending skills encompass your nonverbal behavior. Nonverbal behaviors include eye contact, facial expressions, body language, and even proximity to your client. Egan (2010) developed the acronym SOLER to help understand attending skills. **S** is defined as squarely; taken literally, you should square your shoulders with your client's, taking a posture that is completely facing them. **O** is defined as open; taking an open position rather than closed. Anything that is deemed closed (e.g., crossed-arms) can signal to clients that you are not interested in them or what they are sharing with you. **L** stands for lean; taking a slight lean forward can gesture to the client that you are listening. Egan provided the example of seeing two people in a restaurant who are leaning closely toward each other. What does that signal to you? Most would say that they are actively engaged in communicating, and that is demonstrated by their nonverbal lean. **E** is considered good eye contact with your client. Maintaining eye contact is one of the most important aspects of ensuring that clients know you are paying attention to them. Looking away frequently can signal a disinterest in your client that you want to avoid. **R** is considered your ability to remain relaxed as you portray all these skills. Each of these five SOLER components may look contrived if you do not show a natural position. You must avoid all fidgeting and nervous behaviors that can be distracting to the client. One of the most important aspects to remember about the attending skills is the fact that most are considered North American cultural behaviors and may not be valued in all cultures. For example, some cultures do not value eye contact. In fact, some Asian cultures may view too much eye contact with authority figures as inappropriate (Egan, 2010).

Listening.   When developing a relationship with your clients, your listening skills will be the next step beyond attending. It is the next building block of your skill set and the midsection of the foundation. Without strong listening skills, you may not be successful with future counseling skills, as well as building a relationship with your client. Gladding (2006) provides a clear definition of listening: "Listening involves hearing not only the content of a client's words but also the tone and inflection of what is being said (i.e., the *nonverbal*) . . . hearing what is not being said as well as deciphering patterns" (p. 84).

You may have read or heard different ways to describe listening skills. Some authors have combined the skill of listening with the skill of responding. For example, Okun (1997) used the term *responsive listening* to describe the act of communicating counselor understanding and awareness of client situations. You may also have heard the term *reflective listening* used in motivational interviewing to describe the combination of listening and reflection to direct a client toward deeper self-awareness (Young, 2005). However, more often, counseling professionals use the term *active listening* to understand the skill set. By using the term *active listening*, the process of understanding the client more completely is highlighted to begin the process of helping. According Skovholt and Rivers (2004), listening is "the primary data-gathering method" (p. 136). This describes the fact that active listening is used to learn about multiple client messages.

One of the first elements of active listening is hearing and understanding the client's verbal message. According to Egan (2010), clients often tell stories, share points of view, deliver decisions, and state intentions or offer proposals. More specifically, Egan outlined the verbal message as containing multiple components: experiences, behaviors, cognitions, and affect. Experiences are described as what happens to the client, behaviors as what they do or don't do, cognitions as what they are thinking, and affect as what they are feeling. According to Egan, clients will talk most about their experiences and least about their behaviors. Talking about what happens to them allows them to discuss what is external to them, whereas if they talk about their behaviors, they have to take responsibility for what they did or didn't do. The second component to the client's message is the nonverbal message. When we listen for the nonverbal message, we pay close attention to the aspects of the client such as body language, general appearance, eye contact, facial gestures, and so on. Differences between the verbal and nonverbal message should also be noted. It is commonly believed that if there are discrepancies between the verbal and nonverbal message, most people will believe the nonverbal communication due to the fact that the nonverbal is difficult to fake. Egan also describes another component of the client's message as being the context in which the message is shared. Context can be considered as a client's environment, culture, values and beliefs systems, personality, and/or temperament just to name a few. For example, a message shared by a client who is experiencing domestic violence or mental illness can be very different than a message from a client who has not had these experiences. Kottler (2000) offered several suggestions to help you listen more attentively: clear your mind; empathize; concentrate completely; watch carefully for nonverbal cues; don't just listen, but really hear; ask yourself what the person is really saying; identify underlying feelings, as well as surface content; and use your hearing, as well as your head, to divine meaning.

Listening is the link between your attending and responding skills. One important fact to remember is that if you are listening well, responding will be easy!

Responding Skills

As we continue to discuss the development of a relationship with your clients, we move to the final building block: responding. Although attending and listening are crucial, each of these skills is pointless unless you respond verbally to your clients. They will not know you truly are hearing what they say or understand them unless you tell them with words. Egan (2010) helps us understand the importance of responding skills as three dimensional. To be successful, you must be *perceptive*. This can be accomplished through being intelligent, both cognitively and socially emotionally. You must have *know-how*. In other words, you must develop your skills in this area. The last dimension is the most crucial: assertiveness. Although you can be perceptive and know how to use the skills, unless you actually demonstrate both of those by being assertive, you will not be successful.

There are many verbal responses that you can use to develop the relationship with your client. But using your verbal responses also will be the way you communicate with your clients. As such, the following skills will become staples of your communications with clients: reflecting, paraphrasing, clarifying, summarizing, probing, and questioning. In addition, we will review several advanced skills such as immediacy, confronting, challenging, self-disclosure, and information sharing.

REFLECTION.   According to Gladding (2006), reflection is defined as "a counseling technique similar to a restatement but dealing with verbal and nonverbal expression" (p. 121). Gladding also suggested that reflection can convey empathy (i.e., deep level of understanding), rephrase a client's feelings, or restate the client's content. At some point in your training, you were probably introduced to the reflective formula: You feel (_____) because (_____). This sentence, albeit a very simplistic statement, is also very powerful. It allows you to convey your deep level of understanding of what the client is communicating. This formula contains a stem and the client's feeling(s) connected to the content the client is sharing. The feeling may be expressed either verbally or implied nonverbally. The content typically contains all or some of the client's experience(s), behavior(s), or thought(s). Of course, you should use a variety of different stems to keep your reflections from sounding redundant to the client. However, clients typically do not hear the stem but focus more on your reflection of their personal feelings and content. For sample stems, see Table 3.1.

One key aspect to reflecting is accuracy. The feeling and content are easily understood through the use of your listening skills. Using reflection is your opportunity to convey your understanding of the client. If you are having trouble responding accurately to your client (e.g., he or she is consistently saying, "No, that's not it"), the problem is not with your responding skills but with your listening skills.

TABLE 3.1 Sample empathy stems and probes

Empathy Stems

- You feel (felt) . . .
- So it's a mixture of . . .
- I see. It's (like, more than, not that) . . .
- It's as though . . .
- Sounds like . . .
- What I hear you saying is . . .

Probes

- Tell me more about . . .
- Help me understand . . .
- I'm not sure what you mean by . . .
- What happened when . . .
- Can you be more specific about . . .
- When you say _____, do you mean . . .
- How do you . . .

PARAPHRASING.   Paraphrasing is a skill that focuses on the content the client is sharing, but does not identify the feeling connected with the content. Paraphrasing can use the same stems as in the reflective statement. According to Poorman (2003), a paraphrase contains four components: (a) you must recall the message, which may require repeating or restating the message to yourself; (b) you must identify the content, including key players, the specific situation, and the location; (c) you must put the content into your own words; and (d) you must share the content in a statement. One key aspect when paraphrasing is to avoid parroting or changing the meaning.

PROBES AND QUESTIONS.   Egan (2010) defines a probe as a verbal or nonverbal response with the purpose of helping clients talk more specifically about their concerns or issues. Verbal probes include statements, requests, and questions. Statements can begin with stems such as "I'm not clear about. . . ." Requests can begin with stems such as "Can you be more specific about. . . ." Questions can be either open- or closed-ended questions. Open-ended questions begin with *how, what, when, where, who,* or *why.* Closed-ended questions begin with *is, are, do, did, could, would,* or *have.* There are two important considerations when using questions. First, questions should have a specific purpose, specifically to help clients share more about their concerns or issues. Second, it is better to use open-ended questions and avoid closed-ended questions. Closed-ended questions are those that can be answered with either yes, no, or other single words, thus providing little or no additional information that will help the counselor understand the client. Additional sample probes can be found in Table 3.1.

Nonverbal prompts (also called minimal encouragers) include head nodding, body movements, or gestures that encourage the client to continue sharing. For example, a counselor may lean forward as the client begins to talk about something distressing. By changing body language, the counselor encourages the client to continue talking.

Advanced Responding Skills

SUMMARIZING.   Summarizing is a skill in which the counselor uses several statements, which may be a combination of reflecting and paraphrasing, to report multiple areas of content that the client has shared. Summarizing is considered an advanced skill because of the counselor's need to make a purposeful decision to use the skill for a specific purpose. Summary can be used effectively under at least three circumstances. First, use a summary at the beginning of every session beyond the initial session. This demonstrates to the client that you retained the information from previous sessions and helps move the client forward by not having to repeat details that you clearly understood. Second, use a summary at the end of *every* session. This allows for closure for the client and lets the client know you are retaining his or her personal information. Finally, you can summarize when the session lacks direction or the client cannot move forward. Metaphorically, this can be considered "pushing the reset button."

IMMEDIACY.   Immediacy is defined as the counselor's ability to discuss the dynamics of the relationship developed with a client (Gladding, 2006). This may include the quality of the relationship and/or the interactions between the client and professional counselor. In addition, immediacy can be used to address specific interactions that may be either positive or negative. The best way to conceptualize immediacy is to understand that it is about being honest in the session. It is about you sharing thoughts about the relationship that can be beneficial to the client. Metaphorically, it is often considered to be "talking about the elephant in the room." If certain dynamics, interactions, or issues are ignored, an opportunity to really explore issues on a deeper level is missed. Immediacy can be used with common issues such as when trust is an issue, when an interaction is causing tension between you and your client, or if there are differences between the client and professional counselor, such as race or culture. Immediacy can also be used in less frequent situations, such as when there is dependency or codependency or if an attraction exists between client and counselor (Egan, 2010).

CONFRONTATION.   According to Poorman (2003, p. 130), confrontation "involves offering a client information about discrepancies, conflicts, or mixed messages observed in the client's reports, behaviors, feelings, or thoughts." Although confrontation may have negative connotations, it can be an appropriate intervention to use when clients need a different perspective. However, it does not involve ultimatums. One important consideration is that confrontation should be used purposefully and not arbitrarily.

SELF-DISCLOSURE.   Gladding (2006) defined self-disclosure as "a conscious, intentional technique in which clinicians share information about their lives outside the counseling relationship" (p. 128). Key words in this definition are *conscious* and *intentional*. Although this has been stated with other advanced skills, being purposeful is particularly important when choosing to use self-disclosure with clients. One statement that was made earlier in the chapter was "it is always about your client and never about you." Using self-disclosure is contrary to this statement because self-disclosure is *all* about you. However, in the instance in which you are choosing self-disclosure to achieve a certain goal, it can be appropriate. According to Egan (2010), the main purpose of self-disclosure is modeling. He used Alcoholics Anonymous (AA) as an example. In AA, those who have achieved a certain level of quality of sobriety share their personal experiences, strengths, and hope to motivate others to do the same. Egan offers the following guidelines when using self-disclosure:

1. Do not disclose more than is necessary.
2. Make sure your timing is appropriate.
3. Keep your disclosures focused.
4. Do not use self-disclosure too frequently.
5. Do not overburden with too many personal details.
6. Remain flexible, adapting to different client situations.

Advanced Challenging Skills

Although all the skills reviewed thus far can be considered challenging, this section is designed to help you consider even more advanced challenging concepts and skills. Challenging a client is a way to help him or her see any discrepancies that may exist. These discrepancies may include inconsistencies between two verbal messages, a verbal message and a nonverbal message, a current report and a previous report, a client's view and a helper's view of a particular behavior, a client's judgment about strengths or limitations, inconsistency in self-perception and experience, a client's perception about an "idealized" picture of himself or herself and what is "real" about who he or she is, a client's words and actions, or two nonverbal behaviors that are or seem inconsistent (Poorman, 2003).

ADVANCED EMPATHY. One of the most useful challenging skills is advanced empathy, "a process in which the counselor gets at feelings and meanings in the client's life that are hidden or beyond the immediate awareness of the client" (Gladding, 2006, p. 6). Although advanced empathy does not have a "formula" response similar to reflecting, these challenging responses can take related forms. For example, a client who is expressing sadness about the loss of a parent may also be angry and resentful about losing the loved one. A reflective statement might be "I can see how sad you are about losing your mother." An advanced empathy statement might be "I can see how sad you are about losing your mother, but I am also sensing some anger in your voice too." Advanced empathy also help clients identify themes and make connections (Egan, 2010).

INTAKE SESSION/INTERVIEW

Reviewing Informed Consent

The initial session has many purposes, one of which is an opportunity to ensure that your clients clearly understand their rights and responsibilities, which are typically included in some type of disclosure statement. Disclosure statements can take many forms. An agency will more than likely have a prepared set of documents that clients review and sign, whereas a school counselor may use a personally designed brochure. Informed consent is about your client's right to be educated about the process. It is important to recognize that although informed consent is typically presented in the initial session, it is also an ongoing process and should be reviewed and discussed multiple times as you are working with your clients. Regardless of your work setting, your skill regarding informed consent means being able to effectively explain the informed consent elements that relate to your site and your clients. Informed consent will be addressed comprehensively in Chapter 6.

Confidentiality

Of all the elements to be discussed during the informed consent process, confidentiality could be considered the most important. Confidentiality is a cornerstone of the counseling process. It affords the client the opportunity to discuss intimate details without the risk of having that information shared outside the sessions. Without confidentiality, it is doubtful that clients would choose counseling as a means to helping them resolve issues. However, although we need to make sure that clients understand confidentiality, they must also understand the limits to confidentiality. Confidentiality and the limits to confidentiality need to be reviewed multiple times while working with clients. Counselors must also consider how best to explain confidentiality to their clients, based on the population being served. If you are working with children, you know choosing language they can understand is crucial. If you are working with adolescents, understanding how important confidentiality is to them is crucial. Thus, explaining the limits may be challenging. The limits to confidentiality include (a) client waives privilege; (b) death of the client; (c) sharing information with subordinates for billing or record-keeping purposes; (d) consultation with fellow professionals; (e) protecting someone in danger; (f) counseling multiple clients in the same session; (g) counseling minor clients; (h) court-ordered disclosures; and (i) legal protections for counselors in disputes.

Although you may not choose to discuss all these limits with your clients, you should make sure that you are covering the limits most appropriate for your population. One key consideration is to make sure to provide enough information for your client to understand the information without overwhelming him or her with too much complicated jargon.

What to Do with Parents and Guardians in the Initial Session

If you are working in an agency setting, you should consider how to handle the parents of your minor clients. There are several factors to consider. First, you will need to help parents understand the counseling process. According to the American Counseling Association (ACA) *Code of Ethics* (2005), parents are to be considered a resource for counselors. This differs from previous codes that stated counselors should only act in the best interest of the minor client. Second, you will need to discuss confidentiality as it relates to their children. Considering confidentiality and children, the law and ethical standards may diverge. According to most helping professions' ethical guidelines, children are afforded the same ethical rights to confidentiality as adults. However, the law states that a minor child has no privacy, and that privileged communication belongs to the parents/guardians. This can cause a dilemma for professional counselors. How do you keep your minor client's information confidential while respecting the parent's/guardian's rights to know? The following steps are recommended:

- Determine whether the minor is willing to disclose the information to his or her parents/guardians.
- Try to persuade the parent/guardian that it is in the best interest of the child not to disclose the confidential information.
- Schedule a joint meeting for the minor child and parent/guardian to resolve the issue; assume the role of the mediator.
- If you are disclosing to the parent/guardian, be sure to inform the minor prior to the disclosure.

Depending on the case, there may be a time when you feel that disclosing is not in the best interest of the minor client. In this case, you may decide not to disclose. When choosing this option, you should involve your supervisor to ensure that you are not held liable. Although cases in which you would not disclose to the parents/guardians have been described, it is important to remember that child abuse is always an exception to confidentiality and should be disclosed to authorities immediately.

Gathering Information and Client History

The first session with a client is often more structured and counselor driven than subsequent sessions. The first meeting is the time to conduct an intake. Different agencies have specific policies of how they handle the intake process, and it is important that you understand agency policy prior to your first client visit. Some agencies appoint an intake counselor to conduct the intake interview with all new clientele prior to assigning them a counselor. When gathering information in the intake interview, it is important to remember that this is also a time of relationship building with your client. Explaining the counseling process to them as well as how counseling will be conducted in the future helps to alleviate unnecessary anxiety. Most agencies have a specific intake protocol that includes demographic questions and a psychosocial history of the client. Standardized tests such as symptom and behavior inventories are often used to supplement the intake process to deepen the understanding of the client's treatment needs. Other options for gathering information in the intake include interviewing family members, friends, or teachers, after gaining the permission of the client, or parent/guardian of a minor client.

When gathering information, a professional counselor relies on the basic counseling skills mentioned earlier in the chapter. A heavy emphasis is placed on questioning, and in general, the more open-ended questions the counselor can ask, the more effective the interview will be. It is important to note when a client does not answer a question or hesitates, what a client doesn't say can be just as important as what he or she does say. Do not force a client to answer questions with which he or she is uncomfortable. You can always go back to those more difficult questions at a later date and clarify or explore those issues as needed. Pushing the client turns the intake into more of an interrogation than an interview.

During the intake interview it is crucial to distinguish between the presenting problems and the etiology of the problem. Presenting problems are the symptoms a client is currently experiencing that bring him or her to counseling. These include changes in mood, sleep, eating, thoughts, behaviors, and attitudes, to name a few. In the sample intake that follows, you will see a presenting problems checklist that allows the counselor to explore a wide range and depth of presenting concerns. The etiology, on the other hand, refers to relevant psychosocial factors that have exacerbated presenting symptoms. In the following section is a list of relevant psychosocial factors that need to be unearthed to determine etiological factors.

Psychosocial History

A psychosocial history is a history of the client's social and psychological functioning; it explores the presenting problem, the current context of the problem, as well as resources and barriers to treatment. It also helps the professional counselor to create a case conceptualization and determine the best method of treatment. A comprehensive approach to intake interviews is available in Erford (2013). The psychosocial history usually includes

- *Personal history,* which includes educational background, employment history, military history, family of origin, marital status, current living situation and relationship status with friends and family, and abuse, legal, and religious histories.
- *Drug/alcohol use/abuse history* in self and family. This includes what types of substances are being used, how much, how often, date of first use, and progression of use. Prior treatment for drug or alcohol abuse and family history of abuse are also explored.
- *Counseling history* comprises any past treatment for mental health issues and medications prescribed for such issues. An inquiry into past and current suicidal or homicidal ideations or actions is assessed. Family mental illness is also investigated.
- *Medical history* is important to research from personal and family history perspectives. Oftentimes medical issues can mimic psychological symptoms and need to be ruled out prior to diagnosis.
- *Current symptoms* include what has brought the client into counseling. Assessing the client's beliefs about these symptoms and gaining an understanding of how disruptive they are to the client's current functioning is important. How long have the symptoms been occurring? How often do the symptoms occur? Can you pinpoint when the symptoms began? Is there a time when the symptoms are less intense or seem to disappear altogether?
- *Client resources* consist of social or community supports, client strengths, and motivations. Assessing how the client approaches counseling and how receptive the client is to you as a counselor can be a resource toward change.

Mental Status Exam

As mentioned earlier counselors are listening to both verbal and nonverbal messages in the intake interview. At the conclusion of the intake interview, counselors complete a mental status exam based on their perceptions of a client during the interview process. Seligman (2004) listed 12 categories within the mental status exam that a counselor should be aware of:

1. Appearance: well groomed, adequately groomed, poorly groomed
2. Behavior: calm, psychomotor agitation, psychomotor retardation, poor eye contact, poor impulse control, guarded, poor balance or coordination
3. Speech and language: rate, volume, coherence, abnormalities, deficits
4. Emotions: mood such as euthymic, depressed, irritable, anxious, euphoric, and affect such as appropriate, broad, flat, blunted and the congruencies of mood and affect
5. Orientation to reality: hallucinations, delusions
6. Concentration and attention: attentive, scattered, focused
7. Thought processes: word usage, thought blocking, racing thoughts, flight of ideas, loose associations, magical thinking
8. Thought content: suicidal ideation, fears and phobias, obsessions and compulsions, delusions
9. Perception: hallucinations, illusions, depersonalization, derealization, dissociative
10. Memory: normal, long or short term deficits
11. Intelligence and knowledge: above average, average, below average
12. Judgment and insight: good, fair, poor

Case Study 3.1 and Table 3.2 provide a sample intake for client "Sophie Sheppard" that includes all the preceding information related to intake interviewing.

CASE STUDY 3.1

Sophie

Sophie appears to be a young woman in her mid-twenties and is employed as a marketing manager for a popular clothing company in a large city. She reports that she is single and has no children. Sophie states that the reason she is seeking counseling at this time is to discuss possible options for her future. She states that she is very good at her job and is financially self-sufficient. Now that her career is well underway, Sophie's thoughts have turned toward settling down and starting a family but she has yet to find "the one." She is concerned because her relationships tend to be short term, and she spends a lot of time thinking that she may never find a mate.

TABLE 3.2 Client Intake Form

Date: 9/13/12   Client Number: 28411

I. CLIENT INFORMATION

Last Name ___Sheppard___   **First Name** ___Sophie___   **MI** __O__

Sex: __ Male √ Female   **Date of Birth** ___09/04/84___   **Age** ___27___

Ethnicity: __ Asian __ Black √ Hispanic √ Native American √ White __ Other (_____)

Current Address _____570 W. 4th St., Apt. H_____
                                          Street

                      Rock Hill   SC   27922
                      City   State   Zip Code

Primary Telephone Number (803) 555-1234 **Other Telephone Number** (__) NA

How may we contact you regarding your appointment? *(Check all that apply.)*

√ Primary Telephone __ Other Telephone

May we leave a message on an answering machine or with anyone who answers your phone?

√ Yes or No

In an emergency, whom we should contact: Erica Sheppard   (704) 555-9876

Relationship to you ____Mother_____

Work Telephone (_____) ____NA____ **Home Telephone** (_____) ____NA____

How did you learn about the Community Counseling Clinic? ___Referred by friend, Molly Smith__

II. PSYCHOSOCIAL HISTORY
Educational History

Education: (check all that apply) ___ GED √ HS Grad √ College-# of years ___4___

Degree/Major B.A., Marketing and Management Vocational training ____NA____

Do you have a history of learning difficulties? Yes____ No √

COMMENTS _____

Do you have any barriers to learning such as the inability to read or write? Yes____ No √

COMMENTS _____

Employment History

Employed: (please check one) √ Full time __Part time ___Unemployed-date last worked __/__

Not in labor force: (please check one) _____disabled _____retired _____homemaker _____
student _____living in institution _____other _____

If you checked disabled, please explain further _____

_____

If employed, employer name: ____Urban Utopia_____

Occupation _____ Marketing manager _____

Are you currently under financial distress? Yes ____ **No** √

Military History

Are you now or have you ever been a member of the military? Yes ____ **No** √

If yes, what branch _____

Please list any pertinent duties or trauma experienced during your service _____
_____

Social History

Marital Status:

√ **Single** ___ **Married** ___ **Separated** ___ **Divorced** ___ **Widowed** ___ **Remarried** ___ **Cohabitating**

What is your current living situation? ___ Lives alone _____

Household Members	Relationship	Age	Quality of Relationship

Is there a history of mental illness in your family? Yes ___ **No** √ **If yes, please explain** _____
_____

Are you currently or have you ever been physically, mentally, sexually, or emotionally abused?

Yes √ **No** ____ **if yes, please explain** ___ While in college, CL suspects drink was drugged at a
party, and she was raped by one or more males.

Is there a history of drug or alcohol abuse in your family? Yes √ **No** ___ **If yes, please explain**
Mother is a recovering alcoholic with 5 years sobriety

What do you believe are your strengths? "I am outgoing and friendly. I do really well at my job,
time management, and the structure I create in my life."

Describe what type of support system you have ___ "I'm really close with my family and have a lot
of friends. I believe in God and go to church sometimes."

Drug/Alcohol History

Have you ever had a problem with drug/alcohol abuse? No **If yes, please explain** _____
_____

Illegal drug use past 12 months   ____ **yes** √ **no**

Prescription drug abuse past 12 months   ____ **yes** √ **no**

Nonprescription drug abuse past 12 months   √ **yes** ____ **no**

Alcohol use past 12 months   √ **yes** ____ **no**

Drug/Substance/ Alcohol	Age of 1st use	Date of last use	Frequency	Amount	Method
Benadryl	16	Monday	nightly	2 tablets	orally
Alcohol	16	Monday	nightly	6 oz	orally

III. COUNSELING HISTORY

Have you previously received counseling services? √ **No** ____ **Yes**

If yes, respond to all items below.

Name(s) of Facility _____

Location(s) of Facility (City and State) _____

Type of Facility ____ Outpatient ____ Inpatient (hospital)

Type of Counseling (check all that apply): ____ Psychological ____ Substance Abuse

Dates of Counseling: Start _____ End _____

Previous Problem(s) _____

Success in resolving previous problems (check one):

_____Unsuccessful _____Partially Successful _____Highly Successful

What did you find to be particularly helpful or not helpful about your previous counseling experience? _____

_____

Were you prescribed any medication for dealing with the above issue? Yes _____ No _____

If yes, what medication were you prescribed? _____

IV. MEDICAL HISTORY

Name of *current* physician ___"I don't have one. I go to a clinic."_____

Name of psychiatrist, if one is seen ___NA_____

Please check all *current* and previous medical conditions from the list below.

___Problems with Vision/Hearing	___Headaches
___Thyroid Problems	___Dizziness
___Lung Disease	___Chest Pains
___Stomach Problems	___Joint Pain
___High Blood Pressure	___Diabetes
___Heart Disease	___Seizures
___Weight Loss	___Weight Gain

Physical Exercise: times per week __3__ for how long ___"about 30 minutes"_____

___Pain (explain) _____

___Environmental Allergies: (explain) _____

___Food Allergies: (explain) _____

___Other (explain) _____

Do you *currently* take prescription or "over-the-counter" medications? ____No _√_ Yes

If yes, please provide all requested information below.

Name of Medication	Dosage	Times/Day	Start Date	Side Effects
Valtrex	5 mg	2	as needed	lethargy, headaches

Do you *currently* take vitamins or herbal supplements? ____ No _√_ Yes **If yes, please provide**

Name of Supplement	Dosage	Times/Day	Start Date	Side Effects
Multivitamin		1	age 12	NA
Calcium	200 mg	1	age 12	NA
Vitamin C	10 mg	2	age 25	NA

V. PRESENTING PROBLEM

PRESENTING PROBLEMS CHECKLIST Please rate each of the following items according to the following scale:

1	2	3	4	5
Not at all	A little	Moderately	Quite a bit	Extremely

	1	2	3	4	5
1. School and/or job performance too low.	√				
2. Too critical of others.				√	
3. Unhappy or anxious without knowing why.		√			
4. Have difficulty studying and/or concentrating.		√			

5. Worry about things I have done.			√		
6. Parents or others too critical of my behavior.		√			
7. Have fears that seem unrealistic.			√		
8. Not interested in my courses or job.	√				
9. Problems with sleeping.				√	
10. Worry about my drinking/smoking/drug use.		√			
11. Dislike being dependent on parents/spouse/others.	√				
12. Problems in romantic relationships.					√
13. Parents or others oppose my ideas/values/beliefs.		√			
14. Lack of interest in school or work.	√				
15. Experience frequent mood fluctuations.			√		
16. Don't know what I want out of life.	√				
17. Feel others do not like me/no one seems to care about me.		√			
18. Feel lonely.			√		
19. Have trouble making decisions.			√		
20. Worry about my physical health.				√	
21. Worry about my mental health.			√		
22. Other people disappoint me.				√	
23. Nothing I do seems meaningful or important.		√			
24. Feel very anxious in new situations.		√			
25. Can't seem to control my own thoughts/behaviors.		√			
26. Doubt my ability to meet goals/standards.	√				
27. Concerned about family members.		√			
28. Confused about questions of morals/religion/spirituality.	√				
29. Feel depressed.	√				
30. Concerned about my sexual identity.	√				
31. Feel tired, dizzy, and/or weak.		√			
32. Have difficulty trusting other people.			√		
33. Afraid to speak up in class or at work.	√				
34. Cannot seem to budget my time and/or money.	√				
35. Worry about what others think of me.		√			
36. Concerned with sexual functioning/thoughts/ behaviors.					√
37. Low self-esteem.			√		
38. Thoughts/feelings of ending my life.	√				
39. Easily annoyed or irritated.	√				
40. Feeling hopeless about the future.	√				
41. Having urges to break or smash things.	√				
42. Having urges to beat, injure, or harm someone.	√				
43. Concerned with weight/eating habits/physical appearance.	√				
44. Thoughts of death or dying.	√				

Comments regarding the presenting problem checklist: __Relationship problems. CL is never as interested in men as they are of CL. Since rape incident, has not been sexually active; "I'm afraid to tell my boyfriend about my past because I don't want to lose him."__

What problem(s) brings you to counseling? __CL wants to discuss options for her future, decide whether or not to go forward in her relationship with boyfriend, and figure out why she continues to be awakened by recurring nightmare.__

How *long* have you experienced this problem? (Specify): ___Days ___Weeks _✓_ Months ___Years

How *often* do you experience this problem? (Check one): __Hourly _✓_ Daily __Weekly __Other

How *intense* is this problem? (Check one): ____Mild ____Moderate _✓_ Severe

The following is to be filled out by counselor after the session.

VI. CLIENT STRENGTHS

_✓_ Person states and/or displays **a high degree of motivation** for insight, change, etc.

_✓_ Person has **identifiable skills and/or talents** that may be utilized in the service of coping.

_✓_ Person **relates openly and is receptive in interaction** with interviewer.

_✓_ Person is **verbally articulate** and/or is well **able to identify his/her concerns.**

_✓_ Person appears to display **at least average degree of psychological mindedness** (versus resistant to considering psychological causes and contributions to presenting problems).

_✓_ Person has relatively **few** and **well-defined goals.**

_✓_ Person has identifiable and consistent sources of **psychosocial support** (e.g., family, friends, belief system).

_✓_ Person is **not experiencing significant impairment** in academic/occupational functioning.

VII. MENTAL STATUS and BEHAVIORAL OBSERVATIONS:

A. APPEARANCE (*note height, weight, distinguishing physical characteristics, grooming, hygiene, etc.*):

_✓_ Well dressed/groomed ___ Adequately dressed/groomed ___ Poorly dressed/groomed

B. BEHAVIOR (*note particularly rapport and interaction with interviewer*):

____ Calm, no excesses or deficits   ____ Poor eye contact

_✓_ Displays psychomotor agitation   ____ Shows difficulties of impulse control

____ Displays psychomotor retardation   ____ Reluctant or guarded in interview

____ Poor posture, balance, or coordination ____ Shows abnormalities of gait, limb usage

C. SPEECH (*note rate, volume, coherence, abnormalities or deficits, etc.*):

_✓_ Fluent, no abnormalities or deficits

D. EMOTION:

1. MOOD:

____ Normal/Euthymic   ____ Irritable   ____ Elevated (mild)

____ Depressed/Sad   ____ Angry   ____ Euphoric (moderate)

_✓_ Anxious or Fearful   ____ Pain (emotional)   ____ Expansive (severe)

2. AFFECT:

_✓_ Appropriate/Euthymic   ____ Broad   ____ Labile   ____ Constricted

____ Animated (as in mania)   ____ Flat   ____ Blunted

3. MOOD and AFFECT are

_✓_ Congruent   ____ Incongruent

E. THOUGHT PROCESSES AND CONTENT (*note irregularities of word usage, thought blocking, racing thoughts, flight of ideas, loose associations, delusional or near-delusional ideations, magical thinking, etc.*):

_✓_ No irregularities reported or noted

F. PERCEPTION (*note hallucinations, illusions, depersonalization, derealization, dissociative processes*):

_✓_ No irregularities reported or noted

G. OTHER (*e.g., notable difficulties of orientation, attention, memory, judgment, intelligence, insight*)

Attention/Concentration	Judgment	Intelligence	Insight	Memory
_√_ Intact	_√_ Good	_√_ Above Avg.	_√_ Good	_√_ Intact
____ Distractible	____ Average	____ Average	____ Fair	____ Short-term deficit
____ Impaired	____ Poor	____ Below Avg.	____ Poor	____ Long-term deficit

VIII. CLINCAL SUMMARY:

Client is single, 27-yr.-old biracial (Caucasian/Native American) female of Latin Origin & oldest of 4 siblings (1 bro/2 sis). Good relationship w/immediate family but entire extended family is estranged. Mom is recovering alcoholic w/5 yrs sobriety. CL is employed full time (extremely satisfied). Seeking services for relationship issues stemming from her reluctance to commit to intimate relationship w/BF she "really likes a lot" & thinks he may be "the one" due to overwhelming fear of disclosing her past, which includes a rape, abortion, and STD (Herp II) while in college. CL has remained abstinent since incident. Describes problem as extremely severe. CL also concerned about physical health & spot on leg she fears may be skin cancer but afraid to see medical doctor. CL reports difficulty sleeping & self-medicates w/alcohol & OTC sleep aids to avoid recurrent dream of having forcible sex as a child w/unknown male. Dream has increased in frequency past 6 months. CL relates this to rape incident. CL states readiness to commit to intimate relationship w/current BF but cannot bring herself to disclose her past to him because "he'll leave me" but if she does not tell him or waits too long "he'll get tired of waiting & leave anyway." CL withdraws from BF's pressure to commit by isolating. CL moderately concerned about critical attitude ("being too picky"), realistic versus unrealistic fears, disclosing her past (today is the first time ever), moodiness & tendency to isolate, and difficulty trusting others & making decisions. CL pleasantly dressed & well groomed, articulate, appears above average in intelligence, good insight & thought processes, judgment & (conscious) memory appear intact w/no perceptual irregularities. Displays congruent mood/affect & mostly appropriate/euthymic affect—constricted at times. CL's emotional anxiety & fear displays by psychomotor agitation (heavy breathing, hand wringing, restless legs, squirming). CL stated goals are to explore options for her future & decide how/when/whether to disclose past to BF or just end relationship. CL also wants to be able to sleep w/out having to medicate & wants dream "to go away." CL highly motivated to change, open & receptive w/strong identifiable skills (self-reports "I'm outgoing & friendly"), & few well-defined goals. Strong family support system, no significant impairment noted in job performance but presenting problem does impair significant personal relationship. Limits of confidentiality & emergency services/procedures reviewed w/ CL, who stated understanding.

Rhonda Bradley, LPC
_____   _____
Counselor Signature   Date

LuAnn Sizemore, LPC-S
_____   _____
Supervisor Signature (if necessary)   Date

Understanding the Client's Issues

Counselors-in-training are often overwhelmed by the issues and information a client brings into session. It feels as if the client has come in and given you a handful of random puzzle pieces. If you don't know how to organize the pieces, structure the foundation, and fit the pieces together, you are left with chaos and confusion. In this case, the counselor begins to focus on arbitrary pieces of the puzzle without a clue of how to connect. Case conceptualization is the process counselors use to learn how to organize, structure, and assemble the puzzle.

Case conceptualization is undoubtedly one of the most important aspects in the counseling process. In essence, it is the process of synthesizing and analyzing the data gathered from the client intake, psychosocial history, mental status, and other assessment instruments to create a "framework" for treatment.

When looking at the information gathered as a whole what does it tell us?

- Who our clients are
- What difficulties they are facing
- How they are functioning

- What patterns in behaving they are exhibiting
- What patterns in thinking they are experiencing
- What patterns in emoting they are experiencing and exhibiting
- What patterns of relating they utilize
- What they have tried in the past
- How long the problem has been occurring
- How motivated they are
- How strong a support system they have
- What their trauma history is

So how do we use case conceptualization to make sense of all this seemingly unrelated information? What do we do with it? We choose a model of case conceptualization to generate a plan. H. Stanley Judd said, "A good plan is like a road map: it shows the final destination and usually the best way to get there." That, in effect, is what case conceptualization is to the counseling process. Each conceptualization will detail diagnostic, clinical, and treatment information. Sperry (2005) described three types of case conceptualization found in the literature: symptom focused, client focused, and theory focused. Berman (2010) took this a step further by describing six styles of writing case conceptualizations within a theoretical framework. One of those mimicks Sperry's symptom-focused model; the other styles include (a) historically based, (b) diagnosis based, (c) assumption based, (d) interpersonally based, and (e) thematically based. These will be discussed further in the following section.

SYMPTOM FOCUSED. The symptom-focused model, derived from the medical model of therapy, focuses on the symptomology presented by a client followed by a treatment plan centered on the reduction of these symptoms. The symptom-focused conceptualization is grounded in behavioral modification techniques and employs language consistent with the behavioral approach. Symptoms and treatment objectives are reported in concrete measureable terms. The emphasis is placed on diagnosis and treatment of specific quantifiable symptoms. This type of case conceptualization is straightforward and is rather easy to implement, create, and monitor. Due to the simplicity and ease of monitoring progress, this type of conceptualization is preferred by most third-party payers.

For entry-level counselors this may be the least challenging of the three types of conceptualization. There are also resources available to guide counselors through this process in the way of treatment planning manuals. These manuals provide an outline to: (a) aid in the definition of the problem in behavioral terms, (b) create long-term goals, (c) create short-term objectives, (d) specify treatment in behavioral terms that are easily measured, and (e) offer diagnostic suggestions (Jongsma, Peterson, & Bruce, 2006).

Although a new counselor may be drawn to this type of conceptualization to reduce anxiety and to secure his or her developmental need for concrete explanations and solutions in counseling, there are drawbacks to this type of conceptualization. First and foremost, this type of conceptualization ignores the origins of the symptomology being presented. This leads to treatment that may act as a temporary Band-Aid for the presenting problem, yet may not address the issues needed for long-term symptom reduction. This style is also limited with client issues that are more abstract and ambiguous in nature.

CLIENT FOCUSED. The client-focused case conceptualization is motivated by the client's wants and desires. The information gathered is processed with the client to generate an understanding of the client and treatment for the client that is specific to his or her needs and wants. Sperry (2005) conceded that clients come into counseling with their own schema of how they view their problems, how severely the problem is affecting them, what they anticipate getting out of treatment, and how motivated they are to carry out the strategies identified to reach their therapeutic goals. The client may not be consciously aware of the schema he or she has developed; therefore, it is the counselor's task to work with the client to uncover and explore these schemas. Sperry contended not only that counselors must identify and unearth these schemas but also that they have a duty to collaborate with the client to create a shared schema or conceptualization, which in turns leads to enhanced treatment outcomes.

TABLE 3.3 Teyber's client-focused case conceptualization model

1. Identifying Data
2. Presenting Problem
3. Relevant History
4. Interpersonal style
   a) Is there an overall posture he/she takes toward others? What is the nature of his/her typical relationship?
      1. Moving toward
      2. Moving against
      3. Moving away
   b) How is the client's interpersonal stance demonstrated in the counseling relationship? What is the client's interpersonal orientation toward the counselor?
5. Environmental factors
   a) Environmental stressors affecting the client—both those centrally related to the problem and more peripheral stressors.
   b) Client support system: friends, family, living accommodations, recreational activities, financial situation.
6. Personality Dynamics
   a) Cognitive factors
      1. Intelligence
      2. Mental alertness
      3. Persistence of negative cognitions
      4. Positive cognitions
      5. Nature and content of fantasy life
      6. Level of insight—client's "psychological mindedness"; ability to hypothesize about his/her own and other's behaviors
      7. Capacity for judgments; client's ability to make decisions and carry out the practical affairs of daily living
   b) Emotional factors
      1. Typical or most common emotional states
      2. Mood during interview
      3. Appropriateness of affect
      4. Range of emotions that client has the capacity to display
      5. Cyclical aspects of the client's emotional life
   c) Behavioral factors
      1. Psychosomatic symptoms
      2. Other physical related symptoms
      3. Existence of persistent habits or mannerisms
      4. Sexual functioning
      5. Eating patterns
      6. Sleeping patterns
7. Counselor's conceptualization of the problem:
   What are the common themes identified by the client?
   What ties all the information together?

Source: Teyber (2006).

Edward Teyber (2006) has created a client-focused case conceptualization model based on his interpersonal process approach to counseling (see Table 3.3 and Table 3.4). This model specifically addresses the client's interpersonal style and personality dynamics with others as well as the counselor.

THEORY FOCUSED. Theory-focused case conceptualization uses a theoretical base to formulate the ways you will (a) form a relationship with a client, (b) understand a client given all the information gathered, and (c) determine what interventions to use with a client (Cheston, 2000). The heart of theory-focused conceptualization is determining why a person is experiencing the difficulties they are and how they are perpetuating the symptoms based on your theoretical modality. The answer to this is the driving force toward determining an appropriate intervention. Theory-focused case conceptualization has been criticized for being counselor

TABLE 3.4 Sample case conceptualization using the client-focused model developed by Teyber

Case Conceptualization

During the intake interview, Sophie revealed the following information about herself: While in college, Sophie believes she was drugged and raped by multiple men. The rape resulted in Sophie being pregnant, which lead to her having an abortion. Also, Sophie contracted type II herpes from the traumatic event, and she feels too ashamed to tell anyone, including a physician.

I. Identifying Data

Sophie is 27 years old, is biracial (Caucasian/Native American), and lives alone in a high-rise apartment near the center of the city within walking distance to work. She oversees seasonal sales marketing campaigns for a higher-end clothing chain especially popular with young professionals. Sophie is the oldest of four siblings, and her mother is a recovering alcoholic. While in college, Sophie was raped by multiple men and has had substantial anxiety ever since.

II. Presenting Problems

Sophie wonders why she is unable to commit to a relationship. She indicates that men usually like her more than she likes them. She has turned down two marriage proposals since college. She reports that her family and friends tell her she is "too picky." This adds additional stress and worry to her life because most of her friends have married and started a family, and she feels pressure to do the same. She knows this would please her parents. Though she describes herself as outgoing and friendly, she struggles with feelings of inadequacy.

III. Relevant History

Sophie is the oldest of four children. She was raised Presbyterian in a rural community where her parents still live. Her brother and oldest sister live near their parents in the same town and are married with children. Her younger sister attends college at the local university but continues to live at home. She has German, French, and Native American ancestors. She describes her relationship with her family as close. Her mother is a recovering alcoholic with 5 years continuous sobriety. They gather together almost every Sunday, on holidays, and on birthdays. She remembers a tumultuous family life while she was in high school and, as the oldest, tried to keep peace in the family, often covering for her mother when she was under the influence to reduce household turmoil. Sophie made good grades and was very popular with her peers in high school and college. As a student, she participated in a sorority as well as several clubs and organizations. Mostly, she was determined to set a good example for her siblings by getting a good job after graduation and having a successful career. To her knowledge, no one in her family has a history of mental illness, and only her mother has a history of addiction. Extended family members are rarely mentioned. Sophie is reluctant to commit to her boyfriend due to her overwhelming fear of disclosing her past trauma. Sophie remains sexually abstinent and stated that if her boyfriend finds out the truth about her trauma, he will leave her. In addition, Sophie stated if she doesn't tell him about her trauma, "He will get tired of waiting and leave anyway."

A. Medical: Sophie is a little concerned about her health. She spent a lot of time in tanning beds and for some time has ignored a spot on her leg hoping it would go away, but it seems to be getting bigger. She believes this is the least of her concerns but may see a doctor soon. Sophie has long been troubled by a reoccurring nightmare. In the dream she is a little girl having sex in the dark with an unknown man. She tries but is unable to resist or scream for help. She reports using sleeping pills and alcohol before bedtime in an effort to avoid dreaming.

B. Educational: Sophie has a bachelor's degree in marketing and management. She considered pursuing a MBA but because she has such a good job right now, she decided to postpone furthering her education. She appears to be of above average intelligence and describes herself as responsible and independent.

C. Military: Sophie has never served in the military.

D. Vocational: Sophie was hired for her present position immediately after graduation. After working part time in one of the company's retail stores during high school and completing an outstanding internship in the corporate office during her senior year in college, she required minimal training for her position. She receives excellent performance reviews and has a good rapport with company employees at every level. She rates her job satisfaction as very high.

E. Sexual: Sophie contracted a sexually transmitted disease years ago. She is not sexually active. She aborted one pregnancy. While in college, she remembers passing out at a party after drinking one bottle of beer. She recalls being in and out of consciousness and some males she did not know taking her to her apartment. The next morning she realized she had had sex but could not remember with whom. Several bruises appeared on her body, and she hid them under long clothing until they healed. She did not seek medical attention and kept the incident to herself. After a missed period, a pregnancy test revealed a positive result. She went alone to have an abortion at a clinic using a false name. Several days later, she developed very painful blisters in her genital area and tested positive for type II herpes at a health department. Since then, she manages outbreaks with medication prescribed by a doctor and filled at a pharmacy in another town. She has never revealed this to anyone nor has she had sex since. She has been dating a man for quite some time and is pretty sure he thinks she is "the one" and is ready to commit. His name is Sam, and she really likes him. They are both tiring of the rat race of city dwelling and dream of moving to the country. Recently she has been turning down his invitations to spend time together because he persists in wanting to take their relationship to the next level, which she feels ready to do but is horrified by the thought of telling him about her past. Until now, she has not discussed this with anyone.

F. Counseling: Sophie reports that she has never participated in counseling. She has attended Al-Anon and open A.A. meetings in the past.

IV. Interpersonal Style

Sophie's typical interpersonal style is to move toward others. She likes to please and is an overachiever in the workforce. She avoids confrontation with family and friends. When she is confronted with a situation she cannot handle in that way, she will retreat and become isolated. In counseling Sophie's style is similar to her patterns with others. She is eager to please me as the counselor as displayed by being early and always doing her homework. She becomes quiet when confronted and often tries to explain the contradictions mentioned to settle the issue in her mind.

V. Environmental Factors

Her environmental stressors are limited and her support system fairly strong such that on a typical day, Sophie gets up, usually walks to work, has lunch out with coworkers, walks home, changes clothes, has dinner, and does more work at home. Some evenings she goes out to dinner and/or to the movies with her boyfriend or a group of friends. On weekends, she goes to the library or the park, shops for groceries, cleans house, does laundry, attends church, and often drives to the country to visit her parents, brother and sisters, and their families. Sometimes the man she is dating accompanies her. She reports keeping to a strict schedule and maintaining order as priorities in her life.

VI. Personality Dynamics

a. Cognitive factors: Sophie has above-average intelligence, is mentally alert, focuses on positive cognitions, has an innate ability to understand her own and others' behaviors, and has a high ability to make decisions and carry out the practical affairs of daily living. Sophie has not processed her history of trauma.

b. Emotional factors: Sophie's typical emotional state is anxious, which was displayed during the intake interview. Her affect was appropriate and congruent with her verbalizations and mood; her range of emotions is normal, not blunted.

c. Behavioral factors: Sophie exhibits psychomotor agitation through hand wringing, heavy breathing, restless legs, and squirming. She experiences frequent nightmares, which she tries to avoid through self-medication. She avoids sexual functioning due to her trauma, which has led to embarrassment and fear of rejection. Her eating patterns are normal. Sophie drinks alcohol and ingests sleeping pills to avoid an uncomfortable and reoccurring sexual dream.

VII. Counselor's Conceptualization of the Problem

What are the common themes identified by the client? Sophie shows a common theme of fear of being rejected. She worked hard in every aspect of her life to keep the peace and to avoid confrontation and unease. This is consistent with her growing up in an alcoholic household and being the parentified child and the one to keep the peace.

What ties all the information together? Her personality style of moving toward others and her fear of rejection tie the information together leading to effective treatment possibilities.

driven and forcing a one-size-fits-all mentality. However, integrated theory has become popular to meet the diversity of needs each client brings to the counseling process.

For beginning counselors the first step in theory-focused case conceptualization is identifying a theory. This is an arduous task for some. When learning theories in your counseling program, you are often exposed to a significant variety at a rapid pace, leaving some confused and retaining only surface-level information for any given theory. It is important to spend quality time exploring theories and finding one that is the best fit for you and your personality style. Betan and Binder (2010) referred to the concept of metabolizing theory; they found that with time and experience, seasoned counselors are able to use theory almost unconsciously. It becomes part of the counselor's cognitive process, thereby considerably limiting the time spent on the immense task of case conceptualization. For beginning counselors, this process is slow and cumbersome, requiring much conscious thought, practice, and persistence.

Berman (2010) suggested a two-step process for organizing a case conceptualization by theory. She stated that creating a premise is an important first step to help the reader understand what will be covered in the conceptualization. The second part of the Berman model includes the supporting material that provides evidence for the material written in the premise. Berman suggested this material can be written in a multitude of styles, depending on the counselor's preference and theoretical orientation. Several of the styles she mentioned are (a) symptom focused, (b) historically based, (c) diagnosis based, (d) assumption based, (e) interpersonally based, and (f) thematically based. A description of each follows.

Symptom-focused counseling organizes the information in the case conceptualization in terms of the symptoms the client presents and uses these to guide the long- and short-term treatment goals.

Historically based written conceptualizations organize information in terms of time periods that are relevant to the client's presenting problems. This notes time periods when feelings, behaviors, and patterns emerged and were learned.

Diagnosis-based conceptualizations organize the information based on the five axes of the *DSM-IV-TR*. This is very similar to the symptom-focused model and is preferred in medical settings and for third-party payers.

Assumption-based conceptualizations use the major assumptions from a counseling theory to organize the written format. A sample of an assumption-based conceptualization is shown in Table 3.5.

Interpersonally based written conceptualizations focus on a systems perspective and how the client relates to others in his or her life. The information is organized around the relationships with others, the counselor, and with self.

Thematically based conceptualizations organize the presenting material around the client themes. These themes are identified through the client's behavior or attitudes toward life and the issues presented in therapy, and supporting materials are provided within the context of the theme. Table 3.5 is also an example of a case conceptualization derived from a person-centered theoretical perspective.

Diagnosis

THE DIAGNOSIS DEBATE. There has been some debate about whether counselors should diagnose mental disorders. Traditionally, counselors have used a wellness/developmental model of conceptualization and treatment as opposed to the medical model. However, to communicate with other professionals and to receive third-party reimbursement, diagnosis is necessary. Dougherty (2005) noted several ethical issues associated with diagnosis that beginning-level counselors should be aware of, including time restraints, bias, stereotyping, and lack of consistency from one clinician to another, to name just a few. There is often pressure generated by managed care companies to provide an accurate, speedy diagnosis. Yet, without the proper time to assess the client and consult other professionals, the likelihood of making faulty diagnoses increases. Formulating a diagnosis is not a one-time process; it must be reevaluated often.

Seligman (2004) suggested viewing diagnosis as one part of the person in a holistic context of the developmental model of counseling, providing a guide for the counselor to

TABLE 3.5 Person-centered theoretical case conceptualization written from an assumption-based style

Premise

Client demographics

Reason for referral

- Strengths and weaknesses based on theoretical assumptions

Theoretical supporting material

- Basic tenet: people will move forward in a constructive manner if they have the appropriate conditions fostering growth. Therefore, people who do not have a positive environment around them may grow in unconstructive ways.
- List what aspects of the following conditions are missing in the client's current relationships:
  1. Congruency
  2. Unconditional positive regard
  3. Accurate empathic understanding
- When these conditions are met, people become less defensive and more open to themselves and their world.
- When people are free, they are able to find their own way. What is stopping this person from being free?
- Counseling focuses on the constructive side of human nature, what is right, what assets the client has.
  1. What is blocking the client's growth? (Look within and outside self.)
  2. What is the client doing that is enabling him or her to live an authentic and full life?
  3. How well does this client know himself or herself? Those that know themselves best discover more appropriate behavior.
  4. How much responsibility is the client taking to fully encounter reality?
  5. Focus is on the here-and-now experience. How is the client not keeping this focus?
  6. What masks is your client wearing? These are developed through socialization and enable people to lose themselves.
- During intervention, to assess the case, Rogers (1957) describes four traits of people who are becoming actualized:
  1. Openness to experience
  2. A trust in themselves
  3. An internal source of evaluation
  4. A willingness to continue growing
- Give examples of what you may see or hear from your client that lets you know he or she is becoming actualized.
- The best source of assessment in person-centered counseling is not assessment devices but the individual client.

determine the most effective treatment plan, to understand the course of the disorder, and to help the client identify the symptoms in the context of a disorder. On one hand, a client may feel relief knowing that there is a diagnosis that can explain what he or she has been going through; on the other hand, diagnosis can stigmatize a person and prevent him or her from obtaining certain jobs or insurance policies, as well as allowing the client to perpetuate the problem by blaming the disorder and not taking any responsibility for treatment.

Several assessment guides are available that may help the beginning counselor feel more at ease in the diagnostic process, but one should always proceed with caution because there is no substitute for knowledge and experience. Clients do not want to feel like they are only being assessed based on symptoms and diagnosis, and standardized assessment procedures should be mixed with other interview questions and empathic understanding.

THE ROLE OF DIAGNOSIS IN TREATMENT.   Understanding the diagnostic assessment process is crucial to the formation of the treatment plan. This is a complex topic, and professional counselors ordinarily take entire courses in diagnosis and treatment of mental disorders. As a brief overview, the American Psychiatric Association (2013) proposed providing a view of the client in a holistic context. A sample diagnosis for Sophie on the five *DSM-IV-TR* axes might be as follows: PTSD 309.81/Alcohol dependence 303.90. Herpes zoster is a medical condition under treatment.

VOICES FROM THE FIELD 3.1   **First Impressions in Family Systems Theory, by Guy Shealy**

I have been trained as a pastoral counselor. Later, I adopted Bowen family systems theory as my primary approach to counseling. These two fields of knowledge inform me as I work with the clients I see. When individuals come to see me, I want to listen to what they bring as concerns. They usually are concerned about content issues, such as finances, sex, parenting concerns, in-laws, or communication. The questions I ask serve two functions: to elicit more information about content issues and to help the clients shift to "process thinking." When a content issue is presented, I will ask, "What happens in your head when . . . ?" or "How do you handle it inside you when . . . ?" I want clients to begin to understand process and how it works to creatively make the relationship function more effectively. Oftentimes with a couple, one partner will say something like, "I did not know you thought (or felt) that way." I want to get that kind of thinking into the counseling session.

I begin to look for where the anxiety is in the system. All systems have anxiety. Of course, anxiety does not necessarily have to create problems in the relationship. I look for where the anxiety is and how it is handled. Has this person always been anxious? I also want to know how other people in the relationship deal with this anxiety. Do they get caught up in it? How do they respond? I want to look at how the anxiety is moved around in the system. For example, consider an example where a husband has had a terrible day at work, and he comes home angry and hurt. The wife has already come home from a good day at work, has the kids playing, and is beginning to prepare dinner. The husband comes in, finds something to complain about, and the couple argues. The wife becomes anxious because her good day has been ruined. She is the one with the anxiety now while her husband watches TV or reads the paper or goes to the computer. The wife has now taken on the anxiety from her husband. The idea would be for both to recognize this process and make changes. Perhaps the husband could better contain his anxiety, whereas the wife improves on her ability to stay separate while listening empathically.

Couples often will come into the first session enmeshed. They will say they feel distant, but in reality they are overly involved in each other's lives. I want to create space, a separateness, so they can begin to know and change themselves. I have found the word *space* to be the least offensive and work the best. I will continue to say things like, "I want you to tell me about you, not someone else." I will tell people they are experts on the wrong person. They know what someone else needs to do to make the relationship better. If each partner becomes an expert on himself or herself and what he or she needs to do, the relationship will be better. Space is a difficult concept to grasp because people are concerned they already feel distant. I will continue to clarify what space is. Again, anxiety will be present and will have to be worked through.

I will listen for family-of-origin issues. Somewhere in our discussion something will be mentioned about being "just like your father/mother." That statement rarely is meant as a compliment! That opens the door for further discussion about the family-of-origin issue. Some people will adamantly maintain that what has happened is in the past and should stay there or has no impact on what is happening today. Some can be educated and will learn that our childhood had great impact on who we are, who (or whether) we choose as a partner, and how we raise our children. These family-of-origin issues are very important. At the first session, I will begin to do some education about family-of-origin issues.

I also look for triangulation issues (e.g., when relationships among two partners and a child interfere with direct, effective communication between the couple). People, issues, or things are triangulated into our relationships to keep us from being open with each other. I look for what is being triangulated into the relationship and then help people understand what they have to do to de-triangulate. Here again, space becomes important for the couple to focus on themselves and talk openly about what they are thinking and feeling.

I assess in my first session the differentiation levels of people when they come. Because Bowenian theory says we marry at about the same level, I begin to look for where that level is. We may marry at the same level, but we may not stay at that same level. Events, such as the birth of a child, can create a circumstance where one person grows and changes, but the other person does not. I check for alcohol and drug abuse, when that started, and how much. Do both participate? I also help them differentiate between thoughts and feelings. If they say the word *feel*, they must identify that feeling. Somewhere in the first session, I will ask for their help and say I want them to label the feeling so that I can hear clearly what they mean. For example, if a person says, "I feel like he never listens to me," I will say, "When you think he is not listening to you, what is the feeling?" The response is anger, sadness, or disappointment. I then help the person or the couple to differentiate between thoughts and feelings to be clear. Keeping the space helps the clients focus on themselves rather than the other person.

I must also manage my own anxiety and become a low-anxiety presence with the person or the couple. If I react to what is being said, then my anxiety is poured into the session. If I simply listen and accept, I become the presence that enables clients to accept those parts of themselves they find disgusting and distasteful. As they learn to accept those parts, they grow, and their relationships grow with them.

TREATMENT PLANNING

Treatment planning is an integral, but too often neglected, piece of the counseling puzzle. As mentioned earlier in the chapter, case conceptualization is referred to as a road map for working with your client. Using that analogy, let's consider that the treatment plan is your GPS (Global Positioning System); it actually provides more detail than a map, and if you follow the specific directions, you are much more likely to reach your desired destination. The treatment plan (GPS) should be influenced by your theoretical orientation (road map), but there are many more intricate pieces involved in developing a treatment plan. Ingram (2012) stated that a treatment plan should address the specifics of what will happen in the session, skills that the counselor will use, the type of relationship to be formed, and any specific processes that may be used. Table 3.6 shows an example of a completed treatment plan.

Conceptualizing a treatment plan for each specific client involves several data-gathering steps discussed earlier in this chapter. Whether in the form of an initial intake, a psychosocial history, general questioning to understand the client's story, or some combination of methods, assessment is imperative and must be an early piece of the counseling relationship. All these pieces of information help to clarify case conceptualization, may lead to a diagnosis, and definitely inform the treatment plan.

At this stage it becomes more apparent why it is so important to gain as much accurate information as possible during the assessment phase. Without accurate information, your GPS may take you to Alexandria, Louisiana, when you actually intended to go to Alexandria, Virginia; 1200 miles off course could be very frustrating in a counseling session.

Developing a Treatment Plan

The process of conceptualizing and writing a treatment plan may vary from one client to another and among counselors. In addition to considering your theoretical orientation, the goals of the client, and the setting in which you practice, the plan may also be influenced by the intended purpose (Maruish, 2002). The most obvious use is planning a course of treatment, but the treatment plan may also be used in dealing with third-party payers to support requests for continued services or to meet accreditation requirements with organizations such as TJC (The Joint Commission, formerly The Joint Commission on the Accreditation of Healthcare Organizations). Formalized treatment plans for purposes other than the use of the counselor may require additional information. However, here we will outline the basic steps of treatment planning that are useful for treating a client.

TABLE 3.6 Individualized treatment plan

Client Name (First MI Last): Sophie O. Sheppard				Client # 12345
Goals	Goal #	Linked to Treatment Recommendation # from Intake:		Start Date: 10-5-12
State Goal below in collaboration with client:	Client has read? ☒ Yes ☐ No	Client agrees? ☐ Yes ☐ No	Client's Initial: *SOS*	Target Completion Date: 3-5-12
To ↓ Sx of Anxiety				Adjusted Target Date:
				Reason for Adjustment:
Desired Results in client's words:				
"I want to find out if I have a future with Sam or not and stop feeling trapped and stuck in my life."				
"I want a future with him but he needs to know what he's getting into."				
Strengths and how they will be used to meet this goal:				
CL displays a desire to seek help as evident by confiding in counselor.				
CL values honesty.				
CL is resilient.				
Skills/Knowledge needed:				
CL needs further sexual education in regards to STDs.				
CL needs regular medical care to address health concerns.				
Address sexual trauma; Recognize cognitive distortions.				
Natural/Community Supports needed:				
Family support				
Primary care physician				
Continue w/work				

OBJECTIVE #	Start Date: 10-5-12	Target Date/Duration: 3-5-12
Client will ↓ Sx of Anxiety as evidenced by ↑ exercise level and stress reducing activities		
Client will:		
CL will participate in rigorous exercise for at least 30 minutes once per day.		
CL will research yoga classes and meditation groups.		
CL will engage in 1 pleasurable activity per week.		
Parent/Guardian/Community/Other will:		
☐ Not Clinically Indicated		

Therapeutic Intervention	Service Description	Frequency	Responsible: Provider/ Credential
Identify anxiety relieving activity	Counseling	1x/wk	
Encourage new/ diverse activities	"	"	
Assign/process pleasurable activity	"	"	

Objective #__2__:	Start Date:	Target Date/Duration:

CL will address and process history of sexual trauma as evidenced by ↑ reporting of emotions tied to trauma; identify fears; demonstrate improved coping (↓ in anxiety self-rating).
Client will:
Learn progressive muscle relaxation techniques & practice daily.
Address/process but not relive trauma.
Role-play conversation with b/f.
Parent/Guardian/Community/Other will: ❏ Not Clinically Indicated

Therapeutic Intervention	Service Description	Frequency	Responsible: Provider/Credential
Teach/coach prog. relaxation	Counseling	1x/wk	
Guide in trauma process	"	"	
Role-play inter-/intrapersonal situations	"	"	

Actual Date of Goal Completion:	Goal Discontinued Date:	Reason for Discontinuation or refer to Progress Note of _____ (date):

Other Agencies Involved
Name of Agency: Community Health Clinic
Name and Title: Doctor available
Services Provided: Continued medication monitoring

Transition/Level of Care Change/Discharge Plan	
Level of Care/Transition/Discharge Criteria: For D/C CL needs to report: process history of sexual trauma as evidenced by ↑ reporting of emotions tied to trauma; identify fears; demonstrate improved coping (↓ in anxiety self-rating).	Anticipated Date:

Team Signatures	
Client: Sophie Sheppard	Date: 3-5-12
Client received copy of Individualized Treatment Plan? ☒ Yes ❏ No	Initial to confirm copy:
Parent/Guardian(s) (If Applicable):	Date: 9-15-12
Primary Provider/Credential: *RhondaBradley,LPC*	Date: 9-15-12
Supervisor's Signature/Credential: *LuAnnSizemoreLPC-S*	Date: 9-15-12

Jongsma et al. (2006) suggested six steps for developing a treatment plan that are helpful in providing some guidance. The steps are (a) problem selection (identifying the problem), (b) problem definition (defining the problem), (c) goal development (developing goals), (d) objective construction (developing objectives), (e) intervention creation (selecting interventions), and (f) diagnosis determination (diagnosis). Each of these steps will be discussed in more detail next.

Identifying the Problem

The first step in developing a treatment plan is identifying what the problem is. A familiar concern from counseling interns is, "I don't feel like I'm getting anywhere with this client." To which a supervisor typically responds, "What goals have been identified for counseling?"

Facilitating the client's exploration of possible goals for counseling is an important part of your job as the counselor. Jongsma et al. (2006) pointed out that the client may identify many issues throughout the assessment phase, and it is the counselor's job to help the client prioritize the most important concerns on which to focus in counseling. Some of the issues may need to be "tabled" and dealt with at a later time because the treatment plan should not contain more than a few problems to focus on at any one time. However, it is important to note that the treatment plan should be reviewed and revised over time as goals are achieved and change (Maruish, 2002).

Defining the Problem

The next step in the process is defining the problem as it specifically relates to the client (Jongsma et al., 2006; Maruish, 2002). For example, let's assume that the counselor and client identify the problem to be that the client is depressed. As you know, depression can manifest itself in many ways (e.g., not eating, eating too much, not sleeping, sleeping too much, social isolation, abusing drugs or alcohol, loss of interest, poor performance at work or school). Therefore, it is important to provide a behavioral definition of how the identified problem is manifesting.

Developing Goals

Once the counselor and client have identified, prioritized, and defined problems to be addressed in counseling, the next step is developing long-term treatment goals. Jongsma et al. (2006) recommended setting "broad goals for the resolution of the target problem" (p. 5). In other words, what will it look like if the client achieved the desired effect? Each problem identified for the treatment plan will have a minimum of one goal statement, and each goal will have several related objectives. Maruish (2002) asserted that goals and objectives should be achievable, realistic, measurable, and stated in the positive.

Developing Objectives

There are typically two or more objectives associated with each long-term goal. Objectives can be thought of as short-term goals that are measurable. Therefore, objectives must be written in behaviorally measurable language. Objectives can be thought of as a series of steps that, when completed, will result in the achievement of the long-term goal (Jongsma et al., 2006).

SAMPLE GOALS AND OBJECTIVES.   To help with your conceptualization of goals and objectives, we offer the following examples:

Goal #1—Elevate mood and show evidence of increasing social interaction.

Objectives
1. Identify cause of depressed mood.
2. Specify past or present contributing factors to sadness.
3. Engage in social interaction with family and friends.

Goal #2—Reduce the significance (frequency and intensity) of anxiety so that social and occupational functioning are not impaired.

Objectives
1. Increase participation in exercise activities that decrease level of anxiety.
2. Engage in pleasurable activity with family and friends at least once each week.
3. Participate in relaxation activities such as yoga or meditation.

Selecting Interventions

Interventions are what you, the professional counselor, actually plan to do to achieve the objectives. These are action items, and there should be at least one intervention for every objective identified in the treatment plan. Jongsma et al. (2006) suggested that interventions be selected after taking into account both the client's needs and the counselor's abilities. For example, you should not choose systematic desensitization as an intervention if you have little to no experience with that technique. As counseling interns, you might also take into consideration the experiences of your supervisors when selecting interventions. It's possible to select an intervention that you do not have experience or expertise with if your supervisor is experienced in that technique and willing to supervise you as you are learning new tools for your toolbox.

Diagnosis

Diagnosis may or may not be included in your role as a counselor practicum student or intern. If diagnosis is part of your training placement, the steps you have taken toward assessment and case conceptualization up to this point should inform the diagnosis. Diagnostic categories from the *DSM-5* are typically expected to be included in a treatment plan, especially by third-party payers. You are encouraged to practice this piece of the treatment plan process under supervision, even if it is not required at your internship site.

An Example Treatment Plan

The steps outlined here and included in the Case Study 3.2 example make up the core of any treatment plan. However, it's important to note that, depending on who the treatment plan is being written for, additional information might be included. Maruish (2002, p. 133) identified the following components that may be included in formal treatment plans: (a) referral source and reason for referral, (b) presenting problem, (c) problem list, (d) diagnosis, (e) goals and objectives, (f) treatment, (g) patient strengths, (h) potential barriers to treatment, (i) referral for evaluation, (j) criteria for treatment termination or transfer, (k) responsible staff, and (l) treatment plan review date.

CASE STUDY 3.2

Treatment plan: Problem #1: Depression

Definition: Client reports experiencing decreased appetite (loss of 10 lbs. in 2 weeks without trying), increased sleep (up from 8 hours a night to 14 hours in a 24-hour period), lack of energy or desire to engage in social activities previously enjoyed, feeling worthless.

- *Goal:* Alleviate depressed mood, return to previous level of functioning.
- *Objective:* Describe symptoms of depression client is experiencing.
- *Intervention(s):* Ask client to make a list of symptoms, describing as specifically as possible each symptom; process list in session.
- *Objective:* Identify source of the depression.
- *Intervention(s):* Ask client to identify possible causes of depression, make a list, and process in session.
- *Diagnosis:* Major Depressive Disorder, Single Episode

Summary

When working with clients, there are many details of the first impression. One of your first decisions will be to focus on either building the relationship or gathering information, although both will be a focus in the helping process at some point. In developing the relationship, we focus on building rapport, characteristics of helpers, and counseling skills. When the priority is on information

gathering, we focus on the intake process, informed consent, and treatment planning and diagnosing.

In developing a relationship with clients, the chapter identified such important helper characteristics as empathy, genuineness, unconditional positive regard, self-control, sympathy, flexibility, sensitivity, and an ability to create a safe environment. Basic counseling skills includ attending, listening, and responding skills (i.e., reflection, paraphrasing, probes, and questions). Advanced responding skills include summarizing, immediacy, confrontation, self-disclosure, and advanced empathy.

Initial sessions encompass the legal and ethical aspects of the counseling relationship, defining client rights, confidentiality, and duty to warn through the informed consent process. This chapter also detailed the importance of confidentiality with minors and how to work with parents regarding their child's rights within the counseling relationship.

Although many skills are used with the client in session, there are also more advanced skills related to the counselor's process, which focus on internal processing or working outside the client session. These skills include case conceptualization, treatment planning, and diagnosis. These are imperative for understanding what issues will be addressed, in planning sessions, determining the best treatment, and theoretical modalities to be used.

Many agencies have specialized intake forms to help gather information about the client in a structured format, which is highly recommended for beginning counselors to use while gaining experience in the field. During this initial intake process, counselors are beginning to assess the client's needs, goals, and wants through both formal and informal assessment tools. Gathering a psychosocial history and conducting a mental status exam are the most commonly used tools.

When working with clients, counselors use specific skills to develop the relationship and gather information. These skills should be maintained throughout the relationship even as more advanced skills are used. Another key aspect mentioned in the chapter is the amount of research that shows the person, or the "self," of the counselor is one of the key ingredients in successful counseling, therefore making counselor self-assessment and self-awareness a necessity to becoming an effective counselor.

CHAPTER 4

Integrating Theory into Practice*

BY DANA HELLER LEVITT, ALISSA DARNELL, BRADLEY T. ERFORD, AND ANN VERNON

PREVIEW

The nature and quality of the counseling relationship is more significant than any other factor in counseling. Given this perspective, why do professional counselors study theories? Whether working with individuals, families, or groups, regardless of the setting, professional counselors have a professional responsibility to develop a foundation and clear rationale for their theoretical orientation to serve clients best. Professional counselors operate out of theories that best fit their personal philosophies of human change and the counseling process, but also choose approaches that effectively address the client's issues. Selecting a theoretical orientation is a career-long process that begins during professional training. In this chapter, the significance of integrating theory into counseling practice is explored, and a brief overview of the major theoretical paradigms is presented. You will also begin to explore your own initial preferences for theoretical orientation with the intent of continuing your personal and professional exploration to discover your personal style.

THE SIGNIFICANCE OF THEORY

Theories ground us as professional counselors. They provide a means to understand what we are doing, how we are serving clients, and how to explain counseling to clients. People entering counseling are generally not interested in hearing a detailed description of their counselor's philosophical beliefs about the nature of the counseling relationship and human change. Rather, they are seeking guidance about the change process and how the professional counselor can help accomplish that goal. Theories represent clients' realities and what we know to be important and effective elements of the counseling relationship (Hansen, 2006a). Professional counselors must have a firm sense of the counseling process alongside their own philosophies about what works in counseling and how individuals change and grow.

A firm understanding of your beliefs about counseling can help you explain the process to clients, helping them understand the nature of counseling and what can be expected (Gladding, 2012). This road map for counseling can help you generate new ideas with the client to determine the best course of action and the means to reach goals.

Theories provide a framework for conceptualizing client problems and determining a course of action in counseling (Halbur & Halbur, 2006). For example, a professional counselor who operates from a cognitive-behavioral standpoint would identify a client's struggle with bulimia as faulty logic and plan a course of treatment to reshape thoughts and behaviors. A psychodynamic oriented professional counselor would view the issue through the lens of the client's past and spend counseling time uncovering early triggers and sustaining factors for the disorder.

*The authors wish to acknowledge Tierney Farry for her assistance with revisions and contributions to the chapter.

Ethics of Applying Counseling Theory

One theory does not fit for all clients. A successful approach with one client may be a complete disaster with another. Professional counselors have an ethical responsibility to be culturally competent and to address each client's needs as such. There is no cookie-cutter, "one size fits all," approach to counseling. Despite what some clients may be seeking, professional counselors do not have a handbook of problems and solutions. Professional counselors instead must use their understanding of theory to provide the best possible services to clients. Operating from a clear theoretical framework also means being flexible with that approach to know when it will not work. Self-Assessment Activity 4.1 provides an opportunity to explore some of the theoretical underpinnings of your counseling approach.

SELF-ASSESSMENT ACTIVITY 4.1 THEORETICAL UNDERPINNINGS

A 7-year-old girl is referred for counseling. Recently, she has been having difficulty staying on task during class and difficulty making friends. Her parents were never married and no longer live together. Her teacher reports that the girl came to her the previous day and mentioned something about other students making fun of her on the playground because she does not have a "real" family.

- As a professional counselor, how would you establish rapport?
- What types of questions would you ask her during the first session?
- What strategies would you employ to begin solving some of the problems she is having in school?
- Now, if the student was a 21-year-old male Asian college student with a history of distractibility and poor peer relations, what types of alterations would you make to your approach and strategies?
- Finally, if the client were a 42-year-old woman returning to college or graduate school, and with a history of distractibility and poor peer relations, how might you change your approach and strategies?

From an ethical standpoint, professional counselors must be clear about their professional orientation to serve clients best. As discussed in Chapter 6, the American Counseling Association (ACA) *Code of Ethics* (2005) provides guidelines for professional and ethical counseling practice. All professional counselors and counselors in training are expected to abide by the principles stated in the *Code of Ethics*. Sections of the *Code of Ethics* pertain specifically to learning and practice associated with theories. Professional counselors must be aware of new trends and best practices in the profession. Professional counselors must also be competent to use the theories they choose to employ in counseling and must have a firm foundation for the work they perform with clients.

Closely related, and perhaps one of the most fundamental aspects of professional and ethical practice, is continual counselor self-reflection. **Self-awareness** is crucial to counselor development. Professional counselors must regularly assess their beliefs about the counseling process and their effectiveness with clients. By this manner of self-awareness, professional counselors can determine and strengthen their theoretical beliefs and practices. Self-Assessment Activity 4.2 encourages exploration and refinement of your theoretical approach by exploring the approaches used by practitioners in the field.

What Makes a Good Theory?

In their classic text, Hansen, Stevic, and Warner (1986) suggested that a good counseling theory is (a) clear and easily understood; (b) comprehensive; (c) explicit and heuristic, generating further research; (d) specifically geared to help clients reach their desired outcomes; and (e) useful to practitioners. Theories must be sound to be plausible to professional counselors. Literally hundreds of theories exist, and more continue to emerge (Ivey, Ivey, & Zalaquett, 2010). All these theories can be overwhelming to beginning counselors who are

---

SELF-ASSESSMENT ACTIVITY 4.2 THEORY IN THE FIELD

Interview three practicing counselors about their theoretical orientations. Discuss with them the importance of theory in their current work, how they arrived at their personal theories, and the relationship of their theories to personal philosophies. Are there differences when working with individuals, groups, or families? How do the counselors' theoretical orientations compare and contrast with yours?

---

trying to do what is in the best interests of their clients. Professional counselors need a means of organizing the information about theories, applying what works, and building on natural helping capabilities.

Intentionality, making conscious and intentional decisions, is a necessity in applying the basic helping skills (Halbur & Halbur, 2011). As mentioned in Chapter 5, skill application is both art and science. Technical expertise, although important, will not always make the professional counselor most effective. A firm, philosophical understanding of the counseling profession and practice, and knowledge of the research behind what you do, will help you in your selection of and adherence to a theory that best fits your natural style of helping. Considering theories with respect to their common elements can help professional counselors determine what works best for whom and most notably for you as the counselor.

THEORETICAL PARADIGMS

Through self-awareness, professional counselors strengthen their approaches and learn new ways to work with clients. Theoretical orientation usually remains relatively constant through counselors' development given the connection to personal philosophy. Changes that occur tend to be within the general categories of theories, referred to as **paradigms**. These paradigms are a means of grouping theories based on common characteristics. Multiple theories exist within each paradigm. Table 4.1 provides summary characteristics of the five most

TABLE 4.1 Theoretical Paradigms: Theories and Theorists

Paradigm	Major Theories	Prominent Theorists
Psychodynamic	Psychoanalysis	Sigmund Freud
	Adlerian	Alfred Adler
	Ego Psychology	Carl Jung
Humanistic/Existential	Person-Centered	Carl Rogers
	Existential	Victor Frankl, Irvin Yalom, Rollo May
	Gestalt	Fritz Perls
Behavioral/Cognitive-Behavioral	Behavioral	John Watson, B. F. Skinner, Albert Bandura, John Krumboltz
	Cognitive	Aaron Beck
	Cognitive Behavioral Therapy	Donald Meichenbaum
	Rational Emotive Behavior Therapy	Albert Ellis
Systems	Family Systems	Murray Bowen, Virginia Satir
Emergent	Narrative	Michael White, David Epston
	Constructivist	George Kelly
	Feminist	
	Interpersonal Therapy (IPT)	

prominent paradigms, and Table 4.2 summarizes the techniques and multicultural considerations of the important theories ordinarily associated with each paradigms. Each of these paradigms will be explained in detail throughout the remainder of the chapter.

TABLE 4.2 Theoretical Paradigms: Techniques and Multicultural Considerations

Paradigm	Principles	Techniques	Considerations
Psychodynamic	Predetermined	Free association	Ego and past cultural identity development
	Relationship of events and current functioning	Interpretation	Id, ego, superego development
	Bring unconscious into conscious	Dream analysis	Limited views of women
		Analysis of transference	
Humanistic/ existential	Innate goodness of people	Counseling relationship	Attention to individual's unique perspective
	Self-actualization	Empty chair	Lack of structure
	Freedom and responsibility	Genuineness, empathy, unconditional positive regard	Limited attention to external factors
	Finding meaning	Role play	Common values of love, death, anxiety
	Anxiety	Role reversal	
		"I" statements	
Behavioral/ cognitive-behavioral	Changing behavior, negative thought patterns, beliefs	Specify automatic thoughts	Understanding beliefs as identity
	ABCDEs of REBT	Homework	Structure
	Disputing irrational beliefs	Thought stopping	Caution when challenging belief systems
		Cognitive restructuring	
		Token economy	
Systems	Family provides framework for understanding individual	Genograms	Identity patterns
	Differentiation of self	Questioning	Caution when attempting to change multigenerational patterns
		Coaching	Resistance to external input on family
		"I" position	
		Detriangulation	
Narrative	Retell story to create favorable outcomes	Deconstruct problems	Many cultures emphasize storytelling
	Person is not the problem	Externalize problems	High-level processing required
		Miracle question	
		Sparkling moments	
Constructivism	Personal reality	Card sort	Insight required
	Personal construct	Identify constructs	Challenges test beliefs and principles

Paradigm	Principles	Techniques	Considerations
		Repertory	
Feminist	Application of feminist principles: equality, empowerment	Gender role analysis	Addresses shared experiences of oppression
	Mutuality	Empowerment	Political action may be against belief
	Androgyny	Egalitarian relationship	Limited application with men
		Sociocultural exploration of gender	
Interpersonal psychotherapy	Improve interpersonal functioning, social network	Therapeutic alliance	Flexible and adaptable to unique individuals
	Attachment, social, and communication theories	Communication analysis	
	Present focus	Interpersonal incidents	
		Content and process affect	
		Role playing	

Theories can be described as having specific and common factors. **Specific factors** are the unique characteristics of a given theory. They are elements that distinguish one theory from another and are often the basis of association with a theory. For example, the empty chair technique is a specific factor for gestalt, a humanistic-existential theory. Disputing irrational beliefs is unique to Albert Ellis's rational emotive behavior therapy (REBT) and the behavioral and cognitive behavioral paradigm. **Common factors** are characteristics that appear in most if not all theoretical perspectives. For example, a therapeutic alliance and a healing setting that promotes client trust through professional counselor competence are common factors. A coherent rationale and set of procedures are also common to all theories. These are important principles to keep in mind as you review the major paradigms and begin to formulate and solidify your approach to counseling. To illustrate further the application of theoretical principles, consider the case of Terry in Case Study 4.1, and then answer the questions posed in Self-Assessment Activity 4.3. We will return to this case throughout our discussion of the paradigms and theories.

The following discussion of theories and paradigms is broad in nature. We encourage you to read further about theories in the references provided throughout this chapter and to research in greater depth the specific theories of interest.

CASE STUDY 4.1

Terry

Terry is a 23-year-old graduate student in microbiology. Terry recently relocated to the area to pursue graduate study after completing her undergraduate degree at a small college near her hometown. Now living two states and hundreds of miles away from her family, Terry feels that she is experiencing her independence for the first time.

Terry first became interested in science when she received a science kit for her seventh birthday. Her parents encouraged her to study science throughout high school and pushed her toward a major in biology when she entered college. Terry has heard on more than one occasion that she is the family's "only hope for a doctor." As first-generation immigrants to the United States, Terry's parents feel that their only daughter must be successful to prove their culture's ability to compete in an American environment.

Terry was referred to counseling following the midterm period of her first term in graduate school. Her roommate discovered numerous cuts on her arms and reported that Terry had seemed down over the past few weeks. When she finally agreed to see a professional counselor, Terry reported that she did not perform well on her midterm exams and was questioning whether she could make it in graduate school. She was concerned about disappointing her parents and bringing shame to their family.

SELF-ASSESSMENT ACTIVITY 4.3 PRESENTING ISSUES

Considering the case of Terry, write your initial reactions to her presenting issues for counseling. Specifically:

1. What is the problem?
2. Who is involved in Terry's dilemma?
3. How is the dilemma affecting Terry?
4. What would you hope to see as the goal of counseling for Terry?
5. What might counseling entail?
6. How will you know that counseling is complete?
7. How does your conceptualization attend to Terry's culture?

Keep your responses in a convenient location as you review the remainder of the chapter. These responses may relate to your emerging theoretical orientation.

Psychodynamic Paradigm

At the time of his work, Sigmund Freud was considered revolutionary in his thinking and conceptualizing of the problems experienced by people, primarily women. Today, many theories are based on Freud's work, either additive to what he developed or created as an alternative explanation to a theory heavily focused on the past and the subconscious mind. For this reason, the psychodynamic paradigm serves as an introduction and foundation to the other paradigms of counseling theories.

Theories that fall under the psychodynamic paradigm are based largely on insight, unconscious motivation, and personality reconstruction. The psychodynamic paradigm holds that most problems clients face are the result of unresolved issues from their early development. The focus in counseling from a psychodynamic framework is on the relationship of past events with current functioning. In the case of Terry, the professional counselor may question how childhood messages of expected success are affecting her current performance in graduate school and the subsequent feelings she experiences. The psychodynamic approach is very analytic in nature and may require a good deal of time to uncover past issues and make headway into current and future functioning.

PSYCHOANALYSIS. Freud's psychoanalytic theory is probably the most widely recognized theory in the psychodynamic paradigm. Many people may have the image of a wise therapist sitting behind a couch, on which a client lays and contemplates the meaning of past events. Many popular media depictions do little to ameliorate this stereotype and may perpetuate the public's mistaken beliefs about the nature of counseling in general. Although this image may have been the form of psychoanalysis in early renditions of the theory, much has changed since Freud's groundbreaking approach to counseling to challenge the means by which professional counselors with a psychoanalytic orientation help their clients.

Freud believed that personality is completely formed in childhood, and that challenges later in life are the result of unresolved conflicts. Consistent with the idea that theories emerge from our personal philosophies and experiences, Freud's background demonstrates his emphasis on childhood and the family. The eldest of eight siblings of an authoritarian father, Freud was particularly close to his mother. His upbringing and religious affiliation (a Jew in Vienna, Austria, in the mid to late 1800s) limited his career aspirations to medicine or law. One might see the basis of Freud's intense self-analysis and his subsequent theories of personality dynamics as based on his own life experiences.

In psychoanalysis, the personality is perceived as being composed of three parts: the **id**, or pleasure principle; the **ego**, or reality principle; and the **superego**, or morality principle (conscience). Conflict among these structures creates anxiety in the individual. The subsequent anxiety is often managed by the ego by employing **defense mechanisms**. These mechanisms help the individual to cope with the anxiety and not be overwhelmed. Defense mechanisms can be either adaptive or damaging. For example, Terry may be turning her frustrations with her parents' expectations inward and harming herself, rather than expressing these feelings to her parents. This process of projecting unwanted emotions to oneself in this case is maladaptive in the sense that Terry is being harmed both physically and emotionally.

The goal of psychoanalytic counseling is to bring unconscious drives into consciousness and develop insight into intrapsychic conflicts. Techniques such as free association, interpretation, dream analysis, and analysis of resistance and transference may be employed to assist in the development of insight. As might be expected (and often a criticism of this approach), this process can be quite lengthy and time consuming.

The psychoanalytic counselor is like a blank screen. Listening, analyzing, and attending to **transference** (i.e., a client projects feelings for another person onto the counselor, such as when the client perceives the counselor to be a "father figure") and **countertransference** (i.e., a counselor reciprocates by engaging in interactions with the client similar to what the client experienced in a primary relationship, such as when the counselor behaves as the parent figure would toward the client who perceives the counselor to be a "father figure") issues are essential to successful counseling in the psychoanalytic approach. The therapeutic relationship takes the form of the professional counselor as expert, teaching the client about the intrapsychic processes occurring.

Concepts such as defense mechanisms and transference seem to be relevant for individuals from various backgrounds. The culturally sensitive counselor may encourage individuals from ethnic and racial minority groups to develop an overall ego identity as well as a cultural identity. It is also important for psychoanalytic counselors to address their own potential biases and recognize how countertransference could unintentionally play a part in the counseling process. A limitation for multicultural counseling in psychoanalysis is in the area of gender issues. Women are seen as inferior to men because they do not resolve the Electra complex as completely as it is thought that men resolve the Oedipal complex. This concept and other similar concepts, such as penis envy, have been largely discredited and discontinued. For independent study on psychoanalysis, consult the following foundational resources:

Freud, A. (1936). *The ego and the mechanisms of defense* (J. Strachey, Trans.). New York, NY: International Universities Press.
Freud, S. (1900/1955). *The interpretations of dreams* (J. Strachey, Trans.). London, UK: Hogarth.
Freud, S. (1923/1933). *New introductory lectures on psychoanalysis* (W. J. H. Sprott, Trans.). New York, NY: Norton.
Freud, S. (1923/1947). *The ego and the id* (J. Strachey, Trans.). London, UK: Hogarth.

ADLERIAN COUNSELING.   Alfred Adler, a student of Freud, developed his theory as a result of disagreement with many of the principles his mentor proposed. Adler commended Freud's work on dream interpretation, yet the generalizations Freud drew from dreams and his emphasis on sexual trauma and development did not resonate with Adler. Herein lies another example of the need to formulate a personally relevant theory of counseling. Adler left Freud's tutelage to develop his approach of focusing on the whole person. This holistic viewpoint approached the client as a whole, indivisible being, capable of growth, seeking social interest and connections with others. Similar to Freud, Adler emphasized the role of childhood in personality development and problem (and solution) formation.

Adler's work has been widely used, yet not widely researched or developed. Adler's work is best known for its emphasis and analysis of birth order and sibling relationships. Sweeney (1998) is one of a few modern Adlerian scholars. Traces of Adler's work are evident in the wellness movement in the counseling profession. Commonly used Adlerian-based techniques include use of I messages, "acting as if," and "spitting in the client's soup."

The Adlerian concept of social interest lends to the theory's cultural sensitivity. **Social interest** means individuals are encouraged to move beyond themselves to learn about and understand different cultural groups and how they may contribute to the greater society. Cultures that emphasize the family find that many Adlerian concepts fit with their value systems. However, limitations exist where emphasis is placed on changing the autonomous self and in the exploration of early childhood experiences. Some clients may find it inappropriate to reveal family information or may not want to delve into the past because they may not see the connection to current pressing concerns. For more information regarding Adlerian counseling, the following resources may be useful:

Adler, A. (1927). *Understanding human nature*. Greenwich, CT: Fawcett.

Adler, A. (1964). *Social interest. A challenge to mankind*. New York, NY: Capricorn.

Adler, A. (1969). *The practice and theory of individual psychology*. Patterson, NJ: Littlefield, Adams.

Dreikurs, R. (1953). *Fundamentals of Adlerian psychology*. Chicago, IL: Alfred Adler Institute.

Sweeney, T. J. (1998). *Adlerian counseling. A practitioner's approach* (4th ed.). Muncie, IN: Accelerated Development.

OTHER PSYCHODYNAMIC THEORIES.   Jungian theory, also referred to as ego psychology, and object-relations theory are other approaches that fit within this paradigm. Although many principles of these theories are used today, more modern adaptations of psychoanalysis and Adlerian counseling are seen more readily in practice. Table 4.3 provides a listing of strategies and techniques aligned with the psychodynamic paradigm. To study a foundational work by Carl Jung, refer to:

Jung, C. G. (1961). *Memories, dreams, reflections*. New York, NY: Vintage.

TABLE 4.3 Psychodynamic Strategies and Interventions

- Analysis of transference and countertransference
- Analysis of private logic
- Parent or teacher consultations
- Encouragement
- Analyze Adlerian goals of misbehavior (attention, power, inadequacy) and build social interest through group activities
- Teach "I" statements and other skills
- Encourage insight into unconscious aspects of problem through creative processes
- Adlerian play therapy to discover the child's lifestyle and private logic
- Teach parents techniques for encouraging the child
- Family constellation and family atmosphere
- Lifestyle analysis
- Striving for significance and belonging
- Natural and logical consequences
- Early recollections to understand the child's behavior patterns
- Adlerian family counseling for family to learn to operate cooperatively
- Variation of activities between play and talking can be used such as during sand play or drawing
- The use of metaphor and exploration of developmental themes highlighted in movies, TV, and books
- Focus on helping the student become more self-aware through the use of pictures, stories, and metaphors
- Help the student to accept responsibility for the life choices that come with becoming an adult and to avoid regression toward childhood, where decisions were made on their behalf
- Assist with adult identity formation in a culturally sensitive fashion

- Explore recurrent themes in the child's fantasies and play
- Play therapy techniques may be used to understand the current emotional state of the student
- Acting "as-if"
- Free association
- Determine events of childhood that may have a larger impact later in life
- Empty chair
- Role-play
- Sand tray play and puppets may help younger children project angry feelings outside themselves
- Try a projection game such as "Parallels with Animals" in which the counselor asks the child what different animals look, act, and sound like when they are angry (Vernon, 2004)
- Artwork
- Incomplete sentences
- Psychoeducational lessons/handouts on self-understanding
- Recognizing feelings and basic motivation
- Mutual storytelling
- Draw a tree, and make a branch for each person the student feels he can trust
- Analysis of avoidance (e.g., refusing to come to school)
- Talk about the fears and worries that may be embedded in the unconscious
- Relationship of events and current functioning
- Dream analysis
- Analysis of ego development (fragile ego, under/overdeveloped superego)
- Analysis of anxiety and defense mechanisms (especially avoidance)
- Use of sand tray and symbolic play to better understand conscious and unconscious struggles
- Patterns of similar behavior for family members
- Interpret the reason for behavior based on dialogue, drawings, or dreams
- Explore relationships between current behavior and past or current life events
- Attachment assessment and introduction of stable adult figure
- Explore relationship with teachers perceived as "safe" or "unsafe"
- Explore unconscious themes through use of a timeline to chart significant life events
- Verbally explore the student's past and how this affects current behavior
- Use various art mediums such as drawing or sculpture to allow students to explore and work through early childhood stressors
- List some positive things about self to draw on strengths, encourage, and build self-esteem
- Analysis of relationship with father and mother throughout childhood
- Assist in achieving industry vs. inferiority, identity vs. role confusion
- Expressive techniques in uncovering unconscious struggles
- Uncover and process attachment issues, childhood conflicts, and motivation for behavior
- Explore conflicts regarding maintaining power/status quo in classroom
- Process childhood interests and experiences and how one views family and self roles
- Explore use of emotion (e.g., anger) to mask hurt
- Analyze immature/neurotic defenses (projection, regression, acting out, splitting, devaluation, displacement, rationalization, intellectualization)

Humanistic-Existential Paradigm

In contrast to the subconscious focus in the psychodynamic paradigm, the humanistic-existential paradigm is relationship oriented. Rather than focusing on an individual's unresolved conflicts in the past, the focus here is on current and future functioning. Humanism and existentialism are similar in the belief that human nature is fundamentally good, and people have the freedom and responsibility to grow and develop.

Humanists believe that goodness and worth are qualities that people possess. In the journey toward self-actualization, it is believed that people are purposeful, active, and capable of determining their own behavior. Similarly, existentialists place an emphasis on the importance of anxiety, freedom, values, and responsibilities and on finding meaning in one's actions (Gladding, 2012). Another parallel between humanists and existentialists is that both emphasize the importance of the client–counselor relationship. The professional counselor must enter the client's subjective world to focus on client perceptions of the presenting issue.

PERSON-CENTERED.   Person-centered therapy, developed by Carl Rogers (1951, 1957), is a major theoretical approach in the humanistic framework. Over time, this approach has also been identified as nondirective, client centered, and Rogerian. According to Rogers, the primary motivating force of humans is **self-actualization**, the tendency to move in the direction of growth, adjustment, socialization, independence, and self-realization (McWhirter & Ishikawa, 2005).

Because people have the basic need for a high self-regard, they attempt to organize their internal and external experiences into an integrated self. During this process of self-actualizing, unhealthy psychological or social influences may hinder an individual from realizing his or her potential as an integrated, productive self. In other words, conflicts develop when individuals' basic needs and their needs to obtain approval from others are inconsistent. Terry, for example, is experiencing conflict between her basic needs for self-actualization and her need for approval from her parents. The professional counselor working with Terry will need to be present and congruent to assist her in moving toward the discovery of her true self.

Rogers (1957) identified three essential characteristics a professional counselor must employ for a therapeutic relationship to be established: genuineness (or congruence), unconditional positive regard, and empathy. **Genuineness** is displaying honesty, sincerity, and directness, while avoiding any personal or professional façade. **Unconditional positive regard** is defined as the professional counselor's ability to accept every aspect of the client's personality, while remaining nonjudgmental and nonevaluative toward the client's feelings, thoughts, and behaviors. **Empathy** is the ability to understand the client's world in the way the client understands it. With Terry, the professional counselor must be open to hearing her experiences and acknowledge her challenges with the situation, regardless of personal opinion. Creating a nonthreatening, anxiety-free relationship would allow Terry to resolve conflicts and reach self-understanding.

Person-centered counseling has had a significant impact in the area of human relations with diverse cultural groups. Many countries have adopted person-centered concepts in counseling as well as cross-cultural communication and education. Multicultural limitations include lack of structure, difficulty translating core conditions to practice, and focus on internal evaluation, rather than external evaluation (Corey, 2009a). The following resources provide more information about person-centered counseling:

Rogers, C. (1942). *Counseling and psychotherapy*. Boston, MA: Houghton Mifflin.
Rogers, C. (1951). *Client-centered therapy*. Boston, MA: Houghton Mifflin.
Rogers, C. (1961). *On becoming a person*. Boston, MA: Houghton Mifflin.
Rogers, C. (1980). *A way of being*. Boston, MA: Houghton Mifflin.

EXISTENTIAL.   **Existentialism** stems from Søren Kierkegaard, a 19th-century philosopher who focused on the pursuit of becoming an individual. There are many contributors to existentialism as a therapeutic approach, including Ludwig Binswanger, Fyodor Dostoyevski, Friedrich Nietzsche, and Abraham Maslow. In more recent years, notable figures in existential psychotherapy include Rollo May, Victor Frankl, and Irvin Yalom.

The essence of existentialism is that humans are believed to have the capacity for self-awareness and the freedom and responsibility to make choices that would bring about meaning in their lives. However, along with this freedom comes the reality of living with the consequences of those choices, which could lead to **existential anxiety**. May (1977) asserted that normal anxiety can be healthy and motivational.

Frankl (1963) maintained that despite negative conditions, individuals can preserve their own independent thinking, spiritual freedom, and opportunities for choice. In contrast, an individual who sees life as meaningless and without value would be thought to be in what Frankl termed an **existential vacuum**. A well-functioning person is an individual who authentically experiences reality and expresses needs in a way that is not determined by others. Terry may not be in the existential vacuum, but may be questioning the meaning of her current experiences. While having her first taste of freedom, it will be important for Terry to explore her choices and needs as self-determined and not those of her parents.

Other than concentrating on the client–counselor relationship, there is no systematic way that existential counselors help others. Still, Yalom (2002) was able to emphasize three significant qualities within the existential counseling process: (a) helping clients attend to the **here-and-now** (i.e., being present in the current moment), (b) being open and authentic with clients, and (c) cautiously using self-disclosure.

Specific goals in existential counseling include making clients sensitive to their existence, identifying characteristics unique to each client, assisting clients in enhancing interactions with others, helping clients pursue meaning in life, and promoting present and future decision making that will affect the client's direction in life. Few specific techniques are offered in an existential approach. All interventions are undertaken with the intention of assisting clients to find meaning in their actions.

The existential focus on love, suffering, anxiety, and death, all of which are the universal elements of human life, makes this theory applicable cross-culturally. In contrast, a limitation of multicultural existential counseling involves the emphasis on self-determination and the lack of focus on the environment and the social context. Some clients may feel powerless in the face of external realities such as discrimination, racism, and oppression. Refer to the following resources for more information on existential counseling:

Frankl, V. (1963). *Man's search for meaning*. Boston, MA: Beacon.
May, R. (1953). *Man's search for himself*. New York, NY: Dell.
May, R. (Ed.). (1961). *Existential psychology*. New York, NY: Random House.
Yalom, I. D. (1980). *Existential psychotherapy*. New York, NY: Basic Books.

GESTALT THERAPY. Gestalt therapy began in response to the reductionist emphasis in theories of counseling such as psychoanalysis and behaviorism, which attempted to break an individual's personality or behavior into understandable parts. In contrast, **Gestalt therapy** promoted the idea of wholeness. Frederick (Fritz) Perls and his wife Laura Perls were the major theorists associated with this school of thought.

Similar to person-centered counseling, gestaltists believe that people have the tendency to move toward wholeness or self-actualization. Emphasis is placed on the present as indicated by Perls's (1970) statement: "To me, nothing exists except the now. Now = experience = awareness = reality. The past is no more and the future is not yet. Only the *now* exists" (p. 14).

In contrast to psychoanalysis, which focuses on predetermined and unconscious forces, the gestalt view of human nature is antideterministic; people can become responsible, grow, and change from past events. For example, Terry is experiencing difficulties in her life that are a result of her earlier thoughts, feelings, or experiences. This phenomenon is otherwise referred to as **unfinished business**—in Terry's case, asserting her own interests. The role of the gestalt counselor is to provide an atmosphere that allows Terry to identify and pursue what she needs to grow. Being honest as well as deeply and personally involved with Terry would allow the counselor to help her redirect energy in more positive and adaptive ways of functioning.

Gestalt counselors also directly confront clients with their inconsistencies. They focus on the polarities within people and push clients to correct misconceptions, to genuinely express emotions, and to take responsibility for change. Gestalt techniques may include exercises and experiments such as empty chair, role playing, role reversal, dream analysis, and the use of "I" statements (Erford, Eaves, Bryant, & Young, 2010). Other characteristics of gestalt counseling that help clients develop and become mature in the now include awareness of nonverbal and verbal expressions and shedding neurotic tendencies. Perls (1970) identified five layers of neurosis that were thought to impede a client's ability to be in touch with himself or herself. Only when individuals reach the final, or explosive, layer can they be truly authentic and in touch with themselves and others.

Gestalt counseling can be viewed as a culturally sensitive theory because the experiments employed by professional counselors may encourage clients to integrate the polarities that exist between the cultures to which they belong. Gestalt techniques can also be tailored to fit with a client's distinct perception and interpretation of his or her own cultural framework. In contrast, gestalt counseling has an individualistic focus, which may be a conflict for people from cultures that emphasize group values. Table 4.4 provides strategies and techniques aligned with the humanistic/existential paradigm. Consult the following resources for further study of gestalt therapy:

Perls, F. (1969). *Gestalt therapy verbatim*. Moab, UT: Real People Press.
Perls, F. (1972). *In and out of the garbage pail*. New York, NY: Bantam.
Polster, E., & Polster, M. (1973). *Gestalt therapy integrated: Contours of theory and practice*. New York, NY: Brunner/Mazel.
Zinker, J. (1978). *Creative process in Gestalt therapy*. New York, NY: Random House.

TABLE 4.4 Humanistic/Existential Strategies and Interventions

- Therapeutic conditions (genuineness, unconditional positive regard, empathy)
- Model active listening, congruence, unconditional positive regard and empathy with family
- Use role play and reverse role play to assist student in finding meaning of current behavior while encouraging responsibility
- I-statements
- Focus on the present, immediacy
- Active listening and reflection of feelings
- Building relationship
- Provide opportunity for empathy and safe exploration of thoughts, feelings, and behaviors
- Encourage self-awareness and choice leading to acceptance of self and others
- Gently confront inconsistencies
- Teach family members to (a) focus on the here and now; (b) take responsibility for their own thoughts, actions, feelings, and sensations; and (c) accept personal responsibility for change
- Teach family members to substitute the use of *won't* for *can't* and to substitute the use of *what* and *how* for *why*
- Teach parents to use self-esteem building activities with child
- Encourage self-exploration and self-discovery through a warm, supportive, affirming therapeutic relationship
- Through the relationship, the student can learn to accept himself or herself and begin the journey toward self-actualization
- Provide support around goal setting
- Counseling is seen as a way of *being with*, rather than *doing to* the student
- Culturally sensitive play therapy techniques could be used, giving children the opportunity to *play out* rather than *talk out* feelings
- Appreciation for student uniqueness
- Focus on choice, taking responsibility for actions and the present and future
- Redirect energy or actions
- Focus on the person that the student desires to be through art therapy techniques (mask activity)
- Avoid using desks to be more personal than authoritative
- Respect the student regardless of acting out behaviors
- Create a job or role for the student to feel a sense of meaning

- Create a memory box to feel a sense of accomplishment and connection when he or she adds to the box
- Examination of anxiety and behavioral issues related to safety, belonging, and personal and global responsibility and freedom (to classmates, classroom, school, community)
- Mentoring relationship
- Minimal encouragers and few questions
- Acceptance and trust
- Puppets and expressive art therapies for social issues and familial issues
- Reflective play therapy to process anxiety and substance abuse
- Cautious self-disclosure
- Music and art as adjunctive techniques
- Help parents and staff understand the student's perspective
- Role-play potential scenarios relevant to responsible and irresponsible behavior
- Identify emotions and appropriate expression
- Examination of anxiety and behavioral issues and a sense of belonging to classmates, classroom, school, and community
- Informal "lunch bunches" with student and potential friends to foster relationships among peers and sense of accomplishment and connection
- Redirect energy or actions
- Encourage student to write a letter to his or her ideal self
- Use humor to lighten the mood
- Explore significant changes in his or her life, both good and bad.
- Help to find meaning by having student work with even younger students
- Develop self-awareness
- Demonstrate respect for the student's unique self
- Consultations with familial environments/guardians
- Frame student understanding of self in the context of community
- Help student to find a place through a major life transition
- Develop activities that correct behavior but with respect and regard for the student as an individual
- Explore parent feelings toward students and any incongruence
- Help to provide a sense of belonging by creating a special role for the student (i.e., mentor younger students, special job to complete daily)
- Help the client to work through the feelings of "stuckness" that can accompany transitions
- Explore life scripts
- Allow student to analyze ads for messages
- Consider students' roles in society and the meaning of their choices
- Exploration of conflict regarding future plans
- Provide decision-making models for present and future use
- Explore scenarios using the empty chair technique
- Explore the meaning of place in the world at this time
- Identify and resolve incongruencies

Behavioral/Cognitive-Behavioral Paradigm

Clients seek action. Terry wants to act to change her current dilemma. The behavioral or cognitive-behavioral paradigm is the most action-oriented of the theoretical groupings. Clients are guided to pursue specific tangible changes in behavior and thought. From a practical standpoint, many beginning professional counselors are drawn to this paradigm because of the many tools and techniques it employs. In addition, professional counselors and clients alike can more readily observe progress in counseling from this perspective.

BEHAVIORAL COUNSELING. John B. Watson was one of the first advocates for **behaviorism**, as he was able to establish that human emotions were acquiescent to conditioning. Over time, behaviorism has incorporated various ideas, practices, and theories. Other theorists associated with this approach include Burroughs Frederick (B. F.) Skinner, Joseph Wolpe, Hans Eysenck, Albert Bandura, and John Krumboltz.

Behavioral theory focuses on how to reinforce, extinguish, or modify a wide range of behaviors. Specifically, it emphasizes the association between feelings and environmental stimuli and the learning or unlearning of behaviors accordingly. Professional counselors are mainly concerned with the science of observing behavior with the resulting consequence of whether to reward positive behavior or extinguish negative behavior. This is accomplished by eliminating the cause or condition that triggered the behavior. Terry might be presented with alternatives to handle the emotional and academic stresses she faces, with the goal of developing a new set of more adaptive behaviors that can be used in everyday situations. A specific behavioral technique is the **token economy**, where clients gain or lose tokens depending on whether or not they have reached a mutually agreed-on target behavior. Other behavioral techniques include use of the Premack principle, behavioral contract, time out, response cost, and overcorrection (Erford et al., 2010). Techniques based on social learning theory include modeling, behavior rehearsal, and role play.

Another behavioral approach involves the stimulus-response model. This model applies **classical conditioning**, or learning through the association of two stimuli. The most well-known example of this model is from Pavlov and his laboratory experiments with dogs. He found that when he paired two stimuli, food and the sound of a bell, the dogs would eventually associate the sound of the bell with food and begin salivating in response to the bell before the food was served. Similarly, certain human emotions such as phobias develop because of paired associations. Once these associations are learned, they can be unlearned and replaced in a procedure referred to as counterconditioning or systematic desensitization.

The nature of the client–counselor relationship in behavioral counseling differs dramatically from the humanistic-existential approaches. Behavioral counselors function as active teachers, reinforcers, and facilitators who help clients learn, unlearn, or relearn specific ways of behaving. It is also common for professional counselors to enter into the client's environment to instruct people who are a part of helping the client's change process. Beyond the use of reinforcers, behavioral counselors may use other techniques, including systematic desensitization, assertiveness training, implosion and flooding, contingency contracts, and aversive techniques. The ideal outcome of most behavior modification programs is to have the client's new behavior continue after the program has terminated (**response maintenance**) and to have the desired behaviors generalized to environments outside the counseling setting.

Behavioral counseling has advantages for individuals who are from cultures that do not focus on the experience of catharsis. For example, emphasis is placed on specific behaviors that the client wants to change and the development of problem-solving skills. Behavioral counseling takes into account an individual's environmental conditions that could be contributing to psychological problems, such as sociocultural, political, and social influences. A limitation exists when professional counselors fail to recognize conditions beyond the individual, such as Terry's cultural emphasis on family. Other resources on behavioral counseling include the following:

Bandura, A. (1969). *Principles of behavior modification.* New York, NY: Holt, Rinehart & Winston.

Skinner, B. F. (1953). *Science and human behavior.* New York, NY: Macmillan.

Watson, J. B. (1925). *Behaviorism.* New York, NY: Norton.

COGNITIVE-BEHAVIORAL. In the 1970s, many professional counselors recognized that behavioral approaches were too limited and saw value in combining them with cognitive approaches. Aaron Beck developed cognitive therapy, an approach that focuses on recognizing and changing negative thoughts and maladaptive beliefs into more realistic and constructive thoughts and beliefs. The essence of cognitive therapy is to focus on the cognitive content or automatic thoughts associated with an individual's reaction to an event. Beck asserted that psychological problems were derived from common processes, such as making incorrect inferences on the basis of incorrect information, being unable to distinguish between reality and fantasy, and faulty thinking. In short, he maintained that how people think basically determines how they feel and behave.

Donald Meichenbaum (1995) is one of the founding theorists of the cognitive-behavioral therapy (CBT) approach. Similar to Beck, Meichenbaum thought that helping people change the way they talk to themselves into more constructive cognitions was central to the counseling process. The maladaptive self-statements that affect individuals' behaviors are termed "cognitive distortions." Following are nine ways of mentally assessing a situation: all-or-nothing thinking, catastrophizing, labeling and mislabeling, magnification and minimization, mind reading, negative predictions, overgeneralization, personalization, and selective abstraction (Gladding, 2012).

The CBT counselor collaborates with the client by sharing the responsibility of selecting goals and bringing about change. Specific techniques, such as specifying automatic thoughts, assigning homework, thought stopping, and cognitive restructuring, are useful in identifying and challenging distorted thoughts. With Terry, the professional counselor may address her all-or-nothing perception of success with being a doctor and being accepted by her parents. Homework might include exploration of others' career decision making to challenge cognitive distortions. There are dozens of creative CBT techniques; they are usually active, time limited, and structured (Erford et al., 2010). Consult the following resources for further study on cognitive and cognitive-behavioral counseling:

Beck, A. T. (1976). *Cognitive therapy and emotional disorders.* New York, NY: New American Library.

Beck, A. T. (1987). *Love is never enough.* New York, NY: Harper & Row.

Meichenbaum, D. (1977). *Cognitive behavior modification: An integrative approach.* New York, NY: Plenum.

RATIONAL EMOTIVE BEHAVIOR THERAPY. Rational emotive behavior therapy (REBT) is similar to counseling theories that emphasize behaviors and cognitions by placing emphasis on thinking, judging, deciding, analyzing, and doing. Albert Ellis, the founder of REBT, assumed that people contribute to their psychological problems by how they interpret life circumstances and events. This assumption is based on the idea that there is a cause-and-effect relationship between behaviors, cognitions, and emotions. It is thought that people have the potential for both rational and irrational thinking.

In other words, although people have a tendency to move toward growth, self-preservation, happiness, and self-actualization, they also have a propensity for self-destruction, intolerance, self-blame, and avoidance of actualizing growth potentials. Ellis stresses the point that people generally feel the way they think. Minimizing irrational beliefs and replacing them with practical and effective beliefs is central to REBT.

The REBT counselor encourages clients to identify irrational ideas that contribute to their disturbed behavior, challenges clients to validate their beliefs, uses logical analysis to dispute the irrational beliefs, and teaches clients how to replace their ideas with more rational beliefs. One way to accomplish these goals is to use the ABCDEs of REBT (Figure 4.1). The letter *A* (Activating Event) represents the activating experience, the letter *B* (Belief) represents what the person believes about the experience, and the letter *C* (Consequence) refers to the subsequent emotional reaction or behavioral response to *B*. The letter *D* (Dispute) represents disputing irrational beliefs, and the letter *E* (Evaluation) refers to the development of a new response. Other specific techniques that may be used in REBT include humor, changing one's language, rational-emotive imagery, role playing, and other behavioral techniques.

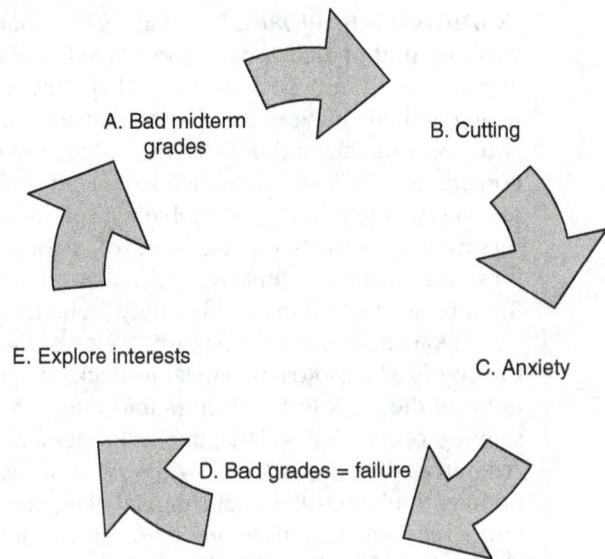

FIGURE 4.1 The ABCDEs of REBT in Terry's case.

The cognitive-behavioral counseling approaches have advantages from a cultural perspective. For example, in the process of identifying and understanding clients' values and beliefs, professional counselors are able to understand fully the clients' conflicting feelings. Also, the emphasis on cognition and behavior and relationship issues and the structure provided can be beneficial for people from various populations. A limitation of these approaches exists when the professional counselor does not fully understand the cultural background of the client. It is important for professional counselors to proceed with sensitivity and caution when challenging beliefs, values, and ideas. For more information on REBT, refer to the following resources:

Ellis, A. (1973). *Humanistic psychotherapy: The rational-emotive approach*. New York, NY: Julian Press.
Ellis, A. (1994). *Reason and emotion in psychotherapy revised*. Secaucus, NJ: Birch Lane.
Ellis, A. (1996). *Better, deeper, and more enduring brief therapy: The rational emotive behavior therapy approach*. New York, NY: Brunner/Mazel.

REALITY THERAPY AND CHOICE THEORY. William Glasser developed choice theory, which is based on the assumption that all behavior is purposeful and is a choice. Glasser contended that most people do not have a clear understanding of why they behave as they do; they choose behaviors they think will help them cope with frustrations caused by dissatisfactory relationships, which constitute many of the problems people have.

Also central to choice theory is that humans make choices based on the physiological need of survival and four psychological needs: love and belonging, power, freedom, and fun. Survival relates to how to maintain good health and a satisfying life. Love and belonging signify the importance of involvement with people and the need to love and be loved. Power refers to the need to be in charge of one's life and to have a sense of accomplishment and achievement. Freedom is the need to make choices, whereas fun is the need to laugh, experience humor, and enjoy life. Individuals attempt to control their world to satisfy these five basic needs, which differ in degree. Importantly, choice theory provides the theoretical underpinnings of Glasser's approach, whereas reality therapy is the counseling application of choice theory.

Reality therapy stresses the present, thereby helping people solve current problems. Instead of emphasizing feelings, the focus is on thinking and acting to initiate change (Glasser, 2000). Reality therapy, whether employed in an individual or a group setting, is active, didactic, and directive; it teaches clients to look at whether their actions are getting them what they want, examine their needs and perceptions, and make a plan for change.

One of the basic premises of reality therapy is that connection and interpersonal relationships are very important, which leads to wide applicability of reality therapy to groups.

With this in mind, a primary role of a counselor is to establish a good relationship with the client by engaging in warm and caring interactions, but also direct and confrontational interactions as appropriate.

According to Glasser (2000), counselors must be responsible individuals who can fulfill their own needs to help others do the same. Furthermore, they must be mentally and emotionally mature, supportive, involved, accepting, and respectful of all. Professional counselors can serve as role models of responsible behavior and help clients to assume responsibility for their own actions. Professional counselors help clients to find effective ways to meet their needs and to develop specific action plans that will help clients make the changes needed to attain their goals. Counselors are active, teaching and encouraging clients to take control of their lives by thinking and acting differently. Of course, professional counselors need to develop their own style so they can employ it with sincerity. It is critical that professional counselors demonstrate openness to their own growth and a willingness to explore their own values with the client.

Wubbolding (2010) identified four techniques commonly employed in reality therapy: humor, paradox, skillful questioning, and self-help procedures. According to Wubbolding, humor helps clients to develop an awareness of a situation and should be used only after considering the timing, focus, and degree of trust. Paradox, where clients are asked to perform the problematic behavior under certain circumstances while restraining the behavior's expression under all other circumstances, can be effective for some clients, but should be used cautiously in school settings. Skillful questioning involves using open-ended questions to help clients explore issues. It is also important to focus on positive behaviors that clients would like to target.

Advantages of reality therapy are that it stresses accountability and includes a structure that helps individuals develop action plans for change. In addition, choice theory is straightforward, flexible, and a relatively brief approach to counseling. Clients learn to accept responsibility for their behavior, realize that they can control themselves but not others, and develop their problem-solving abilities. Clients also learn how to engage in self-evaluation and deal with present concerns in a supportive environment. Limitations of this approach include the de-emphasis on feelings and lack of exploration of the past, and counselors are cautioned against being too simplistic or acting as moral experts. For more information on reality therapy, refer to the following resources:

Glasser, W. (1965). *Reality therapy*. New York: Harper & Row.
Glasser, W. (2000). *Counseling with choice theory*. New York: HarperCollins.
Wubbolding, R. E. (1990). *Expanding reality therapy: Group counseling and multicultural dimensions*. Cincinnati, OH: Real World.
Wubbolding, R. E. (1991). *Understanding reality therapy*. New York: HarperCollins.

SOLUTION-FOCUSED BRIEF COUNSELING (SFBC).   Brief counseling approaches have become increasingly popular since the 1980s due to managed care and other accountability initiatives. Brief counseling approaches go by many names, but currently the most prominent orientation is called solution-focused brief counseling (SFBC). SFBC is difficult to categorize under a specific paradigm and could easily be placed under the emergent theories category. However, given the action-oriented, brief strategies employed in SFBC, we have included it under the behavioral/cognitive-behavioral paradigm.

SFBC is a social constructivist model underlain by the observation that clients derive personal meaning from the events of their lives as explained through personal narratives. SFB counselors value a therapeutic alliance that stresses empathy, collaboration, curiosity, and respectful understanding, but not expertness. de Shazer (1988, 1991) and O'Hanlon and Weiner-Davis (1989) are often credited as scholarly and theoretical forces behind the prominence of SFBC, which de-emphasizes the traditional therapeutic focus on a client's problems and instead focuses on what works for the client (i.e., successes and solutions) and exceptions in the client's life during which the problems are not occurring. Berg and Miller (1992, p. 17) summed up the SFBC approach very nicely by proposing three basic rules on which SFB counselors operate: (a) "If it ain't broke, don't fix it," (b) "Once you know what works, do more of it," and (c) "If it doesn't work, don't do it again." It is easy to see the basic appeal of this commonsense approach to counseling.

Walter and Peller (1992) proposed five assumptions that expand on these three basic rules: (a) Concentrating on successes leads to constructive change, (b) clients can realize that for every problem that exists, exceptions can be found during which the problem does not exist, effectively giving clients the solutions to their problems; (c) small, positive changes lead to bigger, positive changes; (d) all clients can solve their own problems by exposing, detailing, and replicating successes during exceptions; and (e) goals need to be stated in positive, measurable, active terms. Sklare (2005) successfully applied SFBC to children and adolescents using the preceding rules and assumptions to focus on changing student actions, rather than insights. Sklare concluded that insights do not lead to solutions; successful actions lead to solutions.

Five techniques are commonly associated with SFBC (Erford et al., 2010): scaling, exceptions, problem-free and preferred future dialogue, miracle question, and flagging the minefield. Scaling is a very commonly used technique when counseling individuals of nearly any age and from any theoretical perspective. Basically, scaling presents clients with a 10-point (or 100-point) continuum and asks clients to rate where they currently are with regard to, for example, sadness (1) or happiness (10); calm (1) or irate (10); hate (1) or love (10); totally unmotivated (1) or motivated (10). Scaling is helpful in gauging a client's current status on a wide range of issues. It is even more helpful when it is reused periodically to gauge the progress of a client. Scaling is a very quick and helpful assessment technique with wide applicability in counseling.

Exceptions (Erford et al., 2010) are essential to the SFBC approach because exceptions provide the solutions to the client's "problems." Counselors probe and question the client's background for times when the problem wasn't a problem, determining exceptions, and providing the client with alternative solutions to act on. Problem-free and preferred future dialogue is the technique that allows the counselor to turn the counseling intervention from a problem-focused environment to a solution-focused environment. SFB counselors hold the core belief that when clients focus on problems, they become discouraged and disempowered, and any insight they might gain into the origin and sustenance of the problem is not therapeutically valuable. A complementary belief is that finding exceptions/solutions to problematic circumstances encourages and empowers students, leading to actions and successes. The miracle question helps to reconstruct the way a client perceives a problematic circumstance into a vision for success, which motivates the client to pursue the actions that will lead to successes.

The final technique is a treatment adherence technique called flagging the minefield (Erford et al., 2010). Treatment adherence is critical in any field in which individuals seek and receive help. Many, even most, receive the help they seek but then do not follow the treatment regimen, for whatever reason, basically guaranteeing the treatment will not be effective. For example, a patient may go to a doctor to address a medical condition, but then not follow the doctor's advice. If medication is prescribed, the patient may not have the prescription filled or may not take the medication according to the doctor's directions. Flagging the minefield is a technique ordinarily implemented during termination that facilitates clients' thinking about situations during which the positive outcomes and strategies learned during counseling may not work and to think ahead of time about what should be done in those circumstances to persevere and succeed. Treatment adherence is a critical issue in counseling; what good is all that hard work and effort to alter problematic thoughts, feelings, and behaviors if the student will return to problematic functioning shortly after termination?

SFBC is a culturally respectful approach to working with clients of diverse backgrounds because it discourages diagnoses, focuses on the client's personal frame of reference, and encourages clients to integrate and increase actions that have already been shown to be a successful fit for that personal frame of reference. The SFBC approach proposes that the client is the leading expert on what works for the client, and the counselor's role is to help the client recognize what the client knows to already work. The professional counselor then encourages the client to alter actions and "cheerleads" for the client's successes. SFBC approaches are particularly appreciated by clients who prefer action-oriented, directive interventions and concrete goals. SFBC is one of the more effective cross-cultural approaches because it empowers clients' personal values, beliefs, and behaviors and does not try to dispute or alter these. As a brief review of the theoretical approaches described so far, complete Self-Assessment Activity 4.4. Table 4.5 provides strategies and techniques aligned with the behavioral/CBT paradigm. For more information on SFBC, refer to the following resources:

De Jong, P., & Berg, I. K. (2002). *Interviewing for solutions* (2nd ed.). Pacific Grove, CA: Brooks/Cole.

de Shazer, S. (1988). *Clues: Investigating solutions in brief therapy.* New York, NY: Norton.

de Shazer, S. (1991). *Putting difference to work.* New York, NY: Norton.

Metcalf, L. (1998). *Solution focused group therapy: Ideas for groups in private practice, schools, agencies, and treatment programs.* New York, NY: Free Press.

SELF-ASSESSMENT ACTIVITY 4.4 REVIEW OF PARADIGMS

There are numerous action concepts and approaches in the first three paradigms discussed. Test your knowledge by matching the following theorists with the important concepts.

___ 1. Adler	a. wholeness
___ 2. Freud	b. social interest
___ 3. Meichenbaum	c. self-actualization
___ 4. Ellis	d. spiritual freedom and choice
___ 5. Frankl	e. interpretations of life events
___ 6. Perls	f. defense mechanisms
___ 7. Rogers	g. cognitive distortions

TABLE 4.5 Behavioral/CBT Strategies and Interventions

- Positive reinforcement
- Token economy
- Premack principle
- Behavior charts
- Behavior contracts
- Disputing irrational beliefs
- Cognitive restructuring
- Specify automatic thoughts
- Analyze negative self-talk and practice positive self-talk
- Visual imagery
- Modeling
- Behavioral rehearsal
- Role playing
- Time-out
- "Picture in your mind"; what it would look like if …
- Exceptions
- Miracle question
- Overcorrection
- Response cost
- Flagging the minefield
- Behavioral play therapy
- Parent/guardian or teacher consultations
- Brainstorming
- Bibliotherapy/biblioguidance
- Recognize and dispute negative thoughts and beliefs replacing with rational self-talk

(Continued)

TABLE 4.5   *(Continued)*

- Thought stopping
- Behavioral homework
- Develop action plans for change
- Identify positive behaviors and exceptions to the problem and strive to do more of the positive behaviors
- Scaling
- Teach family about basic needs (survival, autonomy, control, belonging)
- Responsibility
- Teach parents about the common irrational beliefs of children and parents
- ABCDE model
- Analyze the client's shoulds, oughts, musts, catastrophizing, and awfulizing
- With children younger than 8 years, focus on concrete skills such as problem solving and behavior rehearsal
- With older children, the therapeutic alliance is essential to help the child to "buy in" to the therapeutic process and establish goals for behavioral change
- Develop coping strategies
- Consider contextual/environmental factors
- Guided imagery/relaxation
- Behavior intervention plans
- Scaling questions to address degree of catastrophizing
- Positive reframing to challenge negative predictions
- Assess triggers through drawing, role play, puppets, or sentence completion
- Postulate different points of view
- Practice healthier self-talk
- "Picture on paper"
- Examine a recent situation in which the student may have made a bad choice and ask him to tell you what a better choice may have been
- Set up a reward system for completed class work and homework
- Develop coping strategies
- Psychoeducation groups (e.g., friendship building, conflict resolution, emotional regulation)
- Positive feedback focusing on resources
- Reframe weaknesses into strengths
- Journaling or drawing about feelings and thoughts
- Understand one's perceptions of the issue and how those perceptions lead to feelings and actions
- Address negative predictions
- Boffey map
- Functional behavior assessment
- Instruct parents to assist in helping the student change the behavior
- Assigning a job to foster a sense of belonging and responsibility
- Students can be taught the stages of change with emphasis placed on timing and choice to modify behavior
- Build on perceived strengths and use culturally relevant examples
- Help students understand that people think (and therefore feel) differently
- Teach about choice theory and help the student make a list of some of the good and poor choices made that have contributed to the current situation.
- Monitor the student to determine compliance with writing homework down and coming to school prepared

- Adopt a strengths-based approach that emphasizes successes not failures
- Make situationally intelligent decisions based on the context and salient cultural factors
- Consideration of the consequences of behavior can help to manage and direct thinking and actions to meet personal goals
- Collaborate to set up clear and tangible goals
- Explore realities of impact of behaviors/circumstances on future life plans (e.g., relationships, family planning)
- Facilitate an increasing awareness of reality testing to discover how the world works

Systems Paradigm

In contrast to the counseling approaches discussed so far, the systems approach focuses on the interactive perspective or the communication patterns within the client's family system or some other societally constructed system. In other words, the family provides the framework for understanding how the client behaves and functions in interpersonal relationships. There are many pioneers in family therapy; Murray Bowen developed one of the most comprehensive views of human behavior of any approach to family therapy. The essence of Bowen's model is **differentiation of self**, which is the ability to maintain one's individuality in the face of group influences—the pressures of a person's family (Nichols & Schwartz, 2005).

Bowen asserted that clients have less emotional autonomy than they imagine, and that clients are more dependent and reactive than we realize. Bowenian theory explains how the family, as a multigenerational structure of relationships, shapes the interaction of individuality and togetherness using six concepts: differentiation of self, triangles, emotional cutoff, nuclear family emotional process, multigenerational transmission process, and societal emotional process (Bowen, 1966, 1976).

Normal family development is thought to occur when anxiety is low, family members are well differentiated, and partners are emotionally sound with their families of origin. This becomes difficult as most people leave home during the adolescence-to-adulthood transformation. The result often is that adults react with adolescent sensitivity in their relationships with their parents and with others who interact in a way that is reminiscent of their parents (Nichols & Schwartz, 2005). This is evident in Terry's struggle to communicate her anxiety and pressure to her parents. Bowen states that individuals are likely to repeat problematic behaviors in their own families that have been passed down from past generations unless they explore and resolve these patterns (Kerr & Bowen, 1988).

To help family members identify intergenerational patterns and to help members differentiate from one another, a professional counselor must remain calm, neutral, and objective and be differentiated from his or her own family. A Bowenian counselor may work with all members of a family, although it is not necessary because it is believed that changing just one family member may have a direct impact on the entire family system. Specific techniques that may be used include genograms, asking questions, going home again, detriangulation, person-to-person relationships, differentiation of self, coaching, and the "I-position" (Gladding, 2012; Nichols & Schwartz, 2005).

The **genogram** can be an appropriate tool for professional counselors to identify cultural aspects that influence family members' behaviors. A genogram is a visual depiction of family structure. Lineage, nature of relationships, and interactional patterns are displayed and analyzed with the counselor to better understand one's current system. The genogram helps individuals and families to see the relationships between familial patterns and present behaviors. Also, evidence suggests that differentiation can be applied to individuals from different backgrounds. In contrast, some concepts may be limited in their application to people from diverse backgrounds. Table 4.6 summarizes some family systems strategies and interventions. For more information regarding genograms, refer to: McGoldrick, M., & Gerson, R. (1985). *Genograms in family assessment.* New York, NY: Norton. For more information regarding family systems counseling, refer to the following resources:

Bowen, M. (1972). *On the differentiation of self.* In J. Framo (Ed.), *Family interaction: A dialogue between family researchers and family therapists* (pp. 111–173). New York, NY: Springer.

Bowen, M. (1976). *Theory in the practice of psychotherapy.* In P. J. Guerin, Jr. (Ed.), *Family therapy: Theory and practice* (pp. 42–90). New York, NY: Gardner Press.

Bowen, M. (1978). *Family therapy in clinical practice.* New York, NY: Aronson.

Table 4.6 provides strategies and techniques aligned with the family systems paradigm.

TABLE 4.6 Family Systems Strategies and Interventions

- Caregiver or teacher training for dealing with relevant behavioral, academic, and social issues and family dynamics
- Play therapy
- Parent/guardian or teacher consultations
- Teacher training on helping children cope with relevant issues
- Reach out to caregivers to engage them in school
- Explore the family system through development of a genogram to identify behaviors and patterns passed down
- Coaching
- "I" position
- Teach family members to recognize harmful communication patterns
- Assist in building each family member's self-esteem
- Teach family members differentiation by modeling "I" statements
- Focus on familial relationships and times when the family successfully overcame difficulties
- Emphasize strengths, community, and resources
- Educate parents on signs, process, and interventions related to issues (e.g., bullying, divorce)
- Focus on interpersonal relationships
- Family as framework for understanding individual
- Use parent skills training for promoting family connectedness and involvement
- Analysis of family rules and expectations
- Evaluation of family communication style
- Exploration of family conflict management techniques
- If family members are unavailable, ask students what they would be doing or saying if family members were there
- Highlight strengths in the existing system
- Use metaphors and narrative to indirectly guide students to healthier ways of behaving and coping
- Miracle question
- Sparkling moments
- Exploring interpersonal incidents
- Role playing
- Exceptions
- Flagging the minefield
- Provide resources in the community to support the family
- Teach individuality despite family pressure
- Collaboration with parents about expectations
- Counseling for siblings and/or parents
- Parent education about school support systems available
- Education and collaboration with school personnel to assist student
- Assess family needs

- Teach caregiver skills to support developmental needs, consistency, and availability and explore alternative solutions
- Autobiography/timeline of family events through sand, art, or play
- Family sculpting
- Analyze family dynamics
- Referral to local agency for family intervention
- Identify triggers
- Coaching
- Assess basic needs of family
- Build a pattern of communication conducive to emotional expression
- Identify key school and community persons who can assist the family in getting an evaluation for student
- Consult with faith-based and community leaders for assistance
- Community member participation in career day
- Get students involved in job shadowing programs
- Teacher training on exposing all students to the college option
- Educate families on the change in family dynamics common in transitional situations
- Link with community resources to support family stability and locate extracurricular activities
- Discuss triangulation and work toward detriangulation
- Help the client to differentiate between self and family and to develop mature peer relationships
- When working with parents, try to reframe misbehavior using a developmental and emotional context
- Use family dynamics as framework for understanding the situation
- Communication analysis
- Try to learn what values are important to the student's family
- Assist student in discussing feelings with parents
- Consult with parole officers, community counselors, and other community service agents working with the student
- Determine student's perceived and actual role in the family, school, and community
- Facilitate healthy peer relationships and connections with mentors
- Revisit discipline policies that continue to affect student academic progress
- Although the student must follow the school protocol, explore ways that school staff, students, and parents can reinforce success
- Encourage adolescent to explore "going home again" and work on differentiation from emotional reactivity in family of origin
- Support the client through identity development
- Help the family to understand changing parent–child relationships and the need for independence that defines adolescence
- Connect the family to resources to support the student in pursuing postsecondary options
- Work with parents to identify possible community resources to assist in understanding student behavior
- Identify cultural beliefs and values that will help contextualize student behavior

Emergent Theories

The theories included in the previously discussed paradigms have the distinct quality of being supported and implemented over time. Theories take time to develop and become empirically validated for use in the profession. A fifth paradigm of counseling theory includes the theories that are newer, or emerging, in the profession. Many can fall into this paradigm, including postmodernism (Hansen, 2006a), decisional counseling (Ivey, Ivey & Zalaquett, 2010), motivational interviewing, narrative or constructivist approaches, and feminist counseling.

Some emergent theories were developed for specific purposes. For example, motivational interviewing is an approach designed to work with individuals struggling with chemical dependency. Many emergent theories have been criticized for lacking empirical evidence that the approach works. Some (e.g., feminist) have even been viewed as lacking specific techniques and being more of a philosophy. Hansen (2006b) has posited that it is some philosophical perspective that makes us most effective as professional counselors. In addition, theories take time to develop. Professional counselors want to avoid the "conference syndrome" approach of applying any new theory they hear or read about in professional development opportunities.

Instead, we propose a more systematic approach to learning about newer theories as they are emerging, seeing what fits with one's personal style of counseling and applying principles as opportunities arise and the theories become more solidified. For the purposes of this chapter, and to avoid overwhelming the reader, only four emergent theories in counseling are addressed: narrative, constructivist, feminist, and interpersonal counseling.

NARRATIVE THEORY.   Terry has a story to tell. She has created a story about her life and present situation, one that she might say needs to be retold. The professional counselor can help Terry to see and create success by helping her to retell her story of wanting to fulfill parental expectations and continual concerns about measuring up to her potential into a story that more accurately fits her desires. Such is the nature of narrative counseling: help clients to retell the stories of their lives to create outcomes that better reflect what they would like to be (Monk, Winslade, Crocket, & Epston, 1997).

One way to conceptualize narrative counseling is to consider a book with many chapters. We can read a book and think we know how it will end in the final chapter. As a metaphor for our lives, we may be comfortable with the opening chapter and a few in between, but we may be dissatisfied with the contents of the book as a whole. Rather than looking to change the problems, a narrative approach suggests rewriting the chapters themselves to create a better perspective on the problems that lie therein. In essence, narrative counseling holds that we are the authors of our own lives (White & Epston, 1990).

Michael White and David Epston are the primary individuals associated with narrative counseling. The concepts of the theory are originally derived from family counseling. White and Epston drew from family therapy expert Gregory Bateson, who suggested that the means for change is to compare one set of events in time with another (White & Epston, 1990). In counseling practice, the goal of narrative counseling is to develop alternative stories for one's life. The counselor would help Terry identify what she would truly like her life to be like, evaluate the possibilities, and determine what must occur in the interim to make this story a reality. The counselor would want Terry to understand that she or her parents are not the problem; rather, the problem itself is the problem. Narrative counseling can assist Terry to shift her perspective of the problem and create a new outlook (story) for her life and circumstances.

The narrative counselor asks many investigative questions to understand what underlies the story and one's self-perception. Techniques used in narrative counseling are encompassed within this idea of questioning and investigating as it relates to retelling one's story. The narrative counselor helps to deconstruct problems, externalizing and separating them from the person and avoiding blame and self-recrimination (Monk et al., 1997). The professional counselor seeks exceptions to the story, times when the outcome of one's actions is inconsistent with what one says or does in the story. These exceptions are referred to as **sparkling moments**, the positive shifts that begin to occur when one can exert control over the problem and begin to create a new story (White & Epston, 1990).

The client and professional counselor work together "against" the problem to identify more favorable stories (Monk et al., 1997). From a cultural standpoint, narrative therapy is consistent with the storytelling nature of some ethnic populations. For example, the Chinese culture is built on a series of stories handed down from generation to generation and appearing in the form of mythical beliefs. For individuals who come from cultures where storytelling is a part of their practice, narrative therapy can feel familiar and productive. The shift to identifying one's role in changing stories can be challenging, and the narrative counselor must exercise patience and caution to deconstruct problems and not beliefs.

Narrative theory tends to provide an overarching and organizing vision of the problem as separate from the person. This approach can be empowering and eye-opening. Narrative therapy requires a level of insight from the client to be able to tell and then retell the story. For more information on narrative theory, refer to the following resources:

White, M., & Epston, D. (1989). *Literate means to therapeutic ends*. Adelaide, Australia: Dulwich Centre Publications.

White, M., & Epston, D. (1990). *Narrative means to therapeutic ends*. New York, NY: W. W. Norton & Co.

VOICES FROM THE FIELD 4.1   Narrative Therapy with Children Who Have Been Abused, by Victoria E. Kress

---

When counseling children and adolescents who have been abused or traumatized, I like to integrate strength-based approaches, such as narrative therapy (NT), with evidence-based treatments for addressing trauma, such as trauma-focused cognitive behavioral therapy. Narrative therapy presupposes our clients possess the inner strengths and resources they need to resolve their own problems. As professional counselors, it is our job to develop, identify, and apply clients' strengths. Children who have been abused often feel a deep sense of shame, guilt, and/or embarrassment and can benefit from approaches that are inherently empowering.

One technique that I often use with this population in individual and group counseling is *Letters from the Future*. In this activity, clients are asked to imagine that they are writing a letter to themselves (in the present) from a future time period when they are much older and wiser. Clients are invited to provide suggestions, advice, and words of hope and wisdom to themselves from this future state.

As a variation of this activity, when I do this activity in a group setting, I often have the group members write a *Letters from the Future to a Friend* (i.e., a friend inside the group, outside the group, or a fictitious person) who has recently experienced sexual abuse. Group members are invited to provide wisdom, encouragement, and direction to their friend. What follows is a letter written by a 12-year-old African-American girl who was sexually abused by her mother's boyfriend for 2 years. She wrote this letter from the future, to a friend, during her third session of a group I facilitated for children and adolescents who had been sexually abused:

Dear Friend,

Hi. How are you doing? Well ... fine? I would like to share something about the sexual abuse which was when I was raped. It was painful, so I talked to my mom about the abuse. It helped but it still hurts but I see I am going strong anyways. And the man is in jail for what he did to me and I thank God for that. I have had the wisdom to talk to people, but before I didn't do that. And even though you have lost a little part in you, I hope that you will keep your self-confidence and always love yourself because whatever happened to you is not your fault. So keep up the good work and keep up having the words of good courage. So keep your mind POSITIVE and look ahead. You have to not do drugs and drink because that is not going to help you neither. When you want to do those things you need to talk to your good friends and to your mom and your counselor. You have to keep going to church and believe God will help you get through this to. Because he will. I promise. Well, bye-bye. See you soon. And just remember, stay POSITIVE and STRONG.

In providing advice from a future orientation, she was able to identify positive coping skills (e.g., the value of talking about her experiences, using her spirituality and faith to ground herself, avoiding substances as a coping mechanism, engaging in positive self-talk, avoiding self-blame) and ways she could evolve and grow secondary to her abuse experiences. A counselor can give a client guidance and suggest adaptive ways of coping, but ultimately our goal is to help our clients connect with and internalize these resources on their own. This narrative therapy technique provides an opportunity for clients to readily connect with solutions and answers to their struggles that fit with their values and beliefs. It is ironic that sometimes getting out of the present can help people better connect with solutions and more adaptive realities.

CONSTRUCTIVIST THEORY. Is one person's perception of a problem another person's reality? How do we derive meaning from our lives, and how do we make sense of this reality? Constructivist theory, based on the work of George Kelly's (1963) **personal constructs**, suggests that people create their own meaning and realities based on personal experiences. Constructivism holds that we create our own meaning, and it is the job of the counselor to respect and work with that reality, not to contradict or deny it (Hansen, 2006a).

Terry believes that she must be a successful scientist to please her parents. She is operating under the belief system that success is equal to parental approval. She also believes that people should have personal responsibility for upholding the expectations of a culture. The constructivist counselor would see that Terry is operating under a set of personal constructs, or belief systems, that guide her actions and goals. Personal constructs, as defined by Kelly (1963), are self-beliefs. They guide us in determining the courses of action we take, the people with whom we associate, and the decisions we make about our own lives. The process of identifying and integrating these personal constructs is at the heart of constructivist counseling.

The constructivist counselor is inquisitive. Constructivism is often paired with narrative techniques such as storytelling and searching for alternative explanations to problems. The goal of constructivism is to create and construe personal reality actively through examination of personal constructs. The professional counselor and client work collaboratively to identify constructs and their origins. Often clients do not emerge with specific strategies to handle situations, but instead focus on personal learning and examination of how they are living authentic lives based on these identified constructs.

One specific technique that stands out from this theory is the use of a card sort. The **card sort** is a means of organizing beliefs into categories to help illustrate the organization of one's system of understanding and operating (Kelly, 1963). The constructivist counselor might help the client to develop a repertory test or grid to illustrate and organize belief systems. For example, Terry might be assisted to determine the major beliefs she has created about family, career, success, and failure. The professional counselor and Terry may identify the basic belief systems to explore further how they are operating in her interactions and decisions regarding her future. In doing so, Terry develops insight and explores the meaning she places on her constructs and the actions she is taking to find meaning in her life.

Similar to narrative theory, constructivism requires significant insight and a higher level of processing than many traditional approaches. The theory may have limitations in its cross-cultural application in that some cultures expect adherence to their principles. Clients engaged in constructivist counseling are questioning and at times even challenging fundamental belief systems. In Terry's case, the exploration of personal constructs may reveal that culture is not as strong a belief to her as it is to her parents. This may contradict her culture's expectation of respect for parents and elders and may challenge Terry in creating a new perspective of her situation. Conversely, proponents of constructivist counseling hold that the exploration of beliefs can be the ultimate goal of the theory and can work effectively with most cultures. Resources for further reading about constructivist counseling include the following:

Kelly, G. A. (1955). *The psychology of personal constructs: A theory of personality*. New York, NY: Norton.

Neimeyer, G. (1992). *Constructivist assessment: A casebook*. Newbury Park, CA: Sage.

FEMINIST COUNSELING. A feminist approach to counseling has been greatly criticized as challenging fundamental cultural beliefs. Feminist counselors operate from the basic philosophy of feminism and support, respect, and highly value the role of culture in one's life.

The feminist philosophy espouses the equality and rights of women. The feminist movement began during the 1800s and abolition, wherein women were fighting for their voices to be heard (Wood, 2005). This movement continued through voting rights and what is more commonly perceived as the start of feminism, the women's rights movements of the 1960s. The principles of feminism held that women should be perceived as equals with men, have equal rights for employment and opportunities, be given certain inalienable rights to make their own choices, and essentially be treated with a fundamental human respect.

Because of this history, one often perceives feminist counseling as benefiting (or being provided by, for that matter) only women. Much of the literature regarding feminist counseling suggests a woman-centered focus. Chester and Bretherton (2001) identified six themes in feminist counseling from their research with practicing professional counselors: woman-centered, egalitarian, feminism as belief, feminism as action, critique of patriarchy, and a positive vision of the future. Gilbert and Scher (1999) further assert elements of feminist counseling to include empowerment, androgyny, and mutuality within the counseling relationship. The latter citation emphasizes the importance of equality in counseling and in one's life and carries a more universal position that can benefit women and men. Gender sensitivity in counseling may be a more accurate (and perhaps more palatable) position in applying feminist principles in counseling (Bartholomew, 2003).

How feminist counseling appears to the observer seems to be more questionable. The fact that this approach is an application of feminist principles makes it difficult to identify key feminist counseling theorists. We may look to the work of Carol Gilligan, a preeminent theorist on women's development, Judith Jordan and her colleagues at the Stone Center, and others who all have had an important role in the creation and proliferation of feminist approaches to counseling. The feminist counselor values the female as well the male perspective—ideally the role of gender in our lives (Bartholomew, 2003).

A **gender role analysis** is one of the primary techniques used from this perspective. The gender role analysis is a means of examining with clients messages they have received about what it means to be male or female, where these messages are derived, and how they have been employed and are affecting one's functioning (Bartholomew, 2003). Gender role analysis may address another important principle of feminist counseling: androgyny.

Based on the pioneering work of Sandra Bem (1981), androgyny challenges the traditional gender roles for men and women. **Androgyny** suggests that we should value individual characteristics for what they are, regardless of a predefined category. Professional counselors addressing androgyny see that stereotypically masculine and feminine roles are valuable within each individual. A woman who is more aggressive in the workplace and athletic with her peers may also be very sensitive and caring with her partner. Feminist counselors employ gender role analysis to examine these roles and to help the individual put them in an historical and societal context (Hoffman, 2001). The client is helped to see that all these attributes create her uniqueness. It is often society's views that perpetuate her beliefs that she is somehow aberrant or unacceptable (Chester & Bretherton, 2001). Feminist counseling addresses the societal perceptions and the means by which the individual can take action to implement change. This sociocultural perspective and action as well as a degree of assertiveness are the goals of feminist counseling.

The sociocultural history and viewpoint of feminism contribute to the multicultural sensitivity of this approach in counseling. Feminism has a rich history of working toward equality. Pioneers such as bell hooks and Alice Walker in the 1970s addressed the concern that feminism addressed the concerns of only White, upper-class women (Wood, 2005). Current feminist movements emphasize and work toward the equal rights of all, including issues of gender, race, ethnicity, and other cultural variables.

Challenges with the feminist theory may be the push for political action. Critics argue that suggesting individuals must see personal issues as political and engage in social change imposes the professional counselor's values, which may be inconsistent with one's cultural beliefs. We instead argue that feminist counselors simply suggest the societal context of issues and explore what, if any, role they would like to have to shape the understanding of one's issues from a broader perspective.

Terry's case is an example of the cultural context and challenges from a feminist perspective. Terry is attempting to fulfill her parents' wishes for her success, a message that may suggest cultural values of parental respect and collectivism. We might also wonder about messages she received about what it means to be female in her culture and in her family. Are there expectations that she will unquestioningly accept her role as a daughter and follow her parents' career aspirations for her? Terry's pursuit of a career in science is nontraditional for women in the United States (even in the 21st century). From a feminist counseling perspective, our gender role analysis might include an exploration of Terry's role in a predominantly male field. This is completed without bias or suggestion that she must stay in or leave the profession. Instead, there is an exploration of what this means to Terry in terms of being female and her identity as a whole. In other words, how does Terry perceive herself and her presenting concern through a gendered lens? Additional resources regarding feminist counseling include the following:

Bem, S. L. (1993). *The lenses of gender*. New Haven, CT: Yale University Press.
Brown, L. S. (1994). *Subversive dialogues: Theory in feminist therapy*. New York, NY: Basic Books.
Enns, C. Z. (1997). *Feminist theories and feminist psychotherapies: Origins, themes, and variations*. New York, NY: Haworth.

INTERPERSONAL PSYCHOTHERAPY. Interpersonal psychotherapy (IPT), originally developed for adults with depression, is time limited and specifically focuses on interpersonal relationships. Goals of IPT include helping clients improve their relationships or their expectations about them and helping clients improve their social support systems to alleviate their presenting distress. For IPT, the view of human nature is based on the assertion that psychological symptoms are connected to interpersonal distress (Stuart & Robertson, 2003). This approach is derived from three theories: (a) attachment theory, (b) communication theory, and (c) social theory.

Attachment theory is based on the premise that individuals have the intrinsic drive to form interpersonal relationships, a result of the need for reassurance and the desire to be loved. Attachment theory describes the way individuals form, maintain, and end relationships and hypothesizes that distress occurs as a result of disruptions in an individual's attachment with others. Problem areas specifically addressed by IPT include interpersonal disputes, role transitions, and grief and loss.

Whereas attachment theory is useful in understanding the broader, or "macro," social context, **communication theory** works on a "micro" level, describing the specific ways in which individuals communicate their attachment needs to significant others. In other words, maladaptive attachment styles lead to specific ineffective communications. The result is that the individual's attachment needs are not met.

Social theory contributes to IPT by placing emphasis on interpersonal factors and how those factors contribute to depression or anxiety. One's social support system may be disturbed as a result of an individual's maladaptive response to a particular life event. The level of social support one has directly influences how one handles interpersonal stress. Social theory hypothesizes that poor social support is a fundamental factor in the development of psychological distress (Stuart & Robertson, 2003).

There are three main goals of counseling for IPT: (a) relieving the client's disturbing psychological symptoms; (b) examination of conflict, loss, and transition in the client's relationships; and (c) establishing the client's needs to aid in more effective use of his or her social support system. In contrast to CBT, where the focus is on the client's internal cognitions, IPT focuses on interpersonal communication. Where IPT may focus on cognitions, they are not the primary targets. Likewise, CBT and the other theories of counseling may touch on interpersonal issues, but they are not the focus.

In contrast to analytically oriented theories, which tend to focus on early life experiences in relation to current psychological distress, IPT has a present, here-and-now focus that helps the client improve the current communication and social support systems. In light of its time-limited approach and its here-and-now focus, IPT aims to resolve psychological distress and improve interpersonal communication, rather than to change the underlying cognitions.

The IPT counselor uses the client–counselor relationship to develop insight into the client's interpersonal functioning and to assess the client's attachment style. In the case of Terry, the professional counselor first would need to establish a therapeutic alliance with her to understand her experiences with school and the pressure from her parents. Together, the counselor and Terry would examine Terry's communication patterns and her social support system. What does Terry need to improve her here-and-now interpersonal relationships to build a more effective social support system? What about Terry's attachment style or communication patterns with her parents need to be addressed?

Common techniques of IPT include establishing a therapeutic alliance, communication analysis, describing interpersonal incidents, using content and process affect, and role playing. Because IPT has a solid theoretical foundation and a solid structure, it can be useful for clients from diverse backgrounds. The process and content of IPT counseling is flexible and adaptable, and highlights the unique needs of individuals. IPT takes into account the components of several theoretical paradigms and creates a unique approach to address the individual needs of the client. Consult the following resources for further reading on IPT:

Bowlby, J. (1969). *Attachment*. New York, NY: Basic Books.

Kiesler, D. J. (1996). *Contemporary interpersonal theory and research: Personality, psychopathology, and psychotherapy*. New York, NY: Wiley.

Sullivan, H. S. (1953). *The interpersonal theory of psychiatry*. New York, NY: Norton.

Weissman, M. M., Markowitz, J. C., & Kleman, G. L. (2000). *Comprehensive guide to interpersonal psychotherapy*. New York, NY: Basic Books.

Table 4.7 provides strategies and techniques aligned with the emergent theories paradigm. These discussions of the various counseling paradigms offer a sampling of the many theories that exist. The information provided can be very challenging to digest and even more challenging to determine what fits you as a professional counselor. Now, complete Self-Assessment Activities 4.5 through 4.7 to begin considering what you would do as a professional counselor and how that fits within the theoretical perspectives. The next section of this chapter addresses the means by which you can apply theory into your counseling practice.

TABLE 4.7 Emergent Strategies and Interventions

- Miracle question
- Sparkling moments
- Empowerment
- Communication analysis
- Interpersonal incidents
- Role play
- Reading stories (bibliotherapy)
- Creating drawings
- Storytelling
- Provide student with age-appropriate information about various aspects of issues
- Deconstruct the problem-laden story, identify unique outcomes, and help students coauthor a new story that is strength based
- Externalize the problem, and work against the problem
- Celebrate success
- Address attachment issues
- Here and now focus
- Work on communication skills and accessing social support
- The process of change results from dialogue between counselor and family members
- Empower each family member to reauthor a more successful story
- Focus on communication skills, building friendships, and development of personal goals
- If the student and family desire it, attend to development of identity and fluency in both the mainstream and native cultures
- Examination of interpersonal relationships
- Social support system analysis and improvement
- Motivational interviewing
- Narrative therapy to deconstruct and externalize problems
- Examine personal constructs
- Identify and improve personal support systems
- Fill-in-the-blank exercises

(Continued)

TABLE 4.7   (Continued)

- Sentence stems
- Word sort activities
- Coat of arms
- Listen to student's story without blame
- Explore gender roles
- Empower student in healthy ways to decrease feelings of helplessness
- Use content of current situations to process affect
- Parent/student collaboration building and negotiating
- Caregiver/teacher training for dealing with relevant behavioral, academic, and social issues
- Explore family, school, and community dynamics
- Write a short story about how the student successfully accomplished a goal
- Bibliotherapy about other students' experiences that are similar
- Explore alternative explanations to problems
- Question and challenge the status quo
- Focus on resiliency factors
- Mentoring
- Encourage student to self-advocate and be competent and confident
- Scaling to determine needs and levels of anxiety
- Use expressive therapies (art, music, play) to tell life stories
- Stress reduction and mindfulness
- Psychoeducational and support groups to construct new realities
- Assist the student in developing positive social networks
- Assist the student in creating a story about the situation and identify a more favorable outcome
- Break problems down into pieces
- Assess ability to code switch in the school environment, if applicable
- Explore beliefs and attitudes toward working with diverse students. What are these beliefs, assumptions, and how do they affect interactions?
- Help school staff ponder multicultural considerations and biases regardless of racial self-identification
- Analyze your expectations of teachers and what historical life events have shaped your expectations or concerns about school staff
- Read stories about different careers and issues
- Create drawings to understand career interests
- Focus on positive relationships with peers and adults
- Provide students with age-appropriate information about various issues
- Improve interpersonal relationships by rehearsing behaviors to achieve desired goals
- Identify someone in the student's life who would be the least surprised to see the student planning for the future
- Shape application of discipline policy
- Identify cultural strengths the student and family bring to the school
- Identify cultural strengths and capital within the family and community and harness these strengths to gain support and encouragement for parenting student
- Share stories about people the student might be aware of, their learning process and how they pursued their careers

SELF-ASSESSMENT ACTIVITY 4.5 REVIEW OF EMERGENT THEORIES

Match the component with each of the emergent theories identified. Expand on your understanding by applying concepts from Terry's case.

___ 1. Family systems

___ 2. Narrative

___ 3. Feminism

___ 4. Constructivism

___ 5. Interpersonal theory

a. personal constructs

b. clients are more dependent and reactive than we realize

c. develop alternative stories for one's life

d. highly value the role of culture in one's life

e. relationships are key to development and wellness

When considering Terry's case, what specific issues do each of these theories indicate?

SELF-ASSESSMENT ACTIVITY 4.6 RELATING SKILLS AND THEORIES

How do the basic helping skills of counseling (e.g., empathy, active listening, reflection of feeling, paraphrasing, challenging, and confronting) fit within the theoretical paradigms discussed? Do all helping skills have a place in all theories, with differing emphasis in each? Attend to your personal preference in using each skill. How do these helping skills fit with your early leanings toward the theories?

SELF-ASSESSMENT ACTIVITY 4.7 REVISITING TERRY'S CASE

Review your previous perceptions of Terry's case. How do your beliefs about her situation and how *you* might approach counseling align with the counseling theory paradigms discussed in this section?

VOICES FROM THE FIELD 4.2   The Picture in Your Mind, by Barb Carlozzi

A client of mine was a 42-year-old Caucasian woman in counseling to deal with her anger toward her husband, who had left her and their two children and married a woman 10 years her junior. It had been 8 years since the divorce, and though the client wanted to get past her anger, she just couldn't let it go. She said, "I just never thought this would happen to me. I'm really angry with him for what he's done to our family." After a discussion about the specifics of this latter statement I asked the woman to describe how she had always imagined her family. At this point the client began to cry, saying, "I just always pictured a whole happy family." Some tears later she explained, "I guess that's it. I hate that phrase 'broken family.' I think I'm over his leaving me, but what I've really been angry about is that I have a broken family. Letting go of that ideal family and what we've lost is just so sad."

Consider the following process questions:

1. Naming the problem can, in itself, be therapeutic. This client has identified her struggle as a lost fantasy about the nature of her family. As the counselor, what would you say next to this client? What function does your statement serve?

2. What emotions and cognitions do you anticipate this client would encounter while processing her reaction to having "a broken family"?

3. Describe an intervention that may help this client get past her feelings of anger and sadness.

INTEGRATING THEORY INTO PRACTICE

These discussions of the various counseling paradigms offer a sampling of the many theories that exist. The information provided can be very challenging to digest and even more challenging to determine what fits you as a professional counselor. After reviewing the paradigms and considering culture, counselors must begin to integrate theory into their counseling practice. As an intern or practicum student, what are the critical components of your approach?

A means of organizing thoughts about theory selection is to consider whether the underpinnings of a theory are aligned with your basic beliefs about counseling. The elements of a theory highlight the specific and common factors, personal philosophy, and multicultural considerations discussed in this chapter. But to be philosophically aligned with the paradigm or theory, professional counselors should consider each of the following elements: view of human nature, goals of counseling, role of the professional counselor, and the techniques or approaches used.

View of Human Nature

How do people change? What motivates people to behave, think, and feel the ways that they do? What do you believe will best help someone grow and develop? These are important questions to ask yourself when considering your own **view of human nature**. The manner in which you believe individuals change will be directly related to the counseling theories to which you subscribe. For example, if you believe that personality is more or less fully constructed in childhood, and change can occur only through regression back to those times, you may be more suited to one of the psychodynamic theories. Conversely, if you believe people are self-determined and control their own destinies, a humanistic-existential approach may be a better match.

Regardless of varying beliefs about how people change, practitioners across settings can agree that change happens only when one is ready to engage in the process. The pioneering work of Prochaska and DiClemente (1982) proposed stages of the change process to explain the manner in which individuals move through changes in thought, behavior, or emotion. Their work originally studied smoking cessation in an adult population and has since been adapted to many issues and populations. Table 4.8 outlines Prochaska and DiClemente's five **stages of change** and how they might appear in counseling practice.

Goals of Counseling

A second important aspect in applying theory to practice is the perceived goals of counseling. Clients may enter counseling wanting immediate answers to difficult problems. We understand

TABLE 4.8 Stages of Change

Stage	Description	Application in Practice
Precontemplation	No intent to change	Identify problem as others have presented it to the individual; create ownership
	Unaware that problem exists	
Contemplation	Awareness of problems, but not yet committed to act to change	Weigh pros and cons of problem and solutions
Preparation	Intent and commitment to take action	Address fears, impact of possible change in life
Action	Modify behavior, experiences, or environment to overcome problems	Discuss experience of the change and subsequent feelings
		Consider means to sustain change
Maintenance	Prevent relapse and sustain gains achieved through change	Monitor and discuss new approach to problem

Adapted from "Transtheoretical Therapy: Toward a More Integrative Model of Change," by J. O. Prochaska and C. C. DiClemente, 1982, *Psychotherapy: Theory, Research and Practice, 20*, pp. 161–173.

that as a profession we are not prone to give direct advice or be problem solvers. Instead, we give individuals the tools to manage their own problems and to apply them in future situations. An overarching goal of all counseling is to help individuals more effectively manage problems in everyday living.

At first glance, the identification of an overarching goal of counseling may seem to answer all our questions about this subtopic. However, further examination shows that theories have different beliefs about what counseling should accomplish. Person-centered counselors believe counseling should result in greater self-awareness, behaviorists want to see physical evidence of change in actions, and REBT-oriented counselors assert that changes in thinking and behavior are the ultimate goals of the counseling experience. Your personal beliefs about what individuals should gain from their time in counseling will dictate your determination of approach.

A word of caution: Many new counselors jump to the conclusion that it is their role to determine specific goals for their clients. Specific goals, such as to stop smoking, build a healthy romantic relationship, stay out of prison, or get into college, must be established by the individual seeking counseling. Goal setting is a collaborative venture between professional counselors and clients. The emphasis on elements of goals and the manner in which counseling can assist in reaching the goals is determined by counselor orientation.

Role of the Professional Counselor

Relative activity or passivity as a professional counselor will help apply theory into practice. As you have read, theories differ in their perceptions of the roles professional counselors play in the therapeutic process. Whether one is collaborator, expert, equal, or indifferent, the role of the professional counselor differs across theories. We have also learned that many theorists were most successful in being genuine and true to their own preferences for interactions with one another. The professional counselor's role must be consistent with the other elements of theory and can in great part be determined by your personality and style of interaction. Some professional counselors teeter on the edge of offering advice, whereas others may utter only a few words throughout their time with clients.

Techniques and Approaches

Professional counselors entering the profession may be drawn to approaches that outline specific techniques to be used with clients. For this reason, we have seen many professional counselors begin with a cognitive-behavioral orientation and gradually shift to approaches that offer more flexibility in the process. This phenomenon may be due in part to the level of ambiguity we are willing to endure as we enter into new situations. So much of what we do as professional counselors does not contain a "how-to" manual. We do not have guidelines suggesting, for example, that if a client states his disdain for his mother, we should offer him the opportunity to role-play a preferred interaction with her. We must instead rely on what seems to be consistent with our beliefs about counseling as outlined in the other elements of theory selection.

Some theories are more heavily laden with techniques, whereas others are more amorphous in providing general guidelines about approaches. As you review the theories, what seems to stand out to you as most meaningful and effective? As you enter into the professional counselor role, what do you notice consistently about your approach? Are there certain techniques to which you are more drawn? Do you work more effectively when you can rely on a general approach and employ techniques as needed? A helpful guide to understanding and applying techniques to counseling practice is Erford et al.'s (2010) *35 Techniques Every Counselor Should Know* (Pearson Merrill).

Flexibility

Beginning to integrate theory into practice requires contemplation of the aforementioned elements. Applying theory also requires flexibility. No two counseling interactions are alike. What works well with one individual may fall flat with another. As we will discuss shortly, few professional counselors operate from truly purist perspectives and instead combine principles that fit best with their goals, beliefs, and desired roles in counseling.

Selecting theory relies on a careful examination of your own personal style. The focus questions presented in Self-Assessment Activity 4.8 are intended to assist you in beginning to consider your counseling style and application of theory. Then complete Self-Assessment Activity 4.9.

SELF-ASSESSMENT ACTIVITY 4.8 RELATING PERSONAL BELIEFS AND THEORY

Answer the following questions as honestly as possible as they relate to each element of theoretical orientation. Consider your own beliefs and preferences as you answer the questions.

View of Human Nature

1. How do people change?
2. Are people able to change (self-determined), or is our destiny determined for us?
3. What motivates people to change?

Goals of Counseling

1. What are the common goals for all people in counseling?
2. What is the possibility of change as the result of counseling?
3. What can be reasonably accomplished in the context of counseling?

Role of the Professional Counselor

1. How do you perceive the relationship between professional counselor and client? Equals? Experts?
2. To what extent are you willing to let the client dictate the direction of the session, and to what extent do you believe the professional counselor should determine the focus?
3. To what degree should professional counselors provide guidance through personal disclosure and perspective?

Techniques and Approaches

1. What tools do you believe will be most helpful in communicating with clients?
2. Which basic counseling skills (i.e., reflecting feeling, challenging) are most appealing to you in counseling?
3. What do you believe would be most beneficial to you if a professional counselor were to help you with a present concern?

Review your answers to these questions and compare them with the information in Tables 4.1 and 4.2 to delineate which theories may be most appealing as you enter into your counseling practice.

SELF-ASSESSMENT ACTIVITY 4.9 A THEORY IN DETAIL

Research a specific theory to discover the basic elements of the theory (e.g., the way of looking at human nature, techniques, goals). You may wish to begin your research with the references listed after each theory discussion in the chapter.

- What types of clients and presenting problems would most likely benefit from the use of this theory?
- For what types of clients and presenting problems would it be inappropriate?
- Would you use this theory? Explain.

THEORETICAL INTEGRATION

With so many sound theories from which to choose, it is challenging to select just one. Many professional counselors, as previously stated, rely on more than one theoretical perspective. **Theoretical integration** is the synthesis of the best aspects of several theories with the belief that doing so will produce richer and more meaningful outcomes (Bradley, Parr, & Gould, 1999). Professional counselors operating from an integrative perspective combine the best of what works for them with intentionality. Although employing diverse perspectives and techniques, the integrative counselor holds fast to one underlying, foundational theoretical orientation. For example, we might at our core believe and operate from the existential standpoint of finding meaning in life and searching for ultimate existence. Yet working with adolescents in an alcohol treatment facility might require that we employ person-centered techniques to build rapport and behavioral techniques to demonstrate change required for discharge. At our core, however, remains the fundamental belief system of existentialism, which guides the use of supplemental approaches.

Integrative Versus Eclectic Counseling

We are intentional in differentiating integrative and eclectic modes of counseling. **Eclecticism**, in contrast to theoretical integration, is more haphazard in nature. The eclectic counselor is a technical expert, relying on knowledge of approaches and applying what seems to fit at a given time. Eclectic counselors select approaches based on client presenting issues and symptoms. Eclectic counselors use techniques from several areas without regard for theory (Cutts, 2011). There is a lack of a unified or guiding theory for the professional counselor employing this approach. In many ways, eclecticism feels safe for beginning counselors who feel that they are "flying by the seat of their pants" every time they are faced with a new client and presenting issue. A challenge with an eclectic approach is a lack of organized understanding of what principles of a foundational theory are most appropriate to a given client (Lazarus & Beutler, 1993). Without the complete knowledge of a guiding theory, it is difficult to know which pieces of the theory to extract and which to apply. Although tempting, always consider more fully what you believe about counseling and use that as your guide.

Why an Integrative Approach?

With myriad research to demonstrate best practices in counseling, there is ironically a lack of consensus on a single most effective theory. Professional counselors rely instead on the "it depends" mentality of counseling. Not to be confused with eclecticism, theoretical integration offers the professional counselor flexibility in working with various issues and presenting concerns. There exists a level of multicultural responsibility to meet clients where they are when they enter counseling. Also, you must be sure that what you do matches what clients need. Professional counselors can remain authentic in so doing, as the application of elements of theories will differ based on one's underlying belief systems. Theoretical integration offers at the core a guiding theory; this guiding theory assists the counselor in making informed decisions about how to proceed in counseling while maintaining flexibility in the techniques used to assist the client in reaching goals (Cutts, 2011).

One must also acknowledge the limitations of a purist approach. As discussed earlier, professional counselors work in settings with specific requirements for their clients. For example, community mental health often requires that individuals reach counseling goals and implement change within a shorter time. How can a psychodynamically oriented counselor work under such managed care dictates? One answer may be simply to maintain the fundamental principles of psychodynamic approaches in selecting cognitive-behavioral strategies to employ in practice. In a school setting, which often offers even more limited time for individual counseling, existentially oriented counselors can help youth explore what is most meaningful in their lives by challenging them to face issues and work in the present-focused framework of reality therapy or gestalt theory.

Integrative counseling was developed initially to help clarify the conceptual understanding of theories and their applications (Norcross & Goldfried, 2005). Being an integrative counselor requires you to be a knowledgeable counselor. Knowledge of the many theories, or at minimum the paradigms, is required to determine consistency in applying varying techniques to support one's foundation. A guiding theory at the core of an integrative approach is necessary in conceptualizing client presenting issues and determining a general direction for counseling (Cutts, 2011). In addition, exploring one's own beliefs about counseling, as in the previous section, builds a better foundation on which to add supporting approaches. Counseling is a profession valued for flexibility and ability to see multiple dimensions of a problem. Professional counselors must put this in practice by employing what works best to meet a client's needs. Complete Self-Assessment Activity 4.10 to explore your personal integrated approach to counseling.

SELF-ASSESSMENT ACTIVITY 4.10 YOUR INTEGRATED ORIENTATION

Using Figures 4.2 and 4.3, indicate the various theories you believe will be part of your integrated style of counseling. Consider not only which theories appeal to you for their consistency in beliefs, but also how they will be used. For example, what do you assume to be your core, guiding theory? On what part of the figure do you identify the core? As a humanistically oriented counselor, I (D.H.L.) would identify my core of existentialism at the midsection, or belly, of the figure because I operate from my "gut" in counseling (Figure 4.2). I tend to "use my hands" as a counselor and supplement my work with approaches in person centered and CBT. Of course, your integration must be consistent. It would not work well to have a core existential approach and supplement with psychodynamic eyes because of the very different philosophies of these two theories. Place your own core theory at your own identified core on Figure 4.3. We have started our own visual depiction of our integrated orientation to help you begin.

As you complete and review your integrated theory, provide a rationale for how these different theories work well together. How do their philosophies complement one another? How is the overall approach depicted here consistent with your own personal beliefs? How is the overall approach depicted here consistent with your beginning beliefs about the counseling process and change?

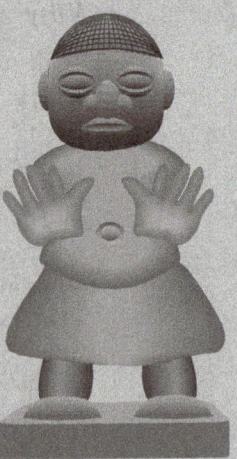

FIGURE 4.2 Author's integrated theory (D.H.L.). Core: belly; theory: existential; tools: hands; supplemental theories: person-centered, CBT.

FIGURE 4.3 My integrated theory. Core: _____; theory: _____ tools: _____; supplemental theories: _____.

VOICES FROM THE FIELD 4.3   How My Counseling Theory Has Informed My Practice, by Randall M. Moate

I recall quite clearly the first day of my counseling theories class in my master's degree program. After taking a look at the syllabus and glancing in the textbook, I asked myself, *"How in the world will this stuff ever help me?"* The material seemed interesting in an academic sense, but far removed from what I envisioned counseling actually being. My thinking was along the lines of *"Real counselors probably don't spend time thinking about this stuff!"*

Through my development as a practicing counselor I have developed a deep appreciation for the importance and utility of connecting with a counseling theory. Reflecting back on my development as a counselor, cultivating a solid theoretical foundation has been invaluable to me. In fact, I cannot envision what it would be like to practice *without* having a counseling theory to work from. The following paragraphs briefly detail how I have come to appreciate and use a counseling theory in my work.

As I began reading about the various theories I approached this experience similarly to how I would approach a first date. I tried to keep an open mind about things and not have any serious expectations, and then see where things went from there. Needless to say, there were several "bad" first dates, but also some pretty good ones. Eventually I came across a theory that was the perfect fit for me—love at first sight, you might say. I recall reading about the theory and found myself nodding my head frequently, and saying to myself *"This totally makes sense to me,"* and *"I have always looked at the world this way."* At this point I wasn't exactly sure how I would use my theory, but I did feel a sort of kinship with it. I felt reassured that there were other like-minded counselors out there.

As soon as I met with my first "real" client in practicum, the utility of espousing a counseling theory or approach became readily apparent to me. I noticed that during a 50-minute counseling session, my client wanted to share a lot of information with me. I also noticed that our conversation wasn't linear, and that my client moved around onto several different tangents. At times I felt like my head was spinning and that the session was moving very fast. What allowed me to persevere through this experience was having my theory to help filter and organize what was being said. My theory functioned like having a personal assistant with me in session. It helped me to organize and prioritize all that was being said.

Typically, when I am working with clients, the first couple of sessions seem to go by rather quickly. In general, clients I have worked with tend to want to focus on their presenting problems, share their story, and have me deeply listen to what they have to say. This generally seems to be a good starting point for our therapeutic relationship, as we build trust, rapport, and understanding. However, as we continue our work together I have several questions that start to tug at the back of my mind: *"How is our work together going?" "Do we have a direction and focus in session?" "Am I helping the client achieve his or her goal(s)?"* and *"Am I doing a good job?"* I am able to fall back on my counseling theory to help me answer these questions. My theory helps to provide a context that I can use as a measuring stick to evaluate how I am doing as a counselor and whether I am helping the client make progress.

"Who am I as a counselor?" "How do I help people?" and *"What are my strengths and weaknesses?"* are questions I frequently find myself reflecting on. During times of doubt and stress, I find answering these questions to be sustaining and comforting. It helps me to reaffirm who I am as a counselor, how the process of change occurs, and what I hope to achieve as a counselor. My counseling theory—in part—influences how I answer these questions. Rather than being left on my own to sort through these things, I have the bulwark of my theory to fall back on.

I have come to regard a counseling theory as a lens through which I see the world. After several years of practicing from a counseling theory, it has become integrated with who I am as both a professional and a person. Looking back over my education experiences, my theoretical development was critical to my development as a counselor. Starting as a skeptical student who was cynical about the "real-world" utility of counseling theories, I have become very appreciative of all the ways in which theories support the work I do as a counselor.

Summary

In this chapter we discussed the significance of integrating theory into the practice of counseling. As mentioned, it is the professional counselor's ethical responsibility to understand theory and to employ techniques with flexibility sensitive to the client's needs. The case of Terry, as well as the self-assessment activities provided throughout this chapter, helps to encourage the reader to apply theory to personal practice by focusing on human nature, goals of counseling, the role of the counselor, and techniques employed with flexibility.

Given the vast array of theories to choose from, this chapter attempted to compartmentalize many theories and their specific factors into larger, more cohesive paradigms. The five major paradigms discussed include psychodynamic, humanistic/existential, behavioral/cognitive-behavioral, systems, and emergent. By providing examples of the major theoretical paradigms in psychotherapy, we emphasized the fundamental principles of each theory and attempted to familiarize beginning counselors with the common factors in these various theories. Without evidence of a single most effective theory, most professional counselors today employ an integrative approach. Integrative approaches rely on the application of theories that work best with a client and attempt to synthesize different treatment strategies to best serve the unique needs of the client, as well as foster growth and development in the personal philosophy of the counselor.

Determining a counseling theory is an involved and lengthy process. The five paradigms discussed here are a starting point to learn more about the counseling theories as you enter into practice. Before foreclosing on a specific theory, we strongly encourage beginning counselors to reflect on their beliefs about themselves, human nature, and counseling. Aside from the ethical and professional responsibilities for using theory in practice, understanding how counseling works will better prepare you to help clients. A unique perspective on your client's issues that is embedded in your beliefs about how people change and develop will enable you to select appropriate interventions to assist clients to reach their goals. An intentional counselor is a successful counselor, employing a unique integration of personal characteristics and counseling theories.

Answer Key

Activity 4.4   1. b, 2. f, 3. g, 4. e, 5. d, 6. a, 7. c.
Activity 4.5   1. b, 2. c, 3. d, 4. a, 5. e.

CHAPTER 5

Record Keeping: What to Include and What to Leave Out

BY JAMES JACKSON AND CHARLOTTE DAUGHHETEE

PREVIEW

Appropriate clinical record keeping is essential to ethical best practice. When documenting counseling services, it is imperative that counselors be mindful of the legal, ethical, and agency requirements regarding documentation. Good comprehensive record keeping promotes quality treatment and also documents that treatment falls within accepted standards of care, thereby providing protection from liability risk. By following standard therapy note-writing formats and by allowing time for note writing immediately following a session, counselors can produce precise yet thorough documentation of their practice. In addition to client records, counselors engage in other types of professional writing, including communication with other professionals and the production of practice marketing materials. The ability to write professionally is vital to professional responsible practice.

THE IMPORTANCE OF RECORD KEEPING

The creation and maintenance of clinical records has been significantly influenced by the climate of managed care and evidence-based practice. One outcome of this influence is that the process of keeping clinical records has taken on increased importance and complexity. Record keeping is an important aspect of providing effective services to clients, documenting that appropriate services were rendered, and maintaining continuity of services when a change in mental health providers occurs (Welfel, 2013). Two primary areas of responsibility that must be considered with regard to keeping clinical records are legal and clinical responsibilities (Gutheil & Hilliard, 2001).

From a legal perspective, the information documented in the clinical record is often the most compelling evidence of the facts when a complaint or legal suit is brought against a professional counselor. Courts and regulatory boards typically give considerable weight to clinical records made during the course of treatment (Gutheil & Hilliard, 2001). Most states require counselors to maintain client records and may have regulations and statutes concerning the content of records. The American Counseling Association's (ACA's) *Code of Ethics* (ACA, 2005) mandates that counselors maintain records in accordance with institutional, agency, and legal requirements. Although inpatient records require specific categories of data with stiff penalties for facilities and clinicians not in compliance, the requirements for outpatient records are generally not as structured or strict (Gutheil & Hilliard, 2001). It is incumbent on counselors in both inpatient and outpatient settings to learn the requirements for and maintain good clinical records.

Good record keeping may help reduce the professional counselor's legal risk of liability by demonstrating that the services provided are within the bounds of a reasonable standard of care; thus, clinical records should document the counselor's decision-making and treatment processes and the response of clients to treatment. Koocher, Norcross, and Hill (2005) identified 14 content domains that should be present in a comprehensive clinical record.

- Identifying information: Client name, contact information, gender, date of birth, marital status, parent/guardian (or next of kin), employment status, and billing information.
- First contact: Referral source and date of the initial contact.
- Legal notifications: Information for clients as required by HIPAA, consent forms, confidentiality, and limits.
- Pertinent history and risk factors: Detailed medical, social, vocational, and educational history, including sufficient information to form a diagnosis and treatment plan. Important to ask in the first session are the questions: "Tell me about the most violent or impulsive act you have ever done" and "Have you had thoughts of harming yourself or others recently?" Obtain permission to contact prior mental health practitioners and secure records of prior treatment.
- Medical or health status: Obtain information regarding medical status, name of the client's primary care physician, and pending medical tests or conditions.
- Medication profile: Identify past and current medications and illicit drugs taken by the client and note any referrals for medication.
- What brought the client to the office? Provide a detailed description of the client's current condition, including presenting problems or symptoms and the reason for the referral. Inquire what brought the client for help at this time and document the reasons.
- Diagnostic impressions: Describe diagnostic formulations and clinical impressions based on the most current edition of the *DSM*. Do not "upcode" or "downcode."
- Treatment plan: Design a treatment plan that includes short-term and long-term goals and a description of planned therapeutic interventions. The treatment plan should be updated as needed.
- Progress notes: Indicate progress toward counseling goals using clear, precise language and observable facts. Write as if the client and client's lawyer were reading the note with a lawsuit in mind, and you are demonstrating you are a dedicated, serious, and concerned professional.
- Service documentation: Document each session and the client's response to treatment.
- Document follow-up: Document any referrals for treatment and missed appointments. Maintain copies of any notices, reminders, and correspondence with clients, and note in the record any significant telephone conversations.
- Obtain consent: Maintain copies of all releases of information and consent forms, including consent for any form of recording (video, etc.).
- Termination: Write a termination summary or discharge note for the client. As termination approaches, make sure that case notes reflect the planning and progress toward the end of treatment.

Koocher et al. (2005) noted that developing a comprehensive record as just described would likely require several sessions. Obviously, certain documentation such as consent forms, HIPAA agreements, and so on should be secured before treatment is initiated, whereas other documentation artifacts will be captured over the course of therapy.

Keeping appropriate case notes is both an important component and indicator of ethical practice. The *ACA Code of Ethics* (ACA, 2005) sections A.1.b., A.5.d., and B.6.g. offer additional guidelines related to maintaining case notes, which include (a) Counselors are responsible for maintaining such records as necessary for providing professional services to clients; (b) Accurate, timely, and sufficient documentation should be kept to facilitate the continuity of services; (c) Interactions of a nonprofessional nature between counselors and clients, including former clients, should be documented in case records and should also include the rationale, possible benefit, and likely consequences of the interaction; (d) After counseling services are terminated, records are maintained to permit future access as required by state and federal statutes; and (e) When records are disposed, this must be done using a method that protects client confidentiality. Although necessarily broad in scope, these guidelines underscore that ethical counseling practitioners are intentional in maintaining appropriate professional records documenting their work with clients.

How to Keep Case Notes

Progress notes serve the dual purposes of documenting both client progress toward counseling goals and the work done during sessions. Piazza and Baruth (1990) identified four components required in a progress note. First, the counselor's goals for the session must be identified. Goals should be linked to the treatment plan and should demonstrate continuity of the work conducted in previous sessions. Second, an evaluation of client progress toward the identified goal for the session should be included, as well as the counselor interventions implemented. Third, clinical impressions based on behaviors observed by the counselor should be noted. The fourth and final component is an action plan, which will serve as the goal of the therapeutic work to be conducted in the following session. Formulating goals for the next session based on the work done in the previous session promotes continuity over the course of treatment.

Process Notes

Under HIPAA, process notes are referred to as **psychotherapy notes**, which may present some confusion due to the terminology. This terminology came about when the federal government included provisions under HIPAA that the client's signature on the Notice of Privacy Practice would allow providers to communicate information required for treatment and payment without the need to secure separate client consent for each contact. Although these provisions greatly streamlined the consent process, this also permitted third-party payers access to the complete clinical record of clients, which presented concerns for mental health practitioners in regard to maintaining confidentiality of client information. In response, professional mental health associations negotiated an exception to such access for documents specified as psychotherapy notes (Welfel, 2013). Thus, process notes differ from progress notes and are not considered part of the clinical record. Due to the special status of psychotherapy notes under HIPAA, these notes are not included under a signed waiver of medical records unless specifically mentioned in the waiver (Koocher & Keith-Spiegel, 2008).

Essentially, process notes consist of information written down by the therapist for the purpose of reflecting on personal reactions to the counseling process such as countertransference, as well as any working drafts of the counselor's impressions concerning treatment (Koocher & Keith-Speigel, 2008). Process notes may be kept for the purpose of increasing counselor competence; for example, reviewing supervisee cognitive processes through the use of process notes can be a valuable supervision technique (Olsen & Stern, 1990). However, due to the impressionistic nature of process notes, after the relevant information has been extracted from these working notes and incorporated into the formal clinical record, it is recommended that these notes be destroyed. Any process notes that are not destroyed may be subpoenaed in legal proceedings (Koocher & Keith-Spiegel, 2008). See Think About It 5.1.

THINK ABOUT IT 5.1

Imagine that a colleague tells you she keeps a separate set of personal notes in her desk at home in addition to the clinical records kept at the agency where she works. What ethical or legal concerns might be associated with such a practice? What, if any, suggestions might you make to your colleague?

Standard Format

Maintaining up-to-date case notes is a challenge for most practicum and internship students, in part because agencies differ widely with regard to the format used for therapy notes. Agencies often are subject to either in-house or external audits and, to ensure compliance, may have guidelines or even training specific to writing case notes. Agencies also commonly have certain expectations for clinical records to facilitate reimbursement for services and demonstrate therapeutic effectiveness. These expectations represent a "learning curve" as interns learn to write the narrative of their work in the session within the structured format of the template used at the site. A good practice for practicum students, interns, and new counselors to follow when first joining an agency is to carefully examine the note format in use at the site and clear up any questions concerning documentation procedures. Even in agencies where guidelines aren't specified, such as schools, supervisors typically have clear ideas about what constitutes a good—and bad—case note.

Agencies with formalized note-writing templates generally include places on progress note forms for information such as Time In, Time Out, Participants, Content, Intervention/Client Response, and Progress. Also, agencies often have specific abbreviations commonly used in writing notes. For example, an agency might have a standardized sentence at the beginning of client notes for each session to indicate client presentation, orientation, and the presence or absence of symptoms of particular concern. This could be noted with an initial sentence such as "Client presented appropriate attire, O x 4, no s/i, h/i, or a/v/h," which would indicate that in this session the client is Oriented to Person, Place, Time, and Situation, demonstrates no Suicidal Ideation, Homicidal Ideation, or Audio or Visual Hallucinations. Examples of exemplary notes (minus identifying client information) and commonly used abbreviations at the site may be available for review and might save the counselor much time by preventing the need to rewrite notes.

SOAP Notes

The acronym **SOAP** stands for Subjective, Objective, Assessment, and Plan and is a standardized format for writing case notes that is part of an organizational system of medical records called the problem-oriented medical record (POMR; Kettenbach, 1990). The SOAP documentation format has been adapted for use across the allied health fields and is a common format used in the mental health field. Cameron and turtle-song (2002) provided an excellent description of the use of the SOAP format for writing therapy notes for mental health practitioners. The information appropriate to include under each heading follows.

SUBJECTIVE. This section and the objective section of the SOAP format are for the purpose of data gathering. Information should be both clear and brief. A common difficulty is deciding whether content is subjective or objective. Content is classified as subjective if it is reported to, versus observed by, the counselor. This includes client perceptions of the problem such as reports of affect, behaviors, cognitions, goals, symptoms (including descriptions of symptom frequency, intensity, and duration), and the impact of symptoms on client relationships. Reports from other outside sources such as client friends, family, as well as information from other agency representatives such as probation officers, and so on should also be included in this section.

Direct quotations of client statements should generally be avoided. Some exceptions to this are situations in which the client makes specific statements of intent to do harm to self and/or others. In this circumstance, it may be important to record the client statements precisely to support the clinical decision to take protective actions, which involve breaking confidentiality. Another circumstance potentially requiring a direct quote includes statements by the client suggesting a change in mental status. Negative statements made by the client about other treatment providers should not be included in the client record (Cameron & turtle-song, 2002).

OBJECTIVE. Information included in the objective section of the note should be factual and quantitative in nature. Two sources of objective data are written records and counselor observations. Counselor observations should be directly witnessed by the counselor and include data that is interpersonal, physical, and psychological in nature. Counselors should strive for precision and clarity and avoid using words with negative connotations and that are open to interpretation such as *manipulative, spoiled,* and *drunk* to describe client presentation. Counselors should generally avoid using terms such as *seemed* or *appeared* to qualify observations and should instead support observations by phrases such as *as evidenced by* (Cameron & turtle-song, 2002).

ASSESSMENT. The counselor's clinical formulations concerning client problems, including *DSM-5* diagnosis (American Psychiatric Association, 2013), should be summarized in this section. Clinical impressions related to diagnostic criteria should also be included to provide a record of information used in diagnosis and treatment planning; such information should be clearly identified as the counselor's clinical impressions. Some authors (e.g., Piazza & Baruth, 1990) contend the inclusion of clinical impressions in the clinical record is inappropriate due to the risk of such information being wrong and recommend such information be kept in the counselor's personal notes. However, keeping clinical impressions in a separate location in the form of personal notes presents serious ethical and legal considerations. Documentation of the clinician's reasoning for diagnostic decisions and the evolution of the treatment is kept most appropriately in the clinical record (Cameron & turtle-song, 2002).

PLAN.   The plan section is divided into two sections consisting of the action plan and the prognosis. The action plan includes information such as interventions, client education, progress of treatment, and the therapeutic work intended for the next session. Any consultation or referrals are also documented in this section. The prognosis is a prediction of the possible outcomes of treatment based on the client's diagnosis, motivation, and resources. Common terms used in prognosis assessments include *excellent, good, fair, guarded,* and *poor.* Supporting information substantiating the prognosis should be provided (Cameron & turtle-song, 2002).

Time-Sequenced Notes

Baird (2010) indicated that the most common format for recording information from counseling sessions is time-sequenced notes. In this format, the significant material that the professional counselor wishes to include in the record is recorded in the same sequence in which it occurred. The counselor may record material as it occurs during the session, or may wait until the session has concluded. The sequence of the material as presented by the client may provide valuable information about the relationship between significant themes. Obviously, the theoretical orientation of the counselor will affect the selection of the material focused on during the session, as well as what is considered important to include in the therapy note. Although this style of note writing is common, additional information (e.g., a treatment plan) is often required to satisfy agency requirements as well as to secure reimbursement from third-party payers (Baird, 2010). Case Study 5.1 provides a context to illustrate how a clinician might capture the essentials of a session using the SOAP and time-sequenced formats.

CASE STUDY 5.1

Jackie

Jackie is a 28-year-old white female who was referred for counseling by her primary-care physician to address her symptoms of anxiety. She arrived for her 4 p.m. intake appointment on time wearing business casual attire. Jackie teaches biology at a local high school. She is single and has lived alone in her apartment for the past 2 months since breaking off a 2-year relationship with her fiancé. She reports that she began experiencing unexpected panic attacks about a month before her fiancé moved out, during which time their relationship became increasingly strained. She describes the main symptoms of her attacks as trembling, dizziness, shortness of breath, rapid heartbeat, a choking sensation, and thinking that she is "going nuts." She said she recognized the symptoms because her mother had experienced panic attacks a few years ago, which were successfully treated with counseling.

Initially, the attacks occurred about once per week, but had increased in frequency to the current level of three per week. A physical examination by her primary-care physician had revealed no medical condition that might explain the attacks. She is very health conscious and exercises regularly. She reports that she is not currently taking any prescription or nonprescription drugs, and she does not smoke, drink, or use illicit substances. Her physician had prescribed an anxiety medication, but Jackie indicates she wants to try a nonpharmacological approach first. Because her mother was able to manage her own panic attacks through counseling, Jackie is hopeful that counseling will be successful for herself as well.

Jackie demonstrated generally positive affect during the interview and described herself as a typically happy person with a "very average" middle-class background. When discussing her work as a teacher, she indicated that she is very satisfied with her career. Although she has not had a panic attack at school, she worries that she might have one and is concerned about how her job might be affected if she did. She appeared calm and relaxed throughout most of the session, but began fidgeting with her hands when the discussion turned to her recent breakup. She indicated that her decision to end the relationship was not due to any single precipitating event and stated that "we were just two independent people with very different goals in life." Jackie is an only child, and she said her mother and father were disappointed when the relationship ended because they were hoping for grandchildren; however, they wanted her to be happy and were supportive of her decision. She indicated she has satisfying, meaningful relationships with several friends, but wants to marry and have children. She noted that her best friend, also a teacher at the high school, had recently gotten engaged. Her eyes grew moist as she continued softly, "I think my biggest fear is the thought of ending up alone." She shrugged, gave a sigh, and said, "I know I let my parents down, and I feel bad about that, especially when they are so supportive. But what really hurts is that I'm starting to think I don't have what it takes to find the right guy. Even with everything else in my life going great, I feel like a loser when it comes to men." She noted that thinking about this causes her stress, and she wondered if this might be related to her panic attacks. She agreed to record in the coming week her thoughts, feelings, and behaviors she experiences in relation to her panic attacks and bring the journal to the next session to discuss.

SOAP Note Format

Subjective (S):

Client is a 28 y/o white female referred by PCP for symptoms of anxiety. Client stated no use of medications/substances, indicated recent physical exam found no general medical condition. Client described unexpected panic attacks occurring over past 3 months, increasing from once/week to current frequency of three/week. Reports onset of attacks occurred around time of relationship difficulties and breakup with fiancé. Symptoms include trembling, dizziness, shortness of breath, rapid heartbeat, a choking sensation, and thoughts of "going nuts." Client reported mother also has past history of panic attacks. Client hopeful symptoms will remit with counseling. Client reports active family and social support systems, satisfaction with career, physically active.

Objective (O):

Client presented appropriate attire and demonstrated appropriate affect; evidenced mild emotional distress and sadness when discussing recent relationship loss. Client stated biggest fear is "ending up alone." Client appears motivated for counseling, as evidenced by being on time for appointment, positive demeanor during intake, and statements expressing belief that counseling might be helpful in ameliorating symptoms.

Assessment (A):

300.01 Panic Disorder Without Agoraphobia. Possible cognitive distortions concerning self and family expectations regarding marriage and childbearing may be related to symptoms.

Plan (P):

Implement cognitive behavioral interventions with client to address anxiety symptoms. Homework: The Client will identify affect, behaviors, and cognitions surrounding the occurrence of panic attacks and record these in a journal to discuss in the next session.
Prognosis: High level of functioning prior to onset of panic symptoms and good insight suggest positive prognosis for treatment.

Time-Sequenced Note Format

Client is a 28-year-old single white female referred by PCP to address anxiety symptoms. Client presented appropriate attire and affect. Client teaches biology at high school. Client lives alone, recently broke off a 2-year relationship with her fiancé. Client began experiencing unexpected panic attacks 3 months ago coincidental with relationship difficulties with fiancé. Client describes main symptoms as trembling, dizziness, shortness of breath, rapid heartbeat, a choking sensation, and thinking that she was "going nuts." Client noted mother has history of panic attacks that were successfully treated with counseling. Initial frequency of attacks once/week, currently three/week. PCP physical examination found no medical conditions to explain the attacks. Client is very health conscious, exercises regularly, reports no use of prescription or nonprescription drugs, does not smoke, drink, or use illicit substances. Client wants to try nonpharmacological approach to ameliorate panic attacks.

Client concerned about having panic attack at her job. Client demonstrated appropriate negative affect when discussing breakup with fiancé, noted parents supportive of her decision but disappointed because they want grandchildren. Client noted good social support system. Identified main stressor as thoughts of ending up alone. Client concerned about her ability to initiate and sustain a successful relationship, good insight into how this relates to panic attacks. Cognitive behavioral interventions indicated per client insight, good prior level of functioning, client cognitive strengths. Client will record in the coming week her thoughts, feelings, and behaviors she experiences in relation to her panic attacks and bring the journal to the next session to discuss.

Current diagnosis: 300.01 Panic Disorder Without Agoraphobia.

THE LINE BETWEEN TOO MUCH AND NOT ENOUGH INFORMATION

A common challenge faced by beginning counselors is deciding what should be included in the therapy note. When writing case notes, style is generally not as critical as brevity, precision, and clarity. The objective with regard to recording essential information is to do so with an efficient use of space and time. By striving for economy of expression, the counselor will save time as well as the time of other professionals who will read the case notes (Baird, 2010).

Although records must contain enough detail to accurately represent the counseling process, counselors should always be mindful that others may view or inspect records in the future. For instance, clients can request copies of records or they may ask that you transfer copies to other professionals. If your records are subpoenaed, they will be viewed by those involved in the case. State mental health authorities might view records at a state agency as part of an auditing visit. Always write with the knowledge that although your records must be thorough, they should not contain unnecessary detail.

Cameron and turtle-song (2002) noted that "few counselors are able to write clear or concise clinical case notes, and most complain of feeling frustrated when trying to distinguish what is and is not important enough to be incorporated in these notes" (p. 287). The difficulty in deciding what should be included and what to omit from the record may be related to the concern of leaving out information that is clinically significant. In the beginning experiences of clinical work, every detail of client verbalizations and behaviors during sessions may appear equally important to include. Deciding what is clinically relevant may be further complicated by unfamiliarity with a theoretical framework that emphasizes certain aspects of treatment; for example, a placement site may approach treatment from a theoretical framework with which the intern is not as well acquainted. Reviewing examples of case notes provided by the placement site may help the new counselor identify the elements of sessions typically included in case notes as well as common phrases associated with these elements; this may in turn facilitate the process of learning to write notes that conform to the protocols of the placement site. As you consider issues around case notes, see Think About It 5.2.

THINK ABOUT IT 5.2

Suppose a colleague confides in you that he is "way behind" on completing his case notes—in fact, he has no written documentation of his work with clients over the last 3 weeks. As your colleague sits down and begins writing his notes from memory, what legal, ethical, and standard of care concerns do you have in relation to his lack of timely documentation?

Instances Where Detail Is Necessary

Certain events in the course of treatment may warrant additional detail to be included in the case note. Baird (2002) noted that one situation requiring special consideration for record keeping is when an abused spouse is receiving counseling, and the abuser does not know. In this case, the record should include some special indicator noting exactly how and where to contact the client and also specific protocols for billing so that it is not possible to inadvertently reveal that the client is coming for treatment. Unauthorized release of client information is one basis for malpractice suits evidenced in case law.

As a source of evidence of appropriate diagnosis and treatment, the information contained in the clinical record is critically important in circumstances when clients threaten harm to themselves or others. If a client expresses a desire to harm self or others, it is important to document the implementation of the appropriate intervention to promote safety. Documentation may include noting compliance with agency protocols, including a record of consultation with outside agencies and resources. Significant client statements that have a direct bearing on the clinician's decision regarding the level of intervention necessary to protect the client or others (e.g., client responses to a risk-assessment) should be included as well (Zuckerman, 2008). If a no-harm agreement is used, a copy of the agreement with accompanying behavioral strategies addressing the risk behaviors should be provided to the client, and the counselor should document that the client received a copy of the agreement. When documenting incidents involving risk of harm, a good rule of thumb to keep in mind is that the only evidence of action taken is that which is written in the record (Harris, 1995), commonly expressed as "If you don't write it down, it didn't happen."

We Are What We Write: The Importance of Professional Written Communication as Keys to Effective Writing

Rawson, Quinlan, Cooper, Fewtrell, and Matlow (2005) noted the importance of professional writing for clear, precise, and succinct communication among colleagues regarding cases and treatment. Professional writing encompasses not only case documentation but also communications between professionals, as well as informational and promotional materials read by the public. Often, the written word is the first contact a counselor has with clients and other professionals. Written expression errors, typos, and an unprofessional tone can create a negative impression that can have an adverse effect on a counselor's reputation and standing. The tone and the requirements of professional writing differ from academic assignments and informal writing. Thus, practice and assessment of professional writing ability is beneficial for all counselors, and writing should be considered a fundamental practice skill. Professional writing involves not only understanding the mechanics of written communication and the use of appropriate terminology to accurately communicate in professional contexts, but it also entails planning and carving out sufficient time to clearly construct text that expresses authentic meaning.

MAKE TIME FOR DOCUMENTATION. A commonly overlooked challenge faced by new counselors related to writing notes is making sure that adequate time is reserved at the end of each session to complete the case note. The therapy record should be written immediately after the session. Although the most obvious advantage of writing notes after each session may be to facilitate recall of significant material from the session (Cameron & turtle-song, 2002), this documentation practice has several other potential benefits, which may include

- Facilitating the processing of reactions to the session, such as countertransference
- Reducing "clutter" in working memory and promoting focus on the client in the following session
- Contributing to a sense of competence as a counselor through demonstrating the ability to appropriately structure sessions within the available resource of time
- Reducing "paperwork fatigue" by completing notes through several short periods of writing one note after each session instead of one long period of writing several notes at the end of the day

- Requiring the counselor to identify significant themes that may assist with case conceptualization
- Reminding the therapist of homework assigned to the client so the therapist will check on this in the next session

OTHER PROFESSIONAL WRITING. In addition to client documentation, writing is required in other facets of a counselor's career. The practice of counseling is often collaborative; therefore, counselors must frequently communicate via letters or e-mail with other professionals, including mental health practitioners, medical personnel, and lawyers. It is prudent to construct such communications with care. First of all, remember that e-mail and faxed documents are not secure communications, and it is essential to protect client confidentiality (Wheeler & Bertram, 2008). Professional communications should never be rushed. Dashing off an e-mail or typing a letter quickly without thought can lead to confusion, embarrassment, or misinformation. Always take time to read over what you have written to make sure you are communicating clearly and competently. Careless mistakes can miscommunicate information about a client and could create a negative impression of a counselor's competency.

Another aspect of professional writing is the development of materials to promote one's practice. Ads, brochures, and other materials are often the initial interface with a new client, and the impression such documents create can make or break a practice. Of course, promotional materials should be eye-catching, but more important, they must be accurate and concise. This is another case where less is more because too much text often ceases to be communicative and simply becomes confusing.

Counselors may be asked to write columns for local newspapers or school newsletters, or they may choose to write informational blogs on their practice websites. Such venues are excellent platforms to communicate general mental health and wellness ideas and can also serve as effective public relations tools. The following tips may be helpful to keep in mind when writing professional letters, columns, and blogs or when developing promotional materials.

- Write and then rewrite. The first draft gives you the basic framework of information that needs to be communicated. Subsequent drafts serve to enhance the readability and style of the document.
- Always proofread carefully. If the information being written is not confidential, it is best to ask a colleague to proofread for you and give you feedback. Another set of eyes can be extremely helpful because people tend to read what they meant to write and may miss actual errors.
- Ask yourself (and your proofreader) if the meaning is clear. Have you clearly communicated your message as you intended? If there is a chance that your meaning could be misconstrued, rewrite.
- When writing promotional materials, you must represent yourself, your credentials, and your expertise accurately. Follow the ethical and legal guidelines of your state regarding promotional material and advertising.
- Promotional materials should be succinct; verbose brochures get tossed aside.
- Avoid using jargon or professional buzzwords that could be confusing to clients.
- When writing columns or blogs, take care that you do not use real-life examples that breach client confidentiality. Examples should be broad, general, and not identifiable as a particular person.
- Read—readers make better writers.
- Relax and enjoy writing. Although you must take care to proofread and have clarity in your writing, you must also let your voice express itself. Allow your genuineness to shine through in your written communication.

Progress Notes and Supervision

Supervisors are responsible for the welfare of their supervisee's clients (Welfel, 2013), and reviewing case notes plays a fundamental role in the supervisory process. By reviewing notes, a supervisor can evaluate the extent to which a supervisee is adhering to standards of care and can monitor client progress. Without examining case notes, supervisors cannot be fully informed on the progress of the client and the skill development of the supervisee (Heller, Gilliam, Chenail, & Hall, 2010). Perhaps more important, Prieto and Schell (2002) highlighted the role case documentation can play in the development of the supervisee's case conceptualization skills. The use of notes in supervision provides an opportunity to help supervisees recognize relevant facts, identify presenting problems, and know when to seek out additional information. Examining notes in supervision strengthens treatment planning and also highlights the importance of examining what is happening within each session and using this information to continually assess and modify treatment. Harris et al. (2009) suggested that graduate programs invite legal experts and practicing counselors as guest speakers in classes to provide students with opportunities to hear about documentation practices and concerns. In addition, programs should have students observe a court proceeding involving counseling records; this would be instructive and would also emphasize the critical importance of following best practice in case documentation and record keeping.

Tips to Avoid Record Keeping Problems

The *ACA Code of Ethics* (2005) is quite clear on the ethical responsibilities of record keeping. As stated earlier in this chapter, client records not only serve to document actions taken within the therapeutic relationship, but they also guide treatment planning and the therapeutic process. Furthermore, in the event a counselor is sued for malpractice or faces a complaint before a licensure board, the case record is the key method by which a counselor can prepare a defense; it is often stated that records are your first line of defense. This is not to say that the only reason one keeps records is in self-defense, but the realization of the possibility of a malpractice lawsuit or a licensure board complaint should keep counselors mindful of the importance of clear and accurate record keeping. Magen and Magen (2010) pointed out that some practitioners, who are overly cautious about possible litigation, may write vague summaries of sessions, noting aspects of the case that could be generalized to most clients. Such nebulous descriptions are not conducive to quality care because this practice fails to adequately describe the counseling process. Magen and Magen provided the following basic guidelines for appropriate professional writing (p. 803):

- Simple, avoid jargon
- Objective
- Parsimony—keep it brief and to the point
- Avoid adjectives
- Write in simple declarative sentences
- Relevant—writing should serve the professional purpose
- Ethical—write in accordance with ethical and legal standards

Not only do records clarify the degree to which a counselor has fulfilled standards of care, but also, according to Wheeler and Bertram (2008), appropriate record keeping is the standard of care: "Counselors have an explicitly stated legal and ethical duty to create and maintain client records on every client" (p. 115). Therefore, if a counselor fails to maintain suitable records, the counselor has violated standard of care.

How long should client records be kept? Ultimately, counselors should be guided by state law regarding how long to keep client records. Basic HIPAA standards recommend a minimum of 6 years after termination of treatment, and for minor clients, a counselor should store records for 7 years past the date the minor client reaches adulthood. State licensure laws may require practitioners to keep records for a longer period of time; thus, counselors should follow the requirements of their licensure. In the event a practitioner has dual licensure, the counselor should keep records for the longest period required by one of their licenses.

DOUBLE-LOCK GUIDELINE. Counselors are responsible for the safeguarding of client records. Records should be stored in a secure locked manner where they will be safe from theft or from dispersal or damage due to a natural disaster such as a tornado or hurricane. Because client records should never be accessible to unauthorized individuals, keeping records under double-lock is best practice. Essentially, the double-lock guideline means that someone must get through two locks to access files. Client files should always be under lock when not in use. Although it may be easier for a counselor to simply leave a file on a desk while he or she pops out of the office for a few minutes, those few minutes could result in a breach of confidentiality that might be harmful to a client and could expose the counselor to litigation.

With the advent of electronic record keeping, counselors must possess technological expertise regarding file security. Confidential files should be password protected or encrypted (Mills, 2012). Counselors should use extreme caution when storing files on laptops or devices such as flashdrives, as these can be easily stolen. Wheeler and Bertram (2008) pointed out the importance of making sure files are secure and having a backup system to guard against loss of information if a computer crashes. There are software systems developed specifically for mental health practice that can assist counselors in setting up a thorough framework for the development and maintenance of client records. Although these systems are extremely useful, it is important that counselors research the security properties of a program before investing in it for their practice. Case Study 5.2 illustrates some security considerations.

CASE STUDY 5.2
Keith

Keith and his colleague Jim have a part-time private practice located in a large office building. Their office space has a waiting area and two offices for counseling. The office building houses several types of businesses and is conveniently located. Keith and Jim see clients in the evening, and although many of the businesses in the building are closed, there are always a few lawyers working late, and the custodial crew comes in around 9:00 to clean, so they are never alone in the building. It has been a good arrangement. Jim has a locked filing cabinet in his office. Keith keeps his client files in the unlocked file drawer of his desk. When confronted by Jim about this practice, Keith noted that because the main door is locked and his personal office door is locked, he is complying with double-lock guidelines. What do you think? Is Keith complying? In what ways could his client files be compromised? Is Jim complying with the double-lock guideline?

CONFIDENTIALITY WITH CLIENT COMMUNICATION. Remley and Herlihy (2010) pointed out that informed consent is linked to the foundational ethical concepts of self-determination and autonomy and is crucial to the development of the counseling relationship. Essentially, a clear explanation of the limits of confidentiality is vital to true informed consent. As a fundamental aspect of the counseling process, informed consent should be accurately documented in the client record with a signed copy of the informed consent document and case file notation that the counselor and client have discussed the document. Informed consent provides clients with all pertinent information about the process of counseling so that clients can know what they are entering into and can make an informed judgment about the counseling process.

One of the most important aspects of informed consent is the explanation of the limits to confidentiality. In most jurisdictions, counselors must breach confidentiality when a client is a danger to self or others or when they suspect abuse or neglect of a child or vulnerable adult. In addition, in states with counselor privilege, a counselor may attempt to quash a subpoena; however, a judge can require the counselor to testify. In some states, counselors do not have privilege and therefore must respond to subpoenas without first attempting to quash them. It is important for counselors to be aware of all their state's laws regarding privilege and confidentiality.

Electronic communications such as phone messages, e-mails, or texts, are not considered secure, and care must be taken to inform clients of this fact. Bradley et al. (2011) suggested that counselors include in the informed consent a discussion with clients about the risks of third parties accessing e-mails that exist even with data encryption and firewalls in place. As part of the informed consent, the counselor should discuss with the client the security limitations of such communications and also clarify if and how counselors should contact clients using e-mails, texts, and phone messages (Zur, 2010). Not only could information be hacked, but more likely, another person may have access to the client's phone or e-mail account and could see confidential information. The counselor has no guarantee that the client is the person on the receiving end of texts and e-mails. However, these types of communications are part of everyday life, and clients may prefer to receive communication via text. Counselors should take precautions to minimize the information imparted in e-mails, texts, and phone messages and communicate simple direct statements such as, "We need to reschedule your appointment."

An important consideration regarding client-generated e-mail, text, and phone message communication is how to appropriately include such artifacts in case documentation. Zur (2010) noted that if a phone message, text, or e-mail has clinical significance, it should be included in the client's record. However, e-mails, messages, and texts that have no clinical significance (e.g., appointment scheduling messages) are not included in the client record. For some messages, the content can simply be noted in the record with the date and time that the message was left. However, counselors might receive voice mail messages where it would be prudent to record the message as part of the clinical record. There are various methods by which client voice mail messages can be saved (VOI or MP3), but counselors must be cognizant of specific security risks with such technologies and include these risks in their informed consent documents. See Self-Assessment Activity 5.1 to reflect on how you would handle such messages.

SELF-ASSESSMENT ACTIVITY 5.1 DOCUMENTING VOICE MAIL

Which of the following client voice mails have clinical significance and should be included in the client record? Could some of these messages simply be documented, or should you record and save the actual message? What ethical and legal concerns might be raised by introducing into the clinical record a verbatim copy of client statements? Do clients know in advance that the message might become part of their clinical record, and should this be a factor in deciding whether or how client statements might be maintained in their files?

1. "Just wanted to let you know that it worked! Timmy did his homework each night this past week."
2. "I was right; the meeting will be over at 3:00 so the 3:30 appointment works fine."
3. "Jim is acting the same way; he isn't doing any of the things you suggested. I'm really getting fed up."
4. "The school counselor signed the release. I'll bring you a copy next week."
5. "I really feel something special happened in our session yesterday. I'm getting so much out of our counseling."
6. "The self-talk statements we worked on just don't ring true. If I say them, I know I'm just lying to myself."
7. "Hey Doc, just wanted to let you know I got the job!"
8. "Susan is on a business trip next week but Jenny and I can make the family counseling appointment."
9. "Sorry I forgot the checkbook. I just put the check in the mail so you should get it in a couple of days."
10. "The insurance people called me, and they got the paperwork, thanks."

Considering that significant voice mail messages may become part of the clinical record underscores the importance of discussing with clients the appropriate content of voice mail as part of informed consent procedures. This discussion might appropriately be part of the process of providing clients with the contact information of agency and community resources to access in times of crisis. Imagine the potential consequences if a counselor neglected to discuss with clients the appropriate use and implications of leaving voice mail messages after agency hours. A client in crisis might call and leave an emotionally charged phone message on the counselor's answering machine with the intent that the counselor listen to the message and assist in processing the crisis with the client in the next session. Such an exchange would resemble the dynamic of asynchronous counseling, which would not be appropriate for a client in crisis (Manhal-Baugus, 2001). Also, if the counselor did not inform the client about the frequency with which the counselor typically checks and responds to voice mail, the client might have the expectation that leaving the voice mail would initiate an immediate response from the counselor to assist with managing the crisis. Consider these questions in regard to this circumstance:

- How might leaving clinically significant messages affect the dynamics of the person-to-person interactions during sessions? How might this impact the counseling relationship? Could this represent a change of service modality?
- If a client calls with the intent of venting on your voice mail and, in the process of venting, becomes even more overwhelmed, what are some other possible adverse consequences?
- If a client leaves information on voice mail that indicates a danger of harming self or others, what might be your responsibility?
- What if a client leaves a message on your voice mail with the expectation you will immediately respond to the crisis and fails to contact emergency services? What if the client follows through and does harm?
- What challenges might the counselor face in appropriately documenting the content of the voice mail in the client record?

As the preceding scenario demonstrates, clients should be provided information during the informed consent process concerning protocols for communicating with counselors via voice mail as well as resources to contact when the counselor is not available.

In addition to providing clients with structure concerning what is appropriate to record on the counselor's voice mail, counselors must also take steps to reduce the likelihood that client phone messages might be accessed by others. For example, a client might leave a message after agency hours on an answering machine. If the machine is located in an accessible place, other staff (e.g., security, cleaning staff) might be able to hear messages as these are recorded or might even be able to play back and listen to recorded messages, thus breaching client confidentiality. To address this risk, voice mail messaging machines should be placed in secured locations.

As noted previously, communicating outside face-to-face interactions via e-mail and text messaging technology also pose significant concerns that should be discussed with clients. If substantial interactions take place between counselor and client through technological means that are not discussed as part of the informed consent process, these interactions could arguably fall outside the parameters of the established therapeutic modality. Clients who interact with their counselors using e-mail through an office network should be made aware that others can directly access their messages. Clients who send e-mail from a shared home computer should also consider that others may also have access to their messages (Recupero & Rainey, 2005). The counselor's limited ability to confirm the identity of clients when using text-based messaging takes on particular significance when considering treating minors and managing crisis situations (Manhal-Baugus, 2001). Even when clients are provided with an identification code to verify identity, the possibility exists that this code could be compromised, and the counselor might unknowingly breach confidentiality while interacting with a person who falsely presents as the client.

A unique challenge presented by text-based interaction is the lack of nonverbal cues facilitating communication. The use of emoticons or other nonverbal expressions such as <laughing> have limited utility in the therapeutic context and do not fully compensate for this challenge. In addition, the therapeutic intervention of calling attention to discrepancies between verbal and nonverbal messages when communicating via text-only interaction might literally be "virtually impossible."

Recupero and Rainey (2005) divided the risks associated with communicating with clients via the Internet into two categories: general security risks and content-specific risks. General security risks are represented by hackers who might intentionally intercept private information through unauthorized means. Also in this category are e-mails sent to the wrong address through inadvertent typos in the "to" field. Content-specific risks refer to "the 'unsanitized' nature of e-therapy communications" (p. 323) represented by exact transcripts of client e-mails. As has been noted previously, these artifacts might include inappropriate, irrelevant, or misleading information that should not be included in the client's clinical record, and the clinician should consider client welfare and best practice in deciding how such information might be appropriately documented.

Electronic records are increasingly being used by agencies and counselor education programs. Electronic record programs designed specifically for mental health professionals, such as Therascribe, assist not only with documentation of counseling sessions, but also with processes such as billing, diagnosis, and treatment planning. Although the benefits of such programs are substantial, so are the potential risks associated with their use. For example, access to client information typically requires the counselor to enter login information such as a username and password. If the counselor's login information is compromised, the client's records would then be accessible.

The process of keeping electronic records has potential risks as well. The ease of editing electronic word processing documents might suggest that making changes to previously documented entries in an electronic clinical record can be accomplished quickly and without detecting the change; however, under HIPAA, such changes could represent a serious violation of standards. HIPAA requires that covered entities protect the confidentiality information stored in electronic records against "reasonably anticipated threats." To address this requirement, electronic record-keeping systems commonly include safeguards to record system activity, identify security violations, and discover when documentation is destroyed or altered. It is critical that electronic health records are kept in compliance with HIPAA rules to avoid substantial penalties.

Another risk associated with electronic records is that when stored on a computer hard drive, any documents may be retrievable by others even if intentionally deleted by the counselor. Conversely, in the event of data corruption or the physical loss or destruction of hard disks, client records that are not also maintained as hard copies could be irretrievably lost. Electronic storage and backup devices should be subjected to the same double-lock guidelines as prescribed for paper-based records.

When Clients Request Their Records

According to the *ACA Code of Ethics* (2005), clients may request access to their records as decreed in B.6.d of the *Code of Ethics*.

> **B.6.d. Client Access** Counselors provide reasonable access to records and copies of records when requested by competent clients. Counselors limit the access of clients to their records, or portions of their records, only when there is compelling evidence that such access would cause harm to the client. Counselors document the request of clients and the rationale for withholding some or all of the record in the files of clients. In situations involving multiple clients, counselors provide individual clients with only those parts of records that related directly to them and do not include confidential information related to any other client. (ACA, 2005)

Welfel (2013) noted that providing clients access to records is based on the foundational ethics principles of autonomy and beneficence; however, access to records does not necessarily mean files are immediately copied. There are several matters to consider. First of all, Welfel pointed out that when writing notes, it is a good idea to remember that a client could one day read the notes. A counselor who has kept this advice in mind will likely not have major concerns regarding the contents of the record. Remley and Herlihy (2010) stressed that records are kept for the benefit of the client, and the client should have access to such records. However, in the event that the counselor believes it would be detrimental for the client to see the records, the counselor can prevent access. In these cases, Remley and Herlihy suggest the following steps: 1. Explain why you believe it would be best if the client did not see the record and the client might retract his or her request. 2. Offer to make a summary of the record for the client rather than a copy. The client could still demand to see or have a copy of the records, and if the client takes legal action, the law will most likely be on the client's side regarding the client's right to record access. Counselors should document their reasons for not wanting to release information and should document that they explained these reasons to the client.

If the records contain confidential information related to other people, a situation that might occur in family or group counseling, the counselor should explain that releasing the records would infringe on the privacy of others. If the client refuses a summary of the part of the records related to him or her and still insists on having a copy of the records, the counselor should expunge from the copy all references to other people. Grossman and Koocher (2012) pointed out that to release unredacted copies of case records of couple or family counseling, the mental health practitioner would need to have written permission of each person discussed in the record. Before releasing any information, counselors must have the consent of the client for release (Grossman & Koocher, 2012; Remley & Herlihy, 2010). In legal situations, a camera review, whereby a judge or other impartial party goes over the records and identifies for release only those parts of the record that are pertinent, might be called for (Gladding, 2011). However, Stansbury (2010) pointed out that a camera review does have "… the disadvantage of providing information to a judge out of context and without any foundation or explanation" (p. 537). Again, it cannot be stressed enough that counselors must be ever mindful of the fact that their client records could one day be read by the client or others. Strict observance of ethical best practice regarding documentation is crucial.

Under HIPAA, when releasing information about a client, counselors should release the minimum amount of essential information and not a copy of the entire file (DeLettre & Sobell, 2010; Grossman & Koocher, 2012). In addition to the protection provided by minimum disclosure, HIPAA also provides protection by allowing state laws that surpass the privacy protection of HIPAA to supersede HIPAA regulations, and by allowing the exemption of "psychotherapy notes" from being released; thus, only requiring the release of the clinical record (Grossman & Koocher, 2012). Grossman and Koocher noted that the clinical record should consist of the following (p. 44): "1. Medication prescription and monitoring; 2. Counseling session start and stop times (i.e. duration); 3. Modalities and frequencies of treatment; 4. Results of clinical tests (including raw test data); 5. Summaries of: a. Diagnosis, b. Functional status, c. Treatment plan, d. Symptoms, e. Prognosis, f. Progress to date" (p. 44).

The Family Educational Rights and Privacy Act (FERPA), which applies to public educational institutions as well as private educational institutions that receive federal funding, must be taken into account when considering records at educational institutions. Regarding educational records, school officials should remain mindful that under FERPA, parents of minor students and students 18 years or older can request to view records and can challenge information contained in such records (Remley & Herlihy, 2010). Counselors may maintain clinical case notes separate from the educational records covered by FERPA and these clinical case notes are not subject to FERPA. FERPA does contain a clause to allow the release of private information in emergency situations in the event that a student is a danger to self or others and the release of such information could protect the health and safety of others.

If a client brings a malpractice lawsuit or a complaint before a licensure board against a counselor, the client must sign a release and relinquish the right to confidentiality, and the client records will be released (Welfel, 2013). Counselors have a right to use client records to defend themselves in a lawsuit or an ethics complaint. However, Welfel stressed that counselors should be certain that the client has signed a release before using case information in a defense. Once again, it is wise to remember that your records could be seen and read by others, and you must have documented your treatment clearly, professionally, and ethically. Your defense will hinge on the extent to which you observed ethical best practice and standards of care. Failure to clearly document what transpired in the counseling relationship will mean that you have no defense. Remember—if it's not documented, it didn't happen.

Other administrative responsibilities. If a counselor works in a school or an agency, the school or agency is the custodian of the records. However, private practitioners must store and eventually properly destroy client records. The length of time a client record should be kept has been discussed previously in this chapter. What happens to the records of a counselor who dies? Again, if the counselor works in an agency or school, continuity of client care and the security of client records are assumed by the agency or school (Mills, 2012). However, private practitioners must address what will happen to their practice in the event of their death. Wheeler and Bertram (2008) pointed out the necessity of private practitioners appointing a records custodian who will assume the secure storage and disposal of client records on a counselor's death or incapacity. This is in keeping with section C.2.h. of the 2005 ACA code, which identifies the need for counselors to prepare in advance a plan by which the records custodian will appropriately carry out the transfer of files and clients. Thus, the designated custodian should also be able to contact clients and provide referrals, thereby ensuring ongoing care. The identity and role of the custodian should be outlined in the informed consent document. If a counselor dies without a custodian, the counselor's clients would be abandoned, and the confidentiality of their records could be comprised if the records are simply tossed into a dumpster or if the counselor's computer is sold with client information remaining on it. These types of actions could result in the counselor's estate being sued for breach of confidentiality.

When it is time to destroy a file, how should this take place? For paper records, the counselor, or an administrative clerk who has been trained in handling confidential information, should shred the documents to ensure that confidential material cannot be obtained. Electronic data should be deleted and then deleted again from the computer recycle bin. In addition, the data should be wiped or overwritten on the hard drive.

Summary

Although record keeping has always been important in counseling, the emergence of managed care and evidence-based practice has emphasized the necessity of appropriate documentation in counseling services. In addition, legal and regulatory requirements actually codify appropriate documentation into law, and the *ACA*'s *Code of Ethics* (ACA, 2005) contains specific directives regarding ethical and best practice in documentation and records. Developing and keeping proper client records is a counselor's ethical, legal, and clinical responsibility.

Progress notes document how a client is progressing in treatment and also provide documentation about what is happening in treatment sessions. Progress notes include goals for the session, which are linked to the treatment plan and can establish continuity of treatment. Progress notes should also include counselor interventions, client progress, and the counselor's clinical impressions. Finally, notes should contain an action goal connecting to the next session.

Process notes, also referred to as psychotherapy notes, are notes written by the counselor for the purpose of personal reflection. They can be useful for analyzing treatment impressions and can also be valuable in supervision. After relevant information has been obtained from process notes, it is recommended that they be destroyed.

A standard record format is the SOAP notes system. SOAP stands for Subjective, Objective, Assessment, and Plan. The Subjective section includes client perceptions of the problem and client report; the Objective section is factual and quantitative and includes written records and counselor observations. The Assessment section is the counselor's clinical and diagnostic impressions. Finally, the Plan section consists of an action plan and the prognosis. Beginning counselors often struggle with writing too much or not enough information. Reviewing examples of notes can help novice counselors to refine their ability to synthesize important elements into notes and also become familiar with agency protocols. It is important to keep in mind that certain situations in counseling call for more detail. For example, cases involving domestic violence or instances where a client indicates harm to self or others.

Clear inclusive documentation is imperative to appropriate practice; counselors should be knowledgeable in documentation procedures and schedule sufficient time for writing thorough notes that accurately reflect client treatment. The therapy record should be written immediately after the session to generate a precise record of therapy. In addition, by making time to write notes after the session, counselors are more likely to identify significant themes, and they also avoid the danger of end-of-the-day paperwork pileup. Consult Self-Assessment Activity 5.2 to hone your documentation skills.

SELF-ASSESSMENT ACTIVITY 5.2 PROFESSIONAL WRITING

The following activities can be done in small groups or in pairs. Practicing common writing situations and obtaining feedback from your peers will strengthen and polish your writing skills. For each of these activities, take your peer feedback and rewrite the activity. Remember, your writing is a reflection of your professionalism.

1. Choose a television show or movie that has psychotherapy scenes. Some suggestions are *Sopranos, In Treatment, Analyze This,* or any television or movie scene that contains a lengthy monologue by a character. View the scene with your activity partner/small group. After viewing, each person should write SOAP notes

as if he or she were the counselor for the character. Exchange SOAP notes, and provide feedback to one another. Did you and your peer(s) emphasize different aspects of the scene? If so, why? Did you write too much? Not enough?

2. Write a flyer describing a new program or group that you will be offering in your practice. This flyer will be displayed publically in local businesses. Exchange with your activity partner/small group and provide feedback to one another. Is your flyer professional yet welcoming to potential clients? Did you portray yourself and your services appropriately?

3. You are an LPC and have opened a private practice, and you want to send a letter to local lawyers and doctors announcing your practice, your credentials, and the services you provide. Write a letter and exchange with your activity partner/small group and give feedback to one another. Is the tone of your letter professional? Does the letter communicate competency to the reader?

4. Have each person choose a wellness or life skill topic (e.g., stress management, self-care, goal setting). Write a brief blog on this topic. Exchange with your activity partner/small group and give feedback to one another. Is the blog informational, and is the information factual? Does it appeal to the reader?

CHAPTER 6

Putting Ethics and Law into Practice

BY LYNN E. LINDE AND BRADLEY T. ERFORD

PREVIEW

This chapter addresses some ethical and legal issues in counseling commonly encountered by counselors-in-training. As a professional counselor, you must always remember that how you conduct yourself personally and professionally reflects not only on yourself, but also on your colleagues. Knowledge and understanding of the issues reviewed in this chapter are only a starting point. Keep up to date with the laws, ethics, policies, and procedures that govern professional practice in your state and workplace. The implementation of your professional responsibilities will require your undivided attention every day of your professional life.

ETHICAL STANDARDS AND LAWS

The cornerstone of the counseling relationship rests on the public's trust in the services provided. Each professional counselor has an enormous responsibility to uphold the public trust and must seek high levels of training, education, and supervision in the ethical application of counseling practices. This is particularly essential in a profession such as counseling because counselors usually work with clients and students as lone professionals, often with little oversight and behind closed doors in confidential circumstances.

One of the greatest challenges facing most professional counselors daily is how to handle appropriately the many different ethical and legal situations they encounter. Because of the nature of counseling, professional counselors must be prepared to help clients who present a variety of challenges. At the beginning of your career, it is often difficult to know all you need to understand and be able to do. Numerous resources and sources of information can help guide professional counselors as they strive to assist clients in an ethical and legal manner. The professional associations for counselors have created ethical standards for professional behavior and provide a wealth of current information, resources, and training. Federal and state governments continually enact laws and regulations that affect counselors, including the judicial branch, in which courts hand down decisions that directly affect counselors' behavior. In addition, agencies, insurance companies, state boards of education and local school systems create policies, guidelines, and procedures that counselors must follow.

Professional counselors are sometimes confused by the difference between ethical standards and laws and what one should do when these seem to be in conflict with each other. It may be helpful to take a look at the origin of both. **Ethical standards** are usually developed by professional associations to guide the behavior of a specific group of professionals. According to Herlihy and Corey (2006), ethical standards serve three purposes: to educate members about sound ethical conduct, to provide a mechanism for accountability, and to serve as a means for improving professional practice. Ethical standards change and are updated periodically to ensure their relevance and appropriateness.

Ethical standards are based on generally accepted norms, beliefs, customs, and values. Codes of ethics ordinarily are based on Kitchener's five moral principles of autonomy, justice, beneficence, nonmaleficence, and fidelity (Forester-Miller & Davis, 1996). Autonomy refers to the concept of independence and the ability to make one's own decisions. Professional counselors need to respect the right of clients to make their own decisions based on their personal values and beliefs, and not impose their values on clients. Justice means treating each person fairly, but it does not mean treating each person the same way. Rather, counselors should treat clients according to the client needs. Beneficence refers to doing good or what is in the best interests of the client. In counseling, it also incorporates the concept of removing conditions that might cause harm. **Nonmaleficence** means doing no harm to others. Finally, fidelity involves the concepts of loyalty, faithfulness, and honoring commitments. This means that professional counselors must honor all obligations to the client.

Laws are also based on these same, generally accepted norms, beliefs, customs, and values. However, laws are more prescriptive, have been incorporated into code, and carry greater sanctions or penalties for failure to comply. Laws and ethical standards exist to ensure the appropriate behavior of professionals within a particular context to ensure that the best interests of the client are met. When ethics and laws seem to be in conflict, the professional counselor must attempt to resolve the conflict in a responsible manner (Cottone & Tarvydas, 2007). Professional counselors must make their clients aware of this conflict. Because there are greater penalties associated with laws, the counselor will often follow the legal course of action if there is no harm to the client. Many ethical standards recognize that other mandates must be followed and suggest that professional counselors work to change mandates that are not in the best interests of their clients. Self-Assessment Activity 6.1 provides an opportunity to explore the nuances of an ethical/legal conflict.

ETHICS IN CLINICAL PRACTICE

Professional codes of ethics form the foundation of effective, moral practice. This section highlights the essential practice elements of the American Counseling Association's (ACA's) *Code of Ethics* (2005), American School Counselor Association's (ASCA's) *Ethical Standards for School Counselors* (2010), American Mental Health Counselors Association's (AMHCA's) *Principles for AMHCA's Code of Ethics* (2010), and American Association of Marriage and Family Therapists (AAMFT; 2012) and International Association of Marriage and Family Counselors (IAMFC; Hendricks, Bradley, Southern, Oliver, & Birdsall, 2011) codes of ethics. Whereas the *ACA Code of Ethics* serves to promote ethical practice across all disciplines and settings of the counseling profession, other associations' codes of ethics and guidelines speak more directly to their specialty area and setting. For example, the ASCA's *Ethical Standards for School Counselors* discusses what ethical behavior consists of in a school setting, whereas the *Principles for AMHCA's Code of Ethics* applies specifically to agency and private practice settings.

Many professional counselors belong to multiple organizations, each of which may have its own code of ethics. They may also hold credentials from organizations or state credentialing boards that have a code of ethics as well. Many counselors are Nationally Certified Counselors, a credential offered by the National Board for Counselor Certification, Inc. (NBCC), which also has a code of ethics. Although most of the specific ethic provisions align across codes, differences do exist. It is often hard to know which code takes precedence. Although each professional will have to make that determination individually, there are two general guidelines. First, what is the setting in which one is practicing (e.g., school, clinic), and is there a particular code that applies specifically to that setting? Second, in what capacity (e.g., licensed professional counselor, marriage and family therapist, certified school counselor) is the professional operating? So, if you are a marriage and family counselor working in an agency, the IAMFC or AAMFT codes may be most applicable, whereas the ACA or AMHCA codes may be most applicable if working in a university counseling center. In addition, all codes are similar, and all concern behaving in an appropriate professional manner, operating in the best interests of the client, and practicing within the scope of one's education, training, and experience. If a professional counselor is doing all these things, the existence of multiple codes of ethics should not be a significant issue. Because the *ACA Code of Ethics* is a more comprehensive and encompassing code, summaries of the main emphases of the ACA code will be provided. However, the practicum student or intern should review the ACA code and the specific applicable practice setting code in depth to become familiar with all expectations for professional conduct.

American Counseling Association Code of Ethics

The ACA revises its *Code of Ethics* about every 10 years. The sixth and most recent revision took effect in 2005. There are numerous significant changes from the 1995 *Code of Ethics and Standards of Practice* to the 2005 *Code of Ethics*. The most obvious change is that the Standards of Practice section, which described in behavioral terms the aspirational ethics set forth in the code, has been incorporated into the body of the *ACA Code of Ethics* and is no longer a separate section. Each section now begins with an introduction, which sets the tone for that section and is a beginning point for discussion (ACA, 2005). Parts of the *ACA Code of Ethics* have been updated to reflect the current thinking and practice in the field, and several new issues were added as was a glossary of terms. The ACA code is currently being revised, and the new code will be effective in 2014 or early 2015. An increased focus on the use of technology and social media in counseling and electronic records will be addressed in this version.

The ACA states that the 2005 *Code of Ethics* serves five main purposes, as follows:

> The *Code* 1) enables the association to clarify to current and future members, and to those served by members, the nature of the ethical responsibilities held in common by its members; 2) The *Code* helps support the mission of the association; 3) The *Code* establishes the principles that define ethical behavior and best practices of association members; 4) The *Code* serves as an ethical guide designed to assist members in constructing a professional course of action that best serves those utilizing counseling services and best promotes the values of the counseling profession; and 5) The *Code* serves as the basis for processing of ethical complaints and inquiries initiated against members of ACA. (p. 3)

The 2005 *ACA Code of Ethics* can be viewed at http://www.counseling.org/Resources/ aca-code-of-ethics.pdf. It addresses the responsibilities of professional counselors toward their clients, colleagues, workplace, and themselves by delineating the ideal standards for conducting one's behavior. All members of ACA are required to abide by the *Code of Ethics* as a condition of membership, and action is taken against any member who fails to do so. In effect, as these are the ethical standards of the profession, all professional counselors are held to the *Code of Ethics* by the mental health community, regardless of whether they are members of the ACA.

The *Code of Ethics* is divided into eight areas: (A) The Counseling Relationship; (B) Confidentiality, Privileged Communication, and Privacy; (C) Professional Responsibility; (D) Relationships with Other Professionals; (E) Evaluation, Assessment, and Interpretation; (F) Supervision, Training, and Teaching; (G) Research and Publication; and (H) Resolving Ethical Issues. Each of these areas details specific counselor responsibilities and standards. In general, the *Code of Ethics* discusses respecting one's client and the background each client brings to the counseling setting; maintaining professional behavior with clients and other professionals; practicing with the best interests of the client in mind; and practicing within the limits of one's training, experience, and education. Section H provides direction for members resolving ethical dilemmas. Highlights from each of these areas are summarized next, but at this point, readers should locate the actual *ACA Code of Ethics* on the ACA website and peruse it in detail.

SECTION A: THE COUNSELING RELATIONSHIP. A key issue addressed in this section is boundaries with clients and dual relationships. The period of time that a professional counselor and former client must wait to engage in romantic or sexual relationships was changed from 2 to 5 years, and the language was expanded to include not just clients, but also romantic partners or family members of former clients. This change highlighted the vulnerable nature of clients in a helping relationship. Although nonprofessional relationships with clients outside the formal counseling relationship ordinarily should be avoided, the current *Code* recognizes that this is not always possible and also recognizes that nonprofessional relationships with clients may even benefit clients (e.g., attending formal ceremonies, hospital visits, membership in community organizations, commerce), albeit when conducted with caution.

Continued emphasis was placed on critical issues, including general client welfare and avoiding harm, appropriate termination of services (see Chapter 14), fees and bartering, and informed consent. The informed consent provision is particularly important because many state counseling boards now require written consent so that clients can choose a counseling relationship with a qualified provider from an informed consumer position. Section A.2.b specifies that informed consent includes, but is not limited to, purposes, goals, techniques, procedures, limitations, potential risks, and benefits of services; the counselor's qualifications, credentials, and relevant experience; the intended use of tests and reports, fees, and billing arrangements; the right to confidentiality and limitations; the continuation of services should the counselor become incapacitated; obtaining clear information about their records; participating in ongoing treatment planning; and the right to refuse treatment at any time and the potential consequences for doing so. In addition, the *Code* addresses the need to balance assent from minors and others incapable of giving consent without the assent of parents and family members who hold the legal rights of consent, protection, and decision making on their behalf. An example of informed consent forms that address these salient points is provided in Table 6.1.

Section A also includes new standards for serving the terminally ill and facilitating end-of-life decisions, making the ACA one of the first national associations to address these issues. In doing so, the ACA directs counselors to receive adequate supervision and seek multiple professional collaborations and help clients to exercise self-determination, establish high-quality end-of-life care, and participate maximally in decision making. Finally, the 1999 ACA *Ethical Standards for Internet Online Counseling* was integrated into A.12, broadening the *Code* to address issues of technology in providing counseling services, record keeping, and research applications.

TABLE 6.1 Professional Disclosure Statement*

Bradley T. Erford, PhD

Address

Telephone Numbers & E-mail

I welcome you as a new client, and I look forward to working with you. The purpose of this form is to let you know about my approach to counseling, what you can expect from counseling, and my background. This form will also give you an opportunity to give consent for counseling or assessment services.

In my view, the relationship of feelings and thoughts to behavior is crucial to understanding the issues that affect being successful in life. I use a variety of strategies that can help people make sense of their world, strategies that are mostly humanistic and cognitive-behavioral in nature; that is, they are strategies based on the notion people often experience personal difficulties because of relationship issues, and that the way people think about and see themselves and the world influences how they feel and behave. You will be encouraged to engage in strategies to address these issues both during and between our sessions.

Individual counseling offers you a chance to express ideas and concerns to understand your situation better and learn new ways to solve problems. However, there are risks and limitations to counseling. At times, you might experience feelings that are uncomfortable and hard to face. I often compare this process to taking medicine: it may not taste great, but it also might be good for you in the long run. I will do my best to provide an accurate and fair assessment and diagnosis that will help guide our treatment planning and goal setting. We will also discuss this assessment/diagnosis and your resulting treatment plan/goals throughout the counseling process. Counseling is a collaborative process done with your best interests in mind, and the ultimate goal is for you to reach a level of healthy and independent personal functioning.

Of course, you have the right to refuse or terminate treatment at any time, and should you believe either of these options appropriate, I hope you will discuss the potential benefits and risks associated with your decision with me. If at any time I become unavailable to continue providing services to you as a result of incapacitation or other cause, I will help transition you to another mental health care provider who can either continue treatment or ensure appropriate referral so that your best interests are served.

(Continued)

I specialize in working with children, adolescents, and their families, and provide psychoeducational assessment, as well as individual, group, and family counseling. I am particularly experienced in working with individuals presenting with disruptive, anxious, and depressed behaviors, as well as individuals experiencing learning, divorce, or grief adjustment difficulties, or in need of stress management.

Everything you discuss with me will be kept confidential by me except matters pertaining to (1) suicide or harm to another person; (2) physical/sexual abuse or neglect of minors, persons with disabilities, and the elderly; (3) legal activity resulting in a court order; and (4) anything else as required by law. For those matters, legally and ethically, I would have to break confidentiality and involve others. Except for these conditions, any written information or report that I possess cannot be shared, orally or in writing, with another individual or agency without your express written permission. Tests are administered and reports are produced to facilitate personal diagnosis and treatment. Of course, I would be willing to share information with any other professional or agency that you wish, provided that you sign a written release-of-information form, which I can provide for you. Alternatively, you may share results from written reports or sessions at your discretion because confidentiality applies to my communications, not yours. Ethically guiding my behavior is the *ACA Code of Ethics* published by the American Counseling Association in Alexandria, VA, the National Board for Certified Counselors (NBCC, Inc.), and the Code of Ethics adopted by the Maryland Board of Professional Counselors and Therapists. Legally, I adhere to U.S. and Maryland statutes.

As for my background, I have been a licensed professional counselor since 1988. I earned my bachelor's degree (BS) in biology from Grove City College (PA), my master's degree (MA) in school psychology from Bucknell University (PA), and my PhD in counselor education from The University of Virginia. I am a member of the American Counseling Association, and I am a Licensed Clinical Professional Counselor (LCPC), which allows me to practice mental health counseling in Maryland. My LCPC state license was issued by the Board of Professional Counselors and Therapists in Baltimore, MD. I also am a National Certified Counselor (NCC), which is a designation given by the National Board for Certified Counselors (NBCC).

As far as counseling/assessment session fees are concerned, I charge $____ per hour. This same rate applies to time spent on providing special services, such as court appearances. Cost for a standard psychoeducational assessment is $_____, which includes a written report and up to 1 hour for a feedback/interpretation consultation session. I do not participate with third-party payers, such as managed care organizations and insurance companies. By signing this form, you are agreeing to pay this fee on the day the service is provided. Missed appointments without a 24-hour notice will have to be paid for, except for genuine emergencies.

I have attached a business card to this letter. Please feel free to contact me at any time during business hours. If I am unavailable, you can leave a message, and I will get back to you as soon as possible. In the event of an emergency, please call 911 or go to the nearest emergency room.

I hope that you will find this counseling experience to be successful and, in some ways, enjoyable. I thank you very much for taking time to read this. Please sign below to indicate your consent to pursue counseling or assessment services.

Bradley Erford, PhD, LCPC, NCC

LC#

Contact Information:

Board of Professional Counselors and Therapists	American Counseling Association
4201 Patterson Avenue	5999 Stevenson Avenue
Baltimore, MD 21215-2299	Alexandria, VA 22304
410-764-4732	800-347-6647

Note: You do not have to sign this; you have the right to refuse counseling or psychoeducational assessment.

I, _____, fully understand what I have just read and offer my consent for counseling or psychoeducational assessment, free of any pressure to do so. Here is my signature and the date of the signature (that expires one year from now).

_____   _____

Signature   Date

_____   _____

Signature of a custodial parent is required in   Date
cases where the child/adolescent is a minor

*This information is required by the Board of Professional Counselors and Therapists, which regulates all licensed clinical professional counselors in Maryland. You can contact the Board at Board of Professional Counselors and Therapists, 4201 Patterson Avenue, Baltimore, MD 21215-2299, or 410-764-4732.

SECTION B: CONFIDENTIALITY, PRIVILEGED COMMUNICATION, AND PRIVACY. Several major changes were made to the confidentiality, privileged communication, and privacy section of the _Code of Ethics_. Standard B.1.a was added to remind professional counselors to maintain sensitivity and awareness in regard to cultural meanings of privacy and confidentiality. Counselors should also be respectful of differing views and inform clients with whom, when, and how information will be shared. Another addition was Standard B.3.e, which took into consideration the transmission of confidential information and reflected the growing use of technology throughout the counseling process. This Standard advised counselors to take precautions to ensure confidentiality when using technologies such as computers, electronic mail, or voice mail. Confidentiality and privileged communication are covered more comprehensively later in the chapter.

A new and important addition was Standard B.3.f, which asserted that professional counselors should maintain the confidentiality of deceased clients as is consistent with legal requirements and policies. Another significant change involved Standard B.4.b, which was renamed Couples and Family Counseling. The 2005 _Code_ stated that professional counselors must clearly recognize who is considered to be "the client," must discuss limitations and expectations of confidentiality during couples and family counseling, and should seek and document an agreement with all involved parties as to their individual rights to confidentiality or obligations to protect the confidentiality of the known information. This differed from the 1995 _Code_, which simply declared that permission was required when disclosing information about one family member to another.

Finally, Section B.5 was expounded on to address confidentiality and privacy when counseling clients who are minors or adults lacking the capacity to give informed consent. Professional counselors are directed to inform parents and legal guardians of the confidential nature of the counseling relationship as well as establish a working relationship with them to serve clients better. Counselors must also seek permission from the appropriate parties to disclose information. When working with this specific population, counselors are reminded to uphold written policies, federal and state laws, and ethical standards as applicable.

VOICES FROM THE FIELD 6.1   Managing Boundary Issues in Counseling, by Victoria E. Kress

As I pulled into my driveway, I noticed someone lying in the grass on my front lawn. My initial reaction was, "That's strange." I went into the house and peered out the window only to realize it was one of my clients. My next reaction was, "Wow, this is creepy. Do I call the police? Do I go and talk to her? How did she know where I live? Why is she on my lawn?" Sadly, in graduate school, no one had taught me what to do when situations like this arise.

When in doubt, peer supervision is always the way to go. So I called my friend who is a counselor, but she didn't answer the phone. I thought about calling the state counseling board to consult, but it was a Saturday and no one there was working. I considered reviewing my ethics textbook from graduate school, but I knew the answer couldn't be found there.

Knowing this client was unpredictable and volatile, worst-case scenarios went through my head: "Is she going to attempt suicide on my lawn? Is she going to harm me and my dog?"

(Continued)

As I pondered my options, she left. She ostensibly wanted me to know that she had been there, and once that end was met, she was able to leave.

What to do next? Naturally, I decided to address the issue with my client. "Tell me about what was going on when you were laying on my lawn Saturday." She was coy in her explanation of why she was at my home, but I was direct in my response. I set boundaries with her and explained the importance to her—and to me—of her honoring those boundaries. We discussed that if she couldn't navigate those boundaries and regulate her affect around our relationship, we would need to explore finding a counselor with whom she could have a more successful therapeutic relationship. As her core issues were related to self and other boundaries, the experience did provide good fodder in helping her work toward reaching her goals. Thankfully, she did not return to my lawn.

SECTION C: PROFESSIONAL RESPONSIBILITY.   This section continues to place emphasis on issues such as professional competence, advertising and soliciting clients, professional qualifications, and public responsibility. One area that was significantly expanded on involves counselor impairment (Standard C.2.g). Professional counselors must be alert to signs of personal impairment and should refrain from providing or offering services if the impairment could potentially harm a client. If the problem reaches the level of professional impairment, the counselor should seek assistance. Professional counselors are now also required to assist supervisors or colleagues in recognizing impairment and, if necessary, provide assistance, intervention, or consultation.

Standard C.2.h was added to address further the issue of counselor impairment or subsequent termination of practice. This new standard states that counselors should follow a prepared plan for the transfer of files and clients when they leave a practice. In particular, counselors need to designate a specific colleague or "records custodian" and create a proper plan for file and client transfer in the case of their incapacitation, termination of practice, or death.

Another major change to this section includes the addition of Standard C.6.e, which acknowledges that professional counselors must use techniques, modalities, or procedures that have a scientific or empirical foundation and are grounded in theory. If not, counselors should note their procedures or techniques to be "unproven" or "developing." The potential risks and ethical considerations of the procedures or techniques should be explained to the client, and counselors should take all necessary steps to protect the client from any potential harm. Counselors are still required to monitor their effectiveness and take any necessary actions to improve as professionals.

SECTION D: RELATIONSHIPS WITH OTHER PROFESSIONALS.   This section stresses the importance of interaction and relationships between counselors and other professionals. Professional counselors should become knowledgeable about their colleagues and develop positive working relationships and communication systems. Generally, the 2005 *ACA Code of Ethics* reorganizes and renames most of the standards in this section. It is also recognized that counselors may often be a part of an interdisciplinary team. Several new standards were created to reflect this development.

Professional counselors are reminded to be respectful of differing approaches to counseling services and the traditions and practices of other professional groups (Standard D.1.a). Inclusion of Standards D.1.b and D.1.c specifically address interdisciplinary relationships and teamwork, respectively. Professional counselors must work to develop and strengthen relationships with interdisciplinary colleagues. Professional counselors must also keep focused on how best to serve their clients when working in a team environment. To do so, counselors can contribute to and partake in any decisions that could potentially affect the well-being of clients by the use of the values, experiences, and perspectives of the counseling profession and other disciplines. Standard D.1.e reminds counselors that when working with an interdisciplinary team, it is their responsibility to clarify the ethical and professional obligations of individual members and the team as a whole. Professional counselors are encouraged to attempt to resolve ethical concerns initially within the team. If a resolution cannot be made within the team, counselors should pursue other means to address the concerns consistent with the well-being of the client.

SECTION E: EVALUATION, ASSESSMENT, AND INTERPRETATION. A noticeable change to this section involves the replacement of the word *tests* with *assessment*, which has a more integrative and broader connotation. In addition, "career assessment" was added to several standards, and further details were included. For example, Standard E.1.a now includes specific examples of measurements, including, but not limited to, personality, ability, interest, achievement, intelligence, and performance. It is still recognized that assessment is only one part of the overall counseling process, and that professional counselors must take into account the cultural, social, and personal factors.

Historical and Social Prejudices in the Diagnosis of Pathology (Standard E.5.c) is a new addition to the 2005 *Code* and states that professional counselors should be aware of social and historical prejudices in the pathologizing and misdiagnosis of specific individuals and groups. In addition, counselors should be cognizant of the role of mental health professionals in the continuation of these problems. Not only does the revised *ACA Code of Ethics* take into consideration historical factors, but it was also changed to reflect the current trends in counseling.

The inclusion of Section E.13, Forensic Evaluation: Evaluation for Legal Proceedings, denotes the increased presence of professional counselors in legal proceedings and subsequent legal matters. This new section outlines the primary obligations for counselors, the consent for evaluation, and the necessity to avoid potentially harmful relationships in regard to forensic evaluations. The primary obligation of professional counselors conducting forensic evaluations is to generate objective findings that are supported by appropriate techniques and information. Counselors are entitled to form their own professional opinions, but must define any limitations in their testimonies or reports.

SECTION F: SUPERVISION, TRAINING, AND TEACHING. This section was heavily revised and expanded in certain sections, such as supervisory relationships and student welfare and responsibilities. Focus still remains on fostering professional relationships and creating appropriate boundaries between supervisors and practicum students or interns. The ethical obligations of both parties are clearly set forth, and counselors should be accurate, honest, and fair during the training and assessment of students.

Areas that were focused on include counselor supervision and client welfare, counselor supervision competence, supervisory relationships, supervisor responsibilities, counseling evaluation and remediation, responsibilities of counselor educators, student welfare and responsibilities, evaluation and remediation of students, roles and relationships between educators and students, and multicultural/diversity competence in counselor education and training programs. As with Section A, Standards F.3.e and F.10.e were included to address the change from dual relationships to potentially beneficial relationships between counselor educators or supervisors and students. Because the revisions to this section are too numerous and beyond the scope of this chapter, individuals are encouraged to go to the ACA website and consult in depth the 2005 *Code of Ethics*.

SECTION G: RESEARCH AND PUBLICATION. An important change to note is the replacement of the term *human subjects* with *research participants*. The revised *Code* also recognizes that independent researchers who may lack access to an Institutional Review Board might also design and conduct research programs. These independent researchers are advised to seek out and consult with researchers who are acquainted with Institutional Review Board procedures to make appropriate safeguards available to research participants.

Further additions or clarifications include the disposal of research documents and records of relationships with research participants when there are intensive or extended interactions. Professional counselors are obligated to take the appropriate steps to destroy any documents or records that contain confidential data or may identify research participants within a reasonable period after the completion of a research study or project. Section G.3 outlines the restrictions on relationships with research participants that include nonprofessional relationships, sexual or romantic interactions, and sexual harassment, as well as potentially beneficial interactions.

Finally, the publication section of the 2005 *Code of Ethics* was expanded. Standard G.5.b was added, which specifically states that professional counselors do not plagiarize or present another person's work as their own. In addition, the standard concerning professional review of documents presented for publication was expanded to include making valid publication decisions, reviewing materials in a timely manner, avoiding biases, and evaluating only those documents that fall within one's field of competency.

SECTION H: RESOLVING ETHICAL ISSUES. This final section provides information and suggestions pertaining to the resolution of ethical issues. Three main changes were made in regard to legal conflicts, unfair discrimination, and reporting ethical violations. Standard H.1.b states that if there is a conflict between ethical responsibilities and laws, professional counselors should make known their commitment to the *Code of Ethics* and work to alleviate the conflict. Counselors may follow legal requirements or regulations if the ethical conflict cannot be resolved in this manner.

The second change included an increase in procedural details for professional counselors reporting a suspected ethical violation (Standard H.2.c). When informal resolution is inappropriate for an ethical violation, or the issue is not correctly resolved, professional counselors are directed to seek further action, such as referring to voluntary national certification bodies, state or national ethics committees, state licensing boards, or any suitable institutional authorities. It is further stated that this standard is not applicable if a professional counselor has been retained to review the work of the counselor who is in question, or if it would violate any confidentiality rights.

The addition of Standard H.2.g is the final major change to Section H. It states that professional counselors absolutely should not deny a person's advancement, admission to academic programs, employment, promotion, or tenure based only on their having made an ethics complaint or their being the subject of an ethics complaint. This standard provides some protection against unfair discrimination for counselors who have made an ethics complaint or been the subject of one. In addition to the ACA, other counseling organizations have established codes of ethics.

AMHCA Code of Ethics

The *Principles for AMHCA Code of Ethics* (2010) can be viewed online at https://www.amhca.org/assets/news/AMHCA_Code_of_Ethics_2010_w_pagination_cxd_51110.pdf. The AMHCA code aligns consistently with the *Code of Ethics* (2005) and is structured into six sections: Section I—Commitment to Clients, which includes counselor–client relationship (primary responsibility, confidentiality, dual/multiple relationships, exploitive relationships), counseling process (counseling plans, informed consent, multiple clients, clients served by others, termination and referral, technology-assisted counseling, clients' rights, end-of-life care for terminally ill clients), counselor responsibility and integrity (competence, nondiscrimination, conflict of interest), assessment and diagnosis (selection and administration, interpretation and reporting, competence, forensic activity), record keeping, fee arrangements, and bartering, and other roles (consultant, advocate); Section II—Commitment to Other Professionals, which includes relationship with colleagues and clinical consultation; Section III—Commitment to Students, Supervisees and Employee Relationships; Section IV—Commitment to the Profession, which includes teaching, research and publications, and service on public or private boards and other organizations; Section V—Commitment to the Public, which includes public statements and advertising; and Section VI—Resolution of Ethical Problems. Interestingly, AMHCA has no ethics committee that enforces or investigates ethical complaints against members. Instead, AMHCA relies on state regulatory boards and other professional organizations, such as the ACA and NBCC, to investigate and, if necessary, sanction professional counselors who violate other applicable ethical codes.

The ethical provisions in the AMHCA code are directed at mental health counselors who work in diverse institutional, agency, and private settings. As a result, the statements often clarify practice behaviors in those settings. For example, AMHCA (2010) states, "Information received in confidence by one agency or person shall not be forwarded to another person or agency without the client's written permission" (p. 2), a provision that fosters compliance with the Health Insurance Portability and Accountability Act (HIPAA) of 1996. The code also specifies that storage of electronic counseling records must be securely maintained for 5 years, at which time the records are to be deleted from the storage system, unless state laws contraindicate this practice.

Mental health counselors do not enter into a counseling relationship with a client being served by another mental health professional unless all parties are aware of and consent to the service arrangement. AMHCA also allows a counseling relationship to be terminated if becomes clear that "the client is no longer benefiting, when services are no longer required, when counseling no longer serves the needs and/or interests of the client, or when agency or institution limits do not allow provision of further counseling services" or "when clients do not pay fees charged or when insurance denies treatment" (AMHCA, 2010, p. 6). Likewise, counselors protect client confidentiality as they create, maintain, store, transfer, and dispose of client records and should plan for client termination procedures due to counselor death or incapacity by assigning a custodian to help transfer clients and files. In each of these instances, clients should be offered appropriate referrals. In addition, AMHCA offers a helpful listing of what supervisors of practicum students, interns, and graduate licensees in training should include in a signed supervision informed consent document (Section III.11, p. 16):

> Supervisors provide written informed consent prior to beginning a supervision relationship that documents business address and telephone number; list of degrees, license, and credentials/certifications held; areas of competence in clinical mental health counseling; training in supervision and experience providing supervision; model of or approach to supervision, including the role, objectives and goals of supervision, and modalities; evaluation procedures in the supervisory relationship; the limits and scope of confidentiality and privileged communication within the supervisory relationship; procedures for supervisory emergencies and supervisor absences; use of supervision agreements; and procedures for supervisee endorsement for certification and/or licensure, or employment to those whom are competent, ethical, and qualified.

A particularly helpful section of the AMHCA code is I.B.7—Clients' Rights. The client informed consent provision indicates that clients must be informed of their rights (I.B.2.b), and the following section provides succinct provisions for a client informed consent document:

> **7. *Clients' Rights.*** In all mental health services, wherever and however they are delivered, clients have the right to be treated with dignity, consideration and respect at all times. Clients have the right:
>
> (a) to expect quality service provided by concerned, trained, professional and competent staff.
> (b) to expect complete confidentiality within the limits of the law, and to be informed about the legal exceptions to confidentiality; and to expect that no information will be released without the client's knowledge and written consent.
> (c) to a clear working contract in which business items, such as time of sessions, payment plans/fees, absences, access, emergency procedures, third-party reimbursement procedures, termination and referral procedures, and advanced notice of the use of collection agencies, are discussed.
> (d) to a clear statement of the purposes, goals, techniques, rules limitations, and all other pertinent information that may affect the ongoing mental health counseling relationship.
> (e) to appropriate information regarding the mental health counselor's education, training, skills, license and practice limitations and to request and receive referrals to other clinicians when appropriate.
> (f) to full, knowledgeable, and responsible participation in the ongoing treatment plan to the maximum extent feasible.

(g) to obtain information about their case record and to have this information explained clearly and directly.

(h) to request information and/or consultation regarding the conduct and progress of their therapy.

(i) to refuse any recommended services and to be advised of the consequences of this action.

(j) to a safe environment for counseling free of emotional, physical, or sexual abuse.

(k) to a client grievance procedure, including requests for consultation and/or mediation; and to file a complaint with the mental health counselor's supervisor (where relevant), and/or the appropriate credentialing body.

(l) to a clearly defined ending process, and to discontinue therapy at any time. (pp. 7–8)

Codes of Ethics from Marriage, Couple, and Family Counseling Organizations

Two marriage, couple, and family counseling organizations have published codes of ethics. The International Association of Marriage and Family Counselors (IAMFC) is a division of the ACA, and the IAMFC code (Hendricks et al., 2011) is consistent with the ACA code. It can be viewed online at http://www.iamfconline.org/public/department3.cfm effective 2011.

The American Association for Marriage and Family Therapists (AAMFT) also publishes a code of ethics (2012), which can be viewed online at http://www.aamft.org/imis15/content/legal_ethics/code_of_ethics.aspx. The AAMFT code outlines eight principles: I, Responsibility to Clients; II, Confidentiality; III, Professional Competence and Integrity; IV, Responsibility to Students and Supervisees; V, Responsibility to Research Participants; VI, Responsibility to the Profession; VII, Financial Arrangements; and VIII, Advertising. The IAMFC and AAMFT codes each addresses the diverse work settings of marriage, couple, and family counselors, but modify the previously discussed codes to the family context.

The American School Counselor Association (ASCA) *Ethical Standards for School Counselors*

The ASCA (2010) has developed a parallel set of ethical standards that specifically addresses counseling practice in the schools. As in the ACA's standards, these standards discuss putting the counselee's best interests first, treating each student as an individual and with respect, involving parents as appropriate, maintaining one's expertise through ongoing professional development and learning, and behaving professionally and ethically. There are seven sections of the ASCA *Ethical Standards for School Counselors*, which are meant to guide the ethical practice of school counselors, provide self-appraisal and evaluation information by peers, and inform stakeholders of responsible counselor behaviors. Although many of the provisions overlap with the *ACA Code of Ethics* explained earlier, what follows is a discussion of additions, extensions, and clarifications provided in the ASCA code.

A. *Responsibilities to Students.* School counselors are concerned with, and make available to students comprehensive, developmental, data-driven programs that address the academic, career, and personal-social needs of all students. They respect and accept the diverse cultural and individual values and beliefs of students and do not impose their own values on the students or students' families.

School counselors disclose the limits of confidentiality and gain informed consent as appropriate. Confidentiality and informed consent are challenging issues when dealing with minor children, and school counselors involve important persons and support networks and consider laws, regulations, and policies, as appropriate to ensure that parents/guardians are active partners in their minor child's school experiences. School counselors acknowledge and support the parent's legal and inherent rights. When students participate in small-group counseling experiences, school counselors notify parents/guardians. As with adult clients, a student's right to confidentiality is surrendered when the student presents serious and foreseeable harm to self or others.

School counselors use brief, solution-focused approaches when possible and strive to maintain an appropriate professional distance from students so as not to engage in a dual relationship that would jeopardize the effectiveness of the primary counseling relationship. School counselors especially avoid online social networking relationships with students through various communication mediums. School counselors also take steps to ensure that students understand the nature of, and how to report the occurrence of cyberbullying.

School counselors separately store sole-possession notes used as memory aids and destroy these notes when the student transfers to another school or school level, or graduates. If the notes may possibly be needed in a future court proceeding, the school counselor uses best judgment in the maintenance of these sole-possession records. This issue of sole-possession notes is covered in more detail later in this chapter.

B. ***Responsibilities to Parents/Guardians.*** School counselors establish appropriate collaborative relationships with parents and respect parental rights and responsibilities. Unless prevented by court order, school counselors honor parental requests for student records and periodic reports. This especially applies to noncustodial parents who may ask for periodic performance reports that the custodial parent may choose not to provide. Legally, a noncustodial parent is allowed access to the student's information, unless a judge has ordered otherwise.

C. ***Responsibilities to Colleagues and Professional Associates.*** School counselors understand the school's "release of information" process and that parents of minor children must provide written permission for this release. School counselors work with their supervisor/director and counselor educators, as appropriate, to implement a data-driven, competencies-based comprehensive school counseling program.

D. ***Responsibilities to School, Communities, and Families.*** As an advocate for all students within the school community, school counselors notify appropriate officials of conditions that systematically limit the effectiveness of the school counseling program or other curricular components. School counselors also engage in community partnerships to obtain resources that support their comprehensive program and promote student success. School counselors advocate for the hiring of only qualified and appropriately trained school counselors and only accept employment for a position for which they are qualified.

E. ***Responsibilities to Self.*** As do all counselors, school counselors function within the boundaries of their training and experience. They are responsible for maintaining physical and mental self-care and wellness and engage in continuous personal and professional growth throughout their careers. This presumes that school counselors will remain current with research and practice innovations in broad areas that influence school counseling practice (e.g., advocacy, cultural competence, technology, leadership, assessment data). Recall that as counselors become more experienced, the standard of care expectations increase. Thus, as school counselors become more experienced, the expectations for their ethical and legal performance also increase. School counselors use culturally inclusive language, create equity-based programs that promote the performance and achievement of all students, and maintain current membership in professional associations.

F. ***Responsibilities to the Profession.*** School counselors follow legal and policy dictates regarding conducting research and program evaluation. They clearly articulate that what they say or write as a private individual is just that, and not as a representative of a school or profession. School counselors also do not use their school counselor position to recruit clients for private practice.

School counselors do provide mentoring and support to school counselors in training, make sure those candidates have professional liability insurance, and ensure that university counselor supervisors conduct at least one on-site visit for each practicum or internship student so they can observe and evaluate the candidate face-to-face.

G. ***Maintenance of Standards.*** This final section provides school counselors with specific guidance on how to handle ethical dilemmas in the field and by colleagues. It is important that school counselors work through the appropriate channels and steps to remedy ethical challenges. Although a colleague who behaves in an unethical manner is problematic and needs to be addressed when evident, ethical codes and hearing committees often serve an educative function to promote high standards and good practice. These procedures are relatively common across ethical codes of conduct and will be addressed more comprehensively in the next section. Self-Assessment Activities 6.1 and 6.2 will help you integrate the information on ethical and legal issues in counseling and apply ethical decision-making principles to numerous scenarios.

SELF-ASSESSMENT ACTIVITY 6.1 DISCERNING ETHICAL ACTIONS

Place a checkmark in the appropriate column. How ethical is it for a professional counselor to?

	Never	Rarely	Sometimes	Usually	Always
1. Barter with a client for services.					
2. Invite a client to a personal party or social event.					
3. Provide counseling to a friend who is in a crisis.					
4. Accept a gift from a client if the gift is worth less than $10.					
5. Accept a gift from a client if the gift is worth more than $50.					
6. Accept a client's invitation to a special event.					
7. Go out for coffee with a client after a counseling session.					
8. Become friends with a client after termination of the counseling relationship.					
9. Give the home phone number to a client.					
10. Share personal experiences as a member of a self-help group when a client is in attendance.					
11. Occasionally hire a client to baby-sit.					

SELF-ASSESSMENT ACTIVITY 6.2 UNDERSTANDING THE *ACA CODE OF ETHICS*

Answer the following questions regarding the *ACA Code of Ethics* (2005).

1. Are the ethical standards sufficiently comprehensive and specific to guide you in working with diverse client populations? Are you aware of any subtle biases you

may have against individuals who are different from you? How can you guard against racial and sexual stereotyping in your counseling relationship with clients?

2. How can you recognize when you are meeting your personal needs at the expense of a client? Do you think it is possible to continue your work as a professional counselor if you do not meet your own needs? Can you think of any values you hold that you might impose on certain clients? If you became aware of personal problems that were negatively affecting your work, what would you do?

3. What might you want to tell clients about the exceptions to confidentiality? Do you think that informing clients about the limits to confidentiality increases or decreases trust? What are your thoughts about confidentiality as it pertains to contagious, fatal diseases? What are your thoughts about confidentiality as it pertains to minor clients?

4. Under what circumstances might you consult with another professional regarding your ethical obligations to a client? How can you determine when a client's condition represents a clear and imminent danger to the client or others? How can you assess the degree of danger?

5. When might you make use of tests as a part of the counseling process? What factors do you need to take into account in selecting, administering, scoring, and interpreting tests? What are the ethical considerations in testing diverse client populations?

6. How can appropriate relationship boundaries between counselor educators and students be determined? What ethical, professional, and social relationship boundaries between counselor educators and students do you see as important? What ethical, professional, and social relationship boundaries between supervisors and supervisees do you see as important?

MAKING ETHICAL DECISIONS

Counseling professional organizations have developed guides to ethical decision making that can be used when a professional counselor is concerned about a particular situation and needs to determine if an ethical dilemma exists. The ACA's model involves seven steps: (a) identify the problem, (b) apply the *ACA Code of Ethics,* (c) determine the nature and dimensions of the dilemma, (d) generate potential courses of action, (e) consider the potential consequences of all options and choose a course of action, (f) evaluate the selected course of action, and (g) implement the course of action (Forester-Miller & Davis, 1996).

C. B. Stone (2009) has taken the ACA model and applied it to the school setting. As Stone and others caution, professional counselors using either of these models or any other ethical decision-making model would not necessarily come to the same conclusion. There is seldom one correct way of handling any given situation, and each counselor brings different background, values, and belief systems to each dilemma. However, if one reflects on the moral principles and continues to practice with these in mind, it is likely that the dilemma can be resolved in the client's best interests.

Remley and Herlihy (2010) suggested four self-tests to consider when a decision has been made. First, in thinking about justice, would you treat others this same way if they were in a similar situation? Second, would you suggest to other counselors this same course of action? Third, would you be willing to have others know how you acted? Fourth, do you have any lingering feelings of doubt or uncertainty about what you did? If you cannot answer in the affirmative to the first three tests and in the negative to the fourth test, perhaps the decision was not ethically sound. It is always appropriate and ethically sound to consult with a colleague when working through a dilemma to ensure that all aspects of the issue have been examined and that all possible problems have been discussed.

Failure to understand the law, and by extension policies, procedures, and guidelines, is an unacceptable legal defense. It is incumbent on the professional counselor to become familiar with all the various sources of information and guidance that are available to perform one's responsibilities in an ethical and legal manner. There are many ways of maintaining current information.

In most work settings, with the exception perhaps of private practice, professional counselors have a supervisor or other individual in authority who can help them become familiar with the regulations, policies, and guidelines relevant to that setting. Most schools and many community agencies have administrative manuals that incorporate all these sources of information into continually updated binders. The ACA newsletter, *Counseling Today*, highlights issues and important, timely topics in counseling, as do other professional journals and newsletters. Many commercially available newsletters cover recent court rulings and their impact in different work settings.

The Internet has become a valuable tool for current information and resources, although one must be careful to authenticate this information. Guillot-Miller and Partin (2003) identified more than 40 sites that include information relevant to ethical and legal practices for professional counselors. The professional associations for counselors and other mental health professionals, institutions of higher education, state and federal government agencies, government-funded organizations, and professional and legal publishers all continuously update their websites and are good sources of current information.

Sometimes mandates seem to be in conflict with each other. In such cases, common sense should prevail. There may be a therapeutically logical reason to follow one particular mandate rather than another one. Professional counselors should follow the logical course of action and document what they did and why. For example, if a counselor is working with a suicidal teenage client but believes that telling the parents would perpetuate an abusive situation, the counselor should handle the situation as an abuse case and also inform child protective services about the suicidal behavior. In addition, if a particular policy, guideline, or regulation is not in the best interests of the clients in the counselor's work setting, as per the ethical standards, the counselor should work to change the mandate.

Two other issues are sometimes confusing for professional counselors. The first concerns the different ways in which counselors in different settings operate. Some mandates cover all counselors, particularly mandates that are the result of federal or state legislation or court cases. For example, child abuse and neglect laws apply to all counselors regardless of the setting in which they work. However, the implementation of some mandates, particularly as they become policy and guidelines, may look different in different settings.

Schools have perhaps the greatest number of mandates under which staff must operate, yet professional school counselors seldom need permission to see students (Remley & Herlihy, 2010), particularly if there is an approved comprehensive developmental program. A mental health counselor, employed by an outside center or agency but working either in a school or in a school-based health center, needs signed, informed consent to see the same students. In some cases, local school systems have mandated an opt-in program, which is a program that requires signed, informed consent for students to participate in different aspects of the comprehensive guidance program. In such cases, professional school counselors working in nearby systems or schools may operate differently, perhaps using an opt-out program in which all students participate unless a parent or guardian has expressly (in writing) forbidden the student from participating.

A second issue concerns professional counselors who hold multiple credentials. A counselor may work as a professional school counselor, but hold state certification or licensure and work as a mental health counselor outside school. The counselor may need permission to do something as a professional school counselor, but not need permission as a mental health counselor, or vice versa. Under which set of mandates should the counselor operate?

The answer to both of these questions is the same: Employees must follow the mandates that apply to their work setting. Professional counselors are required to operate under the mandates of the system that employs them or, in the case of volunteers, the mandates of the entity under whose auspices they are working. If a counselor is employed by an agency or a private practice, he or she must follow the mandates of that entity. If a counselor is employed by a school system as a counselor, he or she must follow the mandates of the local school system. Teachers who have degrees in counseling or another related mental health degree, but who continue to be employed as teachers, do not have the same protections as counselors because they are not employed in a mental health capacity. They need to check the policies of their school system carefully to see if they are covered by any protections such as confidentiality.

COMMON ETHICAL DILEMMAS FOR BEGINNING COUNSELORS

Professional Competence

In addition to being knowledgeable about mandates, as was previously discussed, there are further steps that professional counselors should take to ensure ethical and legal behavior. Several of these are mentioned in the *ACA Code of Ethics* (2005), but it is important to reemphasize them. As reported by Hopkins and Anderson (1990) and Cottone and Tarvydas (2007), professional counselors should

- Maintain professional growth through continuing education. Although counselors must attend continuing education opportunities to renew national credentials, state credentials, or both, it is important to stay current with the theories, trends, and information about clients and different populations.
- Maintain accurate knowledge and expertise in areas of responsibility. Information changes so quickly that professional counselors must ensure they are providing quality and effective services to their clients. One way of achieving this goal is through professional development, but counselors may also gain information through reading, consultation with colleagues, supervision, and other means.
- Provide services only for which they are qualified and trained. The easiest way for professional counselors to get into trouble professionally is to provide services for which they are not qualified, either by training or by education. This is particularly true when using counseling techniques. Counselors should have training in using a particular technique before using it. Reading about a technique is not equivalent to implementing it under supervision. Also, professional counselors should not try to work with clients whose problems go beyond their expertise. If professional counselors are put in a situation where there are no other counselors to whom to refer the client, the counselor should consult with colleagues and ask for supervision to ensure the effectiveness of the counseling.

Misrepresentation

Accurately represent your credentials. As stated in the ethical standards, professional counselors should claim only the credentials they have earned and only the highest degree in counseling or a closely related mental health field. Counselors who hold doctorates in non–mental health fields should not use the title "doctor" in their work as a counselor. This is a particular problem in school settings, where counselors might earn doctorates in administration, supervision, or related fields, but continue to work as counselors and use the title "doctor" in their job. Counselors should not imply in any way that their credentials allow them to work in areas in which they are not trained.

Pressure to "Upcode"

Everyone wants for clients to get the help that they need. In the current culture of managed care and accountability, however, it is not unusual for third-party payers to limit the number of sessions, or even to deny services because a mild mental health concern is not considered serious enough to warrant treatment. To help clients obtain services, some counselors might consider upcoding clients' diagnosis or reported severity. Upcoding means changing a client's diagnosis to a more serious condition, for example, from adjustment disorder with depressed features to dysthymic disorder, or a V-code like bereavement to major depressive disorder. Upcoding also occurs when the client's severity level is changed to make it seem that the client is in more urgent need or in need of longer-term treatment. More sessions means the client has more time to respond to and benefit from the treatment regimen, but it is also skirting the issue of fraud. Fraud is a legal term that in this instance basically means that the counselor is petitioning for services the client is not entitled to and at the same time financially benefiting from the effort. Fraud is a legal issue, and counselors found guilty of insurance fraud face stiff fines, penalties, and even jail.

There are also several ACA ethical clauses that are operational here. Section E.5.a. Proper Diagnosis states, "Counselors take special care to provide proper diagnosis of mental disorders" (p. 12). One of the issues that counselors sometimes do not think about is that an upcoded, improper diagnosis becomes a part of the client's insurance history and may have unintended consequences in the client's future. Looking at the issue from the other side of the coin (i.e., downcoding), Section E.5.d. Refraining from Diagnosis states, "Counselors may refrain from making and/or reporting a diagnosis if they believe it would cause harm to the client or others" (p. 12). Thus, downcoding is ethically allowable if the counselor believes applying the diagnosis may not be in the client's best interest. For example, it may occur that a client with some psychotic phasing and a concomitant mood disorder may be diagnosed with just major depressive disorder or a bipolar disorder, rather than a more serious schizo-affective disorder. Upcoding and downcoding should be avoided when possible, and pressure on a practicum student or intern by an agency to do so should be immediately addressed with a supervisor.

"Can I Be Sued?" and "What Is Malpractice?"

The answer to "Can I be sued?" is, of course, yes. Anyone can be sued for almost anything, particularly in our litigious society. The more important question is, "Will I be found guilty?" The answer to this question is much more complex.

If professional counselors fail to exercise "due care" in fulfilling their professional responsibilities, they can be found guilty of **civil liability**—that is, the counselor committed a wrong against an individual. **Negligence** may be found if the wrong committed results in an injury or damage—in other words, if the duty owed to the client was breached in some way. In counseling, it is more common for counselors to be sued for malpractice. **Malpractice** occurs during performance of a professional duty when either misconduct or an unreasonable lack of skill occurs. Generally, for a counselor to be held liable in tort for malpractice, four conditions have to be met (Stone, 2009): (a) a duty was owed to the plaintiff (client) by the defendant (counselor), (b) the counselor breached the duty, (c) there is a causal link between the breach and the client's injury, and (d) the client suffered some damage or injury.

An example of negligence would be a professional counselor who failed to report an abuse case. The counselor had a duty to the client and failed to fulfill that duty. With malpractice, the client suffered because of lack of skill or inappropriate behavior on the part of the counselor. An example of malpractice would be if a counselor treated a client with an eating disorder through hypnosis when the counselor was not trained to use the technique of hypnosis. The situation may be further complicated if this technique is not recognized as effective for treating eating disorders.

The standard of practice will be used in any liability proceeding to determine if the professional counselor's performance was within accepted practice. The standard of practice question is, "In the performance of professional services, did the counselor provide the level of care and treatment that is consistent with the degree of learning, skill, and ethics ordinarily possessed and expected by reputable counselors practicing under similar circumstances?" and it will be established through the testimony of peers. These peers, who are called expert witnesses, are considered to be experts in the field under question. For professional school counselors, the expert witnesses would be other school counselors (Stone, 2009). For rehabilitation counselors, the expert witnesses would be other rehabilitation counselors. For mental health counselors, the expert witnesses would be other mental health counselors. The standard is an ever-evolving level of expectation and is influenced by two major factors: education and experience. The standard is not an absolute one, but a variable one. It will be much higher for a professional counselor who has practiced for many years and pursued advanced graduate training or professional development than it will be for a counselor in the first year of practice immediately after graduate school. The more training and experience a counselor possesses, the higher the standard to which the counselor will be held accountable. The assumption is that a professional counselor should know more each year he or she practices through experience and training and should be held to a higher standard with each additional year. Using this standard of practice, a counselor will usually be found guilty of malpractice if one or more of the following situations occurs

- The practice was not within the realm of acceptable professional practice.
- The counselor was not trained in the technique used.
- The counselor failed to follow a procedure that would have been more helpful.

- The counselor failed to warn or protect others from a violent client.
- The counselor failed to obtain informed consent.
- The counselor failed to explain the possible consequences of the treatment.

Sexual misconduct is the primary reason that liability actions are initiated against professional counselors. School staff, counselors, and other mental health professionals have been accused of committing sexual abuse or misconduct. It may be that other problems, such as failure to use a more appropriate technique, are actually more common, but that most clients lack the ability to recognize therapeutic problems and may just have a general sense that "it isn't working or helping" and choose to terminate.

Although the number of professional counselors who are sued is increasing, the number still remains small. In schools, parents are more likely to request their child not be included in certain school counseling program activities or to complain to the principal or central administration about a program or behavior. In rare cases, parents may sue. Most cases against school counselors have been rejected by the courts. In school or agency settings, violating or failing to follow mandates would get a professional counselor in trouble faster than almost any other behavior. Depending on the counselor's action, the professional counselor may be reprimanded. In extreme cases, the counselor's employment may be terminated. In clinics and agencies, few counselors are sued over professional practice issues; counselors are more often sued because of sexual conduct or illegal activities. Professional counselors must be knowledgeable about their communities. They may have a legal right to implement certain programs or conduct certain activities, but if the community is not supportive of those activities, they are going to face opposition.

When a professional counselor is faced with any legal action, the first thing the counselor should do is call a lawyer, and then let the counselor supervisor, if there is one, know. Most agencies, clinics, practices, and schools are accustomed to dealing with such legal issues and may even have a procedure for what needs to be done. Professional counselors should never attempt to reason with the client or contact the client's lawyer without advice of counsel. It is important to not provide any information to, or discuss the case with, anyone except the counselor's lawyer or the person designated to help the counselor. Just as professional counselors advise clients to get professional mental health help when they have personal problems, counselors must get legal help when they have legal problems.

Subpoenas

Many professional counselors will receive a **subpoena** at some point in their professional career. Probably the most common reason counselors, and particularly professional school counselors, receive subpoenas is in cases involving custody disputes, child abuse or neglect allegations, and special education disputes. In most cases, the client an attorney is representing believes that counselors may have some information that will be helpful to the case. Professional counselors need to pay attention to subpoenas because they are legal documents. At the same time, consider whether the information being requested is confidential because professional counselors may be limited in what they can share. Under no circumstances should the counselor automatically comply with the subpoena without discussing it first with the client, the client's attorney, or both, or without consulting the agency's or school system's attorney. According to the ACA (1997), professional counselors should take the following steps when receiving a subpoena:

1. Contact the client or the client's attorney and ask for guidance. If you work for a school system, contact the school system's attorney to seek guidance.
2. If the aforementioned parties advise you to comply with the subpoena, discuss the implications of releasing the requested information.
3. Obtain a signed informed consent form to release the records. That form should specify all conditions of release: what, to whom, and so forth.
4. If the decision is made not to release the records, the attorney should file a motion to quash (or, in some areas, ask for a protective order). This will allow the counselor to not comply with the subpoena.
5. Maintain a record of everything the counselor and attorneys did; keep notes regarding all conversations and copies of any documents pertaining to the subpoena.

An attorney who wants information may ask a judge to issue a court order. A **court order** permits the release of confidential information, but does not mandate its release. If both a subpoena and a court order are received, the counselor must release the information with or without the client's consent. Failure to do so may result in the counselor being held in contempt of court.

The important things to remember about subpoenas are do not panic and do consult an attorney. Subpoenas are legal documents, but the counselor has enough time to consider the implications to the client of releasing the information and to seek legal advice.

VOICES FROM THE FIELD 6.2   Garnering a License: A Cautionary Tale, by James R. Rough, Executive Director of the Ohio Counselor, Social Worker, and Marriage and Family Therapist Board

Many licensure applicants struggle to navigate the licensure process because of a lack of understanding or knowledge of a state's laws and rules and regulatory board-related processes. What follows are several examples of licensure-related problems that I commonly see:

1. Graduates with a master's degree in counseling get jobs and hold themselves out as licensed counselors because they passed the NCE exam (even though they are not yet licensed in the state).
2. Students attend CACREP-accredited programs and assume this accreditation will automatically provide them licensure, when in fact many states have additional coursework or training requirements.
3. Students complete their internship in settings that are not acceptable to the regulatory board (e.g., a school setting) or they do mostly case management and little clinical work.
4. Licensure applicants with felony convictions want to get licensed and/or counsel with a license but cannot get a license or find a job.

With regard to the first point, what is the difference between a licensed professional counselor and a graduate of an approved master's counseling program? A licensed professional counselor can legally call himself or herself a counselor and perform services for fees, whereas an unlicensed graduate with a master's degree cannot. To practice without an actual license is a violation of the law in most states and can result in disciplinary action being taken.

With regard to the second point, if you want to be a licensed counselor after you graduate then you need to know the laws in the state in which you want to practice. Each state has its own law, rules regarding which degrees lead to counselor licensure and scope of practice for services counselors can perform. The best way to find the answers to these questions is to use the NBCC website under the "For Counselors"—"prepare for your state licensure exam"—"State Board Directory" or this link: http://www.nbcc.org/directory. There is a link to each state website, which will have the application form and other information you will need.

For example, in Ohio the most common problem for out-of-state graduates is that they need additional clinical course work for Ohio licensure due to a 20-semester-hour clinical course work requirement. In addition, Ohio requires an advanced assessment course focused on the use of assessment instruments in diagnosis and treatment planning. Proper research of the licensure requirements in the state in which you wish to seek licensure will invite an easier licensure process. Do your due diligence to find out the requirements in the state where you want to be licensed, even if it is the state in which your graduate program exists. When it comes to licensure, the five Ps most certainly apply: "Prior Planning Prevents Poor Performance."

CONFIDENTIALITY

For clients to feel free to share sometimes sensitive and personal information during a counseling session, they must feel that they can trust the professional counselor not to share what is disclosed during sessions with anyone else without their permission. This sense of trust and privacy, called confidentiality, is essential for counseling to be successful. **Confidentiality** is the cornerstone of counseling and is what separates the counseling relationship from other relationships in which information is shared. Confidentiality belongs to the client, not to the counselor. The client always has the right to waive confidentiality or to allow information to be shared with a third party.

Counseling minors presents particular challenges to the issue of confidentiality. Every state sets the age of majority; for most states, it is 18 years of age. Most students are minors younger than age 18 years, who are not legally able to make their own decisions. Students have an ethical right to confidentiality, but the legal rights belong to their parents or guardians (Remley & Herlihy, 2010). Most states protect counselor–client confidentiality. Approximately 20 states protect professional school counselor–student confidentiality through statutes (Cottone & Tarvydas, 2007), but many include significant restrictions.

Counselors-in-training often ask what to do if parents want to know what is discussed during counseling sessions with their minor children. Legally, parents have the right to know what is being discussed. However, the child might not want the information shared with the parent. Section B.5.b, Responsibility to Parents and Legal Guardians, of the *ACA Code of Ethics* states that:

> Counselors inform parents and legal guardians about the role of counselors and the confidential nature of the counseling relationship. Counselors are sensitive to the cultural diversity of families and respect the inherent rights and responsibilities of parents/guardians over the welfare of the children/charges according to law. Counselors work to establish, as appropriate, collaborative relationships with parents/guardians to best serve clients. (ACA, 2005, p. 8)

This statement leaves professional counselors with a dilemma. To resolve this dilemma, Remley and Herlihy (2010) suggested that the counselor first discuss the issue with the child to determine if the child is willing to disclose the information to the parent. If the child does not want to disclose, the counselor should try to help the parent understand that the best interests of the child are not served by disclosure. If this does not work, the counselor should schedule a joint meeting with the parent and child to discuss the issue. If the parent is still not satisfied, the counselor may have to disclose the information without the child's consent.

Some professional counselors would suggest that this type of situation may reflect some deeper family issue. Although the parent or guardian has a legal right to the information, there may be an underlying "family secret" that the parent does not want known, and the counselor should be sensitive to any difficulties the child may be exhibiting. Or, this situation may be the result of cultural differences, and the counselor needs to be sensitive to the family's traditions and beliefs.

A related dilemma concerns who has the rights to make decisions for the child and therefore has access to information about the counseling process. In this document, the term *parent* is used to mean the person legally recognized as having responsibility for the child. In many cases this person is the biological parent or parents of the child, but may also be a guardian or someone else designated by the courts. The situation may become more complex when the parents are divorced, separated, or never married. In school settings, under federal law, both parents have the same rights to information about the child unless the courts have limited or terminated the rights of either or both parents. It is not required that the school request a copy of the document from the courts; usually the parent who has the decision-making rights will provide a copy for the school. In clinical settings the counselor would be wise to determine the legal status of custody for the child and to involve all parties having custody in a discussion of confidentiality prior to beginning the counseling relationship (Remley & Herlihy, 2010).

Many professional counselors suggest that at the beginning of the first session of each new counseling relationship, the professional school counselor should discuss confidentiality with the client, explain what it means, and point out the limits of confidentiality. Some counselors choose to hang a sign on the wall of their office that outlines this information as a reinforcement to what is discussed in the first session. Although this issue seems simple on the surface, in reality it is a very complex issue that has generated a significant amount of research and professional discourse. As the use of technology increases in counseling settings, the discussions will continue and expand. There are significant challenges to keeping electronic information confidential.

Limits to Confidentiality

According to section B.1.a of the *ACA Code of Ethics* (2005, p. 2), "Counselors respect client rights to privacy. . . ." Section B.1.c states, "Counselors do not share confidential information without client consent or without sound legal or ethical justification." Section B.1.d states, "At initiation and throughout the counseling process, counselors inform clients of the limitations of confidentiality and seek to identify foreseeable situations in which confidentiality must be breached." There are several instances, however, in which counselors must break confidentiality. These are delineated in Section B.2.a. The most important of these is the **duty to warn**. When a professional counselor becomes aware that a client is in danger of being harmed, such as in instances of abuse or suicide, or when the client is likely to harm someone else, the counselor may break confidentiality and tell an appropriate person.

The basis for the duty-to-warn standard began with the 1974 *Tarasoff* case in California. In this case, the client, a graduate student, told his psychologist about his intent to kill a girl (named Tarasoff) who had rejected his advances. The psychologist told the campus police and his supervisor, but did not warn the intended victim or her family. The majority of the California Supreme Court ruled that the psychologist had a duty to warn a known, intended victim. This case established the legal duty to warn and protect an identifiable victim from a client's potential or intended violence and has formed the basis of many other court decisions across the United States. The *ACA Code of Ethics*, Section B.2.a, now reads, "The general requirement that counselors keep information confidential does not apply when disclosure is required to protect clients or identified others from serious and foreseeable harm . . ." (p. 2).

In the ensuing decades, some cases have extended the duty-to-warn standard to include types of harm other than violence and foreseeable victims in addition to identifiable victims. Several other situations constrain the limits of confidentiality, as delineated in the *ACA Code of Ethics* (2005):

- *Subordinates.* Confidentiality is not absolute when subordinates, including employees, supervisees, students, clerical assistants, and volunteers, handle records or confidential information. Every effort should be made to limit access to this information, and the assistants should be reminded of the confidential nature of the information they are handling.
- *Treatment teams.* The client should be informed of the treatment team and the information being shared.
- *Consultation.* The professional counselor always has the right to consult with a colleague or supervisor on any case. In such instances, the counselor should provide enough information to obtain the needed assistance, but should limit any information that might identify the client.
- *Groups and families.* In group or family counseling settings, confidentiality is not guaranteed. The counselor may state that what goes on in the sessions is confidential, and the members may agree. However, because there is more than one client in the group, it is impossible to guarantee confidentiality.
- *Third-party payers.* Information will sometimes have to be sent to a mental health provider, insurance company, or other agency that has some legitimate need for the information. The counselor must disclose this information only with the client's permission.
- *Minors.* There are special considerations regarding confidentiality and minors; these are discussed in detail in the next section.
- *Contagious, life-threatening diseases.* In contrast to the duty-to-warn standard, the *ACA Code of Ethics* states that the counselor is justified in disclosing information about a client to an identifiable third party if that party's relationship with the client is such that there is a possibility of contracting the disease and the client does not plan on telling the third party. The word used is *justified*, not *should* or *must*. This wording leaves it up to the counselor to decide if the third party is at risk and must be warned.
- *Court-ordered disclosure.* Subpoenas were previously discussed. Even if ordered to reveal confidential information by a judge, counselors should limit what they reveal to only what is absolutely necessary.

In summary, confidentiality is a very complex issue, but it is essential to the effectiveness of counseling. Clients have an ethical right to confidentiality, and counselors must make every effort to ensure this right. There are specific cases, however, in which it is not only permissible but also essential to break confidentiality to protect the client, or others from the client.

Confidentiality and Privileged Communication

The term *confidentiality* is used in discussions about counseling, whereas the term **privileged communication** is the legal term used to describe the privacy of the counselor–client communication. Privileged communication exists by statute and applies only to testifying in a court of law. The privilege belongs to the client, who always has the right to waive the privilege and allow the counselor to testify.

Clients have an ethical right to confidentiality, and the ethical standards for the mental health professions detail the boundaries of confidentiality. Privileged communication is more limited; federal, state, and local mandates determine its parameters. Whether a counselor–client relationship is covered by privileged communication varies widely across jurisdictions. Even within a jurisdiction, a counselor in private practice may be covered by privileged communication, but the school counselors who work in that same jurisdiction may not be. It is essential that counselors become familiar with their local mandates and policies to determine the extent to which privileged communication applies to their situation. Self-Assessment Activity 6.3 provides an opportunity to think ahead and consider how you might handle circumstances when confidentiality may need to be compromised.

SELF-ASSESSMENT ACTIVITY 6.3 LIMITS TO CONFIDENTIALITY

What precautions will you take as a professional counselor to forewarn your clients about the possible limits to confidentiality? Consider how you will approach your client if a breach of confidentiality is necessary, and then practice this approach with a peer.

MINOR CONSENT LAWS

All states have a **minor consent law** that allows certain minors to seek treatment for certain conditions, usually involving substance abuse, mental health, and some reproductive health areas. These laws are based on the federal regulation 42 U.S.C. §§290dd-3; 42 C.F.R. Part 2, which references the confidentiality of patient records for drug and alcohol abuse assessment, referral, diagnosis, and treatment. The law further prohibits the release of these records to anyone without the client's informed consent and includes clients younger than age 18 years, even if they are in school and living with parents or guardians.

Over the past decade, there has been a movement to increase the number of student assistance teams and programs in schools. These teams usually consist of an administrator, one or more student services professionals (e.g., professional school counselor, school social worker, pupil personnel worker, school psychologist, school nurse), and teachers and may include a substance abuse assessor from a local agency or similar professional. School staff members refer students who are suspected to have a substance abuse problem to this team. The team is trained to deal with substance abuse issues and, if they believe the student has a substance abuse problem, have the student assessed and referred for appropriate assistance.

The controversy surrounding this program concerns the role of the parents or guardians in this process. Under the federal law, the student may go from referral through completion of treatment without the parents' or guardians' knowledge. Substance abuse professionals are divided regarding whether it is possible to successfully treat teens who abuse substances without the family's involvement. Other professionals have concerns about the ability of young adolescents to seek treatment without any family knowledge or involvement.

As this federal law has been incorporated into state statute, states have taken different approaches to deciding to whom this law applies and for what. Generally, the patient must be old enough to understand the problem, the treatment options available, and the possible consequences of the problem and the treatment options. Some states may have no age limits and maintain that a minor has the same capacity as an adult to consent to certain services. Some states have decided on a specific age at which the minor may consent to mental health treatment, reproductive or substance abuse services, and treatment for sexually transmitted diseases and AIDS/HIV. According to the Guttmacher Institute's *State Policies in Brief* reports (see http://www.guttmacher.org/statecenter/spibs/spib_OMCL.pdf), various states handle minor consent issues differently.

There is tremendous variation across the 50 states in what is permissible under the law. There is also some question about the applicability of this law to school settings. The laws clearly cover medical personnel and certain conditions. A school nurse is covered, but a professional school counselor or school psychologist may not be covered. It is critical that professional counselors become familiar with the minor consent law in the state in which they work to ensure compliance. A state law may allow a professional counselor to address reproductive issues and substance abuse without parental consent or notification, but a local policy may prohibit such counseling. The laws cover minors seeking advice or treatment or both. If a minor is not seeking help, the law may not apply, and the counselor would follow other policies or procedures in dealing with these issues.

The legal issues aside, this is the law that raises a tremendous number of ethical issues for professional counselors. Numerous professionals have difficulty with the ability of young adolescents, in particular, to access these services without the family's involvement. Should a professional counselor help a 13-year-old with a substance abuse problem seek treatment without the family's knowledge? How successful will the adolescent's recovery be? What about a 15-year-old who is abusing drugs and engaging in risky sexual behaviors? What is the counselor's ethical responsibility in such cases?

The problem this law presents for many professional counselors is that it allows them to assist adolescent clients legally, but may conflict with their personal beliefs. Some professionals believe that behaviors such as these can cause harm to oneself, and they have a duty to warn, which supersedes all other responsibilities. Some professional counselors work with the adolescent to help the adolescent involve the family, whereas others believe that telling the family will work against the adolescent's ability to obtain help.

Another issue is that many parents do not understand that their children can seek treatment in these areas without parental consent. Parents will be understandably angry and distrustful when they discover their child has a sexually transmitted disease or is abusing substances, and that the professional counselor knew but did not tell them about it. Professional counselors need to be prepared to deal with the aftermath of such discoveries. They need to think through their positions on these issues carefully and be honest with clients about their beliefs. Professional counselors should not wait until they are faced with a situation to figure out where they stand on an issue.

RECORDS AND PERSONAL NOTES

Educational Records

Educational records include all records of a student's achievement, attendance, behavior, testing and assessment, school activities, and other information that the school collects and maintains. Schools frequently divide student records into cumulative records, health records, special education records, and confidential records, including psychological evaluations. This division of records is done for the convenience of the school; all these records are considered to be a part of the educational record. The only exceptions are personal notes, reports to Child Protective Services for abuse or neglect, and in some states, reports from law enforcement agencies regarding students' arrests for reportable offenses.

The inspection, dissemination, and access to student educational records must be in accordance with the **Family Educational Rights and Privacy Act (FERPA)** of 1974 (20 U.S.C. 1232g). This law, which is often referred to as the Buckley Amendment, applies to all school districts, preK–12 schools, and postsecondary institutions (colleges) that receive federal funding through the U.S. Department of Education. Nonpublic schools that do not accept federal funding are exempt from this law.

The FERPA has several provisions. The first provision requires that schools or systems annually send a notice to parents or guardians regarding their right to review their children's records and to file a complaint if they disagree with anything in the record. The system has 45 days in which to comply with the parents' request to review the records. There are penalties, including loss of federal funding, for any school or system that fails to comply.

Second, the law limits who may access the records and specifies what personally identifiable information can be disclosed without informed consent—that is, what constitutes directory information or public information. Under FERPA, only individuals "with a legitimate educational interest" can access a student's record. This includes the new school when a student transfers. The sending school may send the records without the parents' consent, but should make every attempt to inform the parent that it has done so. The major exception relates to law enforcement; the school must comply with a judicial order or lawfully executed subpoena. The school must also make whatever information is needed available to the school's law enforcement unit. In emergencies, information relevant to the emergency can be shared (see www.ed.gov/print/policy/gen/guid/fpco/ferpa/index.html). All states and jurisdictions have incorporated FERPA into state statutes and local policies, with some variance among aspects such as what constitutes directory information.

The rights of consent transfer to the student at age 18 years, or when the student attends a postsecondary institution. The law does not specifically limit the rights of parents of students older than 18 years of age who are still in secondary school. For students in higher education, if the child is considered a dependent on the parent's tax returns, the parent may access information about the child. Noncustodial parents have the same rights as custodial parents, unless their rights have been terminated or limited by the courts. Stepparents and other family members who do not have custody of the child have no rights under FERPA, unless the court has granted authority.

The **Protection of Pupil Rights Amendment (PPRA)** of 1978, often called the Hatch Amendment, gives parents additional rights. It established certain requirements when surveys are given to students in preK–12 schools; it does not apply to postsecondary schools because students can consent on their own. If the survey is funded with federal money, informed consent must be obtained for all participating students if students in elementary or secondary schools are required to take the survey, and questions about certain personal areas are included. It also requires informed parental consent before the student undergoes any psychological, psychiatric, or medical examination, testing, or treatment or any school program designed to affect the personal values or behavior of the student. The Hatch Amendment also gives parents the right to review instructional materials in experimental programs.

The No Child Left Behind (NCLB) Act of 2001 included several changes to FERPA and PPRA and continued to increase parents' rights. The changes apply to surveys funded either in part or entirely by any program administered by the U.S. Department of Education. NCLB made minor changes to the seven existing categories concerning surveys and added an additional category. PPRA now requires that:

- Schools and contractors make instructional materials available for review by the parents of participating students if those materials will be used in any Department of Education–funded survey, analysis, or evaluation.
- Schools and contractors obtain written, informed parental consent before students' participation in any Department of Education–funded survey, analysis, or evaluation if information in any of the following areas would be revealed:
  - Political affiliations or beliefs of the parent or student
  - Mental and psychological problems of the family or student
  - Sex behavior or attitudes
  - Illegal, antisocial, self-incriminating, or demeaning behavior

- Critical appraisals of other individuals with whom the student has close family-relationships
- Legally recognized privileged or analogous relationships such as those of lawyers, ministers, and physicians
- Religious practices, affiliations, or beliefs of the student or parent/guardian (newly added)
- Income other than such information as required to determine eligibility or participation in a program (20 U.S.C. 1232h)

The new provisions of PPRA also apply to surveys not funded through the U.S. Department of Education programs. These provisions give parents the right to inspect, on request, any survey or instructional materials used as part of the curriculum if created by a third party and involving one or more of the eight aforementioned areas. Parents also have the right to inspect any instrument used to collect personal information that will be used in selling or marketing. Parents always have the right to not grant permission or to opt their child out of participating in any activity involving the eight previously delineated areas. PPRA does not apply to any survey that is administered as part of the Individuals with Disabilities Education Improvement Act (IDEA, 2004).

As can be seen from the previous discussion, there are many constraints in schools to assessment, testing, and surveying students. Because individual school systems, districts, or colleges may have defined this legislation further, it is essential that professional counselors become familiar with the requirements of the policies and procedures for their specific school system.

The word *parents* has been used in the preceding discussion about student records. The law does recognize the right of students older than age 18 years to access their own records and accords them the same rights as parents of students younger than age 18 years. However, the law does not specifically limit the right of parents whose children are 18 years of age or older to access their child's records, particularly in cases where the child is still living at home and is financially dependent on the parents. The law also gives noncustodial parents the same rights as custodial parents. Unless there is a court order in the child's file that limits or terminates the rights of one or both parents, both parents have the same access to the child's records. School personnel also must provide copies of records such as report cards to both parents if requested.

The word *parent* is used to reference the legal guardian of the child, who may not be the biological or adoptive parent of the child, but some other legally recognized caregiver. Stepparents and other family members have no legal right to the student's records without court-appointed authority, such as adoption or guardianship. This is particularly problematic in situations where a relative provides kinship care—that is, the relative has physical custody 24 hours a day, 7 days a week, but no legal custody of the child. Legally, this person has no educational decision-making rights for the child and cannot access the child's record or give consent. The crack epidemic, incarcerations, and AIDS/HIV have created a situation in which millions of children younger than 18 years of age are involved in informal kinship care situations. Kinship care may be the best situation for these children, but these situations present significant legal implications for schools.

Outside agencies may not access the records of any student without the signed consent of the parent or legal guardian. Some states have worked out interagency agreements wherein a parent signs one form that designates what records may be shared with which agencies, making individual forms unnecessary. Local policies dictate whether signed informed consent is needed to share information at school team meetings, such as student

---

VOICES FROM THE FIELD 6.3   Client Records: A Common Ethics Problem, by William L. Hegarty, JD

For 15 years, I have been the chief investigator for the Ohio Counselor, Social Worker and Marriage and Family Therapist Board. During my time with the board, I have seen every issue imaginable (e.g., counselors having sex with clients, counselors having sex with clients' family members, counselors borrowing money from clients, insurance fraud, counselors acting outside scope of their practice).

One issue that has been a constant yet steadily growing problem over the years is the issue of proper record keeping. More recently, we have seen a sharp rise in counselors backdating case files. This backdating is usually an effort to correct a mistake when the record was originally created. Sometimes the record is backdated to make it appear that services were offered on a date when in fact they were not. The backdating of records is not permissible, and in some states this is considered falsifying records and possibly even insurance fraud. Depending on the type of record falsified, this practice may also invite federal prosecution. A licensee can go back into a file and add or amend a note but the date then has to reflect the date the note was amended in addition to the original date the document was created.

Another problem we are seeing with records is the outright creation of false case notes. These cases almost universally involve licensees who provide home-based counseling services as an employee of an agency. We are increasingly seeing counselors who do not go to a scheduled home-based session yet create a case note as if they had. These faux sessions are then submitted for billing purposes. Of course this action is illegal and harms the clients because the clients are not receiving the necessary services. But these instances also reduce the amount of services the client can obtain because they have reduced the client's entitlement. I have seen agencies have to repay tens of thousands of dollars due to the falsification of notes. The rise in occurrence of this type of situation may be related to the increased agency productivity pressures being placed on counselors; that is, agencies are asking counselors to provide an increasing number of billable hours.

Another issue related to record keeping is their legibility. When records are illegible, client care is compromised. In some client files the treatment plan, client goals, and client statements are totally illegible. When I inquire about the utility of an illegible file, I tend to get blank stares before the realization settles in that the file is of no functional use.

Although record-keeping case violations are not as sensational as, say, sexual violations, they are extremely common. Most of these issues can be avoided by proper supervision and peer review within an agency setting. All counselors must police themselves to ensure that they are devoting the appropriate amount of time to ensuring that their records are accurate, timely, and able to be comprehended by those who may need to review them.

assistance programs, IEPs, or student services meetings, when the agency personnel are regular members of the team.

Personal Notes

Personal notes are notes written by professional counselors to serve as an extension of their memories; they are an impression of the client or session. These notes must remain "in the sole possession of the maker" and cannot be shared with anyone except "a substitute maker." A substitute maker is someone who takes over for the counselor in the counselor's position, in the same way a substitute teacher takes over for the regular teacher. In the case of school counselors, a substitute maker is not the counselor who becomes responsible for the child the next year or in the next school.

Personal notes must remain separate from the educational record. When any information in the personal notes is shared, it is no longer confidential. If professional counselors keep their personal notes in their offices, they should keep them separate from all other records and secure, such as in a locked file cabinet. Some counselors keep them in their car or house, but this is unnecessary, unless there are problems with security in the counselor's office.

As technology becomes more common in counseling offices, professionals may prefer to keep their personal notes on the computer. This is not a good idea, unless the counselor can absolutely guarantee that no one can access the program or break through network firewalls. Even keeping the notes on disk is questionable. Stories of computer hackers breaking codes and paralyzing websites for hours are frequently reported in the news. It is preferable to keep notes separate and not tell anyone they exist, even if there is nothing of particular interest in them. The information is confidential, and the professional counselor needs to ensure its security. Information from the notes would be shared only in cases in which there is a clear duty to warn, or when a judge requires that confidentiality be broken and the information shared.

THE HEALTH INSURANCE PORTABILITY AND ACCOUNTABILITY ACT (HIPAA) OF 1996

The **Health Insurance Portability and Accountability Act (HIPAA)** of 1996 required that the U.S. Department of Health and Human Services adopt national standards for the privacy of individually identifiable health information, outlined patients' rights, and established criteria for access to health records. The requirement that the U.S. Department of Health and Human Services also adopt national standards for electronic health care transactions was included in this law. The Privacy Rule was adopted in 2000 and became effective in 2001. The Privacy Rule set national standards for the privacy and security of protected health information. The rule specifically excludes any individually identifiable health information that is covered by FERPA. Health records in schools that are under FERPA are specifically excluded from HIPAA.

However, the situation is not that simple, particularly in the area of special education. Many schools receive mental, physical, and emotional health assessments of students that have been conducted by outside providers whose practices are covered by HIPAA regulations. In previous years, such assessments and reports automatically became part of the educational record. This may no longer be the case, particularly if the provider requests that the report not be redisclosed. As HIPAA continues to impact health information, agencies and school systems must develop policies and procedures to address any potential conflicts between FERPA and HIPAA. Professional counselors must be aware of these issues and any school policies.

CHILD ABUSE AND NEGLECT

Another issue professional counselors must deal with that has clear legal mandates is child abuse and neglect. Efforts to recognize and intervene in child abuse cases began in the late 1800s and were modeled on the prevention of cruelty to animals laws. In 1961, the "battered child syndrome" was legally recognized, and by 1968, all 50 states had laws requiring the reporting of child maltreatment. In 1974, the National Child Abuse Prevention and Treatment Act (P.L. 93-247) became a federal law. The act was later reauthorized with changes and renamed the **Keeping Children and Families Safe Act** of 2003. The law defined **child abuse** as physical or mental injury, sexual abuse or exploitation, negligent treatment, or maltreatment of a child younger than age 18 years or the age specified by the child protection law of the state in question, by a person who is responsible for the child's welfare, under circumstances that indicate that the child's health or welfare is harmed or threatened (42 U.S.C.S. §5101).

The law is clear regarding who must report cases of child abuse and neglect. Every health practitioner, educator, human services worker, and law enforcement officer must report suspected abuse or neglect, generally within 24 to 72 hours of first "having reason to suspect." It is incumbent on the individual who first suspects the abuse or neglect to call Child Protective Services to report. The oral report must be followed up by a written report in most cases. Each state may have slightly different procedures for reporting; some states allow as many as 7 days for submission of the written report and identify different agencies to which the report must be made. What does not change is the legal mandate to report.

There is no liability for reporting child abuse, even if a subsequent investigation determines no evidence that abuse or neglect occurred, unless the report is made with malice. Most states do have serious penalties for failure to report, however. These penalties may include loss of certification or license, disciplinary action, or termination of employment.

Parents or guardians have no rights to information during this process. The agency, school, or other entity making the report should not inform the parents that a report is being made. It is the responsibility of the department of social services and the law enforcement agency to contact the parent and conduct the investigation. It is critical that professional counselors understand the laws regarding cases of child abuse and neglect and follow the procedures exactly. The individual submitting the report does not have to prove that abuse has occurred; it is enough to have reason to suspect.

Professional counselors are sometimes put in an awkward position when they are not the first person to suspect abuse, but the staff member who does is not willing to make the report and asks the counselor to do it. In such cases, if the staff member will not make the report, professional counselors should do it, but should apprise the administrator of the circumstances surrounding the report. Regardless of who submits the report, the client will need support and assistance throughout the process.

CUSTODY ISSUES*

One of the most common complaints filed against licensed counselors are inappropriate practices in the context of child custody cases. For parents involved in custody disputes, the stakes are high, and the counselor's actions are being scrutinized and well documented through the court system. Most counselors who are sanctioned for custody-related issues unknowingly engage in unethical practices simply because they are unaware of their state laws that relate to counselors' role in custody cases. It is important that counselors know and abide by their state laws related to custody cases.

Many states have language in their counselor practice law that indicates they should not conduct a court evaluation or make a custody recommendation in a case in which he or she served in a therapeutic role for the client or his or her immediate family or has had other involvement that may compromise counselor objectivity. The reason counselors cannot make these recommendations when in this role is because they are unable to be impartial or objective. Any recommendation would be based on limited facts and not within their role as the client's counselor.

With appropriate releases, counselors can testify in custody cases as fact witnesses concerning treatment. In other words, they can report the facts of clients' treatment and their progress in treatment (e.g., how many sessions they have attended, the details of the client's progress, compliance with treatment goals). On the witness stand, counselors are often asked by attorneys, and even judges, to make custody recommendations. In these cases, counselors should clarify to the parties involved their role in the case and the state laws that dictate counselor practice. More specifically, licensed counselors who have a client involved in a custody, visitation, and/or guardianship case, if asked by a client or their lawyer or the guardian ad litem to make a recommendation about custody, visitation, and/or guardianship, should cite their role as the primary counselor for their client. Licensees should inform the requestor that they have not performed a custody, visitation, and/or guardianship evaluation, and it would be unethical for them to make any recommendation outside their role as a treating counselor.

Some counselors may serve in the role of custody evaluator. In these situations it is appropriate for counselors to make recommendations to the court. In addition, during the course of a court evaluation, a counselor should not accept any of the involved participants involved in the evaluation as a therapy client.

HARM TO SELF AND OTHERS

For many years, the standard that was used in the counseling profession for dealing with potential suicide cases was based on the *Tarasoff* case, which was previously discussed. As a result of the *Tarasoff* case ruling, professional counselors had a duty to warn if there was a foreseeable victim. According to Remley and Herlihy (2010), subsequent court decisions interpreted the case differently; some judges ruled that the duty exists even when there is no foreseeable victim, if individuals are unintentionally injured by the client, such as classes of persons of which the victim is a member, bystanders, and other individuals. Generally, when dealing with a potentially suicidal client, the professional counselor conducts a lethality assessment, determines the seriousness of the threat, and based on the seriousness of the threat, decides whether the duty to warn applies.

The *Eisel* case in Maryland changed the standard for many professional school counselors. In that case, two middle school students became involved in Satanism and became

---

*Author Note: We are grateful to Dr. Victoria E. Kress for contributing this section.

obsessed with death and self-destruction. Friends of Nicole Eisel went to their school counselor and told her that Nicole was thinking about killing herself. That counselor consulted with Nicole's school counselor. Both professional school counselors spoke with Nicole, who denied thinking about killing herself. Shortly thereafter, on a school holiday, Nicole's friend, who attended another school, shot Nicole and killed herself in the park behind the school. Mr. Eisel sued the school, the school system, and the professional school counselors. The circuit court dismissed the case. Mr. Eisel appealed to the court of appeals. Its decision of October 29, 1991, stated,

> Considering the growth of this tragic social problem in the light of the factors discussed above, we hold that school counselors have a duty to use reasonable means to attempt to prevent a suicide when they are on notice of a child or adolescent student's suicidal intent. (*Eisel v. Board of Education*, 1991)

Based on the facts of this case as developed to date, a trier of fact could conclude that the duty included warning Mr. Eisel of the danger. The case was remanded back to the circuit court to decide the issue of liability for the school system and the professional school counselors. The case finally concluded 8 years after it began and found the school and professional school counselors had acted appropriately given the circumstances, their training, and the policies in place at the time.

The court's decision had a major impact on professional school counselors in the state of Maryland. This decision removed the counselor's ability to determine whether duty to warn is applicable. As a consequence, professional school counselors in Maryland must always tell the parent whenever there is any indication from a child or someone else that the child is thinking about suicide, regardless of the seriousness of the threat. They must also inform the principal or the principal's designee. Many of Maryland's school systems now apply this procedure to all student services personnel employed by the school system, and other states have implemented similar provisions and policies.

Although this case is legally binding only on professional school counselors in Maryland, it has become the standard by which subsequent cases have been decided. For example, a Florida court subsequently made a similar ruling in a similar case, and several other courts are following suit. Professional school counselors must be aware of the policies within their system. The courts clearly are ruling in favor of duty to warn, as opposed to counselor discretion. Professional counselors practicing outside schools should abide by state statute and policy, but deciding to warn when there is any reason to suspect the client is in danger to self or others is probably a good practice in almost all circumstances, particularly when the client is a minor child.

As this chapter comes to a close, Self-Assessment Activities 6.4 and 6.5 will help you integrate the information on ethical and legal issues in counseling and apply ethical decision-making principles to numerous scenarios.

SELF-ASSESSMENT ACTIVITY 6.4 APPLYING THE ACA *CODE OF ETHICS*

For each numbered situation, indicate whether the behavior is ethical (E) or unethical (U), and cite the *ACA Code of Ethics* Standard or Standards that apply. The person in question in each scenario is underlined.

Situation #1: Judy, a counselor educator at a university, has a colleague named John, who is opening a private practice in addition to his teaching job. John is building his client caseload by offering special rates to recent graduates of the university counseling program in exchange for providing supervision, which is required for licensing.

E   U   Standard(s) _____

Situation #2: A rehabilitation counselor is conducting a research study. Because raw data includes confidential information about individual participants, the counselor deletes all identifying data before giving the material to the secretary for computer entry.

E   U   Standard(s) _____

Situation #3: <u>Larry</u> Adams has a PhD in history and is a university professor. He also has a master's degree in counseling and is an LPC. He wants to open a part-time private practice and has business cards printed that say, "Dr. Larry Adams, Individual and Group Counseling."

E   U   Standard(s) _____

Situation #4: A woman enters into a counseling relationship with a male <u>counselor</u> at a mental health center after finishing a treatment program for alcohol addiction. The woman has a history of violent behavior when intoxicated. Although she has maintained her sobriety for several months, one evening, obviously intoxicated, she calls the counselor and threatens to kill her mother. Despite the client's incoherence, the counselor discerns that she has a gun. The counselor calls the client's mother, but is unable to reach her, and then calls the police.

E   U   Standard(s) _____

Situation #5: A <u>residence hall director</u> who is responsible for hall discipline at a university has a master's degree in counseling. He is approached by students living in his hall who say they would like to address some personal concerns and want him to be their counselor. The residence hall director arranges weekly sessions for counseling with the students.

E   U   Standard(s) _____

Situation #6: A male professional <u>counselor</u> in a mental health center works daily with clients who are taking medications. One of the clients, who is taking Prozac, tells the counselor that she continues to be quite depressed. The counselor says, "No problem, you may need your medication changed. I'll arrange that," and refers the woman to the staff psychiatrist.

E   U   Standard(s) _____

Situation #7: A professional <u>counselor</u> has been encouraging a client to get involved in more social activities to get her out of the house more often. One day, the client unexpectedly shows up at an art class that the counselor is enrolled in, saying that she signed up for the same class. The counselor decides to stay enrolled.

E   U   Standard(s) _____

Situation #8: A professional <u>counselor</u> has been seeing a married couple who have decided to divorce. During the week between sessions, the couple has an argument, and the husband moves out of the house. The wife obtains a restraining order because she fears her husband will harm her or the children as he has in the past. The husband calls the counselor and threatens to bomb the house if his wife does not allow him to see the children. The husband sounds rational, but definitely wants to get even with his wife. The counselor believes the husband is just spouting off.

E   U   Standard(s) _____

Situation #9: <u>Sharon</u>, a counselor in private practice, receives a phone call from a former male friend with whom she has had a sexual relationship. He tells her that he is grieving the death of his father and requests counseling from her. Because Sharon specializes in grief counseling and has not dated him in more than a year, she agrees to counsel him.

E   U   Standard(s) _____

Situation #10: A female <u>graduate student</u> in counseling is doing her internship in a community agency. The administrators tell her that they do not want her to inform clients that she is a student intern. They explain that the clients might think they are getting second-class service if they knew their counselor was in training. The administrators contend that clients are paying (on a sliding scale) for services they receive, and that it would not be psychologically good to give them any information that might cause them to believe they were not getting the best help available. The student did as she was told.

E   U   Standard(s) _____

(Continued)

Situation #11: Robert requests counseling from a counselor in private practice. He indicates that he and his wife are involved in marriage counseling as a couple through an agency in town. Robert says he is undecided about continuing the marriage and would like to sort out his feelings and reach a decision. He intends to continue couples counseling in the meantime. The professional <u>counselor</u> agrees to provide counseling for Robert without requesting permission to contact the other marriage counselor.

E   U   Standard(s) _____

Situation #12: A professional <u>counselor</u> has administered a personality inventory for a Mexican-American client. The counselor is aware that this inventory contains several race-sensitive items, but has decided to use it anyway because this particular client seems so well acculturated.

E   U   Standard(s) _____

Situation #13: A <u>family counselor</u> in a mental health clinic has been having weekly sessions with two parents and their adolescent child, a juvenile offender who is about to be released from a detention center. In the past, the juvenile was known to be extremely dangerous and violent and had made generalized statements of hostility, but with no intended or identifiable victim. The counselor took no action to block his release.

E   U   Standard(s) _____

Situation #14: A professional <u>school counselor</u> is working with a student who is distressed about her family situation, which involves the use of crack cocaine. The counselor has little training in drug counseling, but continues working with the student even though a local family service center has an excellent program for teenagers with parents who abuse substances, and this service is available at no charge.

E   U   Standard(s) _____

Situation #15: As a private practitioner, a professional <u>counselor</u> decides not to purchase malpractice insurance and proceeds to practice without it.

E   U   Standard(s) _____

Situation #16: A high school <u>counselor</u> is contacted by a teacher who reports that Diane, a student in her English class, has written a poem about death. When the teacher talked with Diane, she threatened to kill herself. The counselor calls Diane into her office, and Diane admits to being deeply despondent and wanting to end her life. Diane begs the counselor not to tell her parents or anyone else. The counselor is concerned for Diane's safety, so she calls her parents to tell them of Diane's suicidal ideation.

E   U   Standard(s) _____

Situation #17: A professional <u>counselor</u> is seeing a client who had been sexually abused as a child. The client expresses frustration that she cannot remember the earliest incidents of abuse, and insists that hypnosis would help her break through this barrier. Although the counselor has no specific training in hypnosis, she agrees to purchase a hypnosis audiotape and attempt the procedure with the client.

E   U   Standard(s) _____

Situation #18: Steve, an HIV-infected man, reveals to his professional <u>counselor</u> that he is infected. After the counselor probes the situation a bit, Steve admits to his counselor that he is embarrassed, is confused, and finds it difficult to talk about his condition. Steve admits that he has unprotected sexual relations and does not disclose his condition to his partners. The counselor agrees to continue providing counseling services only if Steve gives a verbal agreement that he will not have sexual relations with others until he is less confused.

E   U   Standard(s) _____

Situation #19: Joe, a 23-year-old college student, was convicted of illegal possession of controlled substances and is now serving a 2-year probation sentence. He is seeing the <u>college counselor</u>. Joe's probation officer contacts the counselor and requests a report. Although Joe has not signed a release of information, the counselor complies, fearing that not to do so might cause the probation officer to file a negative report on Joe to the court.

E   U   Standard(s) _____

Situation #20: Before seeing a family for counseling, a <u>professional counselor</u> gives a written document explaining the process of counseling to the parents. After reading the informed consent document, the parents sign it and bring the family to counseling. The informed consent document is not given to or described to the children.

E   U   Standard(s) _____

SELF-ASSESSMENT ACTIVITY 6.5 REFLECTION ON ETHICS

As a future professional counselor, write a reflection on (a) your ethical decision-making process (with emphasis on self-awareness and analysis of the various codes of ethics), and (b) the implications of your values for counseling practice, including the role of your cultural values in counseling.

Summary

If one were to survey practicing counselors regarding the "hot issues" in counseling, the list would likely include eating disorders, HIV/AIDS, self-mutilation, autism and Asperger's syndrome, bullying, harassment, changing family structures, mobility, cultural diversity, sexual orientation, depression, loss and grief, students with special needs, emotional disturbance, gangs, and a host of other topics. So how does a counselor help a 21-year-old who believes he is gay? Or a 16-year-old who is starving herself to death? Or an incarcerated parent who wants the professional counselor to read his letters to his children because the mother will not let him have any contact with his children?

Here are some final words of wisdom to help guide you as a professional counselor.

- Always document in writing what you did and why you did it.
- If you did not follow a policy, document why you did not (e.g., not calling the parent in a suicide case because it was handled as an abuse case).

- Know federal, state, and local laws, regulations, policies, and guidelines.
- Consult with a colleague or supervisor when you have questions or doubts.
- Read and use resources.
- Consult with a lawyer when appropriate.

Professional counselors must be prepared to deal with these issues and more every day of their professional lives. Many of these areas do not have clear laws, regulations, court cases, or policies to guide counselors toward legal and ethical behavior. Professional counselors need to try to do what is in the best interests of their clients and to help the clients see what that is. They must advocate for their clients because frequently the professional counselor is the only support that the client has. Professional counselors must never stop believing that what they do makes a difference in the lives of clients.

CHAPTER 7

Special Populations and Issues

BY VICTORIA E. KRESS, MATTHEW J. PAYLO, AND NICOLE A. ADAMSON

PREVIEW

Counselors are regularly faced with myriad complex client or student presenting issues that require the synthesis of information spanning multiple areas. The topics presented in this chapter cover a variety of issues and populations that counselors will confront in practice. The topics presented in this chapter are those that were likely not addressed in detail in other areas of the counseling curriculum and, as such, will hopefully prove to be helpful. In approaching these topics, an emphasis was placed on presenting basic, practical information that may help counselors navigate their work with these populations. The presentations provided are intended to serve as a starting point for considering one's work with the indicated populations.

SPECIAL POPULATIONS AND ISSUES

Within this chapter, counseling issues important in working with a number of special populations will be reviewed, including child maltreatment, academic problems, substance use, issues with older adults and the terminally ill, self-injury, intimate partner violence, and issues specific to working with clients with military service. First, child maltreatment, which includes child abuse and neglect, is addressed. Most counselors regularly encounter children who are being maltreated. Consideration is given to counselors' role as mandated reporters and assessors of child maltreatment. Information related to the short- and long-term effects of maltreatment and the related counseling needs of maltreated children are also discussed.

Issues that counselors should consider when working with children who are gifted, have learning disabilities, or are otherwise differently abled are also addressed. An emphasis is placed on how counselors can best support this population in the context of their unique learning and cognitive needs. Psychosocial and developmental counseling issues such as the importance of addressing self-esteem and identity are presented in the context of counseling this population.

Substance abuse counseling will be addressed next, along with a discussion of how co-occurring mental disorders relate to substance abuse and its treatment. The importance of enhancing substance-abusing clients' motivation to want to change is also highlighted.

Counseling considerations related to working with clients who are in violent relationships or relationships involving intimate partner violence (IPV) are also discussed. Safety considerations and safety planning are discussed, as are various counseling considerations that are important to address when working with this at-risk population. Counseling and intervention considerations are presented with a special focus on the value of using evidence-based treatment approaches.

Issues associated with counseling adults who are older or terminally ill are also addressed. The stages of death and dying and their application to counseling terminally ill clients are detailed. Various issues associated with counseling older adults and the terminally ill are also described.

People who self-injure present counselors with a number of unique challenges, and in fact, counselors frequently cite this group as one of the most challenging client populations to counsel. In this chapter, safety and risk management issues that are important to consider when counseling people who self-injure are addressed. Ethics issues (e.g., attempts to force clients to stop self-injuring) and suggestions for ethical practice are also addressed in this chapter. In addition, treatment methods and practical suggestions for counseling those who self-injure are provided.

Military veterans are returning home in record numbers (Hall, 2008), and they bring with them the lasting effects of war-related experiences. Whether dealing with future deployment, PTSD, or anxiety and depression, counselors can benefit from understanding the specific aspects of this population and the common issues they present in counseling. In addition, counselors in training need to be knowledgeable about the specific treatment considerations of this population as well as evidence-based treatment approaches that are beneficial in helping to treat common issues with which they present.

We all come to new relationships with a plethora of past relationship experiences that color our contexts. Counselors and clients are no exception, and it is inevitable that they will, at times, bring these past experiences and reactions into the counseling relationship. Counselors need to be aware of their own internal reactions to clients, as well as clients' reactions to them. These personal reactions are commonly described as transference (i.e., clients' reactions to counselors) and countertransference (i.e., counselors' reactions to clients) reactions. Recommendations are made for how counselors can assess and manage transference and countertransference issues in real-world practice.

Clients with little motivation to change are typically resistant to the counseling process. Legal offenders and court-ordered clients are populations counselors frequently encounter who lack a motivation to make behavioral changes. This section will highlight the nuances associated with counseling these populations and will provide practical applications to aid counselors in their work.

CHILD MALTREATMENT

Counselors frequently find themselves working with children who have, or are experiencing, some type of child abuse or neglect. **Child abuse** includes physical, emotional, or sexual abuse (Centers for Disease Control and Prevention [CDC], 2010a). **Neglect** involves the failure of caretakers to provide adequate emotional and physical care for a child (CDC, 2010b). Child abuse typically receives more attention that neglect, which is unfortunate due to well-documented high rates of neglect. For example, the U.S. Department of Health and Human Services (USDHHS, 2011) reported that of the 3.6 million cases of reported and alleged child abuse and neglect, 78% of the reports involved allegations of neglect.

The effects of child maltreatment are exceptionally diverse and dependent on a number of factors, including the resources and insulating factors available to the child, the duration and frequency of the abuse, the nature of the child's relationship with the perpetrator, use of force or the severity of assault, and the number of perpetrators (Briere & Lanktree, 2012). Possible reactions to child maltreatment may include disruptions to the child's emotional well-being (e.g., lowered self-esteem), difficulty with making and sustaining attachments, anger that can be manifested in behavioral problems, depression and anxiety, and academic struggles (Prosser & Corso, 2007). Posttraumatic stress disorder (PTSD) has also been recognized as a common effect of child abuse, and these symptoms might include avoidance symptoms (e.g., avoiding situations or places that remind them of the abuse, dissociation, or emotional numbing to deaden or block the pain); re-experiencing the abuse (e.g., flashbacks or recurrent nightmares); and a general sense of increased anxiety and emotional arousal. More specifically, children with PTSD may demonstrate the following reactions: worries about dying at an early age, a loss of interest in activities, somatic symptoms such as headaches and stomachaches, moodiness or showing sudden and extreme emotional reactions, sleep problems, irritability or angry outbursts, difficulties concentrating, regression or acting younger than their age (e.g., being clingy or whiny, thumb sucking), showing increased alertness to the environment, and repeating behavior that reminds them of the trauma (e.g., through play or in art).

Children who have experienced chronic maltreatment are especially vulnerable and may have developmental disruptions secondary to repeated maltreatment (Herman, 1997). In addition to the PTSD symptoms previously described, these developmental or complex trauma reactions might include difficulties regulating emotions, alterations in self-perception (e.g., a sense of chronic guilt, shame, helplessness), alterations in relationships with others (e.g., being distrustful, isolating), and alterations in their sense of meaning (e.g., a sense of hopelessness and despair). These developmental reactions can have significant, long-term effects on one's functioning, and it is important that these developmental reactions are addressed in counseling in addition to the traditional PTSD symptoms more typically targeted in treatment.

Certain characteristics appear to insulate children from the long-term potentially deleterious effects of maltreatment, and these factors should be considered when counseling this population. These factors include having at least one supportive relationship, a positive self-regard, a healthy sense of spirituality, possessing external attributions of blame (e.g., "the abuse was her fault, not mine"), and holding to a positive outlook on life (Valentine & Fienauer, 1993). When possible, the aforementioned factors should be identified, developed, and amplified in clients via counseling.

Despite the negative effects that child maltreatment can invite, it is also important for counselors to understand that most children do not develop ongoing trauma reactions secondary to maltreatment; they can and do move forward, adapt, and live productive lives (Tedeshi & Calhoun, 2004). Secondary to their maltreatment experiences, children can even experience posttraumatic growth and develop resources such as additional survival skills, a greater self-knowledge and self-appreciation, increased empathy for others, and a broader and more complex view of the world. It is important that counselors believe that all maltreated children with whom they work can heal and thrive.

Adult victims of childhood abuse seek therapy for a number of reasons, but rarely just because of a history of maltreatment. Most adults fail to recognize the effects past abuse and neglect may have had on their development. Similarly, the caregivers of children who are being maltreated sometimes seek counseling for their children, but they often fail to identify current or past abuse or neglect as related to the child's struggles. Many abusive caregivers do not consider their behaviors to be aberrant, and this can further complicate counselors' efforts to support maltreated children (Cohen, Mannarino, & Deblinger, 2006).

When counseling children, safety should always be a counselor's first priority (Kress, Adamson, Paylo, DeMarco, & Bradley, in press). Counselors should be vigilant about reporting child maltreatment and monitor for any new instances of abuse or neglect that may need to be reported. Attempts to enhance and promote a child's safety should also be a part of the ongoing counseling process.

When working with a client in the child welfare system (i.e., a client who has been identified as being a victim of maltreatment), many professionals will be involved in supporting the child. It is important that counselors work with the child's team to ensure optimal treatment. Team members might include a child welfare system worker, medical personnel who follow the child's growth and development, and if the child has been removed from the home, the team may include foster parents. Oftentimes, an hour a week of counseling is not enough to help a child, and a team approach to helping children can serve to further enhance and supplement the work done in individual counseling.

When working with maltreated children, it is important that counselors provide a consistent, safe space and a nurturing relationship within which the child may experiment with adapting to a safer world. Maltreated children also often do well when counselors work with them in group settings (Kress & Hoffman, 2008). Group counseling can be especially empowering with children who have been sexually abused, as it reduces their feelings of shame and differentness, and depending on the tone of the group, it can help them cocreate a strength-based identity.

Unfortunately, most counseling services provided to maltreated children and their families are not grounded in **evidence-based practices (EBP)** that "promote practices which have been demonstrated to be safe and effective" (Chaffin & Friedrich, 2004, p. 1097). Numerous studies have pointed to the value of using EBPs, which include structured, manualized, and empirically supported models over other methods of treatment (Brassard,

Rivelis, & Diaz, 2009). A variety of EBPs can be used by counselors in school settings (e.g., The Incredible Years, Early Risers Skills for Success, Cognitive Behavioral Intervention for Trauma in Schools; Brassard et al., 2009).

An example of an EBP that can be used with abused children receiving clinical services is trauma-focused cognitive behavioral therapy (TF-CBT; Cohen et al., 2006). TF-CBT is a conjoint child and caregiver psychotherapy approach used with children and adolescents who are experiencing significant emotional and behavioral difficulties secondary to traumatic life events. It is a model that integrates trauma-sensitive interventions with cognitive behavioral techniques, humanistic principles, and family involvement. Through TF-CBT, children and caregivers learn new skills to help them process thoughts and feelings related to traumatic life events; manage and resolve distressing feelings, thoughts, and behaviors that are related to the traumatic life event/s; and develop an enhanced sense of safety, personal growth, parenting skills, and improved family communication (Cohen et al., 2006). A free 10-hour certificate training program on TF-CBT can be completed through TF-CBTWeb (Medical University of South Carolina, 2005). This training program can be completed by counseling interns and is an excellent means of deepening one's understanding of CBT treatment principles in general and trauma treatment in particular.

Counseling maltreated children may arouse complex feelings within the counselor. Counselors may feel anger toward the child's caregivers and/or the perpetrators of the maltreatment. Counselors may feel sadness and a sense of protectiveness of the child. Finally, counselors may feel a sense of anxiety around protecting the child from further maltreatment; they may become overly involved with the child and feel a need to rescue him or her. It is important that counselors working with children who are maltreated seek regular supervision, peer-consultation, and if necessary, personal counseling. Counselors who work with maltreated children should also regularly self-monitor for vicarious trauma, burnout, and compassion fatigue.

VOICES FROM THE FIELD 7.1   The Birth of a Superhero, by Bethany Garr

I remember the first time Cody walked into my office. He bounded in, nearly knocking me over, and proceeded to pick up and examine everything on my desk, the bookshelves, and the table. When he finally sat next to his mother, this little ball of excited energy continued to move frenetically, unable to sit still. But despite the way his excitement and energy seemed to fill the room, as I heard his story, he seemed almost to shrivel and shrink.

Cody was adopted as a toddler; his birth parents had significant mental health and substance abuse issues, and he had experienced a great deal of neglect as a result. When the police came to remove Cody and his brother from his birth parents, he was found in a boarded-up house, wearing a soiled diaper, with no food in the home except for a few bags of chips.

Cody had been drug-exposed in utero, which had resulted in a cleft palate. Cody had been diagnosed with AD/HD, which the doctors also theorized was due to this drug exposure. To compound matters, he had also been diagnosed with Asperger's disorder; although he was quite intelligent and creative, he also had very poor social skills. He had few friends and frequently argued with his peers.

Cody's adoptive mother was frustrated; it seemed that no amount of therapy or medication could alleviate the laundry list of symptoms with which he presented. He had recently been hospitalized for the first time, which greatly upset both Cody and his mother. He had been on multiple combinations of medications, all of which seemed to help for a bit, before the effectiveness would taper off. His adoptive mother stated that she believed Cody was worsening; he rarely slept, seemed depressed, and was extremely defiant.

Initially, Cody was resistant to explore the abuse and neglect he had endured when he lived with his birth parents. Although he had been quite young when he was removed from his birth parents' custody, he still had strong memories about them. Despite his claims to the contrary, it was evident that these thoughts still haunted him. He frequently had nightmares about people chasing and trying to kill him, which caused him to wake up screaming almost nightly. He often obsessed

(Continued)

about stories of child abductions on the news. Although he trusted his adoptive mother, he questioned her ability to protect him.

I attempted to use trauma-focused cognitive-behavioral therapy with Cody. Although he responded well to the skills-based portions, he did not want to write a trauma narrative. Because of his resistance and fear, I knew I had to find an alternative way to approach Cody. He had always been interested in video games and cartoons, especially those involving superheroes. He also loved writing and drawing. So, one day, I asked if he would like to write a comic book, one in which he could be the superhero. He eagerly agreed.

We started by developing a Super-Cody character, one that was equipped to handle the stress of his past. Super-Cody had a strong, protective suit, which was able to repel any weapons used against him. He had several superpowers, including super-speed, invisibility, and the ability to throw fireballs.

We began writing stories about Super-Cody's exploits as he faced all sorts of villains and bad guys, most of whom were trying to steal him away. Even when a villain had trapped Super-Cody, he was always able to summon the strength to save the day. As Super-Cody became stronger and more self-reliant, so did Cody.

One day, I suggested that we write a story about a pair of villains who were trying to abduct Super-Cody. I wondered if we could incorporate the names Tim and Sandy—his birth parents' names—into the villains' names. Cody looked at me with uncertainty, but agreed—although the traditional trauma narrative seemed too daunting for him, it seemed that a comic book version was something he felt capable of doing. It took several weeks for Cody to write the story about his battle against Terrifying Tim and Scary Sandy; at first, he seemed reluctant to write each word and draw each picture, but over time, Cody's fear and hesitation seemed to transform into confidence and excitement. As he finally drew the panel in which he threw the villains into jail, he smiled widely to himself. He shared his comic book with his mother, whose face reflected the pride she felt for a son who had accomplished so much.

I continued to work with Cody on other concerns after we had finished writing about and reflecting on Super-Cody. His alter ego seemed to provide him with a sense of strength and resilience that continued to follow him as he struggled with shaky peer relations and difficult family problems. By the time we terminated, he seemed to be a different child. He had good grades and had even made a few new friends. He no longer argued with his parents or the other children at school. He had a healthy sense of self-esteem and seemed to really believe that he deserved to experience good things in his life. Super-Cody and Cody were no longer two separate people, but one strong, secure being.

CHILDREN WITH LEARNING DISABILITIES OR GIFTEDNESS

Counselors must use a unique set of skills and tools when working with children who are gifted or have learning differences or disabilities. For a counselor to effectively work with any child, it is important to understand children's cognitive ability and their method of processing the information they receive from the world around them. When counseling children, it is important to have an understanding of their cognitive abilities and how this influences children's mental health (Sigelman & Rider, 2012; Stephens, Jain, & Kim, 2010).

Generally, children's cognitive abilities are assessed in relation to their intelligence quotient (IQ), academic performance, and social skill abilities (Rix, Hall, Nind, Sheehy, & Wearmouth, 2009; Sigelman & Rider, 2012). It is commonly accepted that an IQ of 85–115 indicates average intelligence. Intelligence quotients of 70–84 and 116–130 lie outside of the average range, but do not indicate considerable intellectual disability or giftedness. However, an IQ of 52–70 indicates mild intellectual disability, 35–51 indicates moderate, and 20–34 indicates severe intellectual disability. On the opposite end of the spectrum, an IQ of 130 or above indicates intellectual giftedness (Sigelman & Rider, 2012).

When considering how cognitive abilities affect or relate to children's mental health, it is important to have knowledge of their overall sense of well-being. Although a child's sense of belonging, achievement, and personal identity can be heavily influenced by academic achievement, it is also developed through relationships with family, friends, and school personnel (Stephens et al., 2010). By assessing all facets of the client's life, it is possible to determine the area in which counseling can be most beneficial. Counselors work with children, their families, and their teachers to help children learn optimally, develop a strong sense of personal identity, and thrive academically and personally.

Intellectual Disability

Academic difficulty (i.e., an IQ of 70 or below and difficulty with developmentally appropriate behaviors and social cues) can create disruptions in children's sense of self: self-esteem, self-concept, and self-efficacy (Sigelman & Rider, 2012; Stephens et al., 2010). Children's responses to these difficulties may include feelings of sadness and depression, withdrawal, avoidance, or anger. Although these feelings often develop as a reaction to academic struggles, they also further inhibit healthy learning. It is important to help children learn how to address these feelings so that they can develop adaptive behavior patterns both in and out of the classroom (Stephens et al., 2010). Individual mental health counseling can be helpful in allowing some of these feelings to be constructively expressed and validated and to help teach children coping and social skills.

When counseling children, it is important to maintain an active counseling style, avoid prolonged use of silence, and appropriately use self-disclosure (Stephens et al., 2010). These techniques can help children feel more at ease and allow for a more interactive mental health process. Children with intellectual disabilities often experience inattention or difficulty concentrating. It is helpful to reduce distracting stimuli and to be appropriately directive when communicating with these children. Counselors can guide a child with attentional difficulties through any simple, enjoyable task and then process the steps as they apply to other activities that are more difficult for the child.

Some counselor-generated techniques suggested by Stephens et al. (2010) include using group counseling interventions as an effective way to address mental health needs of children with intellectual disability. Stephens et al. reported that it can be helpful to include socially accepted children in these groups to reduce social stigma and to have peers who can model socially appropriate behaviors. Issues of impulsivity can be addressed through games that require physical restraint or activities that clearly explain and rehearse appropriate responses to common situations. This can effectively address behaviors that are further contributing to academic difficulties and can even reduce the use of aggressive coping strategies commonly used by children with intellectual difficulty (Rix et al., 2009; Stephens et al., 2010). Over time, group processes can effectively help children learn to recognize others' emotional and social cues, which can work to reduce anxiety and emotional lability in children with intellectual difficulties. Children's self-esteem is likely to improve as a result of increased social acceptance, which will further promote children's sense of self-efficacy and academic success (Stephens et al., 2010).

School counselors might consider using both individual and group counseling in collaboration with students' teachers (Rix et al., 2009; Stephens et al., 2010). Individual counseling can address clients' overall well-being, group counseling can be used to address specific aspects of difficulty, and collaboration with teachers can be used to identify helpful teaching and behavioral management techniques. Clinical mental health counselors can also be a valuable resource for these students and may find it helpful to work in collaboration with the school counselor and the parents. It might even be possible for some counselors to work with children in their school setting and in their home, as opposed to providing outpatient counseling.

It is also important to consider the social consequences experienced by many who have an intellectual disability. Group counseling can be especially helpful for teaching social skills and normalizing complex feelings that can result from having an intellectual disability (Rix et al., 2009; Stephens et al., 2010). Children with an intellectual disability can address negative feelings in a safe environment that normalizes and validates their feelings, while increasing social interaction.

An additional consideration for children with intellectual disabilities is the child's family and home life. Often, intellectual disability is genetic, which means that one or both parents may experience similar struggles (Sigelman & Rider, 2012). Some parents might have their own mental health challenges that inhibit them from providing fully attentive and responsive parenting. In addition, parents with intellectual difficulties may not have the skills or abilities to help their children with schoolwork, healthy coping skills, or social interactions.

Giftedness

The mental health needs of children who are intellectually gifted (i.e., IQ above 130) are similar to those experienced by children with intellectual disability. These children may struggle with issues of self-identity as they notice that their cognitive ability is different from the majority of their peers (Wood, 2010). In addition, their increased moral awareness may make it difficult for gifted children to relate to their less-introspective peers. Although it seems counterintuitive, children with high intellectual ability might experience struggles surrounding academic difficulties. Gifted individuals have a high need for achievement and stimulation (Wood, 2010). If gifted children are not adequately challenged, they might actually disengage from school activities. In addition, many gifted children are used to easily understanding academic material; if not challenged appropriately, they may begin to doubt their academic abilities and lose some of their identity related to ease of academic success.

When addressing the mental health needs of gifted children, counselors should remember that intellectual giftedness is an asset, but also can be a burden (Peterson, 2006). Boredom and disengagement from schoolwork can lead to negative self-esteem, social isolation, and depression (Peterson, 2006; Wood, 2010). Although intelligence is typically viewed as a protective factor, intelligence can lead to existential thoughts that children are not able to understand or accurately interpret (Peterson, 2006). Consequently, children who are gifted may feel overwhelmed, depressed, and isolated.

When working with gifted children, the primary goal of the counselor is to form a safe, therapeutic alliance with the child through acknowledgment of the child's difficulties, while also facilitating the child's self-awareness (Wood, 2010). Gifted children's intellectual abilities can contribute to some people overlooking the fact that these children progress through the same developmental stages as other children (Sigelman & Rider, 2012). Also, many intellectually gifted children are not used to feeling challenged in an academic setting. When they do encounter demanding academic circumstances, it will be important for counselors to help children develop appropriate organizational and time-management skills (Wood, 2010). In addition, counselors should help children understand that when they struggle or feel frustrated, this is normal and serves to help their character develop, and it is not a sign of weakness (Peterson, 2006).

It is also important to understand the social difficulties some gifted children experience. Parents who do not understand the needs of their gifted children may pathologize behaviors such as underachievement or behavioral expressions of frustration or boredom (Peterson, 2006). In addressing the needs of a gifted child, it is important to help parents gain an understanding of their children's needs and desires. Gifted children also often feel isolated and different from their peers; working with children to develop appropriate social skills and self-esteem will also be important (Wood, 2010).

Although many aspects of mental health are affected by a child's cognitive abilities, it is important to address each one in a systematic way that addresses the child's most serious needs first. It is important to remember that every child is a unique individual who will express his or her mental health needs in a variety of ways. Ultimately, when working with any child, especially those with academic disability or giftedness, it is important to be compassionate, open-minded, and holistic (see Self-Assessment Activity 7.1).

SELF-ASSESSMENT ACTIVITY 7.1 DIFFERENTLY ABLED POPULATIONS

Consider these questions to assess your biases about working with differently abled populations.

1. Consider this statement: "Gifted children sometimes have mental health difficulties." Do you agree or disagree? Why?
2. Consider this statement: "Children with intellectual disabilities are not able to benefit from counseling as much as others." Do you agree or disagree? Why?
3. How would you establish therapeutic rapport with a differently-abled child?

VOICES FROM THE FIELD 7.2   Rose-Colored Glasses, by Emily C. Campbell

We are all human, we are all different, and we all experience struggles. Our differences aren't always negative, and struggles do not necessarily equate to failure. In fact, our challenges can often become our successes.

As a counselor-in-training, I interned in a child and adolescent hospital unit providing mental health and family counseling services to patients and their families. Many struggles brought my 16-year-old client, Beth, to our unit. She had been actively involved in the mental health system, but because of her behavioral issues, many people had struggled to connect with her strengths and frame her situation in context.

Upon completion of an educational evaluation, it became evident that Beth had a preexisting learning disorder that had not previously been identified secondary to the dominance of her behavioral issues. Her learning disability was compounded too by a history of sexual abuse and trauma and subsequent rotations through the foster care system. Due to her lack of social skills, traumatic childhood experiences, and inability to regulate her emotions appropriately, Beth found great difficulty in accepting support from the staff and other patients on the unit, and her learning disability had been overlooked.

My work with Beth was brief, but memorable. Others found her to be negative and disruptive, but I was able to see her untapped skills and talents. Although she was challenging to work with, I provided her with kindness, structure, and patience. She was able to significantly improve socially and scholastically, which was visible even to the hospital staff.

Unfortunately, Beth had not been socialized appropriately or received services such as counseling to help her process through her trauma issues. In counseling, Beth and I worked on processing her traumatic past. We also worked on developing her social and coping skills, especially those that related to interacting with others (e.g., tone and pitch of her voice, eye contact, and other nonverbals). It became a topic of discussion with the clinical staff that it was possible that her learning "disability" was not one that was a product of genetics, but possibly evolved secondary to the circumstances she had endured. If nothing else, it appeared the unresolved trauma symptoms were agitating her learning disability. In fact, as she worked through her trauma issues, the symptoms of her learning disability appeared to diminish.

I have found that when I view clients through a humanistic and strength-based lens, this enables our relationship to flourish and to move toward positive growth. Every person has knowledge and experience to share, and my training and experience as a counselor provided me with the tools deemed necessary to focus on Beth's strengths, rather than her weaknesses. Just like anyone else, clients with learning disabilities have a need to feel heard, accepted, and valued.

NONSUICIDAL SELF-INJURY

Nonsuicidal self-injury (hereafter referred to as self-injury or SI) is the direct and deliberate destruction of body tissue in the absence of suicidal intent (Weierich & Nock, 2008). Although people self-injure in a variety of ways, the most common forms include self-cutting, self-burning, and self-scratching (Whitlock, Eckenrode, & Silverman, 2006). It is estimated that 21% to 80% of clinical samples (Nock & Prinstein, 2004), 13% of high school students (Ross & Heath, 2002), 8% of 6th- to 8th-grade students (Hilt, Nock, Lloyd-Richardson, & Prinstein, 2008), and 11% to 17% of college students (Heath, Toste, Nedecheva, & Charlebois, 2008; Whitlock et al., 2006) have engaged in some form of self-injury, thus making it probable that all counselors will fairly regularly encounter clients or students who self-injure.

There are a variety of reasons people self-injure, and the behavior generally serves various evolving functions that are dependent on time and experiences. Nock and Prinstein (2004) found that the reasons people self-injure can be reduced to two generic functions: it is a form of autonomic reinforcement (i.e., emotion regulation) and/or a means of obtaining social reinforcement (e.g., gaining support from others). Osuch, Noll, and Putman (1999) suggested that self-injury can function (a) as a form of affect regulation; (b) as a means of decreasing feelings of isolation and loneliness; (c) as a method to influence others with the intention of communicating anger, hurt, or rebellion in a manner that does not involve verbally speaking of these emotions; or (d) as a means of self-stimulation with the intention of increasing emotional arousal (e.g., increasing a pleasurable, euphoric sensation).

People who self-injure possess a variety of mental health diagnoses, as well as varied developmental and personal contexts that typically contribute to the development and maintenance of the behavior (Klonsky & Muehlenkamp, 2007). The multifarious nature of self-injury can make it difficult for counselors to conceptualize a client's treatment needs, and they may struggle to know where to begin in helping this population. As such, when working with someone who self-injures, it is important to provide a comprehensive assessment in which the frequency, severity, duration, and onset of the self-injurious behavior is assessed along with the antecedents, consequences, functions, and dynamics of the behavior. More specifically, counselors might inquire about age of onset, course of the behavior, longest period free of behavior, lifetime and current frequency of self-injury, changes in the behavior over time, emotional states when injuring, triggers leading to the self-injurious behavior, immediate and more long-term aftermath of injuring, medical complications (e.g., infections, stitches, surgeries, corrective surgeries), impulsivity of self-injury, dystonicity (e.g., a wish to stop oneself), resistance (e.g., effort to stop oneself), control (e.g., success in stopping oneself), use of substances before and after the behaviors, and past interventions to stop behavior (Kress, 2003).

The literature offers little guidance on effective treatment of SI; empirical research and evidence-supported treatment guidelines are limited (Klonsky & Muehlenkamp, 2007; Muehlenkamp, 2006). In general, therapeutic approaches that emphasize problem solving, emotion regulation, and functional assessment and analysis of the behavior (i.e., developing an understanding of what thoughts, feelings, and behaviors led to the SI, and what behaviors could be altered to preclude further SI) are cited as important treatment elements (Klonsky & Muehlenkamp, 2007). Cognitive restructuring and a strong therapeutic relationship are also suggested as essential to the effective treatment of SI (Muehlenkamp, 2006).

Dialectical behavior therapy (DBT) is one treatment approach that shows promise in addressing SI (Klonsky, 2007). In an attempt to cease SI, a DBT approach focuses on assisting clients in developing alternative coping skills, identifying obstacles to the use of alternative skills, and enhancing skill generalization outside the therapeutic setting (Muehlenkamp, 2006). DBT uses several treatment modalities including group skills training, individual therapy, phone coaching, and supervision or team consulting for the counselor.

The possible health risks (e.g., cutting too deeply, medical complications such as infections) that can occur secondary to self-injury contribute to some counselors feeling intimidated by the prospect of working with this population. Adding to many counselors' apprehension is that many people who self-injure may not view the behavior as problematic and may not elect to select SI cessation as a treatment goal (Kress & Hoffman, 2008). Counselors' challenge when working with clients who do not wish to stop self-injuring is to assess how to best facilitate a client's desire to change while avoiding power struggles and attempts to control the client (e.g., forcing clients to stop injuring, demanding they stop injuring; Kress, Drouhard, & Costin, 2010). Attempts to control clients often increase their resistance to change and are typically considered unethical. Some counselors may want the cessation of the self-injury to be the primary treatment goal, yet clients may not be ready to change. Motivational interviewing (MI) techniques can be helpful in enhancing clients' motivation to want to change and stop self-injuring (Kress & Hoffman, 2008). Motivational interviewing techniques are discussed in greater detail in the section in this chapter on counseling clients who are mandated and/or have a low motivation for change. Case Study 7.1 highlights some of the issues of self-injury.

CASE STUDY 7.1

Mariah

Mariah, a 21-year-old nursing student, presents for counseling at her college's counseling center. She expresses that she would like to receive counseling services to better manage conflicts she is having with her boyfriend. During the interview process, the counselor comes to understand that that Mariah is shy and reserved and has difficulty expressing emotions and needs to her boyfriend. When Mariah cannot express herself or becomes withdrawn, her boyfriend becomes frustrated. In turn, this increases Mariah's inability to express her emotions and thus increases her sense of feeling overwhelmed. Mariah goes on to casually mention that she sometimes uses delicate self-cutting as a method of coping to deal with her unexpressed emotions. Mariah reports that although she feels embarrassed about the self-cutting and self-conscious about her scars, she finds this to be an effective way to manage her frustrations. The counselor is aware of a strong desire to push the client to stop self-injuring and to force her to work on behavioral alternatives to self-injury. The counselor considers several options, including having Mariah evaluated for a psychiatric placement at a hospital. The counselor also considers forcing Mariah to sign a contract stating that she will no longer self-injure.

Based on this information:

1. What are preliminary safety-related questions that should be considered before continuing to provide counseling services to a client who self-injures, like Mariah?
2. In this scenario, the counselor appears to be very uncomfortable with Mariah's self-injuring behavior. What might be your initial personal reactions and attitudes toward working with a client who self-injures? What steps might you take to monitor these reactions?

INTIMATE PARTNER VIOLENCE

Intimate partner violence (IPV), more popularly referred to as domestic violence, is the term used to encompass violence perpetrated by a relationship partner (Campbell, 2003). The scope of IPV is far reaching, with 34% of women spanning varied socioeconomic, age, and racial backgrounds being victims of IPV at some point in their lives (Browne, 1993). Intimate partner violence also affects children, with estimates suggesting that at least that 3.3 million children each year witness IPV, and many of these children experience enduring long-term effects secondary to this exposure (American Psychological Association [APA], 1996).

Intimate partner violence can have serious short- and long-term consequences for its victims. Most seriously, 30% to 55% of female homicides are perpetrated by intimate partners (Campbell, 2003), and IPV is the direct cause of 21% of female emergency room visits each year (Browne, 1993). For victims, the psychological consequences of IPV can include depression, anxiety, an increased risk of suicide, PTSD, psychosomatic complaints, substance abuse, and lowered self-esteem (Bacchus, Mezey, & Bewley, 2003).

The increased risk of psychological problems associated with IPV increases the likelihood that victims will become consumers of counseling services. Counselors' early and accurate assessment and detection for IPV is important. Clients should be routinely asked about relationship experiences with violent and controlling partners (Bacchus et al., 2003). Many clients do not identify or recognize their experiences as abusive, and as such, the first step in completing a thorough assessment of relationship violence is psychoeducation (Lawson, 2003). Clients benefit from having abuse and violence clearly defined, and these efforts may help them to recognize that abuse has occurred. Assessment of IPV should include a determination of the duration, nature, extent, and intensity of violent, controlling, and abusive acts. Inquiries into the following areas can help counselors better identify the nature of the abuse: (a) detailed descriptions of a typical abuse experience, (b) the most severe abuse experience, (c) the most recent abuse experience, and (d) the frequency of the abuse.

A first priority when counseling those in abusive relationships is monitoring and enhancing their safety. One of the most important efforts a counselor can take to minimize risk and facilitate client safety is to help the client draft a safety plan (Kress, Protivnak, & Sadlak, 2008). A safety plan is a detailed plan that highlights the client's role in making the safest decisions possible when managing violent situations. It should be emphasized to clients that although they do not have control over their partner's violent behavior, they do have a choice in how to respond and how to best enhance their safety as well as the safety of their children. Any discussion of safety should be tailored to the unique needs of the individual. For example, a teenager in an abusive dating relationship will require a different safety plan than a woman living with an abusive partner. Safety plans might address the following (Lawson, 2003): (a) an accessible place to store personal items when a quick exit is necessary; (b) safe places to go when the client decides to leave the abuser; (c) telling friends or neighbors about the violence and requesting that they call the police if they hear suspicious noises or witness suspicious events; (d) identifying safe rooms in the house, school, and so on; (e) developing emergency escape routes; (f) where they can go if they fear an argument will develop; (g) storing an escape kit; and (h) processing the safety plan with children (when age appropriate).

In addition to the safety plan, areas of discussion might be exploration of issues related to police protection, legal action, domestic violence shelters, community resources, and social supports (Browne, 1993). Counselors should become familiar with both the state laws that relate to IPV and local resources that may be useful in supporting clients seeking safety. It is also important to discuss with clients the importance of trusting their intuition and judgment related to the violence. Many victims who are experiencing IPV have an excellent understanding of their partner's abuse patterns and sense when more serious harm is a possibility. Encouraging clients to trust their instincts and to do what they can to deescalate the situation may be helpful in promoting client safety and should be discussed in relation to the safety plan.

Many clients who are or have been in an abusive relationship sustain trauma reactions. Golding's (1999) meta-analysis of 11 studies indicated that PTSD is one of the most prevalent mental disorders in women in abusive relationships. The presence of PTSD symptoms can be potentially devastating for victims. When unaddressed, PTSD is related to a risk of future revictimization (Herman, 1997); thus, the resolution of trauma is an important treatment goal. Generally, exposure-based cognitive behavioral approaches are recommended as frontline treatments for people in abusive relationships (Johnson & Zlotnick, 2009; Kubany et al., 2004). Clients not yet living in safe, stable living environments or clients who are managing a great deal of chaos may need to wait to begin exposure-therapy; the exposure-therapy aspect of treatment may be agitating and thus contraindicated during the early stages of treatment (Johnson & Zlotnick, 2009).

SUBSTANCE ABUSE

Because of the complexity of addictions and the high prevalence of co-occurring mental disorders, counseling those who abuse substances is a challenging task. The fifth edition of *Diagnostic and Statistical Manual of Mental Disorders* (*DSM-5*; American Psychiatric Association, 2013) classifies substance abuse separately from substance dependence. The primary difference between the two diagnoses is that **substance dependence** involves a growing tolerance of the substance and symptoms of withdrawal in the absence of the substance. Otherwise, both diagnoses are characterized by clients' use of a substance despite its negative impact on their social, occupational, and financial functioning.

As with any other mental health issue, counselors rely primarily on their clients for information that can lead to an accurate diagnosis and treatment of substance abuse disorders. People who abuse substances tend to be poor historians about their use. There are many reasons why people with substance abuse difficulties are not honest with their counselors about their use. Inherent to all addictions is a strong desire to maintain use of the substance at all costs, even by lying. In addition, the effects of the substances being used may also impair one's ability to connect with their use and its consequences. Perhaps as a psychological defense mechanism that protects them from change, many clients also minimize the extent of their substance use and its consequences, even to themselves. Many clients also receive counseling for substance abuse as the result of a court order. Drug court initiatives operate under the notion that people who are arrested for nonviolent, drug-related crimes have underlying mental health concerns that can be addressed more thoroughly through therapeutic interventions, rather than imprisonment (Brown, 2011). Although Brown found these programs to decrease recidivism in minorities, women, older adults, and people with more serious criminal histories, many people still resent participating in mandated counseling.

In addition to the difficulties associated with mandated substance abuse services, many people who have suffered with substance dependence have suffered significant losses in their lives (American Psychiatric Association, 2013). Some clients fear that truthful discussion about their substance use will further contribute to the loss of their family, social supports, or employment opportunities. This fear can be partially alleviated by the privileged communication between a client and counselor, but many still struggle to be candid about their use (Bohnert, Zivin, Welsh, & Kilbourne, 2011).

At least 60% of people who abuse substances also have other comorbid mental health disorders, and the combination of substance abuse and a second mental health disorder is referred to as **dual diagnosis** (U.S. Department of Health and Human Services, National Institutes of Health, National Institutes on Drug Abuse, 2007). Although it is impossible to say that one causes the other, additional mental health disorders must be addressed when working with substance abuse and dependence. It is imperative to gain clients' trust to fully understand their mental health in the context of their past experiences, personal struggles, and future goals. It is also important to identify the benefits of drug use, such as escape from painful circumstances and social reinforcement.

Most commonly, mood and anxiety disorders accompany substance use (U.S. Department of Health and Human Services, National Institutes of Health, National Institutes on Drug Abuse, 2007). For some clients, it may be helpful to address the substance abuse separately from other mental health diagnoses, but it is often more realistic to address the client in a more holistic way. One therapeutic intervention that is especially helpful with clients who experience comorbid disorders is motivational interviewing (MI; Miller & Rollnick, 2002). This clinical interviewing approach supports clients in enhancing their personal motivation to stop using substances. Using collaboration and encouragement, MI techniques help clients to identify their own desire to change and locate resources to help them modify their lifestyles.

Although MI is a helpful resource when working with substance use disorders, there are many other treatment alternatives, such as cognitive-behavioral techniques and 12-step programs that are helpful in treating clients who abuse substances (Miller & Rollnick, 2002). Ultimately, counselors must understand the complexity of substance use and how it interacts with clients' other mental health needs, their coping strategies, and their motivation to change. See Self-Assessment Activity 7.2 as you begin to think about substance abuse.

SELF-ASSESSMENT ACTIVITY 7.2 SUBSTANCE ABUSE

Begin to reflect on your attitudes about substance abuse:

1. Are substance use issues always caused by other mental health disorders?
2. Would you enjoy the challenge and complexity of working with clients who use substances? Explain.

VOICES FROM THE FIELD 7.3   Success Is Measured in Small Steps, by Kelli Scanlon

Completing my internship at a residential substance abuse treatment program for women and their dependent children was a valuable personal experience. For many of these women, domestic violence, homelessness, prostitution, chronic illness, childhood sexual abuse, and prison time were the norm. Most had lost temporary or permanent custody of one or more of their children and were in treatment at the behest of the local drug court. The women's issues were complex, and process groups were intense. I was quickly enamored with each and every client.

Counseling a soft-spoken, timid, bespectacled client named "Jean" was both rewarding and challenging. Jean had been through treatment twice before, and the odds were she would relapse again. Jean had lost her marriage and her two eldest children to her opiate/cocaine/marijuana addiction. At age 36 years, she had no car, no home, no driver's license, no savings, and very little education or training. But the issue that plagued her most was the death of her mother, which had occurred 1 year prior. Because Jean was high the last time she saw her mother alive, she was flooded with shame and grief at the mere mention of her mom. Unresolved issues with her mother served as a significant relapse trigger for Jean, and it was evident these issues needed to be resolved if Jean was ever to maintain her sobriety.

Gestalt techniques were used to help Jean embrace her mother's understanding, empathy, and forgiveness. She also wrote a letter to her mother and was granted permission by program

(Continued)

staff to leave the facility to read the letter aloud to her mother at the cemetery. It was a gray, drizzly day, but when Jean finished reading the letter, the sky opened and a ray of sunshine illuminated the cemetery, making the experience personally and spiritually meaningful to Jean. We processed the events, and Jean was able to move forward with her mother's death no longer being a focus of therapy.

Few individuals make it out of treatment and remain clean after the first few attempts. Although there is variability in how many attempts it takes to maintain sobriety, most people relapse multiple times. Sadly, around the time of her 9-month sobriety anniversary, Jean relapsed and had to leave the program; she did so with grace and accepted full responsibility for her choices. As a neophyte counselor, I felt I'd failed her, yet I was able to find comfort in knowing that Jean left the program with one less relapse trigger keeping her stuck in the cycle of addiction.

OLDER ADULTS AND THE TERMINALLY ILL

When working with older adults, it is important to consider their cognitive and emotional development, as this may help to illuminate their personal struggles and identify appropriate counseling interventions. Adults over the age of 65 years usually have entered Erikson's psychosocial stage of integrity versus despair (Sigelman & Rider, 2012). A key challenge to this final stage of life is identifying ways in which an individual's life was meaningful and positively influenced the world. This struggle can be addressed in counseling through techniques such as reminiscence therapy, which was supported by Erikson as a natural way to cope with circumstances of older age (Jones, 2003).

Reminiscence therapy techniques invite clients to verbally construct their life stories and identify how they have used the skills and gifts given to them by their ancestors to influence the world (Burnside & Haight, 1992). Furthermore, reminiscence therapy allows older clients to identify how their beliefs and values have been passed on to benefit future generations (Hunter, 2007). Reminiscence therapy may also effectively alleviate symptoms of depression that are often present in older populations (Burnside & Haight, 1992; Hunter, 2007; Jones, 2003). Although many older adults suffer with feelings of isolation and helplessness, countless older adults successfully overcome the challenges of the integrity versus despair stage and find peace in old age (Kübler-Ross, 1969; Sigelman & Rider, 2012). In fact, older adults who perceive that they have good health and low stress feel a certain peace with their situation and may even live more in the moment and appreciate and enjoy life more than they did in their younger years (Myers & Degges-White, 2007).

Many older adults face end-of-life issues, and each person experiences these issues in a unique way. It is important to appreciate and understand people's relationship with death and how they approach death and dying. As they have aged and experienced loss, older adults have had the opportunity to contemplate the meaning of death in a developmentally normal way. In contrast, and depending on a person's developmental stage, some people who experience terminal illness may not progress through natural developmental stages; they may be caught unprepared to cope with the realities of death and dying (Kübler-Ross, 1969; Sigelman & Rider, 2012).

People with terminal illness often learn of their diagnosis from a physician, and for many, this moment can prove to be traumatic, even haunting. As a counselor, it is important to process these disclosure events with clients. Some doctors might be very sensitive about the issue of death and dying, but some may avoid discussing death due to their own denial or anxiety or because of limited ability to communicate such information (Kübler-Ross, 1969). Processing the way in which the client learned of his or her illness might prove to be a helpful step in the therapeutic process. Counselors can learn about the clients' initial reactions to the news, and they can also learn about the client's level of awareness of and relationship with death.

Kübler-Ross (1969) developed five stages of dying, which provide a general framework for working with clients who are terminally ill and/or facing death. Not every person will experience these stages; in fact, some might experience only a few, and others might experience them in a different order. The first stage, denial and isolation, is characterized by clients refusing to believe they will die; this can be psychologically adaptive when the initial shock of receiving a terminal diagnosis may feel as though it pulls too heavily on a person's ability to cope and adapt. Next, clients experience anger; this anger could be directed toward loved ones, themselves, or even a higher power. It is important for counselors to educate clients' loved ones about this stage of dying so that they understand any confusing, or even hurtful, client behaviors. After anger, clients often accept their fate, but attempt to bargain for slightly better circumstances, such as extended time or reduced pain.

After the first three stages, clients often experience depression. The depression stage is multifaceted and is experienced by every person, whether an older adult or the terminally ill, differently. Older adults may experience increased physical limitations, and their depression might lead to consideration of how their lives could have been different or better. In addition, older adults often experience isolation due to the loss of other close loved ones and physical limitations, and this also contributes to depression in older people. People with terminal illness may feel a sense of hopelessness and regret about things that they will not be able to experience. For any person, the reality of leaving loved ones can also be a source of depression (Sigelman & Rider, 2012). Counselors can work with older clients who are depressed by helping them identify their legacy, or their personal accomplishments and relationships that have given their life meaning (Hunter, 2007). As was mentioned with regard to counseling older adults, a review—or reminiscence—of their life allows clients to identify what they have inherited from the world and what they will contribute to future generations. In addition to material possessions, clients' legacies include the values and beliefs that they will leave behind and their relationships and the people they have influenced. Helping clients identify their legacy can allow them to make meaning of their lives, and therefore their deaths.

The final stage in the dying process is acceptance. Regardless of the stage in which a counselor first joins with the client, the goal is to help lead them to a place of acceptance and readiness. Just as with any other mental health issue, it is not always possible to reach maximum gains, and some clients may struggle and not have time to reach a place of full acceptance. It is always necessary to have a treatment goal that reflects clients' personal aspirations.

In addition to working with clients who are experiencing death and dying, it is important to work with their loved ones and, when helpful, to integrate them into the counseling process. Family members can experience feelings of denial, anger, uselessness, and depression as the result of a loved one's dying (Kübler-Ross, 1969). Family members' reactions can inhibit their ability to support the dying person and could result in mental health difficulties of their own. As a counselor, it is important to promote the mental health of clients' loved ones and to make referrals as necessary.

Death and dying lies at the core of human existence and is an issue that every person will eventually face. Counseling this population can prove to be challenging for some counselors. Counseling terminally ill or older adults can be difficult due to time constraints and a lack of control over clients' life circumstances. In addition, to be present and fully available to their clients, counselors must have a firm understanding of their own beliefs and feelings surrounding death. Overall, counselors who have a healthy understanding of their relationship with death, are open and honest with themselves, and are willing to empathize with clients in their greatest time of need will find fulfillment and success in their work with the older adult or terminally ill populations. Case Study 7.2 highlights some of the issues surrounding terminal illness.

CASE STUDY 7.2

John

John is a 78-year-old man who recently learned that he has stage-IV lung cancer. He remarried after divorce ended his first marriage, which produced one daughter, who lives on the opposite side of the United States. He lives with his second wife, Sally, who is considerably younger than he is. John has decided to undergo chemotherapy in hopes of a brief period of "rest" in which he will experience little to no symptoms. After his third treatment, his doctor asked if he would still like to continue, and John asked his wife. With a heavy heart, Sally replied that it may be better to stop the painful chemotherapy treatments. John replied that he wished to continue with the therapy and said to his wife, "We're going to beat this." Two weeks later, John became too weak for another treatment, and hospice was assigned. He passed shortly after in his bed at home with Sally.

1. In what stage of dying was John when he passed away?
   a. Acceptance
   b. Bargaining
   c. Depression
   d. Denial
2. Is it possible for clients to pass from a later stage of dying back to an earlier stage? Explain.
3. In what stage was John when he decided to undergo chemotherapy?
   a. Acceptance
   b. Bargaining
   c. Depression
   d. Denial
4. How aware are you of your own beliefs surrounding death and dying?
5. Could you effectively counsel clients who are older or terminally ill? Explain.

VOICES FROM THE FIELD 7.4   Living with Dying, by Jamie Crockett

Working with a 43-year-old agnostic White woman with rapidly progressing colon cancer was, for me, especially challenging. The client wished to use her time in counseling to cope with her approaching death and address her fears that her two teenage daughters and husband of 25 years "couldn't handle" her illness and end-of-life related issues. Her belief that she had no one else to talk with about her death lent a sense of urgency to the counseling process. It was important that I stayed connected with my role as her counselor; respecting and trusting in her process and ensuring that I did not impose my personal values were critically important.

To meet the client where she was, I had to recognize my own bias that successful end-of-life counseling would include family and legacy work. The client believed that her family did not understand the gravity of her illness, yet she adamantly did not want to work on communicating with them about her dying process. Through self-evaluation and invaluable supervision, I learned to let go of my own hopes for what should be accomplished and instead honored the client's hopes and needs. I had to trust that the client knew what she needed to prepare for her death.

The client emphasized a desire for increased relaxation amid the physical, emotional, and relational pain she was experiencing. She spoke about death, processed her life experiences, and wondered about an afterlife. The client vented about insensitive things that friends and family said to her and appreciated that I did not tell her, "Don't think like that; you have to be positive." As we worked together, she grieved the physical and emotional losses she experienced, including an emerging distance she felt between herself and her loved ones. Yet as her time approached, she also felt increasingly ready to go, and her curiosity about afterlife increased. Though she never stopped hoping for a miracle to prolong her life, she began saying, "I'd rather stay than go, but when it's my time I'm ready."

Our work together was humbling and difficult; it was not about what I wanted for her, it was about what she wanted for herself. As a result of allowing the client to direct her therapeutic process, she felt more confident and relaxed as she passed. Reflecting on our work together, I still find myself second-guessing: *Could I have done more for her and her family? Was it enough?* Although I recognize that this questioning is a good thing and is part of my growing edge as a counselor, I know that the best work happens when I trust and support clients' wishes rather than impose my own beliefs and values.

MILITARY VETERANS

Counseling Military Service Members and Veterans

Counselor exposure to service members and veterans who have experienced difficulties stemming from military involvement continues to increase (Hall, 2008). The sustained involvement of the United States in several wars, as well as the evolution of warfare, technology, and modern medicine, have all contributed to a growing number of military personnel and veterans seeking counseling. In addition, Houppert (2005) contended military members have not only experienced a drastic increase in overall deployment in the past decade (i.e., 300%), but have also had to navigate the issues associated with cutting the general military force by a third. Counselors must understand counseling issues that relate to this growing population and develop appropriate evidence-based treatment plans to be most effective.

As military veterans return to the United States with the lasting emotional and psychological effects of war, there is a significant need for professional counselors' services (Jumper et al., 2006). Hoge, Auchterlonie, and Milliken (2006) noted that 19.1% of service members returning from Iraq reported mental health problems. Combat duty and exposure to combat have been associated with a higher utilization of mental health services and a greater attrition rate in counseling. Conversely, it has also been documented that those with mental health conditions often do not seek mental health treatment; it is estimated that only 23% to 40% of military service members with mental health issues seek mental health care (Hoge et al., 2004).

Stigma continues to be a prevailing theme among veterans, and many hesitate to seek counseling services (Hall, 2008). Pryce, Ogilvy-Lee, and Pryce (2000) contended this stigma is influenced by service members' internalized paradigm that they would not need assistance to cope with the normal demands and stress of the military if internally strong enough. Furthermore, although combat stress (e.g., stress induced by uncertainty, surprise, isolation, sleep deprivation, and/or hardships) is a reality of war; resiliency to this stress is an essential quality for those within the military. If these individuals display evidence of distress from these symptoms, this distress is often equated with personal weaknesses (Hall, 2008). Furthermore, admitting to having distress from combat stress and seeking treatment is like admitting failure and may be seen as shameful, thus reducing the probability of seeking treatment. This lack of disclosure only fuels the probability of military personnel experiencing posttraumatic stress disorder (PTSD) while refusing to seek treatment.

In addition, some military members may believe that the use of counseling services and/or human service programs may adversely affect their military career if confidentiality is not maintained. A service member's records within the military can often be subject to review by that member's commander. This lack of confidentiality and fear of concomitant consequences secondary to breaches in confidentiality may deter the utilization of counseling services within the military entirely. First and foremost, counselors must acknowledge this stigma and make every effort to educate the military service member or veteran of the limits of confidentiality (Kennedy, 2004).

Treatment Considerations

Hall (2008) outlined two concepts that need to be fully considered when working with military members. These concepts include the concept of honor, and the "us versus them" mentality. The concept of honor relates to the idea that getting killed is an honorable choice if it is within the framework of carrying out a mission. Counselors must learn how to respect and even use this concept of perseverance (even through difficulties) to help an individual also honor family and career. The "us versus them" mentality is a sense that civilians cannot possibly understand the military world. Civilian counselors need to assume the "one down position" and allow the service member or veteran to explain the situation. This stance provides the military member with the confidence that one is the expert of one's own life and military experience. In addition, civilian counselors need to be mindful to avoid making statements that suggest they "understand" what clients are going through or have been through because this only undermines and invalidates the clients' lived experience, thus reinforcing the "us versus them" mentality.

Pryce et al. (2000) outlined eight recommendations for civilian counselors who work with this military population. The recommendations are as follows:

(a) seek to understand the individual within the context of his/her military identity (i.e., rank, branch, education, and responsibility);

(b) work to understand the norms and beliefs in relation to service and family;

(c) individualize the "citizen–soldier" (e.g., National Guard and Reserves) as they may have differing commitments to the military and family;

(d) respect the limits of military confidentiality and acknowledge that sensitive issues will remain confidential;

(e) work hard to establish a safe environment in an attempt to increase communication;

(f) work to understand the developmental issues and conflicts especially the ones stemming from the normal separation that may have lead to a number of unresolved issues;

(g) support the limits of self-determination; and

(h) advocate for prevention and intervention by normalizing and facilitating the use of services as a form of self-sufficiency.

These considerations can significantly assist counselors in creating a safe environment and providing the foundation for further treatment with this population.

Treatment Issues

Exposure and the threat of exposure to combat increase the stress and anxiety of service members (Hall, 2008). Recent research suggests that service members who are deployed and enter combat zones continue to display an increased risk of PTSD, major depression, substance abuse, functional impairment in social and occupational settings, and an increase in the usage of health care services (Hoge et al., 2006). Kennedy (2004) contended that deployment and the emotional ramifications of leaving family are the most significant stressor for service members. Hall (2008) suggested that counselors must be prepared to work with veterans on some (if not all) of the following areas: change, grief, and loss; reunion with family and/or children; posttraumatic stress disorder (PTSD) and related combat stress; family violence issues; alcoholism and substance abuse; and stress and anxiety regarding finances. These treatment issues are not always evident during the initial interaction with a counselor; therefore, continued assessment of these issues should occur throughout all phases of treatment.

Evidence-Based Treatment

Much of the evidence-based research on working with military service members and veterans is grounded in cognitive-behavioral therapy (CBT; Foa, Keane, & Friedman, 2009; Hall, 2008). Specifically, the evidence-based treatment literature related to treating PTSD, trauma, and its aftermath in veterans focuses on the use of cognitive behavioral therapy (Brown, Pearlman, & Goodman, 2004; Foa et al., 2009; Salloum & Overstreet, 2008). CBT increased service members' ability to cope with specific trauma symptoms (Foa et al., 2009).

CBT assists service members in forming connections between their thoughts, feelings, and behaviors. It is an evidence-based treatment for addressing the symptoms of PTSD and the associated trauma problems (Foa et al., 2009). CBT is a model that often addresses cognitions and trauma through the use of psychoeducation, stress management, affective modulation, addressing cognitive distortions, trauma/problem processing, and in vivo mastery of trauma reminders. In the final stages of treatment, CBT addresses safety and future personal development. Hall (2008) suggested that when working with military personnel, a family systems approach should also be given consideration and integrated into CBT. Case Study 7.3 provides an opportunity to reflect on the various aspects of working with military service members and veterans.

CASE STUDY 7.3
Chris

Chris is a 23-year-old Caucasian currently seeking treatment for an inability to sleep at night. During the intake phase, Chris disclosed a past sexual assault. Chris discussed that this incident occurred while being enlisted in the Armed Services and during deployment in Afghanistan. The incident in question was not discussed with fellow service members and never reported to authorities. After active duty was completed, Chris returned to work in the electronics field and committed to leave that experience in the past. Due to recent issues with sleep, avoidance of areas that may be difficult to escape from, and recent nightmares about the incident, Chris has increasingly started to isolate from others. After the persistence of a close friend, Chris has decided to talk with a professional counselor.

Questions:

1. What would you need to know prior to working with this veteran?
2. How would you go about establishing a strong therapeutic alliance?
3. Would it matter if Chris were a male or a female? Would your approach to treatment be different?
4. What specific trainings or experiences would be helpful in working with this veteran with this issue?

MANDATED AND UNMOTIVATED CLIENTS

Clients who are mandated to counseling often have a low motivation for change and thus treatment and are frequently noncompliant in attending sessions. Falling into this mandated population are legal offenders and court-ordered clients. However, other initially less obvious populations such as children and adolescents are also frequently forced into counseling by their caregivers and may lack an interest or motivation to make changes. This section will highlight important considerations that may help counselors best approach these often challenging populations.

Low Motivation and Noncompliance

Whether a novice or experienced, it is difficult for professional counselors to work with clients who lack motivation to change. To complicate matters, clients who lack motivation are also often noncompliant with treatment (e.g., they may miss sessions, not follow through on between-session work). Thus, these two concepts have become relatively synonymous as a lack of motivation is usually highlighted by a lack of compliance. It is essential when working with low-motivated, noncompliant clients to create a climate of change and actively engage the client (Cohen, Berliner, & Mannarino, 2010).

When considering a client's level of motivation, a counselor must evaluate whether a client is ready to change, contemplating change, or in a precontemplation stage of change (Miller & Rollnick, 2002). To enhance a client's motivation to change, it is important to address the client's ambivalence around change (i.e., the part of the client that does not want to change), and aid the client by incorporating and increasing change language, while simultaneously seeking agreement on what the problem is that the client wants to change. Resistance is not considered a positive or a negative, only an opportunity to highlight and increase the client's ambivalence in a given situation or process. Miller and Rollnick's approach, motivational interviewing (MI), highlights the importance of *not* attempting to define clients' problems and *not* persuading them that they should change. This approach provides feedback through a nonjudgmental, empathetic stance and seeks to increase clients' ambivalence concerning whether they should change or not. Motivational interviewing allows the counselor to address the issues that brought the client into treatment through a humanizing, collaborative, respectful, and empowering means. The use of MI restores responsibility to clients, thus theoretically increasing their level of engagement in the counseling process.

Aside from assessing the client's motivation, another essential step in the initial stage of treatment is to enhance the climate for change by creating a collaborative working relationship. This is done through the art of engagement and helping clients gain participation and ownership in the counseling process. Nock and Kazdin (2005) described the use of engagement strategies as enhancing clients' motivational self-statements and deepening their commitment to the change process.

VOICES FROM THE FIELD 7.5   Counseling an Unmotivated Adolescent in a Community Mental Health Agency, by Lisa Meyer

In working with adolescents at a community mental health agency, I frequently counseled clients who were forced by others (e.g., parents, guardians, court system) to seek treatment. Consequently, many of my clients lacked the motivation to genuinely examine their situations and behaviors, let

(Continued)

alone consider changing them. They often entered counseling with the belief that it was unnecessary and irrelevant.

In one specific case, on a mother's urgent request, an adolescent who had engaged in serious self-cutting came in for services. The girl spoke very candidly about the cutting and offered to show me her wounds. She went on to discuss her frequent alcohol use, risky sexual behaviors, truancy from school, and elaborate methods for acting on her urges to harm self. I assumed that such a forthcoming disposition would translate into therapeutically rich conversations, the discovery of the roots of her struggles, and accompanying behavior change.

Instead, what transpired were cavalier descriptions of her lifestyle, with minimal insight into her behaviors' function. She expressed that cutting and sex were the best ways she knew to manage her stress. As such, she believed counseling was a futile effort because this was her life, and she could choose how to navigate it. Despite such bold statements, her nonverbal behaviors suggested she was angry, lonely, and hurt. Her body often tensed when particular people or events were discussed, as if releasing her grasp would release her floodgates. She tended to share only when the information portrayed her in a tough and invulnerable manner.

It was my hope that after extensively exploring the functions and disadvantages of her behaviors, she would desire to live in a healthier, more satisfying way. After weeks of exploration, no such desire ensued. It became apparent to me that I was inadvertently imposing my own ideas about where and how change needed to occur. The client was resisting change as she perceived no benefit to altering her behaviors.

With this new realization, I spent the next few months helping the client connect with both the benefits and drawbacks of her behaviors. The main goal with this client was now to help her move from the precontemplation stage (i.e., when clients do not consider their behavior to be a problem and they do not want to change) to the contemplation stage (i.e., when clients begin to think about changing, cutting down, moderating or quitting the addictive behavior by eliciting their own motivators and skills for change). In counseling, I began to focus on my client's autonomy—her ability to make her own decisions about change—which enabled her to take ownership for her actions. As the client settled into the role of being an expert on her situation, she slowly began to see her behavior as problematic. Simultaneously, she began to realize she possessed the strengths to change. I worked with this client for nearly 5 months before she made movements and terminated therapy.

For me, two lessons emerged from this experience. First, a counselor cannot force his or her plan for change on the client; the client may just naturally push back. Second, I learned that if a client continues to be resistant, then perhaps the client has not in fact bought into the idea of counseling. It is then the counselor's responsibility to go back and assess where the client's level of motivation is and aid that client in assuming a greater sense of responsibility for his or her actions and for the direction of the counseling process.

Legal Offenders

Legal offenders are frequently forced into counseling and typically have a low motivation to change. The two central aims when counseling legal offenders are to reduce recidivism (i.e., deviant, criminal behaviors) and to help offenders overcome their conflicts (i.e., internal and external) through the development of more accurate cognitions about themselves and their behavior. Policy makers and the criminal justice system dictate that the counseling services rendered to offenders should increase the public's protection. Ultimately, the success of correctional counseling or treatment revolves around reduction of reoffending behaviors. Failure is measured by recidivism rates as seen through additional legal charges and prosecution (Gendreau, Goggin, French, & Smith, 2006).

Regardless of a counselor's theoretical orientation, sound counseling in a correctional setting must aid offenders in the realization of their cognitions and how those distorted thoughts have maintained and perpetuated their crimes or criminal behaviors. This includes confronting the offenders' mechanisms of normalizing and rationalizing their actions, making them desirable and even reasonable within given circumstances (Cashwell & Caruso, 1997). A legal offender's rationale for deviant offenses can be derived from a host of irrational thoughts and beliefs, and counselors work to address these cognitive distortions. This process of addressing cognitive distortions involves challenging the attitudes and beliefs that maintain the behaviors. It also includes confronting the possible denial or minimization of the severity of the offense.

Court-Ordered Counseling

This section will briefly explore court-ordered (mandated) counseling and some considerations counselors should be aware of when engaging in this type of counseling. Court-ordered treatments can involve required inpatient and/or outpatient treatment and may even go so far as to involve mandates that offenders use medications. Rulings on mandated treatments must come from a judge or magistrate designated for these purposes within a given jurisdiction. Mandated treatments are court ordered, thus providing offenders with an external motivation to comply with proposed treatments.

One often-forgotten mandated treatment modality is university or college disciplinary sanctions against students. In these situations, counselors are asked to educate the student on the norms and rules of the campus (Kiracofe & Wells, 2007). The university holds the student's academic future as a means to get the student to increase compliance with the rules and norms of the campus.

Fully using the external demands placed on the client to receive counseling services may enhance treatment compliance. In other words, although a court-ordered client may be noncompliant and even lack motivation, a counselor should use the external demands of the court to create a sense that a problem may exist and may need to be examined. Often mandated clients are quick to agree that getting out of the arms of the justice system is their personal primary goal of treatment.

Another consideration in working with court-ordered clients is to assess a client's readiness for change and use this information to inform practice. A counselor must select interventions that correspond with the appropriate readiness for change stage. Prochaska (1999) constructed a developmental, stage theory based on a client's readiness for change. These stages are as follows: precontemplation, contemplation, preparation, action, maintenance, and termination.

- In the **precontemplation stage**, a client is not aware that a problem exists and often has little motivation to change any part of her or his current situation. The client may say things like, "I don't have a problem . . . this person . . . or this system has the problem."
- In the **contemplation stage**, a client is able to acknowledge that a problem exists, but is apprehensive about changing anything at this time. Often the client feels as if he or she is at a crossroads because positive and negatives of the behaviors are evident to him or her. The client may say, "I really must stop going out and partying. I know it is really hurting my marriage and my children, but I can't say no . . ."
- In the **preparation stage**, a client is getting ready to change. More ownership of personal responsibility is evident in her/his speech. A client might say, "I've really got to do something about this . . . this is serious . . . something has to change."
- In the **action stage**, a client begins to change his/her behaviors. The client believes that change is possible and acts on this belief.
- In the **maintenance stage**, a client continues to maintain the behavioral change. During this stage a client must avoid temptation to slip back into the old habit, old ways of being. A client in this stage needs to continually remind her/himself how much change has occurred. This stage requires new skills by the client to deal with and avoid relapsing.
- The **termination (or relapse) stage** is when the client returns to older behaviors and abandons the new changes. It is like "falling off the horse," and the best thing to do is to get right back on it. The ideal is that once relapse hits, then the preparation stage starts again. Ideally, the client will not revert back to the precontemplation stage.
- Another term, which is not part of Prochaska's (1999) original model, is the ideal of **transcendence**. This concept refers to the idea that after a good amount of time in the

maintenance stage, a client not only would not return to her/his old ways, but it would also seem abnormal for her/him to do so.

SELF-ASSESSMENT ACTIVITY 7.3 STAGES OF CHANGE

The following statements are from a potential client. Predict the specific stage the client is in using Prochaska's (1999) readiness for change model and prepare a possible response to each statement.

Statement 1: I know I need to stop drinking and partying with my friends . . . . It's really killing my chances at making my marriage work, but I don't know if I can.
Your Responses:
Statement 2: I don't have any problem . . . you should be talking to my husband . . . now he is the one with the problem . . . go talk to him.
Your Responses:
Statement 3: I can make this change . . . but it will not be easy, and I'll need a lot of support.
Your Responses:

These stages of change can be useful in conceptualizing work with any client populations where people have low motivation or are noncompliant clients. See Self-Assessment Activity 7.3 for examples of the stages of change.

TRANSFERENCE AND COUNTERTRANSFERENCE

Counselors must understand and be equipped to deal with transference and countertransference. These concepts are often associated with Sigmund Freud and the classic psychoanalysts, although these terms have recently become common vernacular in clinical supervision relationships and in the field of counseling in general. In this section, these two terms will be explained and presented in the context of real-life situations and scenarios. Self-evaluation will be discussed, and recommendations will be made on how to assess and deal with transference and countertransference reactions.

Transference

Transference, from a psychoanalytic perspective, is when a client projects onto the counselor the attributes, characteristics, and motives reminiscent of another individual (Milne, 1999). More simply, transference is the transferring of the emotions and feelings of the client onto the counselor. This transferring, or projecting, of the client onto the counselor is often based on a real entity, and the client will then respond to the counselor as if she or he is really that individual.

From a psychoanalytic perspective, there is benefit in the counselor transforming him or herself into a "blank slate" and being neutral in presentation. This neutrality allows a transference reaction to become probable thus providing rich therapeutic information. As transference reactions develop, counselors who work from a psychoanalytic perspective believe that repressed material and dysfunctional patterns emerge. With this underlying material exposed, insights may develop, with the client eventually relating to others in a healthier way.

Regardless of the counselor's theoretical orientation, transference can be used to increase the client's level of awareness. Once the counselor realizes that transference is occurring, the use of immediacy is an invaluable technique that can be used to address it. Essentially, immediacy is the counselor's intentional directing of the dialogue to focus on the "here and now" of the session; this moves the conversation to what is currently happening in the counselor–client relationship. Case Study 7.4 offers an example of some aspects of transference.

CASE STUDY 7.4

Karen

Karen is a 28-year-old Caucasian female currently in treatment for severe depression and relational issues. She is a known entity in the community because she has been in and out of a number of treatment facilities and has been diagnosed with Borderline Personality Disorder (BPD). In addition, she has a long history of self-injurious behaviors and some violent, threatening behaviors. Karen displays mixed emotions during the counseling sessions. This emotional polarity is perceived by the counselor as appropriate for an individual who has been diagnosed with BPD. She desires the counselor's attention, admiration, and unconditional regard. When she does not get this from the counselor, she has extreme emotional outbursts. On one such occasion she exclaims, "You never cared for me . . . . You never loved me . . . . Why did you even have me?" The counselor was then able to see that the client was transferring her turbulent relationship with her father onto the counselor. Karen eventually shared with the counselor that the counselor's beard was extremely similar to her father's, and often she would see this counselor as a warm father figure that she had never had in real life.

Questions:

1. How might you have dealt with this client, as she was transferring intense emotions onto you?
2. Write out a script for how you may have addressed this with Karen and how you would have utilized this opportunity to increase her awareness and address treatment goals.

Countertransference

Countertransference is the process of a counselor projecting attributes and motives onto a client based on the client's characteristics or material the client presents within sessions. This can occur for a host of reasons stemming from the counselor's past experiences and can affect counselors at all stages of their development. Often the counselor's first sign that countertransference is occurring is that he or she begins to perceive an internal shift in regard for the client. This shift is often incongruent with the presented material. For example, countertransference within counseling sessions is demonstrated by a counselor taking on too much personal responsibility for the direction of treatment, goals of treatment, and treatment outcomes. This often has an unintended effect on treatment outcomes, as it may invalidate clients' voices and echo to them that they are not able to direct, work on, or be an active member in their own treatment process.

Because countertransference involves the counselor's own internal process, sufficient awareness is needed for a counselor to detect and address it. Self-assessment and supervision are the most useful means to reveal and deal with countertransference. Reidbord (2010) provided counselors with the following four insight-oriented questions that can aid them in the self-detection of countertransference: (a) Is this reaction or feeling characteristic of the way you normally work with clients? (b) Is this reaction or feeling triggered by something outside (e.g., not related to) the client? (c) Is this reaction or feeling related to the client in some obvious way? and (d) Is this reaction or feeling uncharacteristic for the counselor and not evident or obvious to you? The fourth question is the one that sheds the most light on the subtle yet important dynamics of the client and what that material stirs within the counselor. The counselor or supervisor can use these questions to better understand where these reactions and feelings originate.

In addition, a counselor should use supervision to explore one's own unresolved difficulties concerning the client and the client's material. Sometimes counselors are unaware of countertransference, and the use of supervision can aid in its early detection. Often these reactions and feelings can originate from irrelevant characteristics (e.g., physical resemblance), interactional characteristics (e.g., verbally dominated as in a past relationship), by a prior experience or feeling toward a past client, or by material unrelated to the counselor–client relationship (e.g., a fight with a spouse, finances; Reidbord, 2010). Once the counselor becomes aware of where these reactions and feelings originate, the counselor can then identify and address countertransference. To begin to identify countertransference, consider the examples in Self-Assessment Activities 7.4 and 7.5.

SELF-ASSESSMENT ACTIVITY 7.4 IDENTIFYING COUNTERTRANSFERENCE

Is countertransference occurring within the counselor–client relationship in the following scenarios?

Scenario 1: You begin to meet with a client who has had intense trauma experiences involving horrific stories of abuse and neglect. She appears to appreciate your style and the way you create a therapeutic alliance as evidenced by the way she has quickly revealed a great deal of information so early in counseling. You begin to think, "If only this person had a different set of parents, a different upbringing, or maybe if she just knew someone who had shown her love and compassion. . . ." You begin to see her as a victim, and even muster the idea that she just needs to find someone in her life who could save her. If she could just find this person, it could help her heal and move on. . . .

    Question: Is countertransference occurring in this scenario? What could be done to address this situation?

Scenario 2: You have been meeting with a client who has been extremely depressed for the last 3 months. He has denied suicidal ideation, but continues to feel relatively immobilized by his feelings of "worthlessness" and "self-doubt." You have tried ACT (acceptance and commitment therapy) and solution-focused brief therapy as well as CBT. You find that you are starting to dread this appointment each week. You feel frustrated by your client's lack of progress and have found that you are avoiding talking about him during supervision. You always seem to have a more urgent case to discuss. You start to construct statements about the client like: He doesn't want to change . . . He is just resistant . . . No one can help this guy . . . He's hopeless. Then an even quieter voice starts to echo in your mind, "Maybe I'm not good enough . . . maybe I'm not experienced enough to help him."

    Question: Is countertransference happening in this scenario? What could be done to address this situation?

SELF-ASSESSMENT ACTIVITY 7.5 IDENTIFYING POTENTIAL COUNTERTRANSFERENCES

Part 1: Please reflect either historically or currently on the following set of questions.

- Historically
  - List the five most traumatic events that happened to you in your life before age 21 years.
  - List the five most traumatic experiences you have had since age 21 years.
  - List the five most life-altering events that took place in your family of origin.

- Currently
  - List at least five issues that you are currently wrestling with in your life.
  - List at least five issues that your family members are dealing with in their lives right now.

Part 2: Beside each item you have listed, discuss how these events may impact your ability to be objective and emotionally available for a client with a similar situation or problem.

Summary

In this chapter, issues associated with providing counseling to consumers from a variety of populations were addressed. All the populations have in common that their counseling needs are complex; all require that counselors are dynamic and thoughtful in considering their counseling approach. The information presented in this chapter provides a starting place for working with these populations. Counselors will need to conduct additional research and garner more information to ensure a solid understanding of these populations and their counseling needs.

When counseling maltreated children, many important considerations emerge. Among the most important considerations is having a thorough understanding of counselors' role as mandated reporters of child maltreatment. Counselors are not charged with investigating maltreatment and making determinations about whether maltreatment occurred, or if it will occur again. Our role is simply to ensure that we report suspected maltreatment. All counselors must have an understanding of state laws related to counselor reporting of maltreatment. Counselors must also not overlook or fail to report child neglect, the most common form of child maltreatment. Counselors must also vigilantly assess for ongoing maltreatment and report new incidents as warranted.

With regard to child maltreatment, this chapter also addressed the varied and layered effects of child maltreatment. Factors that may insulate some children from the ill effects of maltreatment were also addressed, and readers were urged to consider how these insulative or resiliency factors could be developed or promoted via counseling. It was highlighted that children who experience repeated, ongoing abuse may demonstrate developmental trauma reactions, which include symptoms that are unique from the more traditional trauma reactions that occur after an isolated trauma incident. Because children who are maltreated often need multiple supports and different levels of intervention, the importance of counselors working as part of a team was also discussed.

When counseling maltreated youth, it was emphasized that counselors' interventions should be grounded in evidence-based practices. These evidence-based practices include the use of structured, manualized, and empirically supported models over other methods of treatment (e.g., supportive counseling, play therapy per se). All counselors who work with children and adolescents should become familiar with at least one evidence-based treatment approach (e.g., trauma-focused cognitive behavioral therapy; Cohen et al., 2006).

Counseling issues associated with children who have unique learning needs were also addressed. Although every student has his or her own individual learning needs, additional considerations must be taken when working with those who have learning disabilities or giftedness. It is important to gain a firm understanding of their cognitive abilities and how these affect their overall sense of well-being. Thus, the student's academic identity must be achieved in context to their relationships with family, friends, teachers, and peers. This understanding can be used to inform the counseling interventions that will have the greatest positive impact.

Individual counseling can be an effective way to measure students' identities and can help identify the successes and struggles that are specific to them. However, to address students' needs, it is helpful to implement family or group counseling to create change in the context of the clients' real-life situations. Family therapy can be used to educate parents and relatives of the struggles faced by the student and can promote the presence of healthy supports for the student. Group counseling is especially helpful in addressing issues related to social skills and healthy development, with academic ability being just one part of students' larger personal identity.

Self-injury and issues associated with working with those who self-injure were also discussed in this chapter. Clients who self-injure can be personally activating to counselors, and as such, efforts must be made to ensure counselor personal reactions do not get in the way of effective clinical decision making. Counselors' fear of clients' accidental death and health risks associated with SI can lead some counselors to feel anxious about a client's SI and push them to stop self-injuring. Instead of focusing treatment on pushing a client to stop self-injuring, counselors are encouraged to enhance a client's desire to change (Kress, Drouhard, & Costin, 2010) through the use of motivational enhancement techniques. Peer-consultation, supervision, and education related to self-injury are helpful ways to ensure that counselors' personal reactions are monitored.

With regard to the treatment of self-injury, therapeutic approaches that emphasize problem solving, emotion regulation, and functional assessment and analysis of the behavior may be helpful (Klonsky & Muehlenkamp, 2007). Cognitive restructuring and a solid therapeutic relationship are also important to the effective treatment of self-injury (Muehlenkamp, 2006). Dialectical behavior therapy (DBT), and its emphasis on developing alternative coping skills, identifying obstacles to the use of alternative skills, and enhancing skill generalization outside the therapeutic setting (Linehan, 1993), shows promise in addressing self-injury.

Clients who are in relationships that involve intimate partner violence (IPV) are at a significant risk of being the victims of homicide, and as such, counselors working with this population are challenged with the additional task of considering and supporting their safety. Many people in IPV relationships may not recognize them as such, and counselors must be vigilant about assessing for IPV. Safety plans are an important tool that counselors can use to promote their clients' safety. A good safety plan highlights the client's role in making the safest decisions possible when managing violent situations (Kress et al., 2008). The importance of providing clients with information related to police protection, legal action, domestic violence shelters, community resources, and social supports is also an important element of safety planning.

With regard to treating victims of IPV, research suggests that PTSD is the most common mental disorder in this population (Golding, 1999). Exposure-based cognitive behavioral approaches are considered the best treatments for those who have PTSD secondary to being in abusive relationships (Johnson & Zlotnick, 2009; Kubany et al., 2004). Counselors are cautioned though that clients who are not yet living in safe living environments, or clients who are managing a great deal of chaos, may need to wait to begin exposure-therapy treatment, as cognitive exposure to past abusive incidents may be too agitating (Johnson & Zlotnick, 2009).

Substance abuse is a stigmatized mental health disorder in our society with many people believing that substance use and abuse is a matter of choice and willpower. The complexity of this disorder makes it difficult for the general population and even counselors to fully understand. Due to the complexity of substance abuse issues, high rates of comorbidity with other mental disorders, and high rates of relapse, counselors must be able to accept that multiple interventions over a long period of time might be necessary to produce positive change in this population.

More than half of all people diagnosed with substance abuse or dependence have at least one additional diagnosed mental health difficulty. These findings suggest that people initially begin to use drugs to alleviate the symptoms of their other mental health difficulties. As clients use substances to cope with losses that result from the substance use, a vicious cycle emerges, and substance dependence ensues.

Interventions that have been found effective with this population are motivational interviewing techniques, CBT techniques, and 12-step programs. Counselors who work with this population must have patience and perseverance. It will benefit counselors to assume the perspective of the client to understand the motivations for the substance use and his or her possible recovery. With this ability to understand the client's private logic, counselors might identify a helpful combination of interventions that will be helpful for each specific client.

Death and dying can be an uncomfortable subject, but death lies at the core of human existence. To better serve clients who are experiencing difficulties surrounding death and dying, counselors should take care to evaluate their own struggles and biases related to this natural part of life. Whether it is the client or a client's loved one who is experiencing death and dying, it is important to identify ways in which the individual's life was meaningful and positively impacted the world. Reminiscence

therapy allows clients to identify how they have used the skills and gifts given to them by their ancestors to leave a positive legacy with future generations. This intervention implements verbal storytelling to reduce depression in those who are dying as well as their loved ones.

Some clients encounter the impending reality of dying due to the developmental imperatives of old age. However, issues surrounding death and dying will also accompany a client's diagnosis of a terminal illness. Although distinct spectrums of issues are present in each situation, the five stages of dying developed by Kübler-Ross (1969) are an especially helpful framework for working with clients and their loved ones.

There is no standard way to identify the needs of those facing issues of death and dying, but it is possible to identify how to best help clients by empathically joining with their feelings and allowing them to direct you to the source of their struggle. Whether they are dealing with grief, guilt, denial, anger, or frustration, it is important to normalize clients' feelings and help them to understand that there is no correct way to deal with death and dying. Effective grief counselors have a healthy relationship with death and loss and are willing to serve as a nonjudgmental, helpful presence in their clients' struggles.

Because combat duty and exposure to combat has been associated with an elevated risk of mental health issues (Hoge et al., 2006), there is a significant need for professional counselors trained to work with this population (Jumper et al., 2006). As the exposure and the threat of exposure to combat increases, service members continue to display an increased risk of PTSD, major depression, substance abuse, and functional impairment in social and occupational settings (Hoge et al., 2006). Counselors need to consider that even the unknown potential deployment of a service member can create significant emotional ramifications that should be addressed in counseling (Hall, 2008).

Counselors must be ready to work with veterans in the following areas: grief and loss; reunion with family and/or children; posttraumatic stress disorder (PTSD) and related combat stress; family violence issues; alcoholism and substance abuse; and stress and anxiety regarding finances (Hall, 2008). Most of the evidence-based approaches are grounded in CBT approaches (Foa et al., 2009; Hall, 2008). CBT aids service members in forming connections between their thoughts, feelings, and behaviors. In addition, CBT assists in the reduction of PTSD symptoms (Foa et al., 2009).

Clients who are mandated to receive counseling often have a low motivation for change and are frequently noncompliant with treatment expectations. Mandated clients can include court-ordered clients, legal offenders, or even children and adolescents forced into treatment by guardians/caregivers. A counselor must consider ways to fully use these external demands to enhance the client's treatment compliance. A counselor, at a minimum, should create a sense that a problem exists and needs to be examined. In addition, a counselor must consider the client's readiness for change (i.e., precontemplation, contemplation, preparation, action, maintenance, and termination stages; Prochaska, 1999) and select interventions appropriate to that stage.

Legal offenders are frequently mandated to treatment and typically have a low motivation to change. Regardless of a counselor's theoretical orientation, counseling in a correctional setting must assist the offender in the realization of his or her cognitions and how those thoughts have maintained and perpetuated his or her crimes and criminal behaviors. The aim of this type of counseling is to reduce offenders' deviant behaviors through the development of their awareness of the connection between cognitions and behaviors and to confront distorted thinking.

Whether a novice or veteran, it is difficult for counselors to work with clients who lack a motivation to change. It is essential when working with low-motivated, noncompliant clients to create a climate of change and actively engage the client (Cohen et al., 2010). When considering a client's level of motivation, a counselor must evaluate whether a client is ready to change, is contemplating change, or is not even at a stage to contemplate change (Miller & Rollnick, 2002). In addition to assessing the client's level of motivation, a counselor must enhance the climate for change by creating a collaborative working relationship with the client through the agreement of shared goals and shared expectations of treatment.

Counselors must understand and be equipped to deal with the concepts of transference and countertransference. Regardless of the counselor's theoretical orientation, transference can be used to increase the client's level of awareness. Once the counselor realizes that transference is occurring, the use of immediacy is an invaluable technique that can be used to address transference in the counselor–client relationship.

Countertransference is when a counselor projects attributes and motives onto a client based on the client's characteristics or material the client presents within counseling sessions. This can occur for a host of reasons stemming from the counselor's past experiences and can affect counselors at all stages of development. Often the counselors' first indication that countertransference is occurring is that they begin to perceive an internal shift in how they perceive the client. This shift is often incongruent with the client's presented material. Often the counselor's reactions and feelings are rooted in irrelevant characteristics (e.g., physical resemblance), interactional characteristics (e.g., feeling verbally dominated as in a past relationship), by a prior experience or feeling toward a past client, or by material unrelated to the counselor–client relationship (e.g., a fight with a spouse; Reidbord, 2010). Counselors should consider using supervision to explore their own unresolved difficulties concerning the client and the client's material. Once counselors become aware of, through self-reflection or supervision, where these reactions and feelings originate, they can then identify and address countertransference reactions.

Answer Key

Case Study 7.2   1. d, 3. b.

CHAPTER 8

Multicultural Counseling and Its Multiple Applications

BY JOSÉ A. VILLALBA

PREVIEW

This chapter will enhance the reader's clinical experiences by exploring the historical and contextual nature of cultural sensitivity, examining the development of the American Multicultural Counseling and Development Multicultural Counseling Competence standards, delving into readers' self-awareness and the role their self-awareness plays when working with individuals identifying with different societal groups, and finally, emphasizing the benefits of working with clients from a strengths-based approach. To facilitate readers' heightened multicultural counseling competence while in their clinical placement, each of the four sections of this chapter will conclude with a series of self-assessment activities and case scenarios related specifically to the content of a particular chapter section. Furthermore, the case study included at the end of the first section will be carried throughout the chapter, allowing readers to explore many facets of a hypothetical "encounter with" and "treatment of" the case study client.

DEVELOPING CULTURAL SENSITIVITY: HISTORICAL AND CURRENT CONTEXTS

In 1991 Paul Pedersen acknowledged that Multicultural Counseling should be considered the fourth force of counseling and psychology (after Psychoanalysis, Behaviorism, and Humanism), and the fields have not looked back since. Because multicultural counseling is best carried out by competent and skilled individuals, the push for multicultural counseling competence of clinicians-in-training and mental health practitioners was operationalized shortly after Pedersen's proclamation. To this end, the major professional associations in counseling and psychology (e.g., American Counseling Association [ACA], American Psychological Association [APA]), as well as national credentialing organizations (e.g., Council for the Accreditation of Counseling and Related Educational Programs [CACREP], National Board of Certified Counselors [NBCC]) and state-level licensing boards all include multicultural counseling competence requirements in their bylaws, professional standards of practice and ethical codes. So with most in the field of mental health services advocating for the training and credentialing of multiculturally competent clinicians, why the need for this chapter and this information? Why not leave it at: "Okay. I got it. It's important. I learned about this in undergrad. And I've taken a graduate-level course on this topic. Besides, aren't we all just people, and counseling should focus on the individual?"

As the reader will see in the next few pages, the current "need" for this chapter, in this particular book, is to make sure that clinicians-in-training don't lose sight of the fact that multicultural counseling competence "looks" very different in a clinical placement than it does in books, vignettes, or films. People may think they have already learned, read, and experienced enough in a multicultural sense to relegate more information on the topic as "superfluous," but because the identity development of all clients is influenced by an intersection of their gender, race, ethnicity, first language, religion, sexual orientation, age, ability level, socioeconomic status, immigration status, and so on, the reader's experiences in their clinical placements are precisely the most opportune time to explore the meaning and manifestation of multicultural counseling competence. The information contained over the next few pages should help the reader better understand themselves, their clinical placement clients, and the impact that society has on working effectively with *all* current and future clients.

The process whereby clinicians-in-training grow as multiculturally competent counselors is, quite frankly, different from one trainee to the next. Individuals, in that they are all unique and special in their own ways, will experience multicultural issues from their own worldviews. And though Sue (1978) talks about the development of one's worldview as being unique, he also emphasizes, as have many others since then (e.g., McCarthy, 2005; Williams, 2003), the importance of the era in which one lives, or the city one grew up in, or the background of one's family, as all playing a role in an individual's worldview. In other words, though one's multicultural counseling competence develops at a personal level, it does so, not in a vacuum, but in a series of contexts that are, simultaneously, historical, political, economic, and social. It is within these four contexts, these four "lenses," that the reader must frame his or her cultural sensitivity. And, because it is quite difficult to separate one's cultural sensitivity outside the clinical placement from what happens inside the clinical placement, it becomes paramount for the reader to think of cultural sensitivity as something to which he or she must be attuned at all times.

Historical Context

What does the phrase, "all counseling is historical" mean to you? It is an important question to ponder, specifically as one struggles to find out about a client's history, whether it be his or her family of origin, experiences with peers, academic challenges, or work-related successes, to name a few. When it comes to multicultural competence, however, the phrase "all counseling is historical" also takes into account not only the history of the client, but also how a community's or society's or country's history has influenced the societal groups that make up the identity of the client in question. For example, working with a female client who is an Afghani refugee in the United States will require the counselor to, at the very least, consider how the many military conflicts in Afghanistan have affected the client's personal experiences. Furthermore, the counselor will also have to consider how the United States' past history and current policy toward Afghanistan can influence the perceptions of the client's neighbors, coworkers, or school peers, and how these perceptions may influence the relationship between the client and these individuals. This is not to say that counseling issues related to the client's country-of-origin's history may come up in counseling, but if they do, a multiculturally competent counselor will have already anticipated this possibility and will not shy away from talking about these issues related to the history of both nations.

Probably the most salient, negative historical context for health care, including counseling services, in the United States is the collection of injustices committed against African Americans, from as far back as the pre–Revolutionary War use of slaves in early colonization of what would become the United States of America, through the Civil War, Reconstruction, *Brown v. Board of Education*, and even the current manifestations of health disparities between African Americans and most other ethnic and racial groups (Asim, 2007; Kozol, 2005; Wicker & Brodie, 2004). It is America's ugly and historical treatment of African Americans (and members of other ethnic groups) that has further contributed to lower-than-average usage rates of mental health services, due to a mistrust of the medical and mental health system (Asim, 2007). The sadder and more troubling contexts of certain experiences of the African-American experience also have contributed to a stigma surrounding the use of formal mental health services in the African-American community (Wicker & Brodie, 2004). Counselors and counselors-in-training need not raise their hands and say, defensively, they are not the cause of these issues and that they do not represent the roots of this history; no one is blaming them. However, history, particularly with African Americans, influences mental health and reactions to mental health care, and these issues should not be overlooked for African Americans or any other societal group that may have been marginalized, oppressed, discriminated against, or persecuted.

Current Social, Political, and Economic Contexts

Though any of these three contexts can "stand on their own," social, political, and economic contexts are grouped in this section to encourage counselors-in-training to examine the intricate contexts of their clinical placement. Because each clinical placement and the clientele served by it are affected by the current political climate, social and community-based values, and economic realities, special care should be paid to assessing clients' reactions to these three contexts. These three contexts go so far as to also influence the public policies, budgeting, and provision of mental health services, which are unique to communities and municipalities.

Consider, for example, your current clinical placement setting. What city is it located in? What are some of the local or regional customs? What are the predominant places of worship in this community? What are the racial and ethnic demographics of this community? In other words, how would the "local society and local social norms" influence what is seen as normal and abnormal? The responses to these questions and related questions provide a backdrop of not only the type of counseling issues that clients might present with, but also how potential clients view their current situation.

Similarly, consider the political climate, not only of your local community but also the country at large. For example, what are the hotly debated political issues in your community? Are there controversial public policy debates going on (e.g., immigration reform, availability of financial aid for first-generation college students, construction of a local jail, anti–gay marriage amendment to the state constitution) that clients may feel strongly about, on either end of the political debate? Is there state-level funding of character education programs? What about the current state of health care and health care reform or funding, particularly as it relates to funding mental health services? And, for that matter, are there local, state, or national elections that are arousing strong feelings for or against political parties and ideologies? Again, the responses to these questions may influence some of the questions you ask of your clients, as well as the type of services you provide.

And, finally, the economic status of your clients, as well as national and international fiscal policies, will have some bearing on your experiences at your clinical placement. Consider how your client's income plays a role in meeting economic and/or personal-social needs. What stressors are associated with unmet needs related to income status? How has the local economy helped or hindered your client's ability to remain employed? To what extent is your client's level of education, family history, and health status influenced by past and present economic status? How does the local and state economy support or hinder the ability for your current clinical placement to remain in business, or the funding of the positions held by current colleagues and/or supervisor(s)? How does the local and state economy affect the number of clients on your caseload, or the school-counselor-to-student ratio in your school? As with political and social contexts of counseling, economic contexts have some bearing on the types of issues clients present with, their ability to follow-through on clinical goals, and, in the case of access to health insurance, whether or not potential clients can seek out and pay for the help of a mental health professional.

Exploring Historical and Current Contexts in Developing Cultural Sensitivity

The following experiential activities are designed to facilitate the reader's personal exploration of the importance of contexts in his or her current clinical site. As you read the self-assessment activities and case studies, bear in mind the complexity of each response, and challenge yourself to be genuine about your feelings and experiences. It also helps if the reader can envision current or anticipated clients when reading these activities, in an effort to make the activities and case studies that much more salient. Finally, you should complete all the activities and case studies in a journal to get into the routine of collecting and revisiting multicultural insights gained from the information provided in this chapter, the content and experiences shared in a graduate-level multicultural counseling course, and the overlap between multicultural awareness and the reader's experiences in his or her current clinical placement.

Assessing Your Preconceived Notions

Self-awareness, as you'll see in the second section of this chapter, is one of the most important aspects of multicultural counseling. Therefore, throughout this chapter, you will encounter a series of self-awareness questions, scenarios, and activities that will challenge how much you know about yourself in relation to multicultural counseling issues, as well as where and how you have acquired this knowledge. In this introduction to "Assessing Your Preconceived Notions" please complete Self-Assessment Activities 8.1 and 8.2.

SELF-ASSESSMENT ACTIVITY 8.1 PERCEPTIONS OF CULTURAL SENSITIVITY

In the first section of this chapter, you have been provided with historical events that have influenced the need for health and human service providers, such as counselors, to be more culturally sensitive. Some individuals and societal institutions (like the media and the educational system) use the term "politically correct" or "PC" to be synonymous with "cultural sensitivity." The term "PC," as some of you may know, can have some positive and negative associations. In the space provided, please list at least three ways in which you think being culturally sensitive or "PC" is a <u>positive</u> thing in a clinical setting, and three ways in which you think being culturally sensitive or "PC" is a <u>negative</u> thing in a clinical setting.

Positive connotations of being culturally sensitive:

_____

_____

Negative connotations of being culturally sensitive:

_____

_____

SELF-ASSESSMENT ACTIVITY 8.2 ECONOMIC, POLITICAL, AND SOCIAL ISSUES

In this section, we have explored the current contexts of cultural sensitivity, specifically the reasons why now, just as in critical times of our nation's cultural history (e.g., the Women's Suffrage Movement, the Civil Rights Movement, Farm Workers Rights), it remains important for counselors and human service providers to stay up-to-date on current economic, political, and societal issues. To this end, please list two economic, two political, and two societal factors in your local community (either where you are currently attending school, or perhaps your hometown if you are going to school away from home) that would impact that work that you are doing with clients at your current clinical placement. Then, pick one of the six factors listed and write down your own feelings about why this particular factor is "the most difficult factor for you to deal with in relation to your work with a particular client."

Two political factors influencing your work with clients:

_____

_____

Two economic factors influencing your work with clients:

_____

_____

(continued)

Two societal factors influencing your work with clients:

_____

_____

The most difficult factor to address in relation to your work with a particular client and why:

_____

_____

_____

Assessing Your Multicultural Competence

The following case will be used throughout this chapter. What follows will be a description of a client similar to one you may come in contact with in your current clinical placement. Immediately following the case study you will find two case scenarios to consider related to developing cultural sensitivity (Case Scenarios 8.1 and 8.2). Refer back to this description as you address the case scenarios, both in this section and throughout the chapter. The case scenarios will provide you with opportunities to process different aspects of the case as you seek to increase your multicultural counseling competence. To this end, please make sure to write your reactions to each case scenario on a separate sheet of paper, in an effort to provide you (and peers) with an account of efforts to become more multiculturally counseling competent.

> Consider the case of Sara, to which we will return from time to time throughout the rest of this chapter. Sara is a 22-year-old client of African-American and Latino descent, who identifies herself as a "recovering Catholic" because she no longer practices the religion her parents raised her in. She was born in the United States, as was her mother; however, her father was born in Costa Rica. Her parents divorced when she was 12 years old, during a time that was quite tumultuous for her. She is the oldest of three children in her family, and neither of her parents have children from other relationships. Sara is a first-generation college student, who will be graduating with a Bachelor of Science in Nursing (BSN) degree in the next few months. The university she attends is close to her mother's home, where she has lived since her parents' divorce. Sara has come to talk with you because she feels that the counselors at the university counseling center on campus are only there to "help the rich kids who live on campus" and because she really needs help with talking with someone "impartial" about her fears. Specifically, she reports being "anxious and afraid" of getting a job soon after graduation, as well as worrying that she will "never be happily involved in a relationship." She indicates that she's particularly worried about her potential for a healthy romantic relationship because her parents are not together any more, like "most of her other friends," and because she is bisexual and is unsure how future partners will feel about her sexual orientation. She indicates that both her parents are aware and "fine" with her sexual orientation, though her father's mother (i.e., paternal grandmother) is not pleased with her sexual orientation and has not spoken to her in the 3 years since she shared her sexual orientation with her family, which she did through Facebook. Between her immediate and long-term concerns of getting a job and finding a person to have a "meaningful and long-term relationship with," you are asked by her to "please help me get my life in check before it all comes crashing down around me."

CASE SCENARIO 8.1
Sexual Orientation

What would you do if Sara were to ask you to help her "rationalize" why her grandmother is so against her sexual orientation, particularly because she states that others in her family and support network have made "so many strides in the past few years to recognize different types of couples and partnerships, yet not my grandmother"? Related to this question, how capable do you think you would be of providing the client with a response as free as possible from your opinions or reactions to individuals with similar or different sexual orientations than your own, keeping in mind that you may experience countertransference with the client if you and she share any societal group membership(s) (e.g., same gender, similar ethnic background, both are first-generation college students, both are Catholic)?

CASE SCENARIO 8.2
Multiracial Client

Assume this is your first time working with a client with a multiracial heritage, in this case, African American and Latino. Therefore, because it is your first time working with a multiracial client, you seek supervision from a colleague in your practice. Based on what we have reviewed in this section of the chapter with regard to the historical and current contextual nature of multicultural counseling, how would you respond to your supervising colleague posing the following question: "So, how do you think your client's current goals to find a job right after graduation can be facilitated or complicated by the current economic data?"

THE AMCD MULTICULTURAL COUNSELING COMPETENCIES: ATTITUDES AND BELIEFS, KNOWLEDGE, AND SKILLS

In the spring of 1992, the *Journal of Counseling & Development* published the seminal article by Sue, Arredondo, and McDavis titled "Multicultural Counseling Competencies and Standards: A Call to the Profession." The article was a direct offshoot of the Association for Multicultural Counseling and Development's (AMCD) production of a set of professional standards of practice for clinicians working in an ever-diverse American society. This article came to be seen as the first comprehensive collection of what multicultural counseling competence entailed and how a counselor and counselor-in-training may practice from a position that demonstrates cultural sensitivity. In addition, as the title of the article suggests, the article served as a "grounding point" for the counseling profession to focus on as it strived to become a profession that would serve individuals from all backgrounds. As a "grounding point," the authors wished to not merely outline what multicultural competent clinicians should do, but also what professional counseling organizations, credentialing bodies, and training programs and institutions should do to ensure the training and professional development of multiculturally competent students and learners.

At the core of the AMCD Multicultural Counseling Competencies—which have, to this point, been adopted in one way or another by various professional organizations and credentialing bodies such as the American Counseling Association, the American School Counseling Association, the American Mental Health Counseling Association, and the Council for the Accreditation of Counseling and Related Education Programs (CACREP)—is that clinicians must have self-awareness of their cultural attitudes and beliefs, knowledge of clients' worldviews, and willingness to learn and apply culturally relevant skills and techniques for clients from various backgrounds. A total of 31 competencies are organized under these three general areas, and the competencies are designed so that clinicians can demonstrate an ability to learn about their attitudes and beliefs and those of their clients, to gain empirical and anecdotal knowledge of themselves and clients, and to acquire skills and convey those skills in a manner that is culturally sensitive. This tripartite model of multicultural self-awareness, knowledge, and skills has served as the foundation of many multicultural counseling courses, as well as an effective method for organizing the types of activities clinicians need to engage into continue their growth as ethical and effective practitioners.

Counselors-in-training can increase their understanding of multicultural competence by reviewing both the Sue, Arredondo, and McDavis (1992) and Arredondo et al. (1996) articles. The Arredondo et al. article, published in the *Journal of Multicultural Counseling and Development*, is particularly useful in that it presents explanatory comments and ideas for what counselors, counselors-in-training, counseling instructors, and counseling supervisors can do to improve their multicultural counseling competence. For example, the first multicultural counseling competency under Counselor Awareness of Own Cultural Values and Biases is "Culturally skilled counselors believe self-awareness and sensitivity to one's own cultural heritage is essential" (Sue et al., 1992, p. 484). In the article by Arredondo et al. (1996), seven different explanatory statements are provided, including "[the counselor] can identify the culture(s) to which they belong and the significance of that membership including the relationship of individuals in that group with individuals from other groups institutionally, historically, educationally, and so forth" (p. 56). As is evident from this example, this explanatory statement simultaneously provides a desirable learning outcome for a counseling student, as well as a course or lesson objective for a multicultural counseling course. Because a great portion of Arredondo et al. is devoted to providing the reader with these "ideas" for operationalizing the standards as they were presented by Sue et al. in 1992, it permits the reader the opportunity to devote more time and energy into planning how best to meet the objectives presented in each competency standard.

One last justification for reviewing the Arredondo et al. (1996) article would be the explanation of the dimensions of personal identity model. According to Arredondo et al., an individual's identity is composed of three "dimensions." In Dimension A are factors such as age, gender, language, race, and social class. Next, Dimension B includes less physical and more social attributes such as religion, marital status, geographic location, and citizenship status. Finally, Dimension C is represented by historical moments or eras that provide a context for one's identity. All told, each of these three dimensions and the dimension-specific factors play a role in not only an individual's personal-social development, but also the types of strengths and attributes he or she may possess and the types of counseling concerns he or she may have. Therefore, it benefits a multiculturally competent clinician to consider these three dimensions when thinking about his or her own self-awareness, gaining knowledge of potential clients, and developing a culturally relevant counseling skill set. To this end, the Arredondo et al. article provides various scenarios and examples of when and how the dimensions of the personal identity model can serve to inform clinicians and clinicians-in-training—scenarios that the reader may experience or may have already experienced in his or her current clinical placement.

As with most seminal works, the AMCD Multicultural Counseling Competence Standards were not and have not been universally endorsed. One of the most ardent and cohesive critics of the Multicultural Counseling Competencies was Stephen Weinrach. Specifically, Weinrach and Thomas (2002) presented several reasons why the AMCD Competencies were not useful or necessary to the profession and argued against making them "required" in ethical codes and standards of practice. Some of their main arguments include that the AMCD Competencies are not rooted in empirical validity; that the AMCD Competencies ignore how individuals are actually similar (an etic approach) in an effort to point out how individuals are different (an emic approach); that the original article published by Sue et al. in 1992 focused exclusively on working with clients who are Native American, Latina/o, African American, or Asian American and did not address gender or age or sexual orientation differences, among other societal groups; and perhaps most important, the authors felt that forcing counselors and counselors-in-training to gain multicultural competence might provide them with the false sense of security that they are adequately trained to work with a variety of clients, when this may not be the case. These kinds of ideas and perspectives are what Patterson (2004) used to question "Do we need multicultural competence?" (p. 67).

Considering that the tripartite aspect of the AMCD Multicultural Counseling Competencies stresses the importance of self-awareness, knowledge, and culturally relevant skills, it is imperative that mental health experts and those training to enter the field explore these three concepts in relation to the AMCD Competencies themselves. By doing so, the clinician and preservice student demonstrate an ability to intentionally and deliberately view their present and future clinical placements through the lens of the AMCD Competencies. More specifically, attention should be paid to which of the competencies and exploratory statements are most in line and least in line with the reader's feelings toward the AMCD Competencies. It is precisely because there is some debate about the salience and application of the AMCD Competencies that each clinician and counseling student is encouraged to take the time and effort to become familiar with the information presented from all sides of the debate.

Exploring the AMCD Multicultural Counseling Competencies

The following experiential activities are designed to facilitate the reader's personal exploration of the tripartite aspects of the AMCD Competencies. Specifically, the self-assessment activities encourage readers to place themselves in situations in which they may not be too knowledgeable. The case scenarios further expand on this line of question by considering the many "layers" to the case of Sara, and how working with a client like Sara can push the reader to consider the tripartite notion of cultural competency and perhaps even the dimensions of personal identity model.

Before beginning the exercises in this section, consider a more general idea of exploring the AMCD Multicultural Counseling Competencies. Specifically, read the Arredondo et. al. (1996) article and identify 2 or 3 of the 31 competencies in which you already feel proficient, and 2 or 3 that you see as areas of growth. After you have produced this list, take into account how the competencies in which you are proficient might facilitate the current clinical experience, and identify how the competencies listed as needing to be developed might serve as a limitation in the current clinical experience. This activity is a good precursor for embarking on the more detailed questions and topics presented in the next few pages. Now that you have read about the impetus for infusing self-awareness into multicultural counseling competency presented by Arredondo et al., let's explore a series of questions for enhancing your self-awareness by completing Self-Assessment Activities 8.3 and 8.4.

SELF-ASSESSMENT ACTIVITY 8.3 EXPERIENTIAL ACTIVITIES FOR SELF-AWARENESS

List five experiential activities you could engage in that would help you learn about yourself and preconceived notions *while* you learn about members of other societal groups. For example, suppose you are a Methodist Christian and you want to learn more about Judaism. You want to learn more about Judaism because you recently learned that the Old Testament is, essentially, the Jewish Torah. So you decide to stop by a local synagogue, speak to the rabbi, and ask her if it would be okay for you to come to one of the services. The rabbi emphatically extends an invitation to the following Friday Night Shabbat service, and you decide to attend. At the end of the service, which you are surprised to find out is not on Sunday morning, you take the time to write down some things that you learned from your first experience with a Shabbat service and how these similarities to and differences from your own faith have helped you learn more about yourself and explore your preconceived notions about Jews and Judaism. With this type of activity in mind, use the following five lines to list the type of experiential activities similar to this one that you would complete. You do not need to elaborate on how they would affect you, just the type of experience that you might have.

Experiential Activity 1: _____

Experiential Activity 2: _____

Experiential Activity 3: _____

Experiential Activity 4: _____

Experiential Activity 5: _____

SELF-ASSESSMENT ACTIVITY 8.4 LEARNING FROM BEING WRONG

For this activity, reflect on a time when you were proven wrong about someone because of a preconceived notion you had about his or her gender, ethnic group, second-language ability, sexual orientation, and so on, and how being proven wrong propelled you into

(continued)

learning more about the individual and the societal group(s) he or she was a part of. And, if applicable, share how this experience of personal growth and learning more about others may have affected a particular skill set needed to work with members of this group (e.g., if you were a summer camp counselor and your newfound knowledge about members of a particular group helped you better empathize with or provide services to children who were members of this particular group).

In the following pair of scenarios, you will explore how self-awareness, knowledge of other societal groups, and the establishment of culturally relevant interventions all contribute to the multicultural counseling competence of the clinician. Use Case Scenarios 8.3 and 8.4 as a way to practice what you would say and do when similar opportunities and challenges present themselves in your current clinical experiences.

CASE SCENARIO 8.3
Dissatisfaction

Sara presents a particular "challenge" for you as a client because her direct goals of finding a job after graduation and a fulfilling relationship are affected by several factors outside your control or hers. During your fourth session with Sara, you decide to share these feelings of being challenged with her immediately after she tells you that she's "unhappy with the progress in counseling up to this point" because she's no less "scared or anxious" than she was after the first session. Although there is nothing "wrong" with your response to Sara's opinion of the counseling process to date, she seems put off by your response. Based on what you know about her history and societal groups membership, how might you improve your initial response to her concerns about being unhappy with counseling?

CASE SCENARIO 8.4
Sexuality and Religion

Suppose that Sara told you in your fifth session that she has decided to confront her father and her paternal grandmother about her relationship with her paternal grandmother. However, she would like your suggestions for best talking with them both about how hard the last 3 years have been on her to be so "distant" from her paternal grandmother. She specifically asks you to provide her with tips for convincing her paternal grandmother that "there's nothing wrong with being bisexual." She also mentions that her paternal grandmother also is upset that Sara has "left the teachings of the Church," and that there's no way she's ever "stepping foot in another church as long as she lives." What are your specific reactions to Sara's request that you help "convince" her paternal grandmother on both aforementioned points? And, in addition, what are your feelings with regard to folks "being bisexual" and "never stepping foot in another church," particularly if your views differ from Sara's? How would you reconcile differences in opinion if they do exist *or* how would you maintain objectivity if there is "100% overlap" between your opinion and Sara's?

CONFRONTING ONESELF: SELF-AWARENESS, OVERCOMING BIAS, AND WORKING WITH DIFFERENCES

Although none of the seminal articles in multicultural counseling competence (e.g., Sue et al., 1992; Arredondo et al., 1996) make claims about which of the three parts of the tripartite model are "most important," the information contained in these articles makes clear that clinicians and those in training who fail to acknowledge their cultural identity development, examine their biases, and challenge their notions of comfort will struggle to become multi-culturally competent service providers. Hodges (2011) further expanded on this point by indicating that self-awareness is the first step in developing multicultural competence. From this notion it is quite logical to extrapolate that one must first explore one's own experiences, thoughts, beliefs, values, assumptions, stereotypes, prejudices, and behaviors *before* starting to learn more about members from different societal groups or applying one's clinical skills to diverse populations. As a result, exercises wherein the reader pushes her or his own understanding of what it means to them to be a member of particular ethnic, racial, gender, economic, religious, or sexual orientation groups (to name a few) is paramount to providing culturally appropriate and ethical mental health care.

Expanding Our Notion of Self-Awareness

Where do your ancestors come from? How many generations of your family have lived in the United States, or your particular community? What are the facets of your religious or spiritual beliefs that are most important to you? What privilege do you think your sexual orientation affords you, if any? How have you been discriminated against, and how did you know? When have you discriminated against others, to whom, and what was the context for your behaviors and/or thoughts? Your responses to questions like these go a long, long way toward increasing how much you know about yourself, particularly as a cultural being. This notion of viewing yourself as a cultural being is one that needs to be considered before moving on to personal biases, concepts of privilege, and working with individuals who are different from you or the members of your family.

For years now, researchers and writers in the counseling and psychology fields have argued that we are all cultural beings (e.g., Helms, 1995; Moore-Thomas, 2014; Phinney, 1996). Another way to phrase this is that we all have a culture that influences the way we see the world and our place in that world, specifically in the communities in which we reside, the places in which we work, and the schools we attend. Holding this statement to be true, however, depends on a couple of factors. First, the individual must be willing to see "culture" (e.g., customs, routines, patterns of behavior, ideas handed down from generation to generation, mental schemas, traditions) in many aspects of one's identity. Second, the individual must also acknowledge that culture and how each aspect of culture is affected by messages received from a variety of individuals, including family members, peers, colleagues, and acquaintances, as well as social systems and institutions, such as the media, the judicial system, and the educational system. Combined, these two factors allude to one's ability to self-reflect, which is the cornerstone of self-awareness (Jun, 2010). Once one's ability to self-reflect is taken into account, it becomes much more likely that individuals will become more self-aware, not merely about their own thoughts, beliefs, values, ideas, interests, and skills, but also about the rationale and history behind their thoughts, beliefs, values, ideas, interests, and skills. For counselors, in particular, being self-aware of the cultural lens with which we develop our worldviews is an integral part of being an effective counselor and a more compassionate individual (Sue, 1978; Sue et al., 2007).

The one thing to keep in mind when expanding one's view of oneself as a cultural being is that this realization oftentimes comes with both pleasant and unpleasant consequences (Jun, 2010). Specifically, as a mental health practitioner begins to more intentionally and deeply examine all aspects of his or her cultural identity through increases in self-awareness, it becomes more likely that he or she will find out some deep-seated notions of prejudicial thoughts, or discriminatory behaviors in their past, or the notion that cherished loved ones or pivotal moments in their upbringing were actually manifestations of racism, or homophobia, or socioeconomic privilege. These unpleasant realizations not only clash with the mental health practitioner's notion of what it means to be a helping professional; he or she also may even react to these unpleasant emotions by negating or minimizing the more pleasant realizations, such as a lifelong devotion to altruistic endeavors, or a genuine desire to be an advocate for social justice, or the not-so-common ability to listen to others with dignity and respect.

Overcoming Biases

Once a counselor-in-training or clinician begins to assess and learn from exercises in self-reflection and self-assessment, there exists the possibility that the individual will become so debilitated by unpleasant realizations, that person will be rendered incapacitated to work with future clients. Of course, this should not be the goal of increasing self-awareness as a cultural being. So, to put it in more simplistic terms, how do providers move on without forgetting what they have learned about themselves?

One of the main ways of not stalling the cultural competence developmental process is to not react defensively to the realization that most, if not all, of us have room for growth as culturally sensitive individuals. Exploring our defense mechanisms and realizing our biases and privilege actually increase our abilities to empathize with others, while minimizing the likelihood of intellectualizing reasons behind the biases (Jun, 2010). Examples of intellectualization of the "why" behind our biases include perhaps dwelling too much on the historical nature of racism, or the notion that one has not been the oppressor, or that society is to "blame" for a family member's racist remarks, which keep the practitioner mired in trying to "explain away" the biases, rather than owning up to them and moving on. Anderson and Middleton (2005) elaborated on the importance of "acknowledging and moving on" by encouraging mental health practitioners and those in training to focus more on how to minimize the influence of their biases on their work with clients or potential clients.

An equally effective method to "move on" from acknowledging one's biases is to further immerse oneself in situations that challenge or negate the biases (Hodges, 2011; Hogan-Garcia, 2003). Also known as cultural immersion activities, an individual can make a concerted effort to immerse herself or himself in knowledge, locations, rituals, experiences, literature, cultural festivals, and even foods; the level of how "deep" one is willing to go is truly up to the individual. Some of the activities in this chapter are aimed particularly at increasing the reader's opportunities in this realm, such as visiting places of worship or interacting with members of different societal groups. But the onus truly is on individuals to seek safe experiences outside of their comfort zone to increase the opportunities for growth and learning. The counselor or counselor-in-training may then use this growth toward enhancing work with diverse clients in clinical placements.

Working with Differences

If Hodges (2011) indicated that increased self-awareness and self-reflection are the first steps in multicultural counseling competence, then the obvious next set of steps is to learn more about the individuals with whom one will work, as well as the development of culturally relevant counseling skills. It is in these steps that the counselor and counselor-in-training begin to seek more information, more professional development, and more informal and formal meetings with individuals from different societal groups, all done in an effort to provide the clinician with a foundation for the implementation of clinical skills that will be effective with a wide range of clients and potential clients.

Many writers in the area of multicultural counseling have produced textbooks, articles, and webinars (e.g., Hays & Erford, 2014; Robinson-Wood, 2013; Sue & Sue, 2012) with specific information about a variety of societal groups, including, but not limited to, African Americans, Native Americans, individuals with disabilities, women, older adults, and Muslims. This literature is a great starting place to learn about the types of obstacles and strengths that potential clients representing these societal groups can bring into the counseling relationship. Summative literature of this type also typically provides the reader with a synopsis of research studies that indicate which counseling theories and techniques are better suited for members of certain societal groups. Furthermore, information on identity development and the role that culture plays in the identity development of individuals often is included in this line of literature (e.g., Helms, 1995; Phinney, 1996). Therefore, one can see how consuming this type of information can be very helpful, particularly to novice mental health professionals, as they strive to provide ethical services to clients. However, both the novice and the seasoned counselor should always look at this type of information as a "starting point" for working with diverse clients, lest one runs the risk of acting on or providing services that are or come off as stereotypical. The well-intentioned and multiculturally competent counselor and counselor-in-training are ones that take an open mind to the clinical site, rather than a mind-set that assumes all they need to know about counseling diverse others was learned in a book chapter or from attending a 3-hour professional development workshop. Having an open-minded attitude will go a long way toward establishing effective clinical rapport, as well as getting "buy in" from potential clients to the benefits of engaging in a therapeutic relationship with the mental health worker.

Exploring Self-Awareness, Overcoming Bias, and Working with Differences

The following experiential activities are designed to facilitate the reader's personal reactions to confronting self-awareness and moving beyond the pleasant and unpleasant "aha moments." The self-study activities are designed to illicit self-reflection, which means the reader must be ready for a bit of "honest soul searching." Because "soul searching" can happen in a variety of places and spaces, notice the wide range of possibilities presented in the self-study activities. Building on self-study results, the case scenario encourages the reader to move to the next step of overcoming biases and working with differences by asking the reader to reconsider the case of Sara, the many layers and facets of Sara's identity and presenting counseling concerns, and where the reader might find some challenges as Sara's counselor. As has become the underlying pattern to this chapter and these experiential activities, think of these activities and scenarios within the context of your current clinical setting to increase the usefulness and applicability of your responses.

Up to this point, you have explored your self-awareness and preconceived notions about members of different societal groups. But where do these preconceived notions come from, and what influences the development of your self-concept and self-awareness? Self-Assessment Activities 8.5 through 8.7 are designed to further expand your self-awareness in an effort to better facilitate your abilities to connect with others and improve your current clinical experiences.

SELF-ASSESSMENT ACTIVITY 8.5 SOCIAL INFLUENCES

Think of all the people in your family and group of friends who have contributed to your preconceived notions, both positive and negative, regarding members of different societal groups. Chances are that the number of folks in your family and friend circles, coupled with the many different societal groupings, would make for quite the exhaustive list. So, in the name of efficiency, it would probably be helpful to pick one particular societal group of which you are not a member (e.g., Muslim women, undocumented immigrants, poor families, students from wealthy families, Asian American college students, older adults in the workforce). Now, once you have identified the particular societal group you want to focus on, use a separate sheet of paper to list at least five individuals who are close to you who have influenced how you view members of this group. Next, answer the following questions:

- What was it about these individuals close to you that contributed to the level of influence they had on your opinion of this particular societal group?
- Where do you think they received their ideas about members of this societal group?
- How "right" or "wrong" were they in their opinions of these individuals?
- How did you establish they were "right" or "wrong," and how did your feelings about members of this societal group change once you had time to question certain information for yourself?
- Have there been opportunities in your current clinical experience to work with individuals of this particular societal group?
- How do you think the influence of those close to you has affected your work with members of this societal group in your clinical placement?

SELF-ASSESSMENT ACTIVITY 8.6 MEDIA INFLUENCES

Apart from those close to you, messages we see and hear from the media can have great bearing on our opinions and preconceived notions. For this activity, pick one media source (e.g., television, radio, social networking, Web-based content) that you depend on for information on a regular basis. Now, over a weeklong period, "log" on a separate sheet of paper how many times you notice receiving a "stereotypical" message about members from different societal groups. The group or groups you select, how you choose to "code" messages, their frequency, their duration, and so on is up to you; however, the focus should be on heightening your awareness of the effect of these messages on how you come to construct, "validate," and "negate" your preconceived notions of members of different societal groups. Finally, similar to Self-Assessment Activity 8.5, conclude this activity by reflecting on your work with societal groups at your clinical site and how the media influences your perceptions of members from particular societal group(s) at your clinical site.

SELF-ASSESSMENT ACTIVITY 8.7 CHALLENGING YOURSELF

The final activity in this section is designed more like a "call to action" in that it challenges you to engage in your future self-awareness as it relates to multicultural experiences. In the space provided list five ways you plan to challenge yourself to become more self-aware, specifically about your preconceived notions of members of societal groups, even groups of which you are a member. Think of these self-awareness (SA) exercises as both things you can do in the present **and** in the future, with the end goal of maintaining a high level of multicultural counseling competence (MCC).

Current/future SA-MCC exercise 1: _____

Current/future SA-MCC exercise 2: _____

Current/future SA-MCC exercise 3: _____

Current/future SA-MCC exercise 4: _____

Current/future SA-MCC exercise 5: _____

With the emphasis of this section of the chapter on self-awareness and confronting one's biases, Case Scenarios 8.5 and 8.6 challenge the reader to explore the types of "cultural buttons" that potential clients may "push." The contents in Case Scenario 8.5 are particularly controversial in the United States and tend to energize individuals on both sides of the argument. Clinicians who fall on either side of the argument have the potential to have their effectiveness stunted. As a result, now is the time for you to explore your reactions to "hot-button issues," particularly because the availability of supervision in the university and clinical placement setting provides ample chances to seek out feedback from peers and experienced supervisors.

CASE SCENARIO 8.5
Immigration Status

After meeting for seven sessions, Sara mentions to you that she would like to share something she's "never told anyone before." She shares with you that one of the reasons she decided to move in with her mom after her parents got divorced was because her dad was in the country as an undocumented worker, and she was scared that if she "picked her dad over her mom," she could "get in trouble" if immigration officials ever found out that her dad was in the United

States without proper documentation. She also confides in you that, in retrospect, what scared her more than anything else was that her mother was the one who "planted this seed" about her dad possibly being "deported" and that, in hindsight, this initial information from her mother has driven a long-term wedge between Sara and her father. Knowing what you know now about her dad's undocumented status and her mother's decision to share this type of information with a 12-year-old, how does this information coincide with your own feelings about individuals in the United States without proper documentation, in addition to individuals who would make parental decisions that you may be in agreement or disagreement with? Further, how might your reactions to Sara's new information impact your future work with Sara, if at all?

CASE SCENARIO 8.6
Countertransference

As with Case Scenario 8.2, you have decided to seek supervision with a colleague after your seventh session with Sara. Specifically, you want to share some countertransference issues that you are having with Sara, and you want to be able to explore ways to mitigate the impact of this countertransference. Considering that Sara is a member of several societal groups (e.g., woman, mixed heritage, first-generation college student), what might be some countertransference issues you would discuss with your supervisor, and what recommendations do you envision your supervisor might give you to limit the effects of your countertransference on your clinical work with Sara? Keep in mind that countertransference can have effects where you either overidentify with the client (which limits your ability to be as objective as possible) or negatively judge the actions of your client or their loved ones.

COUNSELING DIVERSE CLIENTS FROM A STRENGTHS-BASED PERSPECTIVE

One of the reasons why AMCD, as documented by Sue et al. (1992), initiated the need for multicultural counseling competence was because traditional psychology was built on the medical model, which assumes that individuals are "sick" and therefore need to be "cured." As one reviews the earliest psychology theories, such as psychoanalysis or behaviorism, it is easy to see how many theorists viewed individuals as "unwhole," "neurotic," or "programmable," which tends to imply that if clients were to follow a certain set of suggestions, or make certain behavioral changes, then these "deficits" could be more easily resolved and/or minimized (Arrendondo et al., 1996). Even the less deficit-based theories, such as Humanism and Existentialism, have a certain set of assumptions, such as the need to find meaning for oneself or the need to be autonomous, which may run contrary to notions of collectivism that readers may have learned about in their multicultural counseling courses (Seligman & Reichenberg, 2010). So, to work with individuals from a strengths-based approach essentially entails that the counselor and counselor-in-training acknowledge that all individuals have the strengths or abilities to solve their own problems and to persevere.

Social Capital as a Framework for Strengths-Based Perspectives

Adding the notion of cultural sensitivity to this framework means that an individual's race, gender, ethnicity, first language, socioeconomic status, age, ability level and challenges, sexual orientation, religion, and so on all contribute to an individual's strength, and that membership and awareness of these societal groupings may provide the client with access to unique skills, perceptions, experiences, and traditions that can facilitate their own mental health and holistic well-being. One way of acknowledging the strengths and benefits of societal group membership is to consider the notion of social capital. Though the origins of social capital as it is used in the literature can be traced to Hanifan (1916), contemporary references to the term typically are credited to Bourdieu (1977). According to Bourdieu, every individual is engaged in a set of relationships, or social networks, that provide her or him with social capital. This social capital is somewhat synonymous with economic capital, so that the social capital generated by group memberships affords each and every one of us with "currency" that helps us solve problems, provides us with a system of support, helps us learn new information, and so on. However, just like some "capital" is valued more than other "capital" in certain situations (e.g., think about the fact that you cannot use the euro to purchase goods in the United States, rather that currency must be exchanged and the rate of exchange varies along several economic variables), the social capital provided to individuals by their religion or gender or ethnicity may be of "more value" in, for example, the home or local community, than it is in a school or work setting. Clients from all walks of life and who value their societal group membership(s) have experienced the valuation and devaluation of their social capital in various settings and may even share some of their unpleasant reactions to and experiences with social capital devaluation in a counseling setting. One example of this devaluation may be a Spanish-speaking client who is learning English as a second language and tells of a time when she was ridiculed at school for speaking in her native language, but who also tells of the time she was offered a receptionist job at a doctor's office solely because of being bilingual and can therefore speak with both English- and Spanish-speaking patients.

With this notion of social capital in mind, the challenge for counselors and counselors-in-training becomes twofold. First, the clinician must be attentive to times when a client's social capital has been minimized, ignored, or worse, viewed by others as a deficit (particularly those in "power," such as a boss, teacher, professor, administrator, politician, or family member). Second, and more salient to the notion of counseling from a strengths-based approach, the clinician must find opportunities in the clinical relationship and discourse to value the social capital that the client possesses. This does not mean the counselor begins to "romanticize" the client's social capital (e.g., "How great is it that you are bilingual!" or "It must be wonderful to have a Jewish mother and a Catholic father because you celebrate both Passover and Easter, right?"); but, rather, that the counselor makes aware to clients the potential for social capital in their societal group memberships and to challenge clients to see if they, too, are aware of their social capital's potential for addressing mental health concerns.

Eliciting Client Strengths through Strengths-Based Counseling

One of the hallmarks of person-centered counseling is the notion that all clients are experts on their own experiences, which provides perspective and insight to address the issues that bring them to counseling (Seligman & Reichenberg, 2010). With this philosophy as a core belief of most counselors and counseling training programs, believing in the client's personal potential to solve some of his or her counseling issues can oftentimes be rooted in some cultural, gender, ethnic, or language proficiency lens through which the client views the world and community. The challenge for the counselor and counselor-in-training is how to elicit the client's ability to share and acknowledge strength he or she can draw from societal group membership, without (a) negating the client's presenting problems, or (b) discrediting the reality that, for most members of different societal groups, group membership oftentimes is at the root of several stressors, negative experiences, or systemic oppression. For example, African Americans have experienced oppression because of their race; some Latinas/os are assumed to be in the country as undocumented residents, even though they were born here; Asian Americans are assumed to be intellectually more capable and, therefore, steered more toward careers in science, technology, and math, even though individuals may want to pursue careers in the arts or humanities. Saleeby (2008) provided a framework for providing strengths-based services that helps the counselor avoid the two aforementioned concerns. According to Saleeby, strengths-based approaches require the clinician to (a) believe that every individual, group, family, and community has the internal strengths needed to solve its problems; (b) believe that the most hurtful and difficult experience can at least present individuals, groups, families, and communities with chances for growth and for problem-solving initiatives to evolve; (c) believe that all individuals are in a process of perpetual growth and development, which points to a limitless potential for growth; (d) believe that clients are best served when counselors collaborate instead of directing clients about what to do and not to do at all times; (e) believe that an individual's, family's, and group's environment and surroundings can provide resources to assist them in problem solving; and (f) believe that individuals, families, groups, and communities are more likely to see the strength in the counselor and the clinical experience if they trust in the genuineness of the counselor. Rothman (2008) expanded on Saleeby's suggestions by stressing the importance of viewing a client, group, or family's strengths from a cultural context, acknowledging that cultures help give meaning to certain events.

For example, if working with an African-American client, a counselor can listen to the individual's concerns, while being attentive to the cause of the problems. If the client fails to indicate that the client's family is at the root of the problems, but rather indicates feeling lost or isolated in the current environment, the counselor may elect to ask the client about the importance being placed on the family unit, collectivism, and support from one's extended network. Because research and the literature on counseling African-American clients points to the power of extended family support for addressing counseling concerns, the counselor is facilitating the client's ability to draw on the social support system through the lens that African Americans, in general, place great importance on the support of nuclear and extended family members (Robinson-Wood, 2013; Rothman, 2008). Inherent in this example is the notion that the counselor must have a working knowledge of the literature as it pertains to counseling African Americans, as well as a level of self-awareness that helps the clinician not "assume" that all African-American clients are going to focus on their family as a source of support. Similar examples of strengths from a cultural perspective also include the bilingual abilities of immigrant clients, the resiliency of many individuals with disabilities to navigate physical and/or systemic obstacles, and the ability for those with economic limitations to find the strength and perseverance to work one or more jobs to provide for their families, particularly during challenging economic times. Again, the emphasis is not for the counselor to ignore the counseling concerns of the client, but rather to understand the successes and resiliency of the client.

Exploring Counseling from a Strengths-Based Perspective

The following experiential activities are designed to facilitate the reader's ability to "see" strengths in present and future clients, where clients may have "seen" only deficits or, at the very least, obstacles. Though the activity and scenarios are designed as "culminating" experiences to this chapter, the challenge for the reader is to use these exercises as templates for experiencing current and future clinical settings, settings that continue to become more and more diverse as our society continues to become more and more culturally rich with diversity. The final self-assessment (Self-Assessment Activity 8.8) is the wrap-up experience to help solidify how much you have learned about yourself in this process and how to continue to push yourself to learn even more through a commitment to a lifelong pursuit of self-awareness activities and the ability to process these experiences.

SELF-ASSESSMENT ACTIVITY 8.8 REPRESENTATIVE CLIENT

Write down the "name" (for confidentiality reasons, use a pseudonym) of the student or client at your current clinical site who you think represents the type of clients you would like to work with the most once you secure postgraduation employment. Next, write down all the different societal groups of which this individual is a member, starting with the group that you think is the most "dominant" factor of the individual's identity. Third, for each societal group, jot down two preconceived notions you had about the particular group, whether these notions are positive or negative. Fourth, write down how your preconceived notions of these particular societal groups positively and negatively influenced your work with the client in question, paying particular attention to the rapport you developed with the individual, the clinical goals you established with the individual, and the type of theoretical orientation you decided to use with this individual. Fifth, share at least three strengths that you now "see" in your client that you may not have "seen" prior to your self-reflection. Sixth, in what ways have you "grown" as a

(continued)

counselor-in-training from your experience with this client, particularly as you've focused on your level of self-awareness in relation to becoming a more multiculturally competent professional counselor? And, finally, how do you plan to "not forget or take for granted" what you've learned from this clinical relationship so that it continues to inform your professional progress and growth after completion of your training program?

A strengths-based approach to multicultural counseling competence calls on the clinician to help the client realize personal strengths and attributes. This is not done in a naïve, myopic manner that circumvents the client's need to talk about fears, inabilities, or concerns, but, rather, in an effort to balance the client's opportunities for growth, success, and accomplishment. Therefore, these last two scenarios (Case Scenarios 8.7 and 8.8) provide you the opportunity to replace possible "deficit-based thinking" with "strengths-based approaches" for working with Sara, as well as present and future clients.

CASE SCENARIO 8.7

Termination

After 9 sessions with Sara, you both realize that the clinical goals have been met and that the time to terminate is upon you both. You decide at the end of this 9th session that the 11th session will be the last one. Even though Sara agrees that the time to terminate the counseling relationship is at hand (in fact, she initiated this line of talk at the beginning of session 9), she still feels a bit anxious about not coming to see you on a regular basis. She no longer feels worried about getting a job after graduation because she has accepted a job offer to work as a nurse for a hospital about 40 miles from home. However, she still feels that her grandmother is no closer to reconciling with her, and she continues to worry about never finding a fulfilling relationship. What might you say to reframe her current worries, based on what you have discussed with her over the past 8 sessions? What are your reasons for pinpointing specific examples of her "strengths," particularly as doing so relates to your own growth as a multiculturally competent counselor over the past few weeks?

CASE SCENARIO 8.8

New Perspective

At the conclusion of the 11th session, Sara thanks you "for everything you've done." You, in turn, say, "you're welcome," and you proceed to thank *her* for all that she's taught you. She appreciates your comment; however, she is intrigued by what exactly it is that you've learned from Sara. As a result, how would you respond to Sara's following, and final, question: "If you don't mind me asking, and I know we are about to part ways, what exactly have I taught you over the past few months that you didn't already know? And thanks for answering my question; it means a lot to me."

Summary

The contents of this chapter, as well as the recommended activities and scenarios, are intended to help the reader get the most out of the clinical placement. Because social, cultural, economic, political, and historical factors all influence the counseling relationship, getting the most out of the clinical placement runs parallel to striving for multicultural competence. To miss opportunities to grow as a multiculturally aware clinician is not only a disservice to the student, but also to clients and colleagues.

Developing cultural sensitivity from historical and current contexts helps the clinician demonstrate honor and respect for experiences of members from different societal groups, as well as the events shared by clients' family and ancestors. Acknowledging and seeking the influence of these contexts on the lives and mental health of clients also positions the culturally competent counselor as a model to other colleagues and mental health practitioners of how to provide culturally respectful service. Part of serving as a model for other mental health practitioners is a commitment to exploring one's own preconceived notions of certain societal groups different from those of which one is a member. As a result, developing treatment plans and establishing treatment goals with clients within the historical, political, economic, and social contexts of a client's reality is one way to demonstrate an intentional development of multicultural counseling competence in a clinical internship setting.

The Association of Multicultural Counseling and Development, through the Multicultural Counseling Competencies (see Arrendondo et al., 1996; Sue et al., 1992), provides clinicians-in-training with clear ideas and standards for providing culturally relevant services in practicum and internship settings. These 31 competencies are organized around clinicians being aware of their own attitudes and beliefs (and their origins), knowledge of members of various societal groups, and developing skills that manifest as culturally appropriate interventions. This tripartite model of multicultural competence, coupled with considering the relevance of Arredondo et al.'s (1996) dimensions of personal identity model, serve as the mental health clinician's springboard for a commitment to multicultural counseling competence.

If there is a first step to the aforementioned springboard, it would be the clinician's and counselor-in-training's need to engage in exercises that stimulate self-awareness. As Hodges (2011) pointed out, self-awareness is the first step toward multicultural counseling competence. For this reason, before a counselor gets too involved or even bogged down in overintellectualizing why members of certain societal groups act in certain ways or choose certain options, the practitioner must pursue activities that increase personal insight. Framing this insight in a genuine manner while confronting potentially unpleasant realities related to stereotypes held by members of other societal groups and related to one's family of origin, is critical to conveying to clients genuine empathy and a willingness to be with the client. Additional work on the part of the clinician to explore the meaning of privilege, times when they have been discriminated against unfairly (or even gained an unfair advantage), and

their own ethnic, racial, and gender identity development (to name but a few societal groups) should serve to enhance the client–clinician relationship, while further cementing the clinician's role within the internship setting as a multiculturally competent counselor.

Although overcoming one's biases is neither a "final step" toward multicultural counseling competence, nor some sort of singular cathartic event, it is nevertheless an important component of providing culturally appropriate services in practicum and internship settings and beyond. Although this chapter includes many different components of biases and methods for overcoming them, it is important to remember that mental health practitioners who react defensively to accusations of behaving in, for example, a racist or sexist manner by clients or colleagues hinder their ability to work effectively with clients and colleagues. Furthermore, mental health practitioner trainees can work to overcome their biases by working with those different from themselves, as they increase their exposure to the experiences, history, customs, and lessons of others. As a result, cultural immersion activities—from those that place the practitioner in an "observer" role to those that provide an opportunity to have a participatory role—are pivotal ways that practitioners can demonstrate their desire to make connections with clients from all backgrounds.

Working with clients from all backgrounds from a strengths-based approach, whether in practicum and internship settings or after graduation, is one of many ways to provide culturally appropriate counseling services. Considering the social capital that all clients and coworkers bring to clinical and professional relationships is an effective way to frame strengths-based counseling approaches. However, all clinicians should remember the importance of balancing the concepts of social capital and providing services from a strengths-based approach with validating the obstacles and negative experiences of clients, for which Saleeby (2008) provided a useful framework. Therefore, clinicians-in-training are encouraged to see all clinical opportunities as openings to practice a strengths-based approach to counseling services.

The content provided in this chapter is but a supplement to the reader's lifelong commitment to the counseling field and the many, many individuals and families who will assist in the professional journey. And, as an added "bonus," the information can help the reader make more meaningful connections in her or his personal life as well, a life that is no doubt enriched by the cultural fabric that continues to cover the schools, campus, and communities in which we all work and live.

CHAPTER 9

Assessing and Intervening with Clients in Danger and Crisis

BY LINDA FOSTER, PAUL HARD, LAURA L. TALBOTT, AND MARY L. BARTLETT

PREVIEW

The focus of this chapter is on assessment and intervention of clients in crisis. Counselors must be prepared to assess and intervene with clients who may be a danger to themselves (i.e., suicidal) or others (i.e., homicidal) or who have experienced traumatic events due to either natural disasters or man-made events. Topics of suicide, homicide, and large-scale shock can be uncomfortable for counselors-in-training, so we have included self-assessment examples and activities to help you gain insight and create a personal philosophy for working with these issues. Also included are Voices from the Field from seasoned professionals to help counselors-in-training learn firsthand from practicing counselors who have vast experience in these areas.

THE IMPORTANCE OF TRAINING IN RISK ASSESSMENT AND SUICIDE AND CRISIS PREVENTION

One of the most traumatic and stressful events that can occur during the counseling relationship is the loss of a client to suicide (Baird, 2010). Research (Granello, 2010) showed that as many as 71% of counselors will encounter a suicidal client during their career and that nearly one fourth of professional counselors have worked with at least one client who completed a suicide. For counselors-in-training, it is vital that training in the assessment of suicide risk is included in preparation programs. For counselor education programs, accreditation standards guide the curriculum and provide rigor and uniformity in training future counselors. The importance of suicide risk assessment and crisis intervention is supported by the Council for Accreditation of Counseling and Related Educational Programs (CACREP, 2009). Suicide prevention and crisis intervention are mentioned throughout the 2009 CACREP standards in several key areas, including (a) Helping Relationships, (b) Counseling, Prevention and Intervention, and (c) Assessment, and this includes both knowledge and skills and practice areas. As a result, this chapter will cover how to assess both suicidal and homicidal clients, identify best-practice crisis intervention strategies with clients, and provide activities to help you assess your views of suicide and ability to work with suicidal or homicidal clients.

Suicide is the 10th-leading cause of death in the United States (Whiston, 2013). Professional counselors must have the ability to accurately assess a client's risk of suicide because it is an essential component of prevention. Given the staggering statistics around death by suicide, including suicide attempts, interns and practicum students can and should be prepared to thoroughly assess and intervene with clients who present with suicidal ideation. Before you read the next section, use Self-Assessment Activity 9.1 to assess your knowledge and perceptions of suicide prevalence.

SELF-ASSESSMENT ACTIVITY 9.1 SUICIDE PREVALENCE

Before reading the next section, answer the following questions according to your current knowledge and perceptions of suicide prevalence in the United States.

1. How many suicide attempts are made each year?
2. How many suicide attempts occur every minute in the United States?
3. How many attempts are made each year for every suicide completed?
4. Do females or males attempt suicide more often?
5. Of the group that attempts suicide the most, at what frequency does this behavior occur?
6. Which age group attempts suicide most frequently: children, youth, or adults?
7. Among college students, what is the most common means used to attempt suicide?
8. Among all suicide attempts, what method is most common?
9. Are sexual minorities (e.g., gay, lesbian, bisexual, or transgender) more likely to attempt suicide than their heterosexual counterparts?

Facts about suicide attempts: And the answers are . . .

1. It is estimated that approximately 500,000 suicide attempts occur each year.
2. It is estimated that one attempt occurs each minute.
3. It is estimated that for each death by suicide in the United States there are 25 attempts.
4. Females attempt suicide more frequently than males.
5. It is estimated that females attempt suicide three times more frequently than men.
6. Youth attempt suicide more frequently than children or adults.
7. The most common form of suicide attempts among college students involve either jumping from a structure or hanging.
8. Firearms are the most common means of suicide across the United States.
9. GLBT persons are not more likely to attempt suicide than their heterosexual counterparts. Although some studies suggest there are higher numbers of suicides among GLBT youth, there are no studies that suggest an increased likelihood due to sexual orientation.

Juhnke and Granello (2005) indicated that suicide is now ranked as the fourth-leading cause of death in the United States for those ages 18 to 65 years. Although the statistics reflect an increase in the number of suicides in the United States, the statistics do not reflect the impact that suicide has on survivors—those left behind after losing a loved one to suicide. Peripheral damage to families and friends is estimated to be almost 1 in 60 Americans (Laux, 2002).

Effective assessment of suicide risk is essential knowledge. Despite best efforts to adequately assess clients for suicide risk, one is never completely certain that a client will not attempt or complete suicide. Still, suicide risk assessment is the first step in understanding clients' difficulties, coping skills, and social support systems (Juhnke & Granello, 2005). Suicide risk assessment is essential to identify treatable risk factors, protective factors, and warning signs that guide counselors in selecting and using interventions.

VOICES FROM THE FIELD 9.1   The Suicidal Mind, by David Litts, Director, Science and Policy, Suicide Prevention Resource Center

Let your clients know you're not afraid to go there. Their suicidal thoughts may be the thing about them they are most afraid to share—even with you, their counselor. You must convey to them in your words, your posture, and sometimes even in your silence, that you are willing to discuss the forbidden topic, something they may well have never revealed to anyone. You must show them you are completely comfortable with the subject and above all, nonjudging. They need you to accept their suicidal thoughts and desires as part of who they are, recognizing that to them, the thoughts make perfect sense. Until you do this, your opportunity to really help them will be minimal.

The assessment process for suicide risk relies on your understanding of the mind-set of clients with suicidal ideation. Suicidal behavior is very difficult to study, for various reasons; sadly, chief among these reasons is the fact that those who complete suicide are not available for any type of assessment or research. Reasons that lead a person to consider suicide generally involve hopelessness and helplessness, a sense of not belonging, and a perception of oneself as a burden (Van Orden et al., 2010).

Historically, Shneidman (1993), founder of the American Association of Suicidology (AAS), coined the term *psychache,* which refers to a state in which an individual experiences extreme and excruciating psychological pain that intensifies the perceived need to take one's own life. The mind aggregates a wide array of negative emotions that perhaps trigger pain, including shame, anxiety, rejection, guilt, threat, unhappiness, and fear-based pressure. The pain experienced by an individual in the state of psychache makes consideration of death by suicide a viable option, and although not all suicidal persons experience psychache, this notion explains the rationale for ending one's life (Shneidman, 1996). Suicidologists agree there are a series of factors that converge, including biological, social, and environmental. Along with those factors, often there is an interpersonal storm that occurs in an individual who becomes suicidal, and the element of psychological chaos and culmination of events leading to death by suicide is difficult to comprehend (Joiner, 2005; Joiner, Van Orden, Witte, & Rudd, 2009; Peterson, Luoma, & Dunne, 2002; Shneidman, 1996, 2004).

The interpersonal theory of suicide further expounds on psychache and describes that the pain resulting from one's own death is perhaps worth more than his or her life. Causal factors associated with an individual's desire to die by suicide may result from self-perceptions of being a burden to others or feelings of disconnection or nonbelongingness (Joiner et al., 2009). Further, acquisition of fearlessness toward death and tolerance of self-inflicted pain may contribute to one's growing capacity of suicide completion. There is an intersection between the factors of burdensomeness, belongingness, and acquired capacity that may overwhelm the psychache, thus resulting in a fatal outcome (Bartlett, Siegfried, & Witte, in press).

Cook et al. (2006) stated that understanding what drives people to suicide is the first step in the counselor's ability to intervene and to gain respect and empathy for clients with suicidal thoughts. Practicum students and interns oftentimes have extreme difficulty putting themselves in the place of a suicidal client. Examination of how one might plan and complete suicide can afford practicum students and interns with a unique chance to understand the emotional and spiritual turmoil involved in suicidal thinking. Understanding the mind-set of a suicidal client will assist in selecting interventions and enhance counselor empathy for clients with suicidal ideation. In addition, practicum student and intern self-awareness of the client's experience will assist in creating interventions and enhance counselor empathy for clients with suicidal ideation.

Part of what complicates the understanding of the suicidal mind is the many misconceptions that permeate society and even the counseling profession. Some commonly identified myths about suicide that have been debunked include (Granello & Granello, 2007; Joiner, 2005):

- Discussing suicide will lead a client to go forward with a plan to die.
- Only severely mentally ill people die by suicide.
- Suicide is a hereditary trait.
- Those who threaten suicide are just seeking attention.
- Suicide is an impulsive act and occurs without warning.
- Suicide is an act of cowardice.
- Suicide is selfish.
- People who die by suicide don't make future plans.
- There is nothing that can stop a person if he or she really wants to die.
- Most suicides occur around the holidays.
- Once a person gets through a suicide crisis (or attempt) there is no more danger.

It is important for you to evaluate the degree to which myths have impacted your understanding of the suicidal mind. The practicum and internship experiences are a unique educational component allowing you to explore the facets of working with suicidal clients. Practicum has been characterized as a "highly individualized learning experience" (p. 30) and promotes an understanding of self, biases, and one's impact on clients (Boylan & Scott, 2009). During the practicum and internship training, students are challenged to view their own patterns of thinking and their own characteristics that may impede the counseling relationship. Further, when students examine their feelings, values, background, and perceptions, practicum and internship can provide enhanced self-awareness. As a result, insights gained contribute to professional growth and development of knowledge.

As mentioned earlier, most counselors will eventually be faced with the care of a suicidal client, a family member struggling with supporting a loved one who has suicidal thinking, or survivors of suicide. It has been suggested that one way to be prepared for client suicide is to be trained early in one's counseling career. Counselor educators debate on how to best provide this training, and various methods have been proposed to enhance student awareness and knowledge about suicide (Juhnke, 1994; Juhnke & Granello, 2005; Laux, 2002). Based on supporting professional literature, examining your values, thoughts, and feelings helps accomplish this goal. Use Self-Assessment Activity 9.2 to begin thinking about your beliefs about suicide.

SELF-ASSESSMENT ACTIVITY 9.2 BELIEFS ABOUT SUICIDE

1. Why do you think people die by suicide?
2. What are your beliefs about suicide?
3. What have you learned about suicide in your life?
4. What type of person kills oneself?
5. Who do you know that has died by suicide?
6. What is your emotional reaction to suicide?

Self-awareness of your attitudes, feelings, thoughts, and values must be addressed in regard to suicide, not just in the training experience, but throughout your professional counseling career. Practicum students and interns may not expect, and therefore may not be prepared for, problems such as suicide or sexual and physical abuse. Initially practicum students and interns may experience extreme distress when such problems are presented. Practicum and internship can provide the opportunity for students to recognize their own reactions and, through supervision, move through their distress.

ASSESSING CLIENT SUICIDE RISK

Although addressing psychache is fundamental to the treatment of suicidal persons, a practicum student or intern may consider that the presentation of symptoms is complex and may include identification, understanding, and mitigation. The use of a multisymptom approach is at the core of effective work with suicidal clients and begins with the assessment process (Granello & Granello, 2007; Shneidman, 2005). Although counselors are not able to predict which client will attempt or die by suicide with complete accuracy, if the situation were to arise, a practicum student or intern should have taken the necessary steps to meet the standard of care in the profession, which includes performing risk assessments and implementing an appropriate treatment plan (Simon, 2002). To provide comprehensive care, counselors should take care to assemble a complete client profile by infusing a risk assessment early on, and throughout the case work to identify warning signs; elicit risk and protective factors to make intervention decisions; elicit information about imminent risk, ideation, and behavior to identify lethality; obtain records to complete the client profile; and consult with experienced practitioners so treatment decisions are not made in isolation (Lee & Bartlett, 2005; Shea, 2002; Suicide Prevention Resource Center and American Association of Suicidology [SPRC/AAS], 2008).

Risk Factors, Warning Signs, and Protective Factors

As mentioned previously, part of the client profile involves gathering information about risk factors, which are those aspects of a client's life that may place the client in a higher risk category but may not necessarily presuppose suicide. Therefore, practicum students and interns must be aware of potential risk factors for suicide and engage a client in conversation to elicit risk factors. Practicum students and interns can find additional information about risk factors, warning signs, and protective factors on the website of the American Association of Suicidology at http://www.suicidology.org (SPRC/AAS, 2008; Worchel & Gearing, 2010). Warning signs are different from risk factors. When warning signs are noted, imminent danger is likely indicated (SPRC/AAS, 2008). It is also important to evaluate protective factors that exist in the client's life. Protective factors strengthen and shield a client from increased suicide risk. Exploring protective factors can yield information the practicum student and intern can use for a rich discussion regarding matters that impact the client's risk. The more protective factors a client can identify, the more fortified a person is against the risk for suicide. Protective factors include, but are not limited to, items such as family and support systems, spirituality, community connections, children, dependents, or a significant other (Granello & Granello, 2007; SPRC/AAS, 2008).

Indicators that suicide is being contemplated may range from overt statements to more veiled remarks. The practicum student or intern should bear in mind that assessment should be based on a holistic examination including the content of client remarks, affect, and other aspects of process. It is not uncommon for clients to make statements that seem passive, but are actually indicators that they may have suicidal ideation. Being alert and tuned into such statements is a way for practicum students and interns to pursue a discussion about suicidality so that an evaluation can be accomplished. A few examples of veiled comments include: "It's all going to be better soon." "It's not worth it." "It doesn't matter." "This is too hard." "I can't do this anymore."

Comments that are more direct may include: "I don't want to live." "I want to die." "I can't live this way." "I (or my family) would be better off if I were dead." "I want to end it all myself." According to the SPRC/AAS (2008), a counselor can begin inquiring about suicide with the following questions: "Have you ever felt that life was not worth living?" and "Did you ever wish you could just go to sleep and not wake up?" Then follow up with specific questions that inquire about thoughts of death, self-harm, or suicide, including: "Is death something you've thought about recently?" and "Have things ever reached the point that you've thought of harming or killing yourself?" and "Do you want to kill yourself?" Whether the client makes a veiled threat or a direct comment, practicum students and interns should not presume to understand what the client means. Asking the client for clarification and detail is critical. Following the protocol of the counseling site is also essential to the safety and care of the client as is consulting with a supervisor to determine the next step in providing quality care.

Evidence-Based Suicide Risk Assessment

Suicide assessment should be clear, unambiguous, direct, and nonjudgmental. It is critical to ask the direct question, "Are you suicidal?" or "Are you thinking of death by suicide as an option?" If asked in a genuine, neutral, open manner, the client will most likely respond honestly. This core question begins a conversation required for an effective clinical suicidal assessment. It should be understood that even a clear denial to the question requires follow-up. It is a clinical error not to ask direct questions (Worchel & Gearing, 2010).

In assessing a client for suicidal ideation, examine these seven areas: (a) demographic data, (b) identified problem and symptom history, (c) current suicidality, (d) suicide history, (e) family and peer suicide history, (f) risk factors, and (g) protective factors. The more detailed the assessment of these areas, the greater the likelihood that an effective plan and subsequent interventions can be implemented. However, it is recognized that it is not always possible to obtain information in all these areas, which makes the assessment process a necessary ongoing event (Rudd, Cukrowicz, & Bryan, 2008).

When examining the seven primary areas, the practicum students and interns should be aware that evidence-based assessments exist and should be used with all clients, rather than relying on best clinical impressions. There are 12 underlying principles of suicide risk assessment proposed by Granello (2010). The principles are not hierarchal (i.e., following a first to last order), and practitioners will develop their own process of implementation.

Suicide risk assessment (a) is unique to each person; (b) is complex and challenging; (c) is an ongoing process; (d) errs on the side of caution; (e) is collaborative; (f) relies on clinical judgment; (g) takes all threats, warning signs, and risk factors seriously; (h) requires asking tough questions; (i) acknowledges that assessment is treatment; (j) tries to uncover the underlying message and pain; (k) is done in a cultural context; and (l) is documented.

The application of risk assessment frameworks begins with assessing for past suicidal behavior, which is often the most potent predictor of subsequent suicidal ideation, suicide attempts, and death by suicide (Bartlett, Siegfried, & Witte, in press). The Suicide Risk Assessment Decision Tree Interview developed by Joiner et al. (2009) is widely endorsed because it is empirically supported. The decision tree involves assessing three "core" indicators of suicide risk: past suicidal behavior, current suicidal desire and ideation, and current resolved plans and preparations. These core indicators guide the practicum student or intern in determining a plan of action based on evaluated risk. It should be noted that with all other risk factors being equal, having resolved plans and preparations for suicide is more concerning than a client expressing only suicidal desire and ideation. A typical interview would include the following questions, moving through the aforementioned interview steps:

1. ***Assessing History of Suicidal Behavior:***   Have you attempted suicide in the past? How many times? Methods used? What happened? Do you have a history of self-injury?
2. ***Assessing Suicidal Desire and Ideation:***   Have you been having thoughts or images of suicide? Wanting to be dead? How often do you think about suicide? What reasons do you have for dying? For continuing to live?
3. ***Assessing Resolved Plans and Preparations:***   When you have these thoughts, how long do they last [look for preoccupation]? How strong is your intent to kill yourself on a scale of 1 to 10, with 1 meaning not at all and 10 meaning definitely? Do you have a plan for how you would kill yourself? Do you possess the means? Do you think you will have an opportunity? Have you made preparations for an attempt? When do you expect to do it? How scared do you feel about making an attempt?
4. ***Assessing Other Significant Findings:***   Has anything especially stressful happened to you recently? Do you feel hopeless? How do you cope when you are feeling badly? Has anyone in your family made a suicide attempt or died by suicide? What are your thoughts and feelings about that attempt/suicide event? Do you feel connected to other people? Live alone? Who do you call when you are feeling badly? Do you believe you are a burden to those significant in your life? In what ways do you believe you contribute meaningfully to those around you?

In addition, the interviewer determines if the client has adequate social support, if there is a presence of any psychopathology, if the person has responsibility to or for others, if the client has cultural and religious beliefs against suicide, and if the client has good problem-solving abilities (Joiner et al., 2009).

Assessment Instruments

A specific assessment instrument is one part of the overall assessment process. A multitude of instruments can be used to assess suicidality. Both the number and complexity may make selection difficult for a practicum student or intern. It is recommended that practicum students and interns have a discussion early into their field placement with their site supervisors regarding preferred suicide risk assessment inventories. In the event the site does not have a preferred instrument, the practicum student or intern should consult a course instructor for recommended evidence-based tools. Factors to consider in selecting an assessment instrument include availability, cost, ease of use, ease of interpretation, and empirical validation. Instruments for use with children, teens/adolescents, adults, and the elderly can be located and evaluated at:

- Buros Center for Testing: Mental Measurements Yearbooks at http://www.unl.edu/buros/
- Neurotransmitter.net: Psychiatric Rating Scales for Suicide Ideation at http://www. neurotransmitter.net/suicidescales.html
- The American Association of Suicidology: Translating Suicide Research into Practice at http://www.suicidology.org/web/guest/current-research

Determining Risk Level

Often, difficulty assessing clients with suicidal thinking involves determining perceived risk level. In part this is because there are no absolute, scientific categories of suicide risk; rather, suicide risk can exist along a continuum (Worchel & Gearing, 2010). The practicum student or intern is encouraged to glean information from the Suicide Risk Assessment Decision Tree Interview to categorize the suicide risk as *low, moderate,* or *high.* Ordinarily, multiple suicide attempts would be assigned to a higher risk category than a nonattempter or single-attempter. The counselor should assess for significant findings (e.g., precipitant stressors, such as a recent divorce) and protective factors (e.g., strong social support). Positive endorsement of additional findings should result in possibly increasing the risk designation of the client (e.g., from low to moderate). In contrast, clients who endorse many important protective factors might be placed in a lower risk category, although it is prudent to err on the side of caution when making the decision to adjust a risk category downward based on protective factors (Bartlett, Siegfried, & Witte, in press; Joiner, Walker, Rudd, & Jobes, 1999).

Once collateral information and evidence is obtained and considered, it must be prioritized. For example, if collateral information indicates a client has attempted suicide multiple times, this client would be considered high risk. The client's current suicide intent and lethality significantly determine the counselor's perception of risk and action steps (Jobes, 2006). The decision tree compares risk factors that are more pernicious than others (e.g., a history of multiple suicide attempts is weighted more heavily than a family history of suicide). These risk categories help the clinician identify the most appropriate actions for interventions.

Having a chart or graph that categorizes risk factors and compartmentalizes them into specific levels is nearly impossible and can be misleading. Each factor has to be evaluated individually as well as in the overall context of the evaluative process. One of the most important things to bear in mind when determining risk level is that although you may use all the information elicited throughout the assessment to make the decision, ultimately, the final determination is subjective. Therefore, a counselor must be able to explain how he or she concluded a client was rated at the identified risk level and how the determination drove the interventions selected from it. This can be very challenging and is why practicum students and interns are advised not to complete an assessment of suicide (i.e., determining risk level and appropriate interventions) without assistance from a field supervisor. The same is true even for experienced counselors. Given that collaborating with other professionals is part of the overall process, no one should work in isolation. This practice helps to best protect the client from suicide and the counselor from liability should the client die (Lee & Bartlett, 2005; Reid, 2010; Simon, 2004).

Risk level determines counselor actions. Counselor actions are informed by the risk assessment. Once completed, and consensus with your field placement supervisor is reached, it would be appropriate to keep clients who have been assessed with a low suicide risk in counseling on an outpatient basis. Should a moderate risk assignment be determined, an outpatient referral and a medication regimen may be considered. In an emergent situation, those presenting with high suicide risk should be referred for medical observation and medication reevaluation (Worchel & Gearing, 2010). In circumstances where a pen-and-pencil assessment instrument is not available or timely, a mnemonic (e.g., acronym) can be used. There are various mnemonics such as SLAP—gathering *Specific* details about suicidal thoughts, gauging *Lethality* level of plan, determining *Availability* of the method, and inquiring about *Proximity* of the client to the method. The AAS (2008) suggests using the "IS PATH WARM" mnemonic device to guide questions in the assessment process:

I – Ideation

S – Substance Abuse

P – Purposelessness

A – Anxiety

T – Trapped

H – Hopelessness

W – Withdrawal

A – Anger

R – Recklessness

M – Mood Change

A mnemonic can help a counselor remember major areas that need to be covered in an assessment when suicidal thinking is introduced. Counselors are advised to identify a mnemonic that comes most naturally for them, whether it is SLAP, IS PATH WARM, or another assessment device (Granello & Granello, 2007). See Case Study 9.1 for practice in identifying aspects of suicide risk.

CASE STUDY 9.1

Alex

Identify risk factors, warning signs, and protective factors in the following case. What level of risk would you assign to Alex?

Alex is a 67-year-old, widowed, Caucasian male, who retired recently. He is coming to counseling on referral from his primary-care physician, who reported that Alex "presented with depressive symptoms." Alex was prescribed an antidepressant by his primary-care physician, which Alex says he only takes on "bad days." The client explained that when he participates in church activities he feels good; however, lately he hasn't been attending church. A change in appetite and sleep is noted, as well as Alex's increasing dependence on taking a sleeping aid for his reported recent sleep disturbance. Alex described having a conflicted relationship with his son, who lives nearby, and a close relationship with his two daughters, who live outside his state of residence. Alex also noted that he had been close to his brother, whom Alex described as mentally ill and who had died some years ago as the result of a suicide. Alex reports concern about his finances and becoming a burden to his children, particularly as his arthritis and chronic pain increasingly prevent him from walking his dog (which he loves to do), and from participating in activities at the senior center (which he recently joined at his daughters' encouragement). Alex indicated that he would return for another visit, but didn't see it as necessary.

Best Practice

Some practices such as no-suicide contracts (NSCs) continue to be used in clinical practice, despite no clear evidence of efficacy with suicidal clients. These practices include the use of suicide risk assessment checklists and no-suicide contracts. Self-report suicide risk assessment checklists may be used in clinical settings, but have not been subjected to rigorous psychometric validation. Checklists may have a place in the counseling setting and may be used for other topics; however, they are not recommended for assessing suicide.

Another practice not recommended is the use of an NSC, which is an agreement in which the client commits not to die by suicide. Literature has suggested the following as potential benefits of including an NSC in a suicide assessment: (a) acknowledges the severity of the situation, (b) reinforces that suicide is a poor choice, (c) affirms a decision not to commit suicide, (d) enhances the working alliance, and (e) provides diagnostic information (Bartlett, 2008; Jobes, 2006; Simon, 2004). However, NSCs have little empirical support in the actual prevention of suicide among clients (Bartlett, 2008; Bartlett, Carney, & Talbott-Forbes, 2009; Rudd et al., 2006). In fact, potential disadvantages include (a) creates an illusion of safety for the counselor and client, (b) may be overvalued as a risk-management tool, (c) is often instigated by the emotional reactions of the counselor, (d) entrusts a disturbed client to adhere to an agreement, (e) has limited effectiveness due to unpredictability, (f) is invalid as a legal contract, (g) a client may sign only to appease the counselor, and (h) it short-circuits a more comprehensive suicide assessment (Bartlett, 2008; Jobes, 2006; Simon, 2004).

It is recommended that practicum students and interns collaborate with clients to create a crisis response plan, which is an empirically driven intervention used in place of a no-suicide contract (Jobes, 2006). A crisis response plan (a) focuses on what the client will do rather than not do; (b) provides direction for collaboration negotiation of stability and client safety; (c) emphasizes mutual give and take; (d) encourages a good faith, time specific, willingness to give treatment a chance; and (e) moves the focus of treatment to increasing pain tolerance, alternative coping skills, and making life worth living (Jobes, 2006).

Interventions with Suicide

Once it is determined that a client is having suicidal thoughts, interventions must be considered. The signs of an effective treatment strategy include (a) a clearly articulated model in which suicidality is the focus; (b) targeting skills deficiencies, self-reliance, self-awareness, and internalized locus of control; (c) ensuring that clients have access to emergency services; and (d) restriction or elimination of lethal means (Bartlett, Siegfried, & Witte, in press). The most effective intervention in terms of preventing death by suicide appears to be a restriction in access to lethal means. Ironically, many practicum students and interns are reluctant to ask clients about available means, in particular firearms, for fear of being too invasive. Just as you are encouraged to ask the core question, "Do you want to kill yourself?" you also are responsible to ask, "Do you own or have any access to firearms?" (Bryan, Stone, & Rudd, 2011; Coombs, Talbott, & Harrington, 2010; Hawton, Townsend, & Deeks, 2001).

It is noted that limited empirically validated treatments exist to prevent suicide. However, the strongest clinical interventions and techniques demonstrated to be effective with clients who present with suicidal ideation include dialectical behavior therapy (DBT; Linehan et al., 2006), problem-solving therapy (PST; Rudd et al., 1996), and cognitive therapy (CT; Brown et al., 2005).

DIALECTICAL BEHAVIOR THERAPY (DBT). DBT is a type of cognitive behavior therapy that, even in the face of intense emotions, facilitates change by assisting the client in achieving a life worth living (Linehan, 1991). The four components of DBT are mindfulness, distress tolerance, interpersonal effectiveness, and emotional regulation. DBT is effective in reducing suicide attempts among clients with recent suicide attempts, self-harm behaviors, and borderline personality disorder (Linehan, et al., 2006). In DBT, clients are taught to: (a) use a behavior chain analysis in which clients dissect their behaviors, identifying urges, thoughts, and situations that contribute to their behavior; (b) engage in live coaching through between-session phone calls, which reduces suicidality by strengthening the client–therapist relationship; (c) use mindfulness to approach situations with perspective rather than emotionality and with a stance of acceptance rather than judgment; and (d) increase distress tolerance to experience and accept intense emotions rather than acting on them in self-destructive ways. The dual focus of DBT on acceptance and change addresses the ambivalence in clients with suicidality. Further, counselor authenticity builds interpersonal connection that may reduce suicidality (Bartlett, Siegfried, & Witte, in press; Joiner et al., 2009; Worchel & Gearing, 2010).

PROBLEM-SOLVING THERAPY (PST). Although some research has shown that PST is no more effective than other treatments for suicidality, other research indicates that it decreases suicide attempts and suicidal ideation (Donaldson, Spirito, & Esposito-Smythers, 2005; McLeavey, Daly, Ludgate, & Murray, 1994; Rudd et al., 1996; Salkovskis, Atha, & Storer, 1990). PST centers on the notion that persons who are suicidal have faulty problem-solving skills and poor interpersonal problem-solving skills (D'Zurilla, Chang, Nottingham, & Faccini, 1998; Sourander, Helstelä, Haavisto, & Bergroth, 2001; Wingate, Van Orden, Joiner, Williams, & Rudd, 2005). The seven steps (i.e., define the problem, identify the goal, generate alternatives, evaluate alternatives, implement an alternative, evaluate efforts, and modify the approach as needed) center on problem-solving skills as alternatives to suicide and may be written on a portable note card (e.g., Crisis Coping Card) for easy accessibility to reduce impulsive coping (Berk, Henriques, Warman, Brown, & Beck, 2004). These cards can be used as part of the client's crisis response plan of what to do when feeling overwhelmed, providing a simple plan of action when the client is overwhelmed or distressed such as calling a friend, focusing on positive statements, or listening to music (Berk et al., 2004; Rudd, Joiner, & Rajab, 2001; Wenzel, Brown, & Beck, 2009).

COGNITIVE THERAPY (CT). Central to cognitive therapy is the concept that behaviors and emotions are a result of meanings a person assigned to events (Wenzel et al., 2009). Cognitive therapy works by addressing depression and hopelessness, rather than focusing on suicide itself (Brown et al., 2005). This approach involves three stages: (a) building a framework for treatment, (b) a focus on behavior that uses cognitive restructuring and behavioral interventions to reduce suicidality, and (c) relapse prevention (Berk et al., 2004; Henriques, Beck, & Brown, 2003). Two specific cognitive therapy techniques are the hope kit and guided imagery. In the hope kit, clients compile mementos, pictures, souvenirs, and reminders of their reasons for living (Henriques et al., 2003). The building of the kit may strengthen hope by correcting cognitive errors regarding reasons to die as opposed to reasons for living. The completed kit serves as a reminder of reasons for living. Guided imagery is a relapse-prevention intervention in which the client is instructed to envision a future suicidal episode and is led through cognitive restructuring, problem-solving, and coping skills. This method acts as a rehearsal for future stresses and creates a vision of self-mastery, which strengthens resilience in preparation for actual events (Wentzel et al., 2009; Worchel & Gearing, 2010).

Documentation of Assessment and Intervention Efforts

Clinical documentation demonstrates the actual work of the practicum student or intern. If a suicide assessment and formulation of risk process is not comprehensively documented, courts may suggest that preventative actions were not established (Granello & Granello, 2007; Remley & Herlihy, 2010; Simon, 2004). "In malpractice litigation, or administrative, or ethics proceedings, an adequately documented, legible patient record is the clinician's 'best friend'" (Simon, 2004, p. 212). Some counselors believe less documentation when treating suicidal clients is more protective when in fact the exact opposite is true. Common risk management intervention errors include not completing an adequate assessment, poor treatment planning, inappropriate management of care, and failure to document (Simon, 2004; SPRC/AAS, 2008). There may be multiple documentation styles used to evidence that an appropriate standard of care was demonstrated. Counselors are responsible to select a documentation format that is setting appropriate. The style of documentation incorporated is often different among agencies and dependent on licensing requirements, mental health governing bodies, and professional organizations.

A widely used and historically established risk-benefit model is that of VandeCreek, Knapp, and Hertzog (1987), who suggested documenting (a) a description of a comprehensive assessment of risk, (b) information obtained alerting the counselor to the risk, (c) indication of which high and low risk factors are present, (d) what questions were asked of the client and responses given, (e) how the clinical information directed the actions of the counselor, and (f) why other actions were rejected. A counselor needs to justify and articulate decisions via detailed client notations (Jobes, 2006) in a timely manner. Assessment and treatment methods are extremely important should a lawsuit arise. Counselors unable to demonstrate how and when assessment information was obtained and used may invite a charge of negligence. The formulation of risk is not possible to prove in court if the appropriate level of documentation does not exist; the request for documentation in court is to be expected, and inadequate documentation of clinical procedures utilized and actions taken leaves the practitioner susceptible to adverse litigation (Bongar et al., 1998; Jobes, 2006; Simon, 2004).

The importance of documenting your work with suicidal or homicidal clients, as noted earlier, can become a legal issue in which you must demonstrate the standard of care provided to your clients. This should not lead you to *fear* working with suicidal clients but to adopt a preventive protocol for documenting your work that fits with your counseling style, your practice setting, and state and local laws (Bongar et al., 1998).

The process for working with a client who may be suicidal would be easier if there was a standard risk management chart or checklist that could be used to assess and treat suicide. Unfortunately, there is not one list because assessing for suicide is complex and multifaceted. Documentation of the standard of care provided by the counselor is vital. One helpful tool for practicum and internship students to learn is the SCATTT mnemonic

(Balkin & Juhnke, 2014). By following SCATTT, counselors can have a step-by-step process to follow utilizing a specific intervention (i.e., Stay, Consult, Apprise, Terminate, Truncate, and Transport):

The SCATTT Mnemonic

- Stay with the client.
- Consult with supervisors and professional peers.
- Apprise the client of assessment findings and your professional judgment.
- Terminate the threat (e.g., remove any identified suicide instruments [e.g., guns, weapons, knives]).
- Truncate threats that cannot be terminated (e.g., remove easy access to medications; ensure only supervised access to cars).
- Transport to the psychiatric hospital or least-restrictive environment deemed best by you and your supervisors (e.g., partial hospitalization, monitored foster care).

SCATTT should be explored in depth by practicum and internship students and is provided here as an overview in recognizing the importance of taking action and documentation of that action as part of the suicide intervention plan. SCATTT is only one helpful tool; there are other approaches as well to minimize counselors' liability. Recommendations from several leading suicidologists include an overall risk management approach, which includes the following checklist (Joiner et al., 2009; Rudd, 2008; SPRC/AAS, 2008):

- Assess for and rule out emergency risk.
- Assess history of suicidal behavior.
- Assess suicidal desire and ideation.
- Assess resolved plans and preparations.
- Elicit warning signs of imminent risk.
- Elicit risk and protective factors.
- Plan to conduct multiple assessments.
- Integrate assessment early and routinely.
- Obtain records from collateral sources.
- Consult with other professionals.
- Formulate risk level.
- Execute treatment and continue assessing.
- Manage treatment and continue assessing.
- Document all work.

POSTVENTION. Postvention, another term first coined by Shneidman (1993), is used to describe helpful acts initiated after a crisis event. Suicide postvention is a concept related to the prevention of subsequent suicides, provision of mental health services, and the community response following a completed suicide. People are affected in different ways by the loss of a family member or person of close connection to suicide. Interns and practicum students should recognize that death by suicide is final for the decedent; however, prevention risk is just beginning for the survivors.

VOICES FROM THE FIELD 9.2   The Impact of Suicide, by Ken Norton, Executive Director of NAMI New Hampshire, Connect Postvention Program

A suicide is the proverbial pebble in the pond, and its impact ripples out to various sectors. It is critical that counselors consider the effects the suicide has on the family, other clinicians, first responders, and society. It is important for counselors to view postvention as a community healing effort.

The survivor, or a person who has lost a loved one to death by suicide, should not be confused with an individual that has survived a suicide attempt. Interns and practicum students should be aware that active postvention should take place immediately beginning with the provision of survivor support group lists. By doing so, survivors can plan to attend bereavement groups and make connections to others who have experienced suicide loss. Suicide survivors often need more care, comfort, and compassion than people who anticipated the death of a loved one, but the needs of survivors are often left unmet (Bartlett, Trippany, & Reicherzer, in press; Jordan & McIntosh, 2011; Talbott & Bartlett, in press).

TREATING SURVIVORS. The responses of parents, spouses, and siblings may vary, with parents often experiencing guilt, spouses suffering the accusation of others, and siblings not receiving adequate support. So familiarize yourself with how suicide affects clients at different ages and stages of life. When providing initial assistance to survivors of suicide, interns and practicum students should be aware of their own reactions to suicide, be familiar with community and national survivor support resources, let the survivor talk at his or her own pace, and refer to the decedent by his or her name rather than saying "your son" or "your husband." Losing someone to suicide is highly personal, and survivors indicate finding comfort when another person refers to their loved one lost to suicide by name. Long-term goals include helping survivors reconcile feelings of anger, to forgive the decedent and others they may perceive were involved in the suicide death, reducing isolation and increasing engagements in social networks, accepting the mysteries of the unknown factors surrounding the suicide loss, and increasing survivors' sharing of the grieving process with others (American Foundation for Suicide Prevention [AFSP], 2010; Jordan & Harpel, 2007).

TREATING RETURNING CLIENTS WHO ATTEMPT SUICIDE. You may face working with a client who returns to counseling following a suicide attempt. For a person who attempted suicide, his or her risk to attempt again remains relatively high even after discharge from a hospital. Further, the stigma associated with the experience; the reactions of family, friends, and peers; and the degree to which the attempt affects the client should be monitored and addressed by the counselor in training. Follow-up questions and statements for use when a client returns after an attempt may include the following: "Have your thoughts about suicide increased, decreased, or remained the same since we last met?" "Since I last saw you, give me an update on your suicide thoughts." "Tell me what you have done this week to deal with your suicidal thoughts more effectively." "How successful were you in modifying your thoughts regarding suicide?" "Describe how effective your thought modification has been." "Do you feel more in control of your thoughts?" Using these questions and statements may help to promote smooth reintegration back into home, work, and social communities and can be an opportunity to rebuild resilience for the returning attempter, affected peers, and family members (SPRC/AAS, 2008). Thus, prevention and intervention without postvention supports fails to complete the cycle of full prevention and potentially undermines the work of the former two efforts (Granello & Granello, 2007; Parrish & Tunkle, 2005; SPRC/AAS, 2008).

LOSING A CLIENT TO SUICIDE. The loss of a client to suicide will affect you on both personal and professional levels. Should client death occur during the field placement, a practicum student or intern may question his or her own competence and self-esteem and may even consider another profession. These feelings are normal and should be discussed with the classroom supervisor. Aside from feelings of guilt, the intern or practicum student may realistically wonder about the potential for litigation (Farberow, 2005; McAdams & Foster, 2000).

Complicating your own recovery from a client suicide is the fact that you may experience discomfort and isolation from other counseling colleagues, staff, and supervisors. Secondary trauma can have a remarkably strong influence on counselors who have experienced suicide of a client (Baird, 2010). This vicarious traumatization can result in counselors being ambivalent about disclosing their own feelings and reactions to the loss of a client to suicide. This kind of loss will impact the continued clinical work of a practicum student or intern. It is important to seek close supervision, individual counseling, and the support of peers who have also experienced a similar loss. Many counselors report increased compassion and understanding about the suicidal crisis and report becoming better educated about suicide following their loss of a client to suicide (Gutin & McGann, 2010). The AAS now has a clinician survivor task force that provides consultation, support, and education to assist in understanding and responding to loss resulting from the suicide death of a client or family member, and it is highly advised that, in addition to the aforementioned recovery suggestions, the intern or practicum student access support through the AAS clinical survivor group (AAS, 2012; Bartlett, Trippany, & Reicherzer, in press). In addition to the risk of having a client die, you may also have other concerns about working with suicidal clients; use Self-Assessment Activity 9.3 to begin to reflect on these concerns.

SELF-ASSESSMENT ACTIVITY 9.3 CONCERNS AS A COUNSELOR

Take a few moments and journal about your concerns with assessing and working with suicidal clients. Consider the following as you reflect:

1. What is your greatest anxiety about this work?
2. What do you believe to be your current knowledge level on working with suicidal clients?
3. What concerns do you have about assessing for suicide in children and teens?
4. What concerns do you have about assessing for suicide in various adult populations?
5. What concerns do you have about assessing for suicide in diverse populations?
6. What do you consider to be your strengths and weaknesses as a counselor in general?
7. How will those strengths and weaknesses affect your capacity to assess and work with clients who may be suicidal?

LEGAL AND ETHICAL ISSUES. Legal standards in treating suicidal clients vary among states, so counselors must exercise additional consideration when treating these vulnerable clients. Comprehensive assessments, risk formulation, and documentation contribute to effective case management. Attention to these details may reduce litigation related to negligence and malpractice should a client die by suicide, which in turn may help to reduce the fear counselors may experience. Interns and practicum students often lack sufficient education on legal aspects of the assessment, management, and malpractice associated with patient suicides. As a result of changing trends and standards, periodic reevaluation of clinical methods is essential, especially given the litigious nature of U.S. society. The best defense against liability tort should a client die by suicide is for the counselor to have followed acceptable standards of care to guide interventions and carefully documented all clinical actions. Through familiarity with evidence-based assessment protocols, professional consultation, and training, interns and practicum students improve their understanding of suicidal clients and legal complications (Bartlett & Talbott, in press; Granello & Granello, 2007).

CULTURAL CONSIDERATIONS. Many populations warrant special attention and require specific training to respond appropriately to a suicidal crisis (e.g., children, young adults, persons with physical illnesses, GLBT). Cultural, racial, and ethnic differences exist among clients who present with suicidal ideation. Successful intervention is accomplished when the differences are considered and treatment adapted. Prevention efforts should be guided by culturally relevant risk and protective factors for suicide and attitudes toward suicide (Worchel & Gearing, 2010). Recommendations for interns and practicum students to achieve cultural competence working with diverse clients who have suicidal ideation include (a) developing an awareness of personal assumptions, biases, and value; (b) understanding that cultural views differ from clients; (c) developing culturally sensitive and relevant strategies when assisting diverse clients (Sue & Sue, 2003); and (d) adapting assessment protocols based on language and cultural customs. Interns and practicum students should be aware that the assessment, intervention, and postvention processes with these and other populations are different, and a review of specific assessment and intervention protocols is essential. Interns and practicum students should seek additional training to ensure they are adequately prepared to meet the special needs of various populations (Bartlett, Trippany, & Reicherzer, in press).

DUTY TO WARN

The sentinel case related to a provider's duty to warn that has resounded throughout the helping professions is *Tarasoff v. Regents of the University of California* (1976). In this significant case, Prosenjit Poddar was seeing a psychologist at the university counseling center. Poddar threatened to kill a female acquaintance, Tatiana Tarasoff, when she returned from a trip. Tarasoff was not warned of the threat to her life, and shortly after her return, Poddar followed through with his threat by stabbing her to death (Cavaiola & Colford, 2006; Corey et al., 2011; Remley & Herlihy, 2010). In the ensuing lawsuit, the California Supreme Court ruled that there are circumstances in which a therapist should break confidentiality, particularly when it is necessary to prevent harm to others. The act of breaking confidentiality in such circumstances is labeled as the duty to warn (Melby, 2004).

The effects of *Tarasoff* continue to impact the counseling profession both ethically and legally. This impact is particularly felt in the wake of widely publicized acts of violence by persons who are or have been in counseling. The American Counseling Association (ACA) *Code of Ethics* (2005) indicates that disclosure of client information is required "to protect clients or identified others from serious and foreseeable harm or when legal requirements demand confidential information must be revealed" (Standard B.2.a, p. 7). This standard was adopted as a direct result of the *Tarasoff* ruling. Following the landmark *Tarasoff* ruling, many state legislatures enacted laws reflecting the concerns of the case. According to Herbert and Young (2002) these states fall into four categories: those with (a) a mandatory duty to warn; (b) a permission to warn; (c) a rejection of a duty or permission to warn (e.g., so-called Anti-*Tarasoff* laws; and (d) those states with no such law. Edwards (2013) noted that the majority of states (33) impose a mandatory duty to warn, whereas 11 jurisdictions give permission to warn at the therapist's discretion. In either case the counselor has some level of legal protection from prosecution arising from the consequences of such a warning. Six states currently have no law regarding a duty or permission to warn, and the Supreme Court of Virginia rejected *Tarasoff*-type laws (Edwards, 2010). States with duty or permission to warn laws vary widely on who may be identified as a victim, what constitutes a viable threat, and how the counselor should proceed to issue a warning. In addition, the application of state laws varies with regard to the responsibilities of the practitioner depending on his or her professional identity (e.g., counselor, psychologist, social worker). Herbert and Young pointed out the absence of any federal law regarding duty to warn; therefore, counselors should be aware of the laws of their own state and the wide differences between state laws as well as the rapidly changing nature of legislation.

HOMICIDAL CLIENTS

VOICES FROM THE FIELD 9.3   Understanding the Homicidal Mind, by Nancy Slicner, Lt Col (ret.) Air Force, Forensic Psychologist and Independent Consultant

People who kill others may look and act completely normal. A counselor has to have an ear tuned into what is making another person concerned about the behavior. Counselors aren't always prepared to ask questions to explore the possibility of homicide. They need to ask, "Are you afraid that your spouse may kill you?" and take a step beyond what is comfortable in the assessment experience.

At some point in your professional career, you will likely encounter a homicidal client. Similar to the fear and stigmatization associated with the suicidal clients, interns and practicum students often feel anxious and uncomfortable working with homicidal clients and the risks they pose. But the duty to warn and duty to protect also apply to the homicidal client. Protection of the public safety is always the primary clinical consideration, and preventing harm to others is imperative. Anticipation of interactions with a homicidal client is not enough. The practicum student or intern must prepare to assess, intervene, and treat this client type. Counselors should individualize their intervention styles and participate in continuing education to ensure a proper response.

Homicide is an act of murder and nonnegligent manslaughter that involves the willful killing of one human being by another (U.S. Department of Justice, 2011a). Over the past decade, a significant decline in homicide rate has been observed in the United States, and consistencies continue to imply that males are most commonly both the victim and perpetrator of these violent acts (U.S. Department of Justice, 2011b). To further illustrate the decline, general homicide rates were 9.1/100,000 (in 1991) in contrast to that of 4.8/100,000 (in 2010; U.S. Department of Justice, 2011c). Of note, homicide rates among young adults aged 18 to 24 years were the highest of any age group reported in 2008 (13.4 homicides/100,000 persons); thus the need for increased prevention and intervention efforts is warranted. Interns and practicum students must take appropriate steps when a client presents with homicidal thoughts or behaviors (Schwartz, 2008). From time to time, counselors may serve persons with a history of mental disorders and violent offenses who pose an elevated risk to the public—and the counselor. The challenge is to balance personal, professional, and public risk while ensuring the client's rights are not violated (Anderson & West, 2011). Interns and practicum students must provide the appropriate level of documentation related to both inpatient and outpatient care provided and the escalation of risk (Rossi, Swan, & Isaacs, 2010).

Assessment of Homicide Risk

The risk of homicide and factors associated with interpersonal violence should be interpreted with caution during the assessment process. A practicum student or intern may encounter a client who exhibits risk factors, but this does not necessarily mean that the individual will become violent. However, it would be naive to think that a client devoid of risk factors could not develop homicidal intentions. The lack of familiarity with violence-based risk assessments should lead the counselor to err on the side of caution and evaluate each case independently (McNiel et al., 2008).

The prevalence of homicide is in some way associated with problem-laden interpersonal relationships, and the majority of victims are killed by someone known to them. The majority of homicide perpetrators are male, and the most common lethal means is the use of a firearm (Papadopoulos et al., 2009). Research supports that males exhibiting a family history of mental illness, family violence, job instability, and impulsivity are more likely to express homicidal tendencies (Flynn, Abel, While, Mehta, & Shaw, 2011; Foster, O'Brien, & Korhonen, 2012).

Violent outbreaks may also be attributed to substance abuse or changes in psychotropic medication but simply cannot be dismissed as acceptable behavior. One may suspect the homicide rate among those with mental illness to be dramatically higher than the general population; however, this is not particularly true (Kleespies & Richmond, 2009). Further, acts of violence such as homicide and war may require deeper explanation and clinical interventions (Liddle, Shackelford, & Weekes-Shackelford, 2012), and client history of military service may be a viable discussion to hold. The increase in homicides by those with schizophrenia and by those with psychotic symptoms at the time may likely be related to drug misuse. The intern and practicum student should be prepared to ask questions of potentially homicidal clients that pertain to the sudden onset of drug use or changes in drug-use patterns (Swinson et al., 2011).

In addition, offenders of homicide may have previously assaulted someone, but that incident may not be on record and documented by the police, community services, shelters, or physicians previously in contact with the client. However, the occurrence of domestic incidents should be assessed and an intimate partner homicide (IPH) risk assessment completed to determine particular risk, as it is unlikely that the initial offense would have raised attention of the police, social services, or mental health systems beforehand (Eke, Hilton, Harris, Rice, & Houghton, 2011).

Comparable to suicide, counselors must be aware of the potential for litigation regarding harm to others caused by a homicidal client. Assessment of the potential threat for homicidal actions among clients requires counselors to stay up to date on professional literature and advances in the assessment process. In doing so, the client, those the client may potentially hurt, and the counselor are better protected. To better assist practicum and internship students, an overall risk management checklist for assessing homicide may include the following items (Collins & Collins, 2005; Foster et al., 2012; Klott & Jongsma, 2004):

- Assess for and rule out emergency risk.
- Assess for interpersonal discord.
- Assess for substance use.
- Determine history of mental illness.
- Gauge access to firearms.
- Monitor impulsivity.
- Explore job instability and termination.
- Obtain details of experiences with justice system.
- Integrate assessment early.
- Refer for evaluation by forensic specialist.
- Obtain records from collateral sources.
- Formulate risk level.
- Execute and manage treatment.
- Document all work.

This checklist is provided to practicum and internship students as an overview of basic steps in the assessment of homicide and risk management. This checklist is not exhaustive, and counselors are urged to be informed and up to date on state laws, professional guidelines, and best practices to ensure a quality standard of care for all clients, especially when assessing for homicide risk.

Media Influence

Depictions of violent acts and terrorism are readily available and sensationalized by traditional media outlets (e.g., television, newspaper) and reinforced by access to violent video games and Internet content (Savage, 2008; Ybarra et al., 2008). The uncontrolled access to violence presented in different forms of media exposes segments of the population to this type of behavior and can have a profound impact on the actions of youth (Ferguson & Kilburn, 2009). Media outlets leave lasting impressions on vulnerable populations. When violent content is not regulated, it normalizes these behaviors and is one reason that acts of violence are underreported (Herrenkohl, Sousa, Tajima, Herrenkohl, & Moylan, 2008; Wolitzky-Taylor et al., 2011). Although seemingly senseless, these acts occur in social networks, families, schools, colleges, the workplace, and all across the country (Smith, 2007).

School Violence

Schools pose a natural gathering place for children, adolescents, and young adults for the purposes of cultural and educational enrichment. Once thought to be a community safe haven, schools have become the focus of violent acts and homicide in recent decades both in the United States and internationally. In particular, events surrounding the Sandy Hook Elementary School (Newtown, CT), Columbine High School, Virginia Tech, and Northern Illinois University tragedies come to mind as heinous acts resulting in the loss of lives at the hands of young homicidal persons in possession of firearms (Borum, Cornell, Modzeleski, & Jimerson, 2010). It is important that interns and practicum students not discount the lethality or intent to harm a student or faculty member. Interns selecting employment in the school setting should be particularly in tune with risk factors for homicide. It is difficult to predict when acts such as these may occur; however, learning from historical responses to school crises can be helpful. Each school and geographic region has differing beliefs about the value of education, and cultural issues around respect for others vary widely (Brown, Osterman, & Barnes, 2009). Administrators, counselors, and concerned others have taken steps to create school threat assessment or crisis plans that perhaps did not exist prior to aforementioned incidents (Allen, Cornell, Loreka, & Sheras, 2008).

Workplace Violence

Ordinarily, a work setting is a public place where individuals can freely enter a facility without restriction. The free range of motion poses a direct opportunity for violent acts should a homicidal individual stalk a victim or carry out homicidal intentions in a particular location. Perpetrators may represent an outside entity, be linked to an external or personal relationship, or be a member of the workplace staff themselves. Increased job stress, uncertain conditions of employment, and disputes with superiors can be factors leading to escalation and homicidal intent (Barling, Dupré, & Kelloway, 2009). If a client is referred by an Employee Assistance Program for exhibiting outward signs of frustration, counselors should determine if there is the potential for threat escalation and ask direct questions.

Intimate Partner Violence

Intimate partner violence (IPV) is the most common form of violence linked to homicide and is defined as "physical, sexual, or psychological harm by a current or former partner or spouse that may occur among heterosexual or same-sex couples and does not require sexual intimacy" (Centers for Disease Control [CDC], 2010c). IPV may involve just one hit, but also can escalate on a continuum to chronic violent beatings. Saltzman, Fanslow, McMahon, and Shelley (2002) described several types of IPV: (a) physical violence, (b) sexual violence, (c) threats of physical or sexual violence, and (d) psychological/emotional violence. According to the National Intimate Partner and Sexual Violence Survey, one in three women and one in four men in the United States will experience rape, physical violence, and/or stalking by an intimate partner in their lifetime (Black et al., 2011). The most documented rationale for IPV as well as homicide is male sexual jealousy (Goetz, Shackelford, Romero, Kaighobadi, & Miner, 2008) and men's partner-directed violence linked to perceived infidelity (Kaighobadi & Shackelford, 2009). Interns and practicum students should be aware that males are most likely to be the victims of homicide and also the offenders (Farington & Lober, 2011). IPV is more likely to occur when couples are cohabitating, and often homicide is a result of more violent beatings (Mize, Shackelford, & Shackelford, 2009). Further, the risk of IPV and homicide increases when a prominent age difference between partners exists, the victim has a child from a previous relationship, and the offender has unregulated access to a weapon (Campbell, 2007; Eke et al., 2011).

Assessing Your Views

Interns and practicum students must be prepared to handle cases involving violence despite varying degrees of training in assessment, intervention, and treatment. Prior to working with violent clients, interns and practicum students must take inventory of their personal and family history, which may also include violence attributed to a friend or family member. In fact, you may have witnessed a particular event or be the survivor–victim of a homicide attempt and could subsequently impede the client–counselor relationship. You must explore personal biases, have an action plan, and be able to show openness and clear judgment because each case is deserving of individual attention and assessment without bias. Although this chapter discusses violence and homicide with an emphasis on interpersonal violence, it is noted that interns and practicum students may also shy away from working with clients who are victims of other personally injurious acts, such as stalking or rape. Use Self-Assessment Activity 9.4 to begin to reflect on how your personal experience with violence may influence your work as a counselor.

SELF-ASSESSMENT ACTIVITY 9.4 YOUR EXPERIENCE WITH VIOLENCE

1. If you have a family history that includes interpersonal acts of violence, how will this affect your willingness to work with clients presenting with homicidal ideation?
2. Would you be suited to seek employment in the criminal court that required clinical evaluation of persons who have completed a homicide attempt?
3. What level of comfort do you have when working with clients presenting with homicidal ideation? Has your curriculum prepared you to handle these situations?
4. What level of trust or mistrust do you have in the legal system and its ability to prevent homicidal acts if you report concerns about a client?
5. What level of continuing education will you seek should you decide to work in the criminal court system as a clinician?
6. What dialogue have you initiated with your course instructor about your desire to work or refrain from working with violent clients?

Counselor Safety Plan

Counselors must exhibit a level of restraint when interacting with potentially violent clients, including projecting a calm, controlled demeanor. A client who senses fear may choose to act on the counselor's vulnerability and become violent. An intern or practicum student may experience anxiety in this situation that is difficult to control; however, careful evaluation of the situation despite fear can help elicit a personal safety plan. If you are new to a clinical setting, complete an assessment of your surroundings that would best protect you from a now-anticipated attack (e.g., sit closest to the door, remove unnecessary objects from the environment that may provide access to means of harm; Stinchfield, Hill, & Kleist, 2010). Although some statements regarding potential harm to others such as "I could just kill someone" are not uncommon and often dismissed, you are responsible for assessing lethality or level of threat associated with these statements by a homicidal client, whether stated or implied.

Threat Level Assessment

Conducting a homicide assessment is paramount in determining the homicidal threat level and intent. The assessment may provide the intern or practicum student with valuable information, such as the names and locations of the people being threatened or targeted. As previously discussed, counselors are required to keep client records confidential under federal laws; however, the duties to warn and protect are altered when a client intends to impose harm on others. Based on the level of threat and violent nature of the information disclosed, counselors are required to notify law enforcement and persons who are the direct target of the proposed violence.

The clinical skill of active listening is important when working with homicidal clients and occurs when a counselor says little to the client but shows a high level of interest in the information disclosed. Active listening clarifies a homicidal client's feelings and attitudes, and may help determine if cognitive distortions are present. Further, open-ended questions allow the homicidal client to provide detailed responses and deeper information (Gekoski, Gray, & Adler, 2012). Many situational factors attribute to violent acts, and the response of the client is in part dependent on his or her stage of developmental cognition, motivation, and environmental cues. Research suggests that counselors should employ violence prevention and reduction tactics rather than violence prediction (Douglas & Skeem, 2005), as there is generally not a single cause of malicious acts. An intern or practicum student must consider a client's family history of violence, stress connected to a particular violent event, use of substances that increased violent responses, client ability to reason in a particular circumstance where an intimate partner is involved, and the client's immediate access to a weapon or other means of force to carry out the harmful behaviors disclosed.

A variety of risk factors are associated with acts of homicide and violence, and the level of risk should be assessed with caution. You should note that each client exhibiting risk factors may not become violent; however, without a working knowledge of risk factors, you may overlook a potentially dangerous situation if the client assessment is not evaluated on an individual basis. A combination of interpersonal, intrapersonal, community, and societal factors contribute to the risk of becoming a victim or perpetrator of IPV (Kantor & Jasinski, 1998; Stith, Smith, Penn, Ward, & Tritt, 2004).

Threat assessment has two parts: (a) an evaluation of the threat itself, and (b) the expression of intent to do harm. Together, these evaluations can help lead to an informed judgment on whether someone who has made a threat is likely to carry it out, causing you to differentiate when someone is making a threat versus posing a threat. The Federal Bureau of Investigation's National Center for the Analysis of Violent Crimes (O'Toole, 2000) states that threat assessment should evaluate the (a) details of the threat, (b) identification of victims, (c) means to carry out a threat, (d) emotional state of the client, (e) affect presented by the client, (f) level of exposure to stressors, and (g) predisposition to violent behaviors. In doing so, the level of homicidal threat can be assessed and the course of action for treatment determined.

A *low level of threat* poses a minimal risk to the victim and public safety and the threat:

- Is vague and indirect
- Contains inconsistent information that is implausible or lacks detail

- Lacks realism
- Suggests the person is unlikely to carry out violent acts

A *medium level of threat* could be carried out, but may not appear entirely realistic. A medium level threat:

- Is direct and more concrete than a low-level threat
- Suggests that the offender has given thought to how the act will be carried out
- Indicates a possible place and time, though the signs still fall well short of a detailed plan
- Gives no strong indication that the offender has taken preparatory steps (e.g., an allusion to a book or movie that shows the planning of a violent act or vague, general statement about the availability of weapons)
- May involve a specific statement seeking to convey that the threat is not empty: "I'm serious!" or "I really mean this!"

A *high level of threat* is defined as an occurrence that appears to pose an imminent and serious danger to the safety of others. A high level of threat occurs when the threat:

- Is direct, specific, and plausible
- Suggests concrete steps have been taken toward carrying it out (e.g., statements indicating that the client has acquired or practiced with a weapon or has had the victim under surveillance)
- Involves the use of warning behaviors offering an escalating perspective in threat assessment

Warning behaviors are acts that constitute evidence of increased risk. The counselor should document acute, dynamic, and particularly erratic changes in patterns of behavior, which may aid in structuring a professional decision that an individual of concern now poses a threat (Meloy, Hoffmann, Guldimann, & James, 2011).

Homicide Survivors

A homicidal crisis may have long-lasting impressions on the community and those involved who are left to figure out how to move forward with life following the tragic event. Counselors should be a referral source for individuals surviving a homicide loss and also involved in community support efforts. Cofacilitation of groups with other mental health professionals can assist interns and practicum students to practice and improve discussion skills with bereaved family and close others. Interns and practicum students should be prepared to offer services to the bereaved family of the victim who is experiencing grief and also offer resources to the family of the homicidal offender who are also grieving the loss of a family member or are faced with the loss of vitality due to imprisonment.

Counselors should note that African Americans are more likely to become the victims and offenders of homicidal events (Currier, Holland, Coleman, & Neimyer, 2007). Loss of a loved one through homicide is very difficult to accept, and it is common that one's faith is used as a primary coping resource (Neimeyer & Burke, 2011). Interns and practicum students must understand that clients grieving the loss of a loved one due to homicide and employing religiosity or spirituality may also experience complicated grief.

Regarding health concerns, men and women who have experienced rape or stalking by any perpetrator or physical violence by an intimate partner are more likely to report frequent headaches, chronic pain, difficulty with sleeping, activity limitations, poor physical health, and poor mental health than men and women who did not experience these forms of violence. Women who have experienced rape, stalking, or IPV are also more likely to report having asthma, irritable bowel syndrome, and diabetes than women who have not experienced these forms of violence.

Homicide survivors may contend with economic stressors, stigmatization, fear of recurrence, anxiety when encountering reminders of the event, negative beliefs about themselves and the world, and feelings of guilt and responsibility. Homicide survivors often face greater intrusion from the media and the criminal justice system, strained relationships, and a preoccupation with revenge (Hertz, Prothrow-Stith, & Chery, 2005; Zinzow, Rheingold, Hawkins,

Saunders, & Kilpatrick, 2009). These stressors may contribute to the risk for mental health problems among homicide survivors.

Little research has examined the prevalence of homicide survivorship or its relationship to psychiatric disorders. However, research has demonstrated that horror, disbelief, and shock give way to devastating grief, and the situation is further complicated by the incomprehensible manner in which a friend or close other died. Murder is an irreplaceable loss without the permission of or any appeals process on the behalf of the decedent, so the feelings of outrage, offense, and helplessness leave a survivor feeling physically violated over a relationship now forever terminated without warning (Blakely & Mehr, 2008).

Legal and Ethical Concerns

Limitations about duty to warn vary according to each state's statutes, and interns and practicum students are well advised to learn applicable state laws, regulations, and agency or school procedures. When the risk level is determined and the decision to break confidentiality is made, the obvious question becomes what legal ramifications exist regarding duty to warn. It is generally not advisable for a counselor to be alone in a room with a client who has a history or perceived risk of violence. Transporting a client at risk for violent acts also poses concerns for counselor safety and the ability to prevent unwanted assaults while retaining control of the vehicle. Counselors are advised to decline such requests providing a rationale that fear for personal safety is of concern. When assessing homicidal clients, it is important to know that forms of documentation may be different than in standard client care, as such notes may need to be immediately shared with law enforcement or the court system.

Counselors-in-training should be equipped with resource information that would facilitate referral of a homicidal client or those experiencing a loss due to homicide. Losses that take place in rural communities are a special challenge because it is sometimes difficult for survivors to locate services that will assist in the recovery and healing processes.

DISASTER: LARGE-SCALE SHOCK

Prior to the terrorist attacks of September 11, 2001, crisis counseling tended to be conceptually limited to individual client needs. Since that devastating large-scale attack, our understanding of disasters and crisis intervention has expanded considerably. Interns and practicum students need exposure to crisis counseling skills so they can quickly respond to the extreme needs of clients when disaster strikes.

A *disaster* is a situation in which both the individual and larger community are faced with circumstances in which normal coping skills and resources are overwhelmed. The forms disaster may take ordinarily are described as natural or man-made. Man-made disasters may be intentional, such as with acts of terrorism, school shootings, or workplace violence. Man-made disasters may also be unintended, as in the case of an industrial accident (Hard & Reynolds, 2011). Large-scale shock is the reaction of the wider community to catastrophic loss experienced through some form of disaster, whether man-made or natural. McGlothlin (2014) described this circumstance as trauma occurring on a communitywide level. For the purposes of this chapter, the terms *disaster* and *crisis* may be used interchangeably and will refer to broader circumstances affecting the wider community, rather than a normal developmental crisis. This section will examine disaster response, reactions, safety issues, interventions, and available trainings, as well as ethical, legal, and cultural aspects of disaster intervention.

Disaster Response Phases

Disaster recovery is developmental in nature. Survivors will experience or process their circumstances based on the phase of the crisis in which they find themselves. It is, therefore, important that practicum students and interns be aware of the client's adjustment through the phases of disaster response. The following phases are an American Red Cross (ARC) adaption of Raphael's (2000) model for envisioning adjustment to disaster:

1. ***Warning or Threat Phase.*** When there is advanced notice of a natural disaster, people may feel unsafe, vulnerable, or a lack of control. Defense mechanisms vary from attitudes of invincibility to despair.

2. ***Rescue or Heroic Phase.*** Citizens may engage in community activities directed at rescue, such as rushing in to save others, self, or possessions.

3. ***Honeymoon Phase.*** Survivors express gratitude at having made it through the crisis, as well as both personal and community pride at how they have handled it. There is a sense of community bonding, and many will be engaged in cleaning, salvaging, and working on their plan of recovery. During this phase many may be heard to say, "We're going to build it back better than it was before!"

4. ***Disillusionment Phase.*** The true impact of the disaster on people's lives is realized as well as how far they must go to actually recover. The limits of helping agencies become apparent. Media moves on to other matters as the disaster becomes "old news." Survivors may feel abandoned, angry, or depressed.

5. ***Reconstruction or Recovery Phase.*** Survivors come to terms with their changed circumstances and the tasks before them. Emotional recovery and the rebuilding of lives and homes may continue for years. Anniversary reactions are common in this phase (American Red Cross [ARC], 2005).

Survivor Responses

Interns and practicum students must be aware that survivors may be in a heightened state of physical arousal, emotional arousal, or exhaustion, depending on both the phase of recovery and their respective individual condition. Routine survivor responses to disaster have been described as normal reactions to abnormal circumstances, and indeed, most survivors do not suffer from mental illness.

Typical responses have been categorized as cognitive, physical, emotional, and behavioral. Common cognitive responses include confusion; poor concentration, memory, or problem solving; reduced self-esteem; blaming; or nightmares. Physical responses are consistent with fight-or-flight arousal and include fatigue, headache, rapid respiration, sweats, reduced libido, fainting, tremors, or weakness. Emotional reactions may run the continuum of human loss and experience, including denial, loss of control, fear, guilt, anger, despair, helplessness, irritation, apathy, sadness, or being overwhelmed. Behavioral responses may include increased drug or alcohol use, isolation, interpersonal conflicts, loss of interest in social activities, poor sleep or appetite, or restlessness (McGlothlin, 2014).

Demographically, researchers (Collins & Collins, 2005) have found that female survivors have more adverse reactions to disaster due to traditional caregiving roles. This reaction tends to be more severe in more traditional cultures. Children's reactions to loss from disaster range across the developmental spectrum. According to the National Center for Post-Traumatic Stress Disorder (Hamblin & Barnett, 2009), children are more profoundly affected by disaster when (a) they are exposed to higher levels of life threat, witnessing death, injury, or calls for help; (b) they are located closer to the actual disaster; (c) they have experienced prior trauma; and (d) their parents have a poor response or are mentally ill. Collins and Collins (2005) noted that younger children tend to express their distress in terms of somatic symptoms, acting out, or regressive behaviors. Older children may evidence some of the same symptoms, but their responses may also include cognitive confusion, self-attribution, and high attunement to parental response.

Adolescents will have many of the same symptoms already described, but will show more advanced emotional responses, anxiety, and even self-injurious behaviors. Although the research (Young, Ford, Ruzek, Friedman, & Gusman, 1998) on older adults is less consistent, interns and practicum students should be aware that the loss clients experience may be compounded due to other age-related losses (e.g., health and roles changes, loss of friends and spouse), potential health concerns, and a higher likelihood of being victimized by criminal elements.

Safety Issues

Disaster circumstances produce a variety of safety and security concerns. When working in a disaster location, counselors must be aware of their own health and safety needs as well as those of the client. These needs include basic safety and nutrition, as well as addressing both environmental dangers and danger from clients or others. Because of the nature of disasters, counselors need to be aware of their environment and possible threats to their personal safety. Harrington and Daughhetee (2014) recommended being prepared for disaster through establishing a crisis plan for the agency or school. Individual practitioners are encouraged to pursue preparedness through some form of standardized training and coordination with crisis teams through a community agency such as the American Red Cross (ARC) or their local Emergency Management Association (EMA). Counselors working in disaster circumstances must coordinate with local authorities to assist survivors in securing access to the basic needs of medical care, safety, shelter, food, and water, as well as mental health care. Counselors are used in these circumstances to provide support and to prevent normal emotional distress due to the disaster from escalating further. Most survivors of a disaster are not mentally ill and do not require more than supportive care. However, disaster mental health workers are vital in identifying those who may need to be directed to more intensive levels of care (Regel, 2007).

VOICES FROM THE FIELD 9.4   Words of Wisdom from a Red Cross Volunteer, by Caroline M. Brackette, Ph.D., LPC, Disaster Mental Health Volunteer, American Red Cross

As a disaster mental health (DMH) relief volunteer with the American Red Cross, it is important to understand your role in working with survivors of a disaster. DMH counselors are trained to assist survivors in coping with the emotional and personal impact of a disaster through performing mental health screenings and triage, making referrals to community resources, providing emotional support, providing education about common reactions and recovery, and listening. Crisis intervention may be necessary to address negative thinking patterns and introduce effective coping strategies. It has been my experience that it is most important to allow survivors the opportunity to tell their story. Listening and using the basic counseling helping skills are critical. I have received many gracious "thank yous" after just being available to listen to individuals express how they were feeling and share their experiences during the disaster. This is not the time to trade "war" stories, but to focus on the client's feelings, experiences, and resiliency. It is also important to be mindful of compassion fatigue and its possible effect on you, your volunteer colleagues, and community workers and members assisting with relief efforts. It may be necessary for you to intervene and advocate for the self-care and well-being of those assisting in relief operations.

Intervention Approaches

It is vital for interns and practicum students to understand that the effectiveness of any disaster or crisis intervention approach is dependent on and unique to the type of disaster, the extent of the disaster response, and the phase of disaster response at which the counselor engages the client. In choosing the best approach in which to address client needs related to disaster, examine multiple models of intervention. Sample models include (a) Crisis in Context Theory (CCT; Myer & Moore, 2006), (b) Preparation, Action, Recovery Framework (PARF; McAdams & Keener, 2008), (c) Resistance, Resilience, and Recovery Model (RRR; Kaminsky, McCabe, Langlieb, & Everly, 2006), and (d) Roberts' 7-Stage Crisis Intervention Model (Roberts & Ottens, 2005). Such models share similar concepts, including stabilization, assessment, and exploration of feelings and identification of effective coping strategies, as well as referral or follow-up. You can use one of these models as a framework for developing a larger understanding of disaster to effectively train in and use intervention techniques. Once you have a conceptual framework for crisis work, being trained in specific disaster approaches will seem more logical. Although a variety of crisis trainings exist, the following have had wide acceptance and are demonstrated to be best practice.

PSYCHOLOGICAL FIRST AID (PFA).   The PFA (Ruzek et al., 2007) approach is a preferred model of disaster intervention (Everly, Phillips, Kane, & Feldman, 2006). PFA is based around eight core actions: (a) contact/engagement, (b) safety/comfort, (c) stabilization, (d) information gathering, (e) practical assistance, (f) connection with social supports, (g) information on coping support, and (h) linkage to collaborative services. This approach is based on the philosophy that when these core actions are provided, clients will be able to return to their normal functioning unless there are other mental health issues that complicate the process. Although this intervention approach is typically designed for individual care, it has been found effective in group settings as well. PFA is designed to be applicable to a variety of critical events, including traumatic crises, existential crises, and psychiatric crises. This application is soundly based on a hierarchy of needs in which the counselor first addresses the basic physical needs (e.g., food, shelter, safety) and then moves on to psychological needs (e.g., emotional support, empathy, consolation).

CRISIS COUNSELING PROGRAM (CCP).   The Crisis Counseling Program (CCP) model is noteworthy for its strength or wellness perspective as a treatment modality (Castellano & Plionis, 2006). Often used for responses to disasters, the CCP model consists of the following five components:

1. *Assess Strengths:*   Identify the human and material resources available to the client in addition to what problems he or she faces.
2. *Restore Predisaster Functioning:*   Reduce the chaos of the disaster by restoring life to what it was before the disaster.
3. *Accept the Face Value:*   Help clients reorganize their lives by accepting the impact of the disaster.
4. *Provide Validation:*   Demonstrate unconditional positive regard, validation, and acceptance.
5. *Provide a Psychoeducational Focus:*   Provide group and individual psychoeducation on the normal and abnormal reactions to disaster thereby enabling survivors to monitor their own recovery.

CRITICAL INCIDENT STRESS MANAGEMENT (CISM).   The critical incident stress management (CISM) intervention approach originated in the early 1980s for the use of emergency medical services personnel in the United States. Critical incident stress debriefing (CISD), also known as psychological debriefing (PD), is a component of the overall CISM and represents a structured group crisis intervention with discussion and review of the traumatic event. Since its inception, many major international humanitarian aid agencies, such as the International Federation of Red Cross and Red Crescent Societies, as well as the United Nations High Commissioner for Refugees, have come to use PD as part of their CISM programs, along with many other law enforcement agencies and emergency service providers across Europe, the United States, and Australia (Regel, 2007). Although as a practicum student or intern you may be encouraged to engage in only the psychological debriefing element, when properly used, CISM actually consists of six components: (a) acute crisis counseling provided by peer counselors, (b) executive leadership program, (c) the multidisciplinary team, (d) acute traumatic stress group training sessions, (e) hotline, and (f) reentry program (McGlothlin, 2014; Regel, 2007).

Controversy has developed around this approach because attention has focused on one component of CISM, which is debriefing. This one aspect of the CISM process became the focus of attention for both intervention and research because it was erroneously perceived that this particular feature of the approach would prevent the development of post-traumatic stress disorder (PTSD) as a stand-alone process. Research does not support a one-time recital of the emotional and factual events of a traumatic situation as effective in reducing the development of trauma-related disorders. Critical incident stress debriefing that is not a part of an overall CISM intervention process may actually be harmful (Collins & Collins, 2005; National Institute of Mental Health, 2002; Regel, 2007). The research does not suggest abandoning debriefing because that intervention has a vital psychoeducational role and is useful in identifying survivors experiencing acute stress reactions that could develop into long-term disorders. However, CISD should be used *only* as a part of an overall intervention (Regel, 2007).

Training Programs

As a future professional counselor you are encouraged to obtain recognized training that is empirically based and provides linkage to nationally and internationally recognized disaster intervention programs. By obtaining training from such programs you not only receive valuable skills but are also provided linkage to an organization that can facilitate their service placement and support in the event of a large-scale disaster. Two such programs are Disaster Mental Health (DMH) training, which is provided by the American Red Cross (ARC, 2005), and Community Emergency Response Team (CERT) training, provided by state and local emergency management agencies (EMA).

DISASTER MENTAL HEALTH (DMH) TRAINING. Disaster mental health (DMH) training is based on the Psychological First Aid (PFA) model that is implemented within the overall ARC intervention strategy. Once you are trained in PFA, you will be eligible to assist in both local and international recovery efforts. Interns and practicum students should contact their local Red Cross chapter for more information (ARC, 2005).

COMMUNITY EMERGENCY RESPONSE TEAM (CERT) TRAINING. Community emergency response team (CERT) training involves a full community-based approach of which PFA is only one part. Based on the concept that community members may be temporarily cut off from assistance and must be self-reliant until help arrives, certified CERT members are taught a wide range of rescue, triage, and assistance skills in addition to PFA. Interns and practicum students should contact their local office of the EMA for more information (U.S. Department of Homeland Security, 2003).

Disaster Legal and Ethical Issues

Ethics and the laws governing client care are more fully explained in Chapter 6. This section is intended to act as a quick guide to just those ethical and legal matters most closely associated with proper practice in crisis and disaster circumstances.

HIPAA AND FERPA. The Health Insurance Portability and Accountability Act (HIPAA) and Family Educational Rights and Privacy Act (FERPA) guard the privacy of client and educational records, respectively. Crisis situations typically occur quickly and often in unanticipated ways, so counselors must respond quickly. Therefore, there may be limited time to obtain HIPAA-required releases when critical care is needed, or it may be impossible to obtain such releases as a result of severe injury, unavailability of family members, or other unforeseen consequences of the disaster. According to the U.S. Department of Health and Human Services (2005), HIPAA is not intended to interfere with the provision of emergency medical care associated with declared emergencies such as Hurricane Katrina. Covered health-care providers may exercise their professional judgment and act, as long as such actions are in the best interests of the patient.

In such circumstances, actions permitted by mental health workers may include disclosure of individually identifiable medical information to government officials, police, emergency first responders, public health officials, or anyone whom the provider deems necessary to best serve the patient. Regardless, the U.S. government has the authority to waive sanctions and penalties associated with violations of the Privacy Rule, even in cases where a public health emergency is not declared (U.S. Department of Health and Human Services, 2013).

Likewise, FERPA is not intended to impede care in a disaster. The U.S. Department of Education (2007) indicates that an emergency situation creates an exception, and schools may release information from records to protect the health and safety of others. However, this exception exists only for the time of the emergency and is not blanket consent to release student information. The information may be released to appropriate health and safety individuals such as law enforcement, medical personnel, and public officials.

DOCUMENTATION. Crisis counselors must keep documentation of their interventions with clients. Of course, disaster conditions (e.g., a fire, flooded area) are not always conducive to writing case notes, but counselors need to clearly document exact dates, pertinent details, assessments, and treatment decisions to the best of their ability. This may mean writing basic notes on returning to a more stable location. Case notes must be specific enough to demonstrate that the treatment reflected prevailing standards of care. The documentation must clearly illustrate the session with details that capture the essence of what occurred and validate treatment decisions. The need for client records to be in a locked and secured location applies during crisis events. Providing for locked and secure confidential file storage in crisis situations must be addressed in crisis planning (Hard, Talbott-Forbes, & Bartlett, 2014).

CONFIDENTIALITY. In situations in which a client is a danger to self or others or where the professional counselor is mandated by law to report abuse or is required by a court of law to disclose information, confidentiality can be legally breached. In situations other than these, a client must give consent for the release of information. In crisis and disaster circumstances provisions for confidentiality are certainly more challenging; however, the ethical standards and requirements of the profession still apply. Counselors should be aware of the latitude that may be allowed for confidentiality in difficult circumstances, yet strive to ensure the protection of client information. Obtaining a written consent in disaster circumstances may be difficult or impossible. In such circumstances oral consent to release information may be accepted (see the preceding discussion of HIPAA), but the counselor should obtain clear communication from the client on what they wish to have disclosed, and to whom, and then only the minimum necessary information should be shared (Hard et al., 2014).

INFORMED CONSENT. In situations of crisis or large-scale disaster, obtaining informed consent will rarely involve a clipboard and paper. Written consent in such circumstances may be impossible, impractical, or, at least, delayed. For example, a counselor may be called on to provide support to a survivor wrapped in a blanket at the scene of a fire. Crisis counselors should introduce themselves, describe their role, explain the basic limitations of confidentiality, and ask permission to speak with him or her. It is possible that the survivor may refuse assistance and in such cases the counselor should withdraw, while offering to be of future service if requested. If the client agrees to work with the counselor the verbal consent needs to be reevaluated throughout the discussion and may be retracted at any point the survivor desires (ARC, 2005; Gamino & Ritter, 2009). The client's privacy should be protected as much as the circumstances of the disaster allow. Protecting confidentiality may simply involve moving the survivor from more public or trafficked areas or lowering one's voice to limit the possibility of being overheard. Often the counselor may be asked to contact others on the survivor's behalf such as community resources or loved ones. In disaster circumstances, it may not be possible to obtain a written release of information. The counselor should clarify with the survivor that he or she gives consent for the contact, whom he or she wishes to have contacted, and what specific information to share, being mindful to share only the minimal amount necessary. A few suggested questions the counselor may ask are, "What would you not want me to disclose when I contact those you have asked me to contact?" "How would you like me to identify myself and my connection with you when I call?" "If I call someone, and he or she is not there, may I leave a recording and identify myself?" Linkage such as this may often be deferred to disaster case managers if necessary (Hard et al., 2014).

Death Notification

There may be circumstances under which you may be asked to provide a death notification to a family member or loved one. Although not a comprehensive treatment of the circumstance, the following are best practice suggestions (Jackson-Cherry, 2014) for this sad, but necessary duty.

- *Get permission.* Never give notice of a death unless you are given permission by a supervisor, team leader, or disaster coordinator.
- *Go in person and in pairs.* Give the notification in person and as a team (e.g., with another counselor, clergy, family member, or loved one of the deceased).

- ***Use plain language.*** Example, "I have bad news. James was in a wreck and was killed." Avoid euphemisms like he was lost, passed away, and so on.
- ***Use compassion.*** Offer support and caring, avoid imposing beliefs or other gestures that suggest the death was "for the best."
- ***Follow up.*** Leave a business card or other contact information and make a follow-up contact to check on the bereaved. They may need other help or direction with the funeral or other arrangements, and this may also facilitate access to mental health care if needed.
- ***Debrief.*** Take time to process the notification with the other team members as soon as possible to evaluate how it went, if other help is needed, and to process any triggers that may have been activated in the team.

Termination

As mentioned previously, termination in a mass crisis or disaster situation should be understood from a special perspective. Formal admission, assessment, and ongoing counseling are normally not possible under disaster circumstances. According to the ARC (2005), victims in need of ongoing care and provision of counseling services should be referred to local counseling services, case managers, and area providers to avoid therapeutic abandonment.

Wellness

The ACA 2003 Taskforce on Impaired Counselors (Lawson & Venart, 2005) observed that counselors working in disaster or crisis circumstances are particularly vulnerable to secondary trauma or compassion fatigue. Such a compromised condition may leave the counselor vulnerable to ethical or legal issues. Therefore a focus on the well-being of the counselor is essential prevention. Pearlman and MacIan (1995) noted 10 strategies for crisis counselors to use to promote and maintain wellness: (a) discussing cases with colleagues; (b) attending workshops; (c) spending time with family or friends; (d) travel, vacations, hobbies, and movies; (e) talking with colleagues between sessions; (f) socializing; (g) exercise; (h) limiting caseload; (i) developing one's spiritual life; and (j) receiving supervision. Not only are these important to maintain ethical practice, but also Lawson and Venart (2005) noted that wellness and self-care are vital to counselors because the care that they provide to others is only as effective as what they give themselves. It is for this reason that many disaster response organizations not only recommend but also require some form of psychological debriefing on leaving the disaster site. This is done to identify any stress reactions that the counselor may be developing and refer him or her to assistance, if necessary.

Large-Scale Shock, Disasters, and Cultural Considerations

There may be a need for interns or practicum students to advocate for cultural minorities in postdisaster circumstances. Researchers have found that disaster is not a social leveler, and marginalized populations will often find their postdisaster reality is worse than before (Enarson, Fothergill, & Peek, 2006). Following Hurricane Katrina, for example, LGBT persons reported difficulty locating loved ones or accessing services because relief organizations' policies or volunteers did not recognize their relationships (Hard & Reynolds, 2011). Counselors may also discover spiritual or religious distress among survivors as they attempt to fit the disaster into their worldview (Zalaquett, Carrión, & Exum, 2009).

The crisis response team should be as culturally diverse as possible. When persons from different cultural groups observe cultural diversity and representation on the crisis team, it enables them to feel connected to mental health professionals. When diverse representation is not possible, the team should adopt an open, accepting approach to limit barriers. For counselors to be effective in crisis intervention with culturally different clients, they must be sensitive to differences in the client's worldview, self-aware, and able to provide interventions that are culturally and contextually responsive. These culturally sensitive components must be applied to the counselor's crisis intervention approach (Bartlett, Trippany, & Reicherzer, in press; Stone & Conley, 2004).

Summary

The focus of this chapter was to give practicum students and interns insight into the assessment process for clients in danger. Clients may be in danger from self-harm or may be in crisis, which results in homicidal behavior. Clients may also be in crisis and experience shock on a large scale resulting from a natural or man-made disaster. Because of the high likelihood that counselors will experience a suicidal client (or family member), assessment of clients who are at risk of suicide is important in your training as a counselor. In addition, because of increased awareness of the impact of disasters, assessment and intervention for clients experiencing large-scale shock is also vital to counselor education.

Assessment of client suicide risk begins with an assessment of the counselor's values and attitudes toward suicide. Topics such as suicide and homicide can often evoke feelings of inadequacy for practicum students and interns, but this can be alleviated somewhat through education and training. Awareness of risk factors, warning signs, and protective factors helps the counselor to recognize the danger for clients and intervene in meaningful ways. Interns and practicum students, as well as seasoned counseling professionals, can benefit from learning as much as possible about evidence-based suicide risk assessment as well as other available assessment tools.

Once suicidal risk has been assessed, interventions should begin quickly, but the novice counselor (and sometimes seasoned professionals as well) may be unsure of which interventions to use. This chapter specifically outlined several approaches that have been shown to be effective with suicidal clients, including DBT, PST, and CT. Finally, documentation of intervention efforts was also addressed because of the legal and ethical issues involving suicidal clients.

Homicidal clients may also be encountered by you as a professional counselor. It goes without saying that the legal parameters and ethical guidelines of our profession dictate our actions with homicidal clients. This chapter highlighted some of the staggering statistics surrounding homicide and some of the influences in our environment that may contribute to homicide. These influences include the impact of the media, which can range from television to movies to newspapers and increasingly social networking. You have no doubt witnessed the evidence of school violence or workplace violence and the impact on communities. A likely impetus for potential homicidal clients coming to counseling might stem from intimate partner violence. These incidences of violence also are a reason for you as a future counselor to assess your viewpoint and ideas about working with violent clients. This chapter provided information on how to assess threat levels and hopefully by understanding the levels of threat you will be able to assess the danger. We hope that this chapter has provided information to help you consider your counseling role with homicidal clients.

Finally, professional counselors need to be prepared to work with clients who have experienced large-scale shock from disasters, either man-made or natural. Information about response phases of disaster recovery, information about survivor responses, and safety issues were provided. Intervention approaches used with disaster response are included, and these intervention approaches include an initial assessment phase to determine the best possible interventions for survivors of disasters. Even disaster response includes adherence to ethical and legal guidelines, and this chapter outlined aspects to consider. We would be remiss if we did not mention the cultural aspects to be considered throughout the assessment and intervention of clients in danger, whether it is suicide or homicide or those suffering from large-scale shock. Culturally competent professional counselors have a duty to recognize the importance of respecting diversity in our clients. We must be social justice advocates in our assessment and interventions with our clients in crisis. We must recognize the impact and intersection of age, gender, ability, race, ethnic group, national origin, religion, sexual orientation, linguistic background, or other personal characteristics as we assess and intervene with our clients to provide effective treatment. Other aspects to be considered as part of our clients' diversity might also be involvement with the military, their legal status, geographic location, previous trauma, communication styles, and cultural differences that may be invisible. Working with diverse populations can run the gamut in terms of differences, but focusing on client well-being and helping our clients move out of crisis is the ultimate goal.

We began this chapter with staggering statistics about suicide, about the prevalence of encountering suicidal clients, and the importance of counselors' ability to assess suicide risk and completion. Our goals for this chapter include helping you as a student and future professional counselor become aware of the potential risk of losing a client to suicide, providing some basic assessment tools, and providing some basic suicide prevention and intervention strategies. Another chapter objective included introducing you to the importance of assessing for homicidal risk and the potential effect. Finally, we introduced the notion of large-scale shock as it impacts our clients from disasters, either man-made or natural. Presented here is a simple list of *rules* designed to help you create a plan for working with clients in danger:

1. ***Ask questions.*** Do not assume you understand what a client means by phrases such as "I'm at the end of my rope." Ask the client to describe in detail what phrases (such as this one) mean specifically to the client. Encourage the client to be open and honest with his or her answers.

2. ***Do not ignore your "gut feeling."*** If you have an inner voice or an uncomfortable feeling in your gut,

follow it. It is critical to follow your intuitive concern about your client. Go *out on a limb* and stretch your comfort zone by checking it out with your client. Refer to #1 above . . . ask questions!

3. ***Go there.*** Approach the topic of suicide or homicide with your client in a nonjudgmental and genuine and caring manner. Let your clients know that you are willing to "go there" with them. Although you may be reluctant to have the conversation, it is your responsibility. Show the client you are willing to talk about the tough stuff.

4. ***Better safe than sorry.*** Always err on the side of caution, and with the client's permission, involve family members or a support network as an intervention. If suicide or homicide is an imminent threat, involving family members (or other supportive people identified by the client) becomes your ethical responsibility.

5. ***Be smart.*** Learn as much as you can about all aspects of clients in danger and particularly how to assess the risk in your clients. Continuing education throughout your career about the risk factors and treatment of suicide and homicide is essential. Being prepared to assist in crisis situations becomes increasingly important for our changing society.

We do not believe that this list is exhaustive when working with clients in danger. We do stress the importance of having a personal plan that works effectively for you and your clients. Creating your own personal protocol for working with clients in danger should happen early in your career and be reviewed often and updated regularly throughout your career. Eagerly anticipate your future as a professional counselor, and continue to gather helpful information, continually adding to your toolbox to provide the best possible counseling outcome for all your clients!

CHAPTER 10

Practicing Professional Responsibility

BY STEPHANIE G. PULEO, CHARLOTTE DAUGHHETEE, AND JASON M. NEWELL

PREVIEW

This chapter explores the theoretical foundations of ethical, proficient counseling practice and the developmental process of ongoing advancement of therapeutic expertise. In particular, the chapter discusses the sacred nature of the counseling relationship and the professional behaviors that are expected of the counselor in service of that relationship. Clients entrust aspects of their lives to counselors, placing a daunting amount of responsibility on them. The counseling relationship and the welfare of the client are contingent on professional, responsible practice by the counselor; therefore, the continuing improvement of one's counseling practice is fundamental to best practice. A major key to proficient counseling practice is the self-awareness of the counselor and the counselor's ability to assess areas of personal and professional growth. It is suggested that counselors seek opportunities for mentoring, consultation, supervision, and professional activity in organizations such as the American Counseling Association (ACA) to enhance therapeutic proficiency. Commitment to continuing competency as a lifelong professional value is stressed, and the importance of advocacy for the profession and for clients is posited as essential to responsible professional practice. The development of the Puleo-Daughhetee Longitudinal Evaluation Objectives (PD-LEO) is discussed, and a description of the 16 resultant professional dispositions is provided. The dispositions are grouped into five categories: microskills, themes and theories, facilitating change, world of work and managing, and caring for the counselor. A thorough description of these dispositions and how the PD-LEO can be used for competency evaluation is offered. Counselors are encouraged to integrate ongoing self-assessment and improvement into their core professional identities.

WHAT DOES IT MEAN TO PRACTICE RESPONSIBLY?

What does it mean to be a responsible professional? Throughout the pages of this text have been discussions of the counselor's role in the counseling relationship, putting theory into practice, attending to the needs of diverse client populations, and adhering to the values, ethical guidelines, and laws that pertain to the counseling profession. Each of these discussions is integral to the concept of professional responsibility. According to the American Counseling Association (ACA) *Code of Ethics* (2005), first and foremost, "the primary responsibility of counselors is to respect the dignity and to promote the welfare of clients" (ACA, 2005, p. 4). The Code further states that to function responsibly, professional counselors must have competence, be nondiscriminatory, advocate for change, employ practices that are grounded in research, engage in self-care, and represent themselves through accurate communication. The topics presented in this chapter are intended to help counselors think about the foundations necessary for practicing professional responsibility.

Many discussions of professional responsibility begin with an examination of professional behaviors, practices, and conduct that are spelled out in codes of ethics and guidelines for practice. *Codes of ethics* reflect the values of a profession and serve to facilitate professional decision making. In general, they are rules that members of the profession agree represent good or acceptable practice and serve as standards against which the behaviors of professionals may be judged (Cottone & Tarvydas, 2007; Remley & Herlihy, 2010). The standards are enforceable and may be used to hold members of the profession accountable. *Practice guidelines* also play a role in professional accountability. They are intended to be motivational and serve as goals to which members of a profession may aspire (Marotta & Watts, 2007). Practice guidelines have been the center of much attention in recent years, as the literature has increasingly called for focus on "best practices." Additional discussions of professionalism and professional behavior highlight professional dispositions. *Dispositions* are the values, attitudes, and commitments that influence behavior toward those served by the professional.

The *Code of Ethics* of the American Counseling Association (2005) is based on five critical principles: nonmaleficence, beneficence, autonomy, justice, and fidelity. These general principles are discussed comprehensively in Chapter 6. Also included in the *ACA Code of Ethics* is an entire section (Section C) outlining professional responsibility. Section C delineates aspirations and expectations regarding competence, credentials and training, nondiscriminatory and nonharassing attitudes toward others, as well as the way counselors represent themselves and communicate with the public and other professionals. These important principles of ethics, standards of practice, and professional dispositions will be woven throughout the discussion of professional responsibility during the remainder of this chapter.

Counseling is defined as "a professional relationship that empowers diverse individuals, families, and groups to accomplish mental health, wellness, education, and career goals" (ACA, 2012). Thus, professional counselors are responsible for the relationship to the clients served. In addition, counselors are responsible for what they bring to the relationship and for how they represent and carry out the intent of the relationship. Key elements revolve around three questions: (a) To whom is the counselor responsible? (b) How should a responsible counselor be? and (c) How do counselors know if they are practicing responsibly?

The Counselor Is Responsible To . . .

THE CLIENT. "The primary responsibility of counselors is to respect the dignity and to promote the welfare of clients" (ACA, 2005, p. 4). This ethical guideline reflects a central value of the counseling profession and provides the basis for ethical decision making. To safeguard client welfare, counselors are responsible for honoring their clients' diversity and autonomy.

A central responsibility of counselors is accountability (Erford, 2014a, 2014b). Counselors are accountable to their clients. Responsible counselors demonstrate their accountability to clients by maintaining their focus on the clients. They establish goals and objectives specific to client needs, implement interventions directed toward those goals and objectives, and measure the results of those efforts. It is imperative that counselors keep their clients' needs, concerns, and goals in focus, while also being cognizant of the contexts of clients' lives.

Many times, clients come to counseling at the request of someone else, perhaps a relative, a teacher, or an employer. Often the request is in the form of an order, and the client faces the choice of being in counseling or suffering negative consequences such as incarceration. In these times, developing counselors sometimes struggle in their roles, aware of participating in a triangle, but unsure of their allegiance or position in the triangle. Very often, consciously or unconsciously, counselors see themselves being more accountable to the referral source than the client. From this stance, however, the client becomes secondary rather than primary, and the counseling relationship will be less than optimal. It is important to consider that although some clients have been "mandated" to participate in counseling, they have, in fact, been given a choice. It also is important to remember that regardless of how the client got to counseling, it is the counselor's duty to do no harm, work toward promoting the best interests of the client, and treat the client with the same level of dignity and respect as any other client.

THE COUNSELING RELATIONSHIP. The therapeutic relationship is of prime importance to the counseling process (Rogers, 1957). Numerous studies have examined the therapeutic relationship from every angle imaginable. The one consistent theme that has emerged from the research is that, regardless of other variables, the outcome of counseling is strongly related to the quality of the therapeutic alliance (Jennings & Skovholt, 2004; Sullivan, Skovholt, & Jennings, 2004). In this context, it seems apparent that counselors are responsible for defining the counseling relationship and for facilitating client engagement (Parsons, 2001).

The counseling relationship is special and different from every other relationship in the client's life. The relationship is intimate, is often intense, and, unlike other relationships, is intended to end. In addition, the counseling relationship is characterized by a power differential. In contrast to other relationships, the manner of sharing in a counseling relationship is predominantly unidirectional; clients disclose intimate details of their lives and have their needs addressed, but counselors do not (Parsons, 2001). Because of the intimate nature of the counseling relationship, the client is vulnerable, and it is the counselor's responsibility to create and maintain a relationship structure that is safe and supportive.

Several interpersonal characteristics and behaviors have been identified in counselors who are considered experts or "master counselors." These counselors are responsive to their clients and seek strong, deep, collaborative relationships. They engage their clients throughout the therapeutic process, and while remaining objective, become agents of change in the relationship (Sullivan et al., 2004).

In using the "self" as an agent of change in the counseling relationship, counselors have a responsibility to make sure that the instrument is in good working order. Counselors have a responsibility to be aware of their own biases, values, and needs. Counselors must be culturally sensitive and must take steps to ensure that their values and needs do not impede the counseling process. Responsible counselors take care of their own needs and are able to participate in the counseling relationship with objectivity (Puleo, 2004). In addition, responsible counselors make efforts to avoid burnout and compassion fatigue by engaging in self-care, issues that are discussed more thoroughly in Chapter 13. The therapeutic relationship will be enhanced if the counselor not only is well, but also is trustworthy, objective, and culturally sensitive.

STRUCTURE. In addition to being aware of what the counselor brings to counseling, it is important for the counselor to accept responsibility for the boundaries of the therapeutic relationship. A *boundary* may be thought of as a structure around a relationship. The structure defines the parameters of the relationship, including its limits and the roles of the individuals in it (Remley & Herlihy, 2010). As noted, counseling relationships are intimate, however, and their structure includes a power differential. Self-disclosure is, for the most part, unidirectional, often leading clients to feel exposed and vulnerable. Boundaries serve the purpose of preserving the integrity of the counseling relationship and safeguarding the welfare of clients. Most responsible counselors are cognizant of potential ways that they might compromise therapeutic boundaries. Confidentiality must be protected, and beneficial multiple relationships are established with caution, consideration, and consent.

In describing their approach to family therapy, Napier and Whitaker (1978) discussed the importance of winning the "battle for structure." They argued that the potential benefit of counseling is greatest when both clients and counselors adhere to clearly delineated terms. The conditions and expectations that must be disclosed and managed include administrative issues as well as boundaries and limitations. Many of these issues can be spelled out in disclosure statements, informed consent documents, or service contracts. See Think About It 10.1.

THINK ABOUT IT 10.1

As you develop as a counselor, what challenges have you had to struggle with to win the "battle for structure"?

INITIATIVE. Issues related to structure sometimes become challenges, as reluctant clients attempt to distract themselves from doing the work of counseling. Napier and Whitaker (1978) also described a "battle for initiative." It was their view that clients must win this battle. It is the responsibility of clients to expend the energy necessary for change. Initiative is seen in clients' motivation, attitude, and movement toward goals. By insisting that clients win the battle for initiative, counselors provide opportunities for clients to make decisions, gain competence, and feel empowered.

Erik Erikson (1963) discussed the concept of initiative as a developmental task to be mastered. Having learned to trust others and construct a sense of autonomy in early childhood, children learn that they can make things happen. If the environment is structured in the right way, and parents and other adults offer appropriate encouragement and support, children develop a sense of initiative. With initiative comes self-efficacy and confidence. In many ways, the concept of initiative that Napier and Whitaker (1978) described parallels this stage of development. Clients need to be supported, but also challenged and encouraged to make things happen for themselves. In this way, autonomy is fostered, and clients are empowered to develop self-efficacy and confidence.

Counselors Are Responsible for Being . . .

COMPETENT. Professional counseling involves the integration of theoretical knowledge, analytical and critical thinking skills, practice experience, and ongoing professional development to maintain the highest level of competency and integrity with clients. According to the ACA *Code of Ethics* (2005), responsible counselors practice within the boundaries of their competence. Determining the boundaries of one's competence might be a difficult task, but suffice it to say that practicing outside those boundaries increases the potential to harm clients and decreases the potential benefit of counseling.

It is often the case that counselors-in-training are hesitant to work with new populations or new client concerns. As a rationale for not entering into counseling relationships in these new situations, they cite the ethical standards and maintain that they are being called on to practice beyond the boundaries of their competence. The spirit of these standards is not intended to be exclusionary, however. The standards allow for the development of new skills so long as there is adequate education, training, and supervision, and clients are protected from harm. It would be irresponsible and perhaps unethical for counselors not to continue to pursue maximum competencies.

Competence may be thought of as an integration of three components: knowledge, skill, and diligence (Welfel, 2006). To be competent, counselors must have a specific knowledge base and must be able to apply that knowledge base in practice. The development and integration of the components of competency occur through education, training, and experience.

KNOWLEDGEABLE. The knowledge base of responsible counselors is rich with information about the history and philosophy of the profession as well as the theories and current research that guide the standards of practice. Professional counselors employ a holistic approach when interacting with clients, which often requires working knowledge in multiple content areas such as medicine, pharmacology, social work, and education. Further, many counselors work from an integrative approach, which requires grounding in a number of theories. Knowledge of the efficacy of various evidence-based treatment approaches ensures that clients are treated with the most appropriate methods given their individual needs and the uniqueness of their situations.

Core knowledge. The Council for Accreditation of Counseling and Related Educational Programs (CACREP; 2009) has identified eight core areas that comprise the knowledge foundation of professional counselors. These areas include professional orientation and ethical practice, social and cultural diversity, human growth and development, career development, helping relationships, group work, assessment, and research and program evaluation. Knowledge in these areas is acquired through graduate degree programs in counseling and validated by examinations such as the Counseling Preparation Comprehensive Examination (CPCE) or the National Counselor Examination (NCE). Knowledge attained through graduate study is only a starting point in the development of competence. Research in counseling continues to evolve, rendering a great deal of information obtained while in graduate school obsolete within a short period of time (Welfel, 2006). Thus, it is the professional counselor's responsibility to be a lifelong learner.

Counseling theory. To help clients in a way that is ethical and effective, responsible counselors are intentional. Counseling theory provides the foundation for intentional counseling (Eaves & Erford, 2014; Halbur & Halbur, 2011). Theory functions as a roadmap that directs the counseling process (Corey, Corey, & Callanan, 2011; Hackney & Cormier, 2013; Halbur & Halbur, 2011). Over 400 approaches to counseling have been identified in the professional literature (Hackney & Cormier, 2013). On closer examination, it would appear that most of these approaches were derived from four or five major schools of thought (i.e., paradigms), demonstrating that theory development is fluid.

Theory is based on a set of beliefs about human nature and the change process. For the most part, the theoretical framework from which a counselor works is a reflection of that counselor's values and personality (Corey et al., 2011; Halbur & Halbur, 2011). Just as a spiritual belief system provides guidance for everyday life, a theoretical belief system related to counseling provides guidance for practice. By working from a theoretical basis, counselors are able to explain how humans develop, learn, and change (Hackney & Cormier, 2013). When working with clients, theory helps counselors organize information they have learned about their clients and generate hypotheses about client behavior and experiences. Further, theory serves as a tool for making predictions that can be applied to choosing appropriate intervention strategies, anticipating client outcomes, and evaluating success.

No one theory stands out in the literature as being better than the others; in fact, studies comparing theories have demonstrated that variation in outcome has little to do with the approach taken. If theory doesn't matter so much, then some developing counselors might question why it is necessary. Although studies have demonstrated that there is little difference in outcome between theoretical approaches, there *is* importance in having some theoretical framework to provide structure for the therapeutic process. As Corey (2009a, p. 3) noted, "Attempting to practice without having an explicit theoretical rationale is like trying to build a house without a set of blueprints." It would not be possible to be intentional without theory.

In part because there seems to be little difference in outcome attributed to theory and in part because there are so many new perspectives and interventions proposed in the literature, many counselors consider themselves to function from an "eclectic" orientation. But to be truly *eclectic* would suggest that counselors change their fundamental beliefs from situation to situation and client to client (Halbur & Halbur, 2011). Thus, it is important to distinguish between being eclectic and applying or integrating a variety of techniques and intervention strategies. Theory and technique are related but distinct. It is most likely that counselors who refer to themselves as eclectic actually work from an *integrated theoretical approach*, one that is woven together from strands of several theories fitting the counselor's values, beliefs, and personality. Responsible counselors, therefore, would maintain strong personal systems of beliefs (theory), but might employ an assortment of techniques in the service of those beliefs. See Think About It 10.2.

THINK ABOUT IT 10.2

What techniques do you frequently employ in your counseling practice? What is the result you anticipate from these techniques? Explain how the techniques should produce the results you anticipate. Is there a common theme or theory?

Research and evidence-based practice. It is important for counselors to participate in the research process, if not as producers, then as consumers. Technology allows counselors to connect and communicate. The launching of new ideas, completion of research, and dissemination of results are facilitated through technology and communication. As the world becomes more connected and populations served by counselors become more diverse, the responsibility of counselors becomes to know and understand "what does and does not work with clients, what techniques and approaches result in positive changes for a diverse clientele" (Erford, 2014b, p. 63).

Counseling involves bringing balance to very difficult and often complex problems of life; given the significance of this charge to the profession, there is an ethical imperative for counselors to treat their clients with validated therapeutic techniques and methodologies. Evidence-based practice (EBP) is the professional skill of actively evaluating and using evidence from the research literature to support the practice methods and techniques employed in the treatment of clinical issues. The philosophy of evidence-based practice originated in the field of medicine under the premise that health care and medicine are ever changing and evolving. Therefore, physicians have an ethical responsibility to be knowledgeable of research and development that could influence the care and well-being of their patients (Adams, Matto, & LeCroy, 2009; Hodge, 2011). This is also true of counseling and other helping professions, as new information and knowledge is continuously developing and circulating into the professional literature. Counseling students in professional training programs often question why an entire course (or multiple courses) in the curriculum is dedicated to learning and understanding research methodology. Students may question, "Do I need to be skilled in conducting research if my goal is to counsel people in a practice?" The answer to this simple question is "yes."

Although many professional counselors, particularly at the master's level, do not actively pursue careers in the field of clinical research, counselors in practice have an ethical obligation to the vulnerable clients they serve to be mindful of the current state of science in the profession. This is particularly important for professional counselors working within specialty care settings (e.g., grief and loss; marital, couples, and family counseling; trauma; children's mental health). In fact, from a consumer's perspective, when seeking services from a professional counselor, there is an understood level of trust between the client and the counselor that the counselor has both intellectual and pragmatic knowledge in a stated area of expertise. It serves to weaken the therapeutic relationship if the consumer is not sure that the interventions used in practice can be validated. Clients have the right to ask the very reasonable question, "How do you know if this is actually going to work; has it been tried before with other people who have this problem?" The way to answer this question and to feel competent when recommending and using therapeutic techniques in practice is to have the professional skills to not only be a good consumer of the research literature, but also to synthesize information from the literature in a concise and meaningful way and to use this knowledge to treat clinical issues efficaciously.

Part of the responsibility for those who conduct large-scale clinical research as a component of their professional practice (e.g., college professors) is to create a public way of knowing findings that influence effective practice methodologies. Once research becomes part of the public knowledge base, the responsibility ultimately falls on the professional counselor to access this knowledge and use it to facilitate clinical practice, which in theory will result in positive client outcomes (Nutley, Walter, & Davies, 2009). One of the essential principles of evidence-based practice is that the professional counselor accepts the responsibility for being consciously and deliberately aware of information in the research literature and applying that information in clinical practice (McNeece & Thyer, 2004). This responsibility is a key feature of ongoing professional development and lifelong learning. See Think About It 10.3.

THINK ABOUT IT 10.3

Is there a technique or practice that you have incorporated into your practice as a counselor that you have learned from reading an article in a professional counseling journal? Share the technique and the journal reference with others.

Another important principle of responsible practice is that professional counselors consider their knowledge in research methodology as an essential part of clinical practice. Although it may not be necessary for professional counselors to conduct clinical research studies, it is important to be able to apply empirical knowledge in a pragmatic way. To achieve this practice goal, professional counselors should have a basic understanding of both qualitative and quantitative research paradigms. These concepts easily can be infused into traditional counseling environments. For example, qualitative methodologies can be useful to assist in learning and documenting client stories as lived experiences. Thematic data on clients and their collective life experiences can be useful tools in understanding individual client or group behavior patterns. Qualitative research methods also can be used in structured interviewing and in interpreting journalist client narratives. Quantitative skills such as use of diagnostic or self-report scales to measure client behaviors add scientific validation to diagnostic and psychosocial assessment work. Also, basic knowledge of data entry and analysis is helpful in analyzing behavioral patterns over time or with large groups of clients and can be done in a time-efficient manner in comparison to most qualitative approaches to client data collection. See Think About It 10.4.

THINK ABOUT IT 10.4

In what ways do you use the skills you learned in your research class in your everyday practice as a counselor?

Basic knowledge of assessment, research, and program evaluation allows counselors to assess their own work as well as the work of others. Counselors should have knowledge of evaluative research practices. Basic evaluative research skills help counselors assess individual practice, program effectiveness, agency or school policies, and overall service delivery. Knowledge of evidence-based practices and ethical standards in scientific research also are an invaluable practice skill for counselors involved with grant writing for agency or program funding and development. Finally, as a profession, embracing the ethical obligation to use evidence-based practices ensures that counseling stays on the "cutting edge" as a leader among the helping professions.

SKILLED. Competency means that the counselor not only has a knowledge base, but also is able to apply that knowledge in practice. A second aspect of competency identified by Welfel (2006) is the responsibility to be skilled. It is important for responsible professional counselors to possess strong relationship skills (Jennings & Skovholt, 2004). Many individuals enter the profession of counseling because they believe, and perhaps have demonstrated, that they have good relationship skills. They have the ability to listen, observe, and care for the welfare of others (Jennings & Skovholt, 2004) while being sensitive and responsive (Sullivan et al., 2004). Through professional training programs, these fundamental skills are shaped and honed until practicum students and interns can successfully facilitate change in clients.

The types of counseling skills necessary to be considered competent include clinical skills, judgment, technical skills, and cultural competence (Hackney & Cormier, 2013; Welfel, 2006). Central to a wide range of clinical skills, responsible counselors are adept at engaging clients in the counseling relationship, facilitating client expression, conceptualizing client needs, and implementing intervention strategies. As these skills are acquired, responsible counselors learn to trust their clinical judgment; they learn to shift their attention to what they are doing and thinking as they work with clients and to use their own knowledge and critical thinking to inform professional decisions. Part of this shift for beginning counselors involves letting go of their self-consciousness and preoccupation with saying the right thing. As developing counselors learn to relax and turn down the volume of their inner critics, they become more present and better able to hear and attend to clients.

Technical skill refers to the ability to choose and implement specific intervention strategies in specific situations. Often this skill is predicated on knowledge of evidence-based practice and research. Cultural competence also calls on counselors to be responsive to the uniqueness of their clients and to choose interventions that are contextually appropriate.

Often this means that counselors must recognize if client concerns originate in societal oppression, marginalization, or discrimination, necessitating that they perform alternate, socially responsible roles such as advocates, consultants, liaisons with community support (Remley & Herlihy, 2010), and agents of social justice.

DILIGENT. Welfel defines diligence as "consistent attentiveness to the client's needs that takes priority over other concerns" (2006, p. 49). This concept ties the ethical principle of competence to the ethical principle of respecting the dignity and welfare of clients, the primary responsibility of counselors. To be diligent, counselors are deliberate in the care they apply to clients. They appropriately conduct assessments and employ interventions fittingly selected for specific clients and client concerns. Diligent counselors are thorough and maintain an appropriate level of care for the duration of the counseling relationship. Being diligent further requires responsible counselors to be self-aware enough to know how their strengths and limitations fit their clients' needs. While maintaining professional boundaries, diligent counselors advocate, consult, and seek further knowledge and training on behalf of their clients. These efforts ensure that individual clients are served effectively while enhancing the counselor's professional growth and ability to serve future clients.

CONTINUALLY COMPETENT. In addition to thinking about diligence as the way that counselors maintain focus and attention on their clients, diligence also may be thought of in terms of the way counselors maintain focus and attention on their own competency. In describing expert counselors, Jennings and Skovholt noted that "continuous professional development seems to be the hallmark of the master therapist" (2004, p. 33).

Competence may be thought of as a developmental phenomenon that crystallizes as developing counselors move through stages from novice to expert. Counselors gain initial, or minimal, competencies as they near completion of requirements for master's degrees in counseling. These competencies are validated by examinations such as the Counseling Preparation Comprehensive Examination (CPCE) or the National Counselor Examination (NCE). Credentials such as the National Certified Counselor (NCC), awarded by the National Board for Certified Counselors (NBCC), are contingent on validation of minimal competencies. Once a credential such as the NCC or state licensure has been awarded, it is the counselor's responsibility to continue to acquire knowledge and to develop further competency.

Whereas validating initial or minimal competencies is accomplished through examinations and the awarding of credentials, validation of continued competency is not so easy. No substantial requirements for postentry level assessment of competence appear to exist (Daughhetee, Puleo, & Thrower, 2010). To ensure that counselors keep their practices and knowledge base current, thereby assuring protection for the public, most state licensure laws, as well as the NBCC, require that counselors participate in continuing education activities. Although the intent of these mandates is admirable, the actual requirements often are too minimal to warrant the desired outcome. Many counselors register for seats in continuing education programs, collect their documentation, and renew their credentials, without being renewed themselves. As their skills and competencies erode, and their lack of awareness of new practices continues, these "stagnant" counselors may present risks to their clients.

Clients will be best served by individuals who are intrinsically motivated to seek out lifelong learning and professional development, regardless of the existence of external regulatory requirements. Daughhetee et al. (2010) have suggested several avenues through which professional growth and further competency may be pursued, including mentoring, supervision, consultation, and professional involvement.

MENTOR. Through mentoring, developing counselors have the opportunity to learn skills and competencies better and quicker than they might have if left alone (Bell, 2000; Taylor & Neimeyer, 2009). In particular, mentoring seems to be an effective way to crystallize competencies related to professional identity (Elman, Illfelder-Kaye, & Robiner, 2005; Taylor & Neimeyer, 2009; Vespia, 2006) as the more experienced professional often represents a model of who the less-experienced counselor wishes to become. The mentoring relationship is an enriching association for both counselors as opportunities for discovery learning are available for both participants (Daughhetee et al., 2010). By providing mentoring, more experienced counselors continue to explore the same issues that perplex beginners and are exposed to different perspectives as they examine the meaning of their own perspective(s) (Puleo, 2004).

PEER SUPERVISOR AND CONSULTANT. A threshold of competency has been crossed when developing counselors no longer consider participation in supervision an academic class exercise and begin to see it as an opportunity for growth and professional development. Peer supervision and consultation are effective vehicles for counselors to acquire specific knowledge, develop skills, and obtain help with difficult cases after they have met the criteria for initial competencies and credentials. These activities are particularly important for counselors who work in isolation and may have limited opportunities to debrief or process with colleagues.

INVOLVED IN PROFESSIONAL ORGANIZATIONS. One of the advantages of membership in ACA, state branches of ACA, Chi Sigma Iota, and other professional organizations is that counselors receive newsletters, journals, and a plethora of digital information and electronic correspondence. Opportunities to expand, enrich, or refresh competencies are ample and include the annual ACA convention, ACA division conferences, annual state conferences, chapter meetings, workshops, seminars, and online courses. Reading and active participation in continuing education exposes counselors to new ideas and perspectives and facilitates professional growth (Puleo, 2004). See Think About It 10.5.

THINK ABOUT IT 10.5

To what professional organizations do you currently belong? What benefits do you enjoy by being a member? If money were no object, what other organizations, divisions, chapters, or groups you would join? Why?

CHALLENGED TO CONTINUING COMPETENCY. There is a wealth of knowledge and practice wisdom to be offered in the professional counseling literature, knowledge that is far too often used only by counselor educators and their students for class projects. After graduating from professional counseling programs, many new counselors inadvertently abandon the valuable skills learned in accessing and synthesizing data from the research literature as an ongoing practice behavior. It can be speculated that this phenomenon in practice occurs for several reasons. First, new counselors may quickly become engaged in daily clinical practice with clients and allow service delivery and client appointments to dominate their daily schedules. New counselors also may find that simply practicing counseling is both liberating and empowering after years of graduate professional training and may see the ongoing practice of research, reading, and learning as more reflective of academic activity. Another challenge to continuing competency is that when professional counselors enter the workforce, whether in schools, agencies, or hospital settings, they often lose access to valuable resources readily available in university settings. Access to comprehensive library systems and online academic databases can be quite costly to maintain independently after graduation. In addition, the developing counselor must take the initiative to actively seek new material as part of lifelong learning, whereas in a classroom setting this information is provided within the context of the curriculum and teaching environment. Therefore, maintaining this important practice behavior after graduation actually becomes more difficult for many professional counselors (see Think About It 10.6). On the other hand, with ongoing advancements in public Internet resources and databases, information on most any clinical issue and treatment methodology is readily available and easily accessible for professional counselors. However, counselors should be mindful that not all online information is scientifically valid; indeed, only a small minority is. Therefore, counselors should be well trained in their professional programs to be "good consumers" of the research literature, especially online information, which tends to be the first, and sometimes primary, source of knowledge for answering practice questions.

THINK ABOUT IT 10.6

How might you recognize a counselor who has not engaged in continuing competency?

GOOD CITIZENS OF THE PROFESSIONAL COMMUNITY.   To be a good citizen of the professional community, counselors need to recognize that they are responsible not only to clients but also to the profession. Counselors who are good citizens of the professional community know who they are, advocate for the profession as well as their clients, and communicate with and represent themselves to others appropriately. In addition, responsible counselors maintain membership in the American Counseling Association along with its divisions and branches and abide by the values and ethical guidelines of the association.

Professional identity.   Being a good citizen of the professional community begins with a clear sense of professional identity. Although there is a great deal of overlap in the work performed by counselors and other mental health professional groups (e.g., psychologists, social workers), counselors with a strong professional identity are able to explain the differences between themselves and these other professionals. Responsible counselors can describe the services they offer, the philosophy that informs their activities, the training that prepared them for practice, and the credentials that validate their training and competency. From a clear sense of professional identity emerges a sense of pride in being a member of the profession (Remley & Herlihy, 2010).

Advocacy.   Compared to other helping disciplines, counseling is a relatively young profession, "still in its adolescence, continuing to develop its identity, and striving for recognition and respect from the public, legislators and other mental health professions" (Eaves & Erford, 2014, p. 19). The maturation of counseling as a profession would not be possible without the advocacy efforts of members of this community. Advocacy involves activities and attitudes that support, justify, and promote a cause (Gladding, 2006; Milsom, 2014). When counselors advocate for the profession, they indirectly advocate for their clients as well. Advocacy efforts may involve simple acts performed by individual counselors or organized group efforts undertaken to influence public policy. Many times, efforts to practice professional advocacy are subtle, as when a counselor encourages someone to seek the services of professional counselors. Other advocacy efforts might be directed at employers who might not otherwise know how professional counselors might contribute to their businesses or organizations (Milsom, 2014). More public advocacy efforts might involve pressing for legislation or public funding that would increase accessibility to qualified professional counselors by expanding opportunities for training, employment, and compensation. All these advocacy activities involve providing information and increasing awareness about the counseling profession. See Think About It 10.7.

THINK ABOUT IT 10.7

How have you engaged in professional advocacy? What are some specific activities that you might initiate during the remaining days of this academic term? In what advocacy activities might you become involved in the future?

Representation.   Advocating for the profession not only requires counselors to have strong professional identity, but they also must communicate and represent their identity properly (see Think About It 10.8). Within the professional responsibility section of the *ACA Code of Ethics* (Section C; 2005), several standards address how professional counselors should interact with others as well as how counselors should represent themselves to the public and to other professionals. When representing themselves, counselors are responsible for being accurate in disclosing the degrees they have earned, whether the degrees were earned through programs that were accredited at the time (e.g., accredited by the CACREP), the credentials they hold, and the professional organizations to which they currently belong. Although the CACREP standards are widely accepted in the counseling profession as the model for counselor training and preparation, the majority of counseling programs in the United States are not accredited by this body (Remley & Herlihy, 2010). Furthermore, degrees awarded for completion of counselor preparation programs vary by institution (e.g., Master of Arts, Master of Science, Master of Education). Credentials also vary. The National Certified Counselor (NCC) credential, awarded by the National Board for Certified Counselors, is recognized across the United States; however, the licenses to practice that are awarded by state governments vary in name and in requirements. Counselors have a responsibility to clarify all this confusion when they introduce themselves to members of the community. Accuracy also is imperative for information disseminated through advertising, media presentations, and reports to third parties. Finally, professional counselors have a responsibility to be socially sensitive and culturally competent. Counselors who are good citizens of the community do not discriminate against or sexually harass others, nor do they condone these behaviors by other counselors.

THINK ABOUT IT 10.8

Suppose you are traveling on a commercial airliner, and the passenger sitting in the seat next to you asks what you do. You tell that person that you are a professional counselor, and the person asks you to explain what you mean. How would you respond?

Networking.   Being part of a community involves being connected to others. Advances in technology augment connections and provide avenues through which information may be shared. Counselors use technology to stay abreast of the latest research and trends in the profession. Mentoring relationships, supervision, and consultation all may be enhanced through communication technology. Communication technologies and social media also provide vehicles through which counselors may reach out to the community. As these advances become more complex and far-reaching, their benefits increase, but opportunities for harm do as well. Counselors who are good citizens of the professional community are connected; however, they must be vigilant about their boundaries.

Given the intimate nature of counseling relationships, along with the power differential and vulnerability of clients, most counselors know that they have a responsibility to protect the structure and boundaries of the relationship. The intimacy and vulnerability aspects of counseling sometimes are confusing for clients, however, and they are uncertain about the limits and boundaries of the relationship. In years past, a clear message about the relationship boundary might have been communicated simply by protecting the counselor's home telephone number. In a digital, wireless, networked society, however, boundaries are much less distinct, and counselors have a responsibility to be aware of the ways in which social media and other technologies may affect the nature and structure of counseling relationships. See Think About It 10.9.

THINK ABOUT IT 10.9

Suppose a client asks to "friend" you on Facebook. How will you respond?

HOW DO COUNSELORS KNOW IF THEY ARE PRACTICING RESPONSIBLY?

Responsibility Is Revealed in Professional Dispositions

Perhaps informed by the *ACA Code of Ethics*, many counselors describe their expectations for professional behavior in terms of professional "dispositions." *Dispositions* can be thought of as behaviors that reflect the values, attitudes, beliefs, and commitment of individuals in the profession. These professional behaviors support growth, empowerment, and change. By having and displaying these positive dispositions, counselors are demonstrating professionalism. Puleo and Daughhetee (2000, 2004) asked counselor supervisors and employers to describe the dispositions they looked for in developing professional counselors. Professional counselors serving in positions as employers and clinical supervisors of developing counselors were invited to participate in focus groups in which they were asked to identify characteristics, attitudes, behaviors, and competencies that represent professionalism. The supervisors and employers described 16 types of behaviors that they thought represented professionalism in counseling. The dispositions identified ranged from relationship building and microskills (similar to the concepts discussed in Chapter 3 of this text), to self-care (discussed comprehensively in Chapter 13) and being proactive in pursuing professional development. Table 10.1 contains a list of the dispositions along with individual objectives that illustrate each. To facilitate discussion, the dispositions are grouped into five categories: microskills, themes and theories, facilitating change, connecting to the world of work, and managing and caring for the counselor.

TABLE 10.1 Puleo-Daughhetee Longitudinal Evaluation Objectives (PD–LEO)

1. Demonstrates appropriate respectful, genuine, empathic, multiculturally competent attitude toward clients.
   - Verbally and nonverbally communicates genuine interest and concern for client(s).
   - Demonstrates genuineness and congruence.
   - Uses humor and self-disclosure appropriately.
   - Maintains focus on client(s).
2. Demonstrates ability to engage clients.
   - Communicates to client the nature of the counseling relationship.
   - Identifies expectations of client.
   - Establishes rapport.
   - Facilitates client expression and self-exploration.
3. Demonstrates facilitative communication skills.
   - Uses specific, concrete language.
   - Appropriately uses probes/questions.
   - Uses clarifying statements appropriately.
   - Summarizes appropriately.
4. Demonstrates understanding of clients' nonverbal as well as verbal communication.
   - Attends to clients' nonverbal behavior.
   - Distinguishes feelings from content.
   - Accurately identifies feelings of client(s).
   - Accurately reflects feelings of client(s).
5. Demonstrates an understanding of clients' presenting problems/concerns.
   - Formulates verbal responses that accurately and concisely reflect the content and feeling of client messages.
   - Communicates understanding of client's perception.
   - Articulates client concerns/problems during supervision.
   - Appropriately applies current record keeping standards.

(Continued)

TABLE 10.1 Puleo-Daughhetee Longitudinal Evaluation Objectives (PD–LEO) (*Continued*)

6. Demonstrates an understanding of themes presented by clients as they relate to the presenting concerns.
   - Challenges client appropriately.
   - Demonstrates advanced accurate empathy.
   - Uses comprehensive responses rather than responding only to the client's last response.
   - Articulates client themes during supervision.

7. Demonstrates the ability to conceptualize client themes/problems within a theoretical framework, exhibiting multicultural competency.
   - During supervision, articulates client themes/problems within a theoretical framework.
   - Within a theoretical framework, articulates relationship between client behavior and themes using principles and practices of diagnosis (current edition of the *DSM*).
   - Using theoretical language, links intervention strategies to themes/problems.
   - Applies theory consistently while working with client(s).

8. Demonstrates ability to develop and implement treatment/program goals.
   - Objectively states treatment/program goals and relates them to presenting concerns/issues including addiction and co-occurring disorders.
   - Communicates treatment/program goals to client(s).
   - Articulates strategies for pursuing treatment/program goals.
   - Demonstrates implementation of strategies for pursuing goals.

9. Articulates a personal theoretical approach for working with clients grounded in relevant research and best practice.
   - Articulates a personal view of human nature and development.
   - Articulates a personal view of the change process.
   - Links intervention and change strategies to theory.
   - Evaluates change process and counselor effectiveness from theoretical perspective.

10. Assesses the counseling process/relationship (with appropriate assessment techniques and instruments), assesses for suicide, addiction, harm to others and making appropriate modifications to benefit client progress, exhibiting multicultural competency.
    - Verbally identifies small increments of change.
    - Responds appropriately and with immediacy to important material as it arises in counseling sessions.
    - Responds appropriately regarding assessment and counseling in crisis situations.
    - Terminates counseling sessions and relationship appropriately.

11. Demonstrates knowledge of organizational structure of site.
    - Articulates program administration issues related to clients (i.e., referral sources, admission criteria, assessment process, policies and procedures . . .).
    - Articulates role of counselor relative to the site.
    - Demonstrates knowledge of site's relationship to families, schools, agencies, or organizations in the community and maintains a resource list for referrals.
    - Recognizes and articulates strengths and challenges of site.

12. Engages in program development.
    - Recognizes and assesses needs of client population.
    - Proposes appropriate prevention/intervention and consultation strategies to meet needs of client population, including referral.
    - Implements program strategies to meet needs of client population with awareness of public or school policy, financing, and regulatory processes.
    - Evaluates effectiveness of program strategies with regard to client population needs.

13. Demonstrates appropriate professional behavior.
    - Honors commitments to clients, site, and supervisors.
    - Presents self in a "professional" manner (including appropriate dress for work setting, identifying self as professional counselor-in-training, etc.).
    - Manages time appropriately with regard to professional responsibilities.
    - Engages in advocacy for the profession and clients.
14. Examines issues of self (values, beliefs, strengths, challenges) in the counselor–client relationship, and in the counselor–supervisor relationship, including ability to recognize limitations.
    - Accepts feedback, constructive criticism, suggestions.
    - Expresses clear understanding of personal needs, values, strengths, challenges, feelings, and motivations that may influence effectiveness.
    - Demonstrates ability to put aside personal concerns to focus on client/program.
    - Appropriately accepts responsibility in counselor–client relationship and in counselor–supervisor relationship, including referral of clients when necessary
15. Demonstrates an understanding of and adherence to the ethical and legal responsibilities of the counselor.
    - Upholds legal standards of professional conduct.
    - Upholds standards of ethical conduct.
    - Applies ethical principles to practical situations in counseling (e.g., informed consent).
    - Demonstrates ability to recognize and articulate ethical dilemmas.
16. Takes responsibility for professional growth and development through identification of specific experiences and opportunities.
    - Meets with supervisor(s) regularly.
    - Demonstrates initiative in selecting professional development opportunities.
    - Identifies learning relative to specific experiences.
    - Demonstrates ability to outline plan of supervision.

MICROSKILLS.   The term *microskills* refers to the basic skills of counseling. These skills are used to enter into and to establish relationships with clients and include behaviors such as attending, active listening, and participating in the therapeutic dialogue. Possessing microskill competency is a central responsibility and disposition of counselors.

   Demonstrating an appropriate professional attitude toward clients.   At the core of professional practice is the counseling relationship. Numerous textbooks written about models of helping and the acquisition of helping skills begin with a discourse on the counseling relationship and what the counselor must bring to it. In his seminal work published in 1957, Carl Rogers identified six conditions that are necessary for the therapeutic relationship to effect change. According to Rogers, the counselor must be "congruent" or genuine and must communicate unconditional regard and empathy to the client. Decades later, these conditions continue to be identified by professional counselors as core dispositions. Participants in focus groups conducted by Puleo and Daughhetee (2000, 2004) considered a professional attitude toward clients as one that is respectful, genuine, empathic, and multiculturally competent. Counselors entering relationships with clients should be genuine and congruent themselves and should demonstrate focused attention and genuine caring for their clients.

   Engaging clients.   Once the counseling relationship has been initiated, it is important for counselors to establish rapport with clients. Clients must feel invited into the counseling relationship. Although legal and ethical standards stipulate that clients must be informed about the nature of the counseling relationship, responsible counselors place value on being certain that the nature of the counseling relationship is communicated in a way that clients understand. It is equally important that counselors understand the perspective and expectations of clients who enter the relationship. Key to engaging clients is facilitating expression and self-exploration.

Facilitating communication.   Professional counselors value effective communication skills. To facilitate client expression and self-exploration, counselors must employ very specific communication skills. By using concrete language, counselors provide clarity and focus and grant permission to discuss sensitive content (Egan, 2010; O'Hanlon & Beadle, 1997). Summarizing statements focus further and communicate to the client that the counselor is listening and engaged.

Understanding communication.   Communication is not just talk. Responsible counselors ask questions and formulate responses that facilitate client expression. Perhaps more important, they hear and understand the answers they receive. Active listening, an important responsibility of counselors, involves being able to discern what clients are communicating without words. Responsible counselors sense what clients are feeling and are able to convey to clients that they understand their feelings.

THEMES AND THEORIES.   Counseling requires more than having a conversation with another person. During the course of therapeutic dialogue, responsible counselors attempt to understand the client from a holistic point of view. They listen for themes, patterns, and relationships among the ideas, content, and feelings that clients express. In essence, responsible counselors look for the "bigger picture." Attending to the bigger picture means developing a comprehensive understanding of clients and their needs in the contexts of their lives. Operating from a theoretical foundation facilitates the conceptualization of client concerns and therapeutic needs.

Understanding clients' presenting concerns.   Counselors must be able to not only hear and understand what clients are communicating, but they must also be able to put that understanding into context. Clients tell their stories in many ways. Some present themselves as "victims," some as complainers, and others as people who do not require help. It is the counselor's responsibility to ascertain what clients are saying about themselves, regardless of the ways in which their stories are told. They must then be able to communicate that they understand the client's perspective. Having a theoretical framework helps counselors explain the relationship between clients' experiences, thoughts, feelings, and behavior. To get at the heart of the matter, responsible counselors must listen with intent and must focus their conversation through challenging and empathic responses.

Conceptualizing.   Case conceptualization requires counselors to be able to see relationships between the client's feelings, behaviors, and thoughts against the backdrop of contextual factors such as culture. Using theory helps counselors understand how clients have arrived at their points of view and how their presenting concerns fit into a diagnostic picture. By using theory as a guide, counselors can anticipate client actions and reactions and can select appropriate intervention strategies to promote change.

Having a personal theory.   It is important for counselors to be intentional in their work, and in being intentional, they must be able to articulate the direction they are going. Theory serves as a road map for counseling, and evidence-based practices serve as vehicles. Responsible counselors are able to articulate their ideas about human nature and the change process. Theoretical framework allows responsible counselors to explain how the practices they intend to employ should work and how subsequent client changes might be identified.

FACILITATING CHANGE.   Case conceptualization is the first step in treatment planning. For change to occur, counselors and clients need to work together in pursuit of goals. Responsible counselors help clients articulate goals for themselves that will be realistic, substantive, and challenging. These goals may be conceptualized as the client's desired outcomes of counseling. At the same time, counselors work toward therapeutic goals that are suggested by their theoretical orientation. Client goals and therapeutic goals, although stated differently, support one another. For example, a client goal representing "anger management" might be a reduction in fight frequency, whereas the therapeutic goal of a counselor working from cognitive theory might be a change in thought patterns that trigger fighting.

Treatment and program planning.   Planning for change involves being able to articulate desired outcomes and to select specific strategies for intervention that would facilitate the desired change. Numerous techniques, methods, and tools are available to counselors, and choosing from this vast array must be done with intention. The choices made by responsible counselors are informed by knowledge of evidence-based practices as well as theory.

Assessing. Responsible counselors assess throughout the entire counseling relationship. Assessment early in the relationship provides information important for conceptualization and diagnosis as well as information about the counselor's and client's suitability for working together. Once engaged, counselors are responsible for assessing whether progress is being made toward goals. They are able to identify small increments of change in their clients and are willing to examine their own choices and effectiveness if no change is noted. Assessment is an ongoing process, and responsible counselors are diligent in their efforts to assess. Small changes as well as critical changes in clients are noted, and the actions of responsible counselors are adjusted accordingly. In addition, to be able to engage in assessment as an informal, ongoing procedure, responsible counselors are familiar with and able to use formal and standardized assessment practices. The results of assessment guide the course of counseling; intervention strategies are adjusted, referrals are made, or counseling is terminated successfully.

Engaging in program development. It is important for counselors to have knowledge of the client populations they serve. Responsible counselors are able to apply their assessment skills, not only to individual clients, but to communities as well. Communities are served when counselors recognize needs of client populations and develop strategies for addressing those needs. Programs should be developed that are culturally sensitive, take into consideration the needs of underrepresented populations, and apply practices that are supported by research.

CONNECTING TO THE WORLD OF WORK. Counselors work in contexts. Some work in school settings; some work in offices and outpatient settings; some work in hospital or inpatient settings. In addition to working in a variety of settings, counselor interests, emphases, and scopes of practice vary. Responsible counselors are aware of their roles within the contexts of their work environments. They understand their own relationships to their work settings and the relationship of their work settings to other systems in the community. By being connected to other professionals in the world of work, counselors are able to consult with others on behalf of clients and make appropriate referrals when necessary.

Socially influencing others. Counselors are responsible for the way they represent themselves and for being aware of how others perceive them. Interpersonal attractiveness is an important source of influence in counseling relationships (Hackney & Cormier, 2013; Strong, 1968). Factors such as demeanor, attitude, and appearance contribute to assessments of attractiveness. Other professional behaviors that make a difference in the way counselors are perceived include honoring commitments made to others. It is important to keep appointments, be punctual, and be prepared, not only with clients, but also with supervisors, colleagues, and other professionals.

Advocating for the profession. Responsible counselors recognize that they not only represent themselves, but they also represent the counseling profession. Counselors with strong, clear professional identities can represent the value of counseling to others. They can describe the services that counselors offer and explain the unique qualities of those services. According to the *Code of Ethics* of the American Counseling Association, "Counselors actively participate in local, state, and national associations that foster the development and improvement of counseling" (2005, p. 9). By being members of the American Counseling Association, counselors have a role in advocating for the values of the profession and for the individual and societal changes that may be brought about by implementing those values.

MANAGING AND CARING FOR THE COUNSELOR. To be effective with clients, communities, and the profession, counselors are responsible for themselves, both professionally and personally. Counselors have a personal responsibility to be well (Puleo, 2004). Counselors are responsible for monitoring and maintaining their own physical, mental, and emotional health.

Counselors also pose a risk of harm to clients if they do not attend to their own professional growth. Counselors have a responsibility to be lifelong learners (Daughhetee et al., 2010). Professional growth is maximized when counselors assume responsibility for continuing the development of their competencies. Numerous avenues for learning and growth are available, including supervision, consultation, mentoring, participating in continuing education activities, and staying abreast of the professional literature, and responsible counselors take advantage of all these opportunities.

Assessment of Professional Dispositions

THE PD-LEO. Puleo and Daughhetee (Attaway, Barnes, Daughhetee, & Puleo, 2002; Puleo & Daughhetee, 2000, 2004) developed the Puleo-Daughhetee Longitudinal Evaluation Objectives (PD-LEO) as a tool for assessing professional development (see Table 10.1). The PD-LEO is a representation of the 16 dispositions identified by supervisors and employers of developing professional counselors. Four behavioral objectives are associated with each area. To assess a counselor's level of professional growth, it is recommended that a 10-point developmental scale (see Table 10.2) be applied to each objective on the checklist. A score at the lowest level of the scale would represent no exposure or growth in a given area. A score of 10 would reflect maximum growth and would be an indication of readiness to teach, mentor, or supervise someone else. By scoring each item individually, a profile emerges that suggests emerging strengths as well as areas of challenge in need of further growth. See Think About It 10.10 to begin considering your own dispositions, and use the PD-LEO to assess the professional development of the early-career counselors in Case Studies 10.1 and 10.2.

TABLE 10.2 Rating Scale For Use With The PD-LEO

- **Level 1**–Does not appear to be familiar with this concept, skill, or practice. Requires didactic instruction or formal coursework to gain knowledge in this area.

- **Level 2**–Has some familiarity with this concept, but has not demonstrated knowledge, skill, or practice.

- **Level 3**–Has attempted to demonstrate knowledge, skill, or practice, but with specific direction and close monitoring and supervision.

- **Level 4**–Has demonstrated this knowledge, skill, or practice with some initiative. Requires close monitoring, training, and supervision to further develop this competency.

- **Level 5**–Demonstrates this knowledge, skill, or practice independently, but at a rudimentary level. Requires monitoring, training, and supervision to further develop this competency.

- **Level 6**–Demonstrates this knowledge, skill, or practice adequately. Requires ongoing training and supervision to further refine this competency.

- **Level 7**–Consistently demonstrates this knowledge, skill, or practice adequately, independently, and with minimal prompting. Requires ongoing supervision to continue to advance this competency.

- **Level 8**–Routinely demonstrates this knowledge, skill, or practice independently and with proficiency. Requires ongoing supervision to continue to advance this competency.

- **Level 9**–Demonstrates expertise in this knowledge, skill, or practice. Could benefit from supervision or consultation to apply this competency in nonroutine circumstances.

- **Level 10**–Consistently demonstrates expertise in this knowledge, skill, or practice. May benefit from consultation. Is capable of teaching others this competency.

THINK ABOUT IT 10.10

Find excerpts from your own counseling activities that reveal each of the dispositions listed in the PD-LEO. Use the rating scale in Table 10.2 to indicate your level of development of each.

CASE STUDY 10.1

Gaining experience in a college counseling center

Anni is a 25-year-old counseling practicum student placed in a counseling center at a large public university. She is very excited about this placement. At the beginning of the semester she helped with various freshmen orientation programs and will begin seeing individual clients after orientation week. Some of the orientation programs provided information about counseling, career development services, and tutoring, and some of the programs were fun social events sponsored by the university's Division of Student Affairs. Anni loved the social events; it brought back memories of her fun days in college a few years ago. Anni believes that college is the best time in life, and she wants to help students adapt to their new environment so they can enjoy these precious years.

After orientation, Anni was assigned a freshman client named Stella. Stella came to the counseling center of her own volition during the second week of classes. Stella is having a tough time and was reminded of the counseling center by her resident advisor (RA). Stella is the youngest of three sisters, and her parents separated the month before she left home for college. In many ways, this separation wasn't a surprise, but it still hurts. Stella is a quiet, introverted person who enjoys writing poetry. She plans to get her B.A. degree in English and go on to graduate school for an M.F.A. degree in creative writing. She is very talented and has had a few of her poems published. Stella's boyfriend broke up with her a year ago, and she is still having a hard time getting over him. She has nothing in common with the other girls in her residence hall and feels very isolated. A part of her just wants to leave and go home, but she knows there's nothing for her there, and she needs to figure out a way to survive here. She is hoping that a counselor can help her.

ANNI:	So Stella, what brings you to counseling?
STELLA:	I don't know. I'm not feeling so great about being here but I also don't want to go back home. I need help in making this college thing work.
ANNI:	Well, homesickness is very common and lots of other people feel the same way. Usually by the third week people have made friends and are involved in activities, and they don't give home a second thought. Maybe you haven't given this enough time? Stella just looks at Anni blankly, so Anni continues.
ANNI:	Were you at the orientation events?
STELLA:	Yes.
ANNI:	Good, so you know about all the clubs and activities you can join. Once you join some groups you'll make friends and this will feel like home. Have you been meeting people, going to games and events?
STELLA:	Well, I'm not much into that sort of thing.
ANNI:	What have you been doing?
STELLA:	Well, I've been reading ahead in some of the novels for my World Lit class, and I've been working on some poems.
ANNI:	Yes, I saw you were an English major. What type of job do you hope to get after graduation?
STELLA:	I don't look upon it as a job.
ANNI:	OK . . . what about friends? Have you met any new friends or any boys you might be interested in?
STELLA:	There is one girl in one of my classes that seems kind of nice. My boyfriend broke up with me a year ago, and I'm still not ready for another relationship.
ANNI:	A year is a long time, there a plenty of fish in the sea you know. Are you going to rush?
STELLA:	No, I'm not into that.
ANNI:	Well, even if you don't join a sorority it's a great way to meet people, and you might be surprised.

The session wraps up with Anni giving Stella a homework assignment to go to two campus events before the next session and to look into sorority rush. Anni also sets up an appointment for Stella in the Career Center. Stella cancels both the counseling and the career center appointments the next day. Anni is surprised and disappointed.

What do you think of Anni's session with Stella? Using the PD-LEO, analyze this session segment. What could Anni have done differently? How might Anni's own experiences be getting in the way of her counseling in this setting?

CASE STUDY 10.2

Gaining experience in the community

Jim is beginning to have doubts about whether or not he wants to be a counselor. He enjoyed many of his counseling classes, but after a semester of practicum, he's not sure if this is for him. He would never tell his site or university supervisor this. He is hoping to just make it to graduation and figure out something else to do with this degree. Work for an art foundation perhaps? Go back to school again and get another degree? He finds the theories and everything interesting; he just doesn't like dealing with his clients. The clients at his practicum site were not like he thought they would be. Jim is interested in using a more analytical, insight-oriented approach with clients, but the client base was not what he was expecting. He realizes that he was expecting clients whose cultural context was similar to his, and not the clients he ended up with—people who were struggling in every way possible and who didn't have any resources you could build on. He is quite proud of his ability to pretend to have unconditional positive regard for these people.

He switched to a new site for internship, but it's not much better. Jim earned a B in practicum, his first B of the program, and he must make an A in internship. He needs to keep his GPA high in case he goes for another graduate degree. It wouldn't look good to have Bs in his clinical courses after making an A in everything else. Jim makes sure to look the part of the professional in all his dealings with supervisors. He is never late to the center or to the supervision sessions. He has been able to feign concern for clients, but in truth he finds them tedious.

Jim is very careful when he chooses sections of video recordings to play for his supervisors. He tries to pick ones where, in his opinion, he does well, but the supervisors are always finding things to pick apart. He tries to control his feelings during supervision, but last week his supervisor commented that Jim seemed defensive. The latest ordeal is the client advocacy project his university supervisor has assigned. Really? How is he supposed to advocate for the clients at his center when they won't do anything to help themselves. Jim puts on a brave face and begins to think about this advocacy project. What does he need to do to impress his professor with this? How can he use this to guarantee an A in internship?

Using the PD-LEO, what do you think of Jim's professionalism, openness to feedback, and examination of self? How could his supervisors and peers help him? What would Jim need to change to receive their help?

Summary

In essence, this entire text is a discussion of professional responsibility. Professional responsibility involves being accountable, being competent, and working well with others. Professional responsibility goes beyond adhering to the *ACA Code of Ethics*; responsible counselors possess dispositions through which they express their professional attitudes, values, beliefs, and commitments.

The questions raised in this chapter were intended to help developing counselors reflect on their own growth and the degree to which they are accepting and practicing professional responsibility. Developing counselors enrolled in practicum and internship are guided toward assuming greater responsibility, but are afforded a level of safety that is provided by their supervisors' responsibility for them and their work. Within this safety net, developing counselors may gain experience, competence, and confidence as professionals.

Counselors are responsible to their clients and to the counseling relationship. To practice responsibly, counselors should be cognizant of the power differential that exists in counseling relationships as well as the vulnerability of clients. Counselors should take caution not to abuse their power and to safeguard the welfare and dignity of all clients. Counselors are responsible for relationships that empower others in the pursuit of their goals. To promote successful outcomes, counselors need to take responsibility for the structure and parameters of those relationships while guiding clients toward taking the initiative to change.

Counselors have a responsibility for being competent. Initial competencies are acquired during graduate training programs, but to practice responsibly once a degree and credentials have been awarded, counselors must continue to gain competency as they mature. Competency includes knowledge, skill, and diligence (Welfel, 2006). Knowledge competencies should include core areas such as those proscribed by CACREP and NBCC, as well as knowledge of research and professional trends communicated through the professional media. As counselors mature, they are responsible for incorporating current evidence-based practices into their repertoires of skill competencies. To function optimally, counselors are responsible for being lifelong learners and for maintaining their own wellness.

Counselors are responsible for being counselors; that is, counselors must know what sets this profession apart from other professions. Counselors are responsible to the American Counseling Association inasmuch as they adhere to the *ACA Code of Ethics*, espouse the values of the profession, and advocate for the profession and the communities they serve. Being clearly identified as a professional counselor is requisite for responsible communication with others.

Professional dispositions are necessary for practicing responsibly. In this chapter, knowledge, skills, and practices that exemplify dispositions were presented as longitudinal objectives for developing counselors. Counselors who practice responsibly will monitor their growth, development, and continuing competencies in a variety of areas to be optimal agents of change.

CHAPTER 11

Wrapping It Up

BY NICOLE A. ADAMSON AND BRADLEY T. ERFORD

PREVIEW

As this text draws to a close, it is essential for practicum students and interns to focus on how best to terminate therapeutic relationships or transition clients from their care to the care of another mental health professional. Clinical experiences also offer opportunities to reflect on what has been learned and to provide formative and summative performance evaluations of the student, supervisor, and training program.

TERMINATION

The process of earning a degree in counseling is extensive, but it does come to an end. After years of coursework and months of internship, counseling students approach the end of their formal education and must terminate multiple relationships they have made along their journey. During the last weeks of class and even at their graduation ceremony, students must bid farewell to their professors and classmates. However, there are more formal relationships that require termination planning, such as those with supervisors and clients. Although it will be difficult to say goodbye, new opportunities will be waiting for you as a counseling graduate (and earning a paycheck will make it worthwhile).

It is important to monitor your own personal reactions to terminations with clients and supervisors. It may be helpful to keep a journal that can be used to express the feelings and worries associated with closing one chapter and opening a new one. It can also be helpful to discuss these thoughts with your supervisors, professors, or other colleagues (Baird, 2010). When used appropriately, some self-disclosure or immediacy with clients can add to the therapeutic value of discussion about termination. Let's review some important facets to consider when terminating relationships with supervisors and clients.

Termination of Supervisory Relationships and Evaluations

The relationships between practicum students or interns and their supervisors are special in that supervisors have the ability to assume many roles throughout the supervision process. A supervisor may act as a mentor, counselor, and teacher over the span of the supervision relationship or even within a single supervision session (Bernard & Goodyear, 2009). In addition, supervisors are responsible for gatekeeping activities and are often required to evaluate the student's performance. This creates a need for the supervisor to assume a careful balance between encouraging the student and realistically evaluating his or her abilities.

Training programs will likely have their own forms for use in student evaluation. Sample forms for school and agency evaluations are provided in Tables 11.1 through 11.4. It is important to provide these forms to supervisors well in advance, so that they have ample time to review the evaluation criteria with the student early in the experience and complete the evaluation thoughtfully and accurately. Some students might find this process awkward, but it is important to view the evaluation process as an opportunity to improve counseling skills, rather than an obstacle to overcome (Hodges, 2011). Invite critical feedback from your supervisor; spend time reviewing areas in which you have excelled and areas for further improvement. It will also be helpful to discuss concrete ways in which you can develop your competency. Your supervisor is a valuable resource; no matter a counselor's age or level of experience, there is still room for growth and improvement.

TABLE 11.1 An Example Criterion-Referenced Counseling Practicum Performance Evaluation to be Completed by a Supervisor

The following counseling experiences must be successfully completed by the end of practicum. Place an (x) beside each outcome achieved and a (−) beside each outcome not fully achieved. Please return to the university supervisor. The practicum student must be able to:

___ Demonstrate high quality personal and professional traits.

___ Describe through observation the role of the counselor as a community liaison and counseling advocate.

___ Demonstrate competence in individual and group counseling through a rotating caseload of at least two individuals and a minimum of one group consisting of at least eight sessions.

___ Use counseling literature to address issues of importance to counseling practice.

___ Use a variety of counseling tools, resources, and strategies to facilitate client growth.

___ Observe and participate in consultation and collaboration with colleagues and parents.

___ Discuss and network with the interdisciplinary treatment team.

___ Demonstrate knowledge of and ability to use a variety of counseling tools.

___ Apply referral procedures for clients in need of specific help.

___ Demonstrate adherence to ethical and professional standards.

___ Facilitate appreciation for cultural, lifestyle, and gender diversity.

TABLE 11.2 An Example School Counseling Practicum Disposition, Competencies, and Skills Rating Scale

Personal Dispositions and Traits	Needs Improvement	Meets Expectations	Above Average	Exceptional
1. Voice quality				
2. Professional appearance				
3. Energy/initiative				
4. Punctuality				
5. Self-confidence				
6. Perseverance				
7. Sense of trust				
8. Sense of humor				
9. Flexibility				
10. Emotional maturity				
Guidance and Counseling Knowledge & Skills				
1. General knowledge of school counseling program				
2. Ability to apply individual counseling skills				
3. Ability to apply group counseling skills				

(Continued)

TABLE 11.2 An Example School Counseling Practicum Disposition, Competencies and Skills Rating Scale (*Continued*)

Personal Dispositions and Traits	Needs Improvement	Meets Expectations	Above Average	Exceptional
4. Ability to plan/conduct developmental guidance lessons				
5. Ability to consult and collaborate with colleagues and parents				
6. Ability to use original and imaginative ideas				
7. Ability to follow up on cases				
8. Ability to work independently				
9. Ability to manage unexpected situations				
10. Ability to work with others				
11. Ability to plan and coordinate				
12. Ability to respect and appreciate the diversity of the student population				
13. Ability to plan and implement a developmental comprehensive school counseling program				
Professional Dispositions and Traits				
1. Rapport with students				
2. Relationships with colleagues				
3. Interest in the total school program				
4. Attitude toward counseling and assigned duties				
5. Response to suggestions				
6. Oral communication				
7. Written communication				
8. Respect for confidentiality				
9. Attitude toward, and respect for, diverse populations				
10. Adherence to ethical standards				

TABLE 11.3 An Example Criterion-Referenced School Counseling Internship Performance Evaluation to be Completed by a School-Based Supervisor

The following school counseling experiences must be successfully completed by the end of the internship experience. Please place an (x) beside each outcome achieved and a (–) beside each outcome not fully achieved. On the completion of the internship, the intern is able to:

____ Demonstrate multicultural competencies in relation to diversity, equity, and opportunity in student learning and development.

____ Engage parents, guardians, and families to promote the academic, career, and personal/social development of students.

____ Provide small-group counseling, consultation, and classroom guidance.

____ Engage in consultation with parents and colleagues.

____ Use current methods of data to inform decision making and evaluation.

____ Use appropriate referral procedures.

____ Understand graduation requirements and facilitate individual student planning.

____ Use a variety of career development tools and strategies to foster career planning.

____ Use procedures for assessing and managing suicide risk as well as other school-based crisis plans or procedures.

____ Implement strategies and activities designed to prepare students for a full range of postsecondary options and opportunities.

____ Demonstrate knowledge of and participate on various interdisciplinary teams.

____ Understand societal problems facing students and suggest possible ways to assist.

____ Develop measurable outcomes for school counseling services and interventions.

____ Understand the relationship of the school counseling program to the total school program.

____ Demonstrate skills in student advocacy.

____ Communicate evaluation results of school counseling services to stakeholder groups.

TABLE 11.4 An Example Counseling Intern Disposition, Competencies, and Skills Rating Scale

Professional and Personal Traits	Needs Improvement	Meets Expectations	Above Average	Exceptional
1. Openness to present one's work for critique				
2. Hears and incorporates feedback				
3. Initiates pertinent discussion in supervision				
4. Demonstrates ability to elicit and understand essential data				
5. Formulates and modifies a working diagnosis				
6. Distinguishes between the presenting problem and underlying issues				
7. Attends/responds empathically, initiates, and accepts clients nonjudgmentally				

(Continued)

TABLE 11.4 An Example Counseling Intern Disposition, Competencies, and Skills Rating Scale (*Continued*)

Professional and Personal Traits	Needs Improvement	Meets Expectations	Above Average	Exceptional
8. Formulates short- and long-term counseling goals				
9. Intervenes in a manner consistent with stated theoretical orientation				
10. Recognizes personal limitations				
11. Shows successful use of therapy to further one's personal and professional growth				
12. Uses countertransference issues in a promotive manner				
13. Reacts in an emotionally appropriate manner in difficult situations				
14. Communicates clearly, routinely and effectively engages clients, peers, faculty, supervisors, and support staff				
15. Displays sensitivity to multicultural issues				
16. Demonstrates an awareness of the multiple levels inherent in each interaction				
17. Functions skillfully as a counselor				
18. Willingness to learn through active participation in individual, small-group, and other supervisory situations				
19. Effectively performs roles in clinical setting				
20. Sensitive to ethical issues as they emerge in the counseling relationship				
21. Respects the confidential nature of the counseling relationship				
22. Establishes, maintains, and respects boundaries				
23. Grasps one's role as a professional counselor				

Professional and Personal Traits	Needs Improvement	Meets Expectations	Above Average	Exceptional
24. Demonstrates knowledge of and use of at least one of the four theoretical approaches (psychodynamic, humanistic, cognitive/behavioral, family)				
25. Demonstrates knowledge of the field of counseling according to student's level of training				
26. Communicates ideas well in reports, summaries, and case studies				
27. Speaks and writes clearly, articulately, and in grammatically correct English				
28. Is prompt, thorough, and conscientious with assignments				

Supervisors are often asked to evaluate university programs as well (see Table 11.5). This evaluation allows training programs to ensure that their students are receiving satisfactory internship learning experiences (Baird, 2010; Hodges, 2011). When completing these evaluations, supervisors should be careful to identify areas in which the program did well and areas in which the program could improve. Likewise, students are often asked to evaluate their site supervisor. It is often difficult to separate any personal biases from the professional relationship, but this practice will prove helpful as a new professional. For example, it is possible that a supervisor and supervisee do not have much in common; perhaps they enjoy different things and have different communication styles. Keep this in mind when objectively identifying overall strengths and weaknesses of the supervisor. This is good professional practice and displays your ability to be objective and work with a variety of people.

TABLE 11.5 School-Based Supervisor Evaluation of a University Counseling Education Program

On the basis of your experience with this university's school counseling intern, please check one response for each area presented below to indicate the level of intern preparedness. This evaluation is not meant to assess any single intern, but rather, is meant to help program faculty more effectively evaluate the effects of the training program. To that end, please feel free to comment on particular strengths noticed in the intern as well as any suggestions the program could use for improvement.

Area	Poor	Fair	Adequate	Good	Exceptional
1. **Managing a Comprehensive Program:** Apply the knowledge base of counseling to develop, implement, and evaluate data-driven, comprehensive developmental school counseling programs. Strengths: Improvements:					

(Continued)

TABLE 11.5 School-Based Supervisor Evaluation of a University Counseling Education Program (*Continued*)

Area	Poor	Fair	Adequate	Good	Exceptional
2. Professional Roles: Assume professional roles and functions of the professional school counselor as described by CACREP, ASCA *National Model*, and MSDE Pupil Services Regulation. Strengths: Improvements:					
3. Effective Interventions: Translate personality theory, learning theory, and normal and abnormal behavior theory into effective research-based interventions for individuals, groups, and families. Strengths: Improvements:					
4. Multicultural Society: Describe and adjust to societal changes and trends in a multicultural society. Strengths: Improvements:					
5. Individual Counseling Skills: Demonstrate the ability to form effective helping relationships with diverse individuals and groups. Strengths: Improvements:					
6. Understanding the Helping Process: Understand the facilitative factors that influence the helping process, including counselor and client characteristics; racial, ethnic, and gender factors that might bear on the success of the helping process; collaboration/consultation skills; and philosophical and theoretical frameworks that undergird the process. Strengths: Improvements:					

Area	Poor	Fair	Adequate	Good	Exceptional
7. Group Counseling Skills: Translate group development, dynamics, leadership styles, and counseling methods and skills into effective interventions with students, parents, faculty, staff, and community initiatives. Strengths: Improvements:					
8. Classroom Guidance Skills: Integrate an understanding of instruction and classroom management into effective classroom guidance interventions. Strengths: Improvements:					
9. Career Counseling and Educational Planning: Demonstrate the capability to apply educational planning, career development and decision theory, and knowledge of sources of career information to student development and aspirations. Strengths: Improvements:					
10. Using Assessments: Use formal and informal assessment procedures to identify needs, focus interventions, and assess counseling interventions and programmatic outcomes and effectiveness. Strengths: Improvements:					
11. Using Counseling Research: Understand and use counseling research and evaluation results to guide counseling practice. Strengths: Improvements:					

(Continued)

TABLE 11.5 School-Based Supervisor Evaluation of a University Counseling Education Program (*Continued*)					
Area	**Poor**	**Fair**	**Adequate**	**Good**	**Exceptional**
12. **Professional and Personal Behaviors:** Exhibit professional and personal behaviors, skills, and attitudes associated with competence in the core areas specified by CACREP Standards. Strengths: Improvements:					
13. **Ethical and Legal Behavior:** Demonstrate ethical behavior based on the ethical standards for ACA and ASCA and understand the legal issues relevant to school counseling. Strengths: Improvements:					
14. **Leadership and Advocacy:** Exhibit the professional leadership and social advocacy skills necessary to serve as an effective change agent and advance the cause of oppressed or underrepresented groups, parents, and students. Strengths: Improvements:					

Evaluations are only one step in the process of terminating supervisory relationships. Be sure to review all necessary termination paperwork that must be completed for the school, agency, or practice in which you are interning. This paperwork might be related to payroll or other agency record-keeping methods. It will also be necessary to identify termination paperwork that needs to be completed for each client on your caseload (Baird, 2010). Termination with clients is a process in itself that will be discussed in further detail in the next section.

The final step in terminating the practicum or internship supervisory experience is reflecting with your supervisor about your experience to become emotionally ready for your next journey. This is a time in which any past difficulties can be resolved and the supervisor and supervisee can celebrate the successful completion of a practicum or internship. It may be helpful to process the emotions that you are feeling about graduation in general, termination of the internship, hopes and fears for the future, and the accomplishments of which you are most proud (Baird, 2010). Self-Assessment Activity 11.1 contains some important internship termination questions to reflect on.

Termination of Counseling Relationships

A wise supervisor suggests that counselors should be thinking about termination during their first meeting with a client and in every session thereafter. Although it is important to be present in the moment with clients and to allow the counseling process to unfold at its own pace, the ultimate goal of counseling is to create client change. Once the client's desired changes have come to fruition, termination is a natural and desirable part of the counseling process. Realistically, not all terminations occur in a planned manner as the result of goal

---

SELF-ASSESSMENT ACTIVITY 11.1 INTERNSHIP TERMINATION

As you reach the end of your internship, reflect on and answer the following questions:

- What have I learned as a result of this internship?
- What are my strengths as a counselor?
- What areas of counseling should be the focus of further growth?
- What qualities of my supervisor do I hope to remember and emulate in the future?
- What would I have done differently as a supervisor?
- Is there any professional relationship that needs to be mended before internship termination?
- Will I have any opportunity to maintain communication with individuals from this internship site after termination?
- Have I completed all necessary paperwork before my last day?
- Whom should I say goodbye to in person and whom should I send a quick electronic goodbye note?
- What is the next step in my plan toward graduation and employment?

---

attainment, and every practicing professional will experience client termination for a variety of other circumstances. Therefore, open and honest discussion about eventual termination allows clients to process this occurrence at their own pace (Baird, 2010; Hodges, 2011).

Questions that may be helpful to ask clients in a first session include the following:

- When our work together is done and you have made the changes you desire to make, how will you know?
- What will look different?
- How will you feel different?
- How will you behave differently?
- How will you think differently?

If clients struggle to develop responses to these questions, you might also ask them: If I were a fly on the wall and was watching you once you'd reached your counseling goals, what would I see and observe?

Although it is possible for clients to realize their desired changes and then continue therapy to gain increased wellness or as a maintenance tool, it should not be assumed every client has this luxury. With the implementation of managed care and insurance companies' reluctance to reimburse for "nonessential mental health services," many clients are not able to receive counseling once their diagnosable mental health difficulties have been solved (Kress, Hoffman, & Eriksen, 2010). In addition, life circumstances often prevent clients from maintaining long-term counseling relationships. Many clients experience housing challenges, have transportation difficulties, or have jobs and other obligations to which they must attend first. Therefore, it is smart for counselors to realize that any session with a client could potentially be the last time the client has the opportunity to receive mental health services.

The counseling process takes time and cannot be rushed; it could take weeks or years to help clients overcome mental health–related difficulties. However, counselors can end each session in a manner that prepares clients to continue their growth between sessions or on their own, if necessary. Counselors might ask clients to articulate one thing they learned from the session. Or, counselors could ask clients to specify one small change they feel comfortable making over the next week. This is a helpful practice because it promotes autonomy and places responsibility on the client. In addition, it allows each client to identify personal progress and a plan to lead to the achievement of actual goals. Additional end-of-session termination strategies may include use of scaling (e.g., On a scale of 1–10 how close are you to achieving [goal]?), sentence completion, process questions, or an assigned journaling activity. Mindful remembrance of the termination goal facilitates the change process and places focus on achieving maximum gains in a relaxed, engaging manner (Baird, 2010).

At the end of each session, counselors might also inquire how clients feel they are moving toward their counseling goals. They might ask questions such as: "How do you feel you are doing in moving toward your counseling goals? How far do you believe you are away from reaching your counseling goals? What can I be doing to better help support you in moving toward your counseling goals?" Counselors can also ask the client to provide a summary of what occurred in that particular meeting. The counselor can add any necessary information, but this helpful tool allows counselors to learn what clients are getting from the sessions, and future meetings can be tailored accordingly. For example, a counselor and client may have spent 20 minutes discussing a relationship, and the counselor might believe that the client resolved to speak with the partner about their difficulty. However, the counselor might learn through the client's summary that the client plans to wait one more week before speaking with the partner. This is valuable information, as it provides clues to the client's internal processes and areas for continued improvement during the next session.

After the client provides a summary of the current session, the counselor could ask the client to describe how things have, or have not, changed since the very first meeting. This allows clients to identify areas in which they have succeeded and provides a sense of hope and control. It also allows clients to verbalize what desires they still have for themselves and how they might achieve their goals. This future-oriented thinking allows the counselor to understand what the client wishes to achieve on completion of the counseling relationship. The counselor can also contemplate termination and visualize a plan for the remainder of the counseling process. Of course, the actual process might look very different from what the counselor visualizes, but it is helpful to operate from a goal-oriented perspective.

Now that the client and counselor have taken 5 or 10 minutes to discuss the client's progress and future goals, the counselor can invite the client to identify one way in which he or she will work for change from then until the next session. This increases clients' self-efficacy, whereas reviewing the client's progress at the beginning of the next session places responsibility on the client in order to facilitate forward progress. This process for terminating an individual session can also be applied to termination of a counseling relationship (Baird, 2010; Hodges, 2011).

Counseling relationships can be terminated for a variety of reasons (Hodges, 2011). Ideally, the client has reached maximum gains in counseling and feels as though more sessions are not needed. It is also possible that extenuating circumstances, such as a counselor or client move or other client obligations, will prevent the counseling relationship from continuing. Another possible reason for termination is that the counselor determines that the counselor–client match is not a good fit, which could occur if the client presented issues outside the counselor's area of expertise or would benefit from a different counseling approach or style. Finally, clients may decide not to return for counseling because they do not feel as though it is helpful, they do not feel as though the counselor is a good fit, or they are not ready to address their mental health issues at the time. For each of these circumstances (whether planned or unplanned), counselors must take necessary steps to ensure they accomplish a satisfactory termination.

In terms of termination paperwork, each agency and private practice will have different procedures and policies in accordance with state laws and rules of affiliated mental health boards or other funding sources. In general, it is important to document the reason for termination and that appropriate referrals have been made, if necessary (Hodges, 2011). In addition, it is important to formally close any terminated case either by having the client sign a termination agreement or by documenting that sufficient attempts have been made to reach the client to have the agreement completed. This protects the counselor or agency; if a case is left open, but inactive, and the client engages in self-harm or harms others, the mental health provider could potentially be held liable for this unfortunate occurrence (Remley & Herlihy, 2010).

In addition to necessary termination paperwork, the counselor has the responsibilities of beneficence and autonomy (Remley & Herlihy, 2010). Throughout the entire counseling process, as mentioned before, the counselor should be working to provide the clients with necessary self-help skills. Upon a planned termination session, counselors can take similar steps to identify the client's current progress, future goals, and how the client will facilitate these goals. Therefore, even the termination session is helpful for the client and promotes his or her own sense of self-efficacy. In the case of an unplanned termination (e.g., the client does not return and cannot be contacted), it is good practice to provide a small-scale termination review at the end of each session, as previously mentioned.

Termination is a natural part of the counseling process; it can be a celebration of the client achieving maximum gains. However, it can also be a difficult process, such as when a counselor's internship is ending or the client wishes to cease counseling despite an obvious need for continuing it. Regardless, it is a necessary part of counseling and can be beneficial for the client and counselor. Counselors should take time to reflect on any termination to identify areas in which they could improve and ways in which they were successful helpers. This information could even be processed with colleagues or a supervisor (Baird, 2010; Bernard & Goodyear, 2008).

To help clients through the termination process, termination should be discussed regularly. For some counselors, discussing termination during the initial intake might feel premature, and counselors might feel concerned they are pushing clients away before they have even begun to work. However, creating a treatment plan implies that the counselor and client are working toward a goal that will hopefully be achieved. Also, research suggests that most clients want to attend counseling sessions only until their presenting problems have been resolved; most clients are not seeking lengthy counseling experiences (Hays & Chang, 2010). The counselor could spend time during the treatment planning session to discuss what will happen on achievement of goals; the client could decide to create new, more challenging goals; or the counseling relationship can be terminated. This is a natural way to assist the client in thinking about termination without feeling rushed. In addition, some clients might like to know that there will be an end to the process and that they can hope to achieve their desired goals.

As a planned termination approaches, the counselor should discuss with the client any final needs (Hodges, 2011). The counselor might also consider a creative way to bring closure to the relationship. The use of symbolic objects or tangible reminders provides clients with an item that he or she can take away and use to reconnect with the concepts learned in counseling (Kress & Hoffman, 2008). For example, if clients responded well to any metaphors used in counseling, a symbolic object such as a picture or a small item representative of the metaphors might be given to clients to help them reconnect with the metaphor once they have moved on from counseling. The client and counselor might also create a book or a picture (using collage, drawings, words, or symbols) that illustrates the change that occurred through the counseling process. Clients might be asked to complete one picture of where they were at during their first session and a second picture that highlights where they are at present. A third picture might depict where the client will be in the future, as the client continues to move forward. Regardless of how the counselor and client choose to spend their last session, a summary of the client's progress and a goal-oriented, hopeful plan for the future should be created.

Counselors are also expected to have thoughts and feelings about termination procedures. As previously suggested, it can be helpful to process these emotions with a supervisor. It is also helpful to use some self-assessment strategies to feel confident in termination procedures. For example, answering the following queries may yield helpful insights about the client's progress:

- What are the client's goals?
- Have these goals been met?
- Do I feel uneasy about terminating this relationship?
- What is different about this client that might be contributing to these feelings?
- Is the client resistant to termination?
- What needs or past experiences might the client have that may be contributing to this resistance?
- What referrals, if any, should be made?

VOICES FROM THE FIELD 11.1   Holding onto Hope,
by Jessica Headley

For over 6 months, a yellow Post-it with the word *hope* written on it rested in my top drawer. Each week, it made its way into the light, as a reminder to my client that I was holding onto her hope. "Are you ready to take your hope back?" I regularly asked her. And in every instance I received similar responses: "Things are never going to get better," "There's no point for hope," and "I wish I didn't exist."

As a beginning counselor, such responses were difficult to hear—especially because our time together was dwindling. I truly believed she was making progress. She had obtained a new job that gave her a sense of purpose, improved her relationships with family members and friends, and had begun to engage in self-care activities. She was even contemplating moving into a new apartment to reclaim her independence. Why wasn't she ready to relieve me of my caretaking responsibility? What was she holding onto?

With a few remaining weeks together, I made sure to give her gentle reminders of when our last day would be. I explained that termination is a process, and together we decided how we wanted to spend our remaining time. The Post-it still sat out as a reminder, but I had stopped asking about it. I had assumed that work still needed to be done, and so together the client and I made arrangements for her to continue seeking therapy with a new counselor.

The week before our final session, she began to cry and I thought, "Oh no, this can't be good." But to my surprise, she told me that she was ready to say good-bye *and* that she was ready to take back her hope. She told me that she was getting ready to pick up the keys to her new apartment. "Why hadn't she told me about this?" I thought. I was hurt. But before the situation became about me she explained that taking back her hope meant that she had accomplished all her counseling goals and that it was time to say good-bye. *She* decided it was time for her to make a new beginning—a beginning that did not include me.

This experience taught me that clients must say good-bye on their own terms and in their own special way. Picking up her hope, and then her keys, signified a new journey for my client. Handing over her hope reminded me of two important things: change doesn't happen on a timeline, and in counseling, change occurs on the client's terms.

METALEARNING: LEARNING FROM WHAT YOU'VE LEARNED

Counseling training programs are compact and intense. The Council for Accreditation of Counseling and Related Educational Programs (CACREP) requires training programs to provide 48 to 60 semester credit hours of coursework in the eight core areas of counseling: human growth and development, social/cultural foundations, the helping relationship, group dynamics/counseling, career development, appraisal, research, and professional orientation/issues (CACREP, 2009). After taking a number of courses that are reading intensive and require an extensive amount of time and energy, it is difficult to step back and truly grasp what was learned throughout the training process.

Metalearning is a concept that encourages people to take control of and integrate their learning. Metalearning encourages learners to understand the ways in which they learn and retain information and methods that allow learners to be aware of their cognitive processes (Biggs, 1985). Metalearning goes beyond metacognition (thinking about the way you think) to encourage learners to think about the ways in which they are learning (Jackson, 2004). Metalearning creates new ways of thinking; as learners begin to ponder the process of learning, their understanding of the learning process is altered, and their attitudes about learning change. As a result of altered thoughts and attitudes, behaviors related to learning, such as study and organizational methods, change in accordance. Finally, knowledge is acquired as the result of thinking about metalearning.

Counselors should use metalearning at all stages of their development. To reach graduate school, students must have identified a basic set of learning techniques that are effective. These techniques were probably further refined throughout their master's education and to accommodate the complex and critical thinking required at this level of study. However, it is possible that students had never thought of the complexity of their learning as is required through metalearning. The process of metalearning requires scholars to actively and mindfully evaluate and alter their learning strategies to maximize their abilities (Jackson, 2004). The earlier this complex thought is integrated in your training program, the better. Use Self-Assessment Activity 11.2 to begin working with metalearning.

SELF-ASSESSMENT ACTIVITY 11.2 METALEARNING

- What is my motivation for learning?
- What emotions do I feel when learning something new?
- In what setting is it easiest for me to learn (e.g., in a classroom, at a work site, online)?
- What behaviors do I alter to increase my learning ability?

Metalearning can be actively applied throughout the internship process. In understanding your organizational preferences, it is possible to acquire the materials needed to best learn in a class. Some people prefer binders, others prefer folders, and some use notebooks. However, it should not be taken for granted that the tools you are currently using are actually maximizing your learning capacity. Analyze your motivation for procuring the supplies (e.g., money, habit, convenience), and identify any other more optimal solutions.

Before entering the classroom or an internship site, analyze the behaviors that allow you to be most present and absorb information the best. For example, some people enjoy exercising before going to class to achieve an attentive sense of calm. Others prefer to read a book or take a car ride to settle their minds into their tasks. In forming an understanding of the behaviors that best help you learn, it is possible to maximize retention of information (Jackson, 2004). In addition, it is more likely that you will be able to identify alternative behaviors to increase learning if the preferred methods are not accessible.

Metalearning is unique to each individual just as each individual's learning style is unique (Jackson, 2004). Learners who are aware of their own personal experiences can better identify the ways in which they make sense of new knowledge. Subjective awareness of these learning biases can allow learners to process new knowledge in alternative ways to gain a different set of knowledge or skills. In addition, understanding the value learners place on a certain type of information and how they will use this knowledge in the future will allow scholars to intentionally retain information that they might otherwise disregard.

The Reflections on Learning Inventory was developed to help students identify their specific metalearning needs (University of South Australia, 2004). Although this instrument is not free, other instruments are available on the Web to help students identify similar constructs, such as preferred study methods (e.g., rereading the text, memorizing, or using repetition). This inventory also measures students' motivation for learning, ways in which learners are able to memorize material, and their motivation for learning. Because the counseling field is constantly expanding, every counselor (regardless of age or educational level) is a perpetual learner; it is never too late to begin exploring metalearning techniques.

When entering an internship, metalearning techniques can allow students to process their surrounding environment in dynamic and informative ways. An awareness of one's biases toward information collection could allow someone to focus on more relevant information throughout the internship process. For instance, an intern could focus on remembering new colleagues' faces and job titles, rather than pairing faces with names. Interns might also focus on retaining clients' treatment goals rather than their home address or mother's name. In understanding our learning biases, we can retrain our brains to retain more helpful information.

As graduating students reflect on their classroom and field experiences, it will be helpful to identify the optimal ways that information can be processed. If students prefer linear processing, it might be helpful to create binders of course information beginning with the first semester's courses and working through the last semester. However, a categorical learner may prefer to file educational materials in a binder according to the eight core areas as defined by CACREP (2009). This will allow students to easily access the palpable information they gained in their program. This level of thoughtful organization might also help students retain the information they have stored in their cognitions, as they will better know how they processed and stored the data (Jackson, 2004).

Often, counselors find their first employment opportunity at an establishment at which they did not complete their internship. It will be important for these new counselors to be able to apply the information they learned at their internship site to their new place of employment. Students who have explored their metalearning are better able to carefully retain information from their internship and generalize that learning to their next job. For example, instead of memorizing the wording of each question on a case note, the learner would internalize the basic categories of data that will need to be explained on any case note in their state (e.g., treatment goal, interventions, client response, and future plans). Learning to retain general data can be much more helpful for interns than focusing on site-specific information.

Metalearning is a helpful concept for counselors at any stage of their career; although it requires a great deal of introspection and self-discipline, the benefits of learning from what you've already learned are endless. Counselors who can understand why they retained the information they chose to retain are able to understand areas in which they need further education and specific aspects of counseling that are most important to them. Counselors who can learn through an objective lens can incorporate new information into their existing cognitions and can retain information in a way that is most beneficial to themselves and their clients. The ability to reflect on past learning to optimize future success will prove to be a valuable skill in a variety of settings. Consider the importance of metalearning for the counselor described in Case Study 11.1, and look back at your own experience using Self-Assessment Activity 11.3

CASE STUDY 11.1

Julie

Julie is a clinical mental health counseling student who is preparing for graduation in 2 months. She is preparing to take the National Counselor Examination (NCE) to become a licensed counselor and feeling a great deal of anxiety. Julie feels as though the past 2 years have been a blur for her; she was working full time and taking classes at night, then she quit work to begin internship and increased her coursework. She has been financially strained and often found herself thinking about expenses and bills during class. She is typically an organized person, but feels disheveled and very stressed about the condition of her course materials. At the end of each semester, she placed the folders for each of her classes on her bookshelf and has not touched them since. Her bookshelf used to be filled with movies that were carefully organized by genre; now, she couldn't find her favorite romantic comedy if you paid her!

Julie used to work in logistics before her company announced financial difficulties. She didn't love her job, but she was good at it. In fact, she could remember 13-digit tracking numbers as soon as the trucking companies shouted them out! Julie is especially stressed about the NCE because she has had some trouble in her classes; no matter how many times she copies her notes or reads the texts, she just doesn't seem to retain the information. Do you think there is anything else Julie can do to pass this test? She really wants to help clients, but she is struggling to help herself!

Discussion

Julie is having difficulty concentrating in class, and she is thinking about life stressors instead of her learning. It would be helpful for Julie to identify her motivation for going back to school. If Julie is able to clearly identify why the class is important, she might find it easier to pay attention. She should also clearly identify what she wants to learn from the class. If she is able to identify aspects of the class that are truly important to her, she can mindfully focus her attention to acquiring those bits of knowledge.

Julie liked to organize her movies in genres, but she is organizing her class material chronologically. It may be helpful for Julie to create a filing system that separates her course material by genre, which would be the eight CACREP core areas. She might purchase eight large 3-ring binders and insert the appropriate class material into each one. This would allow Julie to review the information as she organized her binders and would allow her to more easily access the data when studying for her exam.

It sounds like Julie can remember things very well when they are said aloud. However, she must be unaware of her preference for verbal processing due to her use of written study techniques. Julie probably should study for the NCE through verbal methods such as repetition of key points out loud and listening to audio study guides for the NCE. She might even consider having a fellow student or loved one read information to her and verbally quiz her.

Finally, Julie should work to understand the types of information she finds important. It seems as though she might like to memorize specific numbers, such as dates (as evidenced by her recollection of tracking numbers). However, it may be more helpful for Julie to remember more general information for the NCE. With mindful awareness of her own personal biases, Julie should be able to successfully pass the NCE exam!

SELF-ASSESSMENT ACTIVITY 11.3 PROGRESS DURING CLINICAL EXPERIENCE

1. I feel comfortable confiding in my supervisor about my own thoughts and feelings. True or false? Explain.
2. When would you feel comfortable discussing long-term termination with a client?
3. Termination can be a positive experience for counselors. True or false? Explain.
4. Termination can be a positive experience for clients. True or false? Explain.
5. If clients terminate before reaching maximum gains, they made no progress in counseling. True or false? Explain.
6. I know how I best retain information I learn in the classroom. True or false? Explain.
7. I know how to best retain information I learn at my internship site. True or false? Explain.

Summary

Termination is a sensitive subject and can bring mixed emotions for counselors, supervisors, and clients. It is important to be mindful and deliberate when addressing termination to avoid regret, confusion, or unresolved feelings. Confide in your supervisors and other mentors for guidance in this process.

It may be helpful to view all relationships with clients as temporary. The ultimate goal of counseling is to create change, so planned termination is the sign of success. Take care, however, to carefully prepare clients for this transition and be sensitive and aware of their feelings surrounding termination discussions and actions. It is especially helpful to end each counseling session with a hopeful look to the future and a discussion about the ultimate goal of the counseling process. This helps clients to understand that they are in control of their progress and gives them autonomy and responsibility in the relationship. This practice also makes it clear that termination is a desirable and realistic part of the counseling relationship.

Metalearning is a helpful practice to adopt as a counselor and a lifelong learner. In addition to simply thinking about your thoughts, metalearning is the practice of examining your learning processes. In gaining an in-depth understanding of your learning and retention, your attitudes and practices can be altered to create more meaningful and productive patterns of learning and memory. This technique can be helpful when working through difficult situations, such as terminations, in that students and counselors can be more confident that their practices were helpful and that all necessary tasks have been completed. Metalearning can be helpful for new counselors so they can generalize their skills to new environments, and it is a helpful practice for counselors at any stage of their career. Mindful incorporation of the most salient learning practices will prove to be beneficial for supervisors, counselors, and their clients.

Although there is a great deal of information to learn and process as a counselor-in-training, it is important to work at a pace that is comfortable for you. Most important, incorporate the concepts discussed in this chapter into your daily routine so that it becomes habit, rather than extra stress. In the end these tips and tricks will help you work more reflectively and intelligently!

CHAPTER 12

Other Pertinent Issues in Counseling Practice

BY ELISABETH BENNETT

PREVIEW

Previous chapters have addressed many of the activities, issues, and responsibilities of the professional counselor. This chapter provides an overview of other pertinent issues/roles in counseling practice including consultation, academic advising and career guidance, and advocacy. Supportive and collaborative services such as psychological, educational, and vocational assessment; compliance support for the psychopharmacological regimen set by the medical professional; and practice consistent with the requirements of third-party payers or managed care companies are also discussed. Understanding the role and function of the counselor is imperative in maintaining an ethical position and providing best practice throughout one's counseling career. An examination of each counseling role performed by Meghan in her typical day is provided. A self-assessment at the end of each section will assist the reader in the application of knowledge in each area to the practice of counseling.

A DAY IN THE LIFE OF A COUNSELOR

In considering the role of the professional counselor, many students beginning a graduate degree envision days spent in one-on-one sessions with clients who are extremely motivated and ready to change and grow to alleviate their own and others' suffering. This is a marvelous dream. And some of it is accurate. Most professional counselors, though, do much more than orchestrate the process of growth for individuals, groups, couples, or families. Most play a host of other roles throughout the day. Consider the following typical day of Meghan, a professional counselor at the mental health center in a midsized city where she is employed full time. Throughout Meghan's day she addresses a variety of issues and offers services and resources aimed at increasing the potential for many people to have a more fulfilling life (see Case Study 12.1).

CASE STUDY 12.1

A Day in the Counseling Life of Meghan, Licensed Professional Counselor

8:00 a.m.	Arrive at the office. Respond to business e-mail and phone messages and finish preparations for meeting with Mr. Henderson, Bachelor degree-level supervisor of the mental health center's crisis line volunteers in the Urgent Care Department.
8:45 a.m.	Meet with Urgent Care Team manager, Mr. Henderson. Bring materials for consultation regarding Mr. Henderson's agenda: training of volunteers for suicide hot line and restructuring of volunteer duties.
10:30 a.m.	Work on notes and treatment plans from prior day.

11:00 a.m.	Meet with client, Kevin. Explore results of Myers-Briggs Type Indicator (MBTI) and Strong Interest Inventory (SII) in light of interests and interview. Discuss further assessment as well as potential visit with college counselor.
12:00 noon	Lunch at desk. Catch up on paperwork.
12:30 p.m.	Meet with clients, Raul and Salina, who are raising their grandchildren. They are making progress with grandparenting plans but continue to feel isolated as well as concerned about their abilities to have energy and material resources to meet the needs of their grandchildren. Both want to make connections with other grandparents in this position and not feel alone as grandparents raising their grandchildren. A support group may be very useful, but none presently exist locally. (Fourth set of grandparents parenting grandchildren currently on my caseload.) Make appointment with program manager to discuss beginning a support group for grandparents raising their grandchildren. Schedule meeting with Aging Services Program coordinator to advocate for services in the community for grandparents raising grandchildren.
1:30 p.m.	Meet with client, Kathleen. Celebrate goal attainment (assertive with boyfriend about not smoking in the house). Review symptom reduction since prescription changes. Send note to/call Dr. Brown (MD) with concerns about facial tic and other symptoms since beginning new medications 2 weeks ago.
2:30 p.m.	Supervise interns (Kellie, Jackson, and Maria). Review center protocol for suicide assessment and prevention. Provide contact information for shift supervisors for consultation in case of client crisis. Prepare suicide assessment packages for interns and others at site.
4:00 p.m.	Review student case notes. Complete case notes. Write summary for court case. Prepare treatment plans. Sign documentation for billing department.
5:00 p.m.	End of business day.

THE ROLE OF THE COUNSELOR

The role of a professional is defined by the profession's governing entities, which most often are professional associations and/or accrediting organizations. Such bodies generally prescribe the educational program standards and clinical experiences required of the institution preparing future counselors. The profession's defined practices are aligned with the resulting knowledge and skills (Staton et al., 2007). For the counseling profession, these organizations include the American Counseling Association (ACA) and the Council for Accreditation of Counseling and Related Educational Programs (CACREP). State by state, counseling laws and regulations mandate the requirements for licensure and certification for professional counselors. Professional counselors provide assistance to individuals, groups, couples, families, organizations, and communities across a number of specialties all with the goal of increasing the insights and abilities of the counselee to assist in the resolution of developmental conflicts or to help with challenging day-to-day struggles and decisions.

Nearly 20 years ago, Nugent (1994) defined the role of the counselor as a professional relationship through which the healthy growth and development of a client occurs by way of an increase in the client's self-understanding, as well as the client's understanding of his or her relationship with others. Healthy and accurate understanding would result in the resolution of normal developmental conflicts. Almost a decade later, Altekruse, Harris, and Brandt (2001) proposed that the role of the counselor needed a clearer and more inclusive definition representative of the activities of the counselor, including diagnosis and treatment for disorders that move beyond normal development into the abnormal arena. Another decade of marked efforts toward counseling identity definition clarifies that the activities of the professional counselor are evolving, varied, and critical to the mental health profession. Therefore, it is prudent that counseling students understand the counselor's role in consultation, academic advising/career guidance, advocacy, supporting compliance to medically prescribed psychopharmacology, assessment, and ethical involvement with both public and private insurance providers.

CONSULTATION

In the example of a day in the life of the professional counselor provided in Case Study 12.1, Meghan began her day in the role of consultant. She had been approached by Mr. Henderson to gain her expertise regarding the training of volunteer crisis line workers. Meghan's role was not to provide the training; rather, she was to assist Mr. Henderson in determining *his* actions. This is consultation. Later in the day, Meghan provides instruction and training to interns who must act as directed. This is supervision.

Consultation was defined as early as 1963 by Caplan as a process whereby the assistance of an expert is sought with the goal of increasing the seeker's capacity for addressing a particular issue involving a third party (i.e., target of the consultation). The role of the counselor as a consultant varies in that consultation may be sought by a broad variety of professionals including, but not limited to, teachers, doctors, attorneys, clergy, business leaders, and fellow counselors who are working with students, patients, clients, parishioners, and employees. Anyone who seeks the input of another qualified individual to better address a situation for yet another person or group of persons is a potential consultee (see Figure 12.1).

The counselor-as-consultant's role is not limited to any particular counseling specialty. School counselors are asked by administration, staff, and faculty to provide consultation regarding students, parents, other school personnel, and community members across a wide range of issues. College counselors provide advice and assistance to various

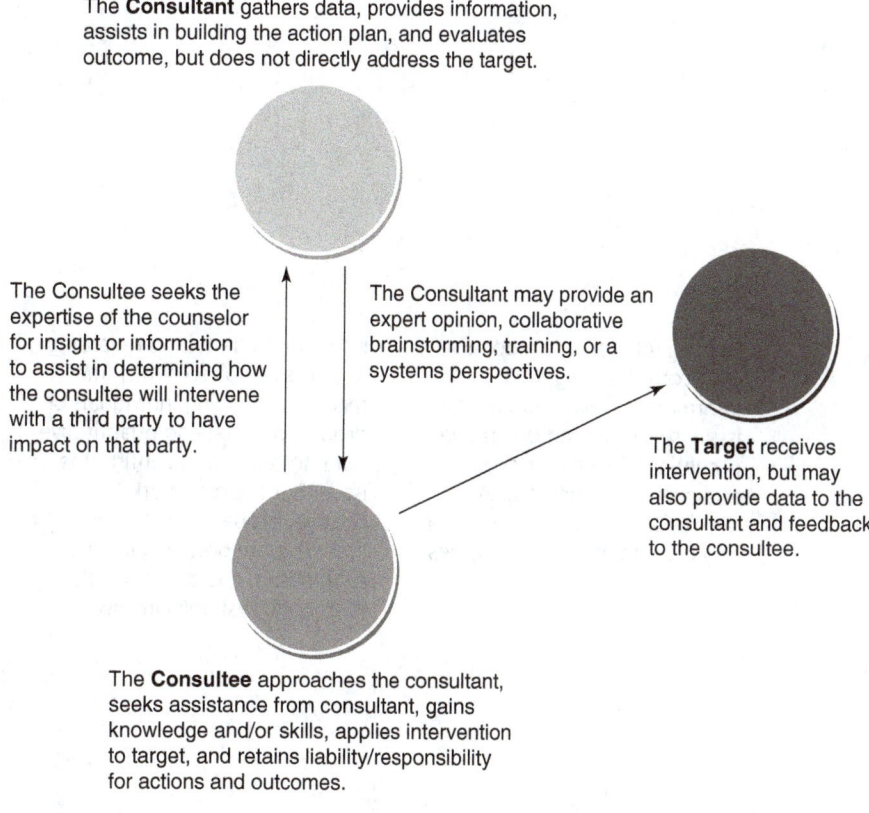

The **Consultant** gathers data, provides information, assists in building the action plan, and evaluates outcome, but does not directly address the target.

The Consultee seeks the expertise of the counselor for insight or information to assist in determining how the consultee will intervene with a third party to have impact on that party.

The Consultant may provide an expert opinion, collaborative brainstorming, training, or a systems perspectives.

The **Target** receives intervention, but may also provide data to the consultant and feedback to the consultee.

The **Consultee** approaches the consultant, seeks assistance from consultant, gains knowledge and/or skills, applies intervention to target, and retains liability/responsibility for actions and outcomes.

FIGURE 12.1 Consultation Roles and Process.

consultees such as faculty, residence life personnel, administration, academic advisors, and student groups. Mental health counselors might provide consultation for parents, schools, businesses, social service agencies, attorneys, doctors, and hospitals as well as for other counselors or mental health personnel in need of the counselor's particular expertise. In any case, the ethical obligations of a counselor to be beneficent and nonmaleficent remain consistent when consulting. Differing from supervision, there is no power to enforce that a consultee behaves as the consultant suggests, and the consultee remains fully liable for actions implemented. The consultant is liable to provide best practice within the scope of the consultant's expertise.

Various models of consultation have been developed and employed placing emphasis on content versus process, expert versus collaborative versus system centeredness, various theoretical foundations, and inward versus outward focus (Keys, Bemak, Carpenter, & King-Sears, 1998). There have been several models of the process of consultation proposed, all of which delineate stages covering entry to exit. Whether the counselor is the expert, a collaborator, or facilitator of a systems-based approach, consultation activities can be categorized into five stages: (a) orientation, (b) design, (c) implementation, (d) review/revision, and (e) follow-up/termination. These stages are noted and applied to associated activities and samples in Table 12.1.

TABLE 12.1 The Consultation Process

Stage	Brief Explanation	Activities	Example
Orientation	Consultee contacts consultant and proposes the issue. Consultant works to build relationship, to understand the issue, and to clarify the conditions of the consultation.	Meet, greet, define issue, set contract defining the roles and responsibilities of each party involved, limitations of expertise with referral where appropriate.	The Dean of Student Life at the university contacts the counseling center regarding the increase in reports from resident directors involving violation of the "no alcohol in the dorms" policy. Opal, a professional counselor, is assigned to consult. Opal has both education and training in chemical dependency and has worked in student life at another university. Opal meets with the dean to gather a clear picture of the issue and assess her expertise to provide consultation. Roles and responsibilities are identified.
Design	Consultant works collaboratively with consultee to gather information, further define the issue, set goals, and determine potential solutions for goal attainment. An action plan is developed as is a means of data collection to measure outcomes.	Information gathering regarding all parties involved, which may mean interviewing individuals or groups, or obtaining quantitative data, to clarify and confirm the issue. Both parties work to discover probable outcomes including the potential impact each option could have on the target and system(s) involved.	Opal meets with a group of resident directors to gather information to assess the details of the issue. Opal also meets with a focus group of residents to discuss their perspectives of the rise in violations of the alcohol policy. After determining a clearer picture of the issue, Opal reviews the most current literature regarding college life and alcohol use with recommended interventions and preventative actions. She meets with the dean to discuss the potential steps the dean could take to assist residents in adhering to the alcohol policy.

Stage	Brief Explanation	Activities	Example
Implementation	Consultee implements the action plan with the target (e.g., individual, group, organization) and connects with the consultant to support/problem solve any issues that may arise throughout implementation.	Consultee implements the action plan and is ultimately responsible for the outcome, whereas the consultant remains responsible for providing best-practice strategies concerning the issue within the consultant's expertise.	The dean implements one of the prevention programs recommended by Opal in addition to weekend late-night campus activities that do not involve alcohol and that are hosted by resident directors. The dean meets with Opal twice to gain her expertise in determining who should be required to complete the prevention program and who may not need the education.
Review/ Revision	Consultant and consultee meet to review and revise the goals and action plan throughout the process (formative review) to ensure ongoing success of consultee's implementation; review is also conducted after the action plan is concluded to evaluate and determine what worked and what did not (summative evaluation) and what could have been done differently to best ensure success.	Consultee provides information regarding the impact of the implementation of the action plan, which may include numerical or anecdotal data. The consultant integrates the data and determines what to retain and what to revise for the next consultation. The consultant further assesses the process and outcome to determine where further education and/or training may be beneficial to maintain expertise in best practice regarding the issue.	The dean meets with Opal and reviews monthly reports of issues related to alcohol use by residents. They brainstorm additional actions the dean could take to assist in reduced alcohol-related issues. They determine that there is a reduction in issues each month and that there appears to be less of an issue when there are more supports available such as the late-night activities and the greater contact with the resident directors. Revisions to increase the number of hosted activities are made within the dean's budget.
Follow-up/ Termination	The consultant lays out a plan with the consultee to follow up after the action plan has been completed to fortify changes that were made during implementation and to provide any further advice or information to secure that the goals that were met are sustained. The consultant concludes the consultation.	The follow-up period is designed to meet the needs of the particular consultation and therefore varies in length and activity. In any case, follow-up includes an analysis of the data, a review of the success or lack thereof with all involved parties, the collaboration between consultant and consultee regarding any unfinished issues, and a formal ending of the relationship once all contracted work is completed.	The dean and Opal meet 6 months later at the end of the academic year and agree that the objectives were met. The consultation is then formally concluded.

The counselor-as-consultant holds an expertise that is sought by a consultee for the consultee to facilitate a change that benefits an individual, group, or community. The consultant and consultee work together to create an action plan that is fulfilled by the consultee, evaluated and revised as needed again in collaboration, and assessed for outcome and process to improve the next consultation (Staton et al., 2007). The most common form of consultation in the counseling profession occurs between helping professionals where one counselor seeks the expertise of another counselor for the first to provide best practice designed for a particular client or type of client. This kind of consultation is a mainstay of the profession, and every counselor must both seek consultation when it best serves the client and be prepared to provide it within one's expertise. As you think about consultation, consider the questions in Self-Assessment Activity 12.1.

SELF-ASSESSMENT ACTIVITY 12.1 CONSULTATION

1. An area of expertise for which I could currently be an effective consultant is _____.
2. Limitations that would lead me to refer a potential consultee to another expert are _____.
3. To develop and/or maintain an expertise necessary for consultation, I would _____.
4. As a graduate student, you are becoming an expert in attentive listening. Assume the local high school has begun a program aimed at student leadership development. It has contacted you for assistance in creating a set of experiences for its students that would increase the students' capacities to be good listeners and effective communicators. Complete the following chart according to your role as consultant.

Stage	Consultation regarding graduate school application
1: Orientation	
2: Design	
3: Implementation	
4: Review/Revision	
5: Follow-up/Termination	

CAREER GUIDANCE

Meghan's day (see Case Study 12.1) included a meeting with Kevin, a college sophomore, to discuss his Myers-Briggs Type Indicator results as well as an upcoming meeting with his college counselor. Kevin came to see Meghan initially because of his increasing uncertainty about his future and the resulting anxiety. In their first meeting, Meghan learned that Kevin had earned a C− in Biology and D+ in Organic Chemistry the prior semester and was in jeopardy of losing his scholarships. Kevin's anxiety occurred as he realized he did not have the requisite skills and motivation to be a medical doctor as he had planned. Meghan helped Kevin realize that he needed to identify a major and develop a career plan that fit his interests, values, and abilities. She helped him understand that his motivation would increase as his academic work and career aspirations aligned. Meghan assisted Kevin in gathering information about his lifetime of career development, and they began formulating a plan for his career in relationship to other life roles.

Counselors across specialties must be prepared to integrate career guidance where needed throughout their counseling practices. As a lifelong critical aspect of human development, career guidance has its place in nearly every aspect of counseling. Career counseling is a required component of the CACREP (2009) standards across all counseling preservice programs. Career counseling also comprises a major section of the National Counselor Examination (NCE; National Board for Certified Counselors & Affiliates, Inc. [NBCC], 2012). The American School Counselor Association's (ASCA, 2012) *National Model* focuses on career development as one of three domains of comprehensive program delivery. This keeps career guidance at the forefront of the school counseling profession. Still, many other specialties spend little if any time in direct focus on career guidance or academic advising, a career counseling component.

Historically, theorists have postulated various approaches to career development. Case Study 12.2 and Table 12.2 illustrate how a range of theoretical approaches might be used to interpret and respond to the situation of the client in the case study. These theories are outlined in the remainder of this section.

CASE STUDY 12.2
Rob

Rob Rutherford is a 57-year-old, married male who has been referred for counseling services after his job as associate vice-president of a small power company was eliminated as the company downsized. He worked for the last 24 years at the same company beginning just after his graduation with a master's degree in business administration. Although Mr. Rutherford has no debt with his mortgage paid and his children completely independent, he states that he must have employment soon or he will not be "the man" of the house—especially given that his wife's income has been the only real source of financial support for the last few months. He states he has scoured the job market for the last 6 months and has found nothing similar to the job he held at the power company. He is not adverse to a new type of employment, but he states he has no idea in what direction he would want to look. Consequently, he feels depressed and has never considered his life less valuable than he does presently. Table 12.2 depicts each theory, the basic premise for each theory, and an application of each theory to Case Study 12.2.

TABLE 12.2 Career Theory Application

Theory (Theorist)	Premise/Foundation	Sample
Trait and Factor Theory (Parsons)	Assesses the client's strengths and interests and considers the job market to assist the client in career decision making.	Counselor assists Mr. Rutherford by assessing his strengths and interests. It is discovered that Mr. Rutherford has exceptional logical and mathematical abilities coincident to his bachelor's degree in mathematics. He enjoys working with numbers and enjoyed the component of budget and projections most in his last job. The counselor assists Mr. Rutherford in finding different access points to the current job market in addition to the local paper and word of mouth. Mr. Rutherford now approaches the possibilities with ideas about other employment related to these interests that go beyond his past career that will fit him. As a result, he has new places to begin to look.
Psychodynamic (Roe)	Parenting styles and emotional climate ultimately result in one of eight orientations to the world of work that combine with gender, physical appearance, temperament and personality, genetics, family background, and economic circumstance to lead to occupational choice.	Counselor engages Mr. Rutherford in talking about his early life experiences and the shaping of his career decisions. Mr. Rutherford shares that his parents were warm, accepting, and loving and that he had enjoyed learning to keep his father's books in their hardware store business during summers while in college. Mr. Rutherford confirms that he is geared toward business and finance in particular and is rejuvenated to continue looking with a scope toward another business/finance venture.
Life-Span Development (Super)	Five predictable and orderly stages of career development across the life span during which humans learn about interests and abilities, developing self-concept, and awareness of the world of work; test their occupational fantasies in leisure, school, and early work; and solidify their preferences in occupational decision making. In later life, humans disengage from work and invest in retirement and leisure/avocation activities.	Counselor determines that Mr. Rutherford has experienced a disruption in his self-concept and developmental progression that has him unsure of his capacities and interests, keeping him from moving forward into a new job. The counselor works to assist Mr. Rutherford in rediscovering his interests and helping him to define more fully these interests and his abilities to make an effective match to the job opportunities that do exist for Mr. Rutherford.

(Continued)

TABLE 12.2 Career Theory Application (*Continued*)

Theory (Theorist)	Premise/Foundation	Sample
Personality (Holland)	Humans play out personalities by career decisions and are content if occupations match personalities (six types including realistic, investigative, artistic, social, enterprising, and conventional). Counselors assess occupational codes comprised of a predominant type and secondary types. Careers are also coded in *The Dictionary of Holland Occupational Codes*. Matching individual code to occupational code leads to satisfaction.	Counselor assesses Mr. Rutherford using the Self Directed Search and determines his Holland code with Enterprising as his primary and Conventional and Social as his secondary types (ESC). Together they perused *The Dictionary of Holland Occupational Codes* to determine a list of potential jobs that would likely be most satisfying to Mr. Rutherford. This rejuvenated Mr. Rutherford and provided direction to him for expanding his job search in a direction fitting him.
Social Learning Theory of Career Decision Making/ Learning Theory of Career Counseling (Krumboltz)	Environmental factors, learning, and task approach skills interact producing self-observation generalizations, an emphasis on task approach, and action outcomes. Positive and negative influences shape career decisions. Interventions include defining/gathering information about problems and goals, identifying solutions/outcomes, and generalizing to new situations. Techniques include modeling, improving and influencing learning experiences, increasing self-observation, task approach, cognitive, and performance skills to enhance self-efficacy. Seven stages: DECIDES. LTCC added emphasis to counselor intervention in shaping decision making. Happenstance added to account for chance, creativity, and exploration.	Counselor works with Mr. Rutherford through the DECIDES model by which they define the issue of his current career decision point, establish a plan to clarify this interests and reestablish his direction concerning his career world, clarify his values by examining his observations of self and the world, identify alternatives to the career path he was just derailed from, discover probable outcomes of the options before him, eliminate alternatives that are not a fit to his desired outcome, and start action aimed toward a resolution of the defined problem. The counselor encourages Mr. Rutherford to see the happenstance of his employment loss as an opportunity for creative exploration of a new direction that might prove to have a silver lining.
Constructive Development (McAuliffe)	One's career challenge adaptability is informed by the meaning one construes throughout one's life span. Each person creates one's own reality via an organized self-created story across the life span dependent on stages of development with more advanced stages allowing for more multifaceted and complex solutions to career problems. Counselors accept clients' stories and gently push for increased development using receptive inquiry, pattern recognition, primacy of life experience, mindfulness, writing, metaphor, and creating meaning through activity.	Counselor encourages Mr. Rutherford to share his life's stories, especially in regard to the formation of his career decisions to date. He listens carefully and affirms Mr. Rutherford's perspectives as they are, yet encourages him to consider stretching outside his current patterns via writing what life would be like with some small changes to his daily interactions with himself, others, and his environment. Mr. Rutherford begins to see himself more fully in relation to his world and begins to think of alternative patterns he could develop that would allow him to maintain his lifestyle as he desires yet to move beyond his job loss. He begins to consider the options that are definitely outside the box he had believed was his work world and has become enthusiastic about the new career adventure that has come via his job shift.

Theory (Theorist)	Premise/Foundation	Sample
Systems Theory Framework (McMahon & Patton)	Considers career issues within the comprehensive context of one's life reflecting content (intrapersonal and context variables) and process (recursiveness, change over time, and chance). Consider the dynamic reciprocal relationship between and with the individual (gender, ability, interests, age, etc.) and social and environmental/societal systems (socioeconomics, political, religious, etc.). Counselors assist clients in examining parts of self in concert with systems and the whole via the individual's sharing of and reconfiguring of story within the counselor assisted accepting environment.	Counselor builds a relationship with Mr. Rutherford in which they explore Mr. Rutherford's patterns of connection within himself, with others, and with the world in which he lives. Mr. Rutherford exposes his unfounded perspectives that his world rests solely on his earning capacity and begins to see the reciprocal relationships with his children and spouse that he has heretofore not noted. He begins to define himself not only as valuable for his income, but he also sees his value as a companion, friend, advisor, and supporter in nonmonetary ways. He begins to consider new career options in addition to the career he has forged within his old employment. He begins talking with his wife and adult children about how they might alter their current environment to better meet what is most valued by each of them and by the family as a family. His job hunt is thereby altered as his desires for potential employment expand to fit his newfound sense of self in his world.

Theories of career development reach at least as far back as Frank Parsons in the early 1900s. He developed the trait-and-factor approach, which involved the rational process of assessing strengths and interests and considering the job market to assist the client in career decision making (Zunker, 2012).

Ann Roe (1956) developed a psychodynamic career theory in the mid-1950s. She postulated that parenting styles (warm/cold) and emotional climate (emotional concentration toward the child, acceptance of the child, or avoidance of the child) ultimately resulted in one of eight orientations to the world of work, including service, business, organization, technology, outdoor, science, general culture, and arts/entertainment. Roe added that additional influences such as gender, physical appearance, temperament and personality, genetics, family background, and economic circumstances contributed to occupational choice.

Donald Super's theory of predictable and orderly stages of career development across the life span has been a marked force in the career counseling world. He proposed that career development occurred across a five-stage (multiple substages) process during which people learn about their interests and abilities while developing self-concept; gaining an awareness of the world of work; testing their occupational fantasies in leisure, school, and early work; and solidifying their preferences in occupational decision making, including specialized education and training (Tolbert, 1974). In later life, people disengage from work and invest their interests progressively more into retirement and leisure/avocation activities.

John Holland's proposed personality theory of occupational choice also helped to frame early career counseling practice by suggesting that humans play out their personalities (preferred ways of social and environmental situations) through their career decisions (Zunker, 2012). He posited that humans would be most fulfilled or content if their occupations were chosen to fit their unique personalities. He conceptualized personality into six types, including realistic, investigative, artistic, social, enterprising, and conventional (RIASEC Model) that are represented along points of a hexagon. By Holland's theory, humans are not bound to personalities of a single type or hexagon point but have occupational codes comprised of a predominant type (strongest point) and secondary types (adjacent two points). Holland proposed that careers could also be typed along the hexagon, and some 12,000 plus jobs have been coded and published in *The Dictionary of Holland Occupational Codes* (Jist Publishing, 2012). Assessing the individual for his/her code and matching codes to occupations of similar code give direction to the options that would lead to the greatest job satisfaction. Indeed, studies have indicated the veracity of the idea (Spokane, 1985).

Recently, theories have emerged that move beyond traits, temperaments, personality, and interests and into *the process* of development of career decision making. Most prominent of the developmental theories are the evolving theories of Krumboltz, constructive development career counseling, and most recently the systems approach. In the seventies, Krumboltz proposed the social learning theory of career decision making (SLTCDM). In addition to one's genetic endowment or personality/trait factors offered in earlier theories, Krumboltz included environmental factors (events and settings) as well as learning histories (associative and instrumental learning experiences) and task approach skills (personal standards, work ethics, emotional responses). Outcomes of the interaction of these factors are self-observation generalizations (one's own evaluation and assessment of performance, values, and interests), an emphasis on task approach, and action outcomes. Krumboltz noted positive (reinforcements, observations of a valued model, access to people and resources) and negative (punishments of self or valued model) influences on career decision-making skills. Social learning theory counseling interventions included defining and gathering information about problems and goals, identifying a host of solutions and potential outcomes, and generalizing the process to new situations. Techniques such as modeling, improving and influencing learning experiences, and increasing self-observation, as well as task approach, cognitive, and performance skills to enhance self-efficacy, were applied. Krumboltz's theory hosted a seven-stage model with the acronym DECIDES as follows: (a) define the problem, (b) establish the action plan, (c) clarify the values, (d) identify alternatives, (e) discover probable outcomes, (f) eliminate alternatives, and (g) start action (Krumboltz, Kinnier, Rude, Scherba, & Hamel, 1986).

Some 20 years later, the Learning Theory of Career Counseling (LTCC) was added to the SLTCDM (Mitchell & Krumboltz, 1996). This addition moved from explanation of the whys of career decision making to what counselors can do to assist in helping clients resolve career-related issues. Since then Krumboltz has demonstrated his belief that theories are strongest when they hold the potential to change on the discovery of new ideas. In line with this notion, his efforts have shifted to the inclusion of "happenstance" or "chance" in the role of career decision making. This addition brings the notion that there are benefits found in unplanned events and that exploration, open-mindedness, creativity, and lifelong learning are essential components to healthy career development and decision making (Krumboltz & Levin, 2004). Krumboltz's theory integrates career counseling and personal counseling, making clear the lifelong process of one's career development. This further validates the importance of all counselors being well educated and trained in the application of career counseling theories.

Constructive Developmental Career Counseling was introduced in the early 1990s by McAuliffe (1993) and Peavy (1992), who incorporated Kegan's theory of constructive development into career practice. The premise was that the meaning one construes throughout the life span shapes one's career challenge adaptability. Constructivist concepts assert that each person creates a reality of his or her own with subjective meaning constructed in organized ways into stories that he or she continually revises over the course of the life span. This formation of meaning is dependent in part on the individual's developmental stage, with later stages allowing greater understanding in more multifaceted and advanced ways. The counselor's role becomes one of acceptance of the client's current developmental stage and cumulative story to lay the groundwork for gently pushing the client's development. As the client develops the capacity to think differently about self in relation to the world (self, work, relationships, career), the client is able to problem solve career issues differently. Counseling activities based in constructive developmental thought might include receptive inquiry, pattern recognition, primacy of life experience, mindfulness, writing, and creating meaning through activity (Peavy, 1994; Stebleton, 2010), all of which aim at supporting development of an altered self-authored story.

The systems approach has been considered fundamental to other career counseling modalities in that this approach considers career issues within the comprehensive context of one's life. Systems theory reflects both content (intrapersonal and context variables) and process (recursiveness, change over time, and chance). The core of systems theory is the individual system consisting of intrapersonal influences such as age, gender, interests, and abilities. Systems theory considers this core within the grander contextual social system and environmental/societal subsystems. The social system consists of those with whom the individual interacts such as family, peers, classmates, and even media. The environmental/societal subsystem includes the whole of the environmental factors within which the individual lives, including location, socioeconomics, politics, and so forth. Interacting systems are not static; rather, they are dynamic, having reciprocal influence on one another. A change in one system or part of a system will create change in others (McMahon, 2005).

Foundational tenets of systems theory include the following conceptual understandings. Just as with constructive developmental theory, systems theory notes that individuals are the experts of their own content. People use language to write multiple stories of their own lives, which produces meaning, which leads to a preferred career. Counselors assist clients in examining all parts possible as they interact within systems, with parts of the system, and with the whole system to understand repeating patterns (recursiveness), change as it occurs over time, and chance. With new information, the client can write different stories leading to new patterns of career decision making. Tools of the system-focused career counselor include the building of connectedness, use of story, and the counseling relationship itself and in relationship to other parts and whole of the system(s), along with genuineness, unconditional positive regard, empathic understanding, and flexibility (McMahon, 2005).

Many tools are available to assess personality traits, interests, values, and abilities in relationship to career decision making. These tools are grounded in theory, have sound score reliability and validity, and should be familiar to the counselor. Table 12.3 depicts some of the most widely used career assessment tools, the theory base of the tool, the publisher, and a brief description.

TABLE 12.3 Career Assessment Tools and Broad Descriptions

Kuder Career Search with Person Match—Identifies interests and aligns interests with most fitting career cluster.

Kuder Skills Assessment—Identifies skills and aligns to the most fitting career cluster.

Super's Work Values Inventory—Identifies values most important to chosen career.

Self-Directed Search (SDS)—Uses test takers' information about interests to determine personality type presented in three-letter Holland code.

Strong Interest Inventory—Measures users' interests based on Holland's six types.

O*Net interest profiler—Educates about occupations based on their code.

O*Net ability profiler—Measures users' skills in nine areas important to many occupations.

O*Net Work Importance Profiler—Measures users' work values in six different categories.

California Occupational Interest Survey (COPS)—168 items, provides activity interests scores to 14 different career clusters. Each cluster corresponds to high school and college curriculum, as well as current sources of occupational information.

Career Beliefs Inventory—Looks at clients' assumptions, generalizations, and beliefs about self related to the world of work.

Jackson's Vocational Interest Inventory—Career assessment and career planning tool that matches interests to careers, job groups, and college majors.

Armed Services Vocational Aptitude Battery (ASVAB)—Originally designed to predict future academic and occupational success in military occupations. Test areas include General Science, Academic Reasoning, Word Knowledge, Paragraph Comprehension, Mathematics Knowledge, Electronics Information, Auto and Shop Information, and Mechanical Comprehension.

Myers Briggs Type Indicator—Allows clients to see how they prefer to behave as opposed to how they actually behave. Preference drives direction of job search.

With the all the ideas of this section in mind, use Self-Assessment Activity 12.2 to explore your thoughts about career guidance.

SELF-ASSESSMENT ACTIVITY 12.2 CAREER GUIDANCE

1. Of the seven theories discussed earlier, which do you find is aligned with your own thought processes about career development and guidance, and why?
2. How might you synthesize the components from each theory that align with your perspectives to provide the foundation for your career guidance counseling work?
3. Belinda is a 15-year-old high school freshman who is considering which courses to take as she contemplates her life beyond high school. Her father and mother are both high school graduates, and she is certain she will graduate from high school. She has always been a good student, and her teachers have been encouraging her to go on to college. She is frightened and intrigued by the prospect, but she feels fairly sure that she doesn't have the capacity to complete college given that no one from her family has ever even applied to college, let alone graduated. She has come to meet with you to get some direction about the decisions she feels she needs to make as she registers for classes. The only thing she has ever considered as a job was a grocery checker because both of her parents work at the local grocery store—her father as a butcher and her mother as a checker. She says she doesn't want to work hard in high school if it isn't going to get her anywhere. What kinds of questions or thoughts come to mind when considering counseling with the following presenting issue?
4. Consider the case of Belinda. Using Table 12.4, complete the sample column with actions the counselor might take if working with Belinda from the theory as noted.

TABLE 12.4 Sample Actions for the Case of Belinda

Theory (Theorist)	Sample
Trait and Factor Theory (Parsons)	
Psychodynamic (Roe)	
Life-Span Life-space Development (Super)	
Personality (Holland)	
SLTCDM/LTCC (Krumboltz)	
Constructive Development (McAuliffe)	
Systems Theory Framework (McMahon & Patton)	

ACADEMIC ADVISING

Your work with Belinda is an example of academic advising in the career guidance process. To effectively advise Belinda, the counselor needs to understand the framework for career development offered at the high school. This includes the courses of study available and the high school's protocols for assisting in college searches and applications as well as applications for scholarships and other financial assistance. An effective tool that may be foundational to the high school's protocol is the ASCA (2012) *National Model*, which contains the key element of individual planning based on assessment and a decision-making process. With this framework in mind, the counselor can assist Belinda in exploring the possibilities in the world of work, in understanding the skills and personal qualities employers want for particular jobs, and in examining Belinda's interests and abilities. The counselor can help Belinda to develop a good decision-making process based on an understanding of the preceding qualities in relationship to the available opportunities. Belinda can then chose from course offerings, experiences within the community such as volunteering or job shadowing in a similar career field to her interests, and other activities such as leadership opportunities that would prepare her for entry into a career or further education or skills training. Once such decisions are made, the counselor and Belinda produce an individualized written career plan that aligns with her high school course of study and career goals beyond high school.

It is clear from this example that *academic advising* involves preparation and planning for the student to select an appropriate direction, a course of study to meet that direction, and a selection of courses to best ensure student success. Academic advising may also include psychoeducation and skill building such as time management, communication skills, test-taking strategies, and effective study habits and skills. Other related counseling activities might include stress reduction/management, test anxiety reduction, communication and social skill building, work readiness skill development, job shadowing, volunteer experiences, service opportunities, and other activities that enhance career maturity.

Academic advising does not begin and end with high school. Academic advising occurs throughout one's education. The National Academic Advising Association (NACADA) states in its guiding principles that academic advising is integral to fulfilling the teaching and learning mission of higher education (National Academic Advising Association, 2006). In the samples of the methods used in academic advising to assess student learning outcomes activities, several are familiar to counselors, including to assist students to

> . . . craft a coherent educational plan based on assessment of abilities, aspirations, interests, and values; use complex information from various sources to set goals, reach decisions, and achieve those goals; . . . cultivate the intellectual habits that lead to a lifetime of learning; [and] behave as citizens who engage in the wider world around them.

The counselor's role over the life span includes assistance in attaining accurate knowledge regarding the client's educational world. This requires using appropriate assessment tools (whether the client is a student in elementary school or retraining in later adulthood). It requires assisting the client in gaining the skills and insight that lead to career choice, including decisions within the academic plan. It includes the skill building and coping strategies listed previously as well as guidance and support in gaining employment such as writing skills and confidence building for interviewing. The counselor who is most effective collaborates with other professionals and uses available career resources and support systems to ensure accurate and efficient guidance throughout the process of career guidance and academic advising.

ADVOCACY IN COUNSELING

Meghan's early afternoon appointment was spent with Raul and Salina, who are grandparents raising their grandchildren (see Case Study 12.1). Meghan recognized a growing need in her community for services related to this population and the lack of resources currently available. She will prepare a rationale for services to present to both her employer and the local Aging Services Program to advocate for resources that would meet the needs of this population. Advocacy work of this kind is a common counseling activity.

The counseling profession was borne out of concern for human beings who were suffering, many of whom were disenfranchised because of little to no access to the kind of assistance that would alleviate such suffering. The meaning of the root word of *advocacy*, voc, is "voice." The counseling profession has been one of "voice" for clients and assisting the client in becoming empowered or finding "voice" for self since its inception (Brooks & Weikel, 1996). The late 1990s gave rise to a renewed call to counselors for social activism regarding a diverse set of client-related issues ranging from antidrugs in schools campaigns to services for the disabled to issues related to sexual orientation to other cultural injustices (Smaby & Daugherty, 1995; Smith & Chen-Hayes, 2003; Torkelson-Lynch & Gussel, 1996). The renewed call was not only extended to social justice concerns, but counselors were also urged to invest in efforts to promote the counseling profession itself (Eriksen, 1997; Myers, Sweeney, & White, 2002).

The response to the call for both social justice and professional advocacy has included advocacy training in counselor education programs. CACREP has required advocacy training in its standards, and counselor educators have developed methodology for the training of effective counselor advocates (Collison et al., 1998; Eriksen, 1997; House & Sears, 2002; Lewis & Bradley, 2000; Steele, 2008). With effective training, education, and dispositions geared to both social justice and the promotion of the profession, the counselor's role can and must include advocacy for both client and profession. A definition of counselor advocacy, an overview of the scope of advocacy with samples of advocacy action and outcomes, as well as a set of advocacy strategies for counselors follow.

Combining the accepted views of *advocacy* in the counseling profession results in the following definition provided by CACREP (2009):

> [a]ction taken on behalf of clients or the counseling profession to support appropriate policies and standards for the profession; promote individual human worth, dignity, and potential; and oppose or work to change policies and procedures, systemic barriers, long-standing traditions, and preconceived notions that stifle human development. (p. 59)

Such a definition provides the foundation for both client-focused and profession-focused advocacy.

Client-focused advocacy may include outreach to deliver helpful services to those who are in need of but not receiving such services otherwise. Outreach promotes and is promoted by the ideal of social justice when the effort is extended to groups of people rather than individual clients, particularly when applied to those who have diminished influence and power. Another client-focused advocacy counselor focus is the empowerment of clients to help clients develop the necessary skills, abilities, and confidence to have more control over their own lives and advocacy within, or influence over, the environment in which they live. Empowerment may include more than community or client changes; in addition, counselors may work toward creating legislative changes such as reworking of regulations developed within the law or in changes to the law at the most basic levels to secure better opportunities and services for clients.

Counselors also advocate for the counseling profession itself. As noted earlier, promotion of the profession generally allows counselors greater potential for successful social change and client advocacy. *Professional advocacy* includes lobbying for extending counseling services to all populations such as the recent addition of counselors serving veterans through the Veterans Administration. Gaining state counseling certification and/or licensure has been a focus of professional advocacy, with California becoming the last of the 50 states to achieve that goal (California Association for Licensed Professional Clinical Counselors, 2012). Each of these changes followed countless hours of devoted efforts of counselors across the nation advocating by establishing a sense of urgency via media communication, supporting existing alliances and creating new ones aimed at collaborative efforts, lobbying legislators and policy makers, and persisting until the vision is realized (Lee & Rodgers, 2009).

Outreach, empowerment, social change, and professional advocacy involve particular counseling dispositions, skills, and activities. Resourcefulness, flexibility, and integrity top the list of counselor-as-advocate characteristics (Kurpius & Rozecki, 1992). Kiselica and Robinson (2001) noted that counselors must have compassionate spirits and a deep sensitivity and commitment to the alleviating of human suffering. Lee and Rodgers (2009) added to compassion, sensitivity, and commitment the characteristics of leadership, a strategic vision, courage, and skills in data collection and use of said data to promote needed change.

Specific steps or strategies assist in securing successful advocacy efforts. Stewart, Semivan, and Schwartz (2009) provided such strategies beginning with the identification of the target including identity, location, and the nature and extent of the issue/injustice. Next, the counselor as advocate hones a rationale for choosing the issue including potential impact on the client or target population. Next, a clear and concise specific identification of the problem and how it fits the role of the counselor is described. Thorough research, both in the literature and from practical experience of individuals and counselors and other professionals who have been involved in the issue, the details and past efforts at resolution of the issue can be gathered. This leads to better determination of resources needed for change. Turning the outcome of the last step into a reference and resource list can assist in educating others who might assist in making changes happen. Goals are then formulated ranging from the global outcome goal to smaller contributory goals that may be refined and readjusted as needed. Finally, steps are delineated in action format so that the counselor-as-advocate can begin intervening driven by the information and resources noted earlier.

The counselor is not always involved in every step of an advocacy strategy. It is often the case that counselors are asked to join efforts for advocacy that are well underway. The advocacy steps as applied to licensure and Veterans Administration roles for counselors are two such actions. Counselors from across the country joined in the efforts to secure these outcomes in the form of letters to senators and representatives of Congress, visits on Capitol Hill, educating key community figures, and rallying other professionals at conferences or via other state and regional organization events. Use Self-Assessment Activity 12.3 to reflect on your ideas about advocacy.

SELF-ASSESSMENT ACTIVITY 12.3 ADVOCACY

1. What is at least one local advocacy opportunity addressing an issue of social justice in which I could participate that would have potential impact on a client population in my area?
2. What is at least one regional or national advocacy opportunity in which I could participate that could impact the profession of counseling?
3. Who are the legislators who represent me at the state and national levels? What stance is each taking regarding the advocacy issues I listed in questions 1 and 2 above?
4. On a scale of 1 to 10, how would I rate myself on each of the dispositions of a counselor foundational to advocacy (e.g., compassionate spirit, resourcefulness, flexibility, integrity, deep sensitivity to human suffering, leadership, a strategic vision, courage, and skills).
5. How can I get involved now, as a graduate student, in advocacy efforts aimed at improving situations for clients or promoting the profession of counseling?

PSYCHOPHARMACOLOGY

Meghan advocated for her client, Kathleen, who struggles with Schizophrenia, Disorganized Type. Meghan encouraged Kathleen's empowerment by assisting her to "find her voice" with her boyfriend regarding his not smoking in their apartment. Meghan also used her own power with Kathleen's medical professional by giving voice to Kathleen's struggles with compliance due to the difficult side effects of her new medication. To do the latter and to collaborate well with the medical professional, Meghan must have an understanding of her role as a counselor in collaboration with medical professionals as well as knowledge of the basics of psychopharmacology.

The counselor as advocate or collaborator does not necessitate major social reform. Most of the advocacy by professional counselors occurs on a much smaller scale such as the preceding efforts made to assist the client in attaining or maintaining consistent and effective psychiatric services from a medical professional. One might argue that psychopharmacology has no place in the day of a counselor given that the counseling degree is not medically based. Counseling is largely based in the social sciences. Still, the reality under managed care is that the medical provider is most apt to see a client only once every 3 to 4 months on average, whereas the counselor often sees the client weekly (Gabbard & Kay, 2001). This gives the counselor much more time to note issues related to medication compliance and impact; hence, the counselor can greatly assist the client by advocating and collaborating with the medical professional.

As noted almost three decades ago, to be an effective advocate and collaborator with medical professionals, counselors need to be prepared with knowledge and the capacity to collaborate with medical professionals (Ponterotto, 1985). This includes understanding basic neuroanatomy, the action of neurotransmitters, the general categories of psychopharmaceuticals including generic and trade names, the side effects of said medications and presentation of side effects notable in the counseling office. Counselors must understand their roles, boundaries, and limitations when collaborating and be able to avoid issues of liability and other pitfalls when providing assistance to the medicated client (King & Anderson, 2004). The following will provide an overview of these essentials of psychopharmacology for the counselor.

The basics of psychopharmacology begin with the lobes and structures of the brain to provide a foundation for understanding the impact of psychotropic medications on the brain and subsequently on behavior, thought, and emotion. Figure 12.2 depicts the lobes of the brain.

FRONTAL LOBE. Toward the back of the frontal lobe is the motor strip, which is responsible for planning and intiating motor movement as well as the controlling complex tasks. The rest of the frontal lobe is responsible for higher-order functions. These include metacognition, cause and effect or futuristic thinking/planning, reasoning, judgment, impulse control, and memory. Broca's area is found toward the back lower part of the frontal lobe and accounts for speech production. The frontal lobe is the last of the lobes to mature, which occurs for women in their early twenties and men in their mid to late twenties. Due to location and size (behind the forehead), the frontal lobe is more susceptible to damage than other lobes (Giedd, 2002).

PARIETAL LOBE. Just behind the motor strip begins the parietal lobe containing the sensory strip. Sensory nerves send messages to the sensory strip, where the messages are processed and sent to specialty areas of the brain for coding and responding. The parietal lobe is responsible for integration of sensory information such as pain, touch, and visual perception as well as for spatial orientation, knowledge of numbers and their relations, and the manipulation of objects (Preston, O'Neal, & Talaga, 2008).

OCCIPITAL LOBE. The occipital lobe controls vision and color recognition. Trauma to this lobe may cause visual defects such as distorted or limited perception fields or misinterpretation of incoming data; however, trauma to this area is less likely due to its location.

TEMPORAL LOBE. The temporal lobe is responsible for hearing, memory, and language comprehension, recognition, interpretation, and semantic processing, These language capacities are housed in Wernicke's area found at the top and center of this lobe. There are eight

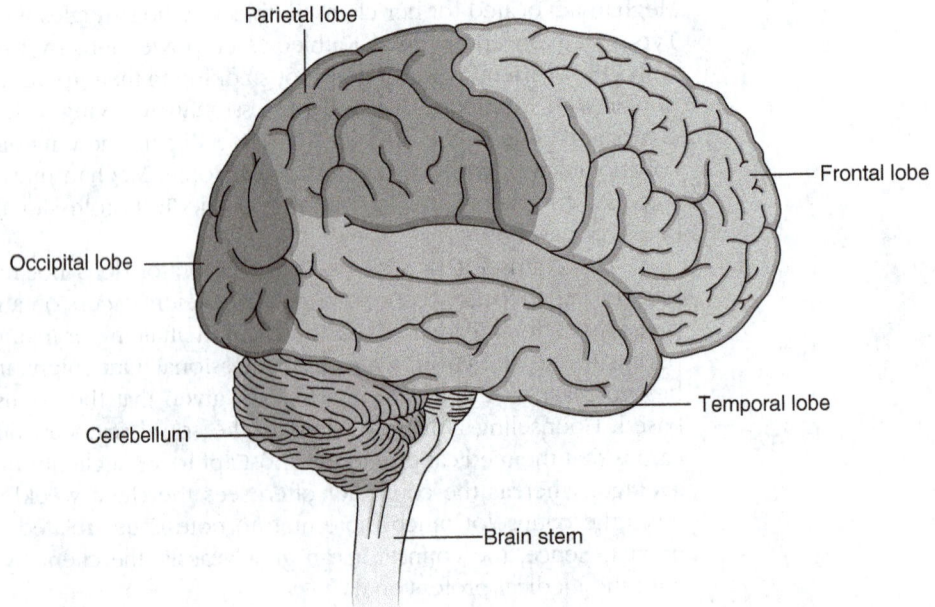

FIGURE 12.2 Right side view of the lobes of the brain.

major signs of damage to the temporal lobe including changes in auditory sensation, perception, and attention to input as well as visual perception issues, impaired verbal organization, decline in language comprehension, long-term memory impairment, and altered personality and sexual behavior (Preston et al., 2008).

LIMBIC SYSTEM. There are a few deep brain structures that appear to work in conjunction with one another to influence behavior and functions such as olfaction, emotion, motivation, motor coordination and behavior, and the autonomic nervous system. The structures include the hippocampus, amygdala, thalamus, cingulated gyrus, fornix, parahippocampus gyrus, and basal ganglia (which include the striatum, pallidum, substantia nigra, and subthalamic nucleus; Preston et al., 2008), some of which are noted in Figure 12.3. Exactly how these structures interact is unclear making it difficult to isolate the process let alone the struggles that result when damage has occurred.

ENDOCRINE SYSTEM. The endocrine system involves brain structures including the thalamus, hypothalamus, and pituitary and pineal glands. Glands producing hormones distributed throughout the body include the thyroid and parathyroid, adrenal, pancreas, and reproductive glands (ovaries and testes). The glands of the endocrine system influence almost every cell, organ, and function of the human body including overall growth and development, mood regulation, tissue function, metabolism, and sexual and reproductive processes (Preston et al., 2008). Likewise, hormone levels are influenced by many factors including infection, changes in fluid and mineral levels in the blood, and stress. These factors make it difficult to determine which emotions are due to neurological issues or to other elements of the environment.

NEURONS AND SYNAPSES. *Neurons* are the basic cells that comprise each structure of the brain. Figure 12.4 illustrates the critical components of the neuron. The cell body houses the nucleus, which functions like the motherboard of the neuron in determining what the cell is and does. This includes the gathering of ingredients for the specific neurotransmitter made in the cell. There are many primary neurotransmitters and modulators that play a role. Of the 10 primary neurotransmitters acetylcholine, dopamine, epinephrine, norepinephrine, serotonin, GABA, and histamine are most commonly targeted by psychotropic medications.

The axon of the neuron (the shaft extending from the cell body to the terminal button) serves as the corridor for message transmission, which occurs at the terminal button at the axon's end. The axon is covered with rings of insulation called myelin sheath, which is produced by nearby glial cells. Myelin assists in making the transmission effective by insulating all

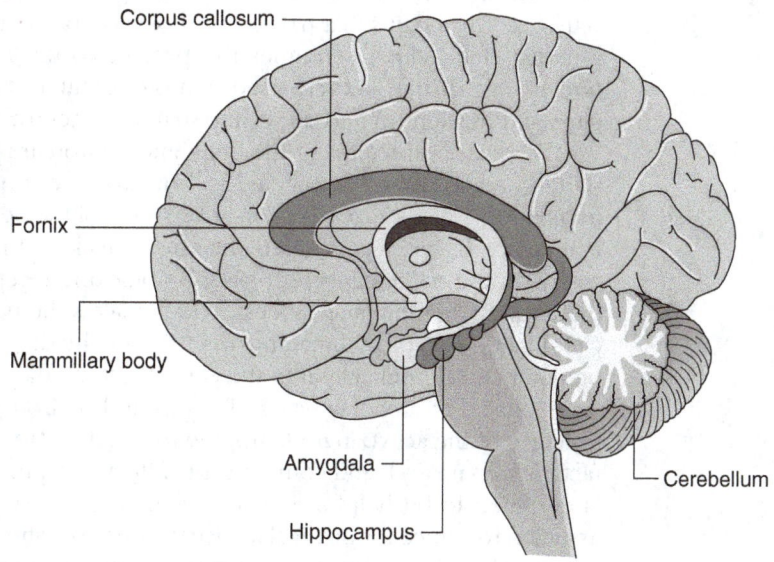

FIGURE 12.3 Limbic system basic structures.

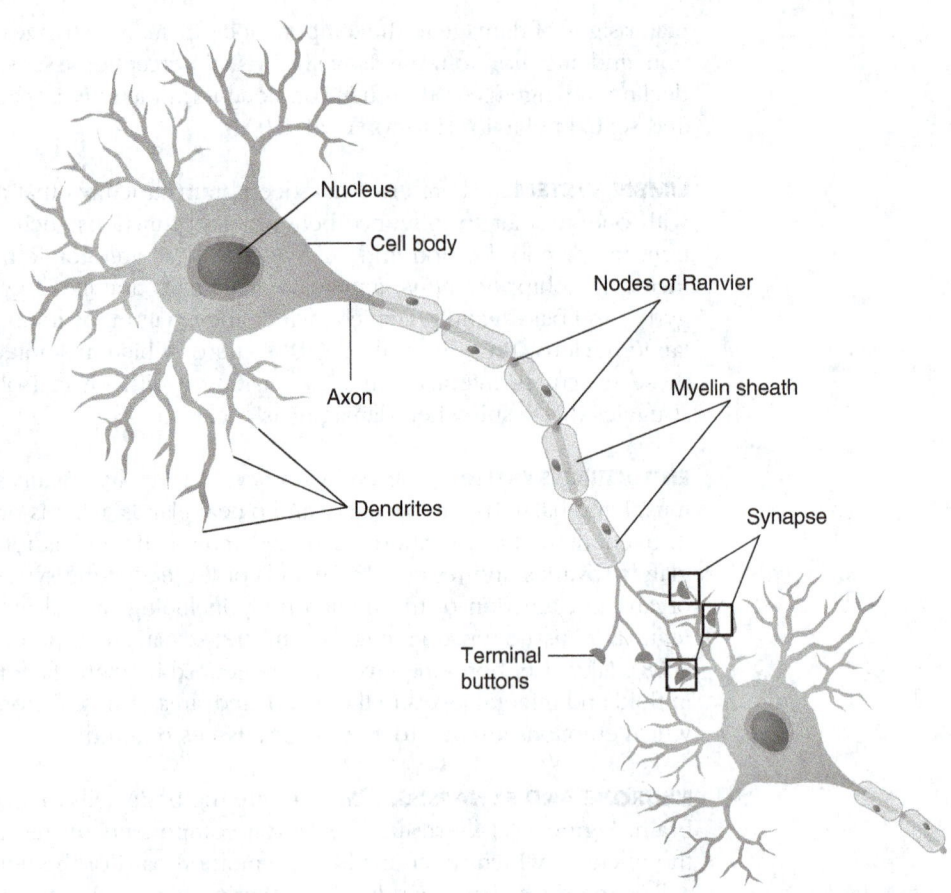

FIGURE 12.4 The neuron and synapse.

but the Nodes of Ranvier (the periodic fraction of the axon that is not insulated by myelin rings) so that the transmission only need occur in those brief spots. The terminal button, or bouton (foot), holds the neurotransmitter in sacs fused to the button until released into the synaptic cleft.

Once released into the synaptic cleft, the neurotransmitter fills in the receptor sites of the neighboring neuron's dendrites (tree branch–like projections coming from the cell body very near the terminal button). When enough dendrite receptors sites are filled, that neuron activates. This begins that neuron's process of transmitting its neurotransmitter into the next synaptic cleft, which continues the process to the next neuron and so on. Neurons are "green" in that they recycle used neurotransmitter, which is broken down into ingredient parts and retaken up into the cell to make the neurotransmitter all over again.

The basic structures of the brain and neuron are important for the counselor to understand to make sense of expected and unexpected drug action and side effects. Each of the psychotropic medications acts on at least one of the neurotransmitters either by providing an abundance of necessary ingredients; by mimicking the action the specific neurotransmitter creates at the specific receptor sites; by blocking receptor sites, which limits cell activation; by blocking the reuptake process, which makes the neurotransmitter remain in the synaptic cleft longer; and/or by breaking apart the sac holding the neurotransmitter so that it cannot be dumped as prolifically into the cleft (Preston et al., 2008).

Table 12.5 denotes types of drugs and their targeted benefits. Generic name (representative of the active ingredient), the trade name (representing the name applied by manufacturing company), and common side effects are provided for each type of drug. This table is designed to be helpful, but it is neither conclusive nor exhaustive and should not be assumed to suffice for medical advice. Counselors should consult with medical professionals such as physicians, physician's assistants, nurse practitioners, and pharmacists for complete, up-to-date, and thorough advice regarding these and all medications.

TABLE 12.5 Psychotropic Medications by Class with Side Effects

Type of Drug Benefits	Generic Name (Neurotransmitters primarily targeted)	Drug Trade Name	Common Side Effects
Anxiolytic Antianxiety, insomnia, muscle spasm—though not all to the same degree	**Benzodiazepines** (GABA)		(In general, as a class)
	Alprazolam	Xanax	• Increased speed of and extent of absorption of ethanol
	Chlordiazepoxide	Librax, Libritabs, Librium	• Increased hostility, irritability, vivid or disturbing dreams, confusion, impaired sexual function, vertigo, lightheadedness, drowsiness, inability to concentrate
	Clonazepam	Klonopin	
	Clorazepate	Azene, Tranxene	
	Diazepam	Valium	• Increased menstrual irregularities, failure to ovulate
	Lorazepam	Ativan	
	Oxazepam	Serax	
	Prazepam	Centrax	
	Miscellaneous		
	Buspirone (Serotonin, Dopamine)	BuSpar	• Chest pain • Dream disturbances • Tinnitus, sore throat, nasal congestion
	Antihistamines		
	Diphenhydramine (Acetylcholine, histamine)	Benadryl	• Drowsiness, dizziness, blurred vision, dry mouth, headache, thickened sputum
	Hydroxyzine HCl/Pamoate (histamine, serotonin, acetylcholine)	Atarax/Vistaril	
	Propranolol (Catecholamines: epinephrine, dopamine, norepinephrine)	Inderal	• Dizziness, tiredness, lightheadedness • Cold hands and feet • Nausea, vomiting, trouble sleeping, unusual dreams
	Herbals		
	St. John's Wort (Serotonin, possible MAOI)		• Phototoxic skin rashes • Inflammation of mucous membranes • Can interact with medications/acts like an MAOI or SSRI
	Passion Flower		• Not considered "safe or effective" by FDA since 1978 • May actually be a stimulant
	Ashwagandha Root	Related to Solanaceaea family	• Has been considered an "adaptogenic" (assisting one to adapt), unproven
Antidepressants Decreased depressed mood, increased sense of well-being, decreased anxiety, improved control of obsessive-compulsive behaviors	**Tricyclics** (norepinephrine, 5-HT, dopamine—but relative selectivity varies)		In general, as a class: • Dry mouth, constipation, sour metallic taste, blurred vision, epigastric distress, tachycardia, palpitations, dizziness, excessive sweating, urinary retention
	Amitriptyline (HT,NE)	Elavil	• Fatigue, weakness, confusion
	Amoxapine	Asendin	• Postural hypotension, edema
	Clomipramine (HT)	Anafranil	• Muscle tremors, extrapyramidal reactions
	Desipramine (NE)	Norpramin, Pertofrane	

(Continued)

TABLE 12.5 Psychotropic Medications by Class with Side Effects (*Continued*)

Type of Drug Benefits	Generic Name (Neurotransmitters primarily targeted)	Drug Trade Name	Common Side Effects
	Doxepin	Sinequan, Adapin	• Vision changes • Weight gain • Jaundice, agraulocytosis rashes • Delay of orgasm, lack of orgasm
	Immiprimine Nortriptyline Protriptyline Trimipramine	Tofranil, Janamine Aventyl, Pamelor Vivactil Surmontil	
	Tetracyclics/Misc.		
	Bupropion (Dopamine, Norepinephrine)	Wellbutrin	• Restlessness, anxiety, dizziness, chronic trouble sleeping, involuntary quivering, heart pounding
	Maprotiline	Ludiomil	• Throat irritation, dry mouth, taste problems, excessive sweating, constipation, frequent urination
		Marplan	• Loss of appetite, weight loss, nausea, vomiting, stomach cramps • Incomplete or infrequent bowel movements • Priaprism
	Trazodone	Desyrel	• Low blood pressure, drowsiness, dizziness, low energy, weak feelings, head pain
	Mirtazapine	Remeron	• Weight gain, increased hunger, high cholesterol
	Monoamine Oxidase Inhibitors (MAOIs) (sympathomimetics, 5-HT)		In general, as a class: • Interference with hepatic metabolism of many drugs
	Isocarboxazid Phenelzine Tranylcypromine	Marplan Nardil Parnate	• Orthostatic hypotension, dizziness, vertigo, headache, dry mouth, blurred vision, inhibition of ejaculation, difficulty in urination, weakness, fatigue, constipation, rashes • Tremors insomnia, hyperhydrosis • Agitation, hypomanic behavior, hallucinations, confusion, convulsions
	Selective Serotonin Reuptake Inhibitors (Serotonin)		In general, as a class:
	Citalopram Duloxetine Escitalopram Fluoxitine Fluvoxamine Paroxetine Sertraline	Celexa Cymbalta Lexapro Sarafem, Prozac Luvox Paxil Zoloft	• Sexual problems, altered interest in sex • Drowsiness, low energy, feeling weak • Headache, dizziness, trouble sleeping, blurred vision, anxiety, tremor • Loss of appetite, weight loss, nausea, gas, constipation or diarrhea, cramps • Rare: extrapyramidal reactions, neuroleptic malignant syndrome, serotonin syndrome, hepatitis, elevated prolactin, skin allergy, mild mania, suicidal thought, hemorrhage

Serotonin Norepinephrine Reuptake Inhibitor

Venlafaxine — Effexor
Desvenlafaxine — Pristiq

- Watch for drug interaction if patient is supplementing Tryptophan (OTC natural sleep aid); reaction consists of headache, nausea, sweating, and dizziness
- Watch for drug interaction (Serotonin Syndrome): with migraine medications (e.g., Imitrex): confusion, agitation, restlessness, dilated pupils, headache, changes in blood pressure and temperature, nausea, vomiting, diarrhea, rapid heart rate, twitching, lack of coordination, shivering, goose bumps, heavy sweating. Can be severe and life threatening: seizures, high fever, irregular heartbeat, unconsciousness.

Antipsychotics (neuroleptics)

Suppression of spontaneous movement and complex behavior; reduction of initiative and interest in environment; reduction of displays of emotion or affect; reduction of agitation and restlessness, aggression, anxiety, and impulsiveness; reduction of psychotic symptoms of hallucinations, delusions, and disorganized or incoherent thinking.

Increase control of tics or Tourette's symptoms.

Atypical Antipsychotics

Aripiprazole — Abilify
Clozapine — Clozaril
Olanzapine — Zyprexa
Paliperidone — Invega
Quetiapine — Seroquel
Risperidone — Risperdal
Ziprasidone — Geodon

As a class, in general:

- In older adults with dementia: may cause fatal side effects such as heart failure, pneumonia
- Somnolence, fatigue, dizziness, anxiety
- Orthostatic hypotension (initially and at dose increase)
- Rhinitis, upper respiratory infection, coughing, fever
- Appetite increase, vomiting, abdominal pain, dyspepsia, constipation
- Urinary incontinence, saliva increase, Parkinsonism, dystonia, tremor, akathesia, Tardive dyskinesia
- Serious/unlikely (report to doctor immediately): yellowing of eyes or skin, painful urination, other eye problems, seizures, difficulty swallowing, signs of infection (fever, sore throat), fast heartbeat, leg swelling, agitation, numbness/tingling of hands/ feet, tremor, trouble walking, pink urine, painful menstrual periods, unwanted breast milk (prolactin increase), breast enlargement, priaprism, inability to produce sperm, decreased sexual ability
- Seek immediate medical attention if these occur: chest pain, weakness on one side of body, sudden vision changes, headache, signs of allergic reaction including rash, itching/swelling (esp. face/tongue/ throat), severe dizziness, trouble breathing
- Blood sugar levels may increase causing or worsening diabetes
- May cause Neuroleptic Malignant Syndrome (NMS) with symptoms such as fever, muscle stiffness, fast/ irregular heartbeat, severe confusion, sweating

Older Antipsychotics

Phenothiazines

Chlorpromazine — Thorazine
Fluphenazine — Prolixin, Permitil
Perphanazine — Trilafon
Thioridazine — Mellaril
Trifluoperazine — Stelazine

Thioxanthines

Thiothizene — Navane

Heterocyclics

Haloperidol — Haldol
Loxapine — Loxitane
Pimozide — Orap

(Continued)

TABLE 12.5 Psychotropic Medications by Class with Side Effects (*Continued*)

Type of Drug Benefits	Generic Name (Neurotransmitters primarily targeted)	Drug Trade Name	Common Side Effects
Attention Deficit Increased ability to focus, decreased distractibility, decreased impulsivity, decreased hyperactivity	**Stimulants** Methylphenidate	Daytrana Methylin Metadate Metadate CD Ritalin Ritalin LA Ritalin-SR	As a class, in general: • Nervousness, trouble sleeping, loss of appetite, weight loss • Dizziness, nausea, vomiting, headache, blurred vision • Fast, pounding, or irregular heartbeat
	Methylphenidate Hydrochloride Amphetamine	Concerta Desoxyn Liquadd Procentra	• Mental/mood/behavior changes (agitation, aggression, mood swings, depression, abnormal thoughts • Uncontrollable muscle movements (twitching, shaking, sudden outbursts of words or sounds) • Report immediately to medical doctor any fainting, seizure, signs of heart attack or stroke, or allergic reaction including rash, tongue/throat swelling, trouble breathing
	Amphetamine with Dextroamphetamine Dextroamphetamine Sulfate Lisdexamfetamine Dimesylate Dexmethylphenidate Hydrochloride	Adderall Dexedrine, Dexedrine Dextrostat, Spansule, Vyvanse Focalin FocalinXR	
	Nonstimulants Atomoxetine	Strattera	• Nausea, cramps, loss of appetite, diarrhea, dry mouth, headache, nervousness, dizziness, trouble sleeping, sweating, weight loss, irritability, restlessness, agitation, aggression, mood swings, depression, hallucinations, abnormal thoughts or behavior, uncontrolled movements, muscle twitching/shaking, outbursts of words/sounds, change in sexual ability/interest, swelling of ankles/feet, extreme tiredness • Seek immediate medical attention for shortness of breath, chest pain, severe headache, fainting, fast/ pounding/irregular heartbeat, jaw/left arm pain, seizures, weakness on one side of body, slurred speech, confusion, blurred vision or for serious allergic reaction such as rash, itching, swelling, severe dizziness, trouble breathing
	Selective Alpha2-Adrenergic Adjunctive Therapy Clonidine Guanfacine	Catapress Tenex, Intuniv	• Dry mouth, dizziness, weakness, headache, stuffy nose, dry eyes, blurred vision, nausea, vomiting, stomach pain/discomfort, diarrhea, constipation, unusual taste in mouth

Antimanic Medications

Mood stabilizers		

Carbamazepine (reduces polysynaptic responses and blocks posttetanic potentiation) — Tegretol

- Vision problems, involuntary eye movement, lack of coordination, dizziness, drowsiness, nausea, confusion
- Immediate medical attention for skin rash, hives, mouth sores, blistering/peeling of skin, fever, sore throat, infections that come and go or do not go away, easy bruising, red or purple spots on body, bleeding gums or nose bleeds, severe fatigue or weakness, new or worsening depression, thoughts of suicide or dying, new or worsening anxiety, agitation, restlessness, anger, aggressiveness, violence, impulsiveness, mania, or other mood/behavioral changes

Divalproex sociaum (valproic acid) — Depakote

- Diarrhea, dizziness, drowsiness, hair loss, blurred/double vision, change in menstrual period, tinnitus, tremor, unsteadiness, weight change
- Seek immediate medical attention for signs of infection such as fever or sore throat, dark urine, persistent nausea and vomiting, severe stomach/abdominal pain, yellow eyes/skin, sudden mental changes, depression, suicidal thoughts, attempts or other mental/mood changes, shortness of breath, chest pain, severe headache, fainting, fast/pounding/irregular heartbeat, jaw/left arm pain, seizures, weakness on one side of body, slurred speech, confusion, blurred vision, or for serious allergic reaction including rash, itching, swelling, severe dizziness, trouble breathing

Gabapentin — Neurontin

- Asthenia, malaise, face edema, anorexia, flatulence, gingivitis, hypertension, purpura, bruising, arthralgia, vertigo, hyperkinesia, parasthesia, altered reflexes, anxiety, hostility, pneumonia, abnormal vision
- Allergy, generalized edema, weight loss, chills, hypotension, angina, peripheral vascular disorder, tachycardia, migraine, murmur, glossitis, bleeding gums, thirst, stomatitis, increased salivation, gastroenteritis, hemorrhoids, bloody stools, fecal incontinence, hepatomegaly, anemia, tendinitis, arthritis, joint swelling/stiffness, syncope, abnormal dreaming, decrease position sense, stupor, decrease/loss of libido, agitation, paranoia, euphoria, psychosis, suicide, apnea, skin reactions from allergy, urinary incontinence or retention, unable to climax/abnormal ejaculation, amenorrhea, dysmenorrhea

(Continued)

275

Type of Drug Benefits	Generic Name (Neurotransmitters primarily targeted)	Drug Trade Name	Common Side Effects
	Lamotrigine	Lamictal	• Headache, flu syndrome, nausea, vomiting/diarrhea, dyspepsia, anorexia, arthralgia, dizziness, ataxia, somnolence, incoordination, insomnia, tremor, depression, anxiety, irritability, convulsion, speech disorder, concentration disturbance, rhinitis, pharyngitis, cough, rash, itching, vision problems, dysmenorrhea, vaginitis, amenorrhea
Lithium Salts (alters sodium transport affecting metabolism of catecholamines) Lithium carbonate Lithium citrate		Eskalith, Lithane, Lithobid Cibalith-S	• Fine hand tremor, polyuria, thirst, nausea, discomfort, diarrhea, vomiting, drowsiness, muscular weakness, lack of coordination, giddiness, ataxia, blurred vision, tinnitus, muscle hyperirritability, hypertonicity, choreoathetotic movements, hyperactive deep tendon reflex, extrapyramidal symptoms, seizures, slurred speech, dizziness, vertigo, nystagmus, incontinence, somnolence, restlessness, confusion, stupor, coma, tics, poor memory, worsening of organic brain syndromes
Topimarate		Topamax	• Tiredness, drowsiness, dizziness, loss of coordination, tingling of hands/feet, loss of appetite, bad taste in mouth, diarrhea, weight loss, mental problems (confusion, slowed thinking, trouble concentrating/attending, nervousness, memory problems, speech/language problems). • Signs of kidney stones, fever, chills, painful/frequent urination, abdominal/back/side pain, bloody or pink urine • Seek immediate medical attention for sudden vision changes, blurred vision, eye pain/redness, shortness of breath, chest pain, severe headache, fainting, fast/pounding/irregular heartbeat, jaw/left arm pain, seizures, weakness on one side of body, slurred speech, confusion, or serious allergic reaction including rash, itching, swelling, severe dizziness, trouble breathing

Sleep Aids

(Not listed elsewhere)

	Zopidem (Ambien)	In general, as a class:
	Flurazepam (Dalmane)	• Similar side effects to the benzodiazepines
	Triazolam (Halcion)	• Retrograde amnesia
	Eszopiclone (Lunesta)	• Next day hangover (worse with flurazepam, triazolam, and temazepam, which contributes to falls in elderly)
	Temazepam (Restoril)	• Sleep driving and other complex behaviors with no memory of event
	Zaleplon (Sonata)	
	Ramelteon (Rozerem) (Melatonin receptor agonist)	• Somnolence, dizziness, fatigue, nausea, insomnia, abnormal thinking, behavioral changes, hallucinations, worsening of depression
		• Not used with fluvoxamine due to metabolism inhibition resulting in increased levels of Rozerem; not used with severe sleep apnea

Herbals/OTCs

	Dimenhydranate (Unisom)	• Sleep driving
	Diphenhydramine (Benadryl, Tylenol PM, Advil PM, others)	• Dry mouth, constipation, blurred vision
	Fo-ti (Chinese remedy)	• Dry mouth, constipation, blurred vision
	Catnip	• Diarrhea, bruising
	Passion Flower	• Probably only affects cats
		• Some varieties may have MAOI properties, blood thinning properties
	l-Tryptophan	• Essential amino acid
	Hops	• Toxic to dogs, direct contact with plant may cause dermatitis
	Valerian	• Stomachache, apathy, mental dullness, mild depression, dizziness, drowsiness, allergic skin reactions
	Melatonin	• Headaches, nausea, irritability, vivid dreams or nightmares, drowsiness, hypothermia, worsen symptoms of orthostatic intolerance including low blood pressure, decreased blood flow

Smoking Cessation Agents

Related to Antidepressants

	Buproprion (Zyban)	• Identical to Wellbutrin (see antidepressants)
	Varenicline (Chantix)	• Neuropsychiatric symptoms including changes in behavior, hostility, agitation, depressed mood, and suicide-related events including ideation, behavior, and attempt. Worsening of preexisting psychiatric illness

Disclaimer: This chart does not represent all side effects for each drug/herb. The counselor should consult with the prescriber for any issues related to the client's medication or potential side effects. The information in this table was compiled from a variety of sources, including Brunton, Chabner, and Knollman (2011), Foster and Tyler (2007), and Awang (2009).

Given that the counselor generally spends a great deal more time both in a single session and over time with the client on medication than does the medical professional, the counselor who can denote side effects, monitor symptoms, and collaborate and advocate with the medical professional can be critical to client medical compliance and ultimate therapeutic success. Suggested strategies for working collaboratively with medical professionals include five guidelines. First is to make certain both the counselor and the medical professional have a signed release from the patient fitting to the collaboration. This step is necessary for all conversations divulging any data about the client to medical professionals except for those involving the client as a danger to self or others that warrant duty to warn or duty to protect. The next is to be ready with a written list of the issues to address to be respectful of the medical professional's time. Third is to be clear about your role regarding the collaborative effort and to not overstep your professional role (e.g., you are not a medical professional, so do not offer medical advice to anyone—especially not the medical professional). Be prepared to offer your opinion when asked, but also make clear what you are not prepared to address. Finally, ask questions that might help you assist the medical professional such as, "What would you like me to watch for?" or "When would you like me to provide a verbal report to you regarding any impact I may notice?" or "Are there any compliance issues you would like me to be aware of or assist with regarding our shared client?"

Occasionally, medical professionals will ask mental health professionals for input regarding medications they have seen to be effective with clients with similar issues to the one under consultation. Counselors may offer an opinion when asked, but must steer clear of assuming any roles belonging to the medical professional and not to the counselor (e.g., counselors do not instruct medical professionals regarding what or how they should or should not prescribe medication or conduct other actions belonging to the medical profession). Furthermore, occasionally the counselor may be aware of prescriptions, over-the-counter medications, or other altering substances (illicit or otherwise, such as alcohol, drug, or herbal remedy) that the client is consuming. A report of such behavior can be critical and should be made to the medical professional when known (King & Anderson, 2004).

It is clear that counselors can be critical components of effective medical treatment when working in collaboration and consultation with medical professionals. That said, there are clear limitations to the counselor's role. Most important, counselors must never assume the roles or responsibilities of the medical profession. Counselors do not alter, in any manner, the regimen outlined for the client (King & Anderson, 2004). Counselors do not prescribe any substance (medical, herbal, or otherwise). Counselors do not instruct clients to begin or end medical treatments or to adjust dosages or timing of medical practices. Rather, counselors support the medical regimen as outlined by the medical professional. Should the counselor note a need for medical intervention (side effects, negative drug interactions, or any other medically managed issue), the counselor makes an immediate referral to the medical professional, sends the client to the emergency room, or calls emergency services as the situation warrants. The counselor never acts in the role of the medical professional. Use Self-Assessment Activity 12.4 to begin thinking about psychopharmacology as it relates to counseling.

SELF-ASSESSMENT ACTIVITY 12.4 PSYCHOPHARMACOLOGY

1. Think about the kinds of symptoms and side effects you might notice a client exhibiting. How do you determine when to contact the medical professional for collaboration? How do you determine when to act more urgently, such as sending the client to the medical professional's office, the emergency room, or even more emergent services such as calling for an ambulance?
2. Practice with a fellow student counselor role-playing a conversation you might have with a medical professional regarding a client who is exhibiting excessive and uncomfortable side effects. How can you make your conversation conducive to collaboration? How can you demonstrate your respect for the medical professional's expertise and role while being helpful and advocating for your client?

3. Suppose a medical professional has just prescribed medication (Alprazolam) for your client presenting with anxiety. Your client explains to you that she is bothered by excessive tiredness and periods where she doesn't feel as "sharp" as she typically does. What might your role as her counselor be in supporting the medical regimen prescribed as well as supporting and assisting your client?

4. Suppose your client has talked to her medical doctor, who has suggested she begin a course of Duloxetine (Cymbalta). Your client is apprehensive because she worries about side effects of medication. How can you educate her about the potential side effects she might experience? How can you assist her in making a decision regarding compliance with the medical doctor's regimen? What must you avoid doing to act ethically?

5. Your client who is diagnosed with Bipolar Disorder has been taking Gabapentin (Neurontin) for 3 weeks. He is threatening to stop taking it entirely and informs you he has missed today's dose. He is doing this because he has experienced diarrhea since beginning it. What would you do to assist your client in being compliant with the medical regimen as outlined by the prescribing professional?

PSYCHOLOGICAL, EDUCATIONAL, AND VOCATION ASSESSMENT

Meghan spent her 11:00 hour with her client, Kevin, reviewing the results of the life planning assessment and information for Kevin. The assessment included a structured interview, observations, client report, review of Kevin's academic record including current transcripts, Myers-Briggs Type Indicator, and Strong Interest Inventory as well as a World of Work review in medically related areas. Meghan has conducted this assessment because Kevin has indicated that the greatest source of his current near-debilitating anxiety is his uncertainty about his academic and career future. They determined together that it would be helpful to assess his interests and personality to determine potential occupational goals to give direction to, and motivation toward, his educational pursuits. Assessment is an ongoing role of the counselor.

Humans spend much of their lives assessing. No matter what the situation may be, humans gather data, consider it, organize it, and construct meaning from the data, which is then used to determine the course of action to be taken. Counseling practice requires an organized means of assessment that involves defining the question, gathering data related to the question from as many sources as reasonably possible, organizing the data and looking for consistent patterns, determining meaning of the patterns, and making recommendations regarding courses of action given the conclusions drawn from the assessment process. Three areas of assessment in which counselors are often involved (conduct or refer for formal assessment) are psychological, educational, and vocational. An overview of the assessment process and a brief examination of each area comprise this section.

The counselor begins the process of assessing the client from the first moment of contact. The astute counselor gathers observations, client report, histories (e.g., social, emotional, medical, educational), reports of others (concerned teachers, spouses, parents, children, coworkers), records (scholastic, medical, past counseling), and many other sources of assessment data to both formulate an assessment question and respond to the question with as much accuracy and helpfulness as possible (Erford, 2013). Most assessment questions center around one or more of three main areas, including the client's psychological functioning, intellectual and educational capacities and achievements, and vocational interests and capacities.

Psychological assessment involves gathering data and developing summaries of the client's mental well-being including personality, cognitive, behavioral, and emotional states (current functioning) and traits (general long-term functioning). In addition to the data sources listed earlier, the counselor may formally assess the client using interviews (structured and unstructured) and psychological tests.

The interview can vary from little structure with more open-ended guidance to a detailed set of questions intentionally chosen by the counselor to assess a particular area of functioning or specific history. A common interview used for over half a century is the Mental Status Examination (MSE), which is often conducted during the first interview. The MSE assesses general appearance, attitude, activity level and quality, mood and affect, speech and language, thought process/content and perception, cognition, insight, and judgment. It provides structure that can lead to the diagnosis in addition to a general understanding of the client's level and style of functioning (Erford, 2013). A very brief and structured mental status examination is the Mini-Mental State Examination (Folstein, Folstein, & McHugh, 1975), which assesses for basic memory, cognitive process, and content issues.

Most psychological tests are standardized; they have structure that details the way in which the test is administered, scored, interpreted, and otherwise used. Most have norms for defined populations that assist the assessor in accurately determining what tests are appropriate to employ given the client's demographics, the question being addressed, and the outcome desired. Most psychological tests require particular education and supervised training of the assessor. Psychological testing can be categorized as projective or nonprojective. Projective tests have little directive stimuli to elicit the client's unconscious thoughts, feelings, or actions. Examples include the Rorschach, the House-Tree-Person, or Sentence Completion tests. Nonprojective tests have more obvious structure that directs the client toward the desired area to be assessed. Examples include the Minnesota Multiphasic Personality Inventory-2, the Beck Depression Inventory, and the Myers-Briggs Type Indicator (Erford, 2013; Gladding & Newsome, 2010).

Educational assessment refers to data gathering and summation regarding the individual's levels of knowledge, aptitude, capacities/limitations, interests, and beliefs. School counselors spend a significant portion of their time participating in the process of educational assessment. Educational assessment involves achievement and ability tests such as the American College Testing Program Assessment (ACT), Scholastic Aptitude Test (SAT), Graduate Record Examination (GRE), Miller Analogy Test (MAT) for entrance to various levels of educational programs. Education assessment can be specific to educational issues such as the improvement of instruction, which is the goal of the Iowa Tests of Basic Skills (ITBS). Another common form of educational assessment is various states' high-stakes testing to determine if students meet levels of knowledge and application required for graduation. The counselor's role in educational assessment can vary greatly from simply proctoring tests, to conducting in-depth observations and testing, to assisting in assessing students' learning disabilities. Time is spent on interpretation and application with students to set goals, plan, motivate, promote the development of self-knowledge, and increase confidence in students as learners. In addition to aptitude and achievement, school assessments include interest, career maturity, and personality inventories.

Vocational assessment is the category containing the example of Meghan and Kevin noted earlier. Clients bring to counseling various issues relating to vocational struggles ranging from unemployment due to downsizing at midlife, to confusion regarding good fit of career choices at high school graduation, to difficulties in retirement planning and adjustment. Literally hundreds of assessment tools are available related to vocational guidance. Those that are most common are listed in Table 12.3 (Career Assessment Tools). General categories of vocational assessment include academic skill, aptitude, interest, intelligence, learning style, occupational skill, personality, transferable skills, and values.

For each type of assessment, the process is consistent. The client and counselor work together to determine the type of assessment needed via a clear statement of the issue at hand. The counselor works with the client to determine the appropriate assessment strategies to employ including both tests and nontest means of data collection. The counselor uses those strategies that the counselor is competent to administer and interpret and seeks assistance from, or refers to, qualified professionals where the counselor is not educated and/or trained to act. The counselor diligently works to gather a well-rounded and complete set of data related to the defined issue. Data is synthesized so that potential answers can be formulated to address the defined issue. The counselor incorporates client feedback and input to ensure that the synthesis has produced accurate results fitting to the client, whether it be a *DSM* diagnosis, clarity regarding educational preparation, or a list of occupational choices that might fit the client. The counselor and client work together whenever possible to determine the action to be taken related to the assessment results, and the counselor assists the client in taking those action steps toward a successful outcome regarding the issue.

All along the assessment path, the counselor remains adherent to professional ethical standards and uses a healthy decision-making model consistent with beneficence and nonmaleficence. The counselor never provides any service beyond the scope of the counselor's education and training without supervision fitting to the level of ethical practice. Critically important to ethical practice is the adherence to the practice of informed consent for assessment, appropriate distribution and retention of results with written release of information when any information is disseminated beyond the client or immediate treatment team within the assessing agency, careful and fitting selection of assessment tools, conditions of assessment administration in accordance with both ethical practice and standardization of specific testing tools, and finally assessment security, keeping assessment tools protected from all inappropriate use or availability (ACA, 2005).

Furthermore, the counselor-as-assessor must be mindful of diversity issues. The counselor must select assessment tools particularly fitting to the purpose of the assessment, ensuring availability of appropriate norm groups for comparison, maintaining awareness of cultural limitations or insensitivity of tools that may impact the client or the accuracy of the summations from the data gathered, and being ever mindful of the impact of assessment on the relationship between the counselor and client (ACA, 2005). Table 12.6 presents the process of assessment with a sample application. See Self-Assessment Activity 12.5 to reflect on your assessment skills, and use Case Study 12.3 to practice them.

TABLE 12.6 Assessment Process with Sample Application

Stage of Assessment	Activities	Sample
1. Orientation	Meet the client, discuss rights of the client and limitations of service as well as fee structure and other policies, build rapport, discuss issue, background, and client's focus.	Sue meets with Jim, a client who, at the recommendation of his boss, is seeking assessment of his depression symptoms that have persisted since his wife passed away following breast cancer approximately 2 years ago. She reviews her disclosure statement and explains the process of assessment to Jim, who understands and agrees to work with Sue and complete a formal assessment. Jim shares his marital history, the period of his wife's illness, and her subsequent death. He states that he has never been an outgoing person and thinks he is probably okay—just not as extroverted as his wife was making him seem. He does divulge his decline following her death and is concerned that he may be clinically depressed, even though he is functioning well at work and with his grown children.

(Continued)

TABLE 12.6 Assessment Process with Sample Application (*Continued*)

Stage of Assessment	Activities	Sample
2. Construct the Question(s)	Formulate the questions to be answered by the assessment. Get specific and concrete. Ensure accuracy with client to ensure buy-in and client rights.	Sue and Jim discuss Jim's and the boss's concerns and determine that Jim could be assessed to determine if his withdrawal from activities is due to a treatable depression or due to his introverted personality that is more prominent now that his extroverted wife is not there to drag him out of his shell.
3. Select the Assessment Tools	Review appropriate available tools for assessment and select those most fitting to the client's demographics, issue, and assessment question(s).	Sue determines that the Beck Depression Inventory (BDI-II) and the Myers-Briggs Type Indicator (MBTI) are useful tests to employ in addition to a detailed structured interview with an embedded mental status examination. She and Jim agree that an interview with his two grown children who live locally might also prove helpful.
4. Administer the Assessment Tools	Administer chosen assessment tools to client, ensuring appropriate testing conditions and following the protocols and procedures of the standardized instructions of each tool.	Jim attends two appointments for his assessment. The first appointment involves an interview with mental status examination for the first 45 minutes and 30 minutes shared with his two adult children. The second session includes both the MBTI and BDI-II.
5. Score, Interpret	Follow all protocols and procedures for scoring and interpreting test results as provided using appropriate norm groups for comparisons. Organize results to discover themes and important outcomes.	Sue scores the MBTI and the BDI and interprets them according to the manuals. She summarized the interview results from both Jim and his adult children and finds themes in each.
6. Write Report	Organize themes and outcomes in structured report concisely and clearly while avoiding professional jargon and unnecessary redundancy.	Sue organizes the results of the testing and the interviews as well as her own observations and writes a detailed, organized report concluding that Jim's testing results do indicate introversion as well as a low level of depression symptoms. She further supports these findings with reports of both Jim and his children that he is functioning well at work and in family gatherings, is keeping his home in good repair and cleanliness, and appears to be enjoying his solitary activities when not with family or at work.

Stage of Assessment	Activities	Sample
7. Share Report with Client	Summarize report and highlight important outcomes with the client, avoiding jargon or complicated language to ensure client understands what you have concluded. Seek input from client regarding conclusions and integrate feedback the client provides in disagreement. Adjust as appropriate.	Sue shares the results with Jim, who states his agreement with the findings. He expresses a desire to branch out a little more in his activities than he has been over the past 2 years and discusses with Sue the option of seeking a few sessions of counseling to work on increasing his activities and contacts with others in a social setting to make his world a bit more fun. Sue includes in her report the recommendation that he may find benefit in counseling to that end.

SELF-ASSESSMENT ACTIVITY 12.5 COUNSELOR AS ASSESSOR

1. What assessment tools are you aware of that are available for your use as a counselor?
2. What are your current skills in using each of these assessments?
3. How might you go about securing increased skills/abilities in using these tools?
4. What are your ethical responsibilities as a counselor conducting assessments?

CASE STUDY 12.3

Casey

Casey is a 16-year-old, 10th grader at the local high school. He is an excellent student, a better than average athlete, and vice-president of the sophomore class. His mother has insisted that he come to see you after noticing that Casey has become somewhat irritable and withdrawn the last couple of months. Casey has refused to talk with her about his struggles, but he has consented to meet with a counselor. He tells you at your first meeting that he thinks he is going crazy because he feels like he is pressured all the time to do things perfectly. He says he feels anxious all the time and cannot sleep at night. He reports being distracted in class and at basketball practice. His symptoms began after a basketball trip with the juniors and seniors (he is on the varsity team) during which time several of them complained about their workloads, college applications, and their pressures to go to college and/or get jobs. Casey came home upset stating he had no idea what he could possibly study in college or what he wanted to do careerwise. Both Casey and his mother want an assessment to see if his anxiety and sleeplessness are as severe as his mother perceives and to assess what he might focus his activities and studies on to prepare for college and his future.

Write up an assessment, following the "Sample" section of Table 12.6, based on your capacities and understanding of the process of assessment. What are the areas for which you are not yet educated and trained, considering this case? What can you do to become prepared?

THE "BUSINESS" OF COUNSELING: THIRD-PARTY PAYERS

The last hour of Meghan's day is spent ensuring all paperwork regarding her workday has been completed. Some of the paperwork completed by counselors promotes quality care, some paperwork documents ethical treatment, and some satisfies the requirements of organizations that pay for the services provided to the client. These organizations (e.g., private insurance companies, government programs, managed care agents, employee assistance programs) are known as *third-party payers*. Third-party payers tend to be diligent guardians of their funds and insist on particular protocols to ensure their clients are receiving necessary care aimed at resolving the issues that led to the need for care or for adequate services that make for the least expensive maintenance for long-term issues.

Private insurance companies make up a large number of third-party payments. From individuals to large corporations, private insurance companies contract to collect premiums from their patrons in return for a guarantee that certain types of health services will be paid for by the insurance company up to a designated amount. Although mental health services have not always topped the list of those services generally covered, most insurance companies now do provide mental health benefits. Recent laws have required that insurance plans serving more than 50 employees provide coverage for mental health services in accordance to the rates of physical health coverage. The federal law providing for this action, the Wellstone-Domenici Mental Health Parity and Addiction Equity Act (MHPAEA), was passed by Congress in 2008 and was enacted initially in January of 2010 and fully in January of 2011. State laws vary, but many require the same parity of plans serving fewer than 50 employees (American Psychological Association, 2012).

Private insurance companies often utilize structures such as PPOs (Preferred Provider Organizations), which require services be provided by panel members or "preferred providers." To become a preferred provider, counselors must complete an application; provide documentation of their education, training, and capacities; and sometimes serve a particular niche the insurance company believes necessary in the counselor's geographic region. Counselors not on provider panels may be allowed to provide services at a lesser reimbursement rate. The rate of payment and number of sessions allotted are generally defined by the policy or plan, and insurance companies keep careful track of "going rates" (average amount charged in an area for counseling services) as well as number of billed sessions. Some insurance companies will consider extending the number of sessions allowed via an appeals process—especially when the appeal documents a savings of funds in the long run. Finally, some insurance companies require preauthorization of services and will not pay for services rendered outside said contract (Foos, Otten, & Hill, 1991).

With the electronic age, billing services have shifted from handwritten bills sent directly to the client, who might then submit the tab to the insurance company for reimbursement, to hand-completed forms the counselor submitted to the insurance company for payment, and often now to electronic payments submitted online with payment systems, including automatic deposits and e-mailed explanations of benefit (EOBs). Many services are now available for counselors in private or group practices or agencies who wish to have another party complete their billing to both clients and third-party providers.

A number of government-run and funded programs function much like private insurance, including Medicare, Medicaid, Labor and Industry Benefits (L&I), and Victims' Compensation. Medicare is a federally funded program that began in the 1960s providing insurance for the aged, blind, and disabled. Medicaid is a similar program with joint federal/state funding extending services to those with financial need regardless of age. Presently, publically funded insurance programs (Medicare) only reimburse master's-level counselors for mental health services under particular circumstances and not under others for which other mental health professionals (e.g., psychologists, psychiatrists, social workers) are reimbursed (Medicaid, 2011). Thanks to the efforts of the American Counseling Association, active house and senate bills are under consideration to extend said reimbursement to services by counselors (ACA, 2011). The inclusion of mental health counselors for Medicaid programs varies by services and differs from state to state. The future of the inclusion of counselors at both state and federal levels provides professional advocacy opportunities. In any case, both federal and state programs provide detailed parameters for the practice and billing of mental health providers as well as a process by which said professionals become Medicare certified. Medicare- and Medicaid-approved fee schedules are markedly lower than most insurance companies and lower still than most private practitioner fees, and certified providers agree to take these fees as full payment (they "take assignment"; Terry-McElrath, Chriqui, & McBride, 2011).

The institutions of Medicare and Medicaid and the growing number of insurance programs offering mental health coverage increased the global costs of mental health services. In response to these escalating costs and resulting concerns, the Health Maintenance Organization Act (HMOA) of 1973 was passed to assist in cost containment while ensuring quality of care. The act required that employers offer managed care alternatives to employees and made available federal money for the development of managed care programs. The impact of the HMOA has progressively grown, and a boom of managed care companies arose in the 1990s and remains a primary factor influencing mental health care today (Gottlieb & Cooper, 2000).

Labor and Industry (L & I) and Crime Victims (CV) are two other government-sponsored third-party payers. L & I provides payment for counseling services to those who have been injured on the job when those services are warranted in relationship to the injury or when those services are deemed necessary for reentry into the workforce. CV is a program intended to assist in amending the psychological harm created via crime on its victims. In many cases, the perpetrator of the crime is required to pay into the system, and CV pays for services to the victim to assist in recovering mental health to precrime levels. Counselors with expertise in each area may contract with L & I and/or CV to become providers of mental health services to these populations.

Employee Assistance Programs (EAPs) are another method by which organizations are attempting to keep costs contained and mental health services available. Some organizations create their own in-house EAP programs, whereas others contract with independent counselors for services through which employees can seek limited assistance with issues ranging from stress to marital issues—each of which may have an impact on the employee's productivity. These services are typically included in employee benefits or offered at very low rates. Most EAPs provide referrals to outside providers for concerns that extend beyond the limited number of sessions allowed or the scope of practice defined for services within the EAP (Gladding & Newsome, 2010; MacCluskie & Ingersoll, 2001). Use Self-Assessment Activity 12.6 to begin to reflect on issues surrounding third-party payers.

SELF-ASSESSMENT ACTIVITY 12.6 THIRD-PARTY PAYERS

1. What ethical dilemmas can you foresee facing as a counselor working within the policies and procedures of third-party payers?
2. How will you ensure quality of care when a client's insurer limits care to a number of sessions you believe are too few, given the client's presenting issue?
3. What are at least five third-party payers you could consider if you were involved in assisting someone with very limited resources in securing mental health services? List the specific resources particular to your area.
4. What challenges might you face in making the business end of a counseling practice work efficiently?

Summary

The activities comprising the role of the counselor have grown tremendously over time. Most counselors now have complex duties, including providing consultation, career guidance, academic advising, advocacy, medical or psychopharmaceutical compliance support, and assessment, as well as business practices with third-party payers. It is critical that counselor preparation include a basic understanding of these activities as well as a foundation for practical application. To review, each role is briefly summarized.

The *counselor as consultant* provides service to a broad range of consultees who seek expert advice, opinions, or information. The counselor as consultant gathers data to ensure that the consultation provides accuracy and current best practices for the consultee to consider. The consultee then determines what services will be provided to yet a third party, or target. The consultant may provide assistance to the consultee in creating an action plan for implementing the decision. Finally, the consultant evaluates the effects of the consultee's actions.

The counselor provides *career guidance* as needed throughout clinical practice, given that career development is a lifelong process. Seminal works in career guidance provide the foundation for assisting clients through the process of career development. These works include the early trait and factor work of Frank Parsons, Ann Roe's psychodynamic career theory, Donald Super's five-stage theory, and John Holland's personality theory of occupational choice, as well as the more recent work of Krumboltz's Social Learning Theory, McAuliffe's and Peavy's constructive development theory, and the systems approach of Patton and McMahon. Many tools have been developed based on these theories to assess clients' needs from, preferences for, and matches to, various potential careers.

A facet of career counseling includes *academic advising*. In this role, the counselor assists the student in ensuring success through planning and preparations in selecting a direction and the course of study to meet that direction. Additional academic advising activities include psychoeducation and skill building such as time management and communication skills as well as testing strategies and study habits. Counselors may also assist students in creating job shadowing, volunteer, and service opportunities that enhance career maturity.

Counselors have acted as *advocates* for the disenfranchised and suffering since the beginning of the counseling profession with a particular emphasis in assisting others in finding their voice. Over the decades, counseling advocacy has grown to include not only social justice issues, but also to advocate for the profession of counseling itself. Indeed, the standards set for professional education and training make clear that counselors must take action on behalf of both clients and the profession to promote human development. Such advocacy has resulted in major changes, including actions to allow counselors positions within Veterans Administration facilities, recent enacting of parity laws, and laws for counseling licensure or certification in all 50 states.

Counseling advocacy has also grown to include having a voice for clients undergoing *psychopharmacotherapy* to ensure effective compliance with the medical professional's regimen and to keep the medical professional apprised of the client's condition. The counselor must understand the basic structures and functions of the brain, its neurotransmitters, and intertwined endocrine and peripheral nervous systems. The counselor must also know the desired and potentially harmful effects of medications prescribed to treat the various symptoms experienced by the client. To be effective in this supporting role, the counselor must build respectful relationships with medical professionals and exercise effective communication with clients, significant others, and the medical professional.

Counselors are in a chronic state of informal *assessment* as they consider the client's symptoms, issues, and desired outcomes of counseling. Formal assessment tends to center around three main areas, including the client's psychological functioning, intellectual and educational capacities and achievements, and vocational interests and capacities. When conducting formal assessment, the counselor is clear regarding the question at hand, the process of gathering data related to that question from as many sources as reasonably possible, the organization of the resulting data into patterns, the determination of meaning or themes of those patterns, and the making of recommendations for a course of action. When psychological tests are employed as part of the assessment process, counselors carefully adhere to the standardization and procedures required of each tool. Counselors work within the professional ethics regarding assessment with particular clarity involving the least invasive protocols and sensitivity to the needs of the client as well as to issues of confidentiality, client rights, and the fit of testing procedures given issues of diversity.

Finally, the role of the counselor involves the *activities of business*—particularly those involving third-party payers. Third-party payers are those organizations, such as insurance companies, government programs, managed care agents, and employee assistance programs, that pay for the services provided to the client. Counselors need to understand the structure and function of third-party payer organizations to become allowable and payable providers and to meet the requirements of each organization including payment systems, record keeping, types of services covered, preauthorization for services, and limitations of coverage.

The counselor's role is varied and complex. Understanding each facet of the counselor's workday requires a solid foundation of knowledge and skill as well as dispositions conducive to the successful practice of counseling. The counselor who stays abreast of the current professional literature will likely find the role of counselor expanding as the profession continues to address the needs of our diverse and changing society.

CHAPTER 13

Counselor Self-Care

BY KERRY THON

PREVIEW

Up until this chapter, the focus has been on your relationship and interactions with clients, how to provide outstanding services, and how to get the most out of your practicum and internship. In these final two chapters, the focus shifts and is now squarely up you as the counselor in training. This chapter reviews the importance for all counselors to have an effective self-care plan to help prevent burnout and to deal with the stressors inherent in the counseling field. Clinical supervision allows you to seek advice and consultation from experienced counselors as you might seek knowledge from others who have gone before you. This can assist you in sidestepping common pitfalls and mistakes made by beginning counselors and provide much-needed support as you push the limits of your competence. Your self-care plan is much like your protective gear, which can help you weather the storms as you navigate through your first counseling experiences. Many professionals have tools of their trade that they need to keep in tip-top shape. As counselors, we are our own best therapeutic tool, so we have an obligation to keep ourselves in shape mentally, physically, and spiritually. Be mindful of the parallel process that happens with stress and wellness. What you learn about stress and wellness applies not only to your clients, but to yourself as well. This chapter will highlight areas to focus on as you create your own self-care plan, but let's first explore stress and its effects.

STRESS AND THE HELPING PROFESSIONS

As I was writing this chapter, I was reminded yet again of the importance of taking care of oneself. This reminder came late one night after I had been writing for several hours in a café. Toward the end of the night the server came by and suggested that I take a break to stretch. Here I was writing about self-care and at the same time ignoring my body signs that I needed a break. The irony of the situation was not lost on me. I decided to heed his advice and felt much better for taking the time to engage in a few self-care practices. Reminders to take a break for our own self-care are all around us. A self-care plan is not just for counseling students; rather, it is a critical tool for all counselors that needs to be reviewed and revised on a consistent basis.

Becoming a counselor is an exciting and rewarding adventure. And just with other journeys and adventures, you must prepare yourself to get the most out of your experience. When traveling I try to anticipate what I may need to bring with me on my journey, so I read up on the locale, gain insights from others who may have traveled there, and pack appropriately for the climate. This is similar to your clinical training in that your classroom knowledge has prepared you with basic clinical tools and skills that you will hone on this journey, but it is always important to keep learning about the population you are serving.

The helping profession is filled with, well, helpers. Some of the personal characteristics of those interested in helping others make them excellent candidates to become counselors. Interestingly, these same characteristics also put those helpers at risk for burnout, secondary trauma, and helper fatigue.

It is critical for counselors, and counseling interns, to understand themselves as a person if they are to grow into competent counselors. Understanding your strengths, areas for improvement, and triggers allows you to know what you are bringing to the counseling session and to better assess your own level of functioning. Counselors are certainly not immune to bad days, relationship troubles, or difficult life situations. It is almost always easier to work on someone else's life, but we also need to apply what we teach to ourselves. There have been many times where I have been working with a client, and the ideas that are being discussed could easily be applied to my own life. Coming up with a self-care plan is not just for those in counseling, it is a necessity for everyone. We should not be asking our clients to do anything that we ourselves are not willing to do. Take some time to explore your relationship with stress by completing Self-Assessment Activity 13.1.

SELF-ASSESSMENT ACTIVITY 13.1 STRESS

- Rate yourself from 1 to 10 (10 being the highest level of stress and 1 being the lowest) regarding how stressed you are feeling in your current life situation. Take the time to jot down what factors you took into consideration when identifying this number.
- Gain an understanding of what triggers stress for you: What life circumstances tend to create the most stress for you (e.g., financial stress, frequent life hassles versus major life stressors, interpersonal conflict)?
- Explore how stress affects your mind, body, and spirit. When you are stressed:
  - What thoughts tend to pop up?
  - What body reactions do you notice (e.g., tight shoulders, headaches, getting run down and sick)?
  - What influence does this have on your mood (e.g., increased irritability, depression, anxiety) and how you express your emotions (e.g., emotionally shutting down, unable to contain emotion)?
  - Which areas of your life do you focus on the most? The least? Does this help you or just lead to avoidance?
  - Do you tend to neglect your own well-being to ensure other aspects of your life are taken care of? How does this help you? How does this hurt you?

OUR OBLIGATION TO HELP OURSELVES

All counselors have an obligation to take care of themselves. If you are not at your best, then you will be less likely to be present and focused for your clients. By taking care of yourself, you are taking care of your best therapeutic tool. As a graduate student you are often pulled in many directions and play a multitude of roles. Your student role may be taking up a significant amount of time, and along with other possible roles of employee, partner, parent, friend, and so on, you may find that you have a limited amount of time to focus on yourself. It is often tempting to put off your own self-care so that you can meet all the other needs around you. As difficult as it may be to take time for oneself, it is a wise investment. You can only put off your own self-care for so long before you feel the effects physically, emotionally, and spiritually.

When talking about stress management to counseling students, their reaction sometimes is, "Yeah, right. Like I have time for exercise or meditation when I'm working, going to school, and taking care of a family." This reaction implies that self-care is a luxury, not a basic need. Finding balance among our life roles is quite difficult, and we all struggle at times to maintain it. There are periods of time when I am successful at setting limits with work and making sure to balance other aspects of my life, and then there are other times when I am putting in many hours of overtime and neglect my personal time. The key is knowing when one area of your life is taking over and you are starting to lose balance.

I see similarities between my need for self-care and when my cell phone battery starts to die. The battery icon on my phone will change colors as it loses power; and when it reaches a certain color, I know I had better plug it in or I will lose use of the phone altogether. This is much like what happens with my body when I am feeling stress, although it is unfortunate our bodies don't come with battery icons. I guess in many ways our bodies do give us warning signs that we are out of balance, such as when we feel the aches and pains, or when we succumb to a virus due to a compromised immune system. Your body can handle only so much, and if you don't recognize the signs, you will lose energy and functioning, much like your cell phone when it has not been properly charged.

In counseling, we may educate our clients about how their seemingly unimportant decisions and the "slippery slope" can contribute to their going down an unhealthy path. It is important to remember this when it comes to our own self-care. Oftentimes we make poor, smaller choices that we don't think will have a significant impact on us. Making one decision to stay up later results in less sleep, which then affects the way you feel the next day, further affecting your decision to work out that next morning. The cycle of poor choices may then contribute to other poor choices throughout the day, eventually resulting in unhealthy habits and patterns in the long run.

As helpers, we may put others' needs before our own, but to assist others we need to have something to give them. It is also important to practice what you preach. If you don't have an active self-care practice, then you won't be able to use it when you really need it. One day while working in a high-end residential treatment facility, I was heading back to my office after an especially difficult meeting about budget cuts and billing quotas when I unexpectedly ran into a client. She stated that she needed to see me right away, which was typical for this client. I explained that I really needed a few minutes to myself and that I would check on her after that. I went into my office and started to use my coping skill of deep breathing. After about three deep breaths I heard a voice coming from the other side of the door saying "You're doing a great job with your breathing!" My client had followed me to my office and had been listening to me engage in this self-soothing technique. My well-engrained coping skill not only helped decrease the amount of stress I was feeling, but it also provided an impromptu role-modeling opportunity.

HELPFUL MODELS FOR UNDERSTANDING STRESS

Stress is a natural part of life, but left unmanaged it can become quite destructive. Hans Seyle (1974, p. 6) defined *stress*, a term that is now widely accepted, as "the nonspecific response of the body to any demand upon it." In other words, regardless of cause, the body will respond and attempt to cope with the demands placed on it to restabilize. Cannon (1929) coined the term *homeostasis*, which refers to the body's drive to return to a previous level of usual functioning after changes are detected. We are constantly making adjustments physiologically and emotionally to deal with outside forces, which highlights our keen adaptive and regulatory abilities; however, when we respond to a perceived threat for a prolonged period of time, we can experience mental and physical illness (Goldstein & Kopin, 2007).

Although stress can have deleterious effects on our mental and physical health, not all stress is unhealthy and leads to distress. Seyle's (1974) term *eustress* describes a more positive psychological response to a stressor, which is often associated with higher levels of hope, energy, and a sense of meaningfulness when coping with that stressor (McGowan, Gardner, & Fletcher, 2007; Nelson & Cooper, 2005). All change to an organism or system involves some level of discomfort or stress, even when the changes are positive or could lead to growth. It requires an evaluation of the stressor, as well as our ability to manage it effectively. Lazarus's (1966, 1999) cognitive-transactional model referred to this phenomenon as the appraisal of demands, in which we assess whether or not the demand is threatening to our well-being. If it is deemed threatening, then we conduct an assessment of the resources we possess to meet this demand. Distress results when we have determined the demands to be greater than our resources. Our interpretation of both the demands and our resources play a significant role in whether or not we experience the negative psychological response of distress.

As you begin your clinical experiences, you may be faced with significant demands that have the potential to lead to distress or significant personal and professional growth. Lazarus and Folkman (1984) posited that when one assesses that one has adequate resources to manage the given demand, one will appraise the demand as a challenge and not as a threat. Whereas appraising a demand as threatening can lead to a high arousal state, appraising a demand as a challenge allows you the opportunity to grow from the experience and leads to a more positive emotional response.

Identifying Personal Stressors

In counseling programs we stress the importance of viewing counselors not only as professionals, but also as persons who inherently bring with them to the counseling session all their own unique characteristics and experiences. As competent counselors and counselors-in-training, it is essential that we understand and recognize our personal stressors and the effects they are having on us in the moment. Counselors are certainly not immune to the same types of personal stressors with which we are often assisting our clients. We too may be dealing with our own interpersonal stressors with family, friends, and significant others. We are also subject to life events that are beyond our control, as well as daily hassles such as getting stuck in traffic, losing items, and technology problems.

Just as you would assess a client at the onset of counseling, so should you assess yourself on the current personal stressors you are dealing with and how they may be affecting your overall functioning. Being able to honestly evaluate your level of functioning in all areas of your life is a skill that needs to be practiced at length. Venart, Vassos, and Pitcher-Heft (2007) identified several important areas for counselor self-care, including physical, cognitive, emotional, social, and spiritual domains. In the next section we will explore each of these dimensions. As you explore each dimension of health, identify any stressors that you have in this area and think about the influence this has on your overall functioning, both as a person and a professional counselor. Identifying possible strengths and resources you have that can assist you in dealing with stressors in this area is also important. As previously mentioned, it is not necessarily the demands that are placed on us, but rather our interpretation of whether or not we have the resources to manage those demands that determines our level of functioning.

COPING WITH PERSONAL STRESSORS—DIMENSIONS OF HEALTH AND INTERVENTION

Once you have assessed your personal stressors and resources, then you need to put your coping skills into action. While in fourth grade, I was in a play called *The GIGO Effect*. GIGO stood for "garbage in, garbage out." Although my only detailed memory of the play is one of an embarrassing dance number, the underlying principle has always stuck with me. This simple concept of what we put into something is directly proportional to what we get out has been invaluable to me both personally and professionally. I have used this concept with numerous clients to illustrate their progress, or lack thereof, in counseling. We often want significant change in our lives without making much personal effort. Just as it is improbable that our clients will make change without effort, we as professional counselors cannot expect to be fully functioning without putting effort into our own self-care. If you find you are lacking in resources for one area or are not using the resources you already have, then you may want to explore the effect this has on your well-being in this particular area, as well as your overall functioning. Use Self-Assessment Activity 13.2 to begin this exploration.

Counselor Self-Care

Many students take on clinical experiences like they would any other class, but there are specific demands related to clinical experiences that make it especially difficult. Up until now you have only read about or practiced your counseling skills with fellow students or volunteers. The pressures of working with real clients, as well as the additional hours in your schedule, can take a toll on your overall health if you are without an adequate self-care plan. As you review the following areas of self-care, think about how you might apply the GIGO

SELF-ASSESSMENT ACTIVITY 13.2 PERSONAL STRESSORS

- Think about what you have been "putting" into yourself, both as a person and as a professional. Where have you been spending your time and energy? How might this affect you in your role as a counselor?
- Next, create a list of your personal stressors and resources. Based on your assessment of the stressors and your personal resources, do you find the stressors to be threatening or challenging?

For any personal stressor you find threatening, determine what resources may need to be gained to turn this threatening demand into an opportunity for growth and learning.

---

effect to each area. As you take on additional responsibilities within your clinical experiences, think about what you are putting into each of these areas.

PHYSICAL SELF-CARE.   Taking care of your body is essential in managing stress and maintaining adequate self-care. Schafer (2000) highlighted daily exercise, healthy eating habits, and adequate sleep as necessary tools to help your body ward off both physical and emotional stress and illness. Although this probably does not come as much of a surprise to you, it is interesting how these aspects of self-care are often neglected. Although simple to understand, it is often difficult to implement, and these basic tools for physical self-care are the first to go when other demands are competing for your time and energy. When you have school, work, and family obligations, it is tempting to stay up late to finish projects, grab fast food on your way to your internship, and skip your physical exercise routine because there just aren't enough hours in the day. Unfortunately, the first areas to be sacrificed when we are overworked and overscheduled are the areas that are most crucial to our own mental and physical well-being. In the long run these healthy activities make us more productive, less fatigued, and less susceptible to burnout. It would be wise to invest time in creating a realistic plan for how you are going to meet your basic physical needs. Try creating a schedule where you first input these key basics into a self-care plan, and then work in your other obligations. Making them a priority can be a difficult transition from your current schedule, but it may be the only way for you to ensure that they are met. Use Self-Assessment Activity 13.3 to take a close look at how you are handling your physical self-care.

SELF-ASSESSMENT ACTIVITY 13.3 PHYSICAL SELF-CARE

- On a scale of 1 to 10 (10 being the best), how would you rate your overall physical self-care?
- What efforts have you been putting into regular physical exercise?
- What efforts have you been putting into getting adequate sleep?
- What efforts have you been putting into maintaining a healthy diet?
- As you evaluate each area of self-care, identify one small action you would be willing to commit to that would make an improvement in that area. These are some examples:
  - *Physical exercise routine:* Take a midday walk break a couple of times a week, take the stairs at work, during commercials do squats/sit-ups/jumping jacks, or other exercises. Although it would be beneficial to have a consistent exercise routine, you can still make progress one step at a time. It is not necessary for you to go immediately from leading a sedentary life to working out 5 days a week. Any activities you add to your routine is progress.

(Continued)

- *Adequate sleep:* Again, you don't have to go to extreme measures if you are a late-night person. Just try going to bed 10 minutes earlier than you normally would and keep moving that up until you reach your target bedtime. Being a late-night person I could come up with a million excuses why it is difficult to get to bed earlier, but in the end if it is negatively affecting me, then I have to make the choice to change or to remain the same.
- *Healthy diet:* This could include drinking more water, eating a healthy breakfast, cutting down on fast food, swapping out one junk food option for nuts, berries, or a healthier snack, skipping dessert 1–2 x/week, and so on. Again, think about small steps that you can build on. It is unrealistic to think you could go from eating fast food frequently throughout the week to cooking all your own meals with organically grown foods every day. If it were that easy, you would already be doing it.

VOICES FROM THE FIELD 13.1   Lack of Self-Care and Lorna Doones, by Nicole Bradley

---

After completing my master's degree in community counseling, I began working full time with children and adolescents at a community mental health agency. I was ecstatic to have found a job close to home and to begin working only weeks after graduation. Previously, I had spent years working with children in multiple noncounseling capacities including day cares, direct care in a residential treatment facility, a center for autism, and school settings. As I tried on the role of professional counselor, I was excited and eager to continue my work with children and use the skills I had worked hard to cultivate over the past 2 years.

In addition to working with children, self-care had also always been a priority for me; I had been a runner since the age of 11 years, maintained supportive friendships, and was always conscious about eating healthy. Despite my attempts to take care of myself, I was not prepared for how emotionally draining counseling could be.

A year and a half into my first counseling position, I was beginning to feel burned out. I was not running as much as I typically did, I was working through lunch, regularly eating the Lorna Doone cookies that I kept in my office, and experiencing guilt about leaving work to go to a safe home, where I had food, heat, and clean clothes and knew that no one would hurt me. Thankfully, I recognized that I wasn't pulling on my healthy coping skills and began to make changes in my life. I look back now and reflect on what a valuable learning experience this was for me.

To overcome the stresses of my counseling job, I created rituals. I committed myself to running with my friends a few days a week—as I had previously done—and asked them to help me be accountable to this commitment. To facilitate focus at work, I began taking my lunch breaks that I had gotten into the habit of skipping. In addition, not only did I take my lunch break, but I would also call a friend or leave the office area to help take my mind off work and my clients. Finally, probably one of the most important changes that I made was the creation of a daily routine to leave my work at work and not bring it into my personal life. Each day before I left the office, I would stand in front of my door after locking it and say to myself out loud, "I am leaving it here until tomorrow." I found that having that concrete behavior at the end of my day really helped me transition into my personal life in a healthier way. Now did it *always* work? No! But it significantly decreased my emotional stress, and it helped me to set a work–home boundary. At present, I work clinically and teach master's-level counseling courses. I make sure to continue to engage in these self-care strategies as well as others, and I actively promote the importance of self-care to my students.

COGNITIVE SELF-CARE.   The area of cognitive self-care relates to our ability to identify and manage our own self-talk, as well as our ability to organize our thoughts and make decisions. As counselors, often we are aware of the importance our cognitions have on our emotional and behavioral reactions. This is the basic tenet of cognitive-behavioral therapy: Our interpretations of events, not the events themselves, influence the way we feel and then react. Accurately assessing situations and our abilities to manage them is part of our cognitive self-care.

Take a moment to complete Self-Assessment Activity 13.4 and reflect on the points in Think About It 13.1 and 13.2. Throughout your career, you will be faced with ethical dilemmas, but during your clinical experiences you may be faced with them for the first time. You also will begin to recognize the expansive gray area of ethics.

SELF-ASSESSMENT ACTIVITY 13.4 COGNITIVE SELF-CARE

- Identify distorted cognitions or negative self-talk that limits your daily functioning. What influences do these distorted cognitions or negative self-talk have on you? Becoming aware of these distortions is a key step to stopping them.
- Identify healthy and realistic cognitions and self-messages that you can use to replace the more negative self-messages. How can healthy and realistic cognitions help you deal with stressors related to practicum and internship?

THINK ABOUT IT 13.1

While in graduate school, I wrote myself a support letter in anticipation of difficult times. This letter identified my strengths, empathized with potential issues my future self might face, and encouraged me to keep going even when things got difficult. You may find it useful to write a supportive letter to yourself that can help ease distress you may feel throughout your clinical experience.

THINK ABOUT IT 13.2

Check out http://www.counseling.org/docx/ethics/practitioners_guide.pdf?sfvrsn=2, and review the Practitioner's Guide to Making Ethical Decisions. *Having a clear understanding of how to make difficult decisions can help ease the pressure when you find yourself in an ethical dilemma.*

EMOTIONAL SELF-CARE. Managing emotions, those of your clients as well as your own, is crucial for all counselors. Oftentimes beginning counselors are not prepared when they are triggered by their client's emotional responses. Working with adolescents with emotional and behavioral problems has taught me a significant amount about managing intense emotions. It is a matter of when, not if, you will be triggered. The ability to manage your own feelings of anxiety, anger, fear, frustration, helplessness, and shame is essential in the counseling relationship. We are less capable of sitting with our clients' emotions if we are already overwhelmed by our own. Later we will review the idea of personal counseling for the counselor, which may be especially helpful for counselors who have a history of depression, anxiety, or personal trauma, but all counselors need an outlet to maintain their emotional self-care. Just as we would promote healthy emotional expression with our clients, we too need to find a healthy balance between shutting down emotionally and becoming emotionally saturated. Use Self-Assessment Activity 13.5 to reflect on the state of your emotional self-care practices.

SOCIAL SELF-CARE. Interpersonal connections are crucial in managing stress. Assessing your own social roles and expectations will be beneficial during your internship. If you can gain an accurate assessment of all your personal and professional roles and obligations, you will be better prepared to balance all these roles. Maintaining healthy and supportive social connections

---

SELF-ASSESSMENT ACTIVITY 13.5 EMOTIONAL SELF-CARE

- How do you typically manage intense emotions you may be experiencing? Do you shut down or feel it so intensely that you become immobilized by the emotion?
- Which emotions tend to be most difficult for you to manage?
- How might you manage intense emotions (your own and others') within a counseling session?
- Although it is important to have a certain amount of comfort being in the presence of emotion, how might you assist a client to manage the intensity of his or her own emotions?

---

will be key throughout your journey as a counselor. Just as we would encourage our clients to seek positive social connections to serve as a buffer to life stressors, counselors too can benefit from strong interpersonal relationships to help them deal with stress and prevent burnout.

Gaining and maintaining social connections are a priority. So are skills related to setting limits and learning when to say "no." This can be especially difficult as we wear many personal and professional hats. As your role of student and beginning practitioner intensifies, you may feel the demands of your professional connections, as well as feel strain on your personal connections. Use Self-Assessment Activity 13.6 to examine your resources for social self-care.

SPIRITUAL SELF-CARE. Myers and Sweeney (2008) originally placed spirituality at the center of their Wheel of Wellness as the most important contributor to well-being. Although not supported empirically to be the basis of well-being, it remains a critical aspect of wellness. Exploring and connecting with our spiritual self is one way to be present and mindful in our everyday lives. Maintaining a mindfulness practice enhances our spiritual and emotional self-care practices. Greason and Cashwell (2009) found connections between mindfulness and counseling students' ability to fully engage and be present in the counseling session. In this study, students were less focused on doing counseling than they were on just being present with their client. This also allowed them to be more tolerant of intense emotions within the session. Attuning to our spiritual center can assist in being genuine and nonjudgmental in a session, as we are less likely to be overly attached to the thoughts and emotions that are evoked throughout the session. Many counseling theory books do not cover issues of spirituality in depth, but Jones-Smith (2012) included an entire chapter in her text on counseling theories due to the increased focus on the significance of this life domain.

Jones-Smith (2012) holds the view that "spirituality influences the way that people interpret their experiences and make meaning out of life" (p. 451–452). Exploring the influence that spirituality may have had on one's purpose and meaning in life, as well as how one perceives the world and oneself in it, would be a valuable exercise for all counselors. Robertson (2010) makes a clear link between spiritual and religious beliefs and one's overall mental and physical well-being, which is helpful as we discuss tools to enhance counselor wellness, but this also has important implications for how we counsel clients. Having cultural competence in the spiritual and religious realms will become ever more present in counselor education and training and the field as a whole. If this is an area of wellness that you have never nurtured or have recently neglected, here are some ideas on how to connect to your spiritual self:

- Start a meditation practice.
- Practice being mindful in everyday activities.
- Take up yoga or tai chi.
- Connect to a spiritual or religious community.
- Spend more time in nature.
- Use prayer or mantras.
- Take time to explore your spiritual journey and purpose in life.
- Attend a kirtan or chanting group.
- Read poetry, books, or articles or watch movies that stimulate your curiosity of spiritual matters.

SELF-ASSESSMENT ACTIVITY 13.6 SOCIAL SELF-CARE

See Figure 13.1, The Social Connections Wheel, and respond to these questions regarding social self-care.

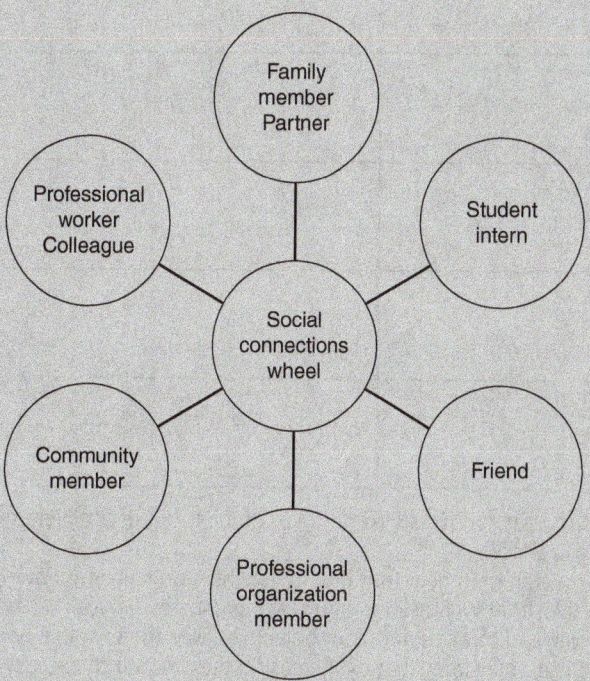

FIGURE 13.1 The social connections wheel.

- Identify the roles and obligations you have in each area. Feel free to add additional social connections.
- Rate each area: 1 = few or no demands, 10 = intense level of demands.
- After reviewing this wheel, which area is most demanding of your resources (e.g., time, energy, money) at this time?
- If there is a need to balance these areas, what is one small step you can take to make that happen?

You cannot make excuses and progress at the same time, so now is the time to get started on your self-care plan. Now see Figure 13.2, where you will find a form to assist as you begin creating your own self-care plan.

Recognizing and Avoiding Burnout

Burnout has become a hot topic in recent years, and you can find many workshops on combating the symptoms and signs of burnout and compassion fatigue. When it comes to burnout, prevention should be the goal, not treatment. We often wait until there are already signs of a problem and then react with a treatment response. Instead of actively working to avoid burnout, we spend time trying to counteract the negative physical and emotional effects it has already had on the individual, as well as the surrounding systems. Primary prevention is a central concept in community psychology, and this approach argues the benefits of taking a more proactive stance, rather than treating emerging or already existing problematic symptoms (Moritsugu, Wong, & Duffy, 2010).

The human services field in general is conducive for stress and burnout reactions. Counselors may face intense billing and budget pressures, long hours, high caseloads, ineffective

I. Demands and Resources: Identify all the stressors or demands you are experiencing in each domain. Then identify all resources and strengths you have that will assist you in meeting the demands. Based on your assessment of the demands/resources ratio, check the box of whether you view the demands on this domain as a threat or a challenge.

Domain of Self-Care	Demands	Resources/Strengths
Physical *Threat* *Challenge*		
Emotional *Threat* *Challenge*		
Social *Threat* *Challenge*		
Spiritual *Threat* *Challenge*		
Cognitive *Threat* *Challenge*		

II. Choose one domain that you would like to focus on first. Please complete the next chart based on this domain. Which domain did you choose? _____

III. Identify a large, overarching goal that describes which domain you have chosen to work on. Then create two to three more specific objectives that will result in you making progress in your overall goal. Finally, identify specific and measurable interventions that will lead to achieving your objectives. See the example here for a model. Remember—think small steps!

The plan in the example states that by increasing the amount of exercise and eating a healthy diet, the person will achieve the goal of improving his or her overall level of physical health. If your objectives don't meet the overall goal, then they should be changed. Once you are sure your objectives will meet your goal, then make sure your interventions have a reasonable chance of meeting your objectives. This is the checks and balances of treatment plans. What you are doing here is creating a treatment plan for yourself, but this format can also be used with clients. Now, it's your turn . . . choose a domain and get started preparing your wellness plan!

Self-Care Plan Example
Large Goal #1: *To improve the overall level of physical health*
Objective 1: *To increase the amount of physical exercise.*
Intervention 1: *Will take the stairs at work at least 3 out of 5 workdays.*
Intervention 2: *Will go for a walk during lunch at least 2 out of 5 workdays.*
Objective 2: *To maintain a healthy diet.*
Intervention 1: *Will plan out weekly meals every Sunday for the following week.*
Intervention 2: *Will have a nutritious breakfast 5 out of 7 days.*

My Self-Care Plan
Large Goal #1:

Objective 1:
Intervention 1:
Intervention 2:
Intervention 3:

Objective 2:
Intervention 1:
Intervention 2:
Intervention 3:

Objective 3:
Intervention 1:
Intervention 2:
Intervention 3:

FIGURE 13.2   Your own personal self-care plan!

policies and procedures, and lack of appreciation. Obviously, there are many reasons why counselors join and remain in the field, but it is important to recognize the most typical stressors that plague the counseling and human services field. Recognizing and targeting organizational factors is one way to intervene before burnout sets in, but it may also be necessary to address individual factors such as your own personal characteristics and motivations for joining the field. Just as knowing how your work culture plays a role in burnout and then taking action to prevent it can be beneficial, so, too, can assessing ways to intervene on a personal level.

Taking the potential stressor of "counseling being a thankless job," let's address this on a personal level. It is important to know that you will not always receive confirmation that you are doing a good job or see the progress you were expecting with clients; therefore it can be helpful for you to prepare for those rough patches when you are questioning your effectiveness. Many beginning counselors equate clients doing well with their counseling skills. They often fail to realize that treatment ebbs and flows, and clients often take one step forward and two steps back. If you solely rely on your client's progress as an indicator of your skill as a counselor, you will be quickly disappointed and discouraged. Further, it can be highly detrimental when we are overly invested in our client's progress as a way to validate ourselves as a counselor, rather than for the sake of our client. Some counselors may overidentify with being a helper and may risk having their clients become dependent on them to serve out their role. The American Counseling Association [ACA] (2005) is clear in its ethical guidelines that counselors should safeguard their client's ability to be autonomous. Self-Assessment Activity 13.7 will help you identify whether you are facing burnout and alert you to some of the related issues.

Ways to manage our personal reactions to clients and our own issues with competence, fear of failing, and desire to help are all worthy topics to explore in supervision. Even if we are aware that our impatience with lack of client progress is our own personal issue, we still need to learn how to manage it. I often tell supervisees that they are planting the seeds for growth in their clients even if they aren't there to witness the end result. Although this can be frustrating, I find it comforting to know that at some time in the future my work with clients will grow into something beneficial and positive for them. I know there have been times when a client quickly progresses, and in part this may be due to the hard work of another clinician, and I just happened to be there when the client finally reached the goal. Savoring the small moments can lift you up and keep you going during times of discouragement. I always found it ironic that during really difficult days when I was contemplating whether or not I was really having an influence on the system, I would receive a call from a previous client who wanted to share with me his or her progress or to tell me about the impact I had on him or her. Those moments remind

---

SELF-ASSESSMENT ACTIVITY 13.7 RECOGNIZING BURNOUT

- Go to www.proqol.org and take the ProQOL (Professional Quality of Life Questionnaire)
- Take a burnout quiz: You can find a free burnout quiz at http://www.mindtools.com/stress/Brn/BurnoutSelfTest.htm. Christina Maslach's burnout assessment is available for purchase at http://www.mindgarden.com/products/mbi.htm
- Assess and improve your time management skills. Lack of effective time management skills can lead to increased stress and burnout. The Mayo Clinic provides numerous suggestions on how to improve your ability to manage your time at the following website: http://www.mayoclinic.com/health/time-management/WL00048. Instead of trying to make too many changes at one time, it suggests you choose one technique and practice it for a couple of weeks. You should determine whether or not this technique has been effective and should be continued. Once you have embraced the technique, then you can start adding additional techniques.

me why I continue to do this work and how special it truly is to have others allow you to take part in their personal journeys.

VICARIOUS TRAUMA, COMPASSION FATIGUE, AND SECONDARY TRAUMA

The term *burnout* is often interchangeably used with secondary trauma, vicarious trauma, and compassion fatigue leading to confusion for counselors on what they are experiencing. There are several key differences among these terms, which are important to note so you can gain an accurate understanding of what you are experiencing. These differences relate to type of onset, the cause of the condition, as well as the effects on the counselor. Whereas burnout and compassion fatigue come about more progressively, the onset of vicarious and secondary trauma tends to be more immediate (Newell & MacNeil, 2010). Let's review the similarities and differences between vicarious trauma, compassion fatigue, and secondary trauma.

Vicarious traumatization, a term credited to McCann and Pearlman (1990), relates to one's exposure to trauma and disrupts one's frame of reference in one of five core areas: safety, trust, esteem, control, and intimacy. Vicarious traumatization targets the counselor's belief systems and self-concept and focuses on the cognitive changes that occur within the counselor as a result of empathic interactions with traumatized individuals. We develop our self-concept over time as we make assessments about the world and our place in it. When a counselor experiences vicarious traumatization, self-concept and overall belief systems change, greatly affecting a counselor personally and professionally. We open ourselves up when empathically engaging with our clients and let the trauma in as a way to assist our clients. When this negatively impacts the way we view the world, then we are experiencing signs of vicarious trauma. Some examples of cognitive shifts that can occur include viewing the world as basically unpredictable and unsafe, others as untrustworthy, and yourself as incompetent.

As a case example, Ann is a 28-year-old, single counselor who is working with Jane in an outpatient clinic. Jane has been diagnosed with PTSD after being sexually assaulted. Both Ann and Jane are similar in age, race, SES, and even live in nearby neighborhoods. As Ann works with Jane on her trauma, she notices some differences in the way she has been thinking. Perhaps due to their similarities Ann started to think that everything Jane was talking about could also happen to her. As Ann leaves work she is suspicious of males around the facility and in her neighborhood. She starts to view the world as more dangerous and less predictable, which alters the way she reacts to her environment. It did not take prolonged exposure to the trauma for Ann to experience these symptoms. She is not feeling burnt out or exhausted, nor is she experiencing actual symptoms of PTSD like her client, but her worldviews have been significantly altered. If you were Ann, what do you think you should do as you noticed the cognitive changes?

Vicarious traumatization and secondary traumatic stress have similarities, but have distinct manifestations. Vicarious traumatization focuses on the cognitive changes that occur after direct work with those who have been traumatized, whereas secondary trauma manifests itself in the behaviors, in particular symptoms of PTSD. Vicarious traumatization and secondary traumatic stress may occur independent of one another or a counselor may both experience a shift in his or her cognitive process and exhibit behavioral symptoms of PTSD (Newell & MacNeil, 2010).

Early in my career I worked with a therapist who was struggling in her work with traumatized individuals. She began experiencing symptoms of both vicarious and secondary trauma, although I did not have a full understanding of these concepts at the time. She began to struggle with her own intimacy with her partner, became hypervigilant, and began to view the world as being unsafe and full of potentially threatening situations. The work she was doing had changed her cognitive schemas, and she also began to report symptoms of PTSD such as hypervigilance, nightmares, a disconnection from others, and avoidance of trauma stimuli. This last symptom greatly impacted her ability to counsel her clients, as she was more avoidant of trauma-related material in sessions, and she more readily allowed her clients to avoid this issue due to her own discomfort. She ended up leaving her position at the facility due to the effect that trauma work had on her.

Now, not all counselors experience vicarious trauma or secondary trauma even though they may do intense trauma work, but it is imperative that if signs are noted that they be addressed early. I do wonder whether or not there would have been a different outcome with my colleague if she received the support and supervision she desperately needed at that time, instead of people perhaps thinking that trauma work was just not for her. There is risk in counselors assuming something is wrong with them if they notice these changes, so talking openly in supervision about changes in cognitive schemas or experiencing PTSD symptoms is imperative. Many times clinicians, both new and experienced, suffer in silence, as there is shame associated with these experiences and fear that others will view them as incapable.

Another related term is *compassion fatigue*, which is similar to burnout in that it develops over time. As counselors we are not just exposed to our clients' suffering; rather, we become a container for it. Working with trauma day in and day out takes great amounts of empathy, and this can take its toll on the counselor's well-being and lead to fatigue. Figley (2002) identified cognitive, emotional, and behavioral effects of the chronic use of empathy and being overexposed to the suffering of one's clients. Cognitively, counselors may experience difficulty concentrating, apathy, increased negativity, and decreased self-esteem. Counselors may begin to feel helplessness and powerlessness, guilt, depression, and emotionally drained. These cognitive and emotional effects may lead to sleep disturbances, impatience and irritability, and somatic complaints (Berzoff & Kita, 2010).

Being cognizant of factors that put one at risk for compassion fatigue is critical to prevention. Craig and Sprang (2010) found that having a high percentage of one's caseload dedicated to clients with PTSD and not using evidence-based practices as significant indicators for compassion fatigue, whereas significant indicators for burnout were "younger age, having no special trauma training, having an increased percentage of individuals on the caseload with PTSD, being an inpatient practitioner, and not using evidence-based practices" (p. 334). Talking from my own experience as a counselor working with trauma, I would agree that these indicators lead to negative effects on counselors. We don't always have control over our caseloads when we work in agencies, but it would be wise to make sure your supervisors are aware of the concepts described if you are frequently dealing with traumatized clients. Making supervisors aware of the potential effects may result in redistribution of caseloads, or at the very least will ensure that everyone is aware of the possible cognitive, emotional, and behavioral outcomes of this type of work.

Make sure to seek supervision, as well as consultation with other colleagues, if you notice any cognitive, emotional, or behavioral changes. As you begin your practicum or even when you start out as a new professional, you may not have all the tools you need to treat your clients, which may lead to the symptoms of compassion fatigue, vicarious trauma, or secondary trauma. If you will be working with traumatized individuals, then seek specific trauma trainings, learn about evidence-based practices, and attend related professional development opportunities. The more you know about trauma and how to treat it, the more prepared and less overwhelmed you will be when working with your clients. It is also helpful to seek consultation on the therapy process. Many new professionals start to question their professional abilities if clients are not making progress. By talking to other professionals about the therapy process, you may be able to combat unrealistic expectations of the therapy process, which could have damaging effects on your sense of self-efficacy. If you are noticing symptoms of PSTD as a result of the work you are doing, then you should consider seeking professional counseling, as well as talking to your supervisor to find ways to assist you in the workplace.

So why in the world would any counselors want to do trauma work if they have all these potential problems to look forward to? Well, first, not all counselors experience these negative effects, so make sure to invest in your prevention efforts so that you limit your risk. Compassion satisfaction might also be a reason for doing this work for many counselors. This refers to the satisfaction one gets from helping others (Bride, Radey, & Figley, 2007). Personally, I have found trauma work to be intrinsically very rewarding. You are assisting clients as they work through intense suffering. They are allowing you to come along on this incredible journey of healing. The intensity of the work can be overwhelming, draining, and yet so very rewarding for both you and your client. It is the intense satisfaction that you get from doing meaningful work that has a direct positive impact on another's life.

COMMON SOURCES OF STRESS FOR THE BEGINNING COUNSELOR

Lack of Delegating

Learning what to delegate to others when you are first beginning your internship can be difficult. You are often the one to whom others delegate and not the other way around. Having an accurate understanding of your skills in time management and problem solving will help you in the area of delegating. Knowing how long it takes you to accomplish tasks is vital when planning projects, as is effectively communicating to your team the resources you will need to complete your tasks and projects. There may be times when it is not feasible to complete all your assigned tasks, so taking initiative to find alternative solutions, such as delegating, will be much appreciated by your supervisors. Taking on whatever tasks are given to you may seem like a great way to be a team player, but this only works if you can realistically accomplish all the tasks.

Difficulty with Boundaries

Many counselors underestimate how difficult it will be to maintain healthy boundaries. Going into graduate school, I held a pretty dichotomous view of ethics where situations were either black or white. Do not have sex with clients … check. There are obviously clear-cut violations of boundaries, but most situations that you will come across will be varying shades of gray that are not always so simple to decipher.

Often, unsuspecting interns go down the slippery slope, eventually finding themselves smack dab in the middle of a boundary violation and not knowing exactly how they got there. Terms such as *SUD*s (seemingly unimportant decisions) are used when working with clients with sexually problematic behaviors or those in recovery from substance abuse. This concept can also be applied to the boundary violations of counselors. The small, seemingly unimportant decisions that we make can lead us down a path that is fraught with ethical dilemmas and boundary violations. Each small decision leads us either closer or further away from high-risk situations and therefore is quite important in the long run.

When I work with clients with significant trauma histories, I often explore the three Ts: how they *talk, trust,* and *touch* others. This can help me assess issues with boundaries as they may talk, trust, and touch others indiscriminately due to poor, diffuse boundaries, or they may have become so rigid in their boundaries that they have difficulty trusting or connecting to anyone. Exploring the three Ts can also be helpful for counseling interns in assessing their own boundaries as they begin to practice. Think about the differences in how you talk, trust, and touch a romantic partner, a friend, a client, and a stranger on the street. You would treat them all differently in the three areas. These areas reflect boundaries, physical and emotional, both in and out of the counseling session. When we start to treat our clients like we would a friend, family member, or significant other, we may be violating boundaries.

Supervision is a great time to explore small decisions you are questioning that may lead to larger ethical issues if left unchecked. This is also a time when you and your supervisor can explore any countertransference reactions you may be having related to these decisions. It is important to note that not all boundary violations are related to countertransference, and not all countertransference leads to boundary violations. Being open in supervision about the reactions you are having toward clients can be uncomfortable, as you want your supervisor to see you as competent, but countertransference reactions that are not openly talked about are likely to be acted on.

Several types of boundaries need to be addressed in a counseling setting such as physical boundaries, which tend to be easier to assess in terms of appropriate versus inappropriate, and emotional and generational boundaries, as well as time boundaries. Physical boundaries relate to how physically close we get to our clients and how close we allow them to get to us. It is important for counseling interns to understand cultural differences that may affect comfort levels related to physical proximity. I have had clients who wanted to give me a hug on meeting me for the first time and others who sit many arm's lengths away. Negotiating physical boundaries can be uncomfortable, as you do not want to offend your clients if you prefer more distance, but you should trust your instinct and respect not just your client's comfort zone of physical closeness, but your own as well.

Some populations of clients struggle more so with healthy, appropriate boundaries. You should know the population with which you are working and ask your supervisor to help you to anticipate possible situations that may come up at your internship site. A client's request for a hug may have an underlying meaning of which you are not aware. When looking at physical contact, I tend to assess my clients in the following areas: gender, age, length of treatment, the context of the situation, treatment issues, and treatment setting. I would assess the request for a hug differently from an 8-year-old client I'd been seeing for 6 months who just found out about a death in the family differently than with the 17-year-old male client with a history of sexually problematic behaviors with whom I have just started working. Every clinical setting will also have expectations related to physical contact with clients. Working in settings such as residential treatment facilities can make maintaining boundaries (physical and emotional) more challenging. You may see your clients frequently outside their therapy sessions as they wake up, go to school, in the hallway, in groups, and even as they get ready for bed. This obviously differs significantly from an outpatient setting where you only see your clients at their weekly therapy appointment.

Looking at countertransference reactions can be helpful when assessing for generational and emotional boundaries. Do you spend more time with a particular client? Do you share more personal information, or specific personal information, with a particular client that you wouldn't typically share with other clients? There may be times when you feel more protective of a particular client or have clients with which building a connection is more of a struggle. Acknowledging and exploring these reactions in supervision is beneficial not only to learn about your triggers, but also to learn how to manage these reactions so that you are effective in therapy. Included in this area are time boundaries, which I've personally found to be the most difficult to manage and the most damaging to one's own self-care. Not being protective of your time and having an unhealthy work–life balance can contribute not only to the decline in self-care, but also potentially to further boundary violations. Robinson (2000) found that those categorized as workaholics were more likely to overcommit to the point of fatigue, resulting in being less productive than what he called *optimal performers*. Although those categorized as workaholics spent more time at work, they were less focused and capable of completing projects. This sounds like a similar result for workers who are experiencing burnout. I was once told by a supervisor that human services would "suck you dry" if you let it. In a field where the demands significantly outweigh the resources, you will be called on to do more with less. As an intern you may be asked to take on additional tasks or to stay later than required to help an overly stressed system. This is the beginning of being "sucked dry," as you are asked to put in more and more until you have nothing left to give. It is our responsibility as counselors to learn what we are capable of giving and to set healthy boundaries with not only our clients, but with our employers as well.

This is another area where it is essential to evaluate yourself as a person and a worker. What role does work have in your life? What motivates you in your work role? Robinson (2000) defined typologies of workaholics and the implications for counselors, but what about when the counselor is the workaholic? His recommendations to moderate workloads, explore underlying work motivations, as well as incorporate time for social, leisure, and family activities into one's self-care plan seem fitting for all workers, including counselors. Use Self-Assessment Activity 13.8 to identify your own perceptions and strategies regarding boundaries.

Inability to Compartmentalize

The inability to compartmentalize our roles as a professional and person often come out in boundary issues as we allow one area of our life to influence the other. At times this may mean that our role as a professional impedes our personal roles. Oftentimes clinical supervision addresses issues of allowing your personal role to impinge on your professional role. At my previous place of employment, the term *detached concern* was used to communicate a need to maintain balance and boundaries. This term implied that as counselors we need to have genuine care and concern for our clients and their success in treatment, but there

---

SELF-ASSESSMENT ACTIVITY 13.8 BOUNDARY ISSUES

- Write out the three Ts (talk, trust, touch), and compare the ways you would treat clients, family members, romantic partners, friends, and acquaintances differently. Explore with your site any expectations it has regarding boundaries. Always bring up concerns with boundaries with your supervisor.
- Think about how you will handle a client trying to break generational boundaries. How might you answer if your clients ask you about whether or not you are married, have a significant other, or about other personal aspects of your life? We do not want to hide behind a professional façade and avoid being genuine with clients, but we do want to maintain healthy boundaries. How might you find a balance between these two when being asked personal questions?
- How can you use your self-care plan to manage time boundaries with your clinical experience and/or work setting?

---

must be a certain amount of detachment so that we do not lose objectivity and perspective. If our personal needs play a significant role in our clinical decisions, then we risk losing objectivity. It can be difficult to enter fully into the world of another and then be able to pull back out without becoming overly attached. It takes practice and supervision, as I found out when I first started counseling and was drawn to a particular client who was in need of intense services. I found myself engaging in small boundary violations such as giving her more counseling time than other clients. Although treatment should be individualized based on the needs of the client, I was providing extended sessions more out of my enjoyment of spending time with this client and feeling personally rewarded by these sessions than by her need for additional services. I felt she was making progress, which made me feel good as a counselor.

In supervision I explored how I could manage my feelings of caring and concern for her well-being, address my need to feel competent in my role as counselor, and yet still maintain healthy boundaries. In the end this experience was invaluable for me as a counselor, and I learned how to recognize when I was acting more out of getting my needs met than meeting the needs of my client. Reinforcing healthy boundaries also allowed me to show genuine concern for my client without connecting my worth as a counselor to her success in treatment. This is not a lesson that one learns once never to be repeated. It involves a constant practice of self-examination.

Two additional areas of compartmentalization are (a) leaving work at work and (b) the inability to compartmentalize different aspects of living. Beginning counselors may frequently think about clients after they get home or have difficulty transitioning to other life roles. It can be helpful to find a transition ritual to signal a switch from a work to personal mode. Some ideas for a transition ritual include the following:

- Change out of your work clothes once you get home.
- Have a period of time to share about your day when you first get home. Once that time period is up, then it is time to move on to other roles.
- Engage in self-care activities on returning home (e.g., journal about your day, listen to soothing music, take a bath, engage in a preferred hobby) to de-stress.

Some counselors may not get the opportunity to engage in self-care activities when they return home because they are immediately thrust into their other role as parent or partner. If this is the case, then use your ride home to ease the transition. Living in Chicago I can take multiple routes back home from work, but when I am a bit stressed I always take Lake Shore Drive. This way my view includes Lake Michigan, which I find very relaxing. Other times I listen to specific music or find a great audiobook so that I can immerse myself in another world. By the time I am home, I am ready to transition from my work mode.

Role Confusion

It is imperative that you know what will be expected of you at your practicum or internship site. Many sites will have orientation activities where you learn about your clinical site, but you can alleviate problems down the road by sitting down with your supervisor to ensure that you both have the same view of your role. Even with clear role expectations, you may be called on to complete tasks not in your job description throughout your clinical experience, which can result in role confusion and blurred boundaries. Some helpful areas to clarify before or as you begin your clinical experience include the following:

- Knowing the days and hours you will be expected to work, whether you will be on call, and the extent of internship hour requirements.
- A review of your primary job duties. Ask about whether or not you will be shadowing other counselors before taking on clients, whether your supervisor will be observing you in individual/group sessions, and your role when coleading groups with other counselors.
- Identifying who will be your primary supervisor and other evaluators of your performance. Also, it can be helpful to identify anyone else on site who will be giving you tasks to complete or to whom you will be reporting. It can become confusing when you are asked to complete tasks for others who are not your supervisor, so clarify how they want you to handle this. At some sites if other professionals would like your assistance, they must first go through your primary supervisor so that your supervisor is aware of all additional tasks that you may be working on.
- What to do if you should find yourself without enough work to do. What other job-related duties would the site like you to work on? I had one practicum student report that she was frequently asked to do non-work-related tasks such as cleaning out closets when she was done with other counseling duties. Although organizing therapeutic materials can be a job responsibility, this was not what she was being asked to do. Your primary role is as a student, and assigned tasks should assist you in further learning about the field. Obviously there may be times when you are asked to pitch in to assist with tasks that are less counseling-based, but this should not become a pattern. As you get settled into your internship, you may have your own ideas on projects you would like to work on. Being proactive and taking initiative is often appreciated by site supervisors, and this can also help avoid situations where you are assigned busy-work to keep occupied.

Being All Things to All People

Ah, the superhero syndrome. For interns, this can be a challenging time as you put into practice all you have learned up until this point. Obviously, we all want to do well when our skills are being evaluated, so we may be tempted to take on additional tasks to demonstrate our competence or show vigor for the field. Knowing your skills, abilities, motivations, and limitations will be key in recognizing and managing any vulnerabilities to being all things to all people. What are the roles and commitments you have already taken on? What motivates you to take on tasks? A desire to please?

Feelings of Incompetence

When I was first starting out, I wanted there to be a structured manual on *How to Be a Great Counselor*. I wanted to read the manual, put it into practice, and voilà be a great counselor. Unfortunately, becoming a competent counselor takes time and practice, and although there are helpful resources out there, you have to work at it. All experienced counselors have struggled with feeling unsure of themselves at one point or another. In the beginning, I had several moments where I thought to myself, "Graduate school did not prepare me for this!" No amount of classroom experience can fully prepare you for the professional journey you are about to embark on, and many beginning counselors feel woefully underprepared as they begin to see clients. It can be helpful to take a few deep breaths and realize that your classroom experience was not a waste of time; it prepared you to critically think about your cases, and during your clinical experiences you will put that knowledge into action. It can be exciting when the interventions you have read about actually work with a real client. But even if they don't, you get the experience of having to adjust your methods or approach. This is why good supervision is such an essential part of your counseling education.

Nothing can bring out feelings of incompetence like an ethical dilemma. Beginning counselors tend to overestimate how much others know and underestimate their own abilities, which leads to beginning counselors doubting themselves. In their attempts to avoid appearing incompetent, some beginning counselors try to handle the ethical dilemma on their own. Seeking consultation and having a firm grasp on how to make ethical decisions can decrease the amount of distress you feel as you begin your work as a counselor. Knowing the steps to ethical decision making and who to turn to for support can prepare you for the inevitable situations that will come up not only in your internship, but also throughout your career. Counselors who are uncertain how to proceed when faced with an ethical dilemma and who feel unsupported can quickly become overwhelmed by the situation. Use Self-Assessment Activity 13.9 to begin to identify your own professional support system.

SELF-ASSESSMENT ACTIVITY 13.9 PROFESSIONAL SUPPORT SYSTEMS

Identify your professional support system, making sure to identify the following types of support people:

- A peer who is at a similar stage of practice as you. This person may be best able to identify with the stressors associated with this stage of practice.
- An experienced counselor working with a similar population.
- An experienced counselor or legal advocate who can assist you in legal and ethical matters.
- A professional who is connected to a professional counseling association or other related professional organization. This person may be able to mentor you and get you connected and involved in professional opportunities within the field. This can lead to writing, teaching, and practicing opportunities in the future.

PERSONAL COUNSELING

I am often asked by my internship students about my opinions regarding personal counseling. There is considerable debate in the field about mandating counseling students to undergo personal counseling as part of their core requirements, although there is consensus on the benefits of personal counseling for counselors. Here are a few assumptions that I have about those entering the counseling field:

- You think that counseling is beneficial and helps people overcome life struggles.
- You understand that going to counseling does not make you "crazy."
- You think those who seek help in dealing with their life struggles, or wanting to explore interpersonal and intrapersonal processes, are showing courage by reaching out for help.

Given these assumptions, it seems natural that counselors would be open to their own individual counseling. Engaging in your own treatment gives you perspective as a client and provides an opportunity for personal growth and a pathway to work on personal issues that may affect your ability to be a competent counselor. A common question is, "Can you ask others to do what you have not done yourself, or are too afraid to do?" What are you reactions to this question?

Feelings of fear are common when deciding to enter into counseling, as it takes a considerable amount of courage to truly explore your inner world. I have heard from both counselors and clients alike that they fear they will fall apart if they engage in the counseling process. This is a legitimate concern, as most people do not feel like they have the time or ability to lose any amount of functioning, although, ironically, this can lead to avoiding significant issues resulting in a loss of functioning. For some, dealing with the surface symptoms without delving deeper is like the old adage "Ignorance is bliss." It has been repeated here, but to be a competent counselor it is important to know yourself as a person. Without this knowledge, you lack insight into your cognitive processes, emotional responses, and significant relationship patterns, which may make you less likely to recognize when you are being triggered in a session.

Whether or not you engage in your own counseling, it is your responsibility to explore how your life experiences affect the way you think and respond to the world. The American Counseling Association (2005) *Code of Ethics* clearly identifies practicing counseling while impaired as an ethical breach in conduct. The question is, how impaired do you need to be before you are no longer meeting ethical standards? As a counselor, how do you know when you have crossed the line? Although supervision can assist the counselor in determining when the line has been crossed, personal counseling allows the counselor an opportunity to explore the impairment or issues that may lead to impairment. Use Self-Assessment Activity 13.10 to explore your views about personal counseling.

SELF-ASSESSMENT ACTIVITY 13.10 PERSONAL COUNSELING

- What are your thoughts about requiring counseling for counseling students?
- If you were to go into counseling, what would your therapeutic work focus on?
- What issues or types of clients are most likely to trigger a countertransference reaction in you? How might you recognize and subsequently manage these reactions when they come up?
- How might counseling help you to become a better counselor?

Summary

By exploring your personal stressors, as well as strengths and resources in each of the wellness domains, you are well on your way to creating your self-care plan. Oftentimes we already know what needs to be done, but yet we fail to make the desired changes or are unable to sustain the improvements we've made. People are often eager to make changes and may become overzealous in their goal setting without a realistic plan on how to maintain their progress. Other times they set lofty goals that are ideal, but difficult to achieve. Corey (2009a) reviewed many theoretical approaches to goal setting, but one that I've found to be particularly useful is the solution-focused brief therapy's focus on "small, realistic, achievable changes that can lead to additional positive outcomes" (p. 381). By starting out with small goals, we are setting the foundation for future progress. These small incremental changes that eventually lead to larger goal attainments further support a successful outcome. Once we get a taste of success, we become more confident in our abilities, increasing our level of motivation. Feelings of empowerment can also result as we feel we have the resources needed to make healthy changes. The goal is to have a long, healthy career in the human services field and to avoid burnout, but first we must invest in our ability to take care of ourselves physically, emotionally, cognitively, socially, and spiritually.

CHAPTER 14

From Envisioning to Actualization: Marketing Yourself in the 21st Century

BY DANIEL S. TESTA, JESSICA A. HEADLEY, AND NICOLE A. ADAMSON

PREVIEW

This final chapter addresses the importance of finding your place in the counseling market as a 21st-century counselor. Section One (*Temet Nosce*) will address the significance of self-evaluation and reflection, utilizing the SELF acronym. Section Two (Understanding the Field Around You) will highlight current trends and opportunities in the field. Section Three (Securing a Job the Old-Fashioned Way) will cover the logistics of the job search and traditional self-promotion strategies. Section Four (Carving Out Your New-Age Niche) will outline how social media can be used to establish counselor identity and credibility. Finally, Section Five (The Advantages of Continued Learning) will discuss how advanced training and postgraduate education can increase your marketing opportunities. Ultimately, the integration of information from all these sections will enhance your ability to promote yourself to potential employers and clients, giving you the edge you need to compete in this current market.

FROM ENVISIONING TO ACTUALIZATION: MARKETING YOURSELF IN THE 21ST CENTURY

In recent years, the job market has changed dramatically, on both domestic and global fronts. Beginning in December 2007, the United States experienced a financial downturn, which has caused a deteriorating effect on the nation's labor market (Şahin, Song, & Hobijn, 2010). The downturn has greatly affected the sustainability and availability of jobs in the manufacturing and construction sectors. However, for mental health practitioners, the U.S. Bureau of Labor Statistics (2012a, 2012b) projects a more optimistic employment outlook, calling for favorable job opportunities.

Although there is a projection that counseling services will be needed in the future job market, Savickas (2012), addressing the current state of employment, asserted that "the new job market in an unsettled economy calls for viewing career not as a lifetime commitment to one employer but as a recurrent selling of services and skills to a series of employers who need projects completed" (p. 13). In the postindustrial technology boom, the selling of services is now dependent on our knowledge of technology-based delivery methods and the use of the Internet as a marketing tool (Anthony, Nagel, & Goss, 2010), in addition to more conventional self-marketing strategies (e.g., business cards, print advertisements, and face-to-face networking).

TEMET NOSCE

As the Latin phrase, *Temet nosce*, goes, "Know thyself." As counselors, if we are to market ourselves in a competitive economic and social climate, it is imperative that we understand who we are as helping professionals. A developed understanding of your professional identity will enable you to select an environment that is personally and professionally stimulating and will be helpful to the individuals you will serve. This initial section will provide a simple way to examine the characteristics that define you as a counselor. We have devised the "SELF" acronym to guide you in this evaluation. The SELF acronym is composed of the following action areas: **S**elect your strengths; **E**xamine your values, biases, and beliefs; **L**ive with limitations; and **F**ormulate your counseling approach.

Select Strengths

Part of developing your professional network as a counselor involves identifying and being recognized for your professional strengths. If other professionals are able to identify your strengths and interests, you are more likely to be sought after for opportunities that will allow you to use and promote your skills and talents. By *selecting* and *developing* your strengths, you are then able to *sell* your strengths. Use Self-Assessment Activity 14.1 to begin assessing your strengths.

SELF-ASSESSMENT ACTIVITY 14.1 PERSONAL STRENGTHS

Take a moment to reflect on your personal strengths and how they fit in the following framework. First, reflect on your basic strengths (e.g., rapport building, punctuality, thorough documentation). Next, reflect on the strengths that make you special or even unique. For example, do you have specialized training or certifications? Or, do you have extensive field experience? Third, reflect on the strengths you would like to further develop. You may ask yourself: Do I want to seek additional education? Do I want research experience? Last, devise some development strategies that you can employ to achieve these desired strengths. If you want to seek additional education by pursuing a doctoral degree, you may consider reviewing programs listed on university websites and talking with current doctoral students. Or if you want to gain research experience, you may want to consider reaching out to faculty or professionals who share similar interests.

Basic Strengths	Special Strengths	Desired Strengths	Development Strategies

The ability to reflect on and acknowledge your strengths will enable you to envision the environment in which you will thrive. For instance, if you find one of your strengths involves working with children in crisis, you should consider focusing your attention on gaining employment that serves this population. Some of the questions you may ask yourself might be: What age group best suits my comfort level or ability? What environment will allow me to practice effectively? And, am I part of a supportive team? Overall, working in an atmosphere that best suits your strengths will allow you to further develop and enhance your skills and talents as a clinician, leading toward a more fulfilling career in counseling.

Last, the ability to verbalize and demonstrate your strengths will allow you to sell yourself with ease and confidence in the interview process. Employers are looking for self-assured and enthusiastic practitioners. Remember, it is not always about the quantity of your strengths or abilities, but rather the quality and how you express them. Imagine that you are in an interview at the present moment and you are asked the following question: "So, what would you say are your clinical strengths?" *What* examples would you provide in response, and more importantly, *how* confidently would you respond? Whether you are interviewing for a position or building an online image, as we will discuss later in the chapter, keep in mind how important it is to deliver a convincing and positive first impression.

Examine Values, Biases, and Beliefs

Along with evaluating your strengths, it is essential to examine your own values, biases, and beliefs and how those may influence your work with clients. Your values, biases, and beliefs are influenced by the sociopolitical and cultural environment in which you live and are shaped by your intersecting identities (e.g., age, gender, ethnicity, religion). The context of your life experiences allow for differing degrees of power and privilege in our society, determining your worldview and ultimately influencing your professional impact on a micro-, meso-, and macrolevel.

When thinking about these levels, you should take an integrated approach. Consider how making a difference on the microlevel (e.g., empowering a client in session) will inevitably influence the meso- (e.g., the client's interaction with community) and macrolevel (e.g., the broader social structure). Broad questions that you should consider may include: Do my values, biases, and beliefs align with the vision of counseling and the standards of practice that guide the profession? Do they mirror the mission of the agency or organization that I see myself a part of? and, Do they interfere with my client's growth and development? Knowing these aspects of your identity will allow you to search for corresponding opportunities in the professional counseling market.

Once you have identified your values, biases, and beliefs—as well as corresponding opportunities—it is time to incorporate them into your self-marketing image. Prospective employers and clients want and need to know where you stand (Corey, Corey, & Callanan, 2011). Discussing these issues is a collaborative effort of both parties to ensure that you are a good fit for either a therapeutic relationship or employment position. Appearing to waiver on your values, biases, and beliefs; seeming unsure of or undecided about them; or having a complete lack of insight into them can all have a negative effect on your marketing image. Therefore, it is important that you take the time to explore your worldview so that you can market yourself with confidence and competence in hand.

Live with Limitations

Reflecting on all that you learned at your field placement, you may feel pressured by high expectations and standards. This may lead to maladaptive perfectionism in which you create self-standards and goals that may be improbable at the moment given your lack of experience. You may find yourself engaging in negative self-talk, telling yourself that you *should* work harder, have *everything* under control, and know *exactly* what to do. These messages will likely lead to self-doubt and criticism, adversely affecting your growth and development.

Instead of focusing on what *should be*, try focusing on *what is* and *what can be*. By doing so, you engage in adaptive perfectionism in which you continue to challenge yourself in the same way, but instead of complying with negative self-talk, you view your experiences as opportunities for self-growth and development without excessive self-doubt and criticism.

In an ever-changing environment, we strive to be the best counselors we can be. Yet, we must accept the same message we impart to our clients: We are human, and each of us has limitations. As you progress through your training, it is crucial to be honest with yourself and admit these limitations. If not, then you risk putting yourself in a position where, despite your best intentions, you may do more harm than good to your clients and self. Remember that recognizing your limitations does not mean you are an ineffective counselor; rather, you become a model for your clients in that you are seeking self-understanding and fulfillment.

In the marketing context, acknowledging your limitations is just as important as promoting your strengths. By acknowledging your limitations, you send a clear message to employers and clients that you are aware of your ethical responsibilities and will not risk putting them in harm's way. Neither your employer nor client want to hear excuses if you make a mistake. Therefore, by taking ownership of your limitations, you convey to them that you are not only aware of your limitations but, more important, are willing to address them. From a marketing standpoint, these qualities of acknowledging your limitations can only increase the positive image you send out to the public.

Formulate Your Counseling Approach

How many times have you been asked about your favorite counseling approach? Chances are that you have had to answer this question often. However, just as with evaluating your values, biases, and beliefs while acknowledging your strengths and limitations, understanding your therapeutic approach will enable you to market yourself toward organizations that share a similar theoretical model. When formulating your therapeutic approach, you will want to consider the following questions: Do I believe individuals have free will over their thoughts and actions, or do our past experiences determine future behaviors? To what extent (if at all) do genetics and past experiences affect development? Is human nature unique or universal? All these are valid questions to consider and will ultimately influence how you view your clients and how you will guide their treatment.

Having a solid theoretical orientation will help you attract agencies, organizations, or clientele who share your beliefs. Remember, an interview is a two-way process: Individuals are not only interviewing you, but you are evaluating your fit with them as well. Take a moment to imagine yourself as a potential employer or client. How important would your applicant's or counselor's theoretical orientation be to you? Chances are that the explicit or implicit response to this question would be an important determinant of how well the applicant would fit into the organization and the likelihood of establishing rapport throughout sessions. Thus, as with the aforementioned aspects of the SELF acronym, be clear about your theoretical orientation, as this will enhance your image when reaching out to network, interviewing for a job, or building your clientele. Use Self-Assessment Activity 14.2 to strengthen your understanding of your own counseling orientation.

SELF-ASSESSMENT ACTIVITY 14.2 YOUR INNER COUNSELOR

1. I am comfortable with self-promotion. True or false? Explain.
2. What are my strengths; values, biases, and beliefs; limitations; and theoretical orientation?
3. How can I become aware of agencies or organizations that share my counseling approach?

UNDERSTANDING THE FIELD AROUND YOU

Typically a counselor is portrayed as a helping professional who works with individuals on a one-on-one basis, whether in a private practice, school, or community agency. This narrow viewpoint overlooks the fact that there is a diverse range of specialty areas within the field, and that within these areas, professional counselors have the opportunity to work in different capacities and settings. A counselor may not just be found in a community agency or private practice. You see professional counselors in schools working with our youth and across college campuses, empowering students of all ages to reach their full potential. Professional counselors can be found conducting workshops and groups for both professionals outside the field of counseling as well as nonprofessionals looking for tools to improve their quality of life. Counselors may be found on the front lines of a natural disaster aiding those in need and connecting them with critical services. If you have a family member who is a veteran of our armed services, a counselor may be working with him or her on a wide variety of issues from reducing trauma symptoms to rehabilitation. We cannot forget how important marriage and family counselors are in improving the quality of interpersonal relationships and bringing struggling families together. These are just a few of the many roles that counselors may take on themselves. If you are still unsure of where you see yourself fitting in among this diverse population of professionals, it may be helpful to look at statistics highlighting growing trends in the field of counseling.

TABLE 14.1 Percentage of Mental Health Counselors by Industry

Individual and family services	18%
Outpatient mental health and substance abuse centers	16%
Hospitals; state, local, and private	12%
State and local government, excluding education and hospitals	11%
Residential mental health and substance abuse facilities	10%

Note. Adopted from the U.S. Bureau of Labor Statistics (2012a).

The remainder of this section will be devoted to providing helpful information on where the field of counseling has been in terms of employment, where it is today, and what the future may hold for careers in counseling.

For mental health counselors, future employment prospects remain positive. In 2010, mental health counselors held about 120,300 jobs with an average salary of $42,590.00 or $20.48 per hour, and marriage and family counselors held about 36,000 jobs with an average salary of $45,710.00 or $23.42 per hour (U.S. Bureau of Labor Statistics, 2012a). The Bureau's job outlook for the years spanning from 2010 to 2020 estimates an increase of 37%, indicating above-average job growth. This results in an increase of around 58,500 new jobs during the current decade. Table 14.1 presents a breakdown of the industries with the highest percentages of mental health counselors in 2010, whereas Table 14.2 presents estimated projected job growth by industry among mental health counselors.

For school and career counselors, future employment prospects remain average despite local and state funding cuts. In 2010, school and career counselors held about 281,400 jobs with an average yearly salary of $53,380.00 or $25.67 per hour (U.S. Bureau of Labor Statistics, 2012b). The Bureau's job outlook for the years spanning from 2010 to 2020 estimates an increase of 19% indicating about as fast as average job growth. This results in an increase of around 53,400 new jobs during the current decade. Table 14.3 presents estimated projected job growth by industry among school and career counselors.

Based on these projections by the U.S. Bureau of Labor Statistics (2012a, 2012b), counseling positions at both the master's and doctoral levels will be in demand throughout the current decade. Although this remains encouraging, it is important to always assess current and future employment trends, as it may be likely that you will not remain in the same position throughout your professional career. Having reliable information on employment trends will better enable you to market yourself toward counseling careers that best fit with the current economic climate. Remember to always keep your options open, be willing to adapt to narrow economic conditions, and remain flexible in choosing which industries you see yourself working in the counseling profession. These traits will allow you to weather less-positive employment conditions while giving you an increased advantage over individuals who have less information or who attempt to target counseling industries with declining projected growth.

TABLE 14.2 Percentage of Projected Job Growth for Mental Health Counselors by Industry

Individual and family services	50%
Outpatient mental health and substance abuse centers	44%
Hospitals; state, local, and private	34%
State and local government, excluding education and hospitals	17%
Residential mental health and substance abuse facilities	12%

Note. Adopted from the U.S. Bureau of Labor Statistics (2012a).

TABLE 14.3 Projected Job Growth for School and Career Counselors by Industry

Community and Social Service Occupations	24%
Educational, Guidance, School, and Vocational Counselors	19%
Total, all occupations	14%

Note. Adopted from the U.S. Bureau of Labor Statistics (2012b).

Using Networking Opportunities and Embracing Mentorship

No matter where you are in your counseling career, a worthy mentor can be a catalyst for marketing yourself to other professionals or organizations. Finding the right match, at times, may require considerable time and effort. For some a mentorship can be initiated with a faculty member in a department, a supervisor from a practicum or internship site, or a professional from the surrounding community. For others, a mentorship can be initiated after networking at a conference, through state or national mentoring programs, or by reaching out to respected professionals in the field (e.g., sending an e-mail to a researcher who shares your interests).

Before you consider reaching out to a potential mentor, consider the following questions: What are my expectations? Are my expectations realistic? How will this professional relationship allow me to market to others? Does my potential mentor have a thorough understanding of the counseling field? Can my mentor connect me with other individuals and organizations that will help me market my skills and abilities? Finding and building a mentoring relationship helps foster professional growth and development in the counseling field. Use Self-Assessment Activity 14.3 to begin thinking about counseling as a professional field.

SELF-ASSESSMENT ACTIVITY 14.3 YOUR KNOWLEDGE OF THE FIELD

1. What are three current trends in the counseling field?
2. Who are several professionals in the field whom I can contact about issues related to my professional growth and development?
3. What are the benefits of counseling to the general public?

VOICES FROM THE FIELD 14.1   Personal and Professional Growth, by Julie Lenyk

I have had a unique experience at every conference I attended, and I think it is important to take the time to attend conferences because they can really benefit you personally and professionally. As I look back, I can mark very important points in my career that involved attending conferences both statewide and nationally. They all offered me the opportunity to network with other professionals in this field, enhance my knowledge of the counseling profession, and develop a professional identity.

One memorable experience occurred at a conference by the American Counseling Association. This conference was significant to me for many reasons, but most important, it led me on the path of my professional goals of being a clinical counselor and obtaining my doctorate degree. Attending the presentations, meetings, and social gatherings gave me the chance to network with many leaders in this field, thus opening the door to many possibilities for my future career. It was these people who really motivated me to pursue my area of clinical work and my

(Continued)

doctorate degree. I established strong relationships with these individuals, and they are people whom I continue to connect with both personally and professionally today.

I think that conferences offer a unique environment because it really is the only time that so many students, counselors, and faculty can all gather together. Conferences are a great way to meet new people and build relationships with other professionals. They can help you to establish new opportunities that can assist you in further achieving your goals.

As I reflect on the conferences I have attended, I realize that each one was vital for my professional development because of the strong relationships I built through networking. I also think they enhanced my personal development as I built strong relationships that continue to influence my life today. I am confident in saying that I would not be where I am today if I did not use the many opportunities conferences offer to network with others, learn about the counseling profession, and develop a professional identity.

SECURING A JOB THE OLD-FASHIONED WAY

Now that you have explored your identity as a counselor and you have a vision of where you want to go, what is the next step? It is likely that the next logical step toward beginning your career as a professional counselor is the job search. Although this may seem simple enough, finding a career that aligns with your needs and goals is a multifaceted process (Hodges & Connelly, 2010). After identifying your personal and professional identify as a counselor and exploring the many employment options that are available for counselors, it is important to approach the job market with knowledge and confidence. In this section we will present the materials you will need to gain entry into the workforce and the knowledge you will need to successfully navigate within it.

Preparing a Curriculum Vita or Resume

In the counseling profession, most counselors-to-be and licensed professionals focus on developing a curriculum vita (CV) or a resume (depending on the employment position). A resume is typically a 1- to 2-page document, whereas a CV is multiple pages. You would use a CV to outline all your academic accomplishments, achievements, and experiences as they relate to your career in counseling. On the other hand, a resume may be more appropriate for employers who desire a more succinct description of your skills and abilities based on your previous work history. This chapter will use the term CV for consistency, but these guidelines can be applied to the creation of either a resume or CV.

The CV should be easy to read, and the major points should be easily found. The language on your CV should be succinct and professional. Given the importance of this document, it is critical that you (a) evaluate whether the information that you choose to include is relevant, (b) ensure that the document is error free, and (c) organize the flow of information using appropriate headings and formatting. A polished CV will set you apart from others and often serves as the first impression that potential employers (or doctoral programs) have of you. It is important to have a wide variety of skills and activities on your CV to display your full range of talents and abilities.

To organize these attributes, it is important to start with a foundation. All CVs are organized with the use of headings. Although there is variation, common headings (and corresponding information) include the following: *personal information* (name, address, phone number, e-mail, Web page address if applicable); *education* (degree, major, minor, institution, graduation dates, program accreditation); *work or related experience* (job title, name of organization, and location; dates of employment; responsibilities, achievements); *leadership experience* (leadership roles, organizational membership, community involvement); *honors or awards* (academic or nonacademic awards, scholarships, fellowships, special recognitions, and year received); *professional affiliations* (on the local, state, national, and international levels); *technical competencies* (computer programs); *licenses or certifications*; *languages* (fluent, conversational, novice); *service* (community involvement, campus involvement, volunteerism); and *research* (grants, publications, presentations). Take care to make sure all information of equal importance is displayed with the same level of headings and maintain the same font and spacing throughout the document.

Begin your CV with your contact information, including your phone number and an appropriate e-mail address. After graduation, it is likely that your school e-mail will no longer be accessible. If you do not have a professional alternative e-mail address, create one. E-mail addresses using your name or initials make it easy to contact you; avoid any slang terms in the address (e.g., flirtygirl@mail.com is not appropriate). After your contact information, you may wish to list some of your most relevant qualifications and an objective statement (Hodges, 2011). However, you could choose to list your education next; take care to indicate if your master's program was CACREP-accredited, as this indicates the focus of your education. Be sure to list any internship positions or other jobs in the helping profession, and make sure your publications and presentations are formatted using the most recent edition of the APA (American Psychological Association, 2010) *Publication Manual*. It is also important to organize your CV so that your most important information is first, which may differ depending on the purpose of your CV.

The next step, after filling in your headings, is to evaluate the message you are sending to the reader. You may ask yourself: Did I overlook anything? Are all of my special strengths highlighted? Is my passion represented? Are there areas for improvement? Some areas that may be particularly important to look at beyond the basic information (contact information, education) are the sections that address your volunteer or professional service. Both emphasize that you are invested in the counseling field for more than just money, and they emphasize your dedication to the mission of counseling, which is helping others. Another area that you may want to turn your attention toward is your involvement in professional organizations, as they are excellent sources of volunteer and professional service opportunities. Your school's chapter of Chi Sigma Iota is a valuable resource; consider running for an officer position, and take advantage of volunteer activities your chapter organizes.

Another great way to build your CV is to join the American Counseling Association (ACA), ACA divisions, or your state ACA branch. You can list your membership on your CV, any conferences that you have attended, and any activities that you have participated in on behalf of your local chapter. Not only is this excellent information for your CV, but also every professional meeting and event is a rich networking experience.

In addition to carefully planning your CV, it is important to include everything that could help explain who you are as a person, counselor, and employee. Although it would be unethical to embellish your accomplishments or activities, it is desirable to present yourself in the most positive light (Hodges, 2011). Do not forget to list the hour you spend every Sunday at the nursing home or the mentoring you have provided to first-year counseling students. These things may seem inconsequential, but they help your reader gain an accurate picture of you.

Ultimately the goal of a CV is to help position yourself in the marketplace. As you can imagine, many CVs will tend to look similar due to similar coursework, trainings, and internship experiences. It is the extra lines on your CV that will help you stand out from the crowd. So, make sure to include extracurricular activities and leadership positions that highlight who you are as a counselor, employee, and coworker. Now complete Self-Assessment 14.4 and peruse Figures 14.1 and 14.2, which include a sample resume and CV, respectively.

SELF-ASSESSMENT 14.4 CVs AND RESUMES

1. How does my resume or CV accurately reflect my personal and professional qualities?
2. Have I planfully participated in local and national activities that reflect my personality and abilities? Explain.
3. What aspects of my resume or CV promote high-quality achievements? What additional experiences should I seek out to enhance my resume or CV quality?

Brandy A. Ackerman

1645 Bowling Court
Greensboro, NC 27455

339-275-9290
baackerman@gmail.com

EDUCATION

M.S. Ed. December 2010	**Clinical Mental Health Counseling** (CACREP-Accredited)	State University City, State
B.A. with Honors May 2008	**Psychology**	State University City, State

CREDENTIALS

- Licensed Professional Counselor, C000098 (January 2011)
- National Certified Counselor (NCC), 980098 (January 2011)

RELEVANT EXPERIENCE

Graduate/Research Assistant   August 2008—December 2010
State University—City, State
Dr. James Don, Supervisor

- **Developed and edited manuscripts for publication**
- **Collected and analyzed research data**
- **Presented at state and national conferences with supervisor**
- **Created documents; updated master's-level syllabi**

Clinical Counseling Intern   January 2010—December 2010
Agency—City, State
Mr. Quinn Pierce, Supervisor

- **Diagnosed and treated mental and emotional disorders**
- **Utilized cognitive-behavioral, trauma-focused, and creative interventions**
- **Served as a behavioral consultant for four Multidisciplinary Student Achievement Teams**

Direct Care Staff   June 2008—June 2009
Agency—City, State
Mr. Ronald Brick, Supervisor

- **Supervised female adolescents**
- **Promoted use of positive coping skills**
- **Implemented concrete, behavioral aspects of therapeutic treatment plans**

SELECTED PUBLICATIONS AND PRESENTATIONS

Ackerman, B. A. (2011). Title of article. *Newsletter Title, 25*(3), 11–12.
Ackerman, B. A., & Peters, R. (2010, November). *Title of presentation*. Poster session presented at the State Conference, City, State.

PROFESSIONAL AND HONORS MEMBERSHIPS

- American Counseling Association
- Chi Sigma Iota (Counseling Academic and Professional Honor Society International)

FIGURE 14.1 Sample resume.

Brandy A. Ackerman

1645 Bowling Court   339-275-9290
Greensboro, NC 27455   baackerman@gmail.com

EDUCATION

M.S. Ed.   **Clinical Mental Health Counseling**   State University
December 2010   (CACREP-Accredited)   City, State

B.A. with Honors   **Psychology**   State University
May 2008   City, State

CREDENTIALS

- Licensed Professional Counselor, C000098 (January 2011)
- National Certified Counselor (NCC), 980098 (January 2011)

RESEARCH AND SCHOLARSHIP

Graduate/Research Assistant   August 2008—December 2010
State University—City, State
Dr. James Don, Supervisor

Developed and edited qualitative and theoretical manuscripts for publication; collected and analyzed research data. Presented at state and national conferences with supervisor and independently. Created documents for the department's counselor training clinic and updated master's-level syllabi according to 2009 CACREP standards.

CLINICAL COUNSELING EXPERIENCE

Clinical Counseling Intern   January 2010—December 2010
Agency—City, State
Mr. Quinn Pierce, Supervisor

Diagnosed and treated mental and emotional disorders in children, adolescents, and families; utilized cognitive-behavioral, trauma-focused, and creative interventions in outpatient and in-home settings. Served as a behavioral consultant for Multidisciplinary Student Achievement Teams at four urban schools

Direct Care Staff   June 2008—June 2009
Agency—City, State
Mr. Ronald Brick, Supervisor

Supervised female adolescents in a residential treatment facility; served meals, created and enforced chore schedule, assisted with online school assignments, developed and implemented leisure activities, promoted use of positive coping skills, and otherwise implemented concrete, behavioral aspects of therapeutic treatment plans.

AWARDS

- **NBCC Foundation Rural Scholarship Semifinalist** 2009

GRANT FUNDING

- 2008—State University–Graduate Studies Internal Grant, Undergraduate Student Research Grant. *Title of Grant.* $500

FIGURE 14.2   Sample CV.

PUBLICATIONS

Ackerman, B. A. (2011). Title of article. *Newsletter Title, 25*(3), 11–12.
Adamson, N. A., **Ackerman, B. A.**, & Lindley, J. L., (2010). Title of article. *Newsletter Title, 2*, 5–7.

PRESENTATIONS

Ackerman, B. A., & Peters, R. (2010, November). *Title of presentation.* Poster session presented at the State Conference, City, State.

PROFESSIONAL SERVICE AND LEADERSHIP

Secretary
Chi Sigma Iota, Our Chapter
State University
April 2009 to April 2010

- Organized workshops for professional continuing education
- Advocated for the counseling profession
- Sponsored social events
- Organized philanthropic endeavors
- Increased chapter participation

PROFESSIONAL MEMBERSHIPS

- American Counseling Association

HONOR SOCIETY MEMBERSHIPS

- Chi Sigma Iota (Counseling Academic and Professional Honor Society International)

FIGURE 14.2 *(Continued)*

Using Your Resume or CV

Your resume or CV will be invaluable when searching for an internship or your first counseling job. It is helpful to e-mail potential interviewers your resume or CV before a face-to-face meeting so that they can study your accomplishments. Also, bring a paper copy to your meeting or interview. It is sometimes nice to use resume paper, rather than regular printing paper, for the first page of your resume or CV. Subsequent pages should be standard printing paper. Resume paper can be found at any office supply store in a variety of professional colors, but white is always appropriate.

Your resume or CV will also be useful to anyone who is writing a letter of recommendation for you. Although this person should know you very well, you cannot expect him or her to know all your accomplishments. Send your resume or CV to those whom you trust to write a supportive letter of reference several weeks before the letter is needed (Hodges, 2011). This allows the writer ample time to create a thoughtful and persuasive letter. There are often many applicants interested in internship, job, or doctoral positions; your resume or CV and letters of reference can set you apart from your competition.

As a graduate student and new professional, you are doing things every day that deserve to be on your resume or CV. It is helpful to update your resume or CV at least once per month so that nothing is forgotten. This practice also prevents you from being caught with an outdated resume or CV when opportunity knocks. As a professional in the job market, it is important to be prepared at all times to secure a job that is right for you. Although there are many job opportunities for counselors, your resume or CV can be used as a reflective tool to help you and an employer gain an understanding of a career choice that would be best for you.

VOICES FROM THE FIELD 14.2   The Course of Life: My Curriculum Vitae, by Ron Del Moro

---

I never knew the difference between a resume and its fancier cousin, the curriculum vitae (more commonly referred to as a CV). I figured if I mumbled both words interchangeably I could not go wrong. As time marched on, though, it became necessary to learn about these documents and how to provide an overview of my life in a few pages or less.

CV is a Latin expression that can be translated to "the course of life." Some say CVs are exclusive to academia, and others will contend they are becoming more popular outside the walls of education. The main difference between a resume and CV is length; resumes typically run one or two pages at most, whereas CVs can go on and on and on. (Consult one of your successful professors' CVs for an example.)

Resumes and CVs are "living" documents that must constantly be updated as your professional identity grows. I find it easiest to update regularly, rather than waiting until I need my CV and then trying to remember what I have done since the last update. It is also helpful to have someone else check it out before sending it.

Resumes and CVs are representations of ourselves; they are often the first impression we leave with others. Countless formats, designs, and styles can be chosen, and there does not seem to be one universally agreed upon "right" design, as long as there are no smiley faces or butterflies! I have learned that this "summation of life experiences" cannot be prepared at the last minute. Do it right the first time, update it regularly, and life will be a lot easier down the road.

Cover Letters

Cover letters are an integral part of your job search. These brief letters act in conjunction with your resume or CV to provide a first impression, clearly explain why you are a viable job candidate, and invite employers to contact you for follow-up (Hodges & Connelly, 2010). Cover letters should be addressed specifically to the person (or group) who will be overseeing the hiring process and should not exceed one page. Ultimately, the cover letter allows you to add personality to your CV, but should also be concise and meaningful. The cover letter provided in Figure 14.3 can serve as a template for your personalized cover letter, which should be written intentionally and specifically for each organization to which you apply.

The Job Search

The job search is a process that intersects your personal desires, practical needs, realistic skill set, and job market availability (Hodges, 2011). Although complicated, this process can be navigated by a prepared counselor. However, luck and chance also play a role in this process, so try not to become discouraged if things do not go exactly as planned—your hard work will pay off soon. If at all possible, choose an internship at an agency or practice at which you would like to work. Many establishments that accept interns also hire their interns, so take your internship seriously. Practica and internships help you gain experience and fulfill graduation requirements, but can also serve as a year-long interview with a future employer. It might be beneficial to have conversations with your supervisor or agency administrators about your graduation date and any possible employment opportunities.

If you find that you do not wish to work at your internship site, or there are no available positions, plan backward from your graduation date. Often, before you can be hired as a professional, you must attain the necessary licensure. Although you may not be able to formally apply until you have graduated, you can take any necessary licensure exams ahead of time. You should begin registering for such exams as you enter the last semester of your program. However, you can definitely start sooner if you feel comfortable doing so.

Each counseling license is associated with different examinations depending on the state in which you plan to be licensed. Currently, there is not a unified licensure process for all 50 states, but there is a way to show potential employers that you have nationally

Tiffany A. Herring
204 Country Rd.
Winston, Ohio 54321

April 2, 2015

Brett Logan, Supervisor of Guidance
Winston City Schools
20 Levitt Street
Winston, Ohio 54321

Dear Mr. Logan:

I am aware of an available school counseling position within Winston City School District, and I would like to convey my interest in this opportunity. Unlike many other candidates, I am a Licensed School Counselor as well as a Licensed Clinical Counselor. My passion for working with inner-city youth combined with my strong academic and leadership background make me an especially valuable school counseling candidate.

As an employee in a residential treatment facility and an intern at Winston Early College, Kale Elementary School, and Sage Counseling Center, I served diverse student populations whose learning and social functioning levels covered a wide spectrum. I particularly enjoyed working with at-risk students to help resolve interpersonal conflicts. One of my greatest strengths is my ability to increase students' academic self-efficacy through individual and group counseling and by paying close attention to the quality of the school environment. I also enjoy professional development endeavors and have made scholarly presentations at the state and national levels.

My experience in the nationally accredited Daley University Counseling Program and my passion for helping students has allowed me to serve as a successful school counseling intern. I have excellent initiative and organizational skills, and I am excited about the opportunity to find employment within your school district. I believe you will discover that my warm personality, strong communication skills, maturity, and honesty are characteristics that make me an outstanding choice for this position. I thank you for your time and consideration and look forward to speaking with you through e-mail or over the phone.

Sincerely,

(Signature)

Tiffany Herring

FIGURE 14.3 Sample cover letter.

recognized qualifications. The National Board for Certified Counselors (NBCC) has developed the National Counselor Examination for licensure and certification (see http://www.nbcc.org/NCE). This exam serves two functions in the counseling profession. First, many state boards recognize successful completion of this exam as an indicator that a candidate should receive a counseling license. In addition, this exam indicates that the counselor is eligible to become nationally certified. National certification is not the same as licensure; it does not allow someone to practice as a counselor. However, it does indicate the candidate has met national standards and is endorsed by NBCC. If this credential can be listed on your CV, it shows employers that you meet national counseling standards.

The credentials that you have chosen to earn are an indicator of the job positions that would be best for you. Once you have created a CV that accurately represents you and displays credentials that indicate your high achievements, it is important to stay abreast of employment opportunities. Opportunities may be sent through listservs (e.g., mass e-mails sent through your state branch of the ACA or from your university or school system), and it is important to take note of these helpful opportunities. Make sure to follow the directions specified in the message and to accompany your CV with a formal cover letter.

Word of mouth is an excellent way to learn of new job opportunities. It is estimated that almost two thirds of all jobs are not formally advertised (Hodges & Connelly, 2010). If you are looking for a job, communicate with other students in your program; ask them if their internship agencies are hiring. This is also helpful because you can find out about the culture of the organization. When attending conferences, make sure to network with your peers and mention that you are looking for a counseling position. It might even be worthwhile to send a CV and cover letter to an agency that is not currently advertising any employment positions, but matches your personal and professional career needs.

When interacting with colleagues in person, business cards are an important networking tool (Hodges & Connelly, 2010). Take care to ensure that your business cards have updated contact information and accurately convey your qualifications. Also, choose a business card format that is simple, professional, and easy to read. It is helpful to exchange business cards when at any networking function. Someone may learn of a job opening after meeting you (although he or she did not know about it when you initially met) and contact you in the future. In addition, if you happen to get an interview at a place with which you are unfamiliar, you might be able to search through your collection of business cards to find a personal contact in the area.

When networking in person, it is especially important to be cognizant of your professional appearance. Remember that you are a counselor at all times of the day; whether you are at church on Sunday or the bar on Saturday, your community now views you as a professional, and it is important not to prove them wrong. Especially when job hunting, but from here on out, think before you act. This applies to activities you do in public and at home, such as Facebook or Twitter. Think about how the things you say or do reflect on you and the counseling profession; you never know who is watching. As a new professional marketing yourself for the best possible employment position, it will be important not to lose any opportunities over events that occur in your personal life.

VOICES FROM THE FIELD 14.3   The Importance of Comfort and Support during the Job Search, by Emily Herman

---

My job as a graduate student was clear: attend classes, work in groups, write papers, and complete internship. However, as graduation approached, the daunting task of the job search loomed ahead. I felt uncertain about finding not only a job, but also a career in counseling. My goal was to work with children and adolescents, but I soon found that there are a limited amount of agencies who work with that population. This realization led me to ask myself, "What would I say to a client who was in a similar position?"

It became apparent that my next step was to identify other options and avenues that could serve as a stepping-stone. After searching local newspapers, online postings, and listservs, I realized that the most useful tool I had was the network of peers, professors, and adjunct instructors that I had worked with and admired for the past 2 years. It was also beneficial that they knew me and my training; this trust led to more personal interactions with people who could help me begin my professional life. I had finally found the comfort and support that I was looking for in the job search.

For me, the most overwhelming part of the job search was questioning if I was making the best decision and feeling isolated in the process. In graduate school and during internship, there was a safety net of advisors, university mentors, and site supervisors to help me with scheduling and internship placement. Although the job search is an individual decision, I used these same resources to search for a job in which I could begin my career. Ultimately, I had to make the final decision, but I found the path clearer when I had support from people I had grown to trust throughout my graduate studies.

Landing the Interview and Following Up

After submitting a carefully constructed cover letter and professional CV, it is important to follow up with the organization. If possible, it is helpful to go to the agency in person to ensure that your information was received. This also serves as an initial meeting during which your personality can be associated with your qualifications. If it is not possible to physically go to the organization, call 3 to 5 days after your resume and cover letter should have been received. Ask to speak with the person in charge of the job search (call him or her by name if possible), but graciously leave a message or speak with someone else in the organization if that person is unavailable.

When you receive a call for an interview, be polite and calm. Make sure to write down the date and time of your interview and confirm the location. Arrive to your interview at least 15 minutes early. If you are unfamiliar with the area to which you are going, take a practice drive a day or two before. Arrive at your interview with proper business attire, minimal jewelry, and no perfume or cologne; it is not worth risking the chance that your scent could offend one of the search committee members. In a dark blue or black folder, carry one or two hard copies of your CV (you may wish to print the first page on resume paper) and your business cards. It is also helpful to bring a portfolio of work that you have done while working in a related position or internship.

Take care to speak and act professionally in your interview; try to avoid slang terms, and sit still if possible (Hodges, 2011). However, it is important to be yourself. It would not be beneficial to falsely represent yourself in the interview, as the employers are sure to learn your true personality if you are offered the job.

In many instances, several rounds of candidates are interviewed for one job opening, so be patient. After the interview, send a handwritten thank-you note to your interviewers. This shows that you are still interested in the position and indicates that you are able to follow through with your commitments. Generally, it would be acceptable to make a follow-up call if you have not heard anything for about 2 weeks. If you are informed that you did not get the position, gracefully thank the interviewer for the opportunity and request that the agency keep your information on file. However, if you are informed that you were selected to fill the position, congratulations!

CARVING OUT YOUR NEW-AGE NICHE

Counseling students and licensed professional counselors who use social networking tools have a unique ability to reach out to thousands and even millions of individuals, groups, and organizations across the globe. Whether promoting the profession, promoting a cause, or promoting oneself, those seeking to self-market have the opportunity to gain from the benefits of social networking tools, as they provide a direct and accessible medium to achieve these aims. However, with increased connectivity comes increased risk and liability. In the sections that follow, we will discuss the most up-to-date and popular social networking tools that you can use to build your professional network and market yourself to potential clients and employers. We will also discuss some of the potential pitfalls of relying too heavily on social media and how it can potentially damage your image and practice.

Reaching Out with Social Networking

As technology expands, more and more social networking tools will become available to the general public. Many of these are user friendly and free of charge. However, perhaps the most enticing incentive to use social networking tools is the ability to connect with, and distribute information to, a larger audience while sitting at your home or office computer. Take, for example, YouTube, one of the most accessed websites across the world. Many visit this site to listen to and watch videos ranging from personal biographies to contemporary and historical media events to professional lectures from esteemed experts. If you were to type the word "counseling" into the search box, there would be over 50,000 unique videos related to this topic, each having the potential to be watched by millions of viewers who have access to this website. Recognizing the advantages of this tool, you as a counselor have endless opportunities to market yourself. Possibilities may include presenting informed consent videos to potential clients, performing a presentation or lecture on a given research topic, or uploading a video diary of your own experience as you work through your master's program and beyond. This is a great way to make a strong first impression and to promote the profession as a whole.

Another social networking medium is Facebook. Originally created as a networking site for U.S. college students, Facebook has gone global. This audience includes everyone from young adults to nationally known organizations. Your Facebook page can allow you to connect with family and friends, but in the context of marketing, it can also serve as an outlet to connect with other professionals in the field, reach out to other mental health organizations, or promote the latest research, depending on your interests. Think of Facebook as a way for your clients, colleagues, or potential employers to perform their own background check on you. Information that you choose to include on your profile can be your education, current employment, trainings and certifications, professional interests, and other organizations that you belong to. Facebook also allows you to post status updates and messages to those who are linked, or "friended," in your profile.

Along with YouTube and Facebook, another website and application called Twitter can allow instantaneous access to spreading information to thousands of individuals. This social networking tool can allow you to post immediate updates to those who "follow" you and share your own interests. If you find yourself traveling and giving lectures or presenting at conferences, you can use Twitter to promote these events. You can also follow the leading experts in the field who have a Twitter account, receiving immediate notifications about the who, what, where, and when of their professional endeavors.

Selling Yourself on the Virtual Job Market

Numerous websites will allow you to search for employment as well as promote your practice and skills. For example, LinkedIn has quickly become one of the largest professional networking sites used around the globe, allowing you to post your professional profile to potential organizations and employers. If individuals type your name into a search engine (for example, using Google Search), your LinkedIn profile will instantaneously be visible to them on their search results page. If they choose to review your profile, you are just one click away from connecting, conversing, and collaborating.

Other websites afford you the opportunity to post your resume and search for jobs specifically tailored to your counseling interests. These sites include, but are not limited to: Monster.com, Careerbuilding.com, and Indeed.com. One option when using these sites is uploading a resume in your account for potential employers to review. If interested, the employers initiate contact. For some, this laid-back approach is ideal; however, for those who are on an aggressive job hunt, this approach may not be beneficial. Thus, the latter group may lean toward option two: searching for positions of interest and sending/uploading their resume to the prospective employer. This is a more direct approach that not only gives the applicant more control, but also shows the employer that the applicant views the position as a professional investment in career development. Using a combination of these options and sites can further enhance your ability to self-market.

A consideration to keep in mind when building your professional profiles on these websites is maintenance. Specifically, you will want to ask yourself: Is my profile up-to-date? Is it accurate? And, does it reflect my skills, abilities, and passions in the field of counseling or related fields? Taking an objective stance will allow you to critically evaluate your online profile and make adjustments based on current trends and the needs of employing agencies or organizations.

Building a Professional Website

So far, we have discussed using other websites as a means to market your practice and professional identity. Now we will discuss using your own website to build on and enhance your professional career in counseling. You may be asking yourself, what are my options if I decide to start my own website? The answer to this question lies heavily on the intent of your website. For instance, if the overall intent of your website is to educate individuals about your professional career and services, you will more likely have a website with fewer features. If, however, the goal of your site is to market your independent practice, then you may have more enhanced features embedded in your website that enable clients to schedule appointments, make and collect payments, or even post comments on a dedicated forum included on your site. Neither example presented should have more appeal than the other. Rather, the success of your website to attract and keep viewers will rely heavily on how well the site functions to achieve its goals.

Beginning a website can be an overwhelming task. Thus, it might be wise to start off slowly by developing your own professional blog. According to Todd (2009), blogs serve two purposes. First, they provide a sense of community to those individuals and organizations that you serve or are trying to attract. Second, blogging allows you to connect with them directly so that you may better understand the services they need and what is most important to them. When developing your blog, you will have the opportunity to incorporate graphics, visuals, and other functions that will not only help stimulate the content of your blog, but will also serve as a foundation for creating tools to enhance the goals of your future website. The experience of maintaining a blog will give you a solid foundation of working within a website and connecting with viewers while preparing you to build your own site.

When you have had some practice in the blogging world and are ready to develop your own website, what are some goals to keep in mind? Todd (2009) stated that your website should accomplish three goals, including making a great first impression to viewers about who you are and your practice, building satisfaction and loyalty, and reducing labor and costs of conducting business. Making a great first impression will help draw viewers in and keep them interested in the information you are presenting. Building satisfaction and loyalty will not only keep them coming back to your site but will also help spread positive word of mouth, thus increasing the traffic on your site. Reducing labor and costs only makes sound financial sense if the intent of your website is to sustain a counseling business or practice allowing you to allocate financial resources to other appropriate business needs. For example, clients may fill out and submit forms via your website instead of your having to pay hundreds of dollars yearly in printing fees.

Although it may be tempting to assume that looks are everything about a website, this could not be further from the truth in the counseling profession. Potential clients are not interested in fancy graphics or animations. They are looking for direct and clear information, so keep your main page organized to reduce confusion. This may be the case if a potential client is in distress and trying to access information quickly about your services to determine appropriateness of fit within your practice. However, it is still important to allow your personality to be reflected through your website.

If you happen to visit counseling professionals with their own website, you may notice common headings on their main page of the site. Here is a list of important headings to consider on your home page, and you may also incorporate others: counselor biography, business information, scheduling, client resources, treatment populations served, and how you approach counseling (Todd, 2009). As we discussed in managing profiles on other social networking sites, it is crucial to keep the information within these headings updated continuously. If viewers visit your website and are met with outdated information, they may develop the impression that you have less interest and commitment to your site and, by extension, to them.

When building your website, remember to have the following criteria in mind to provide a better experience for your viewers and reduce your own frustration when managing your site: keep your site user friendly to allow clients to access and download information with as few clicks as possible. A client or colleague should not have to spend 10 minutes or more searching for your contact information. As you become familiar with your website, you may consider adding videos, links, documents, and podcasts. Depending on the nature of your counseling website, you may consider adding forums or discussion boards so clients or professionals can comment on their experiences or connect with others in a positive and meaningful way.

Ensure that you are always looking ahead when designing your website so you can modify it to your public's liking. Nothing can be more frustrating than trying to build in a feature that viewers are requesting only to find out that it is not functioning properly. For instance, if you decide to incorporate the ability for individuals to view or download documents, make sure they can be converted to a PDF (portable document format); that way the file cannot be manipulated and it is easily accessible (Todd, 2009). Making the website interactive will keep clients and professionals interested and on your site for longer periods of time. However, if viewers are met with confusing information, broken links, or dysfunctional features, they will be more likely to become frustrated and subsequently leave the site never to return.

Virtual Liabilities

Nowadays, all the aforementioned tools can be accessed using a variety of modes—a personal or public computer, your cell phone, and now a tablet computer if you own one. All these tools allow for quick and easy access, along with a cost-effective way to promote yourself to a large-scale audience. However, it is important to note that although self-promotion is just a click away, so is self-destruction. It is essential that you consider the short-term and long-term consequences of what you post on these sites.

Anthony et al. (2010) stated that the ACA (2005) *Code of Ethics* do not address counselors belonging to online communities. In an attempt to address this gap of knowledge, the authors emphasize that although interacting with clients via personal websites may be beneficial for building trust and self-esteem, there are drawbacks worth considering. For example, personally disclosing information (such as posting your views on a particular subject) may potentially harm the therapeutic relationship, blur boundaries, and put a counselor in a position where he or she may cross or violate boundaries. Consider the following questions when evaluating your own presence in the online world: How many online sites do I belong to? How easy would it be for a client to find me on these sites? How will I balance my personal and professional online identity? If my clients reviewed my online profiles, how would that affect our therapeutic relationship?

With the rise of online security breaches and personal data being compromised, it is recommended to always act with caution and safety when presenting personal details to the online world. With the right information, computer hackers may access personal and private information about you and your family. Not only may they access this information but they may also sell it on a black market for their own profit. Therefore, it is prudent to refrain from posting any information about yourself on a website should you feel uncomfortable or unsure.

Overall, there is a variety of positive ways in which your professional identity may grow using social media and websites. However, there are numerous possibilities and events that may occur that can harm the process of building your online image. No matter how well your online image is built, keep in mind the impact of word of mouth. Word of mouth can just as easily ruin your reputation and professional identity as it can launch your career. In the digital age, word of mouth may spread not just from person to person but from blog to blog, online article to online article, chatroom to chatroom, and message board to message board. In the past, news took days and weeks to circle the globe, whereas in the 21st century, information is posted, available, and accessed in seconds.

THE ADVANTAGES OF CONTINUED LEARNING

Part of marketing yourself as a mental health professional includes not only the delivery of content but also the quality of your content. A mistake new counselors may make is feeling like they have to know everything or be all things to all people. According to Diana (2010), counselors become generalists, creating a sense of mediocrity and placing them in the middle of the marketplace. The following section will help guide you in developing your professional skills so the quality of your words and presentations demonstrates expertise, thus positioning you at the front line of the marketplace.

Keep Up to Date

If you are attempting to market yourself in the counseling profession, it is imperative that you keep up to date with the latest information. Otherwise, you risk tarnishing your reputation by appearing uninterested in the profession or incompetent by having the wrong information at hand. There are many ways to keep up to date within the counseling profession. Journals are a great way to stay involved with the latest research and trends. You should visit your state board's website on a regular basis to keep abreast of any changes in laws or regulations. Remember, you are ultimately responsible for seeking this information. Having a thorough knowledge of the latest trends, laws, and regulations will say to others that you take the profession seriously and will help build your marketing image.

Become an Expert

In the field of counseling, there are numerous avenues to explore when obtaining advance training to become an expert. Training institutions and certifications allow individuals to seek additional experience in a variety of formats. For example, institutions and certifications can be tailored to working with specific populations, theoretical approaches, treatment modalities, and in particular settings such as disaster relief training. When seeking these opportunities, it is important to consider the level of commitment required at the time of training and whether there are additional requirements following the initial training, the location of the training, and the financial costs. Some training may only take 1 day, whereas becoming an expert requires a lifetime commitment.

In their journey to become experts, some individuals seek advanced education at the postgraduate level. Pursuing a doctoral degree can seem like an impossible task, especially when you have just finished your master's degree. Whether you choose to pursue the degree immediately after your master's or decades later, a doctoral degree can provide countless opportunities for personal and professional growth. Opportunities include conducting research with faculty in a particular subject, presenting at conferences, teaching counseling-related coursework, and obtaining additional experience and hours toward your counseling and supervision licensure.

VOICES FROM THE FIELD 14.4   Mindfulness: The Personal Becomes Professional, by Andy Davis

---

I can remember starting my master's program and realizing quickly that I had to face many uncertainties and fears: Am I making the right choice? What does it mean to be a counselor? How do I see myself fitting into that mold? What if this does not work out? These were just some of the many questions that plagued my mind. My undergraduate degree was in engineering, and to change careers to counseling felt quite different. I was also faced with confronting my conservative Christian background that had taught me to be suspicious of psychology and its attacks on religious values. Friends were verbally supportive of my decision to change careers, yet I could see from their facial expressions that they too were just as confused as I was. As a source of strength, I could hear my mother, who had passed away one year earlier, saying to me, "Andy, you can be whatever you want to be!"

Up until I began my master's degree program, I had been living up to expectations from others and was now faced with developing my own self-expectations and defining who I was going to be as a counselor. To add to the uncertainty and role confusion, I was getting married and trying to be a father to five children. My life seemed to be moving fast, and I was trying to catch up with it. While working at a mental health practice, I came into contact with clients who were attending a dialectical behavior therapy (DBT) class, where mindfulness is one of the core skills taught. This immediately caught my undivided attention, and I set out to learn more about this clinical approach by attending several workshops and retreats.

One day, while attending a mindfulness workshop, I had a profound and life-changing experience that allowed me to develop an identity as a counselor and approach to my practice with clients. That morning, I was intentionally and slowly eating a bowl of oatmeal. While mindfully consuming the oatmeal, I began to see the beauty in this intricate process of eating that contrasted with my stressful and fast-paced lifestyle. I was overwhelmed with emotion, tears began to flow, and it was at this moment that I experienced mindfulness.

From that moment, I began incorporating mindfulness-based interventions into my own practice and witnessed clients experiencing positive results. Since then, I have had opportunities to run classes for cancer patients, persons suffering from depression, and nonclinical college students. Invitations have been offered to do public workshops and teach a graduate-level course in mindfulness in counseling. In my doctoral program, I have also had the pleasure of connecting with other practitioners interested in research and clinical practice of mindfulness-based interventions. From my own experience, opportunities have seemed to come together based on my own passion for mindfulness and incorporating it into my clinical work. I have allowed my personal experience with mindfulness to transform my professional identity, reaching out to clients and professionals in ways I had not thought were possible.

Although rigorous and demanding, obtaining a doctoral degree in counselor education and supervision will communicate to others that you have gone through advanced training and education in your field. You will have opportunities at the doctoral level that may have never been available to you while in your master's program. Depending on your interest, you can enhance your knowledge by conducting research, writing essays, publishing articles, writing books or book chapters, and even developing your own courses. These are just some of the numerous ways in which a doctoral program can allow you to become an expert in your field and in a particular subject.

Becoming an expert through advanced training will open many networking opportunities. Traveling to conferences, workshops, and meetings will afford you the advantage of networking with other professionals and build stronger relationships with your colleagues, all of which allows you to promote your expertise. Through active promotion, "you will be able to use your expanding knowledge base to build systems and service offerings that will earn you increased credibility, authority, and recognition in the field" (Diana, 2010, p. 76). As a result of successful self-promotion, opportunities will arise; as opportunities arise, you will be afforded new ways to market yourself to others!

Summary

The SELF acronym is a useful tool when going through the job search process and throughout your career. As an ever-changing and growing counseling professional, your personal and professional needs will certainly continue to evolve. By maintaining a clear idea of your strengths and acknowledging your limitations, it is likely that you will enjoy your work as a counselor and will prove to be an asset to your clients and employer. It is important to maintain an understanding of your values as they relate to your personal and professional needs and to maintain employment that aligns with your beliefs and desires.

Traditional methods of networking, such as personal conversation, word of mouth, attending conferences, and sharing business cards, often prove to be successful. However, technology can help professional counselors to access employment opportunities from far distances and allows employers to contact a wide range of potential applicants. Therefore, it is important to remain informed of the latest technological advances. This includes the importance of staying updated with social networking tools that can be utilized to launch your career into the 21st century.

It is important to create a CV that conveys your interests and understanding of counseling skills. Your CV should be organized and succinct to catch readers' attention in a way that showcases a broad range of skills and talents. Take care to list continued education that aligns with your professional interests and the trends in the counseling profession. Consistent revision of your CV allows you to take advantage of job opportunities quickly, which could make quite a difference in your job search. In addition, cover letters should accompany every CV that is sent to a potential employer.

The job search is multifaceted and requires quite a bit of time and energy. If applicants take time during the application process to identify the assets they offer as a professional, as well as the accommodations and opportunities they need from a potential employment opportunity, it will be worthwhile in the end. Careful use of your CV and interviewing skills, in combination with face-to-face interaction and social networking, will result in a fulfilling career and an opportunity to help others in meaningful ways.

REFERENCES

Adams, K. B., Matto, H. C., & LeCroy, C. (2009). Limitations of evidence-based practice for social work education: Unpacking the complexity. *Journal of Social Work Education, 45,* 165–186.

Allen, K., Cornell, D., Lorek, E., & Sheras, P. (2008). Response of school personnel to student threat assessment training. *School Effectiveness and School Improvement: An International Journal of Research, Policy and Practice, 19,* 319–322.

Altekruse, M. K., Harris, H. L., & Brandt, M. A. (2001). *The role of the professional counselor in the 21st century.* Denver, CO: Love Publishing.

American Association of Marriage and Family Therapists (AAMFT). (2012). *AAMFT code of ethics.* Retrieved from http://www.aamft.org/imis15/content/legal_ethics/code_of_ethics.aspx

American Association of Suicidology (AAS). (2008). *Suicide in the USA.* Retrieved from http://www.suicidology.org/c/document_library/get_file?folderId=262&name=DLFE-532.pdf

American Association of Suicidology (AAS). (2012). *Clinician survivor task force.* Retrieved from http://mypage.iusb.edu/~jmcintos/therapists_mainpg.htm

American Counseling Association. (1997, May 31). *Know your rights: Mental health, private practice and the law.* ACA national videoconference. Alexandria, VA.

American Counseling Association. (2005). *American Counseling Association code of ethics* (3rd ed.). Alexandria, VA: Author.

American Counseling Association. (2011). *Medicare coverage of licensed professional counselors—senate bill introduced.* Retrieved from http://www.counseling.org/PublicPolicy/PositionPapers.aspx?AGuid=8194d10b-124f-49db-a843-09b78a1e1382

American Counseling Association. (2012). *Consensus definition of counseling.* Retrieved from http://www.counseling.org/AboutUs/OurHistory/TP/Milestones/CT2.aspx?

American Foundation for Suicide Prevention (AFSP). (2010). *Surviving a suicide loss: A resource and healing guide.* New York, NY: Author.

American Mental Health Counselors Association (AMHCA). (2010). *Principles for AMHCA's code of ethics.* Retrieved from https://www.amhca.org/assets/news/AMHCA_Code_of_Ethics_2010_w_pagination_cxd_51110.pdf

American Psychiatric Association. (2013). *Diagnostic and statistical manual of mental disorders* (5th ed.). Washington, DC: Author.

American Psychological Association (APA). (1996). *Violence and the family: Report of the APA presidential task force on violence and the family.* Washington, DC: Author.

American Psychological Association (APA). (2010). *Publication manual of the American Psychological Association* (6th ed.). Washington, DC: Author.

American Psychological Association (APA). (2012). *Mental health insurance under the federal parity law.* Retrieved from http://www.apa.org/helpcenter/federal-parity-law.aspx

American Red Cross. (2005). *Foundations of disaster mental health: Instructors manual.* Washington, DC: Author.

American School Counselors Association (ASCA). (2010). *Ethical standards for school counselors.* Retrieved from http://www.schoolcounselor.org/files/EthicalStandards2010.pdf

American School Counselors Association (ASCA). (2012). *ASCA national model: A framework for school counseling programs* (3rd ed.). Alexandria, VA: Author.

Ancis, J. R., & Ladany, N. (2010). A multicultural framework for counselor supervision. In L. J. Bradley & N. Ladany (Eds.), *Counselor supervision* (4th ed., pp. 53–95). New York, NY: Routledge.

Ancis, J. R., & Sanchez-Hucles, J. V. (2000). A preliminary analysis of counseling students' attitudes toward counseling women and women of color: Implications for cultural competency training. *Journal of Multicultural Counseling and Development, 28,* 16–31.

Anderson, A., & West, S. G. (2011). Violence against mental health professionals: When the treater becomes the victim. *Innovations in Clinical Neuroscience, 8*(3), 34–39.

Anderson, S. K., & Middleton, V. A. (2005). *Explorations in privilege, oppression, and diversity.* Belmont, CA: Brooks/Cole.

Anthony, K., Nagel, D., & Goss, S. (2010). *The use of technology in mental health.* Springfield, IL: Charles C Thomas.

Arredondo, P., Toporek, R., Brown, S., Jones, J., Locke, D. C., Sanchez, J., & Stadler, H. (1996). *Operationalization of the multicultural counseling competencies.* Alexandria, VA: Association for Multicultural Counseling and Development.

Asim, J. (2007). *The n word: Who can say it, who shouldn't, and why.* New York, NY: Houghton Mifflin Company.

Association for Counselor Education and Supervision (ACES). (2011). *Best practices in clinical supervision.* Retrieved from http://www.acesonline.net/wp-content/uploads/2011/10/ACES-Best-Practices-in-clinical-supervision-document-FINAL.pdf

Attaway, T., Barnes, L., Daughhetee, C., & Puleo, S. (2002, November). *Cutting the muster: Evaluating our future peers.* Paper presented at the Alabama Counseling Association, in Mobile, AL.

Awang, D. V. C. (2009). *Herbs of choice: The therapeutic use of phytochemicals* (3rd ed.). Boca Raton, FL: CRC Press, Taylor and Francis Group.

Bacchus, L., Mezey G., & Bewley S. (2003). Experiences of seeking help from health professionals in a sample of women who experienced domestic violence. *Health and Social Care in the Community, 11,* 10–18.

Baird, B. N. (2010). *The internship, practicum, and field placement handbook: A guide for the helping profession* (6th ed.). Upper Saddle River, NJ: Pearson.

Balkin, R. S., & Juhnke, G. A. (2014). *The theory and practice of assessment in counseling.* Upper Saddle River, NJ: Pearson.

Barling, J., Dupré, K., & Kelloway, E. (2009). Predicting workplace aggression and violence. *Annual Review of Psychology, 60,* 671–692.

Bartholomew, C. (2003). *Gender-sensitive therapy: Principles and practices.* Prospect Heights, IL: Waveland Press, Inc.

Bartlett, M. L. (2008). The efficacy of no-suicide contracts with clients in counseling on an outpatient basis. *Dissertation Abstracts International, 67,* 3438, 06B. (ProQuest [formerly UMI] No. 3225247).

Bartlett, M. L., Carney, J., & Talbott-Forbes, L. (2009). Clients' perceptions of no-suicide contracts. *Journal of Counseling, Research, and Practice, 1*(1),23–31.

Bartlett, M. L., Siegfried, N. J., & Witte, T. K. (in press). Best practice clinical interventions for working with suicidal adults. *The Alabama Counseling Association Journal.*

Bartlett, M. L., & Talbott, L. L. (in press). Legal and ethical issues related to working with suicidal clients. *Journal of Mental Health Counseling.*

Bartlett, M. L., Trippany, R., & Reicherzer, S. (in press). Prevention and crisis intervention services. In D. Sheperis & C. Sheperis (Eds.), *Clinical mental health counseling: Fundamentals of applied practice.* Upper Saddle River, NJ: Pearson.

Bell, C. R. (2000). The mentor as partner. *Training and Development, 54,* 52–56.

Bem, S. L. (1981). *Bem Sex-Role Inventory: Professional manual.* Palo Alto, CA: Consulting Psychologists Press.

Berg, I. K., & Miller, S. (1992). *Working with the problem drinker.* New York, NY: Norton.

Berk, M., Henriques, G., Warman, D., Brown, G., & Beck, A. (2004). A cognitive therapy intervention for suicide attempters: An overview of the treatment and case examples. *Cognitive and Behavioral Practice, 11,* 265–277.

Berman, P. (2010). *Case conceptualization and treatment planning: Integrating theory with clinical practice.* Los Angeles, CA: Sage.

Bernard, J. M. (1979). Supervision training: A discrimination model. *Counselor Education and Supervision, 18,* 60–68.

Bernard, J. M., & Goodyear, R. K. (2009). *Fundamentals of clinical supervision* (4th ed.). Boston, MA: Allyn & Bacon.

Berzoff, J., & Kita, E. (2010). Compassion fatigue and countertransference: Two different concepts. *Clinical Social Work Journal, 38,* 341–349. doi: 10.1007/s10615-010-0271-8

Betan, E. J., & Binder, J. L. (2010). Clinical expertise in psychotherapy: How expert therapists use theory in generating case conceptualizations and interventions. *Springer Science and Business Media, 40,* 141–152. doi: 10.1007/s10879-010-9138-0

Biggs, J. B. (1985). The role of metalearning in study processes. *British Journal of Educational Psychology, 55,* 185–212. doi: 10.1111/j.2044-8279.1985.tb02625.x

Black, M. C., Basile, K. C., Breiding, M. J., Smith, S. G., Walters, M. L., Merrick, M. T., Chen, J., & Stevens, M. R. (2011). *The National Intimate Partner and Sexual Violence Survey (NISVS): 2010 summary report.* Atlanta, GA: National Center for Injury Prevention and Control, Centers for Disease Control and Prevention.

Blakely, T. L., & Mehr, N. (2008). Common ground: The development of a support group for survivors of homicide loss in a rural community. *Social Work with Groups, 31,* 239–254.

Bohnert, A. B., Zivin, K., Welsh, D. E., & Kilbourne, A. M. (2011). Ratings of patient–provider communication among veterans: Serious mental illnesses, substance use disorders, and the moderating role of trust. *Health Communication, 26,* 267–274. doi: 10.1080/10410236.2010.549813

Bongar, B., Berman, A. L., Maris, R. W., Silverman, M. M., Harris, E. A., & Packman, W. L. (1998). *Risk management with suicidal patients.* New York, NY: Guilford.

Borders, L. D. (1991). A systemic approach to peer group supervision. *Journal of Counseling and Development, 69,* 248–252.

Borders, L. D., & Brown, L. L. (2005). *The new handbook of counseling supervision.* New York, NY: Erlbaum.

Borum, R., Cornell, D. G., Modzeleski, W., & Jimerson, S. R. (2010). What can be done about school shootings? A review of the evidence. *Educational Researcher, 39*(1), 27–37.

Bourdieu, P. (1977). *Outline of a theory of practice.* Cambridge, UK: Cambridge University Press.

Bowen, M. (1966). The use of family theory in clinical practice. *Comprehensive Psychiatry, 7,* 345–374.

Bowen, M. (1976). Theory in the practice of psychotherapy. In P. J. Guerin (Ed.), *Family therapy: Theory and practice.* New York, NY: Gardner Press.

Boylan, J. C., & Scott, J. (2009). *Practicum & internship textbook and resource guide for counseling and psychotherapy.* New York, NY: Routledge Taylor & Frances Group.

Bradley, L. J., Hendricks, B., Lock, R., Whiting, P. P., & Parr, G. (2011). E-mail communication: Issues for mental health counselors. *Journal of Mental Health Counseling, 33*(1), 67–79.

Bradley, L. J., Parr, G., & Gould, L. J. (1999). Counseling and psychotherapy: An integrative perspective. In D. Capuzzi & D. R. Gross (Eds.), *Counseling and psychotherapy: Theories and interventions* (pp. 345–379). Upper Saddle River, NJ: Prentice-Hall.

Brassard, M. R., Rivelis, E., & Diaz, V. (2009). School-based counseling of abused children. *Psychology in the Schools, 46,* 206–217.

Bride, B., Radey, M., & Figley, C. (2007). Measuring compassion fatigue. *Clinical Social Work Journal, 35,* 155–163. doi: 10.1007/s10615-007-0091-7

Briere, J. N., & Lanktree, C. B. (2012). *Treating complex trauma in adolescents and young adults.* Thousand Oaks, CA: Sage.

Brooks, D. K., & Weikel, W. J. (1996). Mental health counseling: The first twenty years. In W. J. Weikel & A. J. Palmo (Eds.), *Foundations of mental health counseling* (pp. 5–29). Springfield, IL: Charles C Thomas.

Brown, E. J., Pearlman, M. Y., & Goodman, R. F. (2004). Facing fears and sadness: Cognitive-behavioral therapy for childhood traumatic grief. *Harvard Review of Psychiatry, 12,* 187–198. doi:10.1080/07481180802440209

Brown, G. K., Ten Harve, T., Henriques, G. R., Xie, S. R., Hollander, J. E., & Beck, A. T. (2005). Cognitive therapy for the prevention of suicide attempts: A randomized control trial. *Journal of the American Medical Association, 294,* 563–570.

Brown, R. (2011). Drug court effectiveness: A matched cohort study in the Dane County drug treatment court. *Journal of Offender Rehabilitation, 50,* 191–201. doi: 10.1080/10509674.2011.571347

Brown, R. P., Osterman, L. L., & Barnes, C. D. (2009). School violence and the culture of honor. *Psychological Science, 20,* 1400–1405.

Browne, A. (1993). Violence against women by male partners: Prevalence, outcomes, and policy implications. *American Psychologist, 48,* 1077–1087.

Brunton, L., Chabner, B., & Knollman, B. (2011). *Goodman and Gilman's: The pharmacological basis of therapeutics* (12th ed.). New York, NY: McGraw-Hill.

Bryan, C. J., Stone, S. L., & Rudd, M. D. (2011). A practical, evidence-based approach for means-restriction: Counseling with suicidal patients. *Professional Psychology: Research and Practice, 42,* 339–346.

Burnside, I., & Haight, B. K. (1992). Reminiscence and life review: Analysing each concept. *Journal of Advanced Nursing, 17,* 855–862. doi: 10.1111/1365-2648.ep8530572

California Association for Licensed Professional Clinical Counselors. (2012). *About us.* Retrieved from http://calpcc.org/about-us

Cameron, S., & turtle-song, i. (2002). Learning to write case notes using the SOAP format. *Journal of Counseling & Development, 80,* 286–292.

Campbell, J. C. (2003). Risk factors for femicide in abusive relationships: Results from a multisite case control study. *American Journal of Public Health, 93,* 1089–1097.

Campbell, J. C. (2007). Prediction of homicide of and by battered women. In J. C. Campbell (Ed.), *Assessing dangerous violence by batterers and child abusers* (2nd ed., pp. 85–104). New York, NY: Springer.

Campbell, J. M. (2006). *Essentials of clinical supervision.* Hoboken, NJ: Wiley.

Cannon, W. B. (1929). Organization for physiological homeostasis. *Physiological Review, 9,* 399–431.

Caplan, G. (1963). Types of mental health consultation. *American Journal of Orthopsychiatry, 33,* 470–481.

Carroll, M., & Holloway, E. (1999). *Counseling supervision in context.* Thousand Oaks, CA: Sage.

Cashwell, C. S., & Caruso, M. E. (1997). Adolescent sex offenders: Identification and intervention strategies. *Journal of Mental Health Counseling, 19,* 336–349.

Castellano, C., & Plionis, E. (2006). Comparative analysis of three crisis intervention models applied to law enforcement first responders during 9/11 and Hurricane Katrina. *Brief Treatment and Crisis Intervention, 6,* 326–336.

Cavaiola, A. A., & Colford, J. E. (2006). *A practical guide to crisis intervention.* Boston, MA: Lahaska.

Centers for Disease Control and Prevention (CDC). (2010a). *Child maltreatment prevention.* Retrieved from http://www.cdc.gov/ViolencePrevention/childmaltreatment/index.html

Centers for Disease Control and Prevention (CDC). (2010b). *Child maltreatment: Definitions.* Retrieved from http://www.cdc.gov/ViolencePrevention/childmaltreatment/definitions.html

Centers for Disease Control (CDC). (2010c). *Intimate partner violence: Definitions.* Retrieved from http://www.cdc.gov/violenceprevention/intimatepartnerviolence/definitions.html

Centers for Disease Control and Prevention (CDC). (2010d). Youth risk behavior surveillance—United States, 2009. Surveillance summaries, June 4, 2010. *MMWR 2010; 59* (No. SS-5).

Chaffin, M., & Friedrich, B. (2004). Evidence-based treatments in child abuse and neglect. *Children and Youth Services Review, 26,* 1097–1113.

Chang, C. Y., & Flowers, L. (2009). Supervision and multicultural competence. In J. R. Culbreth & L. L. Brown (Eds.), *State of the art in clinical supervision* (pp. 1–18). New York, NY: Routledge.

Chang, C. Y., Hays, D. G., & Shoffner, M. (2003). Cross-racial supervision: A developmental approach. *The Clinical Supervisor, 22,* 121–138.

Chester, A., & Bretherton, D. (2001). What makes feminist counseling feminist? *Feminism & Psychology, 11,* 527–545.

Cheston, S. E. (2000). A new paradigm for teaching counseling theory and practice. *Counselor Education and Supervision, 39,* 254–269.

Cohen, J. A., Berliner, L., & Mannarino, A. (2010). Trauma focused CBT for children with co-occurring trauma and behavior problems. *Child Abuse & Neglect, 34,* 215–225.

Cohen, J. A., Mannarino, A. P., & Deblinger, E. (2006). *Treating trauma and traumatic grief in children and adolescents.* New York, NY: Guilford Press.

Collins, B. G., & Collins, T. M. (2005). *Crisis and trauma.* Boston, MA: Lahaska.

Collison, B. B., Osborne, J. L., Gray, L. A., House, R. M., Firth, J., & Lou, M. (1998). Preparing counselors for social action. In C. C. Lee & G. Walz (Eds.), *Social action: A mandate for counselors* (pp. 263–277). Alexandria, VA: American Counseling Association.

Cook, K., Juhnke, G. A., Peters, S. W., Marbach, C. R., Day, S., Choucroun, P., & Baker, R. E. (2006). Promoting clinical knowledge, skills, and empathy via a creative self-suicide assignment: Rationale, purpose, and student responses. *Journal of Creativity in Mental Health, 2*(2), 39–46. doi: 10.1300/J456v02_05

Coombs, D., Talbott, L. L., & Harrington, J. (2010). Youth suicides in Alabama: A focus on gun safety. *Alabama State Association for Health, Physical Education, Recreation, and Dance Journal, 31*(1), 31–35.

Corey, G. (2009a). *Theory and practice of counseling and psychotherapy* (8th ed.). Belmont, CA: Brooks/Cole.

Corey, G. (2009b). *Case approach to counseling and psychotherapy.* Pacific Grove, CA: Brooks/Cole.

Corey, G., Corey, M., & Callanan, P. (2011). *Issues and ethics in the helping profession* (7th ed.). Pacific Grove, CA: Brooks/Cole.

Cormier, S., & Hackney, H. (2004). *Counseling strategies and interventions* (6th ed.). Upper Saddle River, NJ: Pearson.

Cottone, R. R., & Tarvydas, V. M. (2007). *Counseling and ethical decision making* (3rd ed.). Upper Saddle River, NJ: Pearson.

Council for Accreditation of Counseling and Related Educational Programs (CACREP). (2009). *2009 CACREP accreditation standards and procedures manual.* Retrieved from http://www.cacrep.org/doc/2009%20Standards%20with%20cover.pdf

Craig, C. D., & Sprang, G. (2010). Compassion satisfaction, compassion fatigue, and burnout in a national sample of trauma treatment therapists. *Anxiety, Stress, & Coping, 23,* 319–339. doi: 10.1080/10615800903085818

Currier, J. M., Holland, J., Coleman, R., & Neimeyer, R. A. (2007). Bereavement following violent death: An assault of life and meaning. In R. Stephenson & G. Cox (Eds.), *Perspectives on violence and violent death.* Amityville, NY: Baywood.

Cutts, L. (2011). Integration in counselling psychology: To what purpose? *Counselling Psychology Review, 26*(2), 38–48.

Daughhetee, C., Puleo, S., & Thrower, E. (2010). Scaffolding of continuing competency as an essential element of professionalism. *Alabama Counseling Association Journal, 36*(1), 15–22.

DeLettre, J. L., & Sobell, L. C. (2010). Keeping psychotherapy notes separate from the patient record. *Clinical Psychology and Psychotherapy, 17,* 160–163. doi: 10.1002/cpp.654

de Shazer, S. (1988). *Clues: Investigating solutions in brief therapy.* New York, NY: Norton.

de Shazer, S. (1991). *Putting difference to work.* New York, NY: Norton.

Diana, D. (2010). *Marketing for the mental health professional: An innovative guide for practitioners.* Hoboken, NJ: Wiley.

Donaldson, D., Spirito, A., & Esposito-Smythers, C. (2005). Treatment for adolescents following a suicide attempt: Results of a pilot trial. *Journal of the American Academy of Child Adolescent Psychiatry, 44,* 113–120.

Dougherty, J. L. (2005). Ethics in case conceptualization and diagnosis: Incorporating a medical model into the developmental counseling tradition. *Counseling and Values, 49,* 132–140. Upper Saddle River, NJ: Pearson.

Douglas, K. S., & Skeem, J. L. (2005). Violence risk assessment: Getting specific about being dynamic. *Psychology, Public Policy, and Law, 11*, 347–383.

D'Zurilla, T. J., Chang, E. C., Nottingham, E. J., & Faccini, L. (1998). Social problem solving deficits and hopelessness, depression, and suicide risk in college students and psychiatric inpatients. *Journal of Clinical Psychology, 54*, 1091–1107.

Eaves, S. H., & Erford, B. T. (2014). Becoming a professional counselor. In B. T. Erford (Ed.), *Orientation to the counseling profession: Advocacy, ethics, and essential professional foundations* (2nd ed., pp. 1–25). Columbus, OH: Pearson.

Edwards, G. S. (2010). *Database of state Tarasoff laws*. Retrieved from http://ssrn.com/abstract=1551505 or http://dx.doi.org/10.2139/ssrn.1551505

Edwards, G. S. (2013). Tarasoff, duty to warn laws, and suicide. *International Journal of Law and Economics, 34*, 1–8.

Egan, G. (2010). *The skilled helper: A problem-management and opportunity-development approach to helping* (9th ed.). Pacific Grove, CA: Brooks/Cole.

Eisel v. Board of Education, 597 A.2d 447 (Md. Ct. App. 1991).

Eke, A. W., Hilton, N. Z., Harris, G. T., Rice, M. E., & Houghton, R. E. (2011). Intimate partner homicide: Risk assessment and prospectus for prediction. *Journal of Family Violence, 26*, 211–216.

Elman, N. S., Illfelder-Kaye, J., & Robiner, W. N. (2005). Professional development: Training for professionalism as a foundation for competent practice in psychology. *Professional Psychology: Research and Practice, 36*, 367–375.

Enarson, E., Fothergill, A., & Peek, L. (2006). Gender and disaster: Foundations and possibilities. In H. Rodriguez, E. Quarantelli, & R. Dynes (Eds.), *Handbook of disaster research* (pp. 130–146). New York, NY: Springer.

Erford, B. T. (2013). *Assessment for counselors* (2nd ed.). Boston, MA: Cengage.

Erford, B. T. (2014a). *Orientation to the counseling profession* (2nd ed.). Columbus, OH: Pearson Merrill.

Erford, B. T. (2014b). *Research and evaluation in counseling* (2nd ed.). Boston, MA: Cengage.

Erford, B. T., Eaves, S., Bryant, E., & Young, K. (2010). *35 techniques every counselor should know*. Columbus, OH: Pearson Merrill.

Eriksen, K. (1997). *Making an impact: A handbook on counselor advocacy*. Minneapolis, MN: Accelerated Development.

Erikson, E. H. (1963). *Childhood and society* (2nd ed.). New York, NY: Norton.

Everly, G. S., Phillips, S. B., Kane, D., & Feldman, D. (2006). Introduction to and overview of group psychological first aid. *Brief Treatment & Crisis Intervention, 6*, 130–136.

Farberow, N. L. (2005). The mental health professional as suicide survivor. *Clinical Neuropsychiatry, 2*(1), 13–20.

Farington, D. P., & Lober, R. (2011). *Young homicide offenders and victims: Risk factors, prediction, and prevention from childhood*. New York, NY: Springer.

Ferguson, C. J., & Kilburn, J. (2009). The public health risks of media violence: A meta-analytic review. *Journal of Pediatrics, 154*, 759–763.

Figley, C. R. (2002). Compassion fatigue: Psychotherapists' chronic lack of self-care. *Journal of Clinical Psychology, 58*(11), 1433–1441.

Flynn, S., Abel, K., While, D., Mehta, H., & Shaw, J. (2011). Mental illness, gender and homicide: A population-based descriptive study. *Psychiatry Research, 185*, 368–375.

Foa, E. B., Keane, T. M., & Friedman, M. J. (Eds.). (2009). *Effective treatments for PTSD: Practice guidelines from the International Society for Traumatic Stress Studies*. New York, NY: Guilford.

Folstein, M. F., Folstein, S. E., & McHugh, P. R. (1975). "Mini-mental state": A practical method for grading the cognitive state of patients for the clinician. *Journal of Psychiatric Research, 12*, 189–198.

Foos, J. A., Otten, A. J., & Hill, L. K. (1991). Managed mental health: A primer for counselors. *Journal of Counseling & Development, 69*, 332–336. doi: 10.1002/j.1556-676.1991.tb01516.x

Forester-Miller, H., & Davis, T. (1996). *A practitioner's guide to ethical decision making*. Alexandria, VA: American Counseling Association.

Foster, K., O'Brien, L., & Korhonen, T. (2012). Developing resilient children and families when parents have mental illness: A family-focused approach. *International Journal of Mental Health Nursing, 21*(1), 3–11.

Foster, S., & Tyler, V. E. (2007). *Tyler's honest herbal: A sensible guide to the use of herbs and related remedies* (4th ed.). New York, NY: Routledge.

Frankl, V. (1963). *Man's search for meaning*. Boston, MA: Beacon.

Gabbard, G., & Kay, J. (2001). The fate of integrated treatment: Whatever happened to the biopsychosocial psychiatrist? *The American Journal of Psychiatry, 158*(12), 1956–1963.

Gallon, S. (2002). *Clinical supervision training manual*. Portland, OR: Northwest Frontier ATTC.

Gamino, L. A., & Ritter, R. H. (2009). *Ethical practice in grief counseling*. New York, NY: Springer.

Gazzola, N., Smith, J. D., King-Andrews, H. L., & Kearney, M. K. (2010). Professional characteristics of Canadian counselors: Results of a national survey. *Canadian Journal of Counselling and Psychotherapy, 44*, 83–99.

Geroski, A., Gray, J. M., & Adler, J. A. (2012). Interviewing women bereaved by homicide: Assessing the impact of trauma-focused research. *Psychology, Crime, & Law, 18*, 177–189.

Gendreau, P., Goggin, C., French, S., & Smith, P. (2006). Practicing psychology in correctional settings. In I. B. Weiner & A. K. Hess (Eds.), *The handbook of forensic psychology* (3rd ed., pp. 722–750). Hoboken, NJ: Wiley.

Giedd, J. (2002). *The adolescent brain—why teenagers think and act differently*. Retrieved from http://www.edinformatics.com/news/teenage_brains.htm

Gilbert, L. A., & Scher, M. (1999). *Gender and sex in counseling and psychotherapy*. Needham Heights, MA: Allyn & Bacon.

Gillam, S. L., & Baltimore, M. L. (2010). Triadic supervision. In J. R. Culbreth & L. L. Brown (Eds.), *State of the art in clinical supervision* (pp. 45–62). New York, NY: Routledge.

Gladding, S. T. (2006). *The counseling dictionary: Concise definitions of frequently used terms* (2nd ed.). Upper Saddle River, NJ: Pearson.

Gladding, S. T. (2011). *Family therapy: History, theory, and practice* (5th ed.). Boston, MA: Pearson.

Gladding, S. T. (2012). *Counseling: A comprehensive profession* (7th ed.). Upper Saddle River, NJ: Pearson Merrill Prentice Hall.

Gladding, S. T., & Newsome, D. W. (2010). *Clinical mental health counseling in community and agency settings* (3rd ed.). Upper Saddle River, NJ: Pearson.

Glasser, W. (2000). *Counseling with choice theory*. New York, NY: HarperCollins.

Goetz, A. T., Shackelford, T. K., Romero, G. A., Kaighobadi, F., & Miner, E. J. (2008). Punishment, proprietaries and paternity: Men's violence against women from an evolutionary perspective. *Aggression and Violent Behavior, 13*, 481–489.

Golding, J. (1999). Intimate partner violence as a risk factor for mental disorders: A meta-analysis. *Journal of Family Violence, 14*, 99–132.

Goldstein, D. S., & Kopin, I. J. (2007). Evolution of concepts of stress. *Stress, 10*, 109–120. doi: 10.1080/10253890701288935

Gottlieb, M. C., & Cooper, C. C. (2000). The future of mental health care delivery: Ideals and realities. *The Counseling Psychologist, 28*, 263–266. doi: 10.1177/0011000000282005

Granello, D. H. (2010). The process of suicide risk assessment: Twelve core principles. *Journal of Counseling & Development, 88*, 363–370.

Granello, D. H., & Granello, P. F. (2007). *Suicide: An essential guide for helping professionals and educators*. Boston, MA: Pearson.

Greason, P. B., & Cashwell, C. S. (2009). Mindfulness and counseling self-efficacy: The mediating role of attention and empathy. *Counselor Education & Supervision, 49*, 2–19.

Grossman, L. R., & Koocher, G. P. (2012). Privacy, confidentiality and privilege of health records and psychotherapy notes in custody cases. *American Journal of Family Law, 24*(1), 41–50.

Guillot-Miller, L., & Partin, P. W. (2003). Web-based resources for legal and ethical issues in school counseling. *Professional School Counseling, 7*, 52–60.

Gutheil, T., & Hilliard, J. (2001). Don't write me down: Legal, clinical, and risk-management aspects of patients' requests that therapists not keep notes or records. *American Journal of Psychotherapy, 55*, 157–165.

Gutin, N. J., & McGann, V. (2010). *Clinicians and suicide loss*. Retrieved from http://app.e2ma.net/app2/campaigns/archived/25465/11e2327ff56588fb1303b45d2c2f3e9b/

Hackney, H. L., & Cormier, S. (2013). *The professional counselor: A process guide to helping* (7th ed.). Upper Saddle River, NJ: Pearson.

Halbur, D. A., & Halbur, K. V. (2011). *Developing your theoretical orientation in counseling and psychotherapy* (2nd ed.). Upper Saddle River, NJ: Pearson.

Hall, L. K. (2008). *Counseling military families: What mental health professionals need to know*. New York, NY: Routledge.

Hamblin, J., & Barnett, E. (2009). *PTSD in children and adolescents*. Retrieved from http://www.ptsd.va.gov/professional/pages/ptsd_in_children_and_adolescents_overview_for_professionals.asp

Hanifan, L. J. (1916). The rural school community center. *Annals of the American Academy of Political and Social Science, 67*, 130–138.

Hansen, J. C., Stevic, R. R., & Warner, R. W. (1986). *Counseling: Theory and process* (4th ed.). Boston, MA: Allyn & Bacon.

Hansen, J. T. (2006a). Counseling theories within a postmodern epistemology: New roles for theories in counseling practice. *Journal of Counseling & Development, 84*, 291–297.

Hansen, J. T. (2006b). Humanism as moral imperative: Comments on the role of knowing in the helping encounter. *Journal of Humanistic Counseling, Education, and Development, 45*, 115–125.

Hard, P. F., & Reynolds, G. (2011, March). *In the eye of recovery: Disaster interventions and considerations with sexual minorities*. Presented at the American Counseling Association annual conference, New Orleans, LA.

Hard, P. F., Talbott-Forbes, L. L., & Bartlett, M. L. (2014). Ethical and legal considerations in crisis counseling. In L. R. Jackson-Cherry & B. T. Erford (Eds.), *Crisis prevention, assessment, and intervention* (2nd ed.). Columbus, OH: Pearson Merrill.

Harrington, J. A., & Daughhetee, C. (2014). Risk assessment and intervention: Suicide and homicide. In L. R. Jackson-Cherry & B. T. Erford (Eds.), *Crisis prevention, assessment, and intervention* (2nd ed., pp. 103–132). Columbus, OH: Pearson Merrill.

Harris, E. A. (1995). The importance of risk management in a managed care environment. In M. B. Sussman (Ed.), *A perilous calling: The hazards of psychotherapy practice* (pp. 247–258). New York, NY: Wiley.

Harris, S. M., Brown, A., Dakin, J. B., Lucas, B., Riley, L., & Bulham, R. (2009). Are clinical records really that important? The dearth of research and practice guidelines in MFT literature. *The American Journal of Family Therapy, 37*, 373–387. doi: 10.1080/01926180902754729

Hawton, K., Townsend E., & Deeks J. (2001). Effects of legislation restricting pack sizes of paracetamol and salicylate on self-poisoning in the United Kingdom: Before and after study. *British Medical Journal (BMJ), 322*, 1203–1209.

Haynes, R., Corey, G., & Moulton, P. (2003). *Clinical supervision in the helping professions: A practical guide*. Pacific Grove, CA: Brooks/Cole–Thomson Learning.

Hays, D. G., & Chang, C. Y. (2010). Termination. In B. T. Erford (Ed.), *Group work: Processes and applications* (pp. 146–170). Columbus, OH: Pearson Merrill.

Hays, D. G., & Erford, B. T. (Eds.). (2014). *Developing multicultural counseling competence: A systems approach* (2nd ed.). Upper Saddle River, NJ: Pearson.

Heath, N. L., Toste, J. R., Nedecheva, T., & Charlebois, A. (2008). An examination of non-suicidal self-injury in college students. *Journal of Mental Health Counseling, 30*, 137–156.

Heller, R. J., Gilliam, L. S., Chenail, R. J., & Hall, T. L. (2010). Three authors, one client: A qualitative description of marriage and family therapy initial case documentation. *Contemporary Family Therapy, 32*, 363–375. doi: 10.1007/s10591-1-010-9130-6

Helms, J. E. (1995). An update of white and people of color racial identity model. In J. G. Ponterotto, J. M. Casa, L. A. Suzuki, & C. M. Alexander (Eds.), *Handbook of multicultural counseling* (pp. 191–198). Thousand Oaks, CA: Sage.

Hendricks, B., Bradley, L. J., Southern, S., Oliver, M., & Birdsall, B. (2011). Ethical code for the International Association of Marriage and Family Counselors. *The Family Journal, 19*, 217–224. doi: 10.1177/1066480711400814

Henriques, G. R., Beck, A. T., & Brown, G. K. (2003). Cognitive therapy for adolescent and young adult suicide attempters. *American Behavioral Scientist, 46*, 1258–1268.

Herbert, P. B., & Young, K. A. (2002). Tarasoff at twenty-five. *Journal of the American Academy of Psychiatry and the Law, 30*, 275–281.

Herlihy, B., & Corey, G. (2006). *ACA ethical standards casebook* (6th ed.). Alexandria, VA: American Counseling Association.

Herman, J. (1997). *Trauma and recovery: The aftermath of violence—from domestic abuse to political terror*. New York, NY: Basic Books.

Herrenkohl, T. I., Sousa, C., Tajima, E. A., Herrenkohl, R. C., & Moylan, C. A. (2008). Intersection of child abuse and children's exposure to domestic violence. *Trauma, Violence, & Abuse, 9*, 84–99.

Hertz, M. F., Prothrow-Stith, D., & Chery, C. (2005). Homicide survivors: Research and practice implications. *American Journal of Preventive Medicine, 29,* 288–295.

Hilt, L. M., Nock, M. K., Lloyd-Richardson, E. E., & Prinstein, M. J. (2008). Longitudinal study of nonsuicidal self-injury among young adolescents. *The Journal of Early Adolescence, 28,* 455–469.

Hodge, D. R. (2011). Using spiritual interventions in practice: Developing some guidelines from evidence-based practice. *Social Work, 56,* 149–158.

Hodges, S. (2011). *The counseling practicum and internship manual: A resource for graduate counseling students.* New York, NY: Springer.

Hodges, S., & Connelly, A. R. (2010). *A job search manual for counselors and counselor educators: How to navigate and promote your counseling career.* Alexandria, VA: American Counseling Association.

Hoffman, R. M. (2001). The measurement of masculinity and femininity: Historical perspectives and implications for counseling. *Journal of Counseling and Development, 79,* 472–485.

Hogan-Garcia, M. (2003). *The four skills of cultural diversity competence: A process for understanding and practice* (2nd ed.). Pacific Grove, CA: Brooks/Cole.

Hoge, C. W., Auchterlonie, J. L., & Milliken, C. S. (2006). Mental health problems, use of mental health services, and attrition from military service after returning from deployment to Iraq or Afghanistan. *The Journal of the American Medical Association, 295,* 1023–1032.

Hoge, C. W., Castro, C., Messer, S. C., McGurk, D., Cotting, D. I., & Koffman, R. L. (2004). Combat duty in Iraq and Afghanistan, mental health problems, and barriers to care. *The New England Journal of Medicine, 351*(1), 13–22.

Holloway, E. L. (1995). *Clinical supervision: A systems approach.* Thousand Oaks, CA: Sage Publications.

Hopkins, B. R., & Anderson, B. S. (1990). *The counselor and the law* (3rd ed.). Alexandria, VA: American Counseling Association.

Houppert, K. (2005). *Home fires burning: Married to the military—for better or worse.* New York, NY: Ballantine.

House, R. M., & Sears, S. J. (2002). Preparing school counselors as leaders and advocates: A critical need in the new millennium. *Theory into Practice, 41,* 154–162.

Hunter, E. G. (2007). Beyond death: Inheriting the past and giving to the future, transmitting the legacy of one's self. *Omega: Journal of Death & Dying, 56,* 313–329. doi: 10.2190/OM.56.4.a

Hutchinson, D. (2007). *The essential counselor: Process, skills and techniques.* Boston, MA: Houghton Mifflin.

Individuals with Disabilities Education Improvement Act. (2004). *IDEA 2004 Resources.* Retrieved from http://www.ed.gov/policy/speced/guid/idea/idea2004.html

Ingram, B. L. (2012). *Clinical case formulations: Matching the integrative treatment plan to the client* (2nd ed.). Hoboken, NJ: Wiley.

Ivey, A. E., Ivey, M. B., & Zalaquett, C. P. (2010). *Intentional interviewing and counseling: Facilitating client development in a multicultural society* (7th ed.). Belmont, CA: Brooks/Cole.

Jackson, N. (2004). Developing the concept of metalearning. *Innovations in Education and Teaching International, 41,* 391–403. doi: 10.1080/1470329042000276995

Jackson-Cherry, L. R. (2014). Death notification. In L. R. Jackson-Cherry & B. T. Erford (Eds.), *Crisis prevention, assessment, and intervention* (2nd ed., pp. 235–245). Columbus, OH: Pearson Merrill.

Jennings, L., & Skovholt, T. M. (1999). The cognitive, emotional, and relational characteristics of master therapists. *Journal of Counseling Psychology, 46,* 3–11. doi: 10.1037/0022-0167.46.1.3

Jennings, L., & Skovholt, T. M. (2004). The cognitive, emotional, and relational characteristics of master therapists. In T. M. Skovholt & L. Jennings (Eds.), *Master therapists: Exploring expertise in therapy and counseling.* Upper Saddle River, NJ: Pearson.

Jist Publishing. (2012). *Dictionary of Holland occupational codes: Overview.* Retrieved from http://jist.emcpublishingllc.com/occupational-data/dictionary-of-holland-occupational-codes.html

Jobes, D. A. (2006). *Managing suicidal risk: A collaborative approach.* New York, NY: Guilford Press.

Johnson, D., & Zlotnick, C. (2009). Hope for battered women with PTSD in domestic violence shelters. *Professional Psychology: Research and Practice, 40,* 234–241.

Joiner, T. (2005). *Why people die by suicide.* Cambridge, MA: Harvard University Press.

Joiner, T. E., Van Orden, K. A., Witte, T. K., & Rudd, M. D. (2009). *The interpersonal theory of suicide: Guidance for working with suicidal clients.* Washington, DC: American Psychological Association.

Joiner, T. E., Walker, R. L., Rudd, M. D., & Jobes, D. A. (1999). Scientizing and routinizing the assessment of suicidality in outpatient practice. *Professional Psychology: Research and Practice, 30,* 447–453.

Jones, E. (2003). Remininscence therapy for older women with depression: Effects of nursing intervention classification in assisted-living long-term care. *Journal of Gerontological Nursing, 29*(7), 26–33.

Jones-Smith, E. (2012). *Theories of counseling and psychotherapy: An integrative approach.* Los Angeles, CA: Sage.

Jongsma, A. E., Peterson, L. M., & Bruce, T. J. (2006). *The complete adult psychotherapy treatment planner* (4th ed.). Hoboken, NJ: Wiley.

Jordan J. R., & Harpel, J. L. (2007). *Facilitating suicide bereavement support groups: A self-study manual.* New York, NY: American Foundation for Suicide Prevention.

Jordan, J. R., & McIntosh, J. L. (2011). *Grief after suicide: Understanding the consequences and caring for the survivors.* New York, NY: Routledge.

Juhnke, G. A. (1994). Teaching suicide risk assessment to counselor education students. *Counselor Education and Supervision, 34,* 52–57.

Juhnke, G. A., & Granello, P. F. (2005). Shattered dreams of professional competence: The impact of client suicides on mental health practitioners and how to prepare for it. *Journal of Creativity in Mental Health, 2,* 205–223.

Jumper, C., Evers, S., Cole, D., Raezer, J. W., Edgar, K., Joyner, M., & Pike, H., (2006). *Report on the cycles of deployment: An analysis of survey responses from April through September 2005.* Alexandria, VA: National Military Family Association.

Jun, H. (2010). *Social justice, multicultural counseling, and practice: Beyond a conventional approach.* Thousand Oaks, CA: Sage.

Kaighobadi, F., & Shackelford, T. K. (2009). Suspicions of female infidelity predict men's partner-directed violence. *Behavioral and Brain Sciences, 32,* 281–282.

Kaminsky, M., McCabe, O. L, Langlieb, A. M., & Everly, G. S. (2006). An evidence-informed model of human resistance, resilience, and recovery. The Johns Hopkins' outcome-driven paradigm for disaster mental health services. *Brief Treatment and Crisis Intervention, 7,* 1–11.

Kantor, G. K., & Jasinski J. L. (1998). Dynamics and risk factors in partner violence. In J. L. Jasinski & L. M. Williams (Eds.), *Partner violence: A comprehensive review of 20 years of research* (pp. 1–43). Thousand Oaks, CA: Sage.

Kaplan, D. M., & Gladding, S. T. (2011). A vision for the future of counseling: The 20/20 principles for unifying and strengthening the profession. *Journal of Counseling & Development, 89,* 367–372. doi: 10.1002/j.1556-6678.2011.tb00101.x

Kelly, G. A. (1963). *A theory of personality.* New York, NY: Norton.

Kennedy, A. (2004). Emotional cycle of deployment: Information for civilian counselors about the military family. *Counseling Today, 47,* 12, 45.

Kerr, M., & Bowen, M. (1988). *Family evaluation.* New York, NY: Norton.

Kettenbach, G. (1990). *Writing S.O.A.P. notes.* Philadelphia, PA: F. A. Davis.

Keys, S. G., Bemak, F., Carpenter, S. L., & King-Sears, M. E. (1998). Collaborative consultant: A new role for counselors serving at-risk youth. *Journal of Counseling and Development, 76,* 123–133.

King, J. H., & Anderson, S. M. (2004). Therapeutic implications of pharmacotherapy: Current trends and ethical issues. *Journal of Counseling & Development, 82,* 329–336.

Kiracofe, N. M., & Wells, L. (2007). Mandated disciplinary counseling on campus: Problems and possibilities. *Journal of Counseling and Development, 85,* 259–268.

Kiselica, M. S., & Robinson, M. (2001). Bringing advocacy counseling to life: The history, issues, and human dramas of social justice work in counseling. *Journal of Counseling & Development, 79,* 387–397. doi: 10.1002/j.1556-6676.2001.tb01985.x

Kleespies, P. M., & Richmond, J. S. (2009). Evaluating behavioral emergencies: The clinical interview. In P. M. Kleespies (Ed.), *Behavioral emergencies: An evidence-based resource for evaluating and managing risk of suicide, violence, and victimization* (pp. 33–55). Washington, DC: American Psychological Association.

Klonsky, E. D. (2007). The functions of deliberate self-injury: A review of the evidence. *Clinical Psychiatric Review, 27,* 226–239. doi: 10.1016/j.cpr.2006.08.002

Klonsky, E. D., & Muehlenkamp J. J. (2007). Self-injury: A research review for the practitioner. *Journal of Clinical Psychology, 63,* 1045–1056.

Klott, J., & Jongsma, A. E., Jr. (2004). *The suicide and homicide risk assessment & treatment planner.* New York, NY: Wiley.

Koocher, G. P., & Keith-Spiegel, P. (2008). *Ethics in psychology and the mental health professions: Standards and cases* (3rd ed.). New York, NY: Oxford University Press.

Koocher, G. P., Norcross, J. C., & Hill, S. S., III (2005). *Psychologists' desk reference* (2nd ed.). New York, NY: Oxford University Press.

Kottler, J. A. (2000). *Nuts & bolts of helping.* Needham Heights, MA: Allyn & Bacon.

Kottler, J. A., & Brown, R. W. (2000). *Introduction to therapeutic counseling: Voices from the field* (4th ed.). Belmont, CA: Wadsworth/Thomson Learning.

Kozol, J. (2005, September). Still separate, still unequal: America's educational apartheid. *Harper's Magazine, 311*(1864), 41–54.

Kress, V. E. (2003). Self-injurious behaviors: Assessment and diagnosis. *Journal of Counseling & Development, 81,* 490–496.

Kress, V. E., Adamson, N. A., Paylo, M., DeMarco, C., & Bradley, N. (in press). Counseling children living in violent environments: Counselors' role in promoting safety. *Journal of Mental Health Counseling.*

Kress, V., Drouhard, N., & Costin, A. (2010). Students who self-injure: School counselor ethical and legal considerations. In M. A. Hermann, T. P. Remley, Jr., & W. C. Huey (Eds.), *Ethical and legal issues in school counseling* (3rd ed., pp. 158–170). Alexandria, VA: American School Counselor Association.

Kress, V. E., & Hoffman, R. (2008). Empowering adolescent sexual abuse survivors: Application of a solution-focused, Ericksonian counseling group. *Journal of Humanistic Counseling, Education, and Development, 47,* 172–186.

Kress, V. E., Hoffman, R. M., & Eriksen, K. (2010). Ethical dimensions of diagnosing: Considerations for clinical mental health counselors. *Counseling & Values, 55,* 101–112.

Kress, V. E., Protivnak, J. J., & Sadlak, L. (2008).Counseling clients involved with violent intimate partners: Mental health counselors' role in promoting client safety. *Journal of Mental Health Counseling, 30,* 200–210.

Krumboltz, J. D., Kinnier, R. T., Rude, S. S., Scherba, D. S., & Hamel, D. A. (1986). Teaching a rational approach to career decision making: Who benefits most? *Journal of Vocational Behaviour, 29,* 1–6.

Krumboltz, J. D., & Levin, A. S. (2004). *Luck is no accident: Making the most of happenstance in your life and career.* Atascadero, CA: Impact Publishers.

Kubany, E. S., Hill, E. E., Owens, J. A., Iannce-Spencer, C., McCaig, M. A., Tremayne, K. J., & Williams, P. (2004). Cognitive trauma therapy for battered women with PTSD (CTT-BW). *Journal of Consulting and Clinical Psychology, 72,* 3–18.

Kübler-Ross, E. (1969). *On death and dying.* New York, NY: Touchstone.

Kurpius, D. J., & Rozecki, T. (1992). Outreach, advocacy, and consultation: A framework for prevention and intervention. *Elementary School Guidance & Counseling, 26,* 176–189.

Lassiter, P. S., Napolitano, L., Culbreth, J. R., & Ng, K. (2008). Developing multicultural competence using the structured peer group supervision model. *Counselor Education and Supervision, 47,* 164–178. doi: 10.1002/j.1556-6978.2008.tb00047.x

Laux, J. M. (2002). A primer on suicidology: Implications for counselors. *Journal of Counseling & Development, 80,* 380–384.

Lawson, D. M. (2003). Incidence, explanations, and treatment of partner violence. *Journal of Counseling & Development, 81,* 19–32.

Lawson, G., & Venart, B. (2005). Preventing counselor impairment: Vulnerability, wellness, and resilience. In G. R. Walz, & R. K. Yep (Eds.), *VISTAS: Compelling perspectives on counseling 2005* (pp. 243–246). Alexandria, VA: American Counseling Association.

Lazarus, A. A., & Beutler, L. E. (1993). On technical eclecticism. *Journal of Counseling & Development, 71,* 381–385.

Lazarus, R. S. (1966). *Psychological stress and the coping process.* New York, NY: Springer.

Lazarus, R. (1999). *Stress and emotion: A new synthesis.* New York, NY: Springer.

Lazarus, R. S., & Folkman, S. (1984). *Stress, appraisal and coping.* New York, NY: Spring.

Lee, C. C., & Rodgers, R. A. (2009). Counselor advocacy: Affecting systemic change in the public arena. *Journal of Counseling & Development, 87,* 284–287.

Lee, J. B., & Bartlett, M. L. (2005). Suicide prevention: Critical elements for managing suicidal clients and counselor liability without the use of a no-suicide contract. *Death Studies, 29,* 1–19.

Lewis, J., & Bradley, L. (Eds.). (2000). *Advocacy in counseling: Counselors, clients, & community.* Greensboro, NC: ERIC Counseling and Student Services Clearinghouse.

Liddle, J. R., Shackelford, T. K., & Weekes-Shackelford, V. A. (2012). Why can't we all just get along? Evolutionary perspectives on violence, homicide, and war. *Review of General Psychology, 16*(1), 24–36.

Linehan, M. (1991). *Cognitive-behavioral treatment of borderline personality disorder.* New York, NY: Guilford.

Linehan, M. M. (1993). *Skills training manual for treating borderline personality disorder.* New York, NY: Guilford.

Linehan, M. M., Comtois, K. A., Murray, A. M., Brown, M. Z., Gallop, R. J., Heard, H. L…Lindenboim, N. (2006). Two year randomized controlled trial and follow-up of dialectical behavior therapy vs. therapy by experts for suicidal behaviors and borderline personality disorder. *Archives of General Psychiatry, 63,* 757–766.

Loganbill, C., Hardy, E., & Delworth, W. (1982). Supervision: A conceptual model. *The Counseling Psychologist, 10,* 3–42.

MacCluskie, K. C., & Ingersoll, R. E. (2001). *Becoming a 21st century counselor: Personal and professional explorations.* Stamford, CT: Thomas Learning.

Magen, R. H., & Magen, J. G. (2010). Revisiting Aunt Fanny: Evaluating professional writing. *Social Work Education, 29,* 792–809. doi: 10.1080/026215471003599327

Manhal-Baugus, M. (2001). E-Therapy: Practical, ethical, and legal issues. *Cyberpsychology & Behavior, 4,* 551–563. doi: 10.1089/109493101753235142

Marotta, S. A., & Watts, R. E. (2007). An introduction to the best practices section in the *Journal of Counseling & Development. Journal of Counseling & Development, 85,* 491–503.

Maruish, M. E. (2002). *Essentials of treatment planning.* Hoboken, NJ: Wiley.

May, R. (1977). *The meaning of anxiety* (Rev. ed.). New York, NY: Norton.

McAdams, C. R., & Foster, V. A. (2000). Client suicide: Its frequency and impact on counselors. *Journal of Mental Health Counseling, 22,* 107–121.

McAdams, C. R., & Keener, H. J. (2008). Preparation, action, recovery: A conceptual framework for counselor preparation and response in client crises. *Journal of Counseling & Development, 86,* 388–398.

McAuliffe, G. J. (1993). Constructive development and career transition: Implications for counseling. *Journal of Counseling & Development, 72,* 23–28.

McCann, L., & Pearlman, L. A. (1990). Vicarious traumatization: A framework for understanding the psychological effects of working with victims. *Journal of Traumatic Stress, 3*(1), 131–149.

McCarthy, J. (2005). Individualism and collectivism: What do they have to do with counseling? *Journal of Multicultural Counseling and Development, 33,* 108–117.

McGlothlin, J. (2014). Emergency preparedness and response. In L. R. Jackson-Cherry & B. T. Erford (Eds.), *Crisis intervention and prevention* (2nd ed., pp. 211–237). Upper Saddle River, NJ: Pearson.

McGowan, J., Gardner, D., & Fletcher, R. (2007). Positive and negative affective outcomes of occupational stress. *New Zealand Journal of Psychology, 35*(2), 92–98.

McLeavey, B. C., Daly, R. J., Ludgate, J. W., & Murray, C. M. (1994). Interpersonal problem-solving skills training in the treatment of self-poisoning patients. *Suicide and Life-Threatening Behavior, 24,* 382–394.

McLeod, A. L. (2008). A phenomenological investigation of supervisors' and supervisees' experiences with attention to cultural issues in multicultural supervision. Unpublished doctoral dissertation. Georgia State University.

McMahon, M. (2005). Career counseling: Applying the system theory framework of career development. *Journal of Employment Counseling, 42*(1), 29–38.

McNeece, C. A., & Thyer, B. A. (2004). Evidence-based practice and social work. *Journal of Evidence-Based Social Work, 1*(1), 7–25.

McNiel, D. E., Chamberlain, J. R., Weaver, C. M., Hall, S. E., Fordwood, S. R., & Binder, R. L. (2008). Impact of clinical training on violence risk assessment. *American Journal of Psychiatry, 165,* 195–200.

McWhirter, B. T., & Ishikawa, M. I. (2005). Individual counseling: Traditional approaches. In D. Capuzzi & D. R. Gross (Eds.), *Introduction to the counseling profession* (4th ed., pp. 155–172). Upper Saddle River, NJ: Prentice-Hall.

Medicaid. (2011). *Mental health services.* Retrieved from http://www.medicaid.gov/Medicaid-CHIP-Program-Information/By-Topics/Benefits/Mental-Health-Services-.html

Medical University of South Carolina. (2005). *TF-CBTWeb: A web-based learning course for trauma-focused cognitive-behavioral therapy.* Retrieved from http://tfcbt.musc.edu/

Meichenbaum, D. (1995). Cognitive-behavioral therapy in historical perspective. In B. M. Bongar & L. E. Beutler (Eds.), *Comprehensive textbook of psychotherapy: Theory and practice* (pp. 140–158). London, UK: Oxford University Press.

Melby, T. (2004). Duty to warn: A question of loyalty varies by state. *Contemporary Sexuality, 38*(1), 3–6.

Meloy, J. R., Hoffmann, J., Guldimann, A., & James, D. (2011). The role of warning behaviors in threat assessment: An exploration and suggested typology. *Behavioral Sciences and the Law, 30,* 256–279. doi: 10.1002/bsl.999

Miller, W. R., & Rollnick, S. (2002). *Motivational interviewing: Preparing people for change* (2nd ed.). New York, NY: Guilford.

Mills, G. (2012). Destroying client records. *Therapy Today, 21*(6), 30–32.

Milne, A. (1999). *Counseling.* Chicago, IL: McGraw-Hill.

Milsom, A. (2014). Advocating for the counseling profession. In B. T. Erford (Ed.), *Orientation to the counseling profession: Advocacy, ethics, and essential professional foundations* (2nd ed., pp. 321–339). Upper Saddle River, NJ: Pearson.

Mitchell, L. K., & Krumboltz, J. D. (1996). Krumboltz's learning theory of career choice and counseling. In D. Brown, L. Brooks, & Associates (Eds.), *Career choice and development* (3rd ed.). San Francisco, CA: Jossey-Bass.

Mize, K. D., Shackelford, T. K., & Shackelford, V. A. (2009). Hands-on killing of intimate partners as a function of sex and relationship status/state. *Journal of Family Violence, 24,* 463–470.

Monk, G., Winslade, J., Crocket, K., & Epston, D. (1997). *Narrative therapy in practice.* San Francisco, CA: Jossey-Bass.

Moore-Thomas, C. (2014). Cultural identity development. In D. G. Hays & B. T. Erford (Eds.), *Developing multicultural* counseling competence: A systems approach (2nd ed., pp. 32–54). Upper Saddle River, NJ: Pearson.

Morgan, M. M., & Sprenkle, D. H. (2007). Toward a common factors approach to supervision. *Journal of Marital and Family Therapy, 33*, 1–17.

Moritsugu, J., Wong, F. Y., & Duffy, K. G. (2010). *Community psychology* (4th ed.). Boston, MA: Allyn & Bacon.

Moster, A., Wnuk, D. W., & Jeglic, E. L. (2008). Cognitive behavioral therapy with sex offenders. *Journal of Correctional Health Care, 14*, 109–121.

Muehlenkamp, J. J. (2006). Empirically supported treatments and general therapy guidelines for non-suicidal self-injury. *Journal of Mental Health Counseling, 28*, 166–185.

Myer, R. A., & Moore, H. B. (2006). Crisis in context theory: An ecological model. *Journal of Counseling & Development, 84*, 139–147.

Myers, J. E., & Degges-White, S. (2007). Aging well in an upscale retirement community: The relationships among perceived stress, mattering, and wellness. *Adultspan: Theory Research & Practice, 6*, 96–110.

Myers, J. E., & Sweeney, T. J. (2008). Wellness counseling: The evidence base for practice. *Journal of Counseling & Development, 86*, 482–493.

Myers, J. E., Sweeney, T. J., & White, V. E. (2002). Advocacy for counselors: A professional imperative. *Journal of Counseling & Development, 80*, 394–402.

Napier, A. Y., & Whitaker, C. (1978). *The family crucible*. New York, NY: Harper & Row.

National Academic Advising Association. (2006). *NACADA concept of academic advising*. Retrieved from http://www.nacada.ksu.edu/Resources/Clearinghouse/View-Articles/Concept-of-Academic-Advising-a598.aspx

National Board for Certified Counselors & Affiliates, Inc. (2012). *Content areas for the NCE*. Retrieved from http://www.nbcc.org/NCE/Topics

National Institute of Mental Health (NIMH). (2002). *Mental health and mass violence: A workshop to reach consensus on best practices*. NIH Publication No. 01-5138. Washington, DC: U.S. Government Printing Office.

Neimeyer, R. A., & Burke, L. A. (2011). Complicated grief in the aftermath of homicide: Spiritual crisis and distress in an African American Sample. *Religions, 2*, 145–164.

Nelson, D., & Cooper, C. (2005). Guest editorial: Stress and health: A positive direction. *Stress and Health, 21*, 73–75. doi: 10.1002/smi.1053

Nelson, M. L., & Friedlander, M. L. (2001). A close look at conflictual supervisory relationships: The trainee's perspective. *Journal of Counseling Psychology, 48*, 384–395.

Newell, J. M., & MacNeil, G. A. (2010). Professional burnout, vicarious trauma, secondary traumatic stress, and compassion fatigue: A review of theoretical terms, risk factors, and preventative methods for clinicians and researcher. *Best Practices in Mental Health, 6*(2), 57–68.

Nichols, M. P., & Schwartz, R. C. (2005). *The essentials of family therapy*. Boston, MA: Allyn & Bacon.

Nock, M. K., & Kazdin, A. E. (2005). Randomized controlled trial of a brief intervention for increasing participating in parent management training. *Journal of Consulting and Clinical Psychology, 73*, 872–879.

Nock, M. K., & Prinstein, M. J. (2004). A functional approach to the assessment of self-mutilative behavior. *Journal of Consulting and Clinical Psychology, 72*, 885–890.

Norcross, J. C., & Goldfried, M. R. (2005). The future of psychotherapy integration: A roundtable. *Journal of Psychotherapy Integration, 15*, 392–471.

Nugent, F. A. (1994). *An introduction to the profession of counseling* (2nd ed.). New York, NY: Merrill.

Nutley, S., Walter, I., & Davies, H. T. O. (2009). Promoting evidence based practice: Models and mechanisms from cross-sector review. *Research on Social Work Practice, 19*, 552–559.

O'Hanlon, B., & Beadle, S. (1997). *A guide to possibility land*. New York, NY: Norton.

O'Hanlon, W. H., & Weiner-Davis, M. (1989). *In search of solutions: A new direction in psychotherapy*. New York, NY: Norton.

Okun, B. F. (1997). *Effective helping: Interviewing and counseling techniques* (5th ed.). Pacific Grove, CA: Brooks/Cole.

Olsen, D. C., & Stern, S. B. (1990). Issues in the development of a family supervision model. *The Clinical Supervisor, 8*(2), 49–65.

Osuch, E., Noll, J., & Putnam, F. (1999). The motivations for self-injury in psychiatric inpatients. *Psychiatry: Interpersonal and Biological Processes, 62*, 334–346.

O'Toole, M. E. (2000). *The school shooter: A threat assessment perspective*. Quantico, VA: National Center for the Analysis of Violent Crime, Federal Bureau of Investigation.

Papadopoulosa, F. C., Skalkidoub, A., Sergentanisc, A. N., Kyllekidisc, S., Ekseliusa, S., & Petridouc, E. (2009). Preventing suicide and homicide in the United States: The potential benefit in human lives. *Psychiatry Research, 169*, 154–158.

Parrish, M., & Tunkle, J. (2005). Clinical challenges following an adolescent's death by suicide: Bereavement issues faced by family, friends, schools, and clinicians. *Clinical Social Work Journal, 33*(1), 81–102.

Parsons, R. D. (2001). *The ethics of professional practice*. Boston, MA: Allyn & Bacon.

Patterson, C. H. (2004). Do we need multicultural competencies? *Journal of Mental Health Counseling, 26*, 67–73.

Pearlman, L. A., & MacIan, P. S. (1995). Vicarious traumatization: An empirical study of the effects of trauma work on trauma therapists. *Professional Psychology: Research & Practice, 26*, 558–565.

Peavy, R. V. (1992). A constructivist model of training for career counselors. *Journal of Career Development, 18*, 215–228.

Peavy, R. V. (1994). Constructivist career counselling: A prospectus. *Guidance and Counselling, 9*, 3–12.

Pedersen, P. B. (1991). Multiculturalism as a generic approach to counseling. *Journal of Counseling & Development, 70*, 6–12.

Perls, L. (1970). One Gestalt therapist's approach. In J. Fagan & I. Shepherd (Eds.), *Gestalt therapy now* (pp. 125–129). New York, NY: Harper & Row (Colophon).

Peterson, E. M., Luoma, J. B., & Dunne, E. (2002). Suicide survivors' perceptions of the treating clinician. *Suicide and Life-Threatening Behavior, 32*, 158–166.

Peterson, J. (2006). Addressing counseling of gifted students. *Professional School Counseling, 10*, 43–51.

Phinney, J. S. (1996). When we talk about American ethnic groups, what do we mean? *American Psychologist, 51*, 918–927.

Piazza, N. J., & Baruth, N. E. (1990). Client record guidelines. *Journal of Counseling & Development, 68*, 313–316.

Ponterotto, J. G. (1985). A counselor's guide to psychopharmacology. *Journal of Counseling & Development, 64*, 109–115.

Poorman, P. B. (2003). *Microskills and theoretical foundations for professional helpers*. Boston, MA: Pearson.

Preston, J. D., O'Neal, J. H., & Talaga, M. C. (2008). *Handbook of clinical psychopharmacology for therapists* (5th ed.). Oakland, CA: New Harbinger Publications.

Prieto, L. R., & Scheel, K. R. (2002). Using case documentation to strengthen counselor trainees' case conceptualization skills. *Journal of Counseling & Development, 80,* 11–21.

Prochaska, J. O. (1999). How do people change, and how can we change to help many more people? In M. A. Hubble, B. L. Duncan, & S. D. Miller (Eds.), *The heart and soul of change: What works in therapy* (pp. 227–255). Washington, DC: American Psychological Association.

Prochaska, J. O., & DiClemente, C. C. (1982). Transtheoretical therapy: Toward a more integrative model of change. *Psychotherapy: Theory, Research, and Practice, 20,* 161–173.

Prosser, L. A., & Corso, P. S. (2007). Measuring health-related quality of life for child maltreatment: A systematic literature review. *Health and Quality Life Outcomes, 5,* 1–17.

Pryce, J. G., Ogilvy-Lee, D., & Pryce, D. H. (2000). The "citizen soldier" and the reserve component families. In J. A. Martin, L. N. Rosen, & L. R. Sparacino (Eds.), *The military family: A practice guide for human service providers* (pp. 25–42). Westport, CT: Praeger.

Puleo, S. G. (2004). Lessons I have learned. *Alabama Counseling Association Journal, 30,* 21–31.

Puleo, S. G., & Daughhetee, C. (2000, October). *Collaborative evaluation of counselor trainees.* Paper presented at the annual convention of the Southern Association for Counselor Education and Supervision, Greensboro, NC.

Puleo, S. G., & Daughhetee, C. (2004, September). *Supervisor empowerment in the evaluation of counselor trainees.* Paper presented at the convention of the Southern Association for Counselor Education and Supervision, Athens, GA.

Raphael, B. (2000). *Disaster mental health response handbook: An educational resource for mental health professionals involved in disaster management.* New South Wales, AUS: New South Wales Institute of Psychiatry.

Rawson, R. E., Quinlan, K. M., Cooper, B. J., Fewtrell, C., & Matlow, J. R. (2005). Writing skills development in the health professions. *Teaching and Learning in Medicine, 17,* 233–239. doi: 10.1207/s15328015tlm1703_6

Recupero, P. R., & Rainey, S. E. (2005). Informed consent to e-therapy. *American Journal of Psychotherapy, 59,* 319–331.

Regel, S. (2007). Post-trauma support in the workplace: The current status and practice of critical incident stress management (CISM) and psychological debriefing (PD) within organizations in the UK. *Occupational Medicine, 57,* 411–416.

Reid, W. H., (2010). Preventing suicide. *Journal of Psychiatric Practice, 16*(2), 120–124.

Reidbord, S. (2010). *Countertransference: An overview. Sacramento Street Psychiatry.* Retrieved from http://www.psychologytoday.com/blog/sacramento-street-psychiatry/201003/countertransference-overview

Remley, T. P., & Herlihy, B. (2010). *Ethical, legal, and professional issues in counseling* (3rd ed). Upper Saddle River, NJ: Pearson.

Reupert, A. (2006). The counsellor's self in therapy: An inevitable presence. *International Journal for the Advancement of Counseling, 28,* 95–105.

Rix, J., Hall, K., Nind, M., Sheehy, K., & Wearmouth, J. (2009). What pedagogical approaches can effectively include children with special educational needs in mainstream classrooms? A systematic literature review. *Support for Learning, 24,* 86–94. doi: 10.1111/j.1467-9604.2009.01404.x

Roberts, A. R., & Ottens, A. J. (2005). The seven-stage crisis intervention model: A road map to goal attainment, problem solving, and crisis resolution. *Brief Treatment and Crisis Intervention, 5,* 329–339.

Robertson, L. A. (2010). The spiritual competency scale. *Counseling and Values, 55,* 6–24.

Robinson, B. E. (2000). A typology of workaholics with implications for counselors. *Journal of Addictions & Offender Counseling, 21*(1), 34–49.

Robinson-Wood, T. L. (2013). *The convergence of race, ethnicity, and gender: Multiple identities in counseling* (4th ed.). Upper Saddle River, NJ: Pearson.

Roe, A. (1956). *The psychology of occupations.* New York, NY: Wiley.

Rogers, C. (1951). *Client-centered therapy.* Boston, MA: Houghton Mifflin.

Rogers, C. R. (1957). The necessary and sufficient conditions of therapeutic personality change. *Journal of Consulting Psychology, 21,* 95–103.

Ross, S., & Heath, N. (2002). A study of the frequency of self-mutilation in a community sample of adolescents. *Journal of Youth and Adolescence, 31,* 67–77.

Rossi, J., Swan, M. C., & Isaacs, E. D. (2010). The violent or agitated patient. *Emergency Medicine Clinics of North America, 28,* 235–256.

Rothman, J. C. (2008). *Cultural competence in process and practice: Building bridges.* Boston, MA: Allyn & Bacon.

Rudd, M. D., Berman, A. L., Joiner, T. E., Jr., Nock, M. K., Silverman, M. M., Mandrusiak, M., Van Orden, K., & Witte, T. (2006). Warning signs for suicide. Theory, research, and clinical applications. *Suicide and Life-Threatening Behavior, 36,* 255–262.

Rudd, M. D., Cukrowicz, K. C., & Bryan, C. J. (2008). Core competencies in suicide risk assessment and management: Implications for supervision. *Training and Education in Professional Psychology, 2,* 219–228.

Rudd, M. D., Joiner, T. E., & Rajab, M. H. (2001). *Treating suicidality: An effective time-limited approach.* New York, NY: Guilford.

Rudd, M. D., Rajab, M. H., Orman, D. T., Stulman, D. A., Joiner, T., & Dixon, W. (1996). Effectiveness of an outpatient intervention targeting suicidal young adults: Preliminary results. *Journal of Consulting and Clinical Psychology, 64*(1), 179–190.

Ruzek, J. L., Brymer, M. J., Jacobs, A. K., Layne, C. M., Vernberg, E. M., & Watson, P. J. (2007). Psychological first aid. *Journal of Mental Health Counseling, 29,* 17–27.

Şahin, A., Song, J., & Hobijn, B. (2010). The unemployment gender gap during the 2007 recession. *Current Issues in Economics and Finance, 16*(2), 1–7.

Saleeby, D. (2008). *The strengths perspectives in social work practice* (5th ed). Boston, MA: Allyn & Bacon.

Salkovskis, P. M., Atha, C., & Storer, D. (1990). Cognitive-behavioural problem solving in the treatment of patients who repeatedly attempt suicide. A controlled trial. *British Journal of Psychiatry, 157,* 871–876.

Salloum, A., & Overstreet, S. (2008). Evaluation of individual and group grief and trauma interventions for children post disaster. *Journal of Clinical Child & Adolescent Psychology, 37,* 495–507. doi: 10.1080/15374410802148194

Saltzman L. E., Fanslow, J. L., McMahon, P. M., & Shelley, G. A. (2002). *Intimate partner violence surveillance: Uniform definitions and recommended data elements, version 1.0.* Atlanta, GA: Centers for Disease Control and Prevention, National Center for Injury Prevention and Control.

Savage, J. (2008). The effects of media violence exposure on criminal aggression: A meta-analysis. *Criminal Justice and Behavior, 36,* 772–791.

Savickas, M. L. (2012). Life design: A paradigm for career intervention in the 21st century. *Journal of Counseling & Development, 90,* 13–19.

Schafer, W. (2000). *Stress management for wellness* (4th ed.). Belmont, CA: Wadsworth Group.

Schermer, M. (2002). Introduction: Colorful pebbles and Darwin's dictum. In M. Schermer (Ed.), *The skeptic encyclopedia of pseudoscience.* Santa Barbara, CA: ABC-Clio, Inc.

Schmidt, J. J. (2002). *Intentional helping: A philosophy for proficient caring relationships.* Upper Saddle River, NJ: Merrill Prentice Hall.

Schwartz, R. C. (2008). Psychosocial symptoms and poor insight as predictors of homicidality among clients with psychosis: Implications for counseling practice and research. *Journal of Counseling & Development, 86,* 471–481.

Seligman, L. (2004). *Technical and conceptual skills for mental health professionals.* Columbus, OH: Pearson.

Seligman, L., & Reichenberg, L. W. (2010). *Theories of counseling and psychotherapy: Systems, strategies and skills* (3rd ed.). Upper Saddle River, NJ: Prentice Hall.

Selye, H. (1974). *Stress without distress.* New York, NY: New American Library.

Shea, S. (2002). *The practical art of suicidal assessment: A guide for mental health professionals and substance abuse counselors.* Hoboken, NJ: Wiley.

Shneidman, E. (1993). *Suicide as psychache.* Northvale, NJ: Aronson.

Shneidman, E. (1996). *The suicidal mind.* New York, NY: Oxford University Press.

Shneidman, E. S. (2004). *Autopsy of a suicidal mind.* New York, NY: Oxford University Press.

Shneidman, E. S. (2005). How I read. *Suicide and Life Threatening Behavior, 38,* 375–386.

Sigelman, C. K., & Rider, E. A. (2012). *Life-span human development* (4th ed.). Belmont, CA: Wadsworth.

Simon, R. I. (2002). Suicide risk assessment: What is the standard of care? *The Journal of the American Academy of Psychiatry and the Law, 30,* 340–344.

Simon, R. I. (2004). *Suicide risk: Guidelines for clinically based risk management.* Washington, DC: American Psychiatric.

Sklare, G. B. (2005). *Brief counseling that works: A solution-focused approach for school counselors* (2nd ed.). Thousand Oaks, CA: Corwin Press.

Skovholt, T. M., & Rivers, D. A. (2004). *Skills and strategies for the helping professions.* Denver, CO: Love.

Smaby, M. H., & Daugherty, R. (1995). The school counselor as leader of efforts to have schools free of drugs and violence. *Education, 115,* 612–622.

Smith, D. L. (2007). *The most dangerous animal. Human nature and the origins of war.* New York, NY: St. Martin's Press.

Smith, S. D., & Chen-Hayes, S. F. (2003). Leadership and advocacy for lesbian, bisexual, gay, transgendered, and questioning (LBGTQ) students: Academic, career, and interpersonal success strategies. In R. Perusse & G. E. Goodnough (Eds.), *Leadership, advocacy and direct service strategies for professional school counselors.* Boston, MA: Brooks/Cole.

Sourander, A., Helstelä, L., Haavisto, A., & Bergroth, L. (2001). Suicidal thoughts and attempts among adolescents: A longitudinal 8-year follow-up study. *Journal of Affective Disorders, 63,* 59–66.

Sperry, L. (2005). Case conceptualization: A strategy for incorporating individual, couple, and family dynamics in the treatment process. *The American Journal of Family Therapy, 33,* 189–194. doi: 10.1080/01926180590932627

Spokane, A. R. (1985). A review of research on person–environment congruence in Holland's theory of careers. *Journal of Vocational Behavior, 26,* 306–343. doi: 10.1016/0001-8791(85)90009-0

Stansbury, C. D. (2010). Accessibility to a parent's psychotherapy records in custody disputes: How can the competing interests be balanced? *Behavioral Sciences & the Law, 28,* 522–541. doi: 10.1002/bsl.949

Staton, A. R., Benson, A. J., Briggs, M. K., Cowan, E., Echterling, L. G., Evans, W. F., . . . Stewart, A. L. (2007). *Becoming a community counselor: Personal and professional explorations.* New York, NY: Lahaska Press, Houghton Mifflin Company.

Stebleton, M. J. (2010). Narrative-based career counseling perspectives in times of change: An analysis of strengths and limitations. *Journal of Employment Counseling, 47,* 64–78.

Steele, J. M. (2008). Preparing counselors to advocate for social justice: A liberation model. *Counselor Education & Supervision, 48,* 74–85. doi: 10.1002/j.1556-6978.2008.tb00064.x

Stephens, D., Jain, S., & Kim, K. (2010). Group counseling: Techniques for teaching social skills to students with special needs. *Education, 130,* 509–512.

Stewart, T. A., Semivan, S., & Schwartz, R. C. (2009). The art of advocacy: Strategies for psychotherapists. *Annals of the American Psychotherapy Association, 12*(2), 54–59.

Stinchfield, T. A., Hill, N. R., & Kleist, D. M. (2010). Counselor trainees' experiences in triadic supervision: A qualitative exploration of transcendent themes. *International Journal for the Advancement of Counseling, 32,* 225–239.

Stith, S. M., Smith, B. D., Penn, C. E., Ward, D. B., & Tritt, D. (2004). Intimate partner physical abuse perpetration and victimization risk factors: A meta-analytic review. *Aggression and Violent Behavior, 10,* 65–98.

Stoltenberg, C. D., McNeill, B. W., & Delworth, U. (1998). *IDM Supervision: An integrated developmental model for supervising counselors and therapists.* San Francisco, CA: Jossey-Bass.

Stone, C. B. (2009). *School counseling and principles: Ethics and law* (2nd ed.). Alexandria, VA: American School Counselor Association.

Stone, D. A., & Conley, J. A. (2004). A partnership between Roberts' crisis intervention model and the multicultural competencies. *Brief Treatment and Crisis Intervention, 4,* 367–375.

Strong, S. R. (1968). Counseling: An interpersonal influence process. *Journal of Counseling Psychology, 15,* 215–224.

Stuart, S., & Robertson, M. (2003). *Interpersonal psychotherapy: A clinician's guide.* London, UK: Edward Arnold Ltd.

Sue, D. W. (1978). Eliminating cultural oppression in counseling: Toward a general theory. *Journal of Counseling Psychology, 25,* 419–428.

Sue, D. W., Arredondo, P., & McDavis, R. J. (1992). Multicultural counseling competencies and standards: A call to the profession. *Journal of Counseling & Development, 70,* 477–486.

Sue, D. W., Capodilupo, C. M., Torina, G. C., Bucceri, J. M, Holder, A. M. B., Nadal, K. L., & Esquilin, M. (2007). Racial microaggressions in everyday life: Implications for clinical practice. *American Psychologist, 62,* 271–286.

Sue, D. W., & Sue, D. (2003). *Counseling the culturally diverse: Theory and practice* (4th ed.). New York, NY: Wiley.

Sue, D. W., & Sue, D. (2012). *Counseling the culturally diverse: Theory and practice* (6th ed.). New York, NY: Wiley.

Suicide Prevention Resource Center and American Association of Suicidology (SPRC/AAS). (2008). *Assessing and managing suicide risk: Core competencies for mental health professionals*. Washington, DC: Education Development Center.

Sullivan, M., Skovholt, T. M., & Jennings, L. (2004). Master therapists' constructions of the therapy relationship. In T. M. Skovholt & L. Jennings (Eds.), *Master therapists: Exploring expertise in therapy and counselling* (pp. 53–76). Boston, MA: Allyn & Bacon.

Sweeney, T. J. (1998). *Adlerian counseling: A practitioner's approach*. New York, NY: Taylor & Francis.

Swinson, N., Flynn, S. M., While, D., Roscoe, A., Kapur, N., Appleby, L. & Shaw, J. (2011). Trends in rates of mental illness in homicide perpetrators. *The British Journal of Psychiatry, 198*, 485–489.

Talbott, L. L., & Bartlett, M. L. (in press). Youth suicide postvention: Support for survivors and recommendations for school personnel. *The Alabama Counseling Association Journal Special Edition*. Birmingham, AL: Alabama Counseling Association.

Taylor, J. M., & Neimeyer, G. J. (2009). Graduate school mentoring in clinical, counselling, and experimental academic training programs: An exploratory study. *Counselling Psychology Quarterly, 22*, 257–266.

Tedeshi, R. G., & Calhoun, L. G. (2004). *Posttraumatic growth: Conceptual foundation and empirical evidence*. Philadelphia, PA: Erlbaum.

Terry-McElrath, Y. M., Chriqui, J. F., & McBride, D. C. (2011). Factors related to Medicaid payment acceptance at outpatient substance abuse treatment programs. *Health Services Research, 46*, 632–653. doi: 10.1111/j.1475-6773.2010.01206.x

Teyber, E. (2006). *Interpersonal process in therapy: An integrative model*. Belmont, CA: Brooks/Cole.

Todd, T. (2009). *Practice-building 2.0 for mental health professionals: Strategies for success in the digital age*. New York, NY: Norton.

Tolbert, E. L. (1974). *Counseling for career development*. Boston, MA: Houghton Mifflin Company.

Torkelson-Lynch, R., & Gussel, R. (1996). Disclosure and self-advocacy regarding disability-related needs: Strategies to maximize integration in postsecondary education. *Journal of Counseling & Development, 74*, 352–356.

U.S. Bureau of Labor Statistics. (2012a). *Occupational outlook handbook, 2012–13 edition. Mental health counselors and marriage and family therapists*. Retrieved from http://www.bls.gov/ooh

U.S. Bureau of Labor Statistics. (2012b). *Occupational outlook handbook, 2012–13 edition. School and career counselors*. Retrieved from http://www.bls.gov/ooh

U.S. Department of Education. (2007). *Safe schools & FERPA*. Retrieved from http://www2.ed.gov/policy/gen/guid/fpco/ferpa/safeschools/index.html

U.S. Department of Health and Human Services. (2005). *Hurricane Katrina bulletin: HIPAA privacy and disclosures in emergency situations*. Retrieved from http://www.hhs.gov/ocr/privacy/hipaa/understanding/special/emergency/katrinanhipaa.pdf

U.S. Department of Health and Human Services. (2011). *Child maltreatment 2010*. Retrieved from http://www.acf.hhs.gov/programs/cb/pubs/cm10/cm10.pdf#page=31

U.S. Department of Health and Human Services. (2013). *Health information privacy: Is the HIPAA Privacy Rule suspended during a national or public emergency?* Retrieved from http://www.hhs.gov/ocr/privacy/hipaa/faq/disclosures_in_emergency_situations/1068.html

U.S. Department of Health and Human Services, National Institutes of Health, National Institute on Drug Abuse. (2007). *Comorbid drug abuse and mental illness*. Retrieved from http://drugabuse.gov/tib/comorbid.html

U.S. Department of Homeland Security. (2003). *Community emergency response team: Participant manual*. Washington, DC: Author.

U.S. Department of Justice. Office of Justice Programs. Bureau of Justice Statistics. (2011a). *Homicide*. Retrieved from http://bjs.ojp.usdoj.gov/index.cfm?ty=tp&tid=311

U.S. Department of Justice. Office of Justice Programs. Bureau of Justice Statistics. (2011b). *Homicide trends in the United States, 1980–2008*. Retrieved from http://bjs.ojp.usdoj.gov/index.cfm?ty=tp&tid=311

U.S. Department of Justice. Office of Justice Programs. Bureau of Justice Statistics. (2011c). *Homicide trends in the United States 1980–2008: Annual rates for 2009 and 2010*. Retrieved from http://bjs.ojp.usdoj.gov/content/pub/pdf/htus8008.pdf

University of South Australia. (2004). *Reflections on learning inventory student profiling services*. Retrieved from www.rolisps.com

Valentine, L., & Fienauer, L. (1993). Resilience factors associated with female survivors of childhood sexual abuse. *The American Journal of Family Therapy, 21*, 216–224.

VandeCreek, L., Knapp, S., & Herzog, C. (1987). Malpractice risks in the treatment of dangerous patients. *Psychotherapy: Theory, Research, and Practice, 24*, 145–153.

Van Orden, K. A., Witte, T. K., Cukrowicz, K. C., Braithwaite, S. R., Selby, E. A., & Joiner, T. E. (2010). The interpersonal theory of suicide. *Psychological Review, 117*, 575–600.

Venart, E., Vassos, S., & Pitcher-Heft, H. (2007). What individual counselors can do to sustain wellness. *Journal of Humanistic Counseling, Education and Development, 46*, 50–65.

Vernon, A. (2004). Counseling children and adolescents: Developmental considerations. In A. Vernon (Ed.), *Counseling children and adolescents* (3rd ed., pp. 1–34). Denver, CO: Love Publishing.

Vespia, K. (2006). Integrating professional identities: Counselling psychologist, scientist practitioner and undergraduate educator. *Counselling Psychology Quarterly, 19*, 265–280.

Walter, J. L., & Peller, J. E. (1992). *Becoming solution-focused in brief therapy*. New York, NY: Brunner/Mazel.

Weierich, M. R., & Nock, M. K. (2008). Posttraumatic stress symptoms mediate the relation between childhood sexual abuse and nonsuicidal self-injury. *Journal of Consulting & Clinical Psychology, 76*, 39–44. doi: 10.1037/0022-006X-76.1.39

Weinrach, S. G., & Thomas, K. R. (2002). A critical analysis of the multicultural counseling competencies: Implications for the practice of mental health counseling. *Journal of Mental Health Counseling, 24*, 20–35.

Welfel, E. R. (2006). *Ethics in counseling and psychotherapy: Standards, research, and emerging issues* (3rd ed.).Pacific Grove, CA: Brooks/Cole.

Welfel, E. R. (2013). *Ethics in counseling and psychotherapy* (5th ed.). Belmont, CA: Brooks/Cole.

Wenzel, A., Brown, G. K., & Beck, A. (2009). *Cognitive therapy for suicidal patients: Scientific and clinical applications*. Washington, DC: American Psychological Association.

Wheeler, A. M., & Bertram, B. (2008). *The counselor and the law: A guide to legal and ethical practice.* Alexandria VA: American Counseling Association

Whiston, S. C. (2013). *Principles and application of assessment in counseling* (4th ed.). Belmont, CA: Brooks/Cole.

White, M., & Epston, D. (1990). *Narrative means to therapeutic ends.* New York, NY: Norton.

Whitlock, J., Eckenrode, J., & Silverman, D. (2006). Self-injurious behaviors in a college population. *Pediatrics, 117*, 1939–1948.

Wicker, L. R., & Brodie, R. E., II. (2004). The physical and mental health needs of African Americans. In D. R. Atkinson (Ed.), *Counseling American minorities* (pp. 105–124). Boston, MA: McGraw-Hill.

Wilkins, P. (2000). Unconditional positive regard reconsidered. *British Journal of Guidance & Counselling, 28*(1), 23–36.

Williams, B. (2003). The worldview dimensions of individualism and collectivism: Implications for counseling. *Journal of Counseling & Development, 81*, 370–374.

Wingate, L. R., Van Orden, K. A., Joiner, T. E., Williams, F. M., & Rudd, M. D. (2005). Comparison of compensation and capitalization models when treating suicidality in young adults. *Journal of Consulting and Clinical Psychology, 73*, 756–762.

Wolitzky-Taylor, K. B., Resnick, H. S., McCauley, J. L., Amstadter, A. B., Kilpatrick, D. G. & Ruggiero, K. J. (2011). Is reporting of rape on the rise? A comparison of women with reported versus unreported rape experiences in the national women's study-replication. *Journal of Interpersonal Violence, 26*, 807–832.

Wood, J. T. (2005). *Gendered lives: Communication, gender, and culture* (6th ed.). Belmont, CA: Wadsworth/Thomson Learning.

Wood, S. (2010). Best practices in counseling the gifted in schools: What's really happening? *Gifted Child Quarterly, 54*, 42–58. doi:10.1177/0016986209352681

Worchel, D., & Gearing, R. E. (2010). *Suicide assessment and treatment.* New York, NY: Springer.

Wubbolding, R. E. (2010). Professional school counselors and reality therapy. In B. T. Erford (Ed.), *Professional school counseling: A handbook of theories, programs, and practices* (2nd ed., pp. 338–351). Austin, TX: PRO-ED.

Yalom, I. D. (2002). *The gift of therapy: An open letter to a new generation of therapists and their patients.* New York, NY: Harper Collins.

Ybarra, M. L., Diener-West, M., Markow, D., Leaf, P. J., Hamburger, M., & Bozer, P. (2008). Linkages between Internet and other media. *Pediatrics, 122*, 929–937.

Young, B. H., Ford, J. D., Ruzek, J. I., Friedman, M. J., & Gusman, F. D. (1998). *Disaster mental health issues: A guidebook for clinicians and administrators.* Menlo Park, CA: National Center for PTSD.

Young, M. E. (2005). *Learning the art of helping: Building blocks and techniques* (3rd ed.). Upper Saddle River, NJ: Merrill.

Zalaquett, C., Carrión, I., & Exum, H. (2009). Counseling survivors of national disasters: Issues and strategies for a diverse society. In J. Webber (Ed.), *Terrorism, trauma, and tragedies: A counselor's guide to preparing and responding.* Alexandria, VA: American Counseling Association.

Zinzow, H. M., Rheingold, A. A., Hawkins, A. O., Saunders, B. E., & Kilpatrick, D. G. (2009). Losing a loved one to homicide: Prevalence and mental health correlates in a national sample of young adults. *Journal of Traumatic Stress, 22*(1), 20–27.

Zuckerman, E. L. (2008). *The paper office: Forms, guidelines, resources* (3rd ed.). New York, NY: Guilford.

Zunker, V. G. (2012). *Career counseling: A holistic approach.* Belmont, CA: Brooks/Cole.

Zur, O. (2010). *Record-keeping of phone messages, email and texts in psychotherapy & counseling.* Retrieved from http://www.zurinstitute.com/digital_records.html

INDEX